Brazil

Life, Blood, Soul

John Malathronas

summersdale

Summersdale Publishers Ltd
46 West Street
Chichester
West Sussex
PO19 1RP
UK

www.summersdale.com

Printed and bound in Great Britain

ISBN 1 84024 350 3

Cover photograph © Stephen Simpson/Getty Images
Map by Bill Le Bihan
www.oldbill.demon.co.uk

Inside cover photos © John Malathronas

Dedicated to:

Esdras Paes de Luna
Marcelo Francisco dos Santos
André Luiz de Oliveira
William Roger Adam Pereira da Silva
Árisson Tavanielli

Acknowledgements

I am indebted to everyone I met in Brazil for providing me with inspiration, especially the people without whose tales there would be no book to write. I would also like to acknowledge the help of the subscribers to the newsgroup soc.culture.brazil who read, commented and answered all my questions and all my Net friends who encouraged me to publish this book. In no particular order a warm thank you to: John Miller, Sílvio Rodrigues Sousa, Marjan Gucek, Mike McKinley, Jim Martens, Chris Viljoen, Emílio Pacheco, Roger Wilcox, Carlos B. Albuquerque, Fausto Arinos de Almeida Barbuto, Marcelo Soares, Sonja Faria Rosa, Sander van Hulsenbeek, Glenn Sahara, Peter Schambil and Rogério Penna. I have to single out João Luiz da Costa Gouvêa who single-handedly taught me Portuguese accents and gave me valuable feedback; my mentor, the author Errol Lincoln Uys who believed in me more than I did; David Herkt for his infectious enthusiasm; Rodney Mello from *Brazzil* magazine whose kind words arrived at the right time; Lise Fernanda Sedrez who helped me with translations, corrected the early drafts and consistently supported me throughout; and, finally, a special thanks to all the nice people at Summersdale, particularly Liz Kershaw for her faith in the book and Kelly Cattermole for turning it into, well, English.

Contents

Prologue 7

Life

Blood

Soul

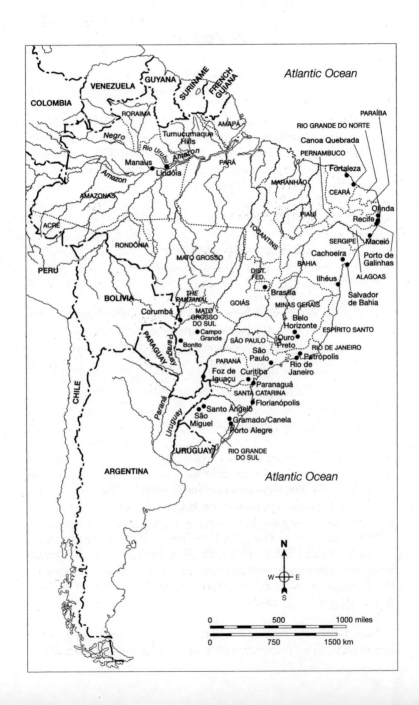

Prologue

Brazil is not a serious country.

– General Charles de Gaulle

It is hard to fathom how a country's image is subliminally imbued in the hearts and minds of the world at large. Is it selective films and newsreels? Is it repeated urban myths? Is it snatches of music heard, recurrent lyrics or an attention-grabbing travel report? Whatever the osmotic process by which it emerges, there is a collective unconscious which crystallises the unseen into a popular concept. Before I first went to Brazil, my image of the country consisted of the usual: the Rio Carnival, the biodiversity of the Amazon rainforest, that legendary 1970 World Cup team, coffee, and the high level of crime. Brazil was a place populated by jaguars and dense forests (destroyed by hamburger chains), by dirty shanty towns and dangerous muggers, by outstanding football players and carousing carnival revellers.

But I had also seen the Brazilian football squad on television. I knew that Brazil's heroes were black, brown and white; I had watched the mixed-colour fans beating the drums together, dancing the samba. That, at a time when the struggle against South African apartheid was at its peak, at a time when racism in the West needed to be named, confronted and fought against, impressed me.

It was thus in the late 1980s I accidentally came across a 900-page blockbuster: *Brazil* by Errol Lincoln Uys, written in the historical-novel style of James Mitchener. I bought it and was immediately taken in by the nuances of Brazilian history he so vividly described. I, too, started reading about the life and customs of the pre-conquest Indians; the saga of the intrepid Portuguese explorers and Jesuit single-mindedness; the invasions of the French and of the Dutch; the slave trade and the stubborn refusal of the subjugated black nations to give up their heritage; the Wild West adventures of the inland expeditions; the momentous tales of the Rich City of Black Gold, which gilded the churches of Brazilian baroque; the stirrings for independence and the formation of the Empire; the Paraguayan War and its aftermath; parliamentarism and the dictatorship of the Estado Novo.

I had to go.

Now I have seen more of Brazil than most Brazilians, and I know a lot more about the country than all those years ago when the mention of

Cabral and Porto Seguro had me searching the atlas for clues. Yes, the popular image of Brazil is not untrue. There is the Amazon, there is crime and Amnesty International condemnations, Rio is a very pretty city indeed, especially during Carnival, they play some mean football and they export a lot of coffee. But that image is one-dimensional. There is much more to this country of 180 million, the fifth largest in the world, than just that.

Which brings me to General de Gaulle's bitchy comment. I don't know what he meant, but I know he didn't make it. It is one of those quotes that were never said, like Humphrey Bogart never said 'Play it again Sam' in *Casablanca*. The person who *did* say this was Brazilian: an ambassador to France, Carlos Alves de Souza. Apparently, during the Lobster War of 1962 (a fisheries conflict between Brazil and French Guyana) he was summoned by the General for a dressing down. When the Ambassador was later interviewed, he made that notorious quote which was somehow attributed to de Gaulle. Still, the arrogant, disdainful General *could* have made that remark, which is why it stuck to him.

Perhaps the Ambassador had in mind Cacareco, São Paulo's beloved female rhinoceros. Cacareco arrived in São Paulo for the inauguration of its zoo in September 1958. She was the daughter of Britador and Teresinha, had a sister called Patachoca and was an Aquarius. I mean, the girl had pedigree! Maybe it was for that reason that a reporter decided to put Cacareco forward as a candidate for the State Parliament as a protest against political corruption. In the forthcoming election Cacareco was the most popular candidate with 100,000 votes, declared null and void by the authorities who had no sense of democracy. She also visited São Leopoldo Zoo for its inauguration, being an old hand at public ceremonies, but her political career there came to nothing. She was a political has-been.

The Ambassador (and the General) would be apoplectic if they were alive today and read some of the National and State Days in Brazil. There is the Day of the Parking Attendant (Belo Horizonte, 14 January), the Day of the Gravedigger (again BH, 17 December), the Day of the Street Peddler (BH once more, 17 August), the Day of the Office Boy (Rio, 19 March), the Day of the Dubbing Actor (São Paulo, 29 June), the National Day of the Sports Referee (on the infamous 11 September) and my favourite, the National Day of the Unrecognised Cadaver (25

September). Everyone, bless them, is remembered, nay *commemorated*, in Brazil.

But if the Ambassador (and the General) were alive today, I would point out to them that if Brazil is not a serious country – whatever that means – in the Eurocentric sense of the word, then this is a strength and not a weakness, for Brazil's strength lies in its people and not in institutions that have been imposed, modified and mutated over the centuries to serve an elite; the ruling classes have failed the Brazilian people who do not deserve the politicians they vote for. But as anyone who has seen how easily they burst into song and dance, as anyone who has been moved by their friendliness, their approachability, their concern and curiosity for strangers, as anyone who has been to a country that moves and laughs and lives life as if there was no tomorrow, I know that Brazilians have something that we in 'serious' countries have lost, perhaps forever.

And this is what my story is about.

LIFE

Chapter 1

Carnaval! (Rio de Janeiro)

Oh, how the attitude of various countries to their colonies betrays national obsessions and quirks! The French tried to civilise the natives by teaching them the secret delights of the subjunctive; the British by providing them with a legal framework so that they could imprison homosexuals; the Spanish turned them into good Catholics by burning the ones who were bad, in the name of God; but the Portuguese – now, the Portuguese were insidious: they tried to pass on their 'master race' genes. In other words, they shagged everything in sight. Hell, even if I were a jaguar, I would be loath to meet a Portuguese sailor in heat.

And if it's good enough for the valiant explorers, it's good enough for me.

....

The Words You'll Need

a dona da casa = housewife – more akin in Brazilian Portuguese to our grand-sounding 'mistress of the house'

caipirinha = the most common cocktail in Brazil: Brazilian rum (cachaça) with lime

Carioca = native of Rio de Janeiro

Carnaval = Carnival (see? Portuguese is easy)

farinha = manioc flour

favela = shanty town

lanchonete = fast-food joint

passarela = stage

picanha = Brazilian steak

Polícia Militar = no, not the military police: this is the state police force as opposed to the federal police force

preciso (ir) embora = I must leave

primo = cousin

real = the basic unit of Brazilian money (the plural is reais)

tem troco? = do you have change?

travesti = transvestite or transsexual

....

Blessed are the meek who can sleep in the seat of a British Airways Airbus, for they shall inherit a full day in their itinerary. I am clearly cursed because I get a bad neck, a bad shoulder, a bad back and a bad temper which put me out for days after a long flight. You have to admit though that they try their best to make you sleep. They turn off the lights even for flights starting in the afternoon, and they either put on the worst film you've seen before, or the most mind-numbing one you haven't. This time it was Kevin Costner emoting about baseball, a game with more innings than moments of excitement – and *Double Jeopardy*, which required a considerable suspension of disbelief. I mean, would *you* bury a woman alive with a loaded handgun so that she could shoot the lid off her marble coffin – and miraculously survive with her hearing intact? Does she know she has a future as a Black Sabbath reunion sound manager?

Some of the people you meet in-flight are also probably plants. There was Daz, an old Indian computer contractor, who tried to put me to sleep by recounting the good old times of the 1960s computers with 32K RAM the size of an aeroplane hangar, or the couple from Barbados who kept offering me their duty-free gin. I tried to warn them that they had far too much gold on their fingers, around their necks and in their mouths.

'You'll bankroll the entire *favela* of Rocinha,' I said. 'I hope you have good dental insurance, or else you'd better tear your teeth out now and put them in the hotel safe. You'll drive down the price of gold in town if you but smile in Praça Mauá.'

The couple seemed to think that being black rendered them immune from mugging.

'Ah,' I said, 'but colour isn't that important in Brazil.'

The novelty amused them.

'Seriously,' I said. 'One of my cultural shocks when I first visited Brazil in '93 was that there were blond street kids in São Paulo as dirty and destitute as the rest.'

They seemed to ignore my advice; it may have been the gin. I don't know what happened to them, but I haven't been watching the price of gold recently.

Finally there was the Italian industrialist who tried to make us slip into catatonia by repetition.

'Do you think we'll find a hotel in Rio? Do you? Do you? We haven't booked. We are arriving on Saturday before *Carnavale*. And it's a *speziale Carnavale* for the five hundred years of Brazil. Do you think we'll find a hotel? Do you? Do you? Because we haven't booked. And it's Saturday before *Carnavale* …'

'Actually, no,' I said, interrupting him. 'I think everything will be booked up.'

'My friend wants to go to the Amazon,' he said. 'I want to see Salvador. So I thought five days in Rio, three days in Manaus, two in Salvador.'

'You won't see the rainforest in three days,' I said. 'Not unless you count your hotel's potted plants.'

'But I only have ten days. I have to be back in Milano Monday week.'

'Then go to Manaus straight away.'

'Hmmm,' he said. 'We haven't booked. And it's Saturday before *Carnavale* …'

*****

Unlike the Italian, I had booked with a B&B at the bottom of Copacabana well in advance. I shared a taxi with Daz.

'Goodness me,' he said. 'It's so green. So green.'

This is the overwhelming first impression of any visitor to Brazil: the light and the vegetation; the sun and the greenness; the open sky and the vast verdant horizon. But in Rio there are other landmarks. Daz was dazzled.

'The hills – the hills have strange shapes,' he remarked, like an extra in *Twin Peaks*.

Yes, the hills have strange shapes: from Sugarloaf Mountain and Morro da Urca to the Morro dos Cabritos and from the Corcovado to Dois Irmãos, Rio is winding and hilly with every wide-open space providing another unique vista.

I was almost asleep as I left Daz and made my way to the ninth floor of a Copa skyscraper to meet my hosts. Jim was a taciturn, softly spoken Australian who was married to beautiful, vivacious Glória.

'You have a choice,' Jim said after the greetings, the smiles and the measuring looks, as he showed me two large rooms at one end of the L-shaped flat. 'And the guests' toilet is all yours.'

As soon as I saw the second room, I was bewitched. My balcony overlooked the Avenida Atlântica by the Copa Fort, and I had a view all the way to Leme. I stood there for a few minutes on my own private belvedere, grinning, taking it all in: the Copacabana curve, the reclining buttock of Sugarloaf Mountain, the sky, the beach, the black and white wavy meeting-of-the-waters pattern of the pavement, more striking from above than on the ground. The fantastic Rio panorama, the warm breeze and my happy heartbeat made me realise that yes, I was in Brazil again, this time in its 500th anniversary year. It was on 22 April 1500 that Pedro Álvares Cabral landed on a beach near present-day Porto Seguro in Bahia. Well, that's what the guidebooks say, so it must be true.

Except that he was not the first, and his name was not Cabral. Start again.

Let's dispense with the name: 'Cabral' was the second of seven children by Fernão Cabral and Isabel de Gouveia and being called Cabral was the privilege of the first-born, Pedro's elder brother. When he discovered Brazil, he was called Pedro Álvares Gouveia. Then his brother died, and he assumed his father's surname. So much for that.

Pedro Álvares Cabral/Gouveia, about 32 or 33 years old at the time, sailed from Lisbon to India on 13 March 1500 with 13 ships and 1,500 men on the route pioneered by Bartolomeu Diaz, who discovered the Cape of Good Hope, and Vasco de Gama, who sailed all the way to India. Their objective was to avoid the Mediterranean–Middle-Eastern route, the monopoly of Turks and various Italians. Bartolomeu Diaz himself was one of the captains in Cabral's fleet. It is a great irony that he drowned in a gale outside the stormy Cape he had discovered (and named prophetically Cape of Storms – it was the Portuguese king who gave the Cape a more sailor-friendly name).

Cabral (let's call him that) was not exactly the brightest of Portuguese explorers. He, ahem, *lost* a ship ten days out of Lisbon. I mean, how daft is that? His caravels looked for two days but couldn't find any trace of it. Presumably the unfortunate captain – Vasco de Ataíde – was on a proper course for India rather than South America, and he expected Cabral to be going his way; we will never know, since he vanished completely. Then Cabral hit Brazil at Porto Seguro, way out west, instead of India, way out east. To top it all, when Cabral anchored off the coast of Brazil, he thought he had hit an island, which he called Ilha de Terra Cruz. An island? South America an *island*? Only in the sense that Eurasia plus Africa is an island, and I don't think Cabral was capable of deep tectonics analysis. Needless to say, he never got another naval commission and died in obscurity.

Cabral may have taken the credit for Brazil's discovery, but he was not the first there. A few months earlier the Spanish navigator Vicente Yáñez Pinzón – who was the captain of *Niña*, one of Columbus's ships back in 1492 – had landed further up in what is now Cabo Agostinho in Pernambuco (although some argue it was Cabo Mucuripe in present-day Fortaleza) and sailed all the way to a huge 'freshwater sea' (*Mar Dulce*), which was clearly the Amazon. Further up the coast he met another Spaniard, Diego de Lepe, who had navigated up a river he called Marañon, which we now know as Pará. No one doubts their word, since they also took captives to show the Spanish court, and a subsequent map of the area by Pinzón's pilot Juan de la Cosa made in 1501 shows the Amazon correctly marked.

But enough of confutations: Cabral had a better spin doctor, and that's why it is his remains that are buried in Rio's church of Nossa Senhora do Carmo. The spin doctor's name was Pero Vaz de Caminha, and he was the voyage's chronicler. He wrote a letter to the Portuguese king, Manoel I, which can be summed up as '*Oh, brave new world, that hath such people in it!*' He described Brazil and the Tupi Indians he encountered in such wondrous tones, combining excitement and rare scientific insight, that he got the Portuguese crown hooked. His account of the naked, peaceful, beautiful Tupi started the myth of the 'noble savage' and inspired many Enlightenment writers, including Thomas More, whose *Utopia*, published sixteen years later, is set on an island off the coast of Brazil.

The best spin doctor of them all was Amerigo Vespucci whose 1503 description to the Medicis of Brazil and the north coast of South America was translated into all the major languages and turned out to be a bestseller of its time: '*If there is Paradise on Earth, it can't be much further from this land.*' It was so successful that people started talking of the new continent not as the New World, but as Amerigo's. In the same way the merchants started speaking of the new territory not as *Ilha* – later *Terra*, as the penny dropped – *de Vera Cruz*, but as *Terra do Brazil*. For this was the place where ships loaded the valuable brazilwood and sold it in Lisbon for the manufacture of the precious red dye. ('I'm off to the Land of Vera Cruz tomorrow.' 'Where?' 'You know, the land of brazil.' 'Ah!')

The merchants' name won.

John Hemming, a renowned historian of the Brazilian Indians, astutely observes that when Cabral sailed from Porto Seguro, he unknowingly performed two acts whose symbolism is hard to beat, for he left the means of destruction of the natives. He gave them alcohol, which they drank '*with great willingness*', and he also left two *degredados* – convicts – behind. They cried and cried, but the naked Indian women provided them with comfort. Thus, the first modern Brazilians were born.

And oh, the Indians offered Cabral's men something called tobacco. Good return, boys …

....

They appear to be people of such innocence that if they comprehended our speech and we theirs they would become Christians instantly, given that they do not seem to believe in anything. Thus if the convicts who are staying back learn their language and understand them, I am in no doubt that they will become Christians according to the Holy Intentions of Your Majesty, and will adopt our Holy Faith […] because these people are of wonderful simplicity and it will be easy to imprint upon them any belief we wish to bestow to them, since Our Lord gave them beautiful bodies and beautiful faces like honourable men. And I believe that he did not bring us here without good cause. Therefore your Majesty who wants to spread the Holy Catholic faith ought to take care of their Salvation. God willing it will be thus with little effort.

They do not work the fields nor raise cattle. There are no bulls or cows, goats, lambs or chicken or any domesticated animals. And they only eat yams of which there are many and such seeds and fruit that lie on the earth and the trees. Despite all this, they are more muscular and lithe than ourselves however much wheat and vegetables we eat.

That day while we were walking with them they danced and pranced with us to the sound of a tambourine like they were more our friends than we theirs. When we asked them in sign language whether they wanted to come to our ships, they were so ready to agree that, if we invited all of them, they would all have come aboard.

– Pero Vaz de Caminha in that famous letter to King Manoel I, bonding with the Tupi who already sound like modern Brazilians.

....

– 2 –

I woke up at 6 p.m. I'd been sleeping for six hours. I felt very tired, but this was Rio, Saturday night during *Carnaval*. I couldn't stay in.

I dressed up and walked towards Ipanema. The gay street party was at Rua Farme de Amoedo. Outside the Cardiac Arrest Hospital the ghetto-blasters were ghetto-blasting samba tunes, and a thousand-strong crowd, dressed only in shorts or swimming trunks and flip-flops, was drinking and dancing. Even the hospital patients were leaning out of their windows shaking their shoulders. I sat down at Bofetada's and had one of those divine Brazilian *picanhas*.

....

Things I Like About Brazil #1: The Beef

It is superb and second in the world only to the Argentinian. The picanha *(steak) is tender, juicy, always medium done and melts in the mouth. In many colonies the outdoors consumption of meat, and especially beef, played an important social role as the local foodie terms give away. American barbecues, South African* braais, *Argentinian* churrascos *or Brazilian* rodízios *betray the cowboy cultures that inspired them. The barbecue is an indigenous American practice: New World Indians used a rack to roast fish and game over an open fire; the word itself comes from Haiti where the natives called this rack 'barbacoa'.*

In a Brazilian rodízio *restaurant you are brought steak, loin, topside, silverside, fillet, brisket, rump and flank, chicken hearts and legs, sausages, turkey, pork – in short, as many meats as you can dream of and as much as you can possibly eat without exploding. I have mental images of me eating that last sausage and bursting open like Terry Jones in* The Meaning of Life.

I have a recipe for Brazilian picanha:
* *Take one bull and cow.*
* *Remove them forcibly from Europe.*
* *Never feed them hormones by law.*
* *Wait for 500 years.*
* *Kill one of their offspring as humanely as you can with the minimum of pain and distress.*
* *Slice the fucker and roast it.*

....

This must be – this must be …

'EMÍLIO!' I shouted, as I spotted a Brazilian friend I knew from London.

'I told you we'd meet in Rio!' he replied.

Emílio was tall, blond and beautiful with a perfect body, white as milk. He is still the whitest, least hairy Brazilian I know. He comes from good German immigrant stock from Brazil's southern-most corner, Rio Grande do Sul. We did not have much to catch up on as we had met only a few weeks earlier. Emílio told me I had missed the procession Carmen Miranda, which draws the biggest bevy of outrageous drag queens in Ipanema; thankfully some of them were still around: Lola Batalhão, with enough fruit on her hat to feed the bird population of a small Caribbean island, and Isabelita dos Patins, with nothing less than a decent-sized tree stuck on her headdress.

'The place to be tonight is X-Demente,' he said. 'They have Paul Oakenfold DJ-ing.'

'I'm going home,' I said. 'Just arrived this morning.'

A second wind came over me.

'Although I may go to Le Boy. That's close.'

'Oh, that was *last* night,' Emílio said. 'Tonight it's X-Demente. The party only happens twice a year!'

'Mmm, Le Boy is only five minutes away,' I said. 'I have good memories of it from my last visit to Rio.'

'You mean you scored there,' Emílio said.

'I wouldn't put it that bluntly, but yes.'

Le Boy is a club with a rectangular bar in the centre where barmen with square shoulders operate. *A very orthogonal arrangement*, I thought, and that was just the security men's jaws. Rio men make you want to hide under the carpet and pray: 'Squash me, Goddess, squash me like an insect, for my pecs are not worthy.' Kafka must have met a Carioca before he wrote *Metamorphosis*. After a few hours in Le Boy, I, too, felt like a cockroach.

The music was, however, as mainstream as I remembered. Rio revels in its samba – everything else is played half-wittedly and danced to half-heartedly. Lounge music on the main floor? Someone tell Gilles Lascar, the French owner who greets everyone with gusto at the door as if this were a private party and not a commercial club. But it's in the shows that Le Boy comes tops, and during *Carnaval* they have specials: '*Seven Days of Total Madness*' featuring Brazilian singing divas. On Saturday, today, there was a night of Bahian music with Simone Moreno. On Monday, the Night of the Millennium Elza Soares, the sexagenarian 'Queen of Samba', would receive the prize of the Singer of the Millennium (and you thought it was Michael Jackson?). Elza Soares is the Judy Garland of the Cariocas: in Brazil's 500th year – and she looks as if she has lived through the best part of that period – she was made the patron of the Movement of Transvestites and Female Impersonators of Rio, which *surely* must be the pinnacle of any entertainer's career. There was a Gala night on Tuesday with Gretchen (Gretchen?) and finally on Wednesday a bye-bye *Carnaval* night with Eloina and her Leopards, who I took to be go-go boys and not the real thing. Multiply all this by every club in Rio and there you have it: ten million revellers, including 300,000 foreign tourists, going ape for a week.

*****

I returned home at 5 a.m. drunk, spent and hungry. I saw an open *lanchonete* stall with several prostitutes hanging about, a common sight in pre-dawn Copacabana. There were only some *kibbés* left: oblong Middle-Eastern meatballs. I was about to order one, but one of the girls looked at me, pointed at them and made a vomiting face.

When a whore tells you not to put something in your mouth, you obey.

– 3 –

I woke up late in an empty flat. On the dining room table, laid out for breakfast, there was a letter:

'John,

Trust you had a good start to Carnival. Please help yourself to whatever you want in the fridge (except Moët et Chandon)! There is fresh coffee in the thermos, bread, butter, cheeses, fruit, cold meats etc. We have a big beach day ahead. We will be in front of Caesar Park Hotel, Ipanema if you want to join us. Banda da Sympatia will be playing near there.

Jim and Glória.'

They had even left me a beach towel …

I had a quick breakfast and left for Ipanema. The sun was hot, and every single square inch of the city beaches had a bum on it. Well, part of a bum really, as the Carioca behind is of considerable circumference. It took me half an hour to find Jim, Glória and an American colleague of Jim's in the crowded area in front of the Caesar Park Hotel, and it took me another half hour to butt-off the space to stretch out my own bottom. Diving in the sea is a no-no. If the waves don't get you (Ipanema means 'bad, disturbed water' in Tupi), the freezing water will put you off more than the new experimental oil rig in the ocean spoiling the view.

It was in Ipanema that Jim and Glória had met five years earlier. Jim had just been posted to Rio and felt so lonely – the city's overwrought sexuality can be intimidating.

'I was walking along the pavement,' he recalled, 'and our eyes met. We each drank a coconut on the beach, and I asked her out for a drink. She accepted.' Dinner followed where he and Glória talked a lot. 'We just couldn't stop, as if we had met already in another lifetime. So I did something mad,' he said.

Mad?

'I took time off, and we went for a long four-day weekend to Búzios. That sealed it.'

They don't call it madness in Rio.

'I wonder what it's like working in Brazil,' I mused.

'It's great. Brazilians are very hard workers. They also have a go-getting attitude. Like their racing drivers and footballers – they don't like losing. And do you know what it means to return home when you've had a bad day at the office and then go to the beach to relax?'

I asked about the Internet-only B&B business.

'We keep it for people "in the know". It's really friends we bring over and charge. We've only had about thirty people since we started, and we've only regretted it once with some girl backpackers who were out of their depth. We've spent a lot of money on the apartment – about $5,000 in renovation, which is a lot for Brazil.'

My attention wandered off to that fantastic Brazilian invention, foot-volley. It's played with normal volleyball rules except that a player can't use his hands to handle the ball: strictly head, chest and legwork. No wonder Brazilian footballing skills are so exceptional, for you need full body co-ordination and expert ball control to hold up your own – and on sandy terrain. The sport has recently been introduced into British footballing schools, but the Brazilians have one up on us – their all-year, 24-7 training ground: the beach.

'One of the few sports that women can't really play,' piped the American. 'They can do the legging and the headers, but it's very hard on their chests.'

'As if *their* game's not impressive enough,' I said, now watching women play some mean beach-volley.

'The Brazilians are very good at beach-volley. The women's teams got the first two tournament places in the world championships.'

I heard that the next day was Jim's birthday.

'Really?' I asked. 'Wow! Your birthday during *Carnaval*! Are we going to have a party? Toga! Toga! Toga!'

'No parties,' said Jim in that serene way of his. 'But would you both join us for dinner? I'll be cooking.'

'Jim is a very good cook,' added Glória. 'Better than me.'

My heart fluttered when I heard it would be a curry.

The American picked up his stuff. 'I'm going,' he said, tipping the man who had looked after our seats. 'We always come here because Rogério is a good man. He guards our clothes and keeps the chairs for us. I always tip him well.'

As we both left he added with a slight wince: 'And because I never forget that I earn four thousand average Brazilian salaries on this assignment of mine.'

....

Things I Don't Like About Brazil #1: Coffee Cups

Why do Brazilians serve their famous black, strong cafezinho *in paper-thin plastic cups? I mean, for a start, when I drink coffee, I need three plastic cups, one inside the other, to avoid second-degree finger burns, which kind of defeats the purpose. How come a litigious American hasn't sued anyone yet?*

....

Rio's southern beaches are divided into sectors, called *postos,* each centred around a lifeguard station. At Posto 8, the designated gay Baywatch, it was standing-room only. Trying to get a *cafezinho* in a thimble-sized plastic cup involved stepping over people and crawling through muscle alleys. I backed into Jean-Paul Gaultier, but then I always do. I first met him in the LA Club in London; I drunkenly went over and said: 'Jean-Paul! Hello!' And looking down at my Levis, I cried helplessly, 'So sorry I'm not wearing one of your creations.'

He took it, I must admit, on the chin.

As I was wearing my Nautica bermudas this time, I thought I'd avoid embarrassing him again and walked on to where the Banda da Simpatia was about to start. That was the plan anyway, because on the Avenida Copacabana I was diverted and joined a lorry with a ghetto-blaster playing music on top, a combination called a *trio elétrico,* with the almost compulsory semi-naked women samba dancers on top. Female nudity is what *Carnaval* is all about.

Brazil is a land where beauty is adored and put on a pedestal. This is a country where men still whistle at women and where women flirt back. This is a country where a special edition magazine featuring the best curvy *Carnaval* buttocks is put on sale and where male transvestites and transsexuals attain adulatory status if they reach and surpass the female form. This is a country where liposuction rules and gossip magazines regularly inform you which famous actress has had a nose-job or boob-job this week. Beauty clinics and plastic surgeons, electrolytic depilation clinics and silicone implants, lip collagen injections and facelifts are not only common, they are expected. Business in the beauty industry booms before every carnival, since the competition in parading nude, with gloss paint the only cover, is fierce. Why? Because the cameras are there, and careers are made and broken on the *Carnaval passarela* every year.

People may recoil at what appears to be shallow behaviour, but worshipping beauty is akin to the adoration of the ephemeral – like the never-to-return moment of a record-breaking run by an athlete at the peak of his form, or the sand-paintings of Tibetan Buddhism which are painstakingly put together, admired for a time and then destroyed to remind the devout of this world's fleeting nature. In the West we go for concrete and permanent values as we bellow with megaphones the eternal immutability of our religious and economic doctrines, divide the Earth into property plots to be inherited ad infinitum and reshape our environment to outlast generations. And yet it is the impermanent, the transient and the purely physical – like beauty or athleticism – that excite us the most. So be in no doubt that in a society that reveres not only the perfection of the few, but also the flirting and the teasing of the many, in a society that elevates the transitory to Zen-like mysticism, that it is in such a society that the thin and the short, the tall and the fat, the curvaceous and the skinny alike have a great, uninhibited sex life; for, I ask you, which activity is more quintessentially evanescent than most?

Perhaps a winning goal.

– 4 –

In ancient Rome old carts resembling boats – *carrum navalis* as they were called – were dished out for parades before spring time. Christianity could not fight certain pagan rituals much beloved by its populace, like the Mithraic festival on winter solstice for instance, or the fun and games of the floats, so it adopted both, as Christmas and *Carnaval* respectively. The latter arrived in the New World with the colonists who lived in their ranches and agrifactories and only congregated in the main towns during big festivals. In Salvador with its fertile hinterland of the Recôncavo, in Olinda with the sugar-cane plantations and in Rio, the port of the mines, the rich colonialists congregated to see and to be seen. No wonder it is in those towns that Brazilian *Carnaval* is traditionally at its most ostentatious.

Modern *Carnaval* really started in 1854 when Rio de Janeiro's chief of police stopped the practice of chucking buckets of water on passers-by, the *entrudo*. From then on the fiesta was dry so people, unafraid of getting wet, could start dressing up. Much, much later in 1916 six friends improvised some tunes in Saúde, the first big Rio *favela*; they thought one song in particular was really catchy. They called it '*O Roceiro*' ('The Country Bumpkin'). Later one of them, Donga, registered the song as '*Pelo Telefone*' ('By Phone'). Its unusual new rhythm became a hit, Donga became rich, samba was born, and Donga's five erstwhile friends sued him for intellectual rights – which they won.

By 1928 samba had won over the Cariocas. One composer called Ismael Silva formed a samba circle, Estácio, in front of the old Rio Teaching Academy in August that year. The group called itself a samba 'school', and all the other groups had to keep up with the Silvas. Shortly afterwards, on 20 January 1929, the first parade of those newly styled schools of samba took place in the house of Zé Espinguela who had co-founded the samba school of Mangueira. Espinguela himself was the judge, and the participating schools were Mangueira, Estácio and Portela (for the record, Portela won). In 1930 the parade took place in the streets of Rio (Mangueira won this time), and five years later it was officially sanctioned by the city authorities.

Seventy years on we have the Sambódromo, a grandiose and bombastic stadium designed by Oscar Niemeyer, with capacity for 88,500 people. Seventy years on at *Carnaval* time 300,000 tourists descend on the city of Rio, which is fully booked for months beforehand, with prices that double and triple and *quadruple*. Seventy years on we have dozens of samba schools (whose links with the provision of educational qualifications are somewhat tenuous) like Beija Flor, Imperatriz (the Y2K winner), the aforementioned Mangueira, Portela, Mocidade, Salgueiro, Tradição, Vila Isabel, Unidos da Tijuca, Império Serrano and more. They select a choreographer, an art director, a composer with a theme song; they use up mountains of cloth and lakes of paint; they sport a cast of thousands including famous actors, actresses and even politicians; they parade in two divisions, one on Sunday and one on Monday; lastly, this being Brazil, when the jury votes are counted, two samba schools are promoted to the first division and the two who came last are relegated.

Seventy years on *Carnaval* is serious stuff.

....

Our party could not let pass this opportunity of being together without practising the amusement of the entrudo, *although the usual time of its celebration was distant one week. On the day subsequent to that of our arrival, dinner was scarcely over before the farinha, the bananas, the rice and the other dainties upon the table*

24

were hurled at each other's heads; soon the smart uniform coats were taken off and in his shirt-sleeves each man began this civil war with heart and soul. Everything was borne with perfect good humour, and at last, fatigued and bedaubed, all of us retired to the hammocks which had been provided for the party. But as our evil stars would have it, a brave captain closed quietly all the shutters (as the moon was shining very bright into the room) and then he placed himself near to an enormous jar of water which stood at one corner of the apartment, and with a small pitcher in his hand soon dealt around him its contents awakening us with repeated showers and obliging us to take shelter under the chairs and tables. This and other jokes allied to it continued until the break of day when we prepared for a continuation of our journey.

– English merchant Henry Koster enjoying *Carnaval* one week early on a plantation in rural Pernambuco in 1810.

....

Before I left, Jim winked at me merrily.

'John,' he said. 'Feel at home. If you want to bring anyone back, do. Just be careful.'

I walked out of the elevator, greeted the porter – we had a morning one too, but I rarely met him and had bonded with the nightshift – and walked out into the sultry night. It was late, I was full and it was hot. When Rio gets insufferably humid, everyone has patches of what seems like post-coital sweat clinging to their clothes.

Outside Bofetada's the semi-naked roistering bodies were formation-dancing the samba in threes and fours. I looked up at the hospital windows where silhouettes were watching the racket.

Don't get ill during Carnaval. *Well, actually do. You'll die, but you'll die happy.*

There was no one I knew (which, if you think about it, is a bit rich to expect, having just arrived in the southern hemisphere) so I went to Le Boy again where the air-con was hardly on, leaving the main room steamy like a sauna. I gasped for air and huddled with others in the cooler corners underneath the impotent fan units. Sandra de Sá came and sang with impressive Eartha Kitt presence. I danced, and I met Alex.

Alex was the epitome of cuteness. He was dressed in a tank top, tight swimming trunks and sneakers, had a slight bleached blond quiff on his light brown hair and a tan. He was on holiday from São Paulo. Alone?

'I'm in Rio with my *primo*,' he said.

'Does he know you're gay?' I asked.

'He's gay as well,' he said.

I chuckled. He guessed my thoughts.

'We met in a club one day. The shock was mutual.'

'Where is he now?'

'Oh, he's here somewhere.'

After some preliminary talk, I dropped a hint. Would Alex come to mine? He would, but …

'I have to tell my *primo*,' he said.

A search to find the *primo* was not fruitful. For a start it was so humid and visibility was so restricted that we needed yellow headlamps to orient us towards the bar. We gave up after a while and returned home.

We entered the flat and tiptoed to my room.

'What about the owners?' asked Alex.

'They'll be going to the beach tomorrow,' I told him. 'Don't worry.'

As if it were that simple.

*****

We woke up at about 11 a.m. 'BREAKFAST!' we heard Jim cry just outside my room.

I half opened the door as Alex rolled under the bed.

'Breakfast? Oh, no, I feel too queasy,' I said. 'I'll eat later. You go to the beach. I'll see you there.'

Alex's pretty, sleepy head emerged from the side of the bed.

'*Preciso embora*,' he said tiredly.

He lived between the Morro de São João and the Morro dos Cabritos, a walking distance away.

'My *primo* will be worried,' he said. '*Preciso embora*.'

I told him to relax, that the owners would go after breakfast, and we went back to half-sleep.

An hour later, I left my room to inspect the situation and reversed into Fatima. Who?

'Hello?' I said, confused.

'Hello,' she said. 'Are you João?'

'Erm, yes,' I replied, looking at the unexpected visitor.

Glória emerged from the kitchen.

'John? Are you better? Jim has gone to the beach.'

She saw me staring at Fatima, perplexed.

'This is Fatima, my cleaner. She comes in three times a week. Have you finished with your room?'

'Ahem, no, no,' I said quickly. 'I came to drink some water. My mouth is so dry.'

Fatima was short, middle-aged, copper-coloured, big-bottomed and came from the interior of Paraíba. She loved the fact that I could speak Portuguese and started singing the praises of Brazil's north-eastern corner: every Brazilian thinks their hometown should be the envy of the world. I feigned a headache and returned to my room.

I explained the situation to an incredulous Alex.

'There is a maid? *A maid?*' He rolled his eyes up. '*Preciso embora.*'

I did everything in my power to silence him – though only one thing proved effective.

*****

We were both asleep when we heard a knock again.

'John? Are you coming to the beach?'

It was Glória. Alex looked at me, scared.

'*A dona da casa?*' he whispered, eyes wide like saucers.

'Shhh,' I said, and then loudly, 'I'll come later, Glória. Go without me.'

We heard footsteps moving away.

Alex was restless. It was one o'clock. The *primo* would by now be forming his own vigilante group to avenge the presumed death of his cousin.

After about fifteen minutes, I opened the door.

'Oh, you are up,' said Glória, emerging from the living room holding the phone. 'I'm trying to get you tickets for the Sambódromo tonight, but everything is so expensive. If you have a bank account in Rio you can get tickets for $30–$50. I wish I'd known. They're asking me for $150–$200 now.'

'Oh, don't worry,' I said. 'Leave it. Jim will be waiting.'

'Just let me try once more,' she said.

Fatima crept up behind me, a big grin on her face. 'Have you finished with your room?' she asked.

'No, no,' I exclaimed. 'That headache has returned.'

I ran back. Alex looked at me and looked up with annoyance. 'What now?'

'She's trying to find me tickets for the parade tonight.'

'We're going to the parade as well,' Alex said. 'Do you want to come with us?'

'That would be nice,' I said. 'But first we have to get you out of here.'

We waited on the bed. Alex told me how he had conveniently split with his Italian boyfriend a week before *Carnaval*. How he worked in a bank and lived near the São Paulo International Airport. We exchanged phone numbers, but I could see he was fretting.

I had to silence him again.

At around two o'clock I heard the outside door slam. I opened mine and had a peek. No one. Fatima was filling the washing machine in the kitchen. Thankfully she was one of those determined maids who only look ahead, walk in one direction, and once started never stop to turn. I waved at Alex. With SAS-like precision, he tiptoed from corner to corner to the outside door and on to the elevator landing.

That's enough French farce for one chapter.

*****

Possibly out of guilt, I had a walk on Copacabana Beach – tired after silencing Alex so many times – and bought a big chocolate cake for Jim's birthday. I also met Daz, the Indian computer contractor from the plane, who was sitting at a beachfront café. He bought me a beer so that he could talk to me. He was travelling alone after losing his wife to breast cancer. He was still carrying a picture of her in his wallet: she was white and blonde, perfectly English.

'My parents didn't want that marriage,' he said. 'They warned me off. "Those white women," they said, "they will divorce you as soon as they get sick of you".' He paused. 'Well, they were wrong. We stayed together and brought up our two kids until truly death did us part.'

He bought me more beer, and we talked about Iguaçu Falls, where he was going next. I advised him to go to the Argentinian side, where he could walk by the waterfalls, and he advised me about the parade.

'Very Brazilian,' he said. 'None of the tour people I was with lasted the full twelve hours. That samba sounds monotonous. The floats and dresses were superb, but after a while it all gets samey. And, you know, the nudity of the women shocked many of the tourists.'

Hey, if you go to a bullfight, are you surprised when the bull gets hurt?

He looked up at the sky as if to ask for forgiveness.

'But it didn't shock me.'

*****

28

When I woke up from my post-Daz siesta Jim and Glória were waiting for me. What had happened? I swallowed hard.

'I'm sorry about this morning,' I started.

'Don't worry,' said Jim – and then: 'I was *so* chuffed about the cake. Thanks.'

Oh, *that*.

'Happy birthday.'

Alex had called and left his number. I called him back. They probably wouldn't have tickets for me, as they were a party of something like twelve people, but he'd call back if they did.

'And the *primo*? Was he crazy from worry? Was he identifying corpses in the morgue?'

'I don't know what you're talking about,' said Alex. 'He was still asleep when I came in.'

The doorbell rang. It was the American with his own crystal whisky glass. He had Jim fill it at once and kept it replenished throughout the night. We walked to the dinner table, all laid out with my cake in a position of prominence. Jim opened one of the best Australian wines, a Tyrell's Vat 47 Chardonnay. At $120 a bottle, it was one of the most expensive wines I have ever tasted, but worth the cost. We had a green Thai chicken curry with rice – too hot for Glória, who, like most Brazilians outside Bahia, disliked spicy food. The three Westerners bemoaned the lack of hot food in Brazilian cuisine.

'When you sit down to eat in a Brazilian restaurant,' said Jim, 'you get salt and toothpicks. If you ask for pepper, you get chilli sauce. You have to explain what you want and how you'll use it for them to get it right.'

How true, we all nodded, watching the parade of the Unidos da Tijuca, a popular samba school. They had caused a storm for having a cross and a priest on a float. The Catholic Bishop of Rio had asked them to remove the sacred symbols from the pagan ritual. In a country that worships *Carnaval*, it was the wrong thing to have demanded. He was loudly ignored.

Alex never called back, and I never got to go to the Sambódromo. I was tired and stayed in drinking post-prandial whiskies. We sat on the balcony looking at the lights below in a city that was buzzing all the way to our ninth floor.

'Well, Jim,' I said, admiring the glittering lights of Copacabana, 'I know many men in their forties who have done much, much worse than yourself.'

'Indeed,' agreed the American.

'I sit here,' said Jim, 'and I do a lot of thinking. There is something about this place that makes me feel warm.'

'It's the heat,' I said.

The silence made me consider my comment again.

'Oh, and the view,' I added quickly.

We nodded, and in a new bout of contemplation I nearly dozed off. Jim spoke first.

'Well, John,' he said, 'you've travelled in many places. You must have had some sex adventures.'

I choked on my whisky.

'What was the strangest one you've ever had?'

I thought of Alex in bed that morning.

'I'll tell you another time,' I said timidly. 'What about yours?'

'It was in Fortaleza,' Jim reminisced.

'You're going to Fortaleza next, aren't you?' the American asked me. I was. Jim was still silent.

'You're gonna tell us or not?' the American insisted.

'It was in Fortaleza,' Jim repeated.

Glória's entrance killed off all this masculine back-slapping to my relief.

– 5 –

The next morning Alex called. I would find him on the gay beach outside the Copacabana Palace Hotel – the most famous in Latin America – inaugurated in 1923 (the hotel that is, not the beach) by a visit from King Albert I of Belgium. Only ten years later it featured in the first Fred Astaire/Ginger Rogers film, *Flying Down to Rio*. This hotel has welcomed Marlene Dietrich and Brigitte Bardot, Princess Diana and Janis Joplin, Walt Disney and Rudolf Nureyev, Liza Minelli and the Rolling Stones. This is the hotel that threw out Rod Stewart for organising a football game in the presidential suite. He was only following in the footsteps of bad boy Orson Welles who, annoyed at a rebuff by Dolores del Rio, threw a chair and a bedside table out of the window.

This is the hotel that made Rio glitzy.

I'm padding up all this because I didn't find Alex. It was impossible to distinguish individuals from the great sun-tanned mass of bodies packed indecently close to each other. So I sat in Maxim's, drank a strong coffee and bought a collapsible shoulder bag, as one does. Oh, and I bumped into Emílio.

'So where's the in-place to be tonight?' I asked him.

'Well, first there is the procession with the band of Ipanema,' he said. 'Then there's only one place to go: the Scala in Leblon. Tonight's Gay Ball is supposed to be the main event of the week. It will be broadcast live on TV.'

'A gay ball live on TV?'

'You'd better believe it! See you there.'

*****

The brass band of Ipanema was celebrating its 35th year, and the 5,000-strong march was full of queens in all attires, for Tuesday of *Carnaval* (the *Terça Gorda* or, in French, *Mardi Gras*) is unofficially the gay night. There were rainbow flags en route, foam spray aplenty, beer and coconut sellers, families with kids, banners, balcony dancing along the way and the usual nudity. A charity was giving away condoms, and people were eager to grab them – only to make balloons and blow them away. Emílio was there, still dressed in a spectacular costume after parading in the Sambódromo with his Carioca friends. They were also going to the Gay Ball – but first we had to drink one more caipirinha together.

In Farme de Amoedo the street party was at its peak. An announcement told us that the hospital was allowing them to play until 1.30 a.m. (applause). Everyone lip-synched to the songs: they knew the lyrics and they knew the dance steps, flawlessly choreographed *Rocky Horror Show*-style. A skimpily dressed woman on a table started strutting her stuff; not long after, a guy got up next to her and did it even better. An 80-year-old grabbed a muscular youth and started gyrating him around in a mad foxtrot. A fat man with five bellies performed a sensual striptease. In Brazil the motto seems to be: if you've got it flaunt it, and if you don't, flaunt it even more. For it was the five-bellies and the 80-year-old who got the biggest whistling and encouragement from the crowd.

By the time I arrived at the Scala nightclub in Leblon I was already drunk, but I sobered up when I saw the queue. It was about 200 yards long and at least ten deep.

Shit. I'll never get in.

I had to jump the queue.

I moved right to the front and slowly wedged myself in. *Strange, this is not like the queues I'm used to jumping. Hey, this is not a queue … this is …* Ouch! The guy in front of me elbowed me in the stomach.

'STAND BACK!' he shouted.

This was not a queue. People were lining up to cheer the *travestis* as if they were Hollywood stars arriving for the Oscars.

'I want to get inside,' I said. 'I want to go to the ticket office.'

A policeman came over. 'You'll have to start from there,' he said and pointed two hundred yards back to where I'd come from.

So I had to swan my way down the human corridor in my plain dancing clothes and shoes, surrounded by beautiful transvestites and guests in many an exotic attire in the full glare of discerning Cariocas. I felt like a fashion terrorist. I could see the perplexed expressions of the crowd. Perhaps I should have pretended that I was a lesbian disguised as Boy Next Door.

Amazingly there was no queue at the ticket office; I paid my $30 and walked in past the clicking of cameras, past the posing of the gleaming drag queens, past the cameras and highfaluting TV presenters into a vast ballroom. A 14-piece band, which included four drummers, three singers, guitar, bass, reeds and brass, was playing on stage. Everywhere you looked there were beautiful people dressed in outrageous costumes and make-up. And so many plumed hats; a parrot during *Carnaval* must feel like a turkey before Christmas. There's a drag queen with a PC on her head and keyboards hanging from her shoulders in a dress made out of CDs. There's another, with a baby face, muscles paralysed by botulin injections. (They had been super-effective: no wrinkles, no smiles, no mouth movement.) Here's an ensemble of four dressed as brides with tiaras and large bouquets. Look at *her* dressed in blue, made up in blue, and – you guessed it – holding a mini blue fan airing herself. She was in the back of a small, ahem, *lorry*, which brought the most extravagant creations to the middle of the room and elevated them to the balconies for the crowd's full appreciation. My eyes had never seen such dress sense. Even the drag queens themselves had small pocket cameras to take pictures of each other in this dragstravaganza.

I spotted Emílio and his friends at the back and ran towards them. But, but … they were in plain clothes!

'Emílio!' I cried. 'Where is your beautiful costume?'

'I should have worn it, shouldn't I?' he said. 'I didn't know what to expect.'

'Oh, look at *those*,' said one of his friends.

The most difficult thing to, well, *swallow* – if you'll pardon the expression – was the silicone boob jobs around me, some as large as that huge millennium tit in Greenwich. Call me old-fashioned, but I am used to seeing big breasts on women. Seeing them on men who were also more beautiful than women took some suspension of disbelief. When everyone started taking their clothes off, we could observe the transplants better. Pity the poor transsexual whose nipples were pointing down like two ripe mangoes, the silicone having descended almost to her abdomen.

I followed Emílio, conga-dancing through the astounding frocks, dodging plush Carmen Miranda headgear, being scratched by strawberry-sized nipples that could cut glass and generally colliding with naked flesh and painted faces for the best part of four hours. Next day I read that the whole *Who's Who* of transvestites had descended on Scala: Marisol, Roberta Close, Verônica, Baby de Montserrat, Tammy La Close, Paulette Pink, Negrine Venturi; most of them household names even amongst Rio's most conservative circles.

Do the scrunch.

In the early 1960s police had to protect famous *travestis* from homophobic attacks when they arrived for the *enxuto* ('pretty boy') balls at the Cinema São José or Teatro João Caetano where their Marilyn impersonations out-Monroed the original. By 1974, even during military rule, Rio's gay *Carnaval* ball had become such an event that it drew personalities like Liza Minelli – fag hag extraordinaire.

Oh, there's Jean-Paul Gaultier again.

'Jean-Paul!' I cried. 'Have you come here for costume ideas?'

He smiled benignly and said nothing. He always does that to me.

By 1982 *travesti* competitions like Miss Gay Universe and swimsuit exhibitions in São José were the toast of the town. Understand this: Cariocas are *proud* that not only their women look like a million dollars, but even their female impersonators kick sand in the face of drag queens from the rest of the world. As the Rio magazine *Fatos e Fotos* – the equivalent of Britain's *Hello* – wrote in its special gay-only *Carnaval* issue under the title, 'The Elite of *Carnaval*': *'It's their party: there's nothing sadder than gays who don't care about* Carnaval *and there's nothing worse than a* Carnaval *without gays. The visual beauty of the pre-Lenten festival is rooted in characters from Italy's* commedia dell'arte: *Pierrot, Harlequin and Columbine. Gays embrace in body and soul the three facets of this comedy: the melancholic air of Pierrot, with his moonlit face; the sprightliness of Harlequin, servant of many masters, and the fickleness of Columbine.*' Hey, who's in that picture at the bottom of the magazine? A sparkling Rock Hudson in Rio's 1958 *Carnaval*, that's who – with a sash saying: *Princesa do Carnaval*. And it was a secret, you claim?

Emílio turned to me enthralled.

'I love it,' he said. 'It's like I remember *Carnaval* from when I was a kid. That's what it was like, not the show-off in the Sambódromo.'

And after a pause: 'You know, London is not that special, if you think about it.'

Yes. In London we take pills to immerse ourselves artificially in the intoxicating exuberance we are experiencing here, high on everyone else's high, for this is a party as it should be: brash, sexy, indolent, loud and carefree.

'You're right,' I said. 'We've lost something in Europe. Dunno, is it lack of spontaneity? Is it too much stress?'

Emílio looked at me seriously for a minute. 'Maybe it was the wars,' he said.

And we both jumped up on a drum roll, our fists high in the air.

– 6 –

I was reading the papers, hangover the size of Corcovado.

'Look,' I said to Glória. 'Two hundred thousand people in São Paulo attended the alternative Christian Carnival where there were no drugs and no drink. Pity it lasted only one hour because it got washed out by rain.'

We looked at each other and chuckled mischievously.

'The fish are dying in Lagoa,' she read out. 'All the sewage is killing them. So sad.'

I was surprised. 'You mean there are still some left?'

The year's spot-the-dumb-gringo story involved a party of four French students who went to Copacabana with their money belts, left them on the beach to dive into the sea and promptly lost them.

'Five thousand dollars!' exclaimed Glória. 'They lost five thousand dollars! John, would *you* leave five thousand dollars lying around on Copacabana?'

I shook my head.

'This sounds like an insurance scam. I wonder how much of the crime is inflated for insurance purposes.'

I went to the balcony outside. My last day in Rio was cloudy and

drizzly to match my mood. Copacabana Beach, where one hundred thousand people were sizzling yesterday, was empty today.

'Won't you go to Sugarloaf Mountain or the Corcovado?' asked Glória.

'I did that first time around: Corcovado, Sugarloaf Mountain, Tijuca,' I reassured her. 'And I had better days than this. I won't see anything in this weather.'

The famous statue of Cristo Redentor (Christ the Redeemer) on Corcovado, which provides the most spectacular views of Rio from Ipanema to Niterói and from the Lagoa Rodrigo de Freitas to the Bay of Guanabara ('The Bay That Resembles A Sea'), is actually part of the forested National Park of Tijuca. This is the largest municipal forest in the world and covers an area of 20 square miles, larger than some island archipelagos. It is criss-crossed by paths, dotted with vista points and washed by streams and waterfalls. Many people visit Corcovado, but fewer venture behind it to see the splendours of what is now a pale shadow of the Atlantic rainforest that covered Brazil's coast before colonisation.

Perhaps I should go sightseeing again.

Every city has an anthropomorphic image: London is a City gent in a striped double-breasted suit, holding his chin up as he rushes by without an umbrella in spitting rain. New York is a loudmouthed, overweight baseball fan, cap and all, who pushes you away from the salt beef deli queue as you fumble for your change. Paris is a chic grand-dame, ex-model, ex-actress, her make-up dextrously applied, who walks her Pekinese in the Jardin de Luxembourg. And Rio is a callipygean copper-coloured beauty, as naked as Eve, dancing in stiletto shoes to the blast of beating drums. But today my beauty is on her comedown after five days of constant carousing, and you can see shadows under her eyes.

I took the bus to the top of Copa and to the last metro station; I got off at Cinelândia in the centre of town. The homeless and the hungry, the street boys and the ragged beggars had emerged once more on to the streets, which had ceased to be a forum for transgressing bourgeois uprightness and sexual mores and had become the domain of the dangerous. Rio was again slipping into its menacing attire, for it is not a city to be taken lightly.

The first time I visited Rio someone tried to mug me. It was outside Maxim's on the Avenida Atlântica and I was traipsing back from a club at 2 a.m., drunk and sleepy. A young kid – no older than thirteen – approached me and asked me in Portuguese for change: *'Tem troco, senhor?'*

I waved him away, but he came closer with a knife: '*Tem troco, senhor?*' he repeated – this time more menacingly.

Maybe it was the drink, or maybe it was the wounded pride (Hey, am I going to get robbed by a *kid*? Am I a man or a mouse?), but I lunged at him suddenly, and he scampered into the darkness. I walked across to a petrol station whose attendants had been lazily enjoying the scene. Next time I'll issue tickets.

'Did you see that?' I asked feverishly. 'He drew a knife on me! That boy!'

'You're lucky his friends in the corner didn't shoot you with their gun,' was their response.

*****

I passed the market by Rua Uruguay and reached Praça Tiradentes, a quiet spot in the mad megalopolis for a change. This is the old Largo do Rossio: one hundred years ago this square was the centre of nightlife in Rio with cafés, bars and French-style high-society brothels. Here also stood the Cinema São José, which had hosted those transvestite balls forty years ago. Nowadays the middle-class flight southwards has left only dingy shops and derelict, unoccupied buildings. I decided to walk across to Avenida Presidente Vargas. Suddenly the urban milieu changed from neutral to menacing. I felt I was being observed. I turned around.

There was no one in the street – except … What was this fifteen? sixteen? year-old boy doing squatting down? *Could it be … oh Goddess. Yes he is,* and he is wiping himself with his hand now, looking at me with an expression of blank forbearance. It's quite a shock to move from the sanitised luxury and comfort of Copacabana to the reality of urban lowlife, a journey from Malibu to Manila all within twenty minutes. I took a deep breath, turned to my right and was confronted by a prostitute. There were others, five – no, six. All old, all black, with red bulging eyes deeply embedded into fungal faces, hair tangled and unkempt, their skeletal bodies dressed in rags and already stinking of alcohol at noon. Perhaps they had been as beautiful as last night's drag queens once, until they were condemned to living as a human rubbish bin by the ravages of time and disease. 'Ten reais,' they shouted as they fought for me, I could have one for ten reais. I would gladly have given them ten reais *each*, but taking my wallet out would have been foolish, I know, so I cold-heartedly pushed them off and made my way to Avenida Passos. There I saw six

policemen of the Polícia Militar jump out of the back of a truck in combat formation and run into a building armed with automatic weapons.

Carnaval was truly over.

*****

Jim was sitting in his customary position on the balcony, staring at Sugarloaf Mountain in the distance. I lay on a chaise longue next to him and followed his stare. We rested there next to each other, silent and thoughtful, slightly surprised by the warmth generated between us in five days.

It was because of this I felt a fraud.

'Jim,' I said, waking him up from his reverie.

He realised this was the end of the silence, turned around and slapped his thighs, his eyes welcoming a chat.

'You remember on your birthday when you asked me what was the strangest sex story I've had in my travels?'

He nodded.

'You remember the day before you said I could bring someone home?' His eyes widened. 'Yes?'

'You remember I wouldn't get up to have breakfast the day after?' 'Yes?'

'Well, then, it was because I *did* bring someone home and was hiding until you and Glória had left and Fatima was busy in the kitchen.' I closed my eyes. 'His name was Alex.'

I took a big breath.

'Listen,' I added. 'I don't need to tell you this, but as it happened in your house, and it involved a bit of deception, I feel bad about it. The bottom line is, I didn't want to embarrass anyone ...'

Jim laughed heartily.

'I'm pleased for you, John,' he said. 'I'm really pleased for you. Good for you! You know Glória and I are very open-minded. This place is open-minded. Don't you worry.'

Phew!

'And I really appreciate you telling me,' he added after a pause.

I was ready to leave for my last night out. I wouldn't see Jim again as I was flying out early next morning. We shook hands.

'If you ever want to work in Brazil,' he said, still holding my hand, 'send me your CV.'

I grinned and made my way to the door.
'Oh, and John –' I heard behind me.
I turned around.
'Thanks for the cake, mate.'

*****

On the way out, I waved goodbye to our night porter.
'No *Carnaval* for you,' I said. 'You've been here every day.'
He shrugged his shoulders sleepily.
'No *Carnaval*, no Sunday, no change.'
'What? Do you work seven days a week?'
With no animation in his voice, he replied: 'Twelve hours a day, seven days a week, *senhor*.'
'Don't you have *any* time off?'
'One Sunday every month.'
'Do you work shifts with the day porter? Do you alternate?'
'No,' he said simply.
That put a dampener on me, as I walked to Bofetada's and saw the street dead and the few clients hung over. The hospital patients were at last sleeping properly. I, too, felt worn out. I was ready to leave, but someone started flyering for Incontru's: free entry before midnight. I had two choices. Either go home and put a tired body to sleep because I needed to wake up at 6.30 a.m. for the flight to Fortaleza or go to the club, stay up all night and subject my liver to further pummelling.
There was no choice, really, was there?

*****

Incontru's is difficult to find as it is in a residential area, looks like the entrance to a flat and is tucked away in a corner. It had taken me half an hour to find it the first time I was in Rio. It was on a night like this, my last night in town then as now, that I walked out of Incontru's to be threatened by that knife-wielding kid. I had a sense of déjà vu as I walked in and the surroundings sprang back from the airy stuff memories are made of and materialised around me in solid walls, sounds and smells.
It's empty. I'll stay for an hour and then leave.
I changed my mind, as in the last fifteen minutes before midnight the place filled up and the DJ started playing some semi-decent dance music.

My ears perked up even more when I heard English spoken behind me. I turned around and introduced myself. It was two friendly trolley-dollies on a night out. One was English and lived in Brighton, and the other one was Danish and lived in Croydon – no prizes for guessing which was their base airport.

The Dane had a problem. The last time he was here he'd met a Brazilian and they had spent a wonderful two days together. That was eighteen months ago.

'I spent the next six months emailing him,' he said.

'Why did you stop?' I asked.

'My boyfriend became jealous. But I've been thinking about him ever since.'

'Have you called your Brazilian yet?'

'No. I don't know whether I should.'

'How long have you known your boyfriend?' I asked.

'Two years.'

'And the Brazilian?'

'Two days.'

'Well?'

The Dane finished his caipirinha. 'You're right,' he said. 'Let's dance.'

And so we did until the drag act came along.

The drag queen was of the old-and-sagging variety whose only attraction is the fascinating revulsion she engenders. None of us understood Portuguese *that* well, but we laughed at her antics, which I can't describe as this is a family read. When she passed around a Madeira cake, we grabbed it and started throwing crumbs at her – tenderly, of course. Soon others followed suit and a genuine food-fight ensued with the drag queen caught in its midst.

'She didn't like *that*,' remarked my trolley-dollies.

Indeed, when she passed by she stared at me fiercely. If looks could electrocute, I would be carbonised.

'She was there yesterday, at the Scala Gay Ball,' I told my new-found friends and went on to describe that night, finishing with my personal leitmotif.

'The Brazilians have got something we don't,' I said. 'Even the poor from the *favelas* dance and parade. They get high on the energy of the crowd. They don't need artificial stimulants.'

'You're right,' said the English guy. 'We wanted to take a taxi to the Corcovado today. But the driver refused to take us, saying, "It's not the day for it. You'll see nothing." In Europe he would have taken us and ripped us off. But he refused! Here people are more genuine.'

'Hmm,' I posited drunkenly. 'Our rational, technologically advanced society with all its rules and sophisticated behaviour needs to take a step back and humanise itself more. Bring in the spirit of Brazil.'

The Dane turned to us angrily.

'No, don't say that! Our societies are more equal, more free. Have you seen the poverty here? We have created the welfare state, we have better healthcare, we have unemployment benefit, we have a poverty safety net. No one in our countries, however poor, lives like the poor in Brazil. No, don't put down our society. We don't have a perfect system, but we have a much more *just* one.'

He was, of course, right.

I have to do better than that, I thought as I joined him on the dance floor.

Chapter 2

The Myths Are Alive (The Amazon)

One of the great joys of travelling is the thrill of the unexpected. It's that magic vision, sound or taste that tingles your spine, slaps your face and disables your speech. It's the event, the person or the place the sheer memory of which shakes you physically by the solar plexus to rapture point. I travel, we travel, for the adventure and the scenery, for the culture and the fun – but ultimately, we all crave an experience. Time is not linear – don't let your senses fool you – and ageing is not a continuous process: we mature in steps, when we have learned something about the world around us or about ourselves. And we know exactly when that happens because we cannot go back; the change is irreversible.

....

The Words You'll Need

arara = *macaw*

caboclo = *literally, copper-coloured; a person of mixed European and Indian origin*

farmácia = *chemist's*

hombre (Spanish) = *man*

igarapé = *Tupi word used in the Amazon meaning sidestream, canal (from ygara-apé meaning the 'path of the canoes')*

jacaré = *cayman; Brazilian crocodile*

macaco = *monkey*

mierda (Spanish) = *shit*

não = *no*

papel higiênico = *toilet paper*

pirogue = *Amazonian dugout*

porta-cerveja = *a protective case for a single large bottle of beer made out of insulating material to keep it cold*

urubu = *Brazilian vulture*

urucu = *an Amazonian plant that provides a red dye*

....

Whenever I let slip that I've been to Brazil, everyone asks the same question. Is it: 'Were you robbed?' Is it: 'Can Rio be as pretty as they say?' Is it: 'What do you think of the murders of the homeless street children?'

No, none of those.

I woke up from my daydream on the long flight to Fortaleza. My excited female neighbour was waiting for an answer.

She repeated: 'So, did you go to the Amazon, then?'

The Amazon and the rainforest that surrounds it has been a totemic archetype since its 'discovery'. It is a place where a Ph.D. can still be had by wandering around a local market and identifying new species of fish laid out on the slab. It is a place where Indians live in the jungle as they did 3,000 years ago, with an estimated twenty-odd tribes uncontacted yet. We have photographed the volcanoes of Jupiter's moons and the cloud formations of far-away Neptune – but we have still not mapped the Amazon rainforest. There are plants and insects and birds we do not yet know about. There are languages we have not heard spoken. There are blank spots on our maps, where the canopy of the trees acts as a shield against spy satellites. And you wonder why it became the location of mythical El Dorado and the lair of the Amazon warrior women, who have provided the most enduring male masturbatory fantasy of all time?

'Yes, I did go to the Amazon when I first came to Brazil,' I said finally. 'Seven years ago.'

'And?'

My terse answer scared her off more than the *Handbook of Practical Egyptian Magic* I was reading.

'The myths are true. El Dorado *does* exist. And yes, the Amazons existed, too.'

I did not jest.

Go back in time.

*****

I arrived in the port of Manaus early in the morning, yet it felt as if the sun was already midway. I was just a few degrees below the equator where the tropical sky is white-hot. My clothes stuck to my skin, encumbering my movements. This must be why the Indians lived stark naked.

There was a bus to the centre of town, so I jumped in. Trouble is, it didn't stop in the centre by the port, which is what I expected: it circled back surreptitiously to the airport. Only when I saw the stretch of highway again – and I'm using the term loosely – did my sleepy mind

wake up to the fact that we were looping the loop. I got off hastily, flagged down a taxi and gave the driver the address of a cheapo hotel.

Ah, a cheapo hotel – not very difficult or rare; in early nineties' Brazil everything was cheap. Inflation was running at about 30 per cent a month, and money transactions were a risky business. Change too much foreign currency and you'd lose half its value if you dithered too long over a restaurant menu. Banks were giving weekly rates: if you give us your money on the 1st of the month and take it out on the 8th you'll receive so much interest; cash it on the 15th and you get more; on the 22nd even more – and if you are naive enough to have your capital locked in for a whole month, we give you a bonus, presumably for bravery. It is one of the unsung tales of economics that such runaway inflation was finally brought under control by a monetary change whose architect, Professor Fernando Henrique Cardoso – the Brazilian chancellor at the time – was rewarded by winning two presidential elections back-to-back.

My five-dollar room looked exactly as if it cost that amount to furnish. It was on the large side, but it was painted dark blue and had no window. I had a thudding ceiling fan straight out of *Apocalypse Now* and my own bathroom with a toilet that didn't flush. I sighed. I was tired and needed a rest.

'I'll take it,' I said and went straight to bed.

Actually no, I went to the toilet first, where I noticed five or six large cockroaches sitting still on the walls mindlessly twisting their antennae. I grabbed whichever bottle was nearest and sprayed them. It was my eau-de-cologne.

At least they died a fragrant death. Horrible, but fragrant.

I was silly to have bothered. Insects rule in Manaus. I should have tried to learn to live alongside the masters.

*****

It was the Spanish who first explored the Amazon, lured by the legend of El Dorado, the 'Golden One', the ruler of a land so rich that he had himself ritually covered in gold dust during an annual ceremony. After the shock of the wealth of the Mexican Aztecs and the Andean Incas such a rumour was not disputed in 1541, when Gonzalo Pizarro and his right-hand man Francisco de Orellana attempted to conquer that fabled kingdom, setting forth from Quito. They were separated somewhere in the Peruvian jungle in circumstances still disputed by historians. After that, Orellana and his party became the first Europeans to travel down the Amazon all the way to the Atlantic. The year was 1542, and it took them seven months.

Orellana's chronicler was a priest, Friar Carvajal. He mentioned a village they'd encountered where there was a big public square and in whose centre there was '*a hewn tree trunk ten feet in girth, there being represented and carved in relief a walled city with its enclosure and with a gate.*' The Spaniards marvelled at the woodcarving and asked what it was. The Indians answered that it was a reminder of their rulers, a fierce tribe of women. Carvajal made the connection with the ancient Greek myths about another tribe of women warriors who reigned in Central Asia and gave them the same name.

Hold on, but Amazons did not exist.

And yet, Carvajal goes on. Not only did he find the same relief in the next village downstream, but he says that they passed through the Amazons' land, where canoes from shiny-white villages came up to them and mocked them, saying that they would seize the Spanish and bring them to the Amazons. Conflict eventually began and Carvajal wants you to have no doubt of their existence: '*We ourselves saw ten or twelve of these women, who were there fighting in front of all the Indian men as women captains and these latter fought so courageously that the Indian men did not dare turn their backs, and anyone who did turn his back, they killed with clubs right there before us and this is the reason why the Indians kept up their defence for so long. These women are very white and tall and have hair very long and braided and wound about their head, and they are very robust and go about naked with their privy parts covered, with their bows and arrows in their hands, doing as much fighting as ten Indian men.*'

Carvajal himself was injured in this battle where seven or eight of the Amazons were also killed by the Spaniards. He also had the chance to cross-examine a captive Indian chief, Quenyuc. It was he who described the Amazons succinctly. They worshipped the sun, had stone houses and, of course, much gold and silver. Their queen was called Coñori, they lived in villages without men, but captured prisoners to keep as sex slaves. They did, however, return them unharmed at their whim. Any male children were killed, but female ones were taught the art of war. In short, male lesbian fantasies mixed with a masochistic streak: Mr Carvajal, you are a sick man! The world and her husband would have left it there, if Carvajal's was the only account.

It wasn't.

*****

I woke up and didn't know what time it was although my clock said six.

No windows – how could I tell if it was night or day? It was still thankfully early evening, so I had just enough time to find myself a travel agency to take me to the rainforest. I rushed into the centre of town past fleapit hotels. You could hear the dull sound of air conditioning emanating from their doors at full blast, occasionally causing a fuse to fail and plunging the hotel into darkness, like Hotel Cheap in the corner buried in litter. It was as if a dosshouse virus had invaded the area and created refuse as it infected it. The smell of the city was of sweet and pungent rubbish. Rats the size of cats, well-fed and fearless, stalked the gloomier corners. Amazonian waste was everywhere: in the bins, in the sewers, on the dried-out riverbeds flowing into the Rio Negro. The boats glittered at night in the old harbour, and the market of the dispossessed at the end of the *igarapé* was lit by candles and the occasional lamp, granting it the medieval appearance of a centuries-old artisan neighbourhood.

I can't remember why I chose the Amazonas Indian Turismo on Rua dos Andradas. Maybe it was the brochure: '*If your dream is to discover the beauty and mystery of the Amazon rainforest then who better to introduce you to it than native Indians for whom the jungle has always been home. Amazonas Indian Turismo is a native agency specialising in exploring the heart of the rainforest. We create adventures for individuals and small groups with the aim of sharing our culture, our knowledge of survival techniques and natural wonders of the jungle.*'

Who could resist that?

My guides were a young, short and scraggy *caboclo* called Chico who spoke some English and a much older, affable native Indian called Avelinho. We would take the morning bus to Itacoatiara and stop at Lindóia, a four-hour drive west of Manaus. We would then travel by boat up the Rio Urubu, a 180-mile tributary of the Amazon, for an hour and a half until we reached a small settlement where we'd spend two nights.

Chico was clear about the level of comfort we were to expect: 'Do you have a hammock?'

'No,' I replied.

'I'll bring you one. Ever slept in a hammock?'

'No.'

If Chico was surprised, he didn't show it.

'How big is the party?' I asked.

'A French couple and an Argentinian guy. Young people. You'll be fine.'

As I made my way out, he reminded me: 'Bring your own *papel higiênico*.'

Back on the street I looked down at my left sandal, which felt uncomfortable. My ankle was swollen, but didn't hurt. I sat by the side of the pavement and touched it. Taut as a cat's paw. *Allergic reaction. Something bit me while I was asleep.* Then I heard the buzz. It was dusk and the mosquitoes were out; I was being devoured alive. *Malaria!* I dashed to my hotel in search of DEET. When I opened my door and turned the light on, I froze.

The place was overrun by cockroaches.

I sprayed them with insecticide; I stepped on them; I chased them from inside my clothes, off my luggage, around the walls. Where were they coming from? I looked at the bathroom. Sealed. The ceiling. Sealed. Outside the door? No, none. I examined my bed carefully: a mattress on a cement base. I pulled out the mattress and recoiled in disgust.

The inside of the concrete structure that held my bed was hollow. It was sheltering a full-blown cockroach nest teeming with brown two-inchers, which became very aggrieved when hit by the light.

Needless to say, I fled.

*****

Fifty-five years after Orellana (who also confirmed Carvajal's reports about the Amazons back in Spain), Sir Walter Raleigh sailed up the Orinoco specifically to reach the 'Inca empire of El Dorado', as he put it in *The Discoverie of the Large and Bewtiful Empyre of Guiana; with a Relation of the great and golden City of Manoa, which the Spaniards call El Dorado*. It's a pity his trip did not end with the discoverie of said Empyre, but why waste a good yarn?

'*I made enquiry amongst the most ancient and best travelled of the Orenoqueponi, and I had knowledge of all the rivers between Orenoque and Amazons, and was very desirous to understand the truth of those warlike women, because of some it is believed, of others not. And though I digress from my purpose, yet I will set down that which hath been delivered me for truth of those women, and I spake with a cacique, or lord of people, that told me he had been in the river, and beyond it also. The nations of these women are on the south side of the river in the provinces of Topago, and their chiefest strengths and retracts are in the islands situated on the south side of the entrance, some 60 leagues within the mouth of the said river.*

'*[The Amazons] which are not far from Guiana do accompany with men but once in a year, and for the time of one month, which I gather by their relation, to be in April; and that time all kings of the borders assemble, and queens of the Amazons; and after*

the queens have chosen, the rest cast lots for their valentines. This one month they feast, dance, and drink of their wines in abundance; and the moon being done they all depart to their own provinces. They are said to be very cruel and bloodthirsty, especially to such as offer to invade their territories. These Amazons have likewise great store of these plates of gold, which they recover by exchange chiefly for a kind of green stones, which the Spaniards call piedras hijadas, *and we use for spleen-stones; and for the disease of the stone we also esteem them. Of these I saw divers in Guiana; and commonly every king or cacique hath one, which their wives for the most part wear, and they esteem them as great jewels.'*

The Irishman Bernard O'Brien participated in an expedition with one of Raleigh's captains in 1620. O'Brien was eventually left in a fort at Pataui amongst a tribe whose language he learned and in whose wars he fought. Out of boredom, one supposes, he attempted to explore the river upstream – until he reached the land of the Amazons, met their queen and spent a week with her. He refers to her as *'Cuña Muchu'* which is 'Great Lady' in Quechua, a language that was the Inca vernacular, but which was not spoken in the Amazon. Now O'Brien had never travelled to the Andes, so explain *that*.

Yet his account, like Carvajal's, has been dismissed; the blarney stone has tainted Irish sailors' tales, especially since he repeated the Greek story about their stunted right breast to aid in archery. Too great a coincidence, historians think.

But there's more still.

*****

One of the things I wanted to do in Manaus was eat a bizarre fish. If you didn't believe me when I said that new species are being identified as we speak, I refer you to *Ichthyology Exploration Freshwater*, Vol. 11 No. 3: pp 241–254 (2000) where four new species of the suckermouth armoured catfish genus *Lasiancistrus* were identified by J. W. Armbuster and F. Provenzano in the Amazon basin. I actually wanted to eat one of those armoured catfish, which are fish that think they're lobsters. I was enraptured by the fact that they build foam nests from debris to lay their eggs on and because they fart: *'The callichthyids inhabit a variety of different habitats in the Neotropical region, from small, swift, oxygen-rich creeks to big rivers and flooded areas, including swampy and muddy habitats where oxygen might be virtually absent. To survive in these habitats, callichthyids perform air-breathing. The air is collected at the water surface and swallowed, since their 'accessory respiratory organ' is the intestine, and is eventually expelled through the anus'* we learn from ichthyologist Roberto Reis. If you think that a farting fish is weird enough, in the Pantanal I'll show you a fish that *howls*.

Restaurant Fiorentina on Praça Roosevelt looked Italian but the sign outside promised fresh pirarucu. That would do: this is the giant of river fish, reaching 8 foot in length and weighing 23.5 stone, which is more the size of a rhino. It was so massive that the stone-age Amerindians didn't have the means to catch it; only the Europeans with their metallic hooks were successful. The fish is so voracious it has been known to leap outside the water and grab small birds. Pirarucu scales are so large that locals use them for sanding furniture. It has a tongue of bone where a set of secondary teeth grow – to enable it to eat those armoured catfish. It also breathes oxygen through its swim bladder, which reaches its mouth. It uses this anatomical oddity to create a vacuum in the water and suck up everything in its path. It is literally the Hoover of the Amazon.

I ordered it with shrimp sauce and it tasted like cod.

– 8 –

Chico picked me up at 6 a.m. from the Hotel Dona Joana where, by paying the exorbitant sum of $8, I had a room with large windows and, relatively speaking, no cockroaches. It was raining heavily; they don't call it the rainforest because it's always dry.

Avelinho was waiting for us in the bus station. There was a French couple on holiday from Curitiba where they were working on a civil engineering project.

And then there was Martin.

Martin was strikingly handsome in a rough, masculine way with blond-brown hair, deep green eyes and a killer smile; he was a well-built medical student in his middle twenties and had the extreme confidence Argentinians show when abroad. It must be in the beef.

The French slept during the four hours it took us to reach Lindóia. I sat with Martin, who at first ignored me and took photos with his expensive Nikon SLR, or rather he looked through his lens every now and again since the light was poorer than London in January.

'I'm doing a round of Latin America,' he said to me in perfect English when he deigned to address me. He recounted how he had travelled from Buenos Aires across to Santiago and up the Chilean and Peruvian coast to Colombia. He had crossed the border in Letitia, the Colombian frontier town famous for its unruliness and contraband.

'I,' he said proudly, 'I have been to Kali and Medellín.'

I wondered whether Martin was a FARC narcotics agent or whether he was just travelling through on sheer chutzpah.

'Next,' he said casually, 'I'm doing the coast of Brazil from Belém to Porto Alegre.'

He rolled over to the window and didn't speak to me again.

Lindóia was three huts, four men and two sleeping dogs. I stomped on my foot getting off the bus. It hurt. It was so swollen, it looked as if I'd worn a ski boot under my sock. As soon as we stopped, Martin ignored me and spent the rest of his time with Avelinho.

'What are they talking about?' I asked Chico as we climbed on the boat. The engine put-putted slowly and rattled every plank aboard. I felt as if I had put my head under a pavement drill and sat on a washing machine during a spin dry 1300 cycle. It was going to be a fun trip.

'Martin specifically wanted a *curandeiro* to show him around.'

'A *curandeiro*?'

'A shaman,' Chico explained. 'A medicine man. Avelinho is the most respected witchdoctor in the area.'

I stared at the thick, impenetrable vegetation enveloping the riverbank, which never reveals its features to intruders like ourselves.

Interesting character, that Martin.

We looked out for the *botos*, the pink river dolphins, and were rewarded with the sight of one: they are not as tame as the ocean kind and have been known to bite humans. They serve a social purpose in Amazonia as they are said to mate with virgins without their knowledge, saving face for girls pregnant out of wedlock. The poor wretches have been violated by dolphins – they should be pitied rather than ostracised. Neat.

Four hours out of Manaus and one hour up the river by motorboat, we reached our, well, *lodge*, deep in the rainforest.

I gasped.

'These – these are the natives?' I asked, feeling betrayed. Like every other tourist, what I expected was nothing less than Indians as Cabral encountered them: naked, natural and primitive, painted with *urucu* dye, bow in hand, arrow dipped in curare at the ready. Instead, a family of a dozen *caboclos*, who wouldn't look out of place strolling by a Manaus *igarapé*, were patiently waiting for us.

Chico read my thoughts.

'You find those Indians only in reservations now,' he said. 'You will not easily get in contact with them. And not all are friendly.'

He pointed at the two straw huts at the edge of the rainforest in a natural river harbour with two *pirogues* moored on the muddy shore.

'These are the real inhabitants of Amazonia,' he said.

Our hosts lived with two large red and green macaws and a small guariba monkey whose only purpose in life seemed to be scaring the city slickers. He jumped on my shoulder and made me squawk like the said macaws. Martin casually picked him up and put him away.

'You are too tense, *hombre*,' he said. 'Be cool.'

The alpha male of the household took us on a tour of the clearing and stopped at a hole partly covered with palm fronds.

'There is a cobra underneath here,' he told us, 'so don't step on it accidentally. Keep off this area at night.'

I got ratty.

'Step on it? Why – can't it move by itself?' I asked. 'What if it climbs up our hammocks in our sleep?'

'It's dead,' said Chico.

I breathed in with relief.

'Dead? So what's the problem then?'

'Dead cobras still have venom,' said Chico. 'If you step on a cobra bone and it pierces your skin, you'll be poisoned.'

I looked at him in disbelief. Disbelief which mounted when I realised that …

'There are no cobras in South America,' I said. 'This is all a joke, innit?'

Martin grimaced.

'*¡Hombre!*' he said, '"*cobra*" in Portuguese means "snake".'

*****

The expedition of Pedro Teixeira up the Amazon in 1637 – at last a Portuguese, you'll exclaim – took ten months and the journo on the boat this time was the Spanish Jesuit Cristóbal de Acuña, a raconteur *par excellence*. He came across a group of coastal Tupi Indians displaced by the Europeans. They too told him of the Amazons: that they only kept the female babies and that they only allowed men once a year for the inevitable orgy. Acuña himself was certain about the existence of the Amazons: '*But the proofs of the existence of the province of Amazons on the river are so numerous and so strong, that it would be a want of common faith not to give them credit […] There is no saying more common than that these women inhabit a province on the river and it is not credible that a lie could have spread throughout so many languages and so many nations with such an appearance of truth.*'

The Tupi told him exactly where they lived: four tribes above, close to the present border of Brazil with Dutch and French Guyana. And it is there where Acuña scores an accidental hit. He mentions that the tribe immediately on the junction of the Amazon with the Trombetas are the Cunuris: the name is far too similar to Carvajal's Queen Coñori to assign to coincidence. Clearly the communication between Carvajal and his informant must have been limited by language difficulties, and Carvajal could have been asking about a sickle and the Indian replying about a hoe. However, the name, repeated by Acuña, is evidence that Carvajal's report is more accurate than it first appeared to be in 1540s Spain. Maybe details were wrong, but the thrust bears the hallmarks of truth.

The French scientist Charles Marie de la Condamine noticed one thing as he read the travel tales one hundred year later when he visited the area. European accounts, centuries apart, conversing with different tribes in distinct languages, all place the Amazons where Acuña's Tupi so carefully located them: the area roughly between the Acaraí and the current reservation of Tumucumaque on the border of the Guyanas and Brazil. For the French eighteenth-century *savant*, the clincher came when he met the tribe of Tapajós who were wearing green stone lip-plugs, first described by Raleigh. These, they said, were bartered from the 'women-without-husbands'. La Condamine knew that these stones could be found in French Guyana, exactly where the Amazons were placed by Carvajal who was shot by them, O'Brien who visited them and Acuña who heard so much about them. You can find green amulets in the shape of frogs – *muiraquitãs* – everywhere in the Amazon basin, a tradition that still continues even today amongst the Borari of the Alter do Chão near Santarem. The collective memory of the people passed on by oral legend is that they were carved and traded by a tribe of women that does not exist any more.

We also know that such green stones are now mined in the Tumucumaque hills.

*****

That first night we ate well. Those real inhabitants of Amazonia were living at subsistence level, but the rainforest and the river provided them with plentiful subsistence like their ancestors before them. The French provided the biscuits; Martin, the wine; Chico, the fruit; Avelinho, the coffee; and our hosts, the eggs, beans and rice, the staple diet of the Brazilian poor. Only I had brought nothing and felt embarrassed, as if I'd crashed a bring-your-own party empty-handed.

I needn't have worried. I accidentally provided the mirth by pouring a lot of what I thought was Parmesan cheese on my rice. Except that it was *farinha*. As anyone who has eaten manioc flour can testify, I might as well have poured cement down my rectum. Given that the grand loo was the rainforest itself, crawling with insects and snakes and vampire bats, being constipated for three days was a blessing.

After I killed a few ticks on the inside of my thighs and swallowed my anti-malarials, I asked Avelinho to examine my swollen foot. He inspected it like a doctor.

'It has the cold of the earth,' he said distantly.

Did he have any remedies for the swelling?

He nodded.

'There are remedies for everything in the Amazon,' he said. 'Even Aids.'

'Yes,' I piped. 'The plant biodiversity still has to be analysed in labs to find cures for diseases.'

Avelinho looked at me benignly.

'Aids is cured by the shock from an electric eel,' he said in all seriousness and took something out of his bag.

'This is for your foot,' he said as he gave me a jar. 'Rub it in.'

I looked at it excitedly.

It was Vicks.

*****

There is one more distinguished explorer who had something to say about the Amazons – Alexander von Humboldt. This was the man who transformed the wandering scientist into a pop star at the turn of the nineteenth century, the man who combined gorgeous looks with an Einstein brain, the man whom Darwin worshipped and the women of Quito found irresistible. According to him, the historical evidence was so strong there was no other conclusion to be reached: the Amazons were women who had escaped the centuries' old yoke of men and lived free and equal in their republic. Pretty strong proto-feminist stuff, Alexander.

La Condamine actually developed a nice theory and Humboldt agreed: a tribe of women warriors conceivably lived first by the Amazon and then retreated to the mountains near the Guyanas. Perhaps they might

have slowly developed a renewed taste for men: the daughters drifted apart from their mothers over three centuries with every successive generation. So as La Condamine hypothesises: *'Although we may no longer find actual vestiges of this republic of women, that would not be enough for us to affirm that it never existed.'*

However much we smile and shake our heads in the twenty-first century, one fact remains true: the people who visited the Amazon between the sixteenth and the nineteenth centuries and interviewed the Indians were convinced that the Amazons existed. It was the Europeans at home who didn't. I have only cherry-picked the accounts. In 1584 Antonio de Berrío heard from the warlike Achagua in the plains of Orinoco that there was a community of Amazons 'five days to the east' who welcomed men to mate; next day if a man had performed well, he was rewarded with poison arrows for his bow. But woe betide those with penile problems: a shabby shag could cost a man his life. I laugh, you laugh – but only months after Orellana's sailing of the Amazon, Philip von Hutten who penetrated Amazonia from Venezuela heard of a place called Ocuarica by a river called Manna where a tribe of Amazons lived. John Hemming wryly comments in his *Search for El Dorado*: '*He [Hutten] could not have known Orellana's tales of Amazons, since Hutten marched inland some months before Orellana's boats reached the Caribbean. The river called Manna sounds like the Manau tribe who lived in the middle Negro: if Hutten was on the Vaupés as is often thought, he would have been within range of the Manau who moved far upstream in their trading missions.*'

So, in the Guyana mountains or the steppes of Central Asia – did a tribe of warrior women exist? Will we ever know?

I do.

*****

We were all tired but couldn't resist a night row on two canoes to see the *jacarés*. I was worried since the canoe was so low it almost rested on the water. If a cayman came up close, it could slide on to my lap without much ado. But no, Amazon caymans are timid, I was told. It was the snakes we had to worry about.

'Sit in the back,' Chico said to me with the lack of tact that characterises the thin. 'You're the heaviest.'

I bore my cross and started paddling. Martin and Chico were at the front, with almost half a length of *pirogue* separating us.

Which is why I was never able to convince them of what happened.

We skimmed the surface through diaphanous lianas, occasionally slamming into tree roots, our heads steering clear of low branches; frogs – poisonous, I presume – croaked around us; mosquitoes swarmed above our heads; fist-sized spiders ran to protect their webs as we wheezed through their silky spins; and occasionally, the eyes of caymans flashed against our searchlight and then slipped into the water. The night in the rainforest was louder than the day. Howler monkeys howled, birds croaked, animals stepped on creaking roots. This was a modern opera cacophony – something like Chian Ching's coloraturas from *Nixon in China* played backwards. And we all tried to hear the sound of the jaguar. I expected a roar, but no, it was a short, sharp grunt. Chico could distinguish it. Martin said he heard it, too.

The incident occurred ten minutes after we had left the camp when our eyes, aided by the moonlight, and, I should add, the starlight, started distinguishing shapes clearly. I saw a large serpentine branch heading towards my forehead. I ducked and tried to avoid it with my arm.

Splash!

The branch fell into the water with a tumultuous *whoosh!* and our subsequent shock movements nearly capsized the canoe.

'A SNAKE!' I shouted. 'A HUGE SNAKE WAS HANGING OVER ME!'

'Don't be stupid,' said Martin. 'It was a tree branch.'

The others agreed, looked at me and shook their heads as the racket would have driven any animals away. I was left at the back sweating pure adrenaline. You see, dead branches fall vertically and this one should have fallen into the canoe; but to this day, I can see the S-shaped branch over my head, lunging *sideways* into the water.

– 9 –

Martin woke me up by pinching my exposed thigh, an episode which in my 6 a.m. warped mind evolved into closet homoerotic lust. Like everyone else, I needed a cold dip in the river to wake up. We changed into our swimming gear where we stood, except Martin who hid behind a bush.

So he is vulnerable, after all.

'Don't jump in the river without swimming trunks,' Chico told the French guy who was walking around naked with Club Med impudence.

Forget about the stingrays and the electric eels, the piranhas and the

anacondas. Chico hammered in the *real* horror of the Amazon: the tiny candiru fish, which swims up the male urethra and anchors in the passage with a spike. In an echo of the legend of the Amazons -- we believe what we want to believe -- many refuse to accept that this fish exists or that it causes the effects attributed to it; the grand Portuguese *Aurélio 2000* dictionary even asserts that these claims have no scientific basis. Yet in October 1997 a proper videotape of an operation for the removal of a candiru from the urethra of a 23-year-old male patient by urologist Anoar Samad was finally released to all doubting Thomases.

The candiru is the most dreaded living thing in the Amazon, way above the elusive jaguar and the misunderstood piranha. There are upwards of sixty articles that describe the candiru, a generic term for many species of small, worm-like, translucent fish. In particular, the fish of the genus *vandellia* are predatory vampires, hiding in the river bottom to attack the gills of other fish and gorge on blood and soft tissue. There exist lab videos of candiru attacking live goldfish in an aquarium and sucking them dry after a few hours. The *New Scientist* reported in 1994 that a lab technician handling a candiru accidentally let it slip through a small cut in his hand and saw it writhing and chomping its way inwards. The candiru are smooth and slimy with spines that point backwards. They are between 1 and 2.5 inches long and only one-tenth of an inch in circumference -- a size 12 catheter which certainly allows them to swim up an engorged, urinating urethra. The stream of urine discharges ammonium salts, like exhaling fish do through their gills, so a dim-witted candiru can easily take the wrong turn, so to speak. It eventually dies because of internal bleeding and, as it is still spiked in, it poisons the blood of its host. I cannot even begin to imagine having a dead decomposing fish inside my precious micturating organ. I bet they won't put *that* smell on flavoured condoms.

As every male reading this will have fainted by now, may I add that the Indians traditionally drink the juice of the *jagua* fruit to dissolve the bones of the fish which can then be, I suppose the phrase is, *pissed off.* The juice is supposed to contain high concentrations of citric acid which accumulates in the urethra and dissolves the calcium of the candiru's tender skeleton. I have difficulty believing that, but if I had to choose between that and a penectomy I think I'd give the juice a chance.

After breakfast we took our first jungle walk armed with the basics: machetes and insect repellent. Some yards later the rainforest enveloped us in a symphony of green: yellow flower green, thin mustard green, reddish bromelia green, sepia decomposing green, olive sunny green, venomous bluish green, faraway camouflage green, pure Islamic green, dry dark maleficent green, expensive emerald green. Some people go to the Amazon to see animals: to them, I say, don't bother. The trees are thick, the light abysmal and the animals know how to hide. No, you go to the rainforest for the flora. There is the telephone tree with a thick trunk, which, when beaten, emits a hollow boom, allowing the tribes to communicate like the bush telegraph; next to it strange fungi are squatting on ageing branches like Rodin sculptures; appealing but deadly berries enmeshed in moss are hiding a giant spider's web; the soil is covered with a carpet of dead brown leaves which yield to the pressure of your foot; a strangler fig tree has sapped out a host hardwood. And everywhere there are insects: large spiders and poisonous millipedes, gigantic beetles (for *titanus giganteus* we're talking ten inches), leaf-cutter ants, see-through aphids, delicate butterflies, red termites, wasps, killer bees, flies and small irritating ticks – plus another million or so disagreeable species I could not name.

We reached a small clearing where a man was laying the foundations of a house. Fancy that – no local authority survey, no dispute about property rights; you just go to the place of your choice and build your house. I presume the problems start the moment you want to plug in your television.

Avelinho and Chico started talking to the guy in a local Indian language. I stood on a hummock to survey the area.

'GET DOWN!' yelled Chico when he saw me.

The light popped in the proverbial cartoon light bulb over my head: I was on a huge ant mound about twelve feet square in area and four foot high, covered with leaves. The red ants, whose purpose in life was to attack any intruder, had found their Nirvana at last and were biting me vengefully, engaged in formic jihad. They were large and their mandibles were sharp and painful. I flipped when I saw them crawling up my legs, ran down the anthill, took off my trousers and squashed every red ant I could find. When I looked up everyone was laughing. Even a family of howler monkeys swung in the branches over my head and emitted ear-splitting screams as they looked at the gringo with his trousers down.

Martin put his arm on my shoulder. 'That looked nasty, *hombre*.'

I should have felt embarrassed and humiliated, but Martin's touch made me feel good. Our eyes met for an instant and I felt even better.

....

Things I Like About Brazil #2: Amazonian Fruit

Guaraná (with the accent on the last syllable) is the seed of a fruit which, when ripe, resembles an eye peering out of the white flesh. The Maué Amazon Indians believe that a child born of the union of a woman and the snake god died for eating the forbidden fruit of the brazil nut tree – only Adam is missing from this story – and that a guaraná plant sprouted from his grave. The child re-emerged fortified, becoming the ancestor of all Maué. It was thus that guaraná became synonymous with the elixir of life, and if we give credence to the accounts of early explorers who regularly spoke of 100-plus-year-old Indian sages, it worked. There was good reason to think that, since the seeds are full of caffeine. Just as the Incas believed they were descended from Mama Coca, the Maué were proud to assign their existence to a stimulant, but then no people in the world loved the states of altered consciousness more than South American natives.

Less known is açaí, a high-carbohydrate cross between blackcurrant and chocolate, which is eaten heated up with guaraná, mashed banana and muesli. You find it in stalls outside health clubs – who wants creatine after that? Another unknown fruit is catuaba, whose juice is a strong aphrodisiac. I had four litres of it in Natal – which is why that chapter is missing, as I daren't publish the results. Take it from me, it works.

In modern Brazil guaraná is sold as a popular carbonated refreshment like Coke or Pepsi or as a syrup mixed with catuaba in a phial for 2 reais a go. Start your night with five of those and you are up until dawn as horny as a fruit bat.

....

'This,' said Avelinho, 'is *the* tree.'

I knew that he meant the rubber tree, that staple of the gomiferous industry of the region which had elevated Manaus into a worldwide money-spinning centre towards the end of the nineteenth century. The Indians used the latex for waterproofing their canoes and made soft syringes to put up their noses and inhale various drugs as well as pump up fluids. That's why it's called the *seringueiro* (syringe tree) in Portuguese.

It was only after 1839 when Charles Goodyear invented the process of vulcanising rubber that the tree started drawing attention. In the Paris exhibition of 1876 rubber was shown to be better for cart-horse wheels; by the time John Dunlop (an Irish vet, of all people) used Goodyear's method to produce the first pneumatic tyre in 1888, rubber fever reigned. Between 1898 and 1900, rubber was responsible for a quarter of all Brazilian exports by value, superseded only by coffee. But the seeds, if I may use the word, of the region's eventual demise had been flown to London from Santarém in 1876. Botanists in the Royal Gardens at Kew were studiously cultivating the *hevea brasilensis*, eventually to acclimatise it for the tropics of South-East Asia. Once the rubber monopoly was broken, two things happened very rapidly: the region's economic prosperity declined and the motor car took off in a big way.

Avelinho made an incision around the tree, and we watched how the white sticky milk ran down the groove and almost instantly started coagulating into a solid. I touched it to test its texture.

'He-he,' said Avelinho. 'There's always a gringo who does that.'

I looked at him and Chico questioningly.

'Smell your hands,' said Chico.

They stank as if I had just fingered a decomposing jaguar kill. *Very* funny!

'This,' said Avelinho a few hundred yards later, 'is a camphor tree,' and gave us its bark to sniff. 'John may want to use this for the smell.' I bet he says that to all the gringos.

'And this,' he said in conclusion, 'is what we'll drink tonight for tea,' and winked at Martin.

'What does he mean?' I asked.

'Avelinho is a medicine man,' said Martin.

'Yeah, so?'

'I paid him specially to brew this potion for me. I've tried many mind-altering substances in my trip around South America: yage, mushrooms, coca leaves; I want to try this hallucinogenic tea.'

I jumped.

'Can I have some too?'

Martin looked me up and down with curiosity.

'*You* want to drink with me?' he said. '*You*? I thought you were a sissy. The French and Chico are too afraid and *you* want to try?'

'Oh, yeah,' I replied. 'I'm quite keen actually.'

Martin marched off, looking at me obliquely over his shoulder.

'And that is a *macaco* tree,' continued Avelinho.

'A monkey tree?' I asked. 'Why is it called that?'

'Because,' said Avelinho, 'if you drink its tea, you become a *macaco*.'

'Let's take some bark home,' said Martin.

'Yeah, let's,' I followed his cue. 'It sounds like fun.'

Avelinho shook his head. 'You don't understand,' he replied sombrely. 'If you drink the tea, then you become a *macaco* – permanently. You never return.'

Pass.

....

Things I Don't Like About Brazil #2: Deforestation

One of the myths is not true. Yes, the Amazon rainforest is disappearing, but no, it is not to satisfy the hamburger appetite of North America. Bradt's guide to Brazil – excellent in most respects – provides the 'hamburger-rainforest equation', quoting Christopher Uhl, a biologist from Penn State. Using back-of-the-envelope calculations on how much grass a cow must consume and how much rainforest must be razed to grow such grass, it affirms that 67 square feet of rainforest must disappear in order to produce a hamburger.

That's all very nice and super but does not fit with the fact that Amazonia is a net importer, not exporter, of beef. According to a UN study, the Brazilian Amazon supplied 0.0007 per cent of US beef in its heyday (1982). In most years, foot-and-mouth disease has prevented the region from competing with southern Brazil, Uruguay and Argentina. The scare has arisen from the Central American connection: in the 1970s a lot of rainforest did disappear there for the raising of cattle for beef exports. It is this deforestation that started the protests against McDonald's and Burger King (who vehemently – and it seems correctly – denied that foreign beef was used in their hamburgers). The rainforest is, sadly, disappearing, but not for such headline reasons. Like in the American Wild West, cattle is the best investment for farmers because it is the most cost-efficient option for land use: in frontier areas workers are scarce and cattle rearing is not labour-intensive.

....

'This is where we fish,' Avelinho decided several miles downstream. We had to catch our dinner. The women were preparing *caldeirada de piranha* and we, the men, were providing the ingredients.

Chico took a piece of red meat, cut it up and made bait. Then he hooked his line away and waited. Not long afterwards, the line became taut, and he started pulling quickly as a large red piranha flapped its way into our boat. Chico unhooked it and showed us its teeth, as sharp as disposable razors. Martin stroked it until it jumped and startled him. Piranhas demand respect even in death.

The Indians caught about half a dozen, Martin caught one and the French did better with three. Guess who caught none.

I blamed Martin: 'You threw all the meat in the water,' I complained.

'I did it for *you*,' he said. 'To attract the piranha.'

'And how would I catch them?' I asked. 'By dipping my arm in?'

'You don't know how to pull the line,' Chico told me, trying to bring peace. 'Have you fished before?'

'Well, no, it's not exactly my number one pastime,' I said. 'Life's too short to catch your own food nowadays.'

Martin turned sharply to me and wagged his finger at my nose.

'And *that*,' he said, 'is the problem with you.'

I was annoyed and felt a strong urge to dump him in the water. But now that I'm writing all this down, I know he had a point – perhaps a major one. That night everyone ate as many fish from the pot as they had caught, sharing them with the women who had cooked the stew. I, having caught none, had just soup and potatoes. If the jungle has a law it is this: if you don't catch food, you don't eat. Chico offered me some of his catch. I refused. If my society has taught me anything it is not to show weakness.

*****

When Avelinho started brewing the tea, I calmed down and drifted towards Martin to check that I was included in the tasting.

'What is this plant called?' I asked.

'*Pacaraná*,' he replied. Or so I wrote down then. From my elementary Tupi I can now deduct that the name is composed of *paca* (an Amazonian rodent, which is edible like Andean guinea-pig) and *raná* ('looks like', 'similar to') – the tree that looks like a rodent, should you care to check it out.

Martin came over in peace, and we each drank a large mug of dark reddish tea. No one else followed suit, not even Avelinho.

We lay on our hammocks staring at the clear, starred sky. I had never seen Orion so close to the horizon. My eyes focused on the constellations and tried to make them out, but in vain. *This is the southern hemisphere; I don't belong here*. I shivered.

It was cold at night, and I pulled a blanket tightly around my body …

… I was falling asleep when I heard Martin's voice close to my ear: '*¡Hombre!* Let's go into the bushes.'

I wrapped my blanket around me and followed him as far as the clearing at the edge of the jungle. He sat on a log, legs astride. I huddled beside him, looking at the felled trees where an awning had been made for some primitive silviculture.

'Deforestation,' he said.

'It's terrible,' I said. 'It's terrible.'

'Are you tripping?'

'Yeah.'

'Me too.'

There was Orion again, its three-stars-in-a-line illuminating our silence which lasted for an eternity and a half.

'Imagine,' Martin said, breaking our tranquillity, 'there could be hostile natives hiding in the trees. They could be watching us undetected.'

'Yeah,' I said.

Orion advanced rapidly in formation like a fleet of spaceships.

'There could be Amazons out there.'

'Yeah.'

'Imagine being abducted and sold as a sex slave to the Amazons.'

I cleared my throat. 'They only have one breast,' I reminded him. 'They cut the right one off to shoot arrows better.'

This put him off.

'Shit, man,' I went on, 'imagine a girl having her right breast cut off and growing up left-handed.'

What a ghastly thought.

'Do you believe the Amazons existed?' he asked me.

I picked up a strange-looking green rock. It was smooth and shiny and to my mind the most precious item I had ever possessed.

'Of course not. Why, do you?'

Martin got up. He was now incredibly tall. He reached the sky. I was shivering violently and pulled my blanket around me. Where did all this light come from?

'*¡Hombre!*' Martin insisted, walking up and down, 'the Amazons did exist. El Dorado exists.'

Where did this green light come from? Had the sun risen? I looked at Orion. Still there, though I wish it would keep still. It must be the moon. Bright moon. Green moon. Like Martin's eyes.

'I can't describe it to you now, *hombre*, but I know they did exist. Will you trust me?'

'I trust you Martin,' I humoured him.

He picked up on my weariness.

'No, it's true. I've read about them. So many people saw them. They just became extinct like so many other tribes. Do you believe me?'

My neck had been gripped by an invisible hand which was pressing at the bottom of my skull. I stepped backwards in time. I followed Martin to the bushes. I got out of my hammock. Martin came to me and whispered in my ear.

'*¡Hombre!* Let's go into the bushes.'

'No,' I replied. 'I want to sleep.'

Perchance to dream?

No perchance there, I've already started.

*****

In the morning we woke up together, heads as heavy as if smeared with El Dorado's own gold dust.

'It was eerie,' I said. 'I dreamt that I was immersed in green. Although my eyes were closed, I could see the forest around me very vividly. And you?'

Martin paused.

'I dreamt that I was watching a man fucking a woman and suddenly the woman turned into a pig. It started grunting and the man was alarmed, but I told him, "It's OK, man. It's cool. Everyone with his vice. You can feel OK about it."'

And his green emerald eyes looked piercingly through me.

– 10 –

Back in Manaus, Chico and Avelinho left us at our hotels; The French disappeared at once, but Martin hung around to drink a beer.

'Tomorrow I'm going to Belém,' he said. 'I've already paid for a passage on a barge.'

I was leaving the day after for Belo Horizonte.

'What are you doing tonight?' he asked.

'Having more of this,' I replied, drinking up thirstily.

He coughed. 'Shall we meet up?'

'Yeah, fine, later.'

There was still something I had to do in town. I had to see that symbol of victorious European values in an imported conflict that involved both class and race: the Manaus Opera House.

I love opera. You have voices singing in unnatural cadences, laterally challenged men and women earnestly pretending to be dashing gay blades and gazelle-like *femmes fatales*, plus scenery from ancient China, Egypt or Valhalla. It is the campest of musical forms, and, like drag, it involves suspension of disbelief and immersion in a pre-arranged fantasy. (It is, of course, this absolute power of the composer as an artist on a pedestal in a well-ordered world, which bore a dozen counter-movements later on.)

I tagged on to a party of Americans who were taking a tour. Americans who reach Manaus are rich. And rich people can be very daft.

'Are these pipes for the acoustics, too?'

'No madam, these pipes are for air conditioning.'

'Oh, they had air conditioning in the nineteenth century?'

'No madam. They were installed five years ago.'

Somehow, the dialogue seemed apt. The Opera House is a folly of monumental proportions. Outside there is cholera and malaria, starving street children, yet we are surrounded by Alsatian tiles, English stone, Venetian mirrors, Italian marble and Portuguese sheet granite shipped to the middle of the jungle at enormous cost.

The Opera House must be seen in the context of its era. The 1890s *belle époque*, when Manaus boomed and the rubber barons ruled, was the apotheosis of the bourgeoisie and opera the apex of its artistic ethos: European, imperial and unquestioned. Rubber and latex were inextricably linked with the car, and the car with a brighter future; there were electric streetcars in Manaus before they appeared in most cities in the United States; there were telephones aplenty; two daily newspapers; three hospitals; special 'ethnic' clubs for the foreigners; chic beaches like the Balneário do Mosqueiro; regular connections via Belém to Lisbon, Le Havre, Liverpool, Antwerp and New York. The latest fashions and consumer fads reached the city on the Rio Negro almost as soon as they reached Rio.

The pink marble opera building in Manaus sealed it all. It is by far the single most famous structure in Brazil this side of the statue of Christ in Corcovado, and it is impressive in its incongruity: it simply doesn't belong there. Hobsbawn called it a 'bourgeois cathedral' and he was not far off: it has, after all, a macaw-coloured green, yellow and blue dome.

And the symbolism continues: one hundred years later, its decline, along with the city of Manaus, personifies the predatory nature of those imperial values it so famously exhorted. The theatre was abandoned as early as 1912 when competition from the stolen rubber-tree seeds of Santarém started hurting, and only on its centenary, in 1996, did it become active again, when José Carreras was invited to sing in a performance whose overall cost reached one million greenbacks.

Opera did not take root in the jungle: it was foreign mimicry, it was espousal of false values – that technological progress equals 'civilisation' – and, like the city itself, it was cruelly deserted by the elites when there was no more money to be made. But what a story, eh? Where is Werner Herzog to film it when you want him?

*****

Martin and I wanted an old-fashioned piss-up. We ended up in a sailors' bar in the port, watching the sun go down on the Rio Negro and the day turn duskless into night. We drank the large Brazilian Brahma beers, complete with *porta-cervejas* to protect them from warming up in the muggy night heat.

'How come you speak English so well?' I asked him.

'I went to an English school in Buenos Aires,' he said. 'I had an English teacher who made me eat with books under my arms. And when I dropped the food then *thwack!* she hit me with a ruler.'

Pity about the Falklands.

'You mean the *Malvinas*. Great pity – many Argentinians look up to the British and their culture. Even the war didn't sour an excellent relationship.'

We drank two more beers. Two fat prostitutes came and sat next to us, eyeing Martin who ignored them. We spoke of our childhood – we both came from broken families: my parents divorced when I was four and his when he was seven.

'My father married again and has two daughters,' he said. 'But my stepmother hates me because I am his only son. My mother married again.'

'You stayed with her?'

'Yes, you?'

'Me too.'

'Yeah, well, my mother married again but my stepfather beat her up.'

The prostitutes started fighting and the bar owner went to separate them.

'At the age of sixteen, I did him in badly.'

What?

'I caught him hitting my mother, so I smashed his face in.'

'And what happened?'

'He was thrown in jail, and I was forced to see a psychiatrist for two years.'

There was only one way I could top that.

'You think *that's* serious?' I asked.

'Why – what happened to you?'

'Well, I turned out gay.'

He looked at me and his eyes shone.

'I guessed it,' he said.

'The dream you had –'

'Exactly. I sensed it.'

'Like you sensed the Amazons around us?'

'You don't believe me,' he said dispiritedly.

'I do,' I replied half-heartedly, but he didn't buy it.

I ordered two more beers which led to more heart-to-heart revelations.

'In Colombia I met this girl,' he said. 'We were together for two weeks. But then I had to go.'

He handed me her picture.

'She looks nice,' I commented.

'Yeah, *hombre*, she was really nice. But what happened, happened. I had to leave, it was inevitable.'

And then rather rapidly: 'Can I ask you a personal question?'

'Go on.'

'Have you ever fallen in love during a journey?'

'I have.'

'And what happened?'

'We split up. It was inevitable, wasn't it?'

He seemed reassured by my repetition of his own words.

More beer. After six large ones each, we decided to call it a night. We traipsed back, leaning heavily on each other's shoulders.

At Martin's hotel, on the way to mine, we stopped by the dark, locked door.

'What time are you leaving tomorrow?' I asked.

'Four in the afternoon. Shall we meet when we wake up?'

'OK.'

He pointed at my cut-off jeans.

'Will you cut my jeans for me like yours?'

'Sure.'

He looked at me for a few minutes.

'My room is a double,' he said finally.

Silence.

'I have paid for a double.'

I held my breath.

'That means I can have a guest.'

My mind was working overtime. He was waiting for me to say something, but I couldn't. I just couldn't. Then the door opened and the receptionist turned on the light, breaking a tender, telepathic thread.

'Bye, Martin,' I said. 'Sleep well.'

His face darkened slightly, but he managed to smile.

'You'll come tomorrow?'

'I will.'

'You'll stay with me all day?'

'I will.'

'Goodnight then, John.'

'Goodnight, Martin.'

*****

Next day, I woke up like a shot when I saw it was midday. I assigned my hangover temporarily to my back pocket as I dressed myself and ran out to Martin's hotel.

I climbed the stairs to his room. He was still asleep. I woke him up.

'*¡Mierda!* I'll have to pay for one more day if I don't leave immediately,' were his first words.

I looked around. Nice room, full of the heavy scent of Martin's sleep, and it had a balcony with a view of the Rio Negro.

'I tell you what – my stuff is still packed from yesterday; I'll leave my hotel and book your room now,' I said. 'It's nicer than mine and costs the same.'

He looked at me with one eye still closed.

'Oh, thanks so much, *hombre*,' he mumbled.

When I came back, all formalities completed, he was coming out of the shower. I stood on the balcony staring at the rising river haze.

'I will never see the *encontro das aguas*,' I lamented. 'Too late to leave now.'

The 'meeting of the waters' is a special natural phenomenon in Manaus; the dark waters of the Rio Negro meet the pale colour of the Amazon and merge like a dark and light marble cake. It is this undulating pattern one can see depicted on many city pavements in Brazil – including Rio's Copacabana.

'Never mind,' I heard his voice say. 'Leave something for next time. Never exhaust a place, because you will never return.'

He walked out in his long blue jeans with a pair of scissors. I kneeled in front of him and slowly cut them above the knee. I could feel him looking down at me, his breathing irregular.

'There,' I said. 'You look boo-tiful.'

We stared at each other, me kneeling, him standing.

It won't happen.

'We have time for a last stroll,' I said getting up. 'Let's go.'

I winced as I put weight on my swollen foot.

'How's your foot?' he asked.

'I'll be OK.'

'Lie down,' he said.

I obeyed, and he removed my shoe. He took an ointment and rubbed it on my ankle.

'Does it hurt?' he asked as he gently massaged my foot.

'No,' I replied. 'It feels numb.'

I felt better, but it was more his concern than the medication.

'That's you sorted,' he said as he put my shoe back on. 'Now me.'

'You?'

We left the hotel, our first stop a *farmácia*. And our second. And our third. Martin was looking for anti-nausea pills for seasickness.

'This is a river you'll be going on,' I reminded him.

'It is rough like a sea,' he said. 'Remember I travelled down all the way from Letitia.'

The river-sea – how apt Pinzón's very first description was …

We walked silently along the various streams and *igarapés*, taking pictures of the river barges; we sat by the central square, the Praça da Matriz, looking at the line of shoeshine boys, waiting in vain for a client in this sandal-wearing town; we admired the *fin de siécle* houses and dined demurely in the Italian restaurant back on the Praça Roosevelt. Yet time always accelerates towards a fixed instant in the future, and we found ourselves walking with Martin's insignificantly small but surprisingly heavy luggage to his boat. We were late in; all the best hammock spaces had been nabbed, and he was exiled to the malodorous spot next to the toilets.

'At least you won't have far to walk if you feel seasick,' I quipped.

He said nothing.

Ah yes, that's where we part.

Martin embraced me, kissed me and held me tight for a very long time.

'Good bye, *hombre*,' he said, 'and good luck.'

'Don't soil those cut-off jeans!' I joked with a lump in my throat and jumped ashore with the rest of the well-wishers.

The boat slid away towards the Rio Negro's confluence with the Big One as Martin, the last of the passengers standing on deck, watched me, immobile, handsome and statuesque until the haze swallowed him abruptly. This is how Martin left my life and at the same time entered it forever, as a ghost. Occasionally I hear his voice in my head, just as we sat alone that night in the clearing, reminding me not to rationalise about legends, that European value judgements have no place in the raw, savage jungle. Yes, the Amazons exist, Martin. I owe it to you, for you opened my eyes which can never close again.

I am now a believer in the myths.

*****

In 1987, the last big gold rush of our times began in the mountains of the Serra Parima where fantastic gold and diamond deposits attracted 40,000 people in a few years and displaced the local Yanomani Indians, leading to massacres, *Time* magazine headlines and the swift issuing of protective decrees by Brazilian President Collor de Melo. It may be an irony to some, a coincidence to others, but I leave it to you, dear reader, to decide why these riches happened to be discovered exactly where Sir Walter Raleigh's quest for El Dorado pinpointed them 400 years ago.

And in 1994, in Kazakhstan, Central Asia, where Greek legend placed them, archaeologists discovered a series of graves. Not one, but several of the skeletons buried in full military regalia were women.

It is a pity we cannot tell if they had a breast cut off to better aim an arrow.

Chapter 3

No Faith, Law or Royalty (Fortaleza)

In the preface to the latest edition of the Spanish language dictionary *Clave*, none other than the great Gabriel García Márquez recalls a wonderful anecdote. He remembers reading the description of the colour yellow as a boy. *'The colour of lemons'*, said the very same dictionary in Márquez's youth. That confused him, for lemons in South America are green. Belying the late acceptance that Spanish has progressed way beyond the mother country, *Clave* has redefined yellow. *'It is the colour of gold'*, it says now – although my simple self would have opted for the colour of an egg yolk.

Travellers clamour for the frisson of the exotic; and yet an equal thrill comes when we stop noticing the differences and descry simple, common truths in mundane human behaviour. It's great when the lemons turn out to be yellow after all.

···

The Words You'll Need

artesanato = local crafts shop
bugueiro = the driver of a beach buggy
embalagem = packaging
falésia = cliff abruptly coming down to the sea
guarda-volumes = place where you store your valuables or clothes (not a coat-check as you'll see)
maloca = Indian hut
noite = night
Nordeste = the north-east of Brazil, from the state of Maranhão to the bottom of Bahia
pargo = a tasty fish like sea bass
pensão = small hotel, B&B
Sem açúcar = no sugar
Tudo bom? = expression close to the French 'ça va?' – the main greeting amongst Brazilians

···

Even on that imperialist Mercator-projection map one can't help noticing that Brazil is bigger than the continental United States. As the southern hemisphere is compressed, a comparison with Australia is much easier; Brazil wins again, and in this case we're talking *continent*. It didn't escape my attention that the flight from Rio to Fortaleza took me almost a quarter of the way back to London.

First impressions always lie, unless you are one of that breed of people who fall in love at first sight, buy a single after the first hearing and explode into gastronomic superlatives with the first smoulder of a barbecue. Now, I *am* like that – after I tasted my first caipirinha my aura could jump-start a lorry – and yet my first impression of Fortaleza was 'what a dump'. The drive to the old port of Iracema under another Brazilian white-hot sky (the city is equilatitudinal with Manaus) bypasses the posh dwellings of the neighbourhoods of Aldeota and Meireles and the eastern coastal strip and crosses the nondescript districts of Bom Futuro, José Bonifácio and the centre, which is best forgotten – I have. If I were a hitchhiker who had decided to stop and check out the town, I might have taken the first ride out: low-rise cement buildings with Amazonian standards of maintenance, bad roads, and stagnant pools by the roadside. Every town wears an outfit the first time you ramble down its streets. Put delicately, Fortaleza wasn't exactly wearing Lacroix for me.

A new name was staring down at me intriguingly from huge advertising billboards: 'Potiguar Oil', 'Potiguar Auto Services', Potiguar this, Potiguar that. Before I went to Fortaleza I had not heard the name. Now I have, and wish I were still blissful in my ignorance.

Fortaleza is the capital of the state of Ceará, more than four times the size of Belgium (a Belgium somehow emerging as the universal unit of measurement of countries, closely followed by Wales). It lies in the romantic Nordeste, where the cognoscenti believe that the true heart of Brazil is beating, and where some of the poorest people live – I wonder if the two are unconnected. Its long dry season may be great for the tourist, but in the even more arid interior it often spells death for the natives. The drought of 1877, followed by a huge famine and a spate of diseases, halved the city's original population of 120,000 souls, causing the Brazilian Emperor Dom Pedro II to burst into tears. No wonder the original natives turned to the sea to feed themselves. So much so that the other Tupi tribes called them shrimp-eaters, *potiguars*.

Ah, I hear you say.

You'll never find a bigger seafood eater in north London than yours truly, so this promise of shrimps, prawns, lobster, crayfish and crab kept me perky during the hot and miserable drive to my hotel; that and the unanimous approbation of everyone I had met who had been to Fortaleza: this was supposed to be a fun city.

I crossed my fingers.

*****

I had a huge room in *pensão* Ondas – and at \$15 the most expensive: TV, double bed, large wardrobe, a view of a small square at the edge of Iracema and a large bathroom with a shower.

Ahem, let me clear my throat, the *shower*.

Cheap showers in Brazil use an electric element for heat exchange, not a well-clad boiler. That means that a wire – with masking tape the only insulation – sticks out to just above your head (or below your eyes if you are that extra inch taller). It scared the beejesus out of me, especially since after my shower I turned the tap off and received a dull shock.

I put on my shorts and ran to Carlos at reception who could easily double for Danny de Vito.

'I got a shock from the shower,' I complained.

He came up and had a look.

'The floor is wet,' he scoffed.

'I know it is,' I erupted. 'It's *supposed* to be. This is the *bathroom*, isn't it?'

Carlos remained unperturbed.

'You touched the tap *and* the wall?'

'What do you mean?'

'If the floor is wet, you turn the tap like this,' he said, and switched the water off with the tips of his fingers. 'If you turn the tap like this,' he added and pretended to palm it so that he touched the wall, 'you create a circuit.'

I opened my mouth to request some capacitor-resistor exercises for a refresher course in Electrodynamics In Your Bathroom, but he was quicker off the mark.

'Are you going to Jericoacoara?'

Jericoacoara, which is a mouthful to say and a bugger to type, is consistently voted one of the top ten beaches in the world. Trouble is, along with Alex Garland's Richard and his demented backpackers in *The Beach*, you have to be mightily determined to set off for it. Jericoacoara ('the bay of the meadow of parrots' in Tupi) is a six-hour drive north of Fortaleza and a further 45 minutes by jeep or lorry. Once there, you are in a primitive paradise with lagoons, caves, dunes and no electricity or running water. There is a local legend that a cave in the vicinity houses a submerged city of riches where a beautiful princess languishes under a spell: she has the head and feet of a woman but the body of a snake, covered in golden scales. She is waiting for her hero who will sacrifice himself and shed his blood to turn her into a human again. The cave can actually be visited, although you must crawl on all fours to make any progress once inside – only those with a victim mentality need apply.

'We organise tours here in the hotel. We have a package that leaves tonight and arrives back Sunday.'

No good – I wanted to experience Fortaleza's infamous weekend nightlife.

'How about Canoa Quebrada instead?' he asked.

Canoa Quebrada had been a secret haunt of travellers in the 1980s and then – horror of horrors – the small fishing village was discovered by mass tourism. The story of its beaches could well have been that in Alex Garland's book, except that you need no secret map to get there: it's off a highway two hours south of Fortaleza, near the colonial town of Aracatí.

'We have a tour on Saturday.'

Good work Carlos: I had forgotten all about the electric shock, and I had a smile on my face because I was down for the day trip to Canoa Quebrada.

That smile was nearly wiped out when I made my way towards the brightly lit hotel skyline at Meireles Beach. The first part of the Avenida Beira Mar to the junction with Monsenhor Tabosa is a dark, drab walk with couples lollygagging in the shadowy recesses and prostitutes parading by the boulder breakers. Only when past the Hotel Praia did the full Fortaleza effervescence hit me: *artesanatos* on the beachfront, open-air restaurants, tourist nuclear families in shorts, sandals and prams, football under spotlights and the inescapable jostling throngs around fire-eaters and jongleurs. One short *caboclo* was ready to dive through a hoop on the other side of which stood a long sharp dagger, balanced blade upwards.

'Put more money in,' he kept urging us. 'But don't give me one real, don't give me two or five. I don't want silly money. I want you to give me ten reais *each*! We're talking about my *life* here!' Either he was an excellent con man with a direct line to the Almighty or a lapsed rain god, for once he had collected enough, a sudden tropical storm broke out and everyone ran for cover.

I entered my first Fortalezan fish restaurant for dinner, the Dom William on Beira Mar. I ordered lobster, shrimp and *sururu* in a mild coconut sauce, which was not unlike Jim's Thai curry in Rio without the chillies. *Sururu* are small mussel-like shellfish with long tails like needles. They look like, oh, large spermatozoa, and as they floated in the coconut sauce, a thousand tasteless jokes came to mind, most of them to do with the liquid assets of a sperm whale.

The rain stopped on cue when I finished, so I walked back towards Iracema and the Ponte Metálico or Ponte dos Ingleses, which is an imitation of an English seaside pier with attractions, kiosks and even more couples holding hands; Fortalezans seemed highly sexed even for Brazilians. I had a beer by a pavilion where a live band was playing *pagode*, one of the better exports of a country whose vast gamut of music still remains to be discovered by the world at large. *Pagode* is a cross between an old-fashioned foxtrot played at a fervent Brazilian tempo and a limberly *lambada* but, unlike the latter, it is more Latin-influenced, with a streak of Cuban cha-cha.

The rain started again – more of a shower than a storm. I pulled my chair under the roof of the pavilion into the middle of a group of sixth-formers. The guys, all handsome, wore no shirts or sandals; the girls, all beautiful, wore bright, tight dresses. The sound system was covered higgledy-piggledy with some plastic sheets for nominal protection. It was just me and the sixth-formers who cared to listen, but still the band played on. A lissom guy with a strong, defined body and his even more stunning girlfriend with a large, almost stuck-on bosom left their sheltered posts and started dancing on the ledge. The rain fell harder, drenching our dancers who were propelling their bodies in unison to the sensuous *pagode* beat. The girl might have been the winner of the night's wet T-shirt contest had there been one; her partner was devouring her with his eyes, his movements enhanced rather than hindered by the rhythm of the raindrops.

Oh, to be young and Brazilian …

Overnight a storm broke. I woke up at 4 a.m. and the street outside was flooded. It was good to see the odd couple – and an odd couple some were – running home in the downpour: it showed Fortaleza slept late in defiance of the elements. You would not believe my 'Wow!' next morning when I got up; all the water had evaporated, which gives you some insight into the prevailing Turkish bath conditions.

....

Things I Like About Brazil #3: Caipirinha

I've talked a lot about this very Brazilian cocktail, so I will give you the recipe:
1 lime (it pays to have a separate word for lemons that are green)
2 measures of cachaça (sugar-cane rum)
1–2 teaspoonfuls of sugar
crushed ice
Cut the lime into four and put in a whisky glass. Add the sugar. Mash the lime quarters coarsely. Add the cachaça. Fill the glass with crushed ice and stir well.

....

What to do on a Friday night?

Iracema was alive again. Unlike the vast expanse of Meireles, you walk the narrow streets shoulder to shoulder with other pedestrians and have to move chairs – and sometimes the occasional diner – from your way. I had hardly sat down on my spot by the pier listening to a Cat Stevens lookalike (version-before-conversion) playing John Denver soundalike songs, when a shower broke out again – is this how it's going to be? I pulled my chair under the pavilion roof.

And so did three guys whom I hadn't noticed before.

It was clear that one of them was stealing glances at me. He was in his early twenties, in faded jeans and a shirt with that distinctive red-and-white Yasser-Arafat-headscarf-cum-Italian-tablecloth pattern. I have one for my dishes, too – whoever has the world copyright on that design must be rolling in it.

'*Tudo bom?*' he asked me.

He looked like a taller version of my Spanish ex, which doesn't help you at all, I know, because you don't know him.

I pointed at the sky. 'Could be better,' I said.

We got talking. His name was Antônio. He was temping in the advert section for the local edition of the Brazilian magazine *Veja*. His two friends were Ab, a short, young guy and an older one, Vicente, who had a permanent who-am-I-why-am-I-here? expression.

Antônio was tipsy-to-drunk and little Ab seemed concerned.

'This is the first time Antônio's been out in weeks,' he said.

Oh. Was he ill?

'Not exactly,' said Ab.

'Ill? I *am* ill,' sighed Antônio.

Ab pinned him with his gaze. I ordered beers for everyone. Was Antônio well enough to drink?

'Yes, please,' said Antônio, avoiding Ab's eyes and, in anticipation of the order, gulped his beer in one.

'You seem like a nice bloke,' he continued. 'I think you'll understand. This is the first time I've been out since I broke up with my boyfriend of five years.'

John, this only happens in your stories.

'I sympathise,' I said. 'Though I split with my last boyfriend four years ago.'

Antônio turned triumphantly to Ab: 'I – told – you,' he said, emphasising every word.

Why did they split up?

Antônio switched to passable English.

'We had become friends,' he said. 'Do you know what that means?'

'Yes,' I answered. 'No more sex.'

Antônio's eyes lit up.

'Is it the same in England then?'

'Yes,' I said. 'It's the same the world over.'

We all pondered over that.

'And you two?' I asked Ab and Vicente. 'Are you together?'

'Since Wednesday,' chirped Ab. 'This is the second time we've met.'

Out of the corner of my eye, I noticed that Vicente seemed a little less enthusiastic.

'And what do *you* do?' I asked him.

Vicente pointed at the pavilion behind us.

'I own the bookshop,' he said.

I turned around. I hadn't noticed that the small circular pavilion housed a book store.

The beers came, travel stories started, and Ab became more concerned with Antônio.

'I've travelled to São Luis, Manaus, Acre, Bolivia, Titicaca, Puno, Cuzco, Lima and back,' Antônio swaggered with bravado.

'How?' I asked.

'By car,' he replied. 'Me and my ex. We drove all the way.'

Only someone who hasn't experienced the roads in Amazonia would be so cocky. From Ab's stunned expression, I gathered that maybe even São Luis, the next big town up, was a porkie.

'I've also travelled to Europe,' Antônio said. 'I have been to London and Holland.'

'Oh,' I said, 'where did you stay in London?'

Antônio squinted.

'West Sussex,' he said. 'My grandmother lives there.'

'Which town?' I asked.

He looked at me.

'The town of West Sussex!'

Oh dear.

'And then I went to Holland. Nijmegen.'

Choosing such an obscure place smacked of veracity. *Or not?*

'What did you do in Nijmegen?' I asked.

'I lived with some friends,' he said. 'And then I took the train to Lyon. In France.'

Ab looked as if he wanted the ground to swallow him up. 'Antônio,' he pleaded, 'don't drink any more.'

'But because it was all flooded,' continued Antônio, 'the train couldn't go in a straight line ...'

That boy must have stopped fingering the dyke.

'... so we travelled via Germany and Switzerland.'

'Antônio,' I asked, 'did you get on the right train?'

'Yeah, yeah,' he said. 'But everything was flooded. So we made a big detour.'

'By train?'

'By train.'

I could picture those Germans, quickly laying the track for the diverted Dutch trains. Such efficiency!

'We're going,' said Ab, standing up simultaneously with Vicente. 'And you owe me some money from yesterday.'

'Here, take this,' said Antônio, giving him his keys and bankcard. 'Use it and take out the twenty reais. I'll spend the night with John.'

The presumptuous effrontery stuck in my throat.

'Take care of him,' said Ab as he winked, leaving me with an Antônio who was becoming more and more legless by the minute.

'Do you like me?' he asked.

'Of course,' I said so non-committally that, even drunk, Antônio looked at me trying to second-guess the sentiment. 'But tomorrow I have to get up early to go to Canoa Quebrada.'

Antônio grasped the sour-tasting reality. 'Can I at least walk you home?' he asked, sobering up. 'As a friend?'

Now that was sweet.

....

Things I Don't Like About Brazil #3: The Portions

A typical prawn dish contains at least twenty-five (of the King variety and not the stunted North Atlantic subspecies) plus rice, manioc flour and sauces. In Brazil you use a small plate to serve yourself, because chefs realise that putting a gigantic kitchen platter immediately in front of their clients would be a source of grand embarrassment.

I have on occasion battled Herculeanly with the terrifying amount of food served in Brazilian restaurants, mainly because of pangs of conscience (all these poor people around and I can't finish my dish?) but the pangs often turned to tummy spasms before the meal was over. It took me ages and eventual linguistic insight to start asking for the 'executivo'. You see, in Brazil, only executives on business trips eat alone – the faithful ones, at least. Females are naturally chaperoned, and every male worth his salt eats with a female companion. It may not be his girlfriend; hell, our male will choose his mother or sister or – dammit – his unmarried second cousin, but not for him the humiliation of dining solo in public.

....

– 13 –

I didn't make it to Canoa Quebrada. At 7 a.m. the street outside was flooded again. Plus, as far as I could see the horizon had taken the dog for a walk. Carlos was irritated.

'You only want to sleep,' he said. 'You always miss breakfast.'

'Hey, the weather's bad! I have an excuse!'

'THIS TIME ONLY!' shouted Carlos, acting every inch like his alter-ego in *Taxi*. 'We have another excursion on Monday. You'll be going then!'

The sky was overcast, but the cloud-covered sun still felt strong. How about a swim at the long stretch of Praia do Futuro, which takes up the whole of the east coast of Fortaleza and runs for miles? It is here that Orson Welles shot his 1942 film *It's All True*, which was thought to be lost, but resurfaced in 1993 with footage of the Rio *Carnaval* – in colour! It is a patchwork of stories, and in the final piece, 'Four Men on a Raft', Welles deals with the story of four Brazilian fishermen from this area who completed a 1,650-mile voyage around the Brazilian coast all the way to Rio to meet the dictator Getúlio Vargas in order to protest about the living conditions in the Nordeste. Despite acting like a vandal in that Copacabana hotel suite, Orson did have an eye for a cinematic setting and in Praia do Futuro he struck gold.

A Brazilian beach is composed of sea, sand and *barracas*, a cross between a French deck-chair rental, a Greek taverna and a Spanish tapas bar. You sit free on the armchairs, but you are obliged to consume something. And when you have a dip, the hawk-eyed proprietor-cum-waiter keeps an eye on your belongings, for which you gratefully give him a tip.

On cue, the *barraca* boy stood next to me.

'Where are you from?' he asked.

You are never alone in Brazil.

'Greece,' I said to disorient him.

'Greece,' he mused, clearly not knowing where it was. And then pointing at my can of beer. 'Do you have those there?'

'Beer?' I asked. 'Of course we have beer.'

'No, I mean the *embalagem*,' he said. 'Do you have cans?'

'Cans? Of course we have cans,' I replied.

This was a revelation to him.

'Is it the same in Greece as in Fortaleza then?'

'Well, we have different brands of beer,' I said. 'But we have cans.'

'But you don't have Antártica,' he scored triumphantly.

'No,' I conceded, 'we don't.'

That seemed to satisfy him.

'Be careful with the sun,' he advised me. 'It's cloudy, but the sun is still strong.'

'Oh, I don't burn,' I replied, and I knew immediately I was betting against the Almighty. I lay down, put on a Tidy Trax compilation tape and closed my eyes.

Guess what: Almighty: 1, John: 0.

*****

BC – that is, Before Cabral – the coastal South American Indians were Tupi/Guarani speakers. The largest and most organised of the Tupi tribes were the Potiguar. It is estimated that they numbered about 100,000 – close to the population of London at the time. Since London numbers about 8 million souls today you would expect them to have bred to this number. Wrong. They are down to 6,120 (1995 count), and they live in the municipality of Mamanguape, on the Baía da Traição in Paraíba. They are all assimilated and speak Portuguese; their language is extinct.

Which is why I wish I was still blissful in my ignorance.

When Brazil was discovered there were 1,500 languages arranged into four major families: the Tupi/Guarani, the Gê, the Carib and the Aruak, with a further 25-odd languages having unclassified roots. There are some words from Tupi in English: *jaguar, cougar* and some from Carib, most notably the word *hammock*. It was the Tupi who first came into contact with the Europeans. In their language the Gê were called 'Tapuia', a term also used by the Portuguese explorers. The fact that 'Tapuia' also means 'enemy' provides an insight into basic human nature, for its exact translation is *'they who speak another tongue'*.

Only about 175 Indian languages remain today, and the Indians who made up 100 per cent of Brazil's population have now been reduced to a quarter of one per cent. It is telling that the two Amerindian languages with the most speakers are Ticuna, an isolated Amazonian language, and Carib Macuxí. Why? Because these tribes did not come into contact with the Europeans until much, much later. The Potiguar who resisted the Portuguese, the French and the Dutch – by playing off one invader against the other – are all extinct, along with the Caeté, Tobajara, Anacé, Cariri, Paiacú, Tarairu, Guengeun, Tremembé, Jucá, Aranhí, Gamella, Urubu-Kaapor, Aranhi, Vidal, Guanaré, Axemi, Tembé, Turiwara, Jacunda, Tenetehara, Pacajá, Uanapú and Camarapim – and these just in the north-eastern corner above Pernambuco, where I was passing through. The Holocaust and slavery considered, the crime of the last millennium has to be the annihilation of the inhabitants of Amerigo's continent. Yes, there were special factors that made the Holocaust particularly gruesome, most of all the dreadful realisation that even technologically advanced populations – I hate to use the term 'civilised' – can act irrationally when imbued by hate. Yes, the legal, commercial and ethical framework which put slavery in place and made it flourish for centuries was exceptionally abhorrent, if only because of its religious hypocrisy. But for sheer numerical scale no crime can compare with the genocide of the native Americans of the South and North which continued well into the twentieth century.

*****

By the Ponte dos Ingleses a solitary Vicente was sipping a beer. As I approached, he looked away nervously.

Was he avoiding me? Why?

I waved and made sure our eyes met.

Vicente had to acknowledge me.

'Did you go with Antônio last night?'

I shook my head. He laughed.

'He was drunk, wasn't he?'

I winced in agreement.

'Is Ab here?' I asked, noticing the second half-empty glass of beer.

He looked me right in the eye.

'No,' he said. 'My boyfriend is, though.'

He pointed at a guy, about the same age as Vicente and about the same cut, talking to the barman.

I see.

'Come to the bookshop sometime during the day and I'll explain,' he said.

'I certainly will,' I replied. 'You give good gossip. Are you coming to Broadway?'

'No, I'm too tired.'

You should be.

Club Broadway in Aldeota, a cool, shaded and leafy middle-class suburb close to the restaurants and clubs of Meireles, was a knockout. Not only was it plush, not only was it huge, but the music was the best I heard in the Nordeste.

Let's start with size, my favourite. There was a large dance floor, which hid an even larger bar behind it and a dimly lit garden. Just the chill-out area was bigger than many a club in Rio or São Paulo. Fortaleza should be a sleepy provincial town, but its nightlife truly transcends its size. It never stops: every night is party night: an air-conditioned Mercedes-Benz from the agency *Fortaleza By Night* can take you to the Clube do Vaqueiro on Wednesdays, to Cajueiro Drink's on Sundays, to the Tropicalia comic show on Tuesdays and to the *axé* rhythms of Bahia in the Barraca Chico de Caranguejo on Thursdays. There's music in the piano bar on Avenida Beira Mar and the odd *barraca* beach fiesta every night. Plus, there is the most famous Monday in Brazil: the Pirata dance in Iracema.

I like this. I like what I see.

And I liked what I heard. The DJs were good, very good: I found myself tapping my foot to an extraordinary version of Fatboy Slim's 'You've Come A Long Way Baby' mixed with The Fall (The Fall in Fortaleza?) and a twenty-minute mix of Yazoo's 'Don't Go' with techno break beats. However, the big moment came when the crowd started belly-dancing languidly to Arab Maghrebi house, the background music of my Nordeste memories: 'El Arbi', a choral, murmured, plaintive melody – I prefer the version by Khaled to the more traditional one by Chakibib – 'Fata Morgana' by the Dissidenten (1980s mix) and 'Simarik' by Tarkik, a most catchy tune that could have been the Israeli entry in Eurovision had it not been, well, Turkish.

I first met a short, scraggy and blond Nordestino, the Franco-Dutch excursions evident in his genetic make-up. He was shy and came from the backlands, the *sertão*, in deepest Ceará bordering Pernambuco. I understood nothing else he said – his singing Nordeste accent was lost in the disco beat. After a while he told me that it was his first time in a gay bar. Some people may find this a turn-on, but it seemed like a pendulous weight of responsibility, so I retreated diplomatically with my textbook London excuses. ('Sorry, I just remembered I have a boyfriend back home.')

Then there was the PE instructor from Belêm, or so he said. He didn't have a place to stay over the weekend – he was moving into a new house on Monday. I was wondering whether I should ask him home, as we were touching third base in the garden, when I found his hand in my pocket. I'm sure he was trying to arouse me rather than rob me, but I quickly made my normal tactful retreats. ('Damn this T-shirt, it's so crumpled. I must iron it at once.')

Towards five in the morning I met Júlio. He was bleach-beach blond, rough-looking, but exceedingly generous (code for 'he bought me a drink'). His apartment was nearby, and he asked me to join him for a post-club chill-out.

I was in no mood for a big afterparty. 'Just the two of us?' I asked.

'And my flatmate,' he said, pointing at a girl.

I liked the girl instantly (code for 'she paid me a compliment') – before the big revelation came, that is.

'Why, didn't Júlio tell you? We're going out together.'

'What?' I stumbled. 'I thought Júlio was interested in me.'

'Oh, he is. We're both bisexual. We like threesomes.'

This time my excuses were more refined. 'THREESOME!' I cried. *'That's* the word I was looking for in that crossword! I must dash home and finish it.'

As I slipped outside into the six o'clock daylight, I noticed that for the first morning since I arrived, the skies weren't flooding the town.

Weather had turned at last.

*****

Why have I chosen to concentrate on the Potiguar out of all the tribes? I could say it is mainly because the name is used in the Nordeste as a sign of belonging and pride in one's roots. I could claim that it's because they were the most organised and the first to encounter and fight the European colonialists – that Spanish Pinzón expedition of January 1500 captured thirty-six of them *'bigger than large Germans'*. However, it is a sexual practice of the Potiguar that aroused – if I may use that word – my interest. Amerigo Vespucci first described it: *'[The Indians] have another custom which seems incredible. Being libidinous, the women make their husbands' members swell so much that they look like those of the animals: they do this by the artifice of the bite of poisonous insects. As a result, many men lose them altogether and are left as eunuchs.'*

This poisonous insect seems to be a giant millipede, black and hairy with a red head if you are curious and yes, Indians apparently still use it to enlarge their sexual organs. I am puzzled that Western science and entrepreneurial spirit haven't caught up with *that.* But don't try this at home, children; beware of what another early traveller, Gabriel Soares de Sousa, said: *'They suffer great pains from this during more than six months that they continue to corrode [their genitals]. In the end their prick becomes so large and deformed that the women cannot wait for it or endure it.'* And the Jesuit Padre Anchieta left this gem for posterity: *'The Indians customarily apply [it] to the genital parts and thus excite them for sensual pleasure. These swell in such a way that in three days they blister. It often results that the prepuce is split in various places and the penis itself contracts an incurable corruption.'*

That, in the immortal words of Beavis and Butthead, sucks.

*****

Bora-Bora was a large outdoors club, half covered in thatch, half open and sandy with a live band which had started a few hours before I arrived and would be playing on for a couple more afterwards. I wore shorts, sandals and a T-shirt and felt overdressed. Most people were still in their Speedos, straight from the day's swim. I tried to check if Ab and Antônio were there (not) but then I met João. In the whole of Brazil, I have never been in a town where it's so easy to talk to strangers.

I was taken in by the brown-haired, brown-eyed João, who would look more at home in Nice than the Nordeste; his surname, which escapes me, was French. The French occupied Rio de Janeiro for a time, dreaming of an Antarctic France and founded São Louis in Maranhão to establish an Equatorial France with 500 settlers sent by Maria de Médicis; of those pompous pretensions only Cayenne remains. It was European dynastic considerations that extinguished the superpower antagonism in the South Atlantic. The Spanish absorbed Portugal for two generations when King Sebastião died childless. The French withdrew because of the marriage of Ana Maria, the daughter of the Spanish king Felipe III to Louis XIII of France. That only left the Dutch fighting everybody else, and for a short period they had the upper hand – but I'm rushing too far ahead.

João could be a son of recently arrived French immigrants; but it was far more romantic to have stumbled upon a genuine descendent of those early daring pirates, so I didn't ask. I looked at his angelic face and tried to imagine his *métier*. What would the descendant of pirates be doing for a living?

'I'm a hairdresser,' he smiled.

My reaction must have been all too obvious, for he rolled his eyes and asked: 'Is it the same in England?'

'Prime gay profession,' I replied. 'It's the same the world over.'

'I wonder why,' he said. 'I share a house with five others. They're all hairdressers and they're all gay.'

'It's part of the secret homosexual agenda,' I replied. 'First we'll annihilate their hair.'

I spent the rest of the evening with João and great fun it was, too. We drank copious amounts of beer and caipirinha. João offered to buy me one first.

'*Sem açúcar,*' I pleaded.

'Oh,' said João. 'Are you diabetic?'

If there was any doubt that João was a true Brazilian, it was dispelled now. No one in the country can accept that bitterness is a taste to savour. Brazilian dentists must be raking it in.

We chatted, we danced and we flirted. But João was tired. He'd been working 12-hour days and the next day we both had to wake up at 7 a.m.

I was finally going to Canoa Quebrada.

– 14 –

Our modern concept of the beach holiday stems from the seventies when the alternative lifestylers started seeking peace, love and understanding on this earth and this lifetime. Beaches offer the chance of introspection (the white noise of the waves quietly breaking on the seashore), relaxation (the eye focusing on the vast marine horizon) and above all hedonism: the sun's rays, the body's sexy tan, the water's womb-like embrace. First there were the beaches close to home: St Tropez and Ibiza, Essaouira and Mykonos, where nude swimming, carefree living and dope smoking begat today's megaclogged superdestinations. In the 1980s it was further afield – Thailand comes to mind along with the Caribbean; Cancun and Pattaya became examples to be avoided.

Brazil's own hippies discovered Ceará and its beaches: in Morro Branco to the east of Fortaleza the first multicoloured *falésias* capture the eye in the 'twelve-colour beach'; Aguas Belas is perched on the mouth of a river with an ever-changing course; Caponga with its 50-foot-high sand-dunes; Iquapé where the fishermen will sell you a kilo of fish for five dollars; Ponta Grossa, vast and deserted, its rocks forming natural sculptures; the S-shaped mouth of the Aracau River at Torrões and Almofala; the legendary Jericoacoara, still without electricity at the turn of the twenty-first century, plus Canoa Quebrada, a prototype of exemplary beach beauty.

My co-travellers were a wealthy, thirty-something middle-class bunch of Paulistas on holiday. There was Rubens and his wife who lived near Congonhas. Rubens, rarely seen without a beer bottle in his hand, could have emerged from a painting by his namesake who loved dimples of fat in his women and layers of lard in his men (that was the only room in the Prado I ran out of, shrieking). His wife was pretty and petite and a fellow screamer – forgive the pun – as I discovered during the scary buggy rides. There was also a banker who was like a fish out of water without his fiancée; they had not been able to synchronise their holiday weeks: oh, the indignity of eating alone. Finally there was quick and quirky Dora, a live-wire lawyer working for A Very Important Computer Company.

Canoa Quebrada is one of those lovely villages where young, dope-smoking tourists wake up late, move on to the nudist beach (where? where?) from midday till sunset and then frequent the small, lively, friendly and picturesque bars, drinking until dawn. It seems Canoa Quebrada has been 'discovered' in a way that has not spoiled its landscape but has certainly enhanced its nightlife. There are irregular sand-dunes, lagoons and bays where *barracas* offer cheap seafood and *jangadas* are moored on the beach in the same way since time immemorial. There are clay houses with makeshift pole hedges tended by black mommas, who have siestas in their rocking chairs. But what makes the area unique and appeals to the hippy side of our inner child are the colours: there are various shades of red, brown, yellow-ochre and coal-black sand which contrast with the deep blue of the ocean and the iridescent cyan of a cloudless sky. The *falésias* – sandy erosion cliffs – slide down abruptly to the coast in a technicolor drop, like the white cliffs of Dover on acid.

....

Nothing this day created as much astonishment on board our ship amongst those who had not been before upon this coast as the jangadas *sailing about in all directions. These are simply rafts of six logs of a peculiar species of light timber lashed or pinned together; a large latine sail; a paddle used as a rudder; a sliding keel let down between the two centre logs; a seat for the steersman and a long forked pole upon which is hung the vessel containing water, the provisions, etc. These rude floats have a most singular appearance at sea, no hull being apparent even when near them. They are usually managed by two men and go closer to the wind than any description of vessel.*

– Henry Koster, defining a *jangada* in the 1820s

....

We climbed down to the beach as the local Potiguar descendants were towing a *jangada* aground using logs as primitive rollers. We sat down by a *barraca* where the waiter demonstrated the glorious three-in-one menu: *pargo*, lobster and king prawns.

I wished I had not taken my large camera along. Where to leave it?

'There is a *guarda-volumes*,' Dora informed me.

I walked up to the bar, asked for and obtained a locker key. I took my camera out, unloosened my money-belt and gave it to the attendant.

'That was quick,' Dora commented as I lay on my towel next to her.

A waiter came running with my camera and money-belt. He was frozen with fear.

'You forgot these,' he said.

'I thought you locked them in,' Dora said, perplexed.

I stood up. The waiters were looking at the gringo who had left his valuables at the counter.

'You are supposed to lock them yourself, silly!' Dora told me. 'You do *not* casually hand away your money-belt like that.'

'I thought it worked like a coat-check,' I mumbled.

'It's different in Brazil,' she scolded me. 'You shouldn't trust anyone where money is concerned.'

Green lemon check: there is paranoia in paradise, after all.

I sat by an old man who was creating sand landscape paintings by skilfully arranging the coloured sand – some natural, some dyed – with a long needle in a clear bottle. I adored them. I wanted a large bottle with an elaborate sand painting.

'Twelve reais,' said the old man.

'What?' I heard the voice of Dora behind me. 'This is robbery. Five reais only.'

I looked up. Twelve reais was not much …

'For five you can have this smaller bottle,' said the old man.

'I don't want the smaller bottle,' I said, looking obliquely at Dora.

'OK, six,' she said.

'Ten.'

'Eight for the two.'

'Done.'

It was all uttered in a time-honoured *staccato allegro* (*ma non troppo*) and it was over in seconds.

*****

The Tupi language did not use the letters F, L or R (rolling R, that is); in Portuguese and Spanish these are pronounced as Fé, Ley and Rey, which translates as 'faith', 'law' and 'royalty', to keep the translation rhyme alive. There: the lack of consonants matching the perceived lack of virtues in a nutshell. Vespucci himself wrote: '*They have no laws or faith and live according to nature. They do not recognise the immortality of the soul; they have among them no private property because everything is common; they have no boundaries or kingdoms and provinces and no king! They obey nobody, each is lord unto himself. They have no justice and no gratitude which to them is unnecessary because it is not part of their code [...] They are a very prolific people* [he means that they have many offspring] *but have no heirs because they hold no property.'*

This lack of ambition and competitiveness touched the sixteenth-century clerics. The values of the Indians seem to have come straight out of Genesis in a society that had not tasted the serpent's apple; after all, they had no idea of their own nakedness (of course, missionaries soon put paid to *that*). Indians hunted, had sex, played and partook in hallucinogenic ceremonies. They had no desire to amass fortunes, nor obligation to work for others. The sixteenth-century capitalists who wanted them to toil in their sugar plantations despaired: enslaved Indians either escaped or committed suicide slowly by eating earth, salt and mud. So black slaves started being transported to America; Africa was still Old World with Old World mentalities. They, at least, *knew* what work was.

The French philosophers were the most impressed. Voltaire, Rousseau, Rabelais – all idealised Amerindian society. Montesquieu rightly concluded that because the Indians had no possessions there was no inequality and thus no robbery or money-related crime. Diderot in his *Encyclopaedia* praised their innocence about natural acts such as sex, *'which involved no false modesty'*. Montaigne wrote an imaginary essay between a Tupi chieftain and King Charles IX where the former's views sound positively insurrectional in the monolithic *ancien régime*.

Nevertheless, the most enduring legacy of the Amerindians was the ritual of bathing in the sea: the roots, if you like, of the modern beach holiday. Swimming also kept their bodies clean and fragrant, unlike the smelly, unwashed Europeans who viewed immersion in water as a violation of their constitution. As Henry Koster observed: *'Though the lower class of Brazilians of all castes have many dirty customs allied to those of savage life, still they are remarkably clean in their persons; one of the greatest inconveniences of a situation when a Brazilian complains of the place he happens to reside in, is the want of a river or pool of water in the neighbourhood for the purpose of bathing.'* Indeed, when the Brazilians started building their new capital Brasília in the middle of a plateau, the first thing they did was create an artificial lake.

Dora woke me up from my reverie, lazing as I was in the sun like the natives of Brazil taught us to.

'Are you coming to the buggy?' she asked.

Normally an open-back buggy sits four plus the driver. We were five, so my right leg had to hang out dangerously and my grip was tenuous at best. Our *bugueiro* – a special breed of *Homo Nordeste*, who thinks he is Ayrton Senna, acts as if he is Ayrton Senna and forgets what happened to Ayrton Senna – started as he finished: foot down as far as the pedal could go.

'Give it some gas. Give it some gas,' Rubens kept crying from the safety of the front seat while the rest of us were holding on for dear life. We drove up and down dune upon dune in all possible permutations: like a catamaran in a stormy sea, like motorcycle showmen pinned down by centripetal forces ready for the *salto mortale*, like Olympic ski jumpers through the air. Riding a buggy is experiencing an endless, do-it-yourself rollercoaster. After a frantic spell of about ten or fifteen minutes, we stopped by a huge ridge with a thirty-foot square drop. A tent housing some soft-drink sellers provided some shade. We looked down just in time to see a kid sitting on a board sliding down the drop into a small puddle at the bottom.

'Sand surfing. One real a go,' said a woman.

Rubens decided to try.

'Lean back,' she said, 'and keep your hands on the ground either side of the board. If you don't, you'll fall.'

Rubens tried to stick to the rules in vain: he rolled and splashed into the water like a sack of potatoes. As he got up and started the long climb up the sandbank using a chain, the rest of us shook our heads politely and closed our ears to the woman's siren enticements to follow suit. I can tell undignified when I see it.

A stop at a reggae bar by a shallow lagoon proved more popular. There were four other buggies there with their passengers dancing in the water, as if attempting aqua aerobics of the unsynchronised kind. I stood under a watermill-cum-ecoshower and chilled. This is as far as fabness can extend without being elevated into a daydream.

Our buggy ride resumed, we travelled miles upon miles of coastline, passing the fishermen's rustic houses, the 900-apartment luxury condominium site of Porto de Canoas (a tragedy) and the nudist beach (where? where?). When we arrived after one hour and forty reais lighter – great value – we were high on adrenaline and very, very hungry. As I took my first bite of my 12-inch lobster, I was grinning like a Cheshire Cat. I made annoying whistling sounds by sucking dry all the crustacean parts except that foul-looking stomach – my autopsy revealed that the lobster had eaten something green and slimy within the last 24 hours.

'Where are you off to tonight?' Dora asked me.

I was going to Pirata's for the evening.

'Watch out. There are many prostitutes who prey on men,' everyone warned me in unison, like a Greek chorus.

*****

No Faith, Law or Royalty: what nonsense. Of course the Indians had laws, believed in gods and were governed by chiefs. The idyllic descriptions, mostly provoked by the sight of so many naked women, were claptrap. Although the Indians of Brazil did not have a society in the manner of the Aztecs, the Mayas or the Incas, they formed tribal groups centred upon reservations with long, communal houses presided over by a chief who achieved his position by showing valour and judgement. They had a *pagé*, a witch-doctor, frequently an effeminate homosexual, who kept the jungle devils at bay with rattles on his ankles and cured diseases with herbs or by sexual intercourse with his patients – males and females alike.

The Indians also smoked; as a result the most rigorous opponents of tobacco were not twentieth-century Californians, but sixteenth-century Jesuit priests. The first Bishop of Brazil, Pero Fernandes Sardinha was sent to Bahia in 1551 and started admonishing the settlers for 'imitating the heathen' – which, in the coded Catholic sin-book meant smoking tobacco. But, as we know, the addiction is strong. The Capuchin priest d'Évreux describes how an Indian sentenced to die tied over the mouth of a cannon asked for a last puff and how, when his remains were found, his right hand was still clutching the pipe. I think all smokers can empathise with *that*.

That first bishop – the grand polemicist of smoking – set sail for Portugal to complain to the king in 1556, but his ship was wrecked near present-day Alagoas and the bishop was captured by the Caeté, the 'men of the forest'.

They ate him.

There was real bad karma in Paradise, and it was not tobacco, religious naivety or shamelessness in sex. Most Tupi tribes practised ritual cannibalism. Their life, although free of money-related crime, was far from being non-violent. Each tribe had a demarcated territory, and raids against other tribes were the norm. There were vendetta wars to avenge the capture and slaughter of some of their own by other tribes – an ever-expanding vicious circle of permanent war and fury. Raids had one purpose: to capture prisoners and eat them. Once caught, a prisoner was ritually goaded, humiliated and then fed and fattened like a turkey. On the specified day and time, he was brought to the place of his slaughter as the women ran about boasting how they would gorge on him. He was forced to tend his own cooking fire. A woman would bring the ritual slaughter baton, the *yware-pemme*, to the designated executioner who would arrive with his face and arms dyed red with *urucu* dye.

'I am he that will kill you, since you and my people have slain and eaten many of my friends,' he would address the prisoner.

The latter was expected to act defiantly: 'When I'm dead, I shall still have many to avenge my death.'

Upon this, the warrior would hold him down with his foot and beat out his brains with the sacrificial club.

The women would then take the body, rub, boil, skin and joint it; the head was given to the executioner who kept the skull as a trophy. The prisoner's flesh was divided amongst the families where it was hung for a day. A big feast would follow. Hans Staden, a German prisoner who escaped this fate by losing weight through a self-imposed diet and by eventually turning native, wrote a remarkable travelogue: '*They eat the innards and also the flesh on the skin, and the tongue, and they let the children eat what they especially enjoy […] Although they all confess that this human flesh is marvellously good and delicate, nevertheless they feast on it more in vengeance than taste […] their main purpose in gnawing the dead down to their bones is to fill the living with fear and horror. Everything that can be found in the bodies of these prisoners is completely eaten by them – from the extremities of the toes right up to the nose, ears and crown of the head. I except, however, the brain which they do not touch.*'

All feasted – all but one. If proof be needed that there was a gut feeling somewhere that the killing of a prisoner and his eating was, well, *wrong*, if I may use this portentous word, in their eyes as well as ours, check this out: the executioner retired to his hammock, abstained from eating the meat and fasted. Cannibalism was the big black spot on the Indian lifestyle and served as the justification used by the Europeans for the enslavement and eventual annihilation of the natives; the Romans had used a similar excuse against the Celts. These were just wars, said the nobles and the priests, and could any be more just than against the peccant Caeté who dared boil our bishop?

The lemons in South America were well and truly green; genocide could safely begin.

No other day exemplifies what is best about Fortaleza than its Monday night. Pirata's is a big outdoor club with a stage, a large dancing area and an aged galleon replica outside. On Monday, traditionally a dead day in Brazil's nightlife, it explodes with the sounds of *forró*, a mutual boy-girl lapdance complete with bosoms touching, hips undulating and legs intertwining. There are two versions of the etymology of the word *forró*: the colourful one is that it started in Natal where the US had a naval base during the Second World War. The American Navy organised balls 'for all' – that is, sailors and locals – and *'forró'* is a corruption of that word. The more mundane version comes from sociologists who claim that it stems from *'forrobodó'* which means confusion or disorder. That killjoy etymology has been adopted by the grand *Novo Aurélio* dictionary, but by none of the Brazil travel guides. Yet the word is documented in the nineteenth century and appears as *'forrobodança'* in a review dated 1913 as a more aristocratic dance than Rio's contemporary *chorão*. The popular and widespread belief has emerged because of a hit, *'For All Para Todos'* released in 1982 by Geraldo Azevedo: if it's in the charts, it must be the truth. Never mind that in Brazilian Portuguese the double R is pronounced as 'H' and if the term had come from 'for all' it would be written and pronounced *foró*. Brazilians are perfectly able to pronounce the R between vowels, but choose to pronounce this one as *fohó* and spell it accordingly.

Whatever its origin, the ball at Pirata's was awe-inspiring in its vivacity. Yes, it cost fifteen reais to get in, quite steep in Fortaleza; yes, there were only two people preparing caipirinha for 1,500 and it took ages to get served, but the frenetic dancing to a live band with hundreds of couples was exhilarating.

I was swept off my feet by Miranda.

'Carmen Miranda?' I joked.

'You are foreign,' she answered back. 'Everyone makes the same joke.'

I was flattered, but weary. I remember what I thought, spurred on by the memories of the Canoa Quebrada gang: she is a pro and she picked me up. Nothing could have been further from the truth. Miranda wanted someone to dance with, to show a foreigner how to wiggle his bottom in her town. She proceeded to drag me to the dance floor, not caring whether I could limber down to *forró*. She was so confident that a man, any man, she danced with would rise to the challenge that her positivity rubbed off on me. I can't remember what she really looked like. She was in her twenties, short and nimble with long black hair, but the particular grey cells which stored her face image must have burnt out since I spent a small fortune in Pirata's drinking as if prohibition had been declared for the next day.

Green ferocious seas of my native land, where the jandaia sings within the carnauba fronds;
green seas which gleam like liquid emeralds in the rays of the rising sun hugging fair beaches shaded by coconut trees;
be serene green seas and stroke sweetly the impetuous waves so that the doughty boat can gently slide on the water's blossom.

I have no idea whether I made a fool of myself or not – I hope not for she hung around with me for hours, and then came back for more; and not once did she even ask me for a drink (I bought her a few, unprompted) or what hotel I was in, or even when I was leaving town, bless her.

My own Iracema …

Iracema the virgin with lips of honey, with hair darker than the graúna's wings and longer than her own frame cut like a palm tree.
The jati's honeycomb was not as sweet as her smile; nor did the fragrant vanilla in the forest scent like the perfume of her breath.

Ceará is the setting of Brazil's Adam and Eve primal romance, José de Alencar's Indianist epic poem, *Iracema* – 'honeylips' in Tupi. José de Alencar was a native of Ceará and one of the nineteenth-century Brazilian romanticists who wanted to cut off the Portuguese influence and amalgamate the native and the European. This, the second of Alencar's Amerindian trilogy composed of *Guarani* (1857), *Iracema* (1865) and *Ubirajara* (1874), is a South American Pocahontas fairytale: Indian maiden meets gentlemanly European captain; Indian maiden falls in love and saves European captain's life; European captain dumps Indian maiden who bears his kid and dies.

Alcides Villaça, a Brazilian critic, wrote that *Iracema* has been categorised as an '*Indianist novel, Brazilian legend, prose poem, romantic epic, American fantasy, Tupi Indian pastoral, Romanesque myth or lyrical novel*'. *Iracema* can be read at many levels and is Brazil's most enduring literary myth; the symbolism of the Tabajara sacred virgin personifying an idyllic past who elopes with the Portuguese captain and gives birth to a son, combining his parents' backgrounds, is an allegory of the birth and development of Brazil itself. The ultimate skill of Alencar, one of the master wordsmiths of the Portuguese language, is to have combined fact – Martim Soares, the captain, his Tupi bosom friend Poti, the Indian chief Irapuã of the Tabajara are all historical figures – and lyrical fantasy to produce a literary original. Ultimately the success of a parable is in its spread amongst popular culture: like *Tarzan* or *Dracula*, not all of us have read the novel but we sure as hell know the plot. From Pará to Porto Alegre, Brazilians believe that Iracema's misfortunes were real: her story is now history, for people demand symbols to revolve around.

By now you may have noticed that Iracema is also an anagram of America.

*****

I entered Vicente's bookshop and said hello and goodbye. I'd be leaving in less than an hour.

'So what's the story?' I asked.

He took a big breath as if wanting to unburden himself.

'It started last Wednesday. I met Ab in a bar and we went home together. I thought he was a one-night stand, but we saw each other again on Friday, and I haven't been able to take my mind off him since.'

'The problem is you have a boyfriend.'

Vicente looked up.

'The problem is that neither Ab nor my boyfriend know about each other.'

Oh dear.

'Which makes you the only person to know about both.'

Oh dear.

'That Friday when we met you, we went to see a friend of his, and there was someone who vaguely knows me – and that's it. Nothing has come back to me, so he may have kept his mouth shut.'

Not likely – I would have gossiped.

'And then, Ab came here yesterday, although I expressly asked him not to. My boyfriend was in the shop. I was terrified.'

I shook my head.

'You have told them nothing about the existence of the other?'

'No.'

'Don't you think that, sooner or later, one of them will find out?'

Vicente lowered his head and said nothing.

'It's make-up-your-mind time, Vicente.'

'I know. But I don't want to. I want them both.'

He looked at me with a fading, bitter smile.

'You may lose them both if you don't tell them the truth,' I said.

I couldn't believe I was advising someone who lived thousands of miles away.

'Start with Ab. He is the one with whom you have the most recent relationship. See what he says and what he decides to do.'

'Why Ab?'

'Because if you lose him, not much will have changed. If Ab terminates the relationship, you may not even have to tell your boyfriend.'

Vicente kept thinking.

'But I don't want to lose Ab,' he said.

'In which case, you have made a choice,' I replied.

'I don't want to lose Ab,' he repeated softly.

I felt sorry for him.

'Is it the same in England?' he asked after a while.

No, our lemons are yellow.

'What did you say?'

'Nothing.'

I could imagine him laughing: 'Yellow lemons? Whoever heard of yellow lemons?'

'Will you ever come back to Fortaleza?' he asked.

'I tell you what, Vicente. Promise me you'll sort your life out, and I promise to return to Fortaleza and come over to your bookshop to find out what happened to your love life.'

We shook hands.

Deal.

*****

So the noble savages of the French humanists had many – literally – skeletons in their *malocas* and the stench of cooked human flesh haunts their reputation as it sealed their karma. But there is a crucial difference between the dressed, civilised European and the naked, savage cannibal as far as History is concerned, and concerned it should be. This conquest was no simple swap of civilisations like the Ottoman excursions in the Balkans or the English Raj in India. When the Potiguar first met the Portuguese, they were surprised at how inept these people were at basic skills like shooting an arrow. How do they hunt? they wondered. And why do they want to own property and slaves?

Now, the inhabitants of the rainforest 'lived in communion with Nature', as documentaries tell you in grand platitudes with low sentimental minor chords in the background. Communion with Nature? They killed animals, they burned the woods and chopped the trees, they loved precious stones, they were in a state of perpetual war, and they ate each other with gusto. Yet there is a difference, a crucial difference. The Indians were as human in their needs, desires and fallibilities as their conquerors. But they did not amass riches. We Old Worlders are exploiting one-off resources never to be replaced and, when we die, we bequeath our property in a line defined and enshrined in law, for we are hoarders, and that is our curse and the curse of our planet.

It's in Brazil we realised this first.

Chapter 4

Univers04 (Recife, Olinda)

I suppose it had to happen. It happened in Recife.

....

The Words You'll Need

agreste = *the semi-arid centre of Pernambuco*
aldeias = *Jesuit villages*
bairro do barulho = *the neighbourhood of noise*
briga = *fight*
canavieira = *pertaining to sugar cane*
chopperia = *bar*
eu sou feliz = *I'm happy*
igreja = *church*
ladeira = *a steep road San Francisco-style. The place is full of them.*
mártires = *martyrs*
mestiços = *of mixed blood*
mirante = *Portuguese belvedere*
Nunca bebeu de coco? = *never drank from a coconut before?*
oração = *prayer*
picante = *hot as in spicy*
vestibular = *university entry exam*
você é muito gostoso = *you are very attractive*
você também = *you, too*

....

– 16 –

How to choose the right location in a state capital first time?

I spent ages dowsing over the map of Recife: would the 6-mile beach of Boa Viagem be isolated? Exactly how hazardous was the centre of town? Which streets would be noisy with traffic? A special package offered by a business hotel in Rua Aurora offered huge discounts for clients who stayed during a weekend and solved the problem. They put me up on the seventh floor with a view of the river Capibaribe, which would become more and more spectacular as the town started sparkling at night. I tried to have a siesta, but the evangelical preacher in the street below my toilet window was screaming his head off and changed my mood to darkest ebony. Like Middle-Eastern muezzins who need louder and louder megaphones, evangelicals like more and more street wattage. As I put in my earplugs and shoved my head under a pillow, I made a mental note to point out to them that they were preaching to people down below and not to the archangels up high.

Pernambuco and Bahia were the centres of early Portuguese colonisation based on latifundiatory sugar-cane monoculture and a parasitic existence: the back-breaking plantation work was conducted wholly by slaves. In the Iberian peninsula there was considerable intellectual resistance to the enslavement of native Indians. Although the Inca and Aztec civilisations were several notches higher than the Stone-Age existence of the Tupi and the Tapuia, the former rubbed off enough respect to all inhabitants of the New World to cause debates about their fate. I suppose we should be grateful to Pope Paul III who decided that, yes, the American Indians were indeed beings of reason – but like children they needed to be guided and patronised by a stream of Jesuits who flooded the continent. One should also be grateful to the various kings of Portugal and Spain who, time after time, prohibited the enslavement of the natives, only for their decrees to be ignored on the ground. There was no Boston Tea Party in South America because the laws from the metropolis were consistently flouted if they didn't suit the locals – even today some would say that this is the norm rather than the exception.

However, the Indians proved totally unsuitable for a sedate, farming environment. Not immune to the white man's diseases, forced to live in Jesuit *aldeias*, and asked to change centuries' old customs in a few generations (most notably, polygamy), they provided an example of what might happen if a benign advanced alien civilisation descended on Earth: they died off. Fortunately for the colonists, there was still one race which was not considered human enough by the Catholic Church. Everyone regarded Africans as subhuman; not only were they a race whose sole function in life was to serve as a slave pool, but they also had the right immunities and farming knowledge. Thus began the cross-Atlantic slave trade for Bahia and Pernambuco, Cuba and the West Indies; sometimes it became illegal, depending on who was advising the king of the time. It was very lucrative and attracted the attentions of other foreign powers; if the sixteenth century saw the French failing to gain a foothold in Brazil, the seventeenth saw the Dutch trying their luck. Like most of

Brazil's history this was decided by events abroad: Portugal had been absorbed by Spain through inheritance and the Dutch were Spain's avowed enemies. They invaded and sacked Bahia, but were eventually routed. They then turned their attentions north, to Pernambuco, where they were rather more successful.

....

Things I Like About Brazil #4: Mangue-Beat

We would call it swamp-rock (I have read the term 'mangroove'), and we would dance to it like it was metal hip-hop: DMC vs. Aerosmith Walking This Way. It started in Pernambuco in the early 1990s with Chico Science and his Nação Zumbi who released a manifesto along with Fred04 (lead vocalist of the group Mundo Livre SA) and the journo Renato Lins. They managed to create a punk-like generational chasm between the dinosaurs of MPB (Música Popular Brasileira) and the vibe of a new generation who synthesised local traditions and international musical genres. Mangrove swamps ('mangues') that abound in Pernambuco were the backdrop, mangue-boys and mangue-girls the fans, screeching guitars and back-breaking thumping alfaia strap-on drums the sound.

But above all, first and foremost, dominating the radical lyrics of Chico Science was 'A Cidade', the Big City: from Macaxeira and Bom Pastor to Boa Viagem, Santo Amaro, Madalena and Boa Vista all the way to Beberibe, Caxangá and Dois Irmãos, the majestic megalopolis of Recife was in the eye of the hurricane that erupted with mangue-beat. This was a city in chronic economic decline, but with a past second to few in the Americas and a rich cultural milieu; so, when the children of the swamp, the self-styled 'carangueijos' – crabs – came to celebrate their unique Nordestino culture, Recife was ready to be raised to the cult status it knew it deserved, like an old diva waiting for her music to be discovered once more by a younger audience. The explosion of talent that followed was dizzying: Mestre Ambrósio, Querosene Jacaré and Cascabulho to name but a few.

Recife rocks.

....

When I woke up I opened my window and was spellbound at once. Not since I looked out of my balcony in Copacabana had I seen such an arresting urban landscape. Recife is called the Venice of Brazil – I suppose calling it the Amsterdam of Brazil would be impolitic – and although the appellation is rather grand, there's no smoke without fire: the city is built on the confluence of the rivers Pina, Jordão, Tejipió, Beberibe and Capibaribe and boasts 39 bridges. Recife and its neighbour Olinda are the most aristocratic of towns in Lusitanian America: in the seventeenth and eighteenth centuries consanguinity in marriage was the norm, not the exception, as cousin married cousin and uncle married niece. Inbreeding may lead long-term to an evolutionary cul-de-sac, but if the original genes are kosher enough, in the short term – say, three or four centuries – they keep the blood pure and the skin white, and that was the main concern was it not? Slaves were there to satisfy the master's urges, to wet-nurse the master's kids, providing them with playmates in the plantation and eventually introducing them to the pleasures of sex, but the family possessions would be inherited by pure family blood. The old colonial adage chillingly cites the pecking order:

> *White woman for marriage,*
> *Mulatto woman for sex,*
> *Negro woman for work.*

On my first foray into Santo Amaro, on my way to Recife Antigo at 10 p.m. ('At your own risk,' I was told by the friendly hotel porter), I was under a heavy impression that this was not Brazil but a distinct, precocious corner of southern Europe or maybe northern Africa. There was no mad I-am-higher-than-thou construction dash for the sky: Recife seemed to grow laterally, like an old-fashioned European burg, rather than vertically, the mark of so many cities in the New World. In keeping with its Old World atmosphere, there was an orgy of restoration, for along with the mangue beats came the confidence of IT technology and the ensuing credit.

The members of the Pernambucan *jeunesse dorée* streaming into town on a Friday night were taller and lighter-skinned than in Manaus or Fortaleza and passed by with an un-Brazilian insouciance verging on Gallic sangfroid. Queues were already forming outside clubs and deep bass sounds were coming out of warehouses. So many people were packed in the picturesque and narrow pedestrian-only streets of the small island, which served as the first settlement on the Rio Beberibe, that movement sometimes resulted in single-file human traffic. Self-proclaimed parking attendants stopped all cars entering the *bairro do barulho* and pointed at parking places in hopeful expectation that they would get a tip.

Squeezed between two freshly painted three-storey antique buildings, but silent and dark in its lack of human patronage, a plain, unassuming edifice attracted my attention. How odd. Prime commercial site and it remains unsold and unexploited. I walked closer and read the inscription: 'Restoration of the building where once existed the first Synagogue of the Americas' in Portuguese, Spanish, English and, I guessed, Hebrew.

Oh – of course – the Dutch.

Now the Dutch weren't, on the face of it, any better than the Portuguese: they used the same methods to Christianise the natives; they, too, thought that the sole purpose in life of the African races was to provide fodder for the plantations; and they considered the European as the main civiliser in a backward, savage country. But they were different in their respect of pluralism then, as they are today. In the Iberian peninsula scores were being settled with the local Jews who were being forced to convert by the Inquisition; God was on the defensive after the age of exploration and with taboos that were falling quicker than saying *'te absolvo'*, religion retreated behind even stricter fundamentalist dogma – like, I suppose, it does today worldwide. But the Dutch allowed the Jews to worship freely and brought Isaac Aboab da Fonseca, the first rabbi to officiate freely in the Americas at the synagogue of Bom Jesus, the silent pride of Recife.

– 17 –

Hindsight is the only perfect science.

If only I knew but a fraction of what I know now that sunny Saturday afternoon, which saw me wandering the streets of old Recife with my camera, snapping at palaces, forts, bridges and riverfronts. Street children were diving in the old port on the Avenida Lisboa by the Torre Malakoff just this side of the *arrecife* (reef) which gave the city its name. I approached to take some photos mindful that I might be hassled for money. No worries: the kids continued their games with that all-pervading breezy aloofness I could sense in the Pernambucan ether. One of them, his back turned to me three feet away, continued his lazy sunbathing, impervious to my presence. Did he see me take his picture or did he simply not care?

Most of the churches were shut, and I had to bribe a street urchin to climb through a window in the Madre de Deus and inform the priest that a gringo had travelled from afar in order to admire its famous decor. I was allowed in and disrupted a wedding practice, but the bride and groom obligingly moved out of the way as I didn't want them in my compositions. Bless.

I waltzed up the Avenida Conde da Boa Vista to browse the shops. Brazil is a country where surfing is practised religiously and Pernambuco has a proud tradition – flyers informed me that the World Surfing Games would be conducted in Maracaípe near Porto de Galinhas that June, when the best waves of the year were expected. In shopping terms this all translates as 'the surf- and street-wear choice is astounding'. I stood salivating at tops, shoes and shorts by UTM, Quiksilver, Bad Boy, Drop Dead, HB (Hot and Buttered), Greenish, Vision StreetWear, Cyclone, Hang Loose, Urban Wave, Dû Hui, OnBongo (Always Ahead), Spy – the glasses only, of course – Rip Curl, Maresia, Mormaii and Redley (big sigh). You notice I didn't mention O'Neil: they've sold out.

I might be too old to be a surfer, but hell, I'm rich enough to afford the clothes. I left the most wonderful Shopping Boa Vista with two HB Bermuda shorts and one white Bad Boy top, which I adored. Back in the hotel, I put it on and on again; it was a beaut.

I had to wear it that night, didn't I?

*****

CATS was a gigantic converted warehouse with a ceiling way too high for the sound which tended to bounce dully in the distance. The punters could climb a two-floor designer split-level structure reached by a spiral staircase. After a few beers the experience was quite intimidating, especially if one looked down on the dance floor – I don't know what was worse: being tipsy looking down or being sober looking up at the leaning drunks above. CATS was spick-and-span sleek and had decent music, although you could still hear the odd Abba song intruding amongst the dance *'choonz'*. Once more there was too much attitude; I was pushed and jostled by drunken youths. I noticed a guy with the body of an Amazonian god – actually this is not a good metaphor, since the tribes there are short and stumpy, but I made it, so there, can't take it back. The god went downstairs to dance. I followed him and took off my T-shirt for good measure, tucking it around my waist. I climbed the podium, struggling to find some space amongst the mass of bodies.

It all happened in a flash.

A fight broke out around me; three guys started exchanging fisticuffs and the rest of us recoiled, forming a circle – a circle around them and around my Bad Boy T-shirt being stomped on the floor.

Aaaaaaaaaaaaargh!

Furious, I followed the bouncers to the exit. I was so enraged I started speaking in English; when a man is angry, he swears in his native tongue to feel fully the weight of the words he utters – which in my case was considerable.

'FUCKING BASTARDS! I BOUGHT THIS TODAY! CHUCK THEM OUT! NOW!'

A softly spoken, tall, lanky guy with an earphone approached me.

'Is there a problem?' he asked in perfect English.

'YES! WHO ARE YOU?'

'Calm down. What's your name?'

'I'M JOHN! I WAS DANCING HAPPILY AND THESE GUYS STARTED FIGHTING AND MY T-SHIRT WAS DRAGGED ON THE FLOOR AND IT'S GOT FOOTPRINTS ALL OVER IT!'

'Calm down,' the guy said again. 'I am William and this one here –' he pointed at another shorter, stockier guy, '– is Evêncio. We are owner-managers of CATS.'

'SOME MANAGEMENT! WHEN I PAY MONEY FOR A CLUB, I EXPECT SECURITY! I DON'T EXPECT A FIGHT!' And for good measure I added: 'THAT'S WHAT HAPPENS IN LONDON!'

'John,' said Evêncio, 'we are dealing with the fight. We are so sorry it interfered with your enjoyment.'

'WHAT ABOUT MY SHIRT? IT'S A BAD BOY T-SHIRT AND IT'S RUINED! I BOUGHT IT TODAY. DO YOU HEAR ME? TODAY! IT COST ME 30 REAIS!'

William rolled his eyes.

'If I give you 30 reais will you leave?' he said.

Leave? Me leave?

I took a deep breath.

'No! Why should I go? What will I wear? And I won't find the same T-shirt in my size: extra-large.'

'Listen,' said Evêncio, approaching me with a concerned expression. 'You are right. It is our mistake. Give me your T-shirt and the name of your hotel, and I will have it washed and sent to your room next week.'

I stayed silent for some time, as Evêncio drew me to the coat-check. He gave me a promo T-shirt for some energy drink and wrote my hotel and room number down.

'Will I see that T-shirt again?' I asked somewhat impolitely.

Evêncio looked me in the eye.

'I am the manager,' he said. 'You can trust me.' He gave me a small keyring with the inscription CATS. 'Please accept our apologies for what happened and give this ticket to the barman to get a free drink of your choice.'

I slowly simmered down, gulping a caipirinha and climbing up and down the club's stairs. My nerves were taut. A short, beautiful, black-haired, brown-skinned guy in his early twenties was eyeing me, but I was still wrapped up in myself and dismissed him. I had to admit that both Evêncio and William were top-drawer material. Any other managers would have chucked me out. Between me and you, I deserved it. I had been terribly rude.

A silhouette leaned next to me to watch the dancers below. It was William.

'Are you OK now?' he asked cordially.

I nodded an embarrassed yes. 'I'm so sorry,' I said. 'I shouldn't have acted like that. I was an arsehole out there.'

'Never mind,' he replied.

We talked for a good while about clubs and clientele.

'Straight guys cause many problems in the club,' he admitted. 'When they drink they want to show off in front of their girlfriends and there are fights. But what can we do? Under Brazilian law we can't discriminate at the entrance. There was a case where someone took a gay club to court and he – or was it a she? – won.'

'Do what they do in London,' I said. 'Use membership. You issue membership cards and only let in members and their friends. Anyone can become a member, but you can screen them. It doesn't matter if they're straight or gay, what matters is that they like the club, and they aren't casual detritus from the street – normally the ones who cause trouble.'

William's face lit up. 'What a great idea,' he said. 'And on Saturdays we can say that it's members only.'

He looked at me admiringly. 'And charge for membership, too!'

I looked down bashfully. It's not every day one single-handedly changes the club scene of an entire city – let alone Manguetown.

I was happier after that and went back downstairs. The short, cute, brown-skinned guy moved next to me. He smiled again, the brightest smile to grace my journey so far. I moved to the bar, looking over my shoulder. He followed.

'Hi,' he said to me.

'Hi,' I replied. I needed to talk.

'What's your name?'

We were entering a carefully balanced verbal choreography.

'John. Yours?'

'Isaías.'

'Like the prophet?'

He laughed. 'Yes. I don't know anyone in Recife with that name.'

'You are from Recife then?'

He shook his head, never letting the smile fade.

'No – I'm studying here for my *vestibular*. I come from a small town two hours into the *agreste* called Limoeiro.' And, pausing: 'You?'

'I come from Athens, Greece,' I replied, 'though I've lived in London most of my life.'

His wide eyes widened more.

'London,' he said in awe.

Everyone in Recife was impressed by my credentials; perhaps a lingering memory of Europe hovered in their genes.

'I had a weird night tonight,' I said to him and told him what had happened. But he wasn't listening.

'*Você é muito gostoso,*' he said when I finished.

It was my turn to smile; my first one all night.

'*Você também,*' I replied.

'Come with me tonight,' he said.

'Pardon?'

'Let me make you forget the *briga*. Come with me.'

I took a good look at him.

'I'll pay for a motel room,' he said.

'What?'

'Motel room. By the hour. We can go there.'

I thought of Antônio in Fortaleza. John, if you turn down another beautiful guy in his twenties you'll be done for blasphemy.

'That's OK,' I said. 'Come with me to my hotel.'

Evêncio was behind the coat-check.

'I'm leaving,' I said.

Evêncio glanced at us. His eyes remained fixed on Isaías for a long time.

'I'm so sorry about the scene earlier on.'

'That's OK,' he said.

'And give me back my T-shirt. I'll have it cleaned at the hotel.'

'Are you sure?'

'Yes. It's better this way. The footprints have soiled it badly, and the hotel cleaners will have more experience.'

'As you wish,' Evêncio said and gave me a plastic bag.

Was something bothering him?

'Perhaps we can have a drink while you're staying in Recife?'

'Call me at my hotel,' I replied. 'You have the details.'

I walked out with Isaías who clung ecstatically to my waist. I stole a look at him, but he saw that and kissed me impishly.

He gives me such a warm tingle in my spine.

'Look,' he said, finger extending to the sky, as we crossed the Ponte Marquês de Olinda.

I knew he was pointing at the full moon about to set.

– 18 –

I was fretting already. *Where is he?* Hell is not other people, hell is other people making me *wait*. Hell must be perpetually waiting for Godot. Patience is such an overrated virtue! Aaargh! It had been six hours since Isaías had left, and I was already missing him. What am I saying? Of course, I wasn't missing *him* – it was the fact that I was waiting for someone who was late, what? five minutes already. *Five minutes!* I bet he's still showering now. Or more likely sleeping. He only left at eight in the morning, and we certainly didn't get much sleep till then. And he's making me miss Olinda. It's Sunday! The churches are open! It's 2 p.m. and I have missed a day, and I will never take pictures of Olinda, and I should never have agreed to see him again. He's going to stand me up, and he's going to make me miss Olinda.

My heart skipped a beat as the telephone rang. It was reception.

'Hey, John?'

'Isaías,' I exclaimed. 'Where are you?'

'I'm downstairs. They won't let me come up.'

'Why?'

'It's a different guy from the night porter. I don't like him. He's bad and he's not letting me come upstairs.'

'I'm ready, OK. I'll come down.'

Isaías was waiting in the lobby wearing a pair of brown chequered Bermudas and a yellow T-shirt, looking more the typical flashy Brazilian youth. What was he wearing in the club? How odd – I couldn't remember after the memory of the intervening night.

I greeted him under the watchful eye of the porter.

'Olinda?' he asked.

'Olinda,' I agreed.

We boarded a bus for the short ride to Olinda – just four miles away, but four centuries apart in feel.

The conductor, of course, had no change.

....

Things I Don't Like About Brazil #4: Lack Of Change

I paid my airport tax in Fortaleza (it has to be paid locally so that it is certain the local authority will receive the money quickly in this bureaucratic country) and wanted seven reais back. The woman at the counter asked me if I had three reais change from a tenner. I said no, so she gave me back five. Confused?

Sometimes you smile when you encounter a refusal from a bus conductor who can't give you change from one real for a ticket costing 80 centavos. Sometimes you blow your cool when you find that even a currency exchange office will not give you smaller notes. Sometimes you panic and plead desperately with aloof and unyielding fast-food cashiers to change your 50-real note so that you can be admitted on the long-distance night-coach which is about to depart – now!

Oh – and if you are lucky enough to come across any change, mindful of the trouble you'll have finding it in the future, you don't give it away. Let the others struggle to find their own! Doh!

....

When the Dutch invaded, Recife was a backwater populated by Brazilian-born, lower-class *mestiços* looked down upon by the inbreeding white Portuguese aristocracy who kept their town houses in Olinda when they were not living in their *Casas Grandes* amongst their plantations. The cool, calculating Dutch saw in Olinda a town in a great setting, but Recife a town in a great *defendable* setting – plus, they liked swamps and knew how to dam them. When they left, Recife had edged ahead and come up trumps.

A century after the Dutch invasions, there was a small civil war between the two cities, called the Mascate War, after the derogatory name the land-owning class of Olinda called the commercial middle-class entrepreneurs of Recife. The war lasted two years and – by historical inevitability Marx might say – ended up with the reduction of the power of the Olindense aristocracy. Recife went on to become the fourth largest city in Brazil and the new capital of Pernambuco, while Olinda remained petite, undulating and cobble-stoned, airy, shadowy and leafy – more and more lovely with age: lovely to visit, lovely to amble through, lovely to photograph and lovely to behold.

I declare Olinda the winner.

The small and recent Igreja dos Milagres is the first church you notice when you reach the town. But it is the stunning twin towers of the Igreja do Carmo, standing tall with coconut trees as a backdrop that provides a taster of the delights still to come: sunny Brazilian baroque on a series of steep hills overlooking the sea, surrounded by tropical vegetation connected by cobbled narrow, winding *ladeiras*. Olinda is a Unesco site, patrimony of all mankind, because its churches, convents, mansions and *mirantes* are pieces of a holistic grand illustration where the glory of the landscape meshes in with the spark of the architectural genius of our species. An apex of the world's heritage in the tropics of Brazil? You bet – and it's not the only one.

'Last time I was here was during *Carnaval*,' said Isaías. 'Everyone was out and you could hardly move for the people. I can't recognise the streets now. I need a map.'

That's what they all tell you in Recife, Rio and Salvador: 'Ours is the better *Carnaval*, you must come.' Admittedly the people of Pernambuco have the longest: for days before the city buzzes with gala nights, club specials, street parties, parades and raves in Boa Viagem on a two and a half-mile stretch by the sea. The Saturday parade in Recife behind the large figure of the Dawn Chicken (you may chortle; I did) is supposed to be the largest in the world with more than one million people in the streets. In Olinda you get more funky chickens – about one hundred large effigies crowd the streets causing hangover havoc. The African note is added on Monday in the *Noite dos Tambores Silenciosos* (Night of the Silent Drums) where the São José district downtown is the place to large it in for *maracatu*. The *maracatu* groups are the Pernambucan equivalent of the Rio samba schools and require up to thirty brightly-clad percussionists marching in front of a black King and Queen and their court retinue – ranging from dukes, counts and princes to servants and ambassadors, down to a slave holding a parasol to shade the royal couple. But at the stroke of midnight the *maracatu* drums suddenly go silent, before the assembled crowds plaintively seek the blessings of the Madonna of the slaves, Nossa Senhora do Rosário, in a centuries-old ritual. Those who have experienced the silence speak in hushed tones of its emotional effect.

The twenty-odd important churches in Olinda, many of them dating from the sixteenth century, are elegant and charming: three storeys high, with red and green window-shutters contrasting with the whitewashed walls and their yellow frames; Doric columns culminating in ornamental mouldings support the structure like wood in half-timbered houses. The perpendicular basilicas are tempered by strange protruding roofs, curving crescent-like upwards – an idiosyncratic Portuguese innovation that they brought from Japan, being the first foreigners there. Certainly the monastery of São Bento alone (so old it was first restored in the 1760s) with its combination of straight lines, curvilinear rooftops and richly decorated interior would be a jewel in the crown of any capital city in the Old World.

We climbed up to the convent of Nossa Senhora das Neves (climbing is the operative word in Olinda) and on to the seminary and the cathedral where the Bishop of Olinda, Dom Hélder Câmara, was being commemorated for his courage. An opponent of the military regime in Brazil during those long sixties, seventies and eighties decades, he was nicknamed 'the Red Bishop' by Pope Paul VI. He was one of those Latin American liberation theologians you have heard about – those who believe equally in the word of God and social justice. Unfortunately, the Vatican's heart has not been big enough to hold both dearly. If there is any space in one's soul it can only be filled with God and God alone, for, as we know from the Ten Commandments, He is a jealous God indeed.

I picked up a paper which was scrupulously folded and left on a seat inside the cathedral. It was a photocopy and it said (my translation, but not my grammar or syntax):

When you encounter a desperate situation, be it a deadly disease or financial or other serious problems, you must know that St Judas Thaddeus is your companion this intermediary note has been around the world through the disciples of St Judas Thaddeus, I ask you to make 81 copies and to deposit them in Catholic churches and say the Lord's Prayer for St Judas Thaddeus and all the souls in the purgatory; this note was sent by one of the millions of people who exist in the world. You must deliver the copies within 13 days one Brazilian President sent the copies but did not pay much attention and after 13 days won the lottery Ezequiel Cortes picked up the note in a church and ordered his secretary to send the copies she forgot and after 13 days she lost her job Izabel Chibam lost the copy and aborted her son after 13 days. As you observe the note changes after 13 days the life of whoever sends the copies changes.

There followed an *oração de São Judas Tadeu* in vernacular Portuguese.

I thought I'd show this to Isaías. I looked around.

Isaías? Where was he? Damn! He was carrying my bag.

I dashed out and saw Isaías sitting under the shadow of a tree in the cathedral square – the Alto da Sé – with its dramatic views over the town. He saw me come out and waved his arms, flashing one of those smiles that were his speciality. As I sat next to him, I felt small, petty and cynical for my suspicions.

A coconut seller passed by. Isaías waved him over and bought a coconut.

'Are you thirsty, John?' he asked me.

'I don't drink from coconuts,' I said.

'What? *Nunca bebeu de coco?*'

'Never.'

'But this is just water.'

He bought a second coconut.

'There. Try it. If you don't like it, I'll drink it.'

I watched the coconut seller deftly hack the top with a machete until he reached the hollow centre. He put a straw inside, and I had my first sip. It was pure cool water. The shell acts as an insulator, keeping the centre at a temperature well below ambient. And it didn't taste at all coconut-ish. I gave Isaías the thumbs up.

'You see?' he said. 'I can also teach you something, can't I?'

We were sitting on the wall at the perimeter of the square, which looked as if it was part of some fortification. On our right was the cathedral, on our left the large complex of the Igreja de Misericordia and the Convent of Conceição, and in front of us a panorama of the reefs, islands, beaches and bridges of Recife.

'This is beautiful,' I said.

'Hey, John, isn't it the best place in Brazil?' Isaías asked.

'There are some I haven't been to,' I replied noncommittally, but then something in me could not stand seeing a shadow in his pretty face so I corrected myself: 'but it must be one of the top two or three.'

Isaías smiled, and I smiled back. We were facing each other, legs apart, knees only a few feet away. I stared at him tenderly: eyes large like chestnuts; lips as if added later with hindsight; ears protruding slightly. Take each individual characteristic and you'll find imperfections. And yet the whole was enchanting. His expression was always calm, happy or bewildered – if he was ever upset he never showed it. His eyes never demonstrated despondency or stress; never fear or worry; he was either happily smiling or registering surprise. For 'sadly' or 'regrettably' he used '*infelizmente*', 'unhappily'. It seemed that for him sadness and regret was the negation of happiness and not a different, new concept. He would have great difficulty with such words as 'gloom', but then he'd never seen the sky in Scotland.

Isaías spoke first. 'Hey, John, what will happen if I can't come up to your hotel room?'

So he was thinking the same thing.

'Dunno,' I said. 'Do you want me to come to yours?'

He shook his head.

'I have a roommate,' he said. 'The place where I'm staying is for students only, and the landlady knows my mother back in Limoeiro. No way.'

'Are you out at home?'

'Oh yes,' he said. 'But bringing someone back is different.'

'What did your parents say?'

'Well, a small town is not the best place to be gay, is it? Here in Recife, studying for my *vestibular*, I'm free. My father is very Christian.'

'Hence the name?'

'Exactly. Old Testament prophet, I ask you! My mother is OK. She writes to me often. She calls me and sends me money. But they wanted me out of town to avoid a scandal.'

Behind us, a boy-girl couple started hugging and holding hands on a bench, a union blessed, I suppose, by the combined 81 letters of St Judas Thaddeus I should deliver in thirteen days – or was it nine? I felt tired – from the sun, the lack of sleep, and finally these feelings inside me.

I like him. I like him very much.

'Hey, John, how long did you say you are staying in Recife?'

'One week. Until next Friday.'

He flashed another smile.

'That's great,' he said. 'That's great.'

'Why?' I asked. 'You want me to leave?'

He laughed.

'No, it's great you're staying for a week.' And then, half pleadingly: 'You will see me again, won't you?'

'Yes!' I heard myself cry out before engaging my brain. I didn't want to speak. I didn't want to think. I just wanted to sit there with Isaías and *react*.

'You know ...' he said.

'I know what?'

'You know that last night was fantastic.'

We looked at each other and there was a lot said in that instant.

I looked at him, looked at Recife in the distance, looked at the freshly painted aristocratic houses that surrounded us, at the trees that grew semi-wild amongst the churches and the belfries, at the two coconuts at our feet with the straws just – *just* – crossing each other, at the couple in love behind us and suddenly Olinda's fulgent beauty overwhelmed me.

This is not now – it is another time, long forgotten.

Something was ripping through me: no, it wasn't the curse of St Judas Thaddeus, no it wasn't anything supernatural, on the contrary, it was mightily human and intensely physical.

My God. I have been alone too long.

'Let's go home,' I said to Isaías, jumping off the ledge, a sudden cheerful spring in my stride.

*****

Enter the Prince of Nassau.

Call him Johann Moritz von Nassau-Siegen because he was German, or Johan Maurits van Nassau-Siegen because he served the Dutch, or João Maurício de Nassau-Siegen, '*o brasileiro*' because he served in Brazil, JM (lovely initials) is the first truly enlightened personality connected with the country. This is even more remarkable since out of his 73 years on this earth, he only spent seven in Pernambuco where he was governor from 1637 to 1644. But during those seven years, he fortified the city of Recife, rebuilt Olinda, constructed hospitals, bridges and gardens (including a zoo), allowed complete religious freedom amongst the Catholic, Calvinist and Jewish settlers, created – wait for it – the first astronomical observatory in the New World, and extended Dutch rule not only from Fortaleza to Bahia, but also across the Atlantic to Portuguese Angola to control the slave trade. The Renaissance arrived in Recife: the naturalist Georg Marcgraf von Liebstadt created a natural history of Pernambuco with 200 plant and 222 animal woodcuts plus an ethnographic study of the various tribes; Frans Post painted the earliest Brazilian landscapes; and Zacharias Wagener created the 'Animal Book' (*Zoobiblion*), one of the best albums of sketches we have from Brazil.

It was because of the Prince's census in the lands of New Holland that we have a record of the decimation of the native tribes in the Nordeste. In Ceará the Potiguar had been reduced to five villages; in Natal and Paraíba only ten and in Pernambuco six. In just over a century, the Potiguar, like all the coastal Tupi, had diminished from hundreds of thousands to about 10,000 souls. The Prince was appalled by the conditions he found the Indians living and working under, and he demanded that the landowners pay the natives who toiled in the fields a decent salary – in modern terms one could say he introduced something resembling a minimum wage, way ahead of its time. He went as far as creating a special post: Protector of the Indians. This was an ombudsman-like figure who travelled from village to village registering complaints and stopping abuses. The second of them, Johan Listry, presided over a daring experiment unparalleled in European colonialism: he called for a meeting of representatives of the Indian villages under Dutch control. Remarkably the assembly proved both workable and dignified. It elected three Indian 'councillors', who were the local warlords, gave a list of requests to the Dutch administration and boldly affirmed the fundamental desire of a people to be free: *'Liberty should be conceded to any of our race who might possibly still be kept as a slave.'*

Johan Maurits became too successful, too popular, too powerful, too quickly. Unsurprisingly, he was recalled back to Europe and within five years the Dutch had been expelled from the Nordeste. Yet he remained forever under its spell, writing missives ever on the side of the Indians: *'The quiet and preservation of the colony of Brazil depends on part on the friendship of the Indians. With this in mind they should be permitted to enjoy their natural freedom. Orders should be issued that they are not outraged by their commanders, hired out for money or forced to work in sugar mills against their will. Each one should on the contrary be allowed to live in the way he understands and to work where he wishes like men of our nation.'*

Over 350 years later, we still have not fully accomplished the dream of the Prince of Nassau.

*****

I kissed Isaías goodbye that evening and asked: 'One o'clock?'

Isaías went to his college every day from nine to twelve, so we were meeting after lunch.

'*Sim*, one o'clock.'

I couldn't let him go like that. I wanted to give him something of mine; something tangible, afraid of the impermanence of feelings. I had bought so much new surf stuff, I could give away something I arrived in: one tight navy Lycra D&G top fitted him perfectly. How I enjoyed that glint in his eye as he posed happily in front of the mirror.

And then he was gone.

I lay back on my bed. Here was a guy I had spent less than 24 hours with – and yet …

I got up and walked to my window. Night was coming down and the sunset colours blended with the pastel shades of the Recife buildings by the river.

… and yet, he dominates my thoughts and plays thimblerig with my emotions without even trying.

John, there is a word for this …

My eye fell on the message the evening porter had handed to me upon our return from Olinda – not the 'bad' porter who didn't let Isaías in this afternoon. It read: 'Called in at 6 p.m. You weren't there. Please call back. Evêncio' – his mobile number scribbled next to his name.

Evêncio had come to the hotel? Well, that explained his expression yesterday when I left with Isaías. He wanted a date. I was in a mood to throw the note away, but on second thoughts perhaps a dinner with Evêncio might tone down this intense relationship with Isaías.

I called his mobile number.

'*Olá?*'

'Evêncio, it's me, John.'

'Oh, nice to hear from you, John. Listen – can't talk much, I'm in a movie.'

Movie?

'Yes, in the cinema next to you. *Meninos Não Choram.*'

I remembered: the cinema on the other side of the Conde da Boa Vista was showing *Boys Don't Cry.*

'I popped over to see if you were interested in an early dinner and then a movie.'

Bingo! I was right.

'Oh, that's OK. I was in Olinda most of the day.'

'Listen, John. You know that guy you left with last night?'

I jumped.

'Who, Isaías?'

'That short young guy.'

I can't believe he is talking to me on his mobile in the cinema.

'Yes, Isaías. We spent the night together, and he came to Olinda with me today.'

'Oh. So you know him well.'

'On the contrary, I only met him yesterday.'

'Well, this is what I wanted to tell you – I thought I had better tell you.'

'What? Tell me what?'

'Do you know he was involved in the fight that ruined your T-shirt? That he started it?'

My knees went weak. I sat down.

'No, I didn't know that.'

'He didn't tell you?'

No.

'No, he didn't.'

'Well, that's why I called. William said he comes to the club and causes trouble. Since you are new here, I thought I'd … bring this to your attention.'

Bring it to my attention.

'Thanks, Evêncio. You did well.'

'I must go. I'll call you tomorrow.'

'Yes, thanks. Bye.'

'*Ciao.*'

I put the phone down and lay on my bed silent and immobile – just breathing, for just breathing is the sum total of the exertion I could muster at that moment. I was afraid – afraid that the Olinda dream would disappear and a lorryload of grief would take its place.

Isaías caused the fight – why?

He didn't tell me about it – why?

He must have heard me shout. He knew I wasn't Brazilian when he tried to pick me up. That I was a tourist. Maybe a rich one.

I haven't paid for anything. He hasn't asked for money. What's his game?

I got up and found the Bad Boy T-shirt, which I had chucked carelessly in a corner of the room. I looked at it. Only 24 hours ago I didn't even own this beast and look what it's done for me. Maybe it's the curse of St Judas Thaddeus, 13 days too early.

There was only one thing to do. I picked up the phone with great determination and dialled a number.

'Is that room service?' I asked looking at my mega-soiled T-shirt. 'I have a job for you.'

– 19 –

It was 1 p.m. sharp next day when Isaías called me from reception. The bad porter was on duty again. This time I had a plan.

'I want to go to Boa Viagem,' I said. 'Another dry and sunny day – for the beach.'

As I expected, he didn't have his swimming trunks with him.

'Well, we'll just have to go to your place and pick them up,' I said. 'Any problem?'

'No,' he said, with just a little apprehension.

I had to see where he lived and whether more lies were in store.

We wound our way to one of the backstreets of Boa Vista, behind the famous church of La Matriz; he lived only fifteen minutes away. He seemed a bit sheepish when he unlocked the house-gate railings and let me in.

A big matron appeared in no time, the object of his uneasiness. Her piercing, silent look gave me the jitters too.

'We'll only be a minute,' Isaías said. And as if to underline our purpose even more emphatically: 'We'll be off right away.'

'How many people live here?' I asked.

'Twelve, two to a room. Almost everyone is a student,' Isaías answered.

His room was tiny and reminded me of my undergraduate residence lodgings when I occupied a cubby-hole. (If by any chance I entertained a guest, I could not open the wardrobe.) Isaías's room was similar, except that there were two small beds in the same space, two small sideboards with every drawer individually padlocked and two small portable televisions on top of two commodes – everything symmetrically and uniformly arranged around a virtual central bisecting plane.

'You have two televisions?' I asked.

'Yes,' he answered. 'One for me and one for my roommate.'

'And you watch different programmes at the same time?'

Isaías shrugged his shoulders. 'Yes, why not?'

I see.

'How much do you pay for this?'

'One hundred reais a month.'

I looked at the books on his sideboard. One Jorge Amado novel, and several self-improvement books in the line of 'how to convince people'. But the most striking feature was the lack of the usual pre-university primers one would expect.

'Do you have any pictures from home?' I asked.

He unlocked a cupboard and picked up an envelope. He started sifting through the photos for me.

'I want to see them all,' I demanded.

Isaías looked at me questioningly. 'OK,' he acquiesced and gave me the bundle.

There were pictures of his brother, his mother and his house in Limoeiro. There were also pictures of him and another guy on a beach.

'That's my ex-boyfriend,' Isaías said. 'We went together to Porto de Galinhas a few years back. Have you been there, hey, John? You should go. It's really nice.'

'So what happened to him?' I asked.

'He moved away, and I lost touch. But, but –'

He struggled to find the words. He had clearly sensed my chilliness. 'What's this – this inquiry?' he asked.

Time for confrontation.

'Remember Evêncio's note last night when we came back?'

'Yes.'

'Well, I called him.'

'So?'

'So he told me that it was you who started the fight in CATS. That I should be careful with you. That you are trouble.'

A streak of incomprehension shadowed Isaías's coffee-bean pupils. He sat slowly on his bed and looked down at the floor as if he was about to cry.

'I can't believe you found out before I told you,' he whispered.

So it was true.

'There were two of them, straight boys hopping around their girlfriends. They were pushing me and shoving me to make more space – so I turned around and pushed them back and they fell on me.'

He showed me a slight cut on his inside lip. Surprisingly, I hadn't noticed.

'That much is true,' Isaías said. 'I saw you, and I wanted so much to meet you and be with you, but you were so mad about your T-shirt I couldn't own up to being in that fight or else you wouldn't speak to me.'

'The owners don't think much of you,' I said.

'I know. But they're wrong. I haven't caused any trouble. If I had, why didn't they chuck me out like the others?'

That was a good argument. Evêncio and William had let him stay. Was Evêncio peppering it all up?

'Hey, John, I'm sorry. God, how I wish I could turn the clock back. But it's done. I'm sorry about the fight, I'm sorry about your T-shirt, I'm sorry I didn't tell you. Believe me, I *was* going to tell you today. If only I had spoken to you about it sooner, you'd see that I'm an OK guy.'

'Is there anything else I should know?' I asked.

He shook his head.

'Nothing. Nothing. I'm a sincere guy, John, and I really, really like you.'

Was he shamming?

'Do you hate me?' he asked.

'Don't be silly!'

He sighed.

'But you don't fully believe me. That's why you wanted to come here. You don't believe anything I say, do you?'

I stayed silent.

'Well, I said I'm sorry,' he said. 'I don't want to go to the beach. I want an answer now. Do you want to continue with me? Do you want us to part? Do you want to leave?'

His expression became more and more pained as he followed his thoughts to the inevitable conclusion.

'Do you think I am … dangerous – or violent?'

I tried to gather my scattered thoughts; the spectre of suspicion had come between us. Actually no – it was the not insubstantial shadow of the landlady who had appeared silently on the doorstep.

'He's leaving,' said Isaías. 'He's leaving.'

I stood up.

I couldn't fight this.

I didn't want to fight this.

'*We're* leaving,' I said, putting my arm around Isaías, who had hunched his back and looked smaller and more vulnerable. 'Come Isaías.'

Our eyes met. His vacant stare became fuller and more animated when he took in the full meaning of my words.

'Come on,' I helped him up.

He made a small choking noise.

*****

Isaías and I did go to Boa Viagem that day. We wandered around a mall, the grand Shopping Recife, and lazed about on the beach. I gazed at the expanse of ruler-sharp coastline protected by the famous reefs. As surfers abound, this is the stretch with the greatest number of shark attacks in Brazil. I was half listening to Isaías, not always paying attention until –

'You had a maid?' I jumped. 'A maid?'

'Yes,' he sighed. 'My father had a business. We had a big house. But not anymore.'

I looked him up and down and up again.

'Why?'

'He can't work.'

'Why? Is he ill?'

'He is.'

Is this a sob story?

'What's wrong with him?'

I was pushing. I wanted to see how far I could go before Isaías clammed up. But he didn't. I could see him clenching his jaws and swallowing hard – but he answered, albeit softly.

'He's schizophrenic.'

I cleared my throat. I had gone too far.

'That's OK,' Isaías said. 'That's OK. I know what you're thinking.'

'I'm sorry.'

'That's OK. I know what you're thinking,' he repeated.

That it's hereditary.

'My aunt had it. I used to be afraid of catching it when I was sixteen. But not any more. It's becoming less likely as I grow older. And no, when I had the fight in CATS I wasn't a different person from the guy you are talking to now.'

'I'm really sorry,' I said, feeling vaguely guilty.

'The important thing is that he is stable. They give him drugs that keep him in check. He is now only suffering from acute depression.'

He stared at a Bahian woman dressed in white with her pots and pans steaming in the corner. 'Do you want a snack?' he asked, providing a much-needed diversion from our topic. 'Have you tried Bahian food?'

'A São Paulo street-vendor put me off years ago.'

'Oh, you *must* have some. You must try *acarajé*.'

Acarajé looks like the disastrous result of a biochemical experiment. It is a bun made out of bean flour, fried in palm oil and contains tiny soft-shelled shrimps in pepper sauce. About 12 million of these are consumed every month in Bahia alone.

'*Picante?*' asked the woman.

To Isaías's horror, I asked for mine to be *very* hot.

'I like hot curries,' I reassured him.

The woman spread the hot sauce liberally.

I bit and braved back the tears. Normally I can feel spicy food sliding down my oesophagus and zigzagging around my intestines. This appeared to drop vertically through my insides like a shot of molten metal.

'Is it good?' asked Isaías with apprehension.

'Deh – goh – bah,' I mumbled. I couldn't feel my tongue.

He finished his *acarajé*.

'You're going to Bahia, aren't you?'

'After Maceió,' I replied, wiping my mouth. Boy, this *was* good.

'I have always wanted to see Salvador,' he said. '*Axé*. Olodum. Daniela Mercury.'

'I want to see a candomblé ceremony.'

Isaías laughed.

'And dance the god's dances?' he replied.

He adopted the teapot posture and revolved around a bus stop.

'This is the dance of Xangó,' he said.

He joined his two index fingers together and moved them up and down.

'This is the dance of Yemanjá –'

'You know,' I said suddenly, 'we should go somewhere together.'

'Like where?'

'I don't know. Where you went with your ex. Porto de Galinhas, perhaps?'

'I have college to attend,' he reminded me.

'Only for one night,' I said, overexcited. 'Let's go, find a hotel and stay two days together.'

'Hey, John,' he said carefully. 'My mother sends me three hundred reais a month for me to study, and one hundred goes to my landlady. I don't have much money.'

'Don't worry about money,' I reassured him. I explained that he would cost me next to nothing. He was already saving me money on taxis with his knowledge of buses. Portions in restaurants are for two people; I could never finish them anyway. And a double room outside town would cost as much as one night in my Recife hotel.

'But most of all,' I said, 'most of all, we *owe* this to each other.'

He beamed. 'Fine, then. Porto de Galinhas. It's a really nice place, you know, with natural swimming pools amongst the rocks.'

Our bus came, and we got in. He stretched in his seat next to me and touched the inside of my calf with his knee.

'I'm so glad you've forgiven me,' he said.

Francisco de Assis França, better known as Chico Science, died on 2 February 1997 in a car accident on the short stretch of highway between Olinda and Recife. He died young, still at his artistic peak without incurring the scars of possible middle-age failure or commercial compromises. He died pure in heart, high-riding in fame and, most importantly, wrinkleless. The sum total, as we know from Jimi Hendrix and Jim Morrison to Sid Vicious and Kurt Cobain, is the stuff legends are made of, for what they have left behind is a grand, melancholy 'if only'.

Chico Science and Nação Zumbi made two albums when he was still alive: *Da Lama Ao Kaos* (From Mud to Chaos) and *Afrociberdelia*. They wore their influences outside their pants by sampling Mark E. Smith in *'Rios, Pontes e Overdrives'* (what with my experience in Fortaleza, The Fall must be Very Big in the Nordeste), reworking local *maracatu* songs in *'Maracatu Atômico'* and titling one of their songs *'Samba Makossa'* – a reference to the exquisite *'Soul Makossa'* by Cameroon tenor sax player Manu Dibango: English punk, Pernambucan folk, soul, samba and African music in case the critics were too thick to comprehend.

A double CD, *CSNZ*, quite rare nowadays, was released posthumously with tracks recorded before his death and tributes from other artists, including the Talking Heads' David Byrne and Jamaican dub master The Mad Professor. Unlike the sparse guitar and drum beats of the first album, *CSNZ* indicated that a jazzier, fuller sound was in store for the future, with prominent musical ideas being floated in the studio, but the live tracks are still lean, mean and skeletal with an inflection not unlike the manic resonance of Rage Against The Machine. God knows what the audience felt that summer in 1995 when the group played the Montreux Jazz Festival. They would have felt more comfortable with their later offerings without Chico Science and an unrecognisable line-up. It's not just like The Doors without Jim Morrison; it's like The Doors without Jim Morrison, Ray Manzarek, Robbie Krieger and John Densmore – but, I have to admit, with the original two-fingers spirit still floating amongst the acid jazz melodies.

Tributes on the Net attest to the fact that hearing *'Da Lama Ao Kaos'* for first time for someone fed on samba, Brazilian MOR and formulaic regurgitated rhythms produces a heartbeat similar to that which accompanies the appearance of an overwhelming new emotion.

Like, well, like falling in love.

*****

I walked across Recife to the bus terminal at the bottom of Rua Dantas Barreto to buy the tickets for Porto de Galinhas, checking out the various churches of Santo Amaro in the process: small, pretty Santo Antônio, squashed amongst the commercial buildings surrounding it, Nossa Senhora do Carmo with its imposing façade opposite the cathedral of São Pedro de los Clérigos. I was close to getting altar fatigue, and on my way back I almost ignored the church and museum of São Francisco. This was built by the Venerable Third Order of São Francisco, a powerful and rich lay Catholic brotherhood that was very prominent in the religious and political life of Pernambuco, with many churches still prospering under their aegis. The church itself is ornate, but what makes it well and truly unmissable is its golden chapel, the Capela Dourada, completed in 1725. The opulent interior, composed of gilded cedarwood in dizzying Louis-Quinze baroque, represents the zenith of the financial power of the affluent Pernambucan *fidalgos*. Things would never be the same thereafter for the plantation owners as world competition for the crop intensified and new mineral wealth was discovered in the south, permanently shifting the political centre of gravity to this day.

A bunch of papers, carefully equispaced on the chapel seats, were facing downwards. I picked one up.

'When you encounter a desperate situation, be it a deadly disease or financial or other serious problems, you must know that St Judas Thaddeus is your companion …'

Tsk, tsk. The note specifically said that you must spread nine notes in nine different churches and not the whole lot in a single one! Unless, of course, there were many faithful operating at once, which was more than likely.

Two paintings at the end of the chapel depicted the martyrdom of Christians by aborigines; I guessed at the time that they were the *mártires do Pará*. I guessed wrongly, as I found out later. The paintings are called 'The Martyrs of Morocco' and 'The Martyrs of Japan', but as the artist had never visited those places, the landscape and the faces looked distinctly Brazilian. But what was unusual about these paintings was that they had been vandalised: the faces of the executioners had been scratched out by human fingers unable to distinguish the image from reality.

I got angry. Very angry.

Minds who fear, hate, and conversely, minds who hate, fear. You must pray to St Judas Thaddeus and spread the message 81 times or else in 13 days you will lose your job, your children, your life. No wonder the same people who gouged out the eyes of the baddies in those religious paintings were the same who tormented the Jews, considered Africans subhuman and burned homosexuals at the stake. People who follow a moral code because of fear of punishment – in this or another life – can only think in terms of crime and castigation. All outsiders, be they Indians, black slaves, Jews or homosexuals, are depraved and corrupt and must be eliminated not for what they believe, but for what they don't – *they do not fear what we fear*: a disciplinary chastisement in the netherworld. The thought that someone may follow a moral code for following a moral code's sake is not entertained by minds who fear, for what you see outside is a reflection of what you are within. I collected the St Judas Thaddeus notes, crumpled them together and stuffed them in my pocket. If nobody else does, I will clean the church of rubbish out of respect for the toil and the faith of the people who built this golden temple and for him who died on the cross preaching love and peace and being nice to each other. He – and they – don't deserve this.

I left the church and immediately entered a scene from a thirties' newsreel. A soup kitchen was operating outside the convent of São Francisco and a ragged, dirty, smelly queue of silent people with hungry eyes and scaly skin was being served by a couple operating from a van. The stench was so revolting I stepped back, but not too far: I was transfixed and appalled by the sight of so many skin diseases. I watched the black scarring on a woman's wrinkled face. Her hand was missing several fingers. Was it leprosy? Were those growths on the old man's head syphilitic? Were these guys thin because they were undernourished or did they have full-blown Aids? I thought I'd take a picture because no one, no one would believe me, but when I saw the quiet, suffering nobility in the zombified crowd's eyes, on par with the more fortunate denizens of Recife, I decided to respond with deference. Some misery is too strong even for voyeurism.

I meandered aimlessly. The scratched-out paintings amongst the golden magnificence of the Capela Dourada and the army of the decrepit poor amongst the architectural splendour of Recife obscured the processing of live images in my brain. I found myself browsing in a Christian bookshop. Perhaps I could find something on those martyrs – which I still thought were those of Pará.

'Do you have anything about the *mártires do Pará*?' I asked a lady with a glossy expression in her eyes and a taut shiny smile. She remained so motionless, I thought she might be deaf.

'Do you have anything about the *mártires do Pará*?' I repeated.

'This is an evangelical shop,' she replied with eerie cheerfulness. 'The *mártires* are Catholic, no?'

'I don't know,' I replied. 'I'm an atheist, myself.'

'And you want to find out about the *mártires*?'

'Erm, yes.'

Her expression changed to one of deep suspicion. I could read 'troll' in the stretching of her nostrils. She put her hand on my shoulder and escorted me out, applying an imperceptible but firm uniform pressure.

'I'll give you directions to the Catholic bookshop,' she said.

....

Extinct Languages of Brazil: Pernambuco Region

Fulniô: 2,788 ethnic population in Pernambuco. Macro-Gê language. Everyone in the ethnic group is bilingual in Portuguese. The Fulniô language is mainly used in an annual three-month religious retreat.

Kambiwá: 1,108 in ethnic group living in Pernambuco. Unclassified language. The ethnic group now speaks Portuguese. Extinct.

Kapinawá: 354 in ethnic group living in Pernambuco. Unclassified. The ethnic group now speaks Portuguese. Extinct.

Kirirí: 1,800 in the ethnic group living in Pernambuco and Serra de Urubá (Arobá) near the city of Cimbres, Bahia. Unclassified. The people are monolingual in Portuguese. Apparently distinct from Karirí-Xocó. Extinct.

Pankararú: Ethnic group: 3,676 spread in Pernambuco, Alagoas. Language isolate. The people are highly acculturated and monolingual in Portuguese. Possibly related to Kirirí. Extinct.

Truká: Ethnic group with numbers unknown living in Pernambuco and Bahía. Unclassified. People are monolingual in Portuguese. Extinct.

Tuxá: Ethnic group comprise 900 living in Bahía and Pernambuco. Language isolate. Ruhlen and others classify it as Equatorial. People are monolingual in Portuguese. Extinct.

Uamué: Ethnic group: 3,900 living in Pernambuco in the vicinity of Floresta. Unclassified. Ethnic group now speaks only Portuguese. Extinct.

(All numbers based on the 1995 census. From www.ethnologue.org)

....

When it was time for the Prince of Nassau to leave Recife, all the townspeople – Catholic, Protestant and Jewish – gathered to see him off. As his brothers had both died during his tenure in Brazil, he was to assume the family stewardship and claim the patrimonial palaces and castles in Siegen and Cleves. The Prince rode slowly on horseback through the throngs who were lamenting his departure. In the seventeenth century any departure on a long sea-voyage was akin to a gentle death. When he reached the sea he saw that the May surf was strong; it was difficult to reach the boat that would carry him to the ship moored outside the reefs.

Suddenly the crowd parted to let hundreds of naked, painted Indians through. We don't know whether they were Pankararú or Fulnió, Kambiwá or Kapinawá, Truká or Tuxá, Kiriri or Uamué. Some had been sent by the village chiefs to plead with him to stay. Many more asked to leave with the Prince. But it wasn't up to him. If only Holland had not engaged in war with Cromwell's England, if only the directors of the Dutch West India Company had not suspected him of personal empire-building, if only his brothers had not both died leaving the ancestral lands leaderless … well, that's what the Dutch adventure in Brazil has been reduced to: an 'if only' footnote in history.

Like those tribes would soon become.

I wonder if the Indians – those wild, bloodthirsty savages – knew that as they carried the Prince of Nassau on their shoulders through the raging surf to his boat, so that their beloved governor would not wet his feet.

– 21 –

I was sitting with Isaías in Pit Hausen on Rua Jeriquiti eating toasted sandwiches and drinking beer. I was reading an article in a newspaper about mangue-beat. The previous night a documentary had made history in the Rua da Moeda in Pina. The production company that made the award-laden *Central Station* was shooting a documentary about Brazilian music in the last 30 years in which Manguetown featured prominently. After interviewing the protagonists, a jam followed with Nação Zumbi, Naná Vasconcellos as a mixture of old *tropicalismo* and new mangue-beats resounded in the streets.

Damn, I wish I had known about that.

I read there was a blip on the screenplay: Fred04 from Mundo Livre SA, the only musician still living who had signed the original *mangue* manifesto, refused to participate. No co-habitation in celluloid of the *mangue* spirit with the star-studded Brazilian music establishment where Caetano Veloso and Gilberto Gil have reached divine status in academia as well as on *Top of the Pops*: hell, if it's studied in universities, it ain't rock'n'roll. Nice to see the torch of disobedience and innovation carried on defiantly by Fred04 now that Chico was dead.

Tomorrow we were going to Porto de Galinhas and Isaías was excited. He had, as was his wont, chosen my dish: a sweet made of fried cheese, banana and cinnamon sugar.

Pit Hausen was not the poshest of establishments.

'*Homens ordinarios,*' Isaías scoffed.

Ah, a false friend.

'Do you know how that translates in English?' I asked.

'How?'

'Ordinary – *comum* – people. In Portuguese an "ordinary" person means a person of bad character, doesn't it?'

He nodded.

'The expression is called a "false friend". You think you know what it means, but you don't. False friends lead to many a misunderstanding.'

Isaías was looking at me approvingly.

'You like languages, don't you John?'

'I do. Languages provide us with concepts we didn't know we had. There is no equivalent word for *saudade* in English: the feeling of missing something or someone. In English we use a verb, so we associate it with the passing of time and the therapeutic connotations time carries. In Portuguese, it's a feeling akin to nostalgia and has a more permanent quality, which affects the character of the people who speak the language, doesn't it?'

And every extinct language impoverishes our common perception even more.

'Is there an English word that is untranslatable?'

'Many, and you don't have to dig deeply to find one. "Unpredictable", for instance, has a nuance of excitement, and it's a positive term to use in art criticism, as it brings to mind images of innovation. In other languages it means simply "unforeseen".'

I paused for emphasis.

'If we don't have a word for it, do we have an image of a concept beforehand?' I asked rhetorically.

'What do you mean?'

'Do you know what *Angst* means?' I asked. 'It's a German word for a peculiarly German concept: existential fear. Do you suffer from existential fear, Isaías?'

He seemed perplexed.

'Yes, you do. You were worried about inheriting your father's illness. But you didn't have a word for it. German provides you with one, and bingo! it illuminates what you didn't know you knew.'

I stopped. Chico Science's mournful love ballad 'Risoflora' had started playing over the PA.

E quando estou um pouco mais junto eu quero te amar
E aí te deitar de lado como a flor que tinha na mão
E esquecí na calçada só por esquecer
Apenas porque você não sabe voltar pra mim

'Hey, John, are you happy?' Isaías asked.

What a question.

'I am content,' I said. 'I don't believe in happiness as a permanent state. If you manage your life correctly, you can generally be content and have spurts of happiness in between. If you can manage a few more spurts than average, you are a lucky man.'

Isaías sighed.

'*Eu sou feliz,*' he insisted.

'Isaías,' I said, 'I'm leaving on Friday. The more we stay together and the closer we become, the more difficult it will be to part. You know that.'

He stared away in the darkness.

Em meus braços te levarei como uma flor
Pra minha maloca na beira do rio meu amor
Oh Risoflora!
Vou ficar de andada até te achar
Prometo meu amor vou me regenerar
Oh Risoflora não vou dar mais bobeira dentro de um caritó
Oh Risoflora não me deixe só.

There was still something I had to ask.

'Your father ...' I started.

He stiffened.

'... was he ever violent?'

He nodded, still looking away.

'Is that … is that why you left your village?'

Isaías turned around and looked me in the eye.

'Yes. That and the Other Thing.'

'Being gay?'

'John,' he said, 'I know three gay people in my town, and they're all married with kids.'

'Will you also get married?'

He smiled, put his fork down, looked at the stars and asked back, 'Will you marry me, John?'

I didn't reply.

If only.

Well, God or no God, or whatever god, we of the human race are collectively blessed with the gift of exploring alternative universes where 'what if' and 'if only' questions materialise: that gift is called a dream, and if there's anything I learned in Recife it is that we in the West have lost our capacity to dream, to conjure up images in our heads to serve as foundation for future hope, because it is only he who can have a dream that may attain it. And that night in Rua Jeriquiti, I had a real dream for the first time in years. And you know what? The more impossible the dream, the more satisfying the feeling.

So I dreamt in my alternative universe, say Universe04, that the Prince of Nassau had not been recalled to Holland so quickly, but spent enough time in Pernambuco to imbue its people with the ideals he espoused; no, not to make Brazil Dutch – that could never be, and it is improper even to think that it should be so with the weight of centuries hanging so heavily in the land – but to allow a better understanding between the colonists and the Indians, between the Jews and the Catholics and to leave a legacy of tolerance and mutual respect, avoiding the extinction of peoples and their languages. I dreamt that Chico Science had not been killed and that what I was listening to was a track from his masterpiece-yet-to-be, an album that had taken the world by storm and turned him into the most influential artist to emerge from South America.

And I dreamt that I did not have a prepaid Varig air-pass ticket in my suitcase, but stayed instead in Recife with Isaías, living happily ever after …

Chapter 5

Red Moon (Maceió, Porto de Galinhas)

Wonderful Life – or to give it its English title, *Afterlife* – is a 1998 Japanese cult movie, scripted and directed by Kore-eda Hirokazu, rated highly by the members of the Internet Movie Database. It has won several awards including Best Film in the Buenos Aires International Festival of Independent Cinema and the FIPRESCI Award in the prestigious Festival of San Sebastian 'for its universal theme, its empathy for nostalgia and its homage to cinema as transcending life'. It is certainly based upon a very unusual plot.

Ah, yes, the plot ...

....

The Words You'll Need

alvará = *royal decree*
bandeirante = *that will take a later chapter to explain – take it as a slave-hunter for the time being*
bofe = *hunk*
boite = *club*
Cerveja? Bem gelada, senhor? = *Beer? Ice cold, sir?*
como está? = *how are you?*
cruzeiros = *the Portuguese currency before the real*
fidalgo = *Portuguese aristocrat*
galinha = *chicken*
legal = *cool*
macaco = *monkey*
maconha = *dope, marijuana*
mocambo = *black rural community*
piscinas naturais = *naturally formed swimming pools*
polígono = *polygon*
yungas (Spanish) = *the cocaine-cultivating valleys in Bolivia*

....

I was dead when I arrived in Maceió.

Still at the airport and still dead, I made my way to the Varig desk to confirm the next flight out. The operator was a beautiful, bored blonde who was catching flies before I came and, I presume, relapsed into the habit after I left.

She was taking her time confirming.

'Is there a problem?' I asked.

'Only a slight one. Did you add the Curitiba flight later?'

I had indeed. What was the problem?

'The time of the connection in São Paulo precedes the flight in. I'll fix it straight away.'

I stood there waiting.

'Do you have a place to stay in Maceió?'

'No, I'll look around.'

'I can organise one for you,' she offered. 'As a Varig esteemed guest.'

Esteemed guest?

'Yes, it entitles you to a discount in the best hotels.'

I gently dismissed her surely futile attempt. 'I don't care much for the best hotels. My very top limit is $50 a night.'

She dialled a number, fired up with determination.

Well, cor blimey …

'I got you Hotel Tambaqui Praia,' she said. 'It's a modern four-star hotel in Ponta Verde. Normal price is $120 per night, but you get a special Varig discount to $50.'

Oh, to be off-season in Brazil.

'Is Ponta Verde inside Maceió city limits?' I asked for confirmation as images of an idyllic gringo-only exile flashed before my scared eyes.

The blonde returned my airpass with a why-don't-you-have-faith-in-me look.

'Yes it is. Trust me, you'll like both the hotel and the area,' she said. 'Come and let me know when you leave on Monday. I'll be here.'

And that's my plug for Varig.

*****

Maceió, the capital of the state of Alagoas, is an oddity: a Nordeste town seemingly at peace with itself. It may be because it's a sleepy, relatively modern capital with not much to show except its stunning beaches (yes, more of them); it may be because its ex-mayor, subsequently the state governor, became President of the Republic, so it was allocated extra attention when the pork-barrel politics started rolling; or it may simply be that the people of Alagoas have learned from past mistakes and are determined not to repeat them.

Alagoas used to be part of Pernambuco for most of Brazil's lifetime, until the hapless Recife revolution of 1817. Brazil was then still a Portuguese colony and secret societies in Minas Gerais, Bahia and Pernambuco plotted for independence. However, this was not to come for several years yet, and the leaders of the 1817 revolution were summarily executed, although the banner of independence they designed is now the official state flag of Pernambuco. For punishment, and to reduce the power of the sugar-cane barons, a state just under the size of our dear Belgium was carved from Pernambuco and named after the town of Alagoas. Don't look up the town on a map – it's been renamed Marechal Deodoro.

So what does this grand phrase I used – 'at peace with itself' – mean in practice?

Well, it means people queuing at bus stops. It means cycle lanes next to the freshly asphalted streets. It means special ramps for disabled access. It means a reasonable, modern bus system. It means bathers daring to wear watches on the beach, something unheard of in Copacabana or Boa Viagem. It means having villas without high walls or barbed wire for protection. The state contains seven out of the bottom ten poorest Brazilian municipalities, but you can walk around at night without worries.

Finally, it means respect for minorities.

Alagoas prides itself on being the most gay-friendly state in Brazil. Katia Born, Maceió's mayoress, sanctioned Law 1999/4898 which declares 28 June as Day of Homosexual Consciousness in commemoration of the New York Stonewall riots of 1969, which gave birth to the modern Gay Rights movement. Law 4920 followed, which established a civil entity: the Grupo Gay de Alagoas (GGAL) funded by the Alagoas taxpayer to stand up for gay rights and help disseminate information about sexually transmitted diseases, such as Aids.

It wasn't always so.

As the GGAL website informs us, on 20 January 1993 Renildo Santos, the city councillor for the district of Coqueiro Seco in Alagoas, publicly declared his homosexual orientation in an interview with Rádio Gazeta. His political foes accused him of lack of decency and suspended him from his political functions in the City Council. Feeling threatened, he asked the police authorities for protection. Brazilian leaders of the gay movement tried to transfer him from Coqueiro Seco to the south of Brazil.

They were not quick enough.

At dawn on 10 March 1993, Renildo was kidnapped from his house. Taken to an unknown location, he was beaten up violently and his ears, nose and tongue were mutilated. His fingernails were ripped out, and then his fingers were sheared off. His legs were broken. He was castrated, and a piece of wood was inserted into his anus and then broken while still inside. He was then shot in both eyes and both ears. His body was burned, because his murderers wanted to make his identification impossible. Finally, as if all this was not enough, his head was cut off and thrown into a river.

Renildo's murderers are still at large.

*****

Hotel Tambaqui Praia, need I say, was *fabulous*, and its location on the road parallel to the waterfront, ten minutes from the beach of Sete Coqueiros was *super*. A party of German tourists was reassuringly busy placing towels on the deckchairs, for Germans, like North Americans, are hard to please comfort-wise. This was easily one of the best hotels I have stayed at in Brazil, and one that normally I could not afford. My solar-powered shower was so high-tech it was impossible to operate – like all those super-duper video recorders where you end up taping the wrong channel, if at all. I was too embarrassed to ask for instructions and ended up like a pupil at a nineteenth-century boarding school, forced to have cold showers. At least mine was not communal.

My eyes fixed on the phone. Should I call?

No, wait until Sunday, as agreed.

Things I Don't Like About Brazil #5: Telenovelas

The nation is addicted to telenovelas, the raison d'être of a whole media industry. University research fellows have blamed them for the halving of the birth rate. They are TV drama mini-series that are blitzed into the television-owning households for several months and monopolise the tabloid news by turning their protagonists into superstars who then burn out like supernovas. The actors and actresses emote on the improbable scripts with all the charisma of a cream cheese bagel; the directors churn out the episodes in a Soviet-industrial manner; and the camera operators move from face to face in tear-jerking close-ups. Torsos are where the human body ends for the telenovela masters – but since that includes cleavage, we're all in good stead.

Sometimes they are based on famous novels – Jorge Amado being the most cinematic author, he is the one most savaged. Sometimes the photography does take in the splendour of the panoramic Brazilian landscapes and pushes a region up the country's conscience, like it did with the Pantanal back in 1990. But mostly it is soma for the masses who deserve bread and circuses but are only fed the latter.

In this chapter, you get three.

....

I switched on the telly.

The telenovela which was the rage at the time was *Terra Nostra*. It had shot into prominence Thiago Lacerda, a Carioca swimming champion who played Matteo, an Italian immigrant. Thiago was so gorgeous even I had picked up the hearsay that he was gay. That week, one of the tabloid magazines carried an interview in which he denied all rumours. (And to leave no doubt whatsoever, he got married two weeks afterwards.) Thiago's face was everywhere. Even the reputable *Jornal do Comércio* was offering a CD of Thiago 'full of intimacies' and a poster with the extra incentive of entry in a lucky draw. The winner and a friend of hers (the advert used the female gender to address the reader) were going to fly to Rio for dinner with the desirable hunk.

I switched off, fell back on the bed and stared at the ceiling, a bright red disk in front of my eyes.

– 23 –

Maceió was catapulted into the consciousness of Brazil in 1990 when its former mayor and later governor of the state of Alagoas, Fernando Collor de Mello, became the first democratically elected president after the long shadow of military dictatorship. By the time of my first trip to Brazil, he had been impeached, resigned and was subject to 140 court actions. By the year 2000, he had returned to politics and was running for mayor of São Paulo. In a nation hooked on soap operas with impossibly scripted and appallingly acted scenarios, no one could have predicted how lavishly the real-life telenovela of Fernando Collor's presidency would furnish the Brazilian appetite for juicy drama.

Even if politics bore you, stay with me for this one.

He started well. He used his position as chairman of the most popular football team in Alagoas to obtain the votes of its supporters. The rest of Brazil learned about him when, a week before he assumed the state governorship of Alagoas, he tried to block the payment of sinecures to state officials in court. He immediately earned the reputation of a corruption-busting Batman (and he was only 33, Boy Wonder!). He was part of the ruling elite of the Nordeste, but during his presidential bid he started as an outsider. He advertised heavily on TV – by controversially buying off the political broadcast time of smaller parties – and was supported by the big Globo network.

However, after his inauguration at the tender age of 40, the 'Plano Collor' came into effect and stunned the country: the President was freezing everyone's bank accounts and investments of more than 50,000 cruzeiros for 18 months in a radical and autocratic attempt to reduce the money supply and lower inflation. Although he sort of succeeded, temporarily, the fear he put into the man in the *Avenida* created the 1993 hyperinflation which I witnessed, and no one – Brazilian or foreign traveller – can easily forget *that*. This measure attracted the most attention, but looking back there were some lasting reforms: he liberalised the country's trade by lifting import controls, started the process of privatisation of ailing state companies, and moved to protect Indians by creating reserves. In a country which had lived under the paternalistic corporate state custody of the military he created powerful enemies – very powerful, indeed.

Fernando Collor was, and still is, a charmer, an 'Indiana Jones of politics' (© George Bush Sr.), who was photographed playing tennis, football and volleyball. He wore smart, flashy suits, could fly a plane, ride jet-skis and just *had* to drive a Ferrari. To top it all, he was married to gorgeous, pouting Rosane.

In typical soap opera fashion, it was his own brother, Pedro, who stabbed him in the back. Pedro made allegations of corruption in an interview with the magazine *Veja*, and much wilder ones in a book he published later about cocaine, LSD abuse and black magic ceremonies where Fernando Collor, all dressed in white, was supposed to offer animal sacrifices. 'Foul!' cried the President and his supporters: Pedro was jealous, because he suspected that Fernando and Pedro's wife, Teresa, might be having an affair. Fernando denied it; he had only been a vocal admirer of his sister-in-law's legs, that was all.

The really meaty scandal, though, was being slowly unveiled by Congress. A plan 'PC' was alleged, where irregularities and favours were granted to industrialists via Fernando's electoral campaign treasurer, Paulo César ('PC') Farias, who fled to – of all places – Thailand. Another interview with the chauffeur of Collor's secretary confirmed that monies were siphoned to a secret fund. The sum of seven hundred million dollars was floated.

From then on, events went ballistic. Congress started impeachment proceedings. The people, shocked, stunned and betrayed, started marching against their President. PC Farias was extradited from Thailand. Rosane was accused of nepotism and abuse of public money – in one celebrated case, she was alleged to have used public funds to stage her friend Eunícia's birthday party. Fernando and Pedro's mother, upset at the scandals, had a stroke and entered hospital in a coma.

Now things become outright confusing: since the new, post-dictatorship 1988 constitution had not made provision for impeachment, the proceedings were based on the *previous* one (the Collor defence concentrated on such technicalities). Then Collor resigned minutes before the impeachment vote was due to be taken, but it was taken anyway in December 1992 and went against him; he was banned from holding public office for eight years. But as he had resigned just before the vote was taken, how could Congress impeach a non-President? He challenged this at the Federal Supreme Court which was tied 4–4 at its verdict. So, in a baffling move, the Supreme Court decided to co-opt three judges from the Appeal Court to break the deadlock. The latter voted 2–1 to withhold the ban, allowing Collor to keep protesting that such an important decision was in reality made by a lower court.

Teresa, his sister-in-law, divorced his brother Pedro and made a fortune from those famous legs by advertising women's tights. Soon after, Pedro was diagnosed with a brain tumour and died. Their comatose mother died in 1995. Paulo César Farias was convicted of various financial crimes and went to jail, but as soon as he got out he was murdered in Maceió.

After an exhausting investigation by the Brazilian police and Interpol, Fernando Collor was never indicted of any crime for lack of evidence. He insists that it was all a plot by his enemies who never swallowed his liberalisation of the economy. What most people believe is that he was a politician out of his depth who may have been a good provincial governor, but should never have had a stab at higher office. The Nordestino part-authoritarian, part-paternalistic wheeling and dealing conducted in smoke-filled rooms (and Fernando Collor *adores* Cuban cigars) is different from the scrutiny and standards expected from higher office in

Brasília. And, more than that, there is a Brazilian establishment which presidents have to work *with*, not against.

But the soap opera goes on regardless. On Christmas Day 1999, José Carlos Guimarães, husband of Eunícia whose birthday party provoked such outcry, was found drowned in his swimming pool before he was due to appear in court to face 14 accusations of corruption. Dumb-bell weights were tied to his feet and heavy stones to his chest, and he left behind a – let me clear my throat – *suicide* note. If black magic was indeed involved, it seems to have worked.

The years in political wilderness ended in 2000: Collor returned from his exile in Miami, and, good as his word, ran for mayor of São Paulo. He lost dramatically – but hey, this is South America. From Argentina's Peron, and Brazil's own Vargas to Bolivia's Banzer and Venezuela's Chavín, the history of the continent is jam-packed with unlikely presidential comebacks.

It's the jam that seems to attract them …

*****

Life in Maceió has shifted away from the old centre and waterfront of the port of Jaraguá to the hotels, villas and beaches of Pajuçara, Ponta Verde and Jatiúca. But in defiance of the modern, at night the inhabitants flock to party in the narrow and atmospheric bars of Jaraguá, which has an air not unlike Lisbon's own decomposing Bairro Alto.

Seculu's is also in Jaraguá. A drag queen door-whore was posing in front inviting people in. Not many had taken up the offer by midnight: the club was almost empty, and after trying to engage the two bored barmen in conversation, I ended up talking to Patrícia, the hirsute lesbian owner. After this trip, I will have made friends with all the club promoters of the Nordeste.

Her male friend was ogling me.

'*Olá bofe,*' he drunkenly interrupted us.

'You're speaking to me?'

'Yes, big guy.'

Now, if anyone described me as *petit*, I would slap them in the face and shout: 'Truth Police, arrest this individual!' but I expect to be called 'muscular' rather than 'big'. I don't get those eating disorders for nothing! After a stabbing stare, I turned back to Patrícia.

'The good thing about a large town such as Recife is that there is a choice of gay clubs. Unlike Maceió where you only have one.'

The man with the size fixation piped up immediately: 'We have *two* gay clubs. Number One is further up the road.'

It was Patrícia's turn to stare at him murderously.

'Oh,' I chirped cherubically (OK, read a big cherub in the metaphor), 'can I pop over and have a look?'

I did not return. Number One was full to the brim, playing house music with the occasional Maghrebi tune in the same style as Fortaleza's Broadway. There was a square bar in the middle, a small dancing area in front, and a small stage for the occasional performance.

Since I was a new face in a small-town club, I attracted some attention. His name was Tony and he was tall, thin, long-limbed and black; a typical Maceiota if ever I saw one. He was dressed immaculately in a white frilly pirate shirt (circa 1981) and a black velvet jacket. He was beautiful, and he knew it with an arrogance that verged on rudeness.

Tony was a 'social organiser'.

'What the hell is that?' I asked. 'Marketing?'

Tony shook his head, demurely weighing his job's demands.

'Not really. I organise meetings and conventions in the city. Everything from hiring a room to the meals and lodgings of the participants.'

'That is – administration?'

'Not quite. I study economics,' Tony said. 'I'm working in the afternoons until I get my degree.'

'Are you out at work?'

He looked at me.

'No one is *out*, out in Maceió,' he replied. 'But everyone knows, and no one talks about it.'

'Don't ask, don't tell.'

'Precisely.'

'So what is there to do in this place?' I asked.

'Weekdays it's all dead. Fridays it's Number One. Saturdays it's Seculu's. Sundays it's the sauna or the beach.'

'Which beach is that?'

'Garça Torta. It's up north and rather difficult to find. But it's nice. There's a lesbian bar which serves food and drink.'

I was getting more and more dizzy-drunk by the minute.

'I should take you home,' Tony offered.

I needed to forget.

We ordered a taxi to my hotel, passed the woman receptionist who pretended she didn't notice, took the lift upstairs to my room and got up to some serious mischief. But when Tony asked to spend the night, I shot up like a bolt and surprised him with the venom in my voice.

'*NO WAY!*'

When he left, I felt relieved.

– 24 –

Maceió's beaches are its pride. I thought I had seen it all in Natal and Fortaleza, but in Maceió it's different: the sea is a gentle demulcent green, calm and imposing. The Chinese combine two characters to denote an ocean: the character that denotes 'green' and the one that denotes 'distant'. In Maceió you understand the inference – here the Atlantic becomes the Mahavishnu Orchestra's Emerald Beyond. In Fortaleza and Natal you have the sand-dunes; in Recife and Maceió you have the *piscinas naturais* where you splash around in rocks outside the coastal stretches of sugar-fine sand with the tropical fish circling, puzzled, around you.

I lay down on the beach at Ponta Verde next to a party of Germans who are always the first to discover such well-kept secrets.

'Tomorrow we are going to União de Palmares,' their rep was informing them. 'This is where the largest and last *quilombo* existed – the *quilombo* of Palmares.'

I stretched on the sand and mentally cut him off. He was only partly right. Palmares was the largest *quilombo* but certainly not the last.

Brazilian *quilombos* were small villages where runaway slaves from the plantations fled their masters and their humiliations in order to live as free men. The jungle and bush of the interior were a barrier to Europeans, but a natural refuge for the African slaves. Palmares was huge, and at its height in the 1680s, its territory extended for about 220 miles, it had a population of 30,000, and it fought off the Portuguese and Dutch colonial armies for sixty-odd years.

Contrary to popular belief, *quilombos* were never wiped out. It was the abolition of slavery in 1888 – and Brazil was the last country in the world to abolish this heinous practice – that turned them licit. When the Brazilian Ministry of Culture decided to count them one hundred years later, it found 672 sites that could be classed as remnants of old *quilombos*: most of them in the Nordeste, nine of them in Alagoas. The majority are composed of a few dozen families – but Chapada do Norte in Minas Gerais has a population of 16,000 souls. The *quilombos* are now treated like indigenous areas. This means that the land, which the slaves toiled for centuries, is officially and communally owned by their descendants. A process of regularisation has started and many *quilombos* now legally possess the land that sheltered their ancestors.

You cannot imagine a society more different from colonial Pernambuco than that in the black republic of the backlands. The former was white, capitalist, patriarchal, theocratic. The latter was black, communist, matriarchal with an admixture of Catholicism and African beliefs. I presume one word caught your eye there. Yes, as women were scarce, they were the head of the household. When a slave arrived, he was allotted a hut headed by a woman whom he had to share with other men and whom he had to obey. (This lack of women also bolstered male-to-male sexual relationships.) As for the other word that caught your eye: I said that the society was communist, but only in the sense that the social order was based on togetherness, communal cultivation and fraternal equality, since Palmares had a king who organised the *quilombo* in a stratified Angolan manner, for that was the primary cultural influence. '*Kilombo*' is a Bantu African word and denotes a male initiation camp. Palmares, whose inhabitants called it *Angola Janga* – Little Angola – was modelled on such traditional Bantu camps that turned into military compounds composed of fighting units of men who were roughly of the same age, ideal for perpetual war.

The 'Great Lord' of Palmares, in Bantu '*Nganga a nzumbi*', was transliterated in Portuguese as Ganga Zumba: '*As the king or lord, he enjoys everything produced in Palmares in addition to imported goods. He has a palace and a royal cloak, and is attended to by guards and officers who are accustomed to royal houses. In all respects, he receives a king's treatment and the ceremonies proper for a lord. People immediately kneel in his presence, applaud him and affirm his excellence. They speak to him as His Majesty and obey him out of admiration. He lives in the royal city called Macaco, a common name for death, which they associate with an animal. This city is the metropolis among the rest of the cities and settlements. It is fortified entirely by a wall of wattle and daub, with openings aimed so that the combatants might harm your safety. The area outside the wall is entirely planted with iron spikes and such clever traps that even the most vigilant will be imperilled. This city occupies a wide area and is composed of more than 1,500 houses. Among the residents are ministers of justice for the necessary execution of laws. They imitate everything found in a republic.*

Although these savages have completely forgotten bondage, they have not entirely lost recognition of the church. In this city crowds have recourse to a chapel and entrust their worries with images. At the chapel's entrance is a very perfect image of the child Jesus and others of Nossa Senhora da Conceição and St Bras. They choose one of the smartest to revere as the priest who baptizes them and marries them. However baptism does not follow the form determined by the church, and marriages are not the special events that the law of nature still demands.'

So we read in a 1670s report by an anonymous administrator in Recife. I don't know about you, but I noticed the phrase 'imported goods'. This was a full-blown trading state, a state composed of many *mocambos* and the document goes on to enumerate them.

*****

I'm lying there on the beach at Ponta Verde, the sun's rays bringing out my melanin by the gallon, watching the world stroll by, and the world wants to sell me something. There are peddlers of cheap sunglasses which can't compete with my Ray-Bans; kite-flyers who have their wares flip and flap off a single line; cooked shrimp, raw oyster and toasted cashew vendors; soap-bubble blowers who attract the kids' attention and their parents' *centavos*; serious traders who flaunt 21-carat medallions (as if); silly plastic trinkets or Nike baseball caps (does Nike have a trading standards officer in Alagoas?) plus the inevitable coconut and Coca-Cola sellers. Yes, I'm lying on the beach, listening to the petty gossip of the German tourists behind me – it appears I am missing out on the Tambaqui Praia breakfast buffet with all my late nights; I wake up from my daydreaming, fending off beer sellers (*'Cerveja? Bem gelada, senhor?'*); I'm swimming slowly, being entertained by children who splash around on inflatable tyres. And all the time, my mind is miles away.

I'm dreading tomorrow.

Things I Like About Brazil #5: Telenovelas

C'mon: they're so camp and over the top, so ineptly shot and acted, so grotesquely improbable, they appeal to connoisseurs of kitsch. If you are a B-movie fan who thinks that They Stole Hitler's Brain *is a forgotten masterpiece of bad taste, that* The Wild Women of Wonga *is a classic of the exploitation genre and that director Ed Wood (Great Be His Name) should be canonised, then Brazilian telenovelas are an unmissable treat.*

Telenovela alert again.

Palmares was unique because it bred the myth of Zumbi, the valiant black hero who has become a symbol of Black Pride. Incidentally, he is Number 50 on the list of prominent homosexual Brazilian historical figures compiled by the Grupo Gay da Bahia.

Francisco Zumbi was born in 1655 in Palmares but was captured in that year and sold to a Catholic priest, Padre Antônio de Melo, who later wrote a monograph about his famous 'possession'. Apparently he taught Zumbi Latin and Portuguese, but at the age of 15 the ungrateful boy disappeared, leaving a note behind saying that he was off to join Ganga Zumba and his merry men. According to the Padre, he returned to visit him three times during his later life.

Zumbi became a famous warrior, while Palmares was being slowly bled to death. It had to be defeated as it was acting as a magnet for newly arrived slaves. In the campaign of 1676–7 a number of Ganga Zumba's family were captured in Amaro. He was ready to negotiate – and negotiate he did in 1678. The government of Pernambuco ordered him to leave Palmares and move to the less easily defendable Cucau Valley. They would let his people live in peace under one condition: they would return any new runaway slaves to the colonial authorities.

It's at this point that Zumbi made the transition from history to heroism: he refused to obey the king and led a palace coup that ended in Ganga Zumba's regicide. Zumbi occupied Macaco and assumed the leadership of Palmares to lead his people in a desperate, doomed but defiant last campaign, holding his head high with his principles intact, for no slave would be returned to the Portuguese as long as he lived. Historians are divided on this. Wasn't the survival of the Palmarinos under an imperfect peace preferable to annihilation in short-lived freedom? Other communities in the Americas (most notably the Saramaca of Suriname) went through similar treaties and survived with their identity intact.

People, however, have hardly acted with logic throughout history; they have acted with emotion. Zumbi might have been a hothead, but he was a heroic hothead. He resisted for six more years, finally succumbing to the old fox Domingos Jorge Velho, a Paulista *bandeirante* who made his living out of enslaving Indians and capturing runaway slaves. One point of interest was that Jorge Velho's Portuguese was minimal and he preferred to communicate in Tupi; the other is that he was well into his seventies when he started the campaign against Palmares. The letter from the governor of Pernambuco to Jorge Velho regarding '*the conditions for the conquest and destruction of the Negroes of Palmares*' reads like a blank cheque – which it was. Not only did the governor furnish the expedition with ammunition, food and money, not only did the authorities relinquish any share in the future loot, but the Crown also gave away the lands in the region to Velho's gang. The only thing the governor wanted was the fugitives. An *alvará* tells us what the punishment was for any slave caught after an ambush in a *quilombo*: he was branded with the letter F – for *fujão*, 'runaway' – and had one ear cut off. He wasn't killed; that would be destroying another person's property.

The first round in 1692 was Zumbi's, but the subsequent ones belonged to the old *bandeirante*. Macaco fell after a long siege where 400 prisoners were taken, 500 killed and 200 committed mass suicide, hurling themselves from the precipice of the Macaco fortifications.

Despite that, Zumbi escaped; for another eighteen months, he fought a guerrilla campaign against the Portuguese. In true Messianic manner, he was betrayed by one of his retinue, and when Jorge Velho ensnared Zumbi and his pitiful band of faithful, he gave no quarter. Zumbi's head was taken back to be displayed in Recife as proof, since for the slaves and for a few whites, too, he was an immortal black Spartacus – a vengeful, nocturnal *zombie* spirit, fighting indefatigably for his people's liberty. We do not know the day of his birth, but because of his notoriety Jorge Velho noted the exact day of his death. And in the twenty-first century, the Zumbi Nation or *Nação Zumbi* – comprising, like Reverend Jesse Jackson's Rainbow Coalition, African-Brazilians, landless peasants, left-wing ideologists and *favela* slum-dwellers – celebrates the day of Zumbi's death, 20 November, with a reverence normally reserved for saints.

He never really died, did he?

*****

At night I went to Seculu's again, where Patrícia let me in for free. Now, I have a confession to make: all this time, and I haven't described to you my secret weapon in clubland: my flashing Cyberdog top. It's a blue T-shirt with a hole in the front where you can wire in a flashing plastic spiral stuck to the outside by velcro and operated by a battery in an inside pocket (which can be removed before washing). If I feel less chatty than usual, I wear the shirt and the crowd comes to me instead.

Like Roberto was doing now.

'*Muito legal*,' he said. 'How does it work?'

I touched my breast.

'With the power of my heart,' I answered.

He laughed. He had beautiful black eyes, not as pretty as Tony, but with a sexy approachability.

'It's my birthday today,' he said.

'*Bom aniversário*,' I said. 'How old?'

He grimaced. 'Twenty-nine. One more year and then …'

My turn to wink mockingly.

'So the rest of us are only fit for the scrap heap?'

Roberto was flirtily drunk. So was I.

'Well, us older men will now retire hurt,' I announced and kissed him on the cheek.

I traipsed to the bar. The music had turned Brazilian, and the crowd was going ape. A guy climbed on a chair and started blowing a shrill whistle attached to his neck with a shell necklace.

'Ouch,' I said. 'Go away. You are uncool. This isn't happy hardcore!'

I don't think he understood, because he called his friend and they both blew their whistles at me. I moved. They moved with me, right into my personal headspace.

I got angry.

Without thinking of the implications, I grabbed the guy's necklace and twisted it round his neck until it broke. Then I grabbed his friend's whistle and pushed him on the floor. Within seconds, before the two were able to react from the shock, the bouncers were escorting us to the exit.

Why do I get into such situations when I'm drunk?

Aha, but at the exit was Patrícia. Or, should I emphasise, my *friend* Patrícia?

The two guys were more effusively out of it than I was.

'HE BROKE MY NECKLACE!' yelled one.

'HE STOLE MY WHISTLE!' shouted the other.

'HE NEARLY CHOKED ME!' cried the first.

'HE PUSHED ME DOWN ON THE FLOOR!' shrieked the second.

I sobered up and pretended to be a paragon of virtue.

'They were whistling in my ear,' I complained. 'I asked them to stop. But they wouldn't leave me alone.'

'HE BROKE MY NECKLACE!' the first started again.

'I'm sorry,' I lied. 'But it was only a reaction.'

'HE STOLE MY WHISTLE!' continued the other.

Patrícia had already made up her mind.

'All right!' she ruled. She turned to me. 'Give him the whistle.'

I gave the second guy his whistle.

'Now, go back in and keep off each other,' she said. 'And let no one whistle in the other's ear.'

I thought I did well there with such an oblique rebuke, especially since I was one necklace up on the others. They knew that as well, and once inside they made a slight cut-throat gesture to me. I assessed the situation quickly, looked around and attached myself to Roberto's party, which numbered about half a dozen – hell, if I had a tail, I'd wag it.

*****

The receptionist was the same one who had greeted me and Tony the day before. She was still expressionless and polite as she gave me the key.

When we got upstairs, Roberto complained that he was too sweaty and disappeared into the shower. I waited wondering … two minutes … three minutes …

He emerged on cue.

'How does your hot water work?' he asked. 'I can't figure it out.'

Him too.

I proceeded to lie. 'I don't care; I like it cool and refreshing.'

He bought it.

When he'd finished in the shower, we sat on the bed and had some beer. Bad move, because Roberto was putting me to sleep telling me shaggy-dog stories.

'… four years into my psychology course …'

A psychologist who talks? Rare species.

'… and no one knows. Not even my parents …'

Roberto was boring me, so I made a move.

'Hey, don't rush me,' he said. 'Is sex the only thing you want?'

Ahem, yes.

He got up and started pacing around the room.

'I can't *just* have sex,' he said. 'I am interested in *you*. I want to find the personality behind that flashing T-shirt.'

'Roberto,' I reminded him, 'I'm flying to Salvador the day after tomorrow.'

'So? I want to know the person I'm sleeping with.'

I snapped: 'Is that why you've been talking on your own for the last half hour?'

There was an uncomfortable silence. I made an effort.

'Go on, since it's your birthday, I'll give you a present,' I said and attempted to smile.

'YOU RUINED MY BIRTHDAY!' he bellowed at me.

That's it. This isn't working …

I started getting dressed.

'What are you doing?'

'I thought we might get back to the club,' I said. 'It's still early.'

'Back to the club? You want to pick up someone else, don't you?'

I counted to ten. Actually no – to two.

'Roberto,' I said, 'it's for the best. I'll pay for the taxi. It's only 4 a.m. – your friends will still be there.'

He looked at me with mounting desperation.

'But I don't want to go to the club. I want to be here with you.' He looked down, dejected.

If it wasn't his birthday I'd have chucked him out ages ago.

A thought passed swiftly through my mind.

'Roberto,' I said, 'how long has it been since you've, well, you've come out?'

He looked at me. 'Not long.'

Goddess, give me strength!

'OK,' I relented. 'We'll stay here.'

I lay back on my bed, tired.

'But you still want sex,' he chirped.

'I'm not sure now,' I replied dozily.

'I put you off don't I? I put you off. This *always* happens to me.'

My patience exploded with an audible glass-shattering crash. I looked down. I had thrown the large painted sand bottle from Fortaleza on the floor and smashed it. There was coloured sand everywhere.

'Roberto,' I said furiously, 'please GO!'

He finally grasped that things had passed the point of no return.

'Fine,' he said, and politely, but icily, helped me sweep up the sand.

We left my room in a hurry. We didn't speak in the lift, and when I turned to the night receptionist Roberto turned the other way and fled.

The receptionist's eyes, full of opprobrium, said to me openly: *'Isn't it late to be going out again?'*

Mine replied curtly: *'None of your business.'*

Her pupils dilated even more and said, *'Aren't you tired for goodness' sake?'*

Mine threw daggers: *'There are at least two more dancing hours left.'*

Hers looked aside mockingly. *'Oh, that's what we call it now, is it?'*

My eyes were now throwing meat-cleavers at her.

'I am an esteemed Varig guest, remember?'

'Esteemed Varig slut, more likely!'

I gave her my room key.

'Thank you, sir,' she said.

I smiled clumsily and walked out.

– 25 –

Sunday. Today was the day.

I missed that wonderful hotel breakfast again, but managed to take the two buses to Garça Torta for the *barraca* called Beco da Garça. I lay on the beach; I listened to my Club Privilege house tape; I spoke to the bubbly waitress who had heard from Patrícia about last night's shenanigans in Seculu's; I ate a bowl of *siri* – freshwater crab cooked in a thick broth; I tried to kill time, before it slowly killed me.

I returned to my hotel at 6 p.m. I turned the TV on and saw an advert for a CD of Maghrebi house called *Arabian Nights*. I had bought the CD the day before. The shop owner had sold his whole stock of 75 that week alone; world music, indeed.

6.30 p.m. I called Glória and Jim in Rio. Glória was gushy, not expecting to hear from me. 'Where are you? Maceió? Are you enjoying yourself? Are the beaches as good as they say?'

7 p.m. I called Tony. I got his fax machine.

7.30 p.m. I figured out how to turn on the hot water and had a shower.

8 p.m. sharp. I waited five more minutes before I dialled the number.

'Olá,' I heard the voice on the other end. Albeit familiar, it sounded strange behind the wires' attenuation.

'Hello Isaías,' I said.

*****

As Woody Allen once mused, life doesn't imitate art – it imitates cheap television. So on to my own little telenovela. If it is ever filmed, I want Thiago to play me.

*****

The bus trip from Recife to Porto de Galinhas allowed me my first glimpse of those sugar-cane fields which become more and more plentiful as you approach Alagoas. Now the major sugar-cane producer of the Nordeste, Alagoas accounts for 50 per cent of the total, Pernambuco having diversified into floriculture, fruit and, last but not least, marijuana. The area occupied by the frontier formed by Pernambuco, Bahia and Alagoas is called the *'Polígono da maconha'* by the Brazilian authorities. This makes excursions into the interior of the *agreste* as dangerous for tourists as the odd trek in the Bolivian *yungas*.

The interstate BR-101 joins with the state PE-60 which degenerates into the smaller B-road of PE38 to the small community of Nossa Senhora do Ó, a village straight out of the Oscar-winning road movie *Central Station*, all overflowing rain sewers, stray dogs, pecking chickens and square-boxed, low-rise, concrete houses with no solid doors.

'It's a strange name, Nossa Senhora do Ó,' I said. 'What is special about the Ó? What does it signify?'

Isaías explained.

Mariolatry is a feature of all Catholic countries, but the Portuguese did not swallow the Virginal doctrine until much later, unlike the Spanish. This is the reason why in Spanish Latin America you will hear of the *virgen* this and the *virgen* that, whereas the Portuguese speak of 'Our Lady', *Nossa Senhora*. The role of the Virgen de Guadeloupe in Spanish-speaking America is assumed in Brazil by Nossa Senhora da Conceição, Our Lady of Conception, with the underlying fertility theme. In a place where child brides of fourteen and fifteen were given in marriage to men frequently three times their age and often died in childbirth in the remote plantations of the interior, the cult of Mary became totemistic: there is Nossa Senhora das Dores (Our Lady of the Pains), Nossa Senhora dos Anjos (Our Lady of the Angels – 'angels' being the name given to stillborn children or those who died soon after birth) and finally Nossa Senhora do Ó; the big, rotund capital vowel is a lexical restraint for Our Lady Pregnant with Child.

Porto de Galinhas welcomes you with a large papier mâché carnival-like figure of a Foghorn-Leghorn rooster. But I doubt if the tourists lounging in the beautiful, chic resort are aware of the eerie connotations of the name. The port of chickens? Firstly, why did chickens need to be imported? Answer: because in colonial Pernambuco every inch of the soil was cultivated for sugar cane at the expense of foodstuffs – monoculture meant exactly that. Beef, pork, chickens, sheep, goats had to be imported (where would they graze?) and, as they cost so much, they were not for the consumption of slaves. (In Bahia, the governor had to put in the statute book an obligation for every landowner to cultivate '*a thousand mounds of manioc for every slave he possesses*'.) Now, in times past the slave trade was not always officially sanctioned, especially after Great Britain declared it illegal, so slave trading ships moored clandestinely on the shores of Pernambuco and Bahia. The code used at the time to inform the interested parties was '*Tem galinha no porto*': 'There are chickens in the harbour' – because slaves were disguised as chicken cargo. In Brazil there are chilling reminders of the past even in the most idyllic of places.

Isaías and I settled for an unpretentious *pensão* fifty yards from the beach. We had a large room with a double bed, fridge, and Laura Ashley floral curtains plus –

'An air conditioner!' shouted Isaías with delight. 'I've never stayed in a hotel with an air conditioner.'

He turned it on full. I smiled benignly and put on a long-sleeved shirt.

The unique feature of this coastline is the occurrence of natural swimming pools formed in the reef just outside the beach. Flat *jangadas* take you there and back for a fee, but I was tall enough to walk the couple of hundred yards, keeping my camera out of the water. It was a bit hairier returning as the tide had started coming in.

'Why are those *piscinas naturais* so famous?' I asked.

Isaías walked carefully amongst the sharp reef surface.

'Here,' he said and squatted, dipping his index finger inside a pool.

So what? I thought, until …

… until a myriad of small fishes emerged from the reef and swam around Isaías's finger checking for something edible. He looked up, smiled, and dipped it elsewhere, prompting the formation of a new piscean chorus line. So we splashed about in the holes, scared the crabs, marvelled at the colours of the coral, picked up the starfish and avoided stepping on the spiky sea-urchins. The reef is so large, it's easy to find your own personal crystal-clear waterhole to explore and forget about the rest of the world – and that is exactly what we did.

*****

Isaías was putting on the D&G top I'd given him when he heard me sigh in bed. He turned around.

'Are you crying?' he asked.

I wasn't.

'Aren't you happy?' he asked instead.

'It's great being here together,' I said. 'But I'm dreading Friday when I have to fly to Maceió.'

He presented me with one of his smiles.

'At the moment, John, I am living a dream. I am enjoying the Now. I am not thinking about Friday.'

'But I am. In every situation, I can think only of how it will end.'

'It doesn't have to end,' he whispered.

I had thought of that. Maceió was only five hours away from Recife by bus. I dismissed it; it would only prolong the agony. What right did I have to come barging into Isaías's life with his *vestibular* exams and mess it all up for a few weeks? This was my holiday, but it was his life.

'The longer we stay together, the more difficult it will become to separate,' I answered back.

It was early evening and the day-trippers had left; Porto de Galinhas had become more intimate as fishermen returned with their catch and the few lights of the restaurants turned the large, boundless beach into a smaller and more manageable stretch. We sat at a bar and sipped cold caipirinhas, feet up, watching the sun set into the sea with dozens of other revellers scattered on chairs and mats – all fixated on the large red disk about to disappear.

'This is the life,' I said to Isaías. 'Sitting back, drinking alcohol, watching the sunset.'

Isaías laughed and before he said anything, I realised: the north-eastern coast of Brazil was, well, facing *east* last time I checked the map.

'It's not the sun, John,' said Isaías. 'It's the moon.'

'Amazing,' I murmured.

I had heard of this before: when the moon reaches the bottom of its ecliptic – and it doesn't happen very often – it appears large and red like the sun. The moon was not full; that happened on the night I had met

Isaías, but it now appeared on the horizon, red and gibbous, like a second sun about to set; a bravura celestial vernissage I never expected to witness. We watched, hypnotised, as the moon rose; and the more it rose, the more it lost its colour and the smaller it became until there came a time when it turned into its normal pale, silvery self.

'I'm happy,' said Isaías.

'So am I,' I said, surprised to hear my mouth utter those words.

He took a deep breath. 'Hey, John, we have a saying in Brazil: *the happiness of the poor does not last long.*'

I rose before he got too soppy.

'Let's move to a restaurant for dinner.'

I let Isaías order a *cabidela* for two. 'Hey, John, this is what my mother cooks at home. It's a real Pernambucan dish.'

'Consisting of …'

'It's a chicken cooked in a sauce of its own blood.'

I didn't quite fancy the thought of it, but when the meal came it was delicious. I was thinking of black pudding and what I got was pot roast with thick gravy. A bit heavy.

'Let's have a stroll,' I proposed.

We walked on the beach under the strong moonlight, but because of that moonlight we had to walk past the last restaurant, past the last expensive beach villa with dogs barking at us; past the fishermen who were mending their nets under an oil lamp; past the boy-girl couples embracing each other under the palm trees. We walked for forty-five minutes to be able to hold hands, to sit down and kiss and cuddle, for we were gay and society doesn't like what we like and actively persecutes us for it. Our behaviour merits different legal and religious restrictions because our kisses are considered depraved, our love diseased and our embraces aberrant in the pleasure they give us. But that night in Porto de Galinhas, if there was any shame to be had, it stood wholly on the other side.

*****

Isaías was coughing and sniffing.

'I shut down the air conditioning,' I said at breakfast. 'You were shivering during the night. I much prefer ceiling fans myself.'

Isaías wasn't cheery.

'I've fallen ill many times with air conditioning,' I added. 'If you don't maintain the water tanks properly, you end up breeding microbes.'

The landlady came in and heard me speaking Portuguese.

'How did you learn?' she asked.

'I already spoke Spanish, so I started with BBC cassettes,' I said, 'and went on from there.'

That made Isaías chuckle and the lady disappear.

'What did I say?' I asked.

'You said *cacete* not *cassete*.'

The fine distinction eluded me. 'So?'

'You don't know what *cacete* means?'

'No – what?'

'It means your *pênis*.'

I jumped and looked towards the kitchen. 'NO!'

'Yes!'

'No!' I had been mispronouncing the word during the whole trip!

'Tell me all the swear words – now. First for *cacete*.'

Isaías started thinking, I started writing.

'*Pica. Pau* – like wood.'

'We say wood, too.'

'*Peia. Bimba. Bilola. Caralho.*'

He stopped.

'How do you say queer? I only know *bicha* and *entendido*.'

'*Frutinha*,' he laughed. '*Boiola. Baitola. Veado. Pederasta.*'

'No,' I said, 'that's paedophile.'

'No,' he insisted. 'That is *pedófilo*. You say *pederasta* for queer.'

Like in French, I thought.

'And the female bit.'

If he could blush he did.

'I can't say *that*. I can't,' he repeated. 'It's *very* bad.'

'Go on,' I prompted him. 'I might mispronounce something again.'

'I can't.'

It's always the words for female genitalia that are taboo.

'Go on.'

He relented.

'*Boceta*,' he said and cringed.

I saw the landlady coming in from the kitchen.

'OK, OK. Enough,' I said.

Isaías thought I was getting embarrassed and started enjoying it.

'*Vagina! Chochota! Cona!*' he continued.

Unbeknown to Isaías, the landlady did a sharp U-turn out of the room again.

'*Pipí!*'

I got up. 'Let's go, shall we?'

As we walked to the beach, we fell silent again with only Isaías's occasional sniff breaking the monotony. We sat on a couple of deckchairs.

'So, what do you think you'll study when you pass your entrance exam?'

He looked at me bitterly.

'I don't know, John. I'm not sure I'll pass.'

'Nonsense. You'll study and you'll pass ...'

'I have so much to cover ...'

'So, you'll cover it.'

Isaías shook his head in a you-don't-understand manner.

'The university entrance exam is a sham. Only the rich middle-class kids succeed.'

'But it's the same for everyone.'

'Hey, John, in Brazil nothing is the same for everyone.'

'Well, OK, but exams are exams. Are you saying they're fixed?'

He shook his head wearily.

'No, they're not. But it's the rich who go to schools that are able to teach them the full syllabus. Some state schools don't even touch some subjects. What about the teachers – do you think the best teachers prefer to work in decaying buildings? Then there are the books – who can manage to buy them? And do you think the poor who need to work to live can afford time to study?'

I remembered Isaías didn't have exam books in his room: oh, the presumptions of the First World. He continued, his grievance undiminished.

'So you end up with the middle-class boys going to universities that don't charge tuition fees whereas the poor can't improve themselves.'

'But you're going to a private school. Your mother is paying.'

He did not reply.

'You *are* going to school, aren't you?'

He remained silent for a minute, but it was not the silence of guilt.

'So much to cover ...' he repeated distantly. 'So little time.'

'There's never enough time,' I commented. 'That is our curse.'

We said nothing for a while.

One more thing bothered me.

'Isaías?' I asked.

'What?'

'If I give you the money, could you pay the landlady yourself?'

*****

When we returned to Recife, we had our last dinner together in a *crêperie* in the fashionable Galeria Jeanne d'Arque in Pina washed down with a bottle of my favourite Chilean red – Casillero del Diablo.

'See this?' I pointed at the label. 'Concha y Torro, just outside Santiago. I've been there. I've been to the actual Casillero, the vault where they keep the wine!'

Isaías was watching me nonplussed.

'They call it the Vault of the Devil in order to frighten off the workers, because that is where they keep their best wine.'

Isaías was far away.

'So, you'll leave Recife and you'll fly tomorrow and goodbye Isaías.' I jumped.

'Hey, what happened to that "Don't worry about Friday, John"?'

'Friday is *tomorrow*.'

I flinched. 'Don't remind me.'

'You'll have a nice memory of Recife and you'll have fun with the boys in Maceió.'

'Isaías,' I said mockingly, 'it's not as if you'll be alone in Recife yourself.'

I fixed my eyes on him and tried to read his thoughts. There was a hidden side of him I didn't know. For instance, I had never met any of his friends. Was he a bit of a hustler after all or was he genuine?

'We are at a stage in our relationship when one is wondering whether the other one is indeed special,' I said. 'I'm thinking: *Does he always do this with tourists?* and you are probably thinking: *Does he always have affairs on holiday?*'

Isaías grinned.

'How true,' he said. 'How true.'

'And …?'

He smiled mischievously.

I stuck out my tongue.

*****

Friday.

There was a knock on my hotel-room door at 7.30 a.m. It was Isaías. Without a word we fell into each other's arms and stayed there for what should have been forever, but forever is a long time indeed and, well, there's never enough of it.

'When do you have to go?' asked Isaías.

'In half an hour.'

'Half an hour,' he repeated, biting his lip.

'Hey, John,' he said after a while.

'What?'

'Will I see you again?'

'I don't know.'

I moved towards the window for one of my last views of the Recife panorama over the Rio Capibaribe.

He squirmed.

'Tell me anything, tell me you don't love me, but don't tell me I won't see you anymore.'

'Do you really want to?' I asked. 'You are so much younger than me. If we meet again, you'll still be young and handsome, but I'll be older and will have lost my looks. Isn't it better to remember me like this?'

'You're stupid,' he said and walked over to me. 'Call me then. Will you?'

'OK, I'll do that.'

'Tomorrow.'

'No,' I said. 'Let a few days pass.'

'Sunday then. Eight o'clock. I'll be waiting.'

'OK, I promise.'

He looked away through the empty room to my luggage that had grown so much I had to send some of it back home by surface mail. Blame those Pernambucan surf shops.

'Did they clean your T-shirt?' he asked.

'Actually, no, there are still some shadows around the shoulder. I'll try one more time.'

We lay back on the bed in a tight embrace. I remembered the cynic's definition of love: two animals each with its teeth sunk into the other's neck, both scared to let go in case they bleed to death.

But this old cynic's had it.

'Isaías,' I whispered.

'Yes.'

'You remember the night in Porto de Galinhas when we were sitting by the beach watching that red moon rise?'

'How can I forget?'

This was getting harder. I spoke slowly.

'There was this Japanese film that was released in England not so long ago. I can't remember its name. Something about the *Next Life* or *Wonderful Life* or something.'

'Yes?'

'Well, its plot is very peculiar. It's about Heaven. People die, and they wait in the antechamber of Paradise and the angels try to help them remember the one moment in their life when they felt truly happy, the moment they would like to relive in all eternity. That would be their Heaven.'

'Yes?'

I hesitated.

'Well, if this was true, and if it was me up there for all my sins, I would choose that night in Porto de Galinhas under that big red moon.'

This time Isaías didn't answer. He lay there looking at the ceiling. When he finally turned around, and I saw his moist eyes, I knew he'd be forever mine.

– 26 –

'*Olá John. Como está?*'

It was strange hearing Isaías's voice, me sitting in a different hotel room, in a different town.

'Fine. And you?'

'I'm well.'

'What did you do for the weekend?'

'I went to CATS.'

There was a pause.

'I didn't enjoy it because you weren't there.'

I said nothing.

'And you? Have you forgotten me?'

I thought of Tony and Roberto.

'I did my best to forget you, Isaías. But no, I haven't.'

'How is Maceió?'

'Much smaller than Recife. More touristy.'

'Will you call me again?'

'From Salvador?'

'Yes.'

I said nothing.

'I'd love to see Salvador,' he said.

The pause sounded like an invitation. He was so needy, he made my heart bounce.

'Listen Isaías,' I started without thinking, 'I must follow my airpass flights, but towards the end, I just might try to delay my departure and fly over to Recife.'

I was improvising to keep the flame of hope alive.

'It costs a lot,' he replied. 'Plane tickets cost so much.'

He was right, of course. I swallowed hard.

'Anyway, even if you come, I won't be here.'

I jumped. The thought that I might lose contact with Isaías gave me stomach cramps.

'What do you mean?'

'I'm going back to Limoeiro.'

'And your *vestibular*?'

'I don't stand a chance.'

'But ... but ...'

'I am missing my village,' said Isaías. 'My family.'

Something, something in this story doesn't tally.

'Will you write to me?' I was now the beggar.

Something in this story doesn't fit, and I will never find out what.

'Maybe,' I heard him say.

He's playing games. What a time to play games.

'Hey, John. I must go now. But remember this ...'

And then he said something that still haunts me.

'... you are your own slave.'

*****

When the Europeans encountered the natives, they were shocked at their 'laziness' – their inability to think beyond tomorrow. The Indians didn't care much for backbreaking work: they hunted when they were hungry; they moved on when their small clearings went fallow; their *malocas* were built and rebuilt; their ornaments were portable, and they wore no clothes to covet. I am a product of my culture: insidiously Christian – the ultimate religion for hoarders, preaching as it does repayment in the afterlife; Graeco-Judean – all the arrogance and presumption of the know-it-all; materialistic – with all the imposition of reflected dreams that the work ethic entails.

Yet somewhere along the line we lost the plot and started putting a price on everything.

Yes, I am a product of my culture. I've been taught it's the apex of human achievement. I'm told that if I can buy what I want, that will make me happy and content. Therefore, if I cannot find happiness it's my own fault, so I am forever finding excuses: I'm ugly, I'm lazy, I'm gay, I'm old, I'm poor, I'm fat, I'm unlovable, and I'm reinforcing these beliefs in a negative feedback loop. But the ones who taught me this are the ones who are really having a ball, because they know I can never be satisfied and that if I ever realised how to really be content, I'd be out of the loop, like that one who flew out of the cuckoo's nest. He was a North American native, wasn't he?

They killed Zumbi for a reason: they want you to be in the loop.

It is the greatest of ironies that in this country of the longest institutionalised slavery I discovered that I myself was a slave, for I carry too much baggage and my shoulders ache from the weight. But I am not content with being content any more; a big red moon in Pernambuco will be my oriflamme to remind me that happiness is attainable – because for a night, for just one night, I did not care about tomorrow. I made time stand still.

And that, as a film from a remote culture points out, is the quintessence of Heaven.

BLOOD

Chapter 6

The Day of Ogum (Salvador)

Back in time, when Kings were Kings and Gods were Gods, the mythological African city of Irê, composed of seven different villages, was conquered by a superhuman warlord named Ogum. After leaving one of his sons as governor, Ogum departed for more glorious and successful military campaigns. One day he returned to Irê expecting adulation and recognition. But no one spoke to him, for he returned on a special festival when everyone had taken a vow of silence. Ogum was unaware of this – in his eyes here was a crime of *lése-majestè*, so in an act of rage, he embarked on a terrible massacre of the seven villages of Irê. When he found out what his choleric temper was capable of, the great leader stood back horrified, for this was not a first. His explosive temperament had led him to many acts of fury, but none so impetuous. Blood, especially innocent blood, demands blood in return. So he took out his sword, the sword that had slain so many enemies in so many battles, and killed himself in an act of such transcendent emotional intensity and remorse that the warlord became an *orixá*, an African god, the god of war, of iron and of the number seven.

If Ogum had been white, Roman and called Mars, his star sign would have been Aries, his pathos would have been turned into an opera by Gluck, and the sons of Ogum would find their horoscopes in the *Daily Trivial*. But because he's black and African the followers of the candomblé religion had to endure Roman-style persecution. In the 1930s, they came under the jurisdiction of the Vice Squad, which dealt with drugs, illegal gambling and prostitution. Until recently in Brazil their religious functions had to be authorised by the Secretary for Public Security.

Ógun méjeje lóòde Irê.

....

The Words You'll Need

azulejos = *tiles*
Baiano/a = *native of Bahia*
baião = *Bahian ballroom dancing*
camareiras = *cleaning ladies*
com leite frio = *with cold milk – the Brazilians make white coffee with hot milk*

com licença = excuse me
consulta = consultation
lembrança = memento
lomito = pork fillet
mal-educado/mal-educada = crass; it's an insult to Brazilians to tell them they've had no education. Amazingly, this is a source of pride for the self-made entrepreneur in Britain.
muito prazer = glad to meet you
negro/preto = black. Unlike in English, the word 'negro' has been reclaimed in Portuguese (like the word 'queer' in English) and has no offensive connotations.
pai/mãe-de-santo = father/mother of the saints – chief priest/priestess of the terreiro
rapaz-de-programa = rent boy, escort
Recôncavo = the country backlands of Salvador
senzala = slave quarters
sucos naturais = fruit juice
terreiro = candomblé place of worship
Um real só! = only one real
uma fita = a tape

....

– 27 –

Òkàn

I can think of no place other than Salvador where the airport bus eschews the direct autoroute and winds its way through the best parts of town, providing you with a sense of the city's measure. I was going to Hotel Palace on Rua Chile, which meant that I travelled from the airport to the main bus city terminus for over an hour; but this was an hour well spent, map in hand, judging distances, stamping visual images on sights underlined in blue ink and breathing in the names of neighbourhoods as they rolled by. We entered Avenida Dias da Silva – this must be Pituba; the zoo – here's Ondina; this stretch of sand with all those windsurfers – *black* windsurfers I had to pinch myself – must be Barra; these are the old aristocratic areas of Vitória and Canela, and we're going up, up to the High City – the *Cidade Alta* – through the Praça Castro Alves – I tried to imagine the gate to the city which stood here – into the bus terminus off the Praça da Sé.

Like many visitors to Salvador I got lost in clichés: I was in the capital of Bahia, the most African of Brazilian states (forget Belgium, Bahia is the size of France), cultural hub of the country, seat of the most famous *Carnaval* outside Rio, first capital of Brazil, founded in 1549, earlier than some European ones (say, Madrid or St Petersburg), breeding ground of half the musical talent of the country, and the source of serious crime warnings by every travel guide. Where did they say it was most dangerous? Near the Elevador Lacerda and the Ladeira da Misericordia.

About where I am now, I suppose.

I looked around. It was one o'clock in the afternoon, Monday, and there were plenty of people and police about. Relatively safe.

Anyway, there was no turning back, for Hotel Palace was the one I'd decided upon. It gets a name check (and action) in Jorge Amado's *Dona Flor and Her Two Husbands*, and I am a big Amado fan – believe me, magical realism did not start with Salman Rushdie. I will never suss out those Swedish bestowers of Nobel literature prizes and their obsessive hatred of commercial success. Winston Churchill has won and not Graham Greene; Rudolf Eucken and not Bertold Brecht. And when the Portuguese language came to be honoured in 1998, who got the prize but José Saramago and not Jorge Amado. Frankly, I know how their obscurantist, elitist minds work: as the Swedish Academy's press release reveals, Saramago's first major success didn't come until he was 60, whereas there is hardly any language Amado's work has not been translated into. Hey, don't start me off on this subject, because I'll take off and land on another planet. Where was I? Another planet – oh yes, Salvador.

I took up my fifteen-dollar room on the top floor – fifties in its ampleness and design, with an old *haut-bourgeois* air about it: strong, wooden wardrobes, large taps on deep washbasins, heavy curtains on tall, narrow windows, embroidered sheets on uncomfortable beds – and left almost immediately, camera in my backpack, photocopy of my passport in my back pocket, money stuffed down my sock. I wanted to see Salvador while it was still light, for I was at my most apprehensive. Dammit, those warnings from the travel guides eventually creep under your skin.

I met Nelson in the Terreiro de Jesús, the old Jesuit Square, outside the church of São Pedro. He followed me inside. I saw him and checked my camera as if he were able to steal it by telekinesis. Back to *The Beach*: you know the scene when the guys just *know* that Leonardo DiCaprio's backpacker would want to try cobra's blood and offer him a glass? I must have been emanating similar vibes for Nelson picked me out of the tourists admiring the tame rococo interior.

'Hello,' he said in English as he introduced himself. 'I'm Nelson. I'm a guide.'

I studied him carefully. His features were West African: short, oval face the colour of espresso with a tiny moustache and straight black hair. He treated everything, including my comments, with a sense of urgency and seriousness that verged on opaque antagonism. He wore a white shirt, black trousers and black polished shoes. Shoes are important – the poor in Brazil (and the not so poor) walk around if not barefoot, at least with primitive springy flip-flops; Nelson at least appeared respectable. I decided to ignore him but then he offered me the glass of cobra blood: 'Do you want to come to a candomblé ceremony?' he asked.

If there was one thing guaranteed to hold up my interest it was that.

'What ceremony?' I asked back in Portuguese. This threw him, but he recovered well.

'A normal ceremony. Not a tourist one. In a proper *terreiro*. Today is the day of Ogum.'

The rococo around me diminished in importance.

'What's your name?' he asked, switching into his mother tongue and taking advantage of my hesitation.

'John. And I thought the day of Ogum is Tuesday,' I replied. 'Or Wednesday. Today it's Monday.'

Was that admiration in his eyes?

'You *will* want to come,' he said. 'Today is the special day of Ogum. His feast day. You are very lucky. We don't have such a ceremony every week. Actually, we do. For the tourists. Would you rather go to that?'

In another city, another country, Nelson would be a highly successful second-car salesman.

'How much will it cost?'

'Nothing to get in. I'll take you there. For twenty reais?'

Good grief. Only a fiver.

'Will there be others?'

'There will be locals but not many tourists. You won't be able to take pictures.'

I stood there with mixed feelings. Despite all my scepticism, I thought he was genuine.

'Is it in Salvador?'

'Yes, yes, not too far, in Federação. Fifteen minutes by car. Tonight around eight o'clock.'

John, how brave are you?

'OK,' I heard myself say. I knew I was rolling head-first into some kind of adventure, but I had no idea that soon I'd be living inside a real Poppy Z. Brite horror story.

Nelson took out a pencil and paper: 'John, write down your name, hotel and room number.'

I wrote it down.

'Oh, the Hotel Palace,' smiled Nelson. 'I know it. Be ready for seven tonight.'

He patted me on the back.

'Don't worry, John. You'll like it. Let's have a walk together around the area.' And with a pause for emphasis: 'This is not a nice church. Come with me.'

We walked down the Praça Anchieta to the church and convent of São Francisco, which contains the greatest ballast of gold and silver in all of Brazil: one whole metric ton of gold is used, and the silver chandelier alone weighs twelve and a half stone. The Franciscan brothers were not as contemptuous of wealth as their patron: the eighteenth-century interior is sumptuously gold-leafed and the ceiling, inlaid with jacaranda wood, is illusionary baroque at its best.

'See that bird on the ceiling?' asked Nelson, who had got in free while I had to pay a ticket – so he might be a guide, after all.

'Yes.'

'Move about and see what happens.'

I walked back and forth looking up. Not only did the bird's gaze follow me wherever I went, but it turned its head as well!

'Now come over here.'

He showed me a courtyard full of large blue *azulejos* dating from the sixteenth century, each panel depicting a different parable or myth. Outside we passed by the unique plateresque façade of the church of The Third Order of São Francisco formed wholly from chiselled stone. I had seen this in Seville's cathedral and in Mexico City, but this early Renaissance style, which uses stone to mimic the excessively elaborate filigree work of a silversmith, is Spanish, not Portuguese.

'This is Spanish baroque!' I exclaimed.

'The only example in Brazil,' Nelson replied. 'It was only rediscovered in the 1930s. It had all been covered by plaster for centuries.'

Nelson was enjoying my speechlessness.

'Have you been to the historic district of Pelourinho, yet?' he asked.

'I literally walked from my hotel to the Terreiro de Jesus and met you,' I said.

'Well then,' he replied and took me to the irregular expanse of the Largo do Pelourinho, walking far too quickly amongst the kaleidoscope of colours, smells and sounds of its backstreets, each of which I could have spent hours in. When I stood outside the Casa Jorge Amado looking down on the hill past the elegant mauve Church of the Black Slaves and up towards the Carmelite monastery, I understood why this area is a vast Unesco monument containing 3,000 dwellings. This is a snapshot of life in times past and no Internet café in the corner or reggae club posters on a building site can alter the fact that you have walked into a time bubble. Yes, there are other places where you can peek through the mist of centuries: Pompeii in Italy, Mistra in Greece, Machu Picchu in Peru, Fatipur Sikri in India, but this time bubble is alive and thumping with the throbbing vitality of the original.

I felt Nelson's hand on my shoulder. How long had I been standing there?

'Let me show you one last thing,' he said.

We walked through a yard passing Hotel Pelourinho, a converted student house where a young Jorge Amado wrote his book *Suor*. Nelson climbed nimbly up a tight flight of stairs to a balcony. I was too dizzy to figure out whether there was public right of way: I just followed Nelson who stood on the roof and showed me the view.

'Look,' he said simply.

I was high on the High City – and I was looking down on the Low City – the *Cidade Baixa*: on my left the Elevador Lacerda, the gigantic 236-foot public lift connecting the two towns; below me the bustling Comércio with its yellow bazaar building; on my right the never-ending port of Salvador ...

But in front of me the sun lay low on the Bay of All Saints – the original *Bahia*, which gave the city and the state its name; vast, calm, imposing, unconquerable. So yes, I was back in time, and I was a follower of Mem de Sá, the iron governor of the new colony; I was a young priest in the entourage of the first Jesuit bishop, Manuel de Nóbrega; I was Toledo Osorio, sent by the Spanish king to defeat the Dutch – for what I saw had hardly changed in the centuries since they stood up here and gazed west. My imagination aflame and my cheeks in a teenage rush, I turned excitedly to Nelson who was enjoying my wonderment.

I wanted to tell him that, for a moment, I felt all-powerful like the old colonial masters.

I froze.

That would make him … that would make him …

I gritted my teeth. I mustn't forget. This was the place where slaves were stripped naked and whipped and tortured and put in stocks for punishment. In every new Brazilian town, according to the old Portuguese custom, a pole was erected in its principal square as a symbol of authority: the *pelourinho*, the whipping post. And all the saints of the bay can never atone for the injustices perpetrated on Nelson's ancestors for they weigh heavily on his shoulders and when he looks down, he can never *ever* feel like I did then, and that, by itself, is a crime.

Embarrassed, I toned down my excitement to a simple, whistling 'Wow!'

Méjì

Do you know proportionally how many African slaves were transported to North America out of the whole three-hundred-year transatlantic slave trade? Only 4 per cent. The rest went to the Caribbean and South America, with the lion's share landing in Brazil: a whopping 38 per cent, accounting for just under 4 million souls.

Where did they come from? Mostly from three tribes: the Angolans who spoke Quimbundo and have given the world the words 'zombie' and 'tanga' (which now means a G-string, but originally meant a loincloth); the Nagô speakers of Yoruba who provided the main religious language and rites for candomblé; and the Gége or Juju of Dahomey (now Benin) whose main contribution to world religious awareness was the fetish puppet. But as the Greeks and Romans had different names for the same deities (Zeus/Jupiter, Venus/Aphrodite), so did the nations of Africa. The Yoruba Ogum is the Juju Gu and the Angolan Mucumbe. The devil Exú is the Angolan Bombogira and the Juju Elegbá. A Yoruba spirit-god *orixá* (literally 'ruler of the head') is a Juju *vodum* – voodoo, the word which has come to describe the whole spectrum of New World African ceremonies. Bahian candomblé, like Rio's Umbandá or Cuban santería is – historical and geographical distances notwithstanding – the same as our more familiar Haitian voodoo: African religion syncretised with Catholic beliefs.

Why did it not take root in North America? Simply because the Protestant churches did not tolerate the worshipping of statues and offerings like the Catholics did. In Brazil one could easily keep a statue of Yemanjá (a kind of female Neptune) in the *senzala* and pass it off as Nossa Senhora da Conceição. Ogum was St George with the lance; Oxalá the creator, the very original Angolan 'zombie', was our own resurrected Jesus Christ; Iansã (a close match would be goddess Diana of the forests) was Santa Barbara and so on. For in the minds of the devotees, we are all one and we all believe in the same values, so the Catholic cult of the saints was mixed with the *voduns*, the statues with the fetishes, the Sunday mass with the trance dance and holy communion with ritual sacrifice.

*****

'Will there be any animal sacrifice?' I asked Nelson, who had arrived promptly, only twenty minutes late. Since no dark colours, especially black or red are allowed in a candomblé ceremony, I was wearing *that* white Bad Boy T-shirt with light khaki combats and was wondering whether I would be drenched in goat's blood. 'If I'm going to get muck on me, I have a cheaper T-shirt I bought in Fortaleza.'

'No, this is perfect,' said Nelson.

'Will there be any animal sacrifice?' I repeated.

Nelson shook his head. 'No. And you wouldn't be allowed to participate. Only affiliates are allowed in those. There was probably a ceremony earlier in the day, and they prepared the *orixá*'s food to be distributed afterwards.' He waved me to a parked taxi.

'Oh,' I said getting in, 'what food is it going to be?'

'Black cock,' said Nelson.

I should never have asked.

'But a special Angolan one – imported and then bred in the *terreiro*.'

I noticed the taxi meter stayed off. 'Can you put it on?' I asked.

Nelson dismissed me. 'It's only going to be about fifteen reais,' he said. 'I had trouble getting a taxi at this time of day and arranged the price with him in advance.'

'I thought twenty reais would include you taking me there and back,' I protested.

'Yes,' said Nelson, 'but my friend with the car let me down so we have to take taxis.'

Small-time hustler, but I should be OK as long as he thinks he can get more out of me.

We took a right from the central artery of Avenida Reitor Miguel Calmon, and I gasped. It wasn't just the change of scene with the bright lights of cars giving way to the semblance of a drive in a country road – it was the suddenness of it as the maze of narrow, unpaved roads with no street lighting started unfolding. One minute you're in the central thoroughfare of Brazil's third major city and the next in an impoverished *favela*. Nelson had to direct the taxi driver through the barely lit, deserted streets, flanked by decrepit dwellings and watched by mute silhouettes, until we reached a clearing on top of a hill.

'The *terreiro* of Oxumarê,' said Nelson, pointing at a large, white bungalow.

The *terreiro* was rectangular, like a low-ceilinged basilica. Inside, a single set of benches was arranged in a U, broken only by a small corridor to the door. At the other end there was an alcove where the musicians, the *ogãs*, all male, would play the ritual music, their only instruments three conical *ketu* drums. In the middle of the room stood a large floor-lamp with a stone base and a stuffed armadillo, Oxumarê's beloved animal, stuck halfway up, its legs forced around the pole like an overweight koala in a gladiator suit. The colour scheme was overwhelmingly cyan and the decor neutral and nondescript, especially after the golden ostentatiousness of São Francisco. Leaves were strewn on the floor; paper flags and plastic swords hung from the blanched walls. There was nothing that could not be bought in a Pound Shop where every piece of bric-a-brac costs a quid.

I took my seat on the right bench facing into the centre of the U: the sexes were strictly segregated – men sat on the right and women on the left. There were seven other tourists apart from myself: an elderly French-Swiss couple and their son, three Austrian guys and a German girl. After the *terreiro* started filling up, ours were the only European faces in what would eventually turn out to be a 200-plus capacity crowd. I saw an entrance on the musicians' right and a sign: *Reservado p/eguns* – reserved for spirits.

'Where does that lead to?' I asked Nelson.

'To the inner chambers of the *terreiro*,' Nelson said. 'For initiates only. That's where the sacrifices take place.'

I tried to be droll.

'Are there ever any human sacrifices?' I asked.

'Not in candomblé. In Quimbandá. Have you ever wondered where all those disappearing street children end up?'

Quimbandá is the black magic aspect of Umbandá, which is a modern spiritualist candomblé-style religion practised in Rio: the forces unleashed by spirits can be used constructively or destructively, leading to white or black magic. I dismissed the thought; this was scaring the gringo.

'Although,' he added, 'there is this *terreiro* in the Recôncavo –'

'What about it?'

'You noticed that the land around here is clear? *Terreiros* need to be built in an environment resembling nature. They can't be in the main square like Christian churches. It's much easier in the country than in the city. To reach this *terreiro* in the Recôncavo you have to walk eleven kilometres through the forest. Not even the authorities know about –'

He shut up abruptly.

'Are you Christian?' I asked after a while.

'Of course,' said Nelson. 'I was baptised Catholic.'

'And you also believe in candomblé?'

'I am an initiate myself.'

'But – but …'

'Candomblé accepts that every religion points to the true God. There are no contradictions.'

'And what do your Catholic priests say?'

Nelson's expression hardly changed.

'They don't like it so I don't tell them,' he answered with impeccable logic.

An effeminate old man dressed in a gold costume emerged from the reserved area.

'Who's that?' I asked.

'He's the *pai-de-santo*. He is the chief priest of the *terreiro*, along with Dona Tania. She's the *mãe-de-santo*, famous in all of Salvador. She's very powerful.'

'He's *white*,' I remarked. 'I thought this was an African-only religion.'

Three young white men in their twenties dressed in white linen robes emerged behind him.

'It's an African religion most of the time,' said Nelson, 'but there are exceptions.'

Several elderly women sat on plastic chairs opposite, and the men showed great deference by kneeling in front of them and kissing their hands.

'Is Dona Tania one of them?' I asked.

Nelson shook his head.

'No. These are *mães-de-santo* from other *terreiros*. There she is.'

There was no questioning Dona Tania's hierophantic presence: once she walked in, the room felt full. She was younger than I had thought; I reckon she was still in her late thirties – but African men and women are notorious for ageing gracefully, so I could be wrong. She was tall, handsome, big, very big, and dressed like all the others in a maid's uniform with a white lace apron that reached to the bust and functioned as a bra, leaving the shoulders bare. She scrutinised the surroundings, and her stare crossed mine for a moment. Was that a calm, regal nod I detected before she averted her eyes to embrace and kiss the *pai-de-santo*?

'Notice that the *pai-de-santo* is homosexual,' said Nelson.

I feigned surprise. 'It never crossed my mind.'

He missed my sarcasm.

'Fifty per cent of men in candomblé are homosexual,' he went on.

'Why?'

Nelson's expression, always serious and unsmiling, became puzzled. He thought for a bit.

'No one knows,' he said. 'But especially in the temple of Oxumarê you have many male homosexuals. It's the *orixá* who is homosexual.'

Pardon me?

Dona Tania led several barefoot women ranging from a septuagenarian to a twelve-year-old (guessing again) to the door. They knelt and kissed the floor with reverence.

'They're asking permission from Exú, the guardian of the threshold,' whispered Nelson in my ear.

'Permission for what?'

'For the ceremony. Tonight the spirits will enter the bodies of the dancers summoned by the drums. Exú will lead the way, then most likely Ogum. He's rather impatient.'

'Isn't Exú the Devil?

The drums started thumping and made my chin twitch.

'According to the Christian church. But no, think of him more like an angel. He intercedes. When he intercedes with evil intent, he can be the Devil.'

'Isn't it dangerous being possessed by a god, let alone the Devil?'

'It is. These mediums' – he pointed at the women – 'are very experienced, even the little ones.'

The drums echoed harder and harder playing the *oró*, the invocation to each spirit, and drowned Nelson's words. The first and smallest drum is the *lé*, the one that mutates the rhythm; the second, taller one is the *rumpi*, used for the sharp counterpoint that characterises all African-rooted music from syncopated jazz to the off-beat of reggae; and the big standing one is the *rum*; this keeps the beat, which becomes faster and faster as the entreaties to the deity grow more determined. These are the sacred drums, each of which has been generously sprinkled with the blood of a specially decapitated chicken. Candles, palm oil and offerings have stood a whole night in front of each one so that the drum can be infused with their strength. For these drums summon gods – and if any recalcitrant deity is moody and doesn't want to party, a double cowbell, the *agogô* is rung to sap the deity's disfavour, for its sound is irresistible, piercing through the battery of bongo-drummery like a whistle.

The women started rotating in a circle and around their own axis, slowly at first, eyes closed, feet and shoulders bare, layers of long, white, frilly undergowns swirling and bustling, light blue headkerchiefs demarcated by beads of sweat. The antiphonal chanting began: the call to Ogum '*Ogum je*' and what is this – yes, they are all dancing privately, the dance of Ogum summoning down the iron spirit of a bygone age. '*Ora Yeyê-o!*' – they're calling Oxum, the Black Venus, who is always pictured holding an *abebê*, a golden mirror-fan; '*Okê Arô*' – the dance of Oxóssi, the king of Ketu who became the spirit of the forest, green and blue like the jungles and the streams; '*Epa Babá*' – *terreiro* calling Oxalá, the god who fell asleep when Olodumaré asked him to create the world, letting Odudua steal his thunder, though Oxalá woke up in time to create us humans at the end; '*Odô Iyá*' – the dance of Yemanjá, the Lady of the Sea, the Great Mother of all spirits; '*Kawô Kabiyesile*' – 'Long live the King,' the cry to bring Xangô, the king with the three wives, the symbol of justice in an unjust land; '*Ora Yeyê-o!*' – again? Is Oxum not listening to our signals and has to be called again? Bring on the *agogô*! Yes!

I looked at my watch: how long had I been sitting there? It had been an hour: the repetition dulls your senses. We were all sweltering in the heat. The Swiss looked as if they'd been dipped in a pool with their clothes on. I wiped my forehead – this wasn't exactly boring, but it soon might be.

Then the youngest of the girls squatted in front of me, twisted her mouth as if to spit out a large stone and growled like a jaguar.

Métà

Back in time, when Kings were Kings and Gods were Gods, there lived a tall, strong man called Saboadã, the Oxumarê (king) of the Nagô nation. He fell in love with the beautiful Goddess Oxum, who had just left her husband Oxossi to live with Xangô. But the attentions of Saboadã sparked jealousy in Xangô, so a duel was in store with the inevitable result – the death of the mortal. Oxalá his father and Nanã his mother took away the body of Saboadã and transformed him into a serpent, the Oxumarê of the astral constellations, to pass his time amongst the stars. This serpent turns into a rainbow when the rain is over to transport water to the palace of Xangô in the sky and spends six months as a man – the serpent of the Earth – and six months as a woman – the serpent of the waters. Oxumarê is the god of duality: the Brazilian yin and yang embodied in one. He lives in waterfalls; his colours are those of the rainbow and his acolytes are the sexually unorthodox of this world. I was startled at the coincidence of the rainbow flag, the symbol of Gay Pride all over the globe, being the image of an African bisexual god-spirit for centuries before – but not as much as when I found out that Oxumarê is a full-blooded macho male in the original Yoruba culture.

It is only in Brazil that he's bisexual.

*****

The shock of seeing a possession at first-hand over, I watched raptly while the crowd started ululating as a spirit possessed each dancer in turn. The heat, the cries and the repetitive, ingressive rhythm of the drums took their toll on the German girl first and the Austrians second. The Swiss left soon after, summoned by a bossy guide. By 10.30 p.m., two hours after the ceremony had started, I was the only white face left, tapping my feet. Where the untrained ear only hears the common denominator of the percussive hypnotic beat, someone who likes Jamaican dub like me picks out the underlying synthesis of mutating tunes as they erupt to the fore and then disappear under the gradual unfolding of new beats. The monotony was broken by a frail old man who lunged at the dancers, eyes closed, movements unsteady. He was caught by the *pai-de-santo*, who took the man's shoes off and laid him down to rest.

I waved Nelson over. 'Has he been possessed as well?' I asked.

'Some god is playing tricks. This old man is untrained.'

'What will happen to him?'

'The *pai-de-santo* will direct the god to someone who is trained to receive him.'

'Can I talk to the *pai-de-santo* later?' I asked. 'I'm fascinated by this homosexuality business, especially because it runs counter to Christianity.'

'Sure,' said Nelson. 'You can have your future told by Dona Tania, too.'

I wasn't sure about *that*, but a huge communal wail filled the room and interrupted our conversation. From the inner entrance there came the gods – or the *eguns* dressed like gods. I recognised Ogum in pale cyan attire and a cheap, plastic sword; Exú in red and black with a pitchfork trident; Oxum in yellow and white; Omolú with a reed scarecrow dress covering his body; Iansã with her holy featherduster (no, I am not making this up); Oxalá in white, his long and multi-levelled handmade sceptre wrapped in glorious Bacofoil. There followed new initiates, men in suits with cyan sacred symbols, what seemed like a wedding couple and a woman offering sweet blue cakes all around. The drums grew climactic and the audience started participating harder; they reached out to the dancing *eguns*, palms open as if to keep them inside their enclosure. The *pai-de-santo* stood by the door turning away any straying gods who might want to escape – didn't they know this was a *controlled* trance? There were many embraces; between Dona Tania and the *eguns*; between the *eguns* and the audience. Ogum himself came up to me and asked for a hug. I stood up, embraced him and felt the divine breath on my cheeks. Take it from me, His Holiness suffers from halitosis.

Two kids behind me – nine? ten? years old – gave me the thumbs up. Apparently it is a great honour for a god to bless you. Before I knew it a plate of food had been placed on my lap. So this was the hallowed cock that had been ritually sacrificed earlier on to provide the *ebó*, the sacred nourishment for Ogum, who likes chicken, black beans and rice. I passed on the plate to the kids, remembering that candomblé ceremonies were also used to feed the poor in times past and, I suspect, in times present.

The *eguns* were now circling the audience, folding their dresses up like receptacles, and the ululating crowd started throwing in money.

Not unsurprisingly, they eventually assembled in front of me, beckoning me to reward them. They should have known that Nelson was their agent and gone to him to demand their cut, but there were far too many gods for me to resist their combined power and I succumbed, although Oxalá kept insisting for more and wouldn't take no for an answer. *Enough is enough!* I felt something land on my shoulder from the direction of the two kids. It was a bean dipped in tomato sauce. One of them pointed at the other who was holding up a fork with a guilty expression. Dammit, I should have given Oxalá those five reais or else this Bad Boy T-shirt will never get clean.

I stepped outside where about half of the faithful were chilling after their encounters with the Divine. Nelson dragged me to a corner where the younger *pais-de-santo*-to-be were leaning on a wall in a tight embrace. He introduced me. They smiled in what can only be described as a stoned manner and tightened their grip on each other's bodies.

'Many men in candomblé are homosexual,' said Nelson for the umpteenth time.

'I'm interested,' I said. 'I'm gay, too.'

Nelson, as usual, didn't register any emotion. 'You've come to the right place – Bahia. All the major politicians and leaders of the arts and sciences in Bahia are gay.'

'How does one become a *pai-de-santo*?' I asked.

Nelson looked at me as if he didn't understand why I couldn't. I saw the cavorting libidinous *pais-de-santo* on the wall, and it came to me in a flash.

'Like *that*?' I said, opening my eyes wide.

'How else? It's transmission of knowledge from male to male.'

I laughed flippantly. Nelson shook his head.

'Don't laugh. Candomblé is much more serious than that. And candomblé is for life. In some religions miracles or spells happen because you believe in them. In candomblé it doesn't matter. The spells will happen anyway.'

'How does one do spells?'

'Dona Tania can do some for you.'

I didn't like that.

'I don't want to see Dona Tania. I want to see the *pai-de-santo* and talk about homosexuality in the religion.'

'OK,' said Nelson, 'I'll manage that. Are you ready to leave?'

I was. We boarded one of several taxis parked outside the *terreiro* and returned to Rua Chile. I looked at my watch. It was 1.30 a.m. It had been a long day.

'Is there anything open at this time of night?' I asked Nelson.

Nelson said something to the taxi driver who let us off next to the Elevador Lacerda. There was a 24-hour diner with *lomitos* and *hamburguesas* and *sucos naturais*, eaten and sipped by Salvador's nocturnal *demi-monde*, which in my frightener scale comes between Vampire and Undead. There were prostitutes and their pimps, lone young crackheads with red eyes, and small gangs of, well, *gangsters* out on a run in town. The ubiquitous day police were nowhere to be seen – they probably think that anyone walking around the Elevador after midnight deserves a good mugging to cut them down to size. I paid for a couple of *sanduíches* and *sucos naturais* for myself and Nelson; I pretended to tie my laces and used the extra money rolled up in my sock rather than flash my wallet.

We left and made our way towards Hotel Palace, munching slowly. But then I felt uneasy; I turned around and saw a man, pumped up on drugs, walking towards us. He was holding a rolled-up newspaper pointed at our chests.

A gun, I thought, and nudged Nelson with my elbow.

Nelson waved me to walk on. He stayed back, faced the red-eyed would-be mugger and said something to him. They quibbled momentarily, but Nelson won the argument and the guy walked away.

When Nelson caught up with me, I bowed respectfully. 'That was very good,' I said. 'Candomblé magic scared him off?'

Nelson seemed miles away. 'Ah, nothing. You don't have to worry about anything when you're with me.'

'You are my Exú,' my joke went on.

He looked at me, seriously as was his wont, but then, for the first time, I saw him crack a smile.

Mèrin

Exú is always teasing, playing practical jokes, pushing the limits of divine tolerance and human patience. Although he is identified with Hermes/ Mercury, the messenger of the gods or a Christian archangel, the Catholic Church sees him, with his mischief-making and interfering old nature, as the Devil incarnate. Was not the Devil, after all, a full-time archangel before his fall?

One day Exú painted his body in his two favourite colours, taking care to stain one half of his body in red – up to his profile – and the other half in black. Then he asked the gods what colour he was. The gods on one side saw the black and the ones on the other side saw the red, so they all guessed wrong.

Exú laughed: 'In order to judge me,' he said, 'you have to check both my sides.'

*****

I missed most of the next day because I slept like a log except for the bit where I had to fend off stubborn hotel cleaners who insisted on doing my room even though I just wanted to snuggle and sleep and roll around and sleep again. I hate conscientious *camareiras* who don't recognise scruffy night owls and keep knocking at the door reminding them of breakfast. *Breakfast?* Excuse me, if Oxalá wanted us to be early birds, He would have given us beaks and wings!

I sat down at noon at the Cantina da Lua on the Terreiro de Jesús where I bumped into last night's Swiss tourists. They were up in arms when I told them that they missed the costume show and the ritual food banquet – their guide was concerned that they shouldn't hang around in Federação too late; why, even their taxi might be ambushed. Talking about guides, Nelson appeared out of nowhere carrying a large packet of Pampers. He answered my questioning look with a 'For my daughter. She's eighteen months old.' He suggested we meet later.

I gave him short shrift, using the Swiss as an excuse.

'Remember, I arranged for you to see Dona Tania tomorrow,' he said.

'I wanted to see the *pai-de-santo*,' I replied.

'It's all the same. You can talk to Dona Tania instead.'

I made a gesture of acquiescence if only to make him go away.

The Swiss and I spent most of the day walking down the Pelourinho streets starting from the old town gate, now part of the Museum Portas do Carmo. This was next to Nossa Senhora do Rosario dos Pretos, a church built brick by brick by slaves and freed blacks who were not allowed to worship freely in the European churches – all the gold of the church of São Francisco was not for their eyes, as they entered backwards and crouched at a specially designed enclosure averting their gaze from Mass.

At the top open V-neck of the Largo de Pelourinho, the Casa Jorge Amado reigns. We were bombarded with biographies, photographs, videos and editions of Amado's books on sale – plus a wallpapering of sleeves of his hardbacks in all the languages they have been translated into. At the bottom of the gentle Pelourinho declivity we started ascending the abrupt Ladeira do Carmo again to reach the Carmelite church and monastery. The original exterior of this church is quite fetching with its curved Mediterranean railings and simple neo-classical surfaces; the garden provides another Tardis-like glimpse of matters past with the original, unreconstructed catacombs leading into the netherworld of the runaway slaves, part of a maze network connecting crypt to crypt and cellar to cellar. 'You can go all the way to Nossa Senhora do Rosario,' the cleaner told me as I peeked into the hole, which looks as unkempt and hastily dug today as it must have done three centuries ago.

The treasury contains, amongst the bejewelled chalices and silver cruet sets, the *sui generis* attraction of Salvador, the Senhor Morto: an early eighteenth-century cedar statue of Christ laid to rest with thousands of rubies scattered about his body representing drops of blood shining triumphantly in death. For death was an occasion of celebration in Catholic Salvador with great libation and merriment taking place around the corpses buried inside the church walls. It was later, when various epidemics struck the city, that fear of the dead body began to emerge along with burial in new, specially designated areas – called cemeteries. When the Brazilian government decreed in 1836 that persons would henceforth be interred in the cemetery of Campo Santo (with a typically Brazilian bent, the rights went to a private monopoly which could raise charges at will) the whole population – rich, poor, white and black revolted and overturned the gravestones of Campo Santo. This was the ultimate setback for a city which, having lost its capital status to Rio back in 1763 and its sugar-cane and tobacco power to the southern states with their mineral and coffee wealth, was condemned to sink further and further into the quicksand of epidemics that would diminish its pre-eminence.

*****

Tuesday night, and I am stuck at a police checkpoint between the Praça da Sé and the Terreiro de Jesús, scrambling to get into Pelourinho with dozens of other hopefuls. The police did not allow anyone without an identity card to enter. I showed my tattered passport photocopy – I wasn't going into Pelourinho at night with my *real* passport. The policeman let me in and a small kid was also able to squeeze through. I looked back at the pleading throng. Were they all pickpockets about to be unleashed onto the unsuspecting tourists? Hardly. They were merely poor and would tone down the festive, upbeat face of the square.

A *baião* group was controlling the action on a stage in the Terreiro de Jesús with tourists dancing cheek to cheek with colourfully dressed Baianas – a dollar a picture. Food stalls, beer barrels and caipirinha lemon crushers were all touting for my attention. I could hardly move for the people. This was like trying to cross Rua Farme de Amoedo in Ipanema at the height of the Rio *Carnaval*. And this happens every Tuesday?

Outside the Casa Amado a reggae singer was contorting his body to Bob Marley songs: '*Get up! Stand up! Stand up for your rights.*' In front of the reggae singer stood a *batería*, a drum orchestra: the Swing do Peló, all seventeen of them, with two conductors – one for the top snares and bongos and one for the timpani and drums at the back. '*Ratatata! Ratatata!*' The conductors were yelling, impelling, chiding, scolding, pushing the sweating musicians into higher levels of concentration. The rhythm penetrated my eardrums, dispensed with the singer's attempts to provide a melody to the pulsing nerve of the batons – which ranged from drumsticks to long rubber hoses – and splattered the nerve endings on my spine. If this was a tourist attraction, then it failed, for I was in the middle of hundreds of gyrating locals: African women in white candomblé vestments and Muslim-like headgear swaying unobtrusively; big mommas with bosoms that could smother the Elevador Lacerda shaking their hips; sexually charged, dreadlocked young couples splashing their pheromones onto older men and women who grabbed the next passer-by for a dance. This was Fortaleza's Pirata's in the streets; this was Rio's *Carnaval* in miniature. Yesterday the sacred drums were doleful and respectful, but today – *Ratatata-tata-tata* – they are joyful, voluptuous and profane, exploding into my solar plexus. This is percussive concussion pulverising my brain, digging down, digging deep. I could not imagine my straitlaced Swiss friends enjoying this physical intensity. It is this lack of drums, the lack of a beat, that made European classical music – and ergo European civilisation – what it is: we are cerebral creatures; we crave melody or harmony to capture the mind; we have simply lost the rhythm. I wonder if we ever had it in us anyway. And yet, when the instinctive minimalism, the raw stomp and the choppy manic jerk of drums did arrive in the West and a gentle 4/4 rock 'n' roll beat started shaking the shoulders of Western teenagers, that beat was ultimately responsible for scenes of mass hysteria unseen before or since.

Amongst the multitude I spotted a guy so handsome as to make the incessant drum beat fade from my ears. He looked like a tanned Richard Gere circa *American Gigolo*; he was dressed like a male model out of *GQ*: a red open shirt with tight black trousers and a tight gold necklace. Suddenly our eyes met amongst the bobbing crowd. They stayed fixed for a minute as he puffed out smoke from his cigarette cinematically.

Then I lost him as a tourist asked me to take a picture of her with the drum orchestra. Cursing slightly, I obeyed. She put the camera back in her bag and held it tight against her body. Yes, there were many tourists around, and they were all afraid. I saw a guy with his backpack worn forwards looking apprehensive, keeping a safe distance from the crowd. Not for him the bonhomie of dancing in a line shoulder to shoulder or the sharing of a bottle of beer. Two white girls shook off – violently – the offer of a hand by a black youth to enter the dancing circle. So to the $64,000 question – and it's not a pleasant one: are we afraid of Salvador more than the rest of Brazil because it's more African, more *black*?

By now the Swing do Peló drummers and their constantly gesticulating conductors – who at one point, drunk on the passion of the rhythm, ever hypercritical of their retinue, nearly came to blows – were jogtrotting up the street with the reggae singer trying to flog recordings: '*Uma fita. Uma fita cinco reais. Dois reais. Um real só!*' As the drum sounds vanished one by one, my senses started rushing in to fill the void the resonance was abandoning. I looked at my watch. I had been pummelled for 50 whole minutes.

I returned to the Terreiro de Jesus where the more gentle *baião* band was still bopping strong and bought a beer. As I turned around, I saw the red shirt before I saw his face. Richard Gere was next to me, and he was smiling.

Game on.

'Hi,' I said. '*Tudo bom?*'

Richard Gere introduced himself as Emerson.

'I have no connection with Salvador,' said Emerson with a friendly but vacant air. 'I'm a Carioca.' He pointed at another immaculately dressed man next to him. 'Henrique, here, is Paulista. You?'

I told them the general stuff about my name, where I came from and where I'd been in Brazil.

'You went to a candomblé ceremony?' Emerson asked in disbelief.

'Yeah, it was good. I'm going to meet the *pai-de-santo* again tomorrow.'

'Don't. You don't know what you're letting yourself in for.'

'Why?'

'They are very powerful and dangerous,' Emerson said. 'You haven't given them anything of yours, have you?'

'Money.'

'I mean something like your name, your address.'

In my mind's ear I heard Nelson intone: *John, write down your name, hotel and room number.*

'Well, I did write down my details on how to find me. What's wrong with that?'

Emerson shook his head. 'They have you now.'

A sense of unease crept over me. 'What do you mean?'

'Now they can put a spell on you. They can control you.'

I bit my lip.

'What are you going to do after this?' asked Emerson.

Was that an invite? I stayed silent for a minute while Emerson made an excuse and ran off to talk to a girl standing nearby.

His mate, Henrique, approached me.

'Do you like my friend?' he asked matter-of-factly.

I looked at him.

'He is a *rapaz-de-programa*,' said Henrique. 'You got that didn't you?'

Huh? What? Erm, of course, of course.

'We are male models, and we were doing a shoot today for *Elite* magazine. Have you heard of it?'

'No.'

'It's very popular. We're also looking to earn some extra money.'

I must have looked very shocked so Henrique waved Emerson back and whispered something in his ear.

'You know what? You can have us both tonight,' said Emerson.

A huge bout of clapping resounded around the square. The band had finished their last song.

'I know what you're thinking,' said Emerson. 'Am I too old? Am I too ugly? No, nothing of this. We are professionals and we choose who we go to bed with. Believe me, we wouldn't offer this to you if we didn't like you.'

I just *had* to ask. 'How much?'

'Fifty dollars. Both of us. We live in a hotel nearby,' and he pointed towards the darkness of the backstreets. 'If you don't like it you don't pay.'

He paused to make a point.

'We can make all your dreams come true,' he added, not realising how pathetic his banter was: only losers have dreams that come true for fifty dollars. There was no way I was going to be seduced into the backstreets of Pelourinho by a couple of rent boys.

'Sorry,' I said. 'I'm not tempted. I don't normally have problems getting sex and I'm not going to start paying now.'

Emerson looked at me in disbelief.

'You'll go back to your hotel *alone*?'

'Watch me,' I replied and started walking away without looking back.

My tribulations were not over. Suddenly it seemed that everyone in the square was after my body. The police had disappeared and the square had been transformed into a cathouse ante-room. A plump Baiana emerged behind her even plumper pimp, who was wearing a '100 per cent NEGRO' T-shirt, breathed on me and gave me a bibulous kiss. One elderly matron, buttwise overendowed, slapped my bottom. '*Olá gringo*,' she cried. A cinnamon-coloured leggy beauty stepped overzealously in front of me and squeezed one of my nipples under my vest. Hell, the natives were getting restless, nay, *perfervid*. My walk turned into a scamper towards the passage to the Praça da Sé, which had in store the most tragic vision of the night: a ten-year-old girl, dirty and barefoot, dressed in a single white piece of cloth that came down to above her knees. She winked at me suggestively in a disturbingly premature sexualised way. What was her price? A sorbet?

*****

Márùn

There are many ways of divining the *búzios*, sixteen cowrie shells cut in half. Only the halves with the original cleft are held; the other halves are discarded. After ablutions and sacrifices, the shells remain a sacerdote's own tarot cards; consecrated and personal. When they are thrown up and fall down, they are considered closed if they fall on the cleft (uncut) side – else they are open. There are sixteen open/closed ways they can fall, each associated with an *orixá*. But for a good *dafa* (consultation) you need the diviner – normally a *mãe-de-santo* – to detect one of those sixteen ways through the candomblé cosmogony for you. She starts with all sixteen shells in her closed palms and moves them from one to the other. She stops and picks up rapidly with the right hand as many as she can while holding them on the left. If one remains, she draws a single line on the floor. If two remain, she draws a double line. If more than three remain, she repeats the exercise, swapping between right and left until four lines (single or double) have been drawn – a pattern like, say, I, II, II, I or I, II, II, II. A single line represents a universe expansion/light; a double one represents universe contraction/darkness. In candomblé, events unfold through the struggle of light and darkness without any value judgement assigned to the opposites, as in: Light = Good, Darkness = Evil. Each of the resulting patterns has a Yoruba name and shows a way forward; the first pattern I drew is called *Odi-Meji*, the second is *Obara Meji*. Of course if candomblé was called Taoism we'd name the cowrie shell consultation I-Ching, write serious theosophical books about it and practise it along with reflexology and shiatsu in Islington alternative workshops. But since we are all racists, we call it black magic.

Note the value judgement.

*****

Nelson appeared at 11 a.m. at my hotel, although nothing had been arranged.

'Dona Tania is not ready for her *consulta*,' he informed me.

'I don't want to know my future, thank you, Nelson,' I repeated. 'I want to have an intellectual discussion with the *pai-de-santo*. Now arrange *that*.'

While he was on his mobile phone, we walked up the Saúde hill, which must be what Pelourinho looked like before the late 1990s restoration spree. I could have been in the backstreets of Lagos for all I knew: semi-naked boys ran up and down the *ladeira* and housewives' furtive looks behind dirty curtains followed my steps.

'This is our house,' said Nelson, and directed me to a door.

Odd. Nelson had always been awkwardly semi-detached and never chummy.

His house was not poor or dirty; it was terraced (imagine – on a steep *ladeira*) and small to claustrophobic, but it had a modern, aluminium kitchenette, cheap wooden furniture, carpets, a TV with an inside aerial and a toilet with a flush. Nelson's wife was short and pretty. His daughter, sitting on her lap, started crying instantly. His mother, suspicious of anyone who made her granddaughter cry, was reading letters by the window. I was introduced and given a slice of stale Madeira cake which I accepted, and water which I refused. ('Not thirsty,' I lied as the cake bestodged my mouth.)

'How big is your family?' I asked Nelson.

He counted mentally.

'I have three half-brothers and two half-sisters. My mother was a bit wild in her youth,' he said with indifferent innocence.

'So what do your wife and mother do?'

'My wife looks after our daughter Iracema.'

How Brazilian: a fictional Potiguar princess's name for a Yoruba Bahian girl.

'My mother manages three houses for an absent landlord.'

'How much does a property cost to rent? Like your house.'

'About 150 reais a month,' Nelson answered. 'Most houses are modern inside. This is not a *favela*. It is a normal black neighbourhood.'

'Poor?'

'Only relative to Barra and Ondina. But compared to Federação …'

'Is there crime?'

'Not if you're a local,' answered Nelson. 'People who live here have jobs.'

He looked at his watch.

'We'd better go,' he said. 'We don't want Dona Tania to wait.'

I took my leave of his family and followed him up the *ladeira* and down again to a bus stop.

'So now you've seen my family,' said Nelson.

'Nice,' I commented as the bus came and we climbed in. Of course, I paid for both of us.

'You should try and see the area around the bay,' said Nelson. 'The Recôncavo, Cachoeira. I took a Portuguese couple there earlier this month. We rented a car. I am an excellent driver.'

So he *did* want to be chummy. Were we friends? I asked myself. No, I decided, for despite the level of trust that had been established, there was still an overwhelming commercial aspect to our relationship. Nelson wanted more work off me. I looked at him again as we sat down on two empty seats. He had offered to hold a set of books for a girl student standing next to him.

··

Things I Don't Like About Brazil #6: Holding Someone's Books on the Bus

Not quite a 'don't like' this one – more of a 'don't understand'. I have seen this, especially in the Nordeste. If you are sitting down on a bus and a student carrying books stands next to you, you are supposed to offer to hold the books for them. This is baffling. OK, it is polite. But when you don't give up your seat to an elderly lady or when you don't offer to do something similar to someone with heavy shopping, it's obvious that the custom is very specific. Why? Won't you trust your cabbages to a stranger but you would your books? Are school books terribly heavy, modifying your centre of gravity and thus considered dangerous when the driver suddenly brakes? Are books supposed to be more worthless than your fruit and veg? And have those students never heard of daypacks? Or shoulder bags? Are they too poor? Or is it unsafe to walk with a backpack? Anyway, I refuse to carry anyone's stuff on the bus, and I am considered a 'gringo mal-educado'.

I wish I knew the finer points of why. Answers on a postcard please.

···

Now, John, you can tell people you've been to a *favela*.

We got off in Federação to visit Nelson's uncle whose house was on our way to the *terreiro* down a rocky, muddy street with dwellings that seemed to have been scrambled together without any regard for the horizontal and the vertical. Some were solid and amorphous, made out of cement and corrugated iron. Some were plain spaces demarcated by chicken-coops. Some were just towers of rubbish. What was disconcerting was the lack of people. The sun was up and it was hot and the old Brazilian custom of sleeping on your portico was conspicuously absent.

'Stay close to me,' said Nelson.

I knew what he meant when I spotted the big, barefoot man clothed only in dusty cut-off jeans walking towards us. I clung close to Nelson.

'*Olá*,' Nelson said to the guy. He didn't answer back, his eyes fixed on me.

'*Olá*,' I said, too.

'We're going to my uncle's,' said Nelson, who'd stopped. 'You know him,' and he mentioned a surname which the other guy understood. He pointed at me. 'We're *both* going to see him, and then we're going to the *terreiro*.'

The semi-naked man let us pass, but his eyes never left mine for a second.

'You go to your uncle,' he said to Nelson. 'And then' – he pointed in my direction – 'YOU leave.'

After this, any thought of a long social visit to Nelson's relatives was gone. But oh, his uncle seemed so delighted to see me; his house consisted of two rooms with a mattress and a few basic articles of furniture, which did not extend to high tables or wardrobes. He pulled together his only two chairs, offered me the safest-looking one, on which my weight was precariously poised, and started asking me how I liked Salvador. He was very friendly, but he had clearly just woken up. Was he unemployed? Possibly, as today was Wednesday. Had he been drinking the previous night? He certainly looked rough.

'My uncle knows all you need to know about candomblé,' said Nelson.

Then I got the sting. I was supposed to pay the uncle to learn about the religion instead of the *pai-de-santo*. And if I left the house, I would be in immediate danger. No wonder the uncle was pleased to meet the goose who would lay the golden egg.

I stood up.

'We'll be late for Dona Tania,' I said. 'Nelson, have you finished here?'

Nelson looked at me like a child caught stealing chocolate biscuits from the tin. 'Yes, I have, but I thought my uncle who has more time and knows a lot about candomblé could fill the time ...'

I turned to the uncle.

'*Muito prazer*,' I said in the firmest tone I could muster. 'Let's go, Nelson.'

I walked out alone as Nelson ran behind me. I turned to remind him that I was not a pushover.

'Nelson,' I said, weighing my words angrily. 'Don't betray my trust.'

Although his expression remained unchanged, he must have understood, for he said nothing.

I felt I had the upper hand. This was the time to strike while the iron was hot.

'And something else,' I added. 'Do you have the paper I gave you with my address on?'

At a loss to understand my animosity, Nelson opened his wallet and fumbled through a wad of pieces of paper with addresses and names. He found mine and gave it to me with a questioning look. Was it my impression or had someone torn off a piece of it? Had I not included my room number originally? There was no room number on the slip.

Overreacting or not, I tore it to pieces.

'You know where to find me,' I said.

'What did you do *that* for?' he asked.

I left the question hanging and paced ahead, but out of the corner of my eye I noticed a glint of respect in his coal-black pupils.

*****

We had to climb the *terreiro* hill on foot. Steps, some wooden, some created from makeshift soil, led ever upwards. We passed the sacred tree where the food of the gods was deposited; I noticed the fresh offerings from Monday's fiesta. Further up we met the cages where the sacrificial animals were kept – not much difference from a bog-standard farmhouse where animals are slaughtered for food on special occasions.

At the top I saw how the hill imposed itself on the surroundings. The view over Salvador was vast and uninterrupted; this was a small organic oasis in a concrete desert. The *terreiro* door was closed. There were only a few women about and a proud Angolan cockerel, which took a dislike to me. I noticed another pair of eyes following its movements. I recognised the twelve-year-old who had first snarled at me in the trance. Nelson picked her out, too.

'Hey, how you've grown,' he said. 'My grandfather was your godfather, you remember?'

I left Nelson trying to establish blood vertical or non-blood lateral ties and asked the oldest woman there whether I could take a picture.

'We have to wait for Dona Tania,' she said and sat on a stone under a tree.

'John was here on Monday night,' Nelson announced.

The little girl and the old woman looked up with interest – forced or genuine, I could not tell. This world I had entered was quasi-oriental in its inscrutability. My normal judgement of character and body language was ineffective.

'Did you like it?' asked the old woman.

'Very much,' I said.

'Yes, it was good,' she said, nodding her head. 'It was long.'

'When did you finish?'

'Oh … when the sun came up,' she said.

That must have been four or five in the morning ...

We sat waiting. I studied the extension of rooms behind the *terreiro* where the women and initiates-to-be lived. *Terreiros* subsist on the contribution of the faithful. One way of making money – especially in Umbandá – is to train initiates to tell fortunes by throwing the *búzios* and performing charms. But mostly the *terreiro* survives on alms and donations.

'Is the *pai-de-santo* in?' I asked.

The twelve-year-old looked at me, expressionless as usual.

'The *pai-de-santo* is not in today'

I turned to Nelson.

'No *pai*, no *mãe*,' I said. 'I feel like an orphan.'

'Wait,' he said. 'Dona Tania will come.'

'And I will ask her about the association between gay men and candomblé.'

Nelson looked up.

'She will do your *búzios*,' he said. 'That's what I told her.'

I pounced.

'That is *not* what I wanted.'

The little girl leapt up.

'There is Dona Tania,' she announced.

The majestic, burly queen of Monday's trance walked up the hill with her shopping. She nodded to us in acknowledgement and went into the back quarters.

'And how much will this *consulta* cost me?' I asked, becoming increasingly pissed off with Nelson.

He wavered a trifle too long.

'For you, 150 reais,' he said.

The rent of a house in Saúde for a month.

I went ballistic.

'That's it,' I said. 'I'm going. Sorry Nelson, you've been wasting my time. Goodbye.'

The old woman and the girl stood by blankly.

I rushed down the steep hill steps. Nelson and the Angolan cock ran behind me.

'Dona Tania is the best,' Nelson cried.

'I don't care. I'm not paying through the nose for something I don't want.'

'Dona – Tania – will – be – upset,' I heard his voice dictate gravely.

By then we had reached the bottom. I confronted him.

'If she knows everything, she'll know it's *your* fault,' I said.

Nelson looked dejected. At last, an emotion.

'How much do you want to pay?'

'*You* should pay *me* for wasting my time! Do you know how much I charge per hour back home?'

'What about *my* time?' asked Nelson. 'I took you to my home, the *terreiro.*'

I pulled twenty reais from my sock so hard I nearly ripped it.

'Take that and disappear from my life,' I said. 'JUST GO!'

'Only twenty reais?' insisted Nelson.

I flagged down a cab.

'Do you know something Nelson? You constantly try to rip me off and make me do what you want. Why? Because I'm just a source of money to you. This is not the basis of a friendship or even of a commercial relationship. I suggest you start seeing the tourists with the same positive attitude and respect they try to approach you with.'

I moved inside next to the driver. 'Now get out of my life. I don't want a guide in Salvador.'

The last I heard Nelson shout was: 'DONA TANIA WILL BE VERY UPSET.'

Mèfà

....

To you a candle is only a piece of wax with a wick down the middle. But tell me my son, is a candle lit during a blackout and a candle offered to a god exactly alike? One is filled with your hopes, the other with your anger at being left in the dark. What really counts is what you put into things. Human beings are not aware of all their powers. Not a single gesture you make is without consequence, without effect. Every motion, every action, has invisible repercussions which create a presence that surrounds you. One day this presence which you create by yourself will reveal itself to you in broad daylight. It's odd, you have no problem in accepting the existence of ideas such as liberty, will and so on. But you can't understand the idea of power. Yet right under your nose every single day are examples of relationships between forces and their results. I suppose it's primarily a question of vocabulary. You were taught to classify things under a certain label, and now you no longer see the things themselves.

– From '*Macumba*' by Serge Bramly: *mãe-de-santo* Maria-José talking
to the author.

....

The taxi left me on Campo Grande, the big, unmanageable, featureless square at the bottom of the old town. I wandered aimlessly until I found myself by the Museum of Arte Sacra. The edifice itself is much more interesting than the exhibition, and a huddle of design students were squatting around in the extensive gardens with their sketchbooks and pens. A few barefoot young males hidden in door thresholds observed me and my backpack as I walked down the salubrious Ladeira da Conceição. I was descending to the Low City and the houses were leaning on the rock, multiple-storeys high, like skyscraper fronts for troglodytes. You might think that they looked smart and chic, but favelisation has long gnawed away any grace the façades might have had even 50 years ago, when Dona Flor descended those same *ladeiras* – I mean *would* have done had she not been a fictional character. I walked into the startling canary-yellow 1930s Mercado Modelo municipal market, a tropical version of Istanbul's main bazaar. *Olodum* T-shirts, linen, *acarajé* paste in powder form, spices, art galleries, clothes, sacred herbs for *orixás*, necklaces, drinks, tacky souvenirs, gems, more clothes, wooden sculptures, plastic trinkets, paintings, pendants, Brazilian football kits, Renaldo tops – all in stalls whose proprietors seemed to have been rooted at the spot for decades and who could suss you out in a second ('Is he a potential buyer – is he not?') like this old, mean and mingy Baiana in white robes – she must be an initiate – who saw me checking out her wares.

Then her pupils turned white, she suddenly moved forward and hissed at me like a caged rat.

*****

I withdrew to my hotel after an early dinner in the Largo Teresa Batista – *bobó de camarão*, that exquisite king prawn dish of coriander, tomatoes, mashed yams and palm oil which epitomises Bahian cuisine. Pelourinho looked empty after Tuesday's drum extravaganza and resembled an armed camp even at seven in the evening. I had spent my day walking around the lower city, trying to shake off the still vivid memory of the scary spectacle I had witnessed in the Mercado Modelo. Unsurprisingly, I had developed a headache. I took two Solpadeines. Normally their combination of paracetamol, caffeine and codeine works wonders – but to no avail: my pain was sinus pain, deep below the eyes. When I walked into the bathroom to clear my head, I crashed my skull into the shower.

Fuck! By the time I was towelling myself, I had a bump large enough to harbour a botfly. I lay on my bed with a sense of unease compounded by the unexpected pain.

I closed my eyes; I was a child in Athens – I was ill, and I was crying. My mother was crossing my face, murmuring some tune and slightly touching her teeth with her tongue three times, as if spitting without saliva. '*Ptumas*,' she said. 'Someone's jealous of you my darling, you're so cute, and they're jealous.' She put a pendant with a single blue bead around my neck and put me to sleep, which cured whatever symptoms I might have had. I learned later that she'd performed a kind of exorcism – common in the Mediterranean, where the evil eye is a fact of faith as unshakeable as sunrise and sunset – an exorcism transmitted and performed only by female relatives, which had ruled me out. I wondered if it worked long-distance.

'Sleep,' I said loudly to myself. 'Sleep.'

The spell will happen anyway, Nelson had said.

*****

The noise woke me up in the middle of the night. *Tok-tok-tok*. I turned over. *Tok-tok-tok*. I looked at my watch. It was 2 a.m. Are they doing roof repairs at night? I tried to go back to sleep. *Tok-tok-tok*. The clanking noise went on at staggered intervals. There was no doubt. Someone was hammering on the roof and more fool me for being on the top floor *and* next to the elevator shaft, which acted as a noise amplifier. What kind of hotel was this, planning its maintenance at night?

I turned the light on and called reception. Reception didn't answer. And didn't answer. And didn't answer.

Tok-tok-tok. The noise was driving me nuts.

I jumped out of bed, dressed my nakedness in shorts and sandals, left the room and took the lift to the ground floor.

To my surprise, there was someone at reception. My call must have woken him up.

'Excuse me,' I said angrily. 'I was ringing for ages; why didn't you answer the phone?'

The receptionist was unruffled.

'The phone didn't ring,' he said. 'Are you sure you dialled reception and not, say, the washroom?'

I let it pass.

'There's a lot of banging on the seventh floor,' I said. 'Are there any workers on the roof?'

He seemed genuinely surprised. 'At this time of night? Certainly not on ours. Let me come up with you.'

We took the lift up to my floor and stood listening.

Nothing.

'They must be taking a break,' I said. 'Believe me, they've been knocking for at least half an hour.'

'Well, they've stopped now,' said the receptionist, shrugging his shoulders. 'Is there anything else I can do?'

I was going to say 'Give me your strongest painkiller' as my headache was still raging, but I thanked him and sent him down.

I turned the light off and curled back into bed.

When I was about to drift halfway between consciousness and alpha-wave emission, the noises started again – *tok-tok-tok*. This time, however, they appeared to be emanating from within me: I was about to dream I couldn't sleep because of noises coming from the roof. I felt unable to stop the slide into semi-consciousness; the more I was sucked in, the louder the noises became. Where before there was just a whiff of suspicion regarding their presence, there now existed a near-audible reality. That's it: I was to fall asleep but dream of the noise that would not let me rest.

There is a word for such a state.

I jumped up all sweaty. I listened for the clanging and the hammering. Not a sound. If I went to sleep they'd start again; I was sure of that. My watch showed that an hour had passed since I was last fully awake. I stood there and breathed in a couple of times. I picked up the phone and carefully made sure I dialled reception. They answered promptly this time. I cleared my throat. How much of what I remembered was true and how much a vivid dream?

'This is the gentleman from 713,' I said. 'Remember I complained about some noise?'

'They started again?' the receptionist asked.

I breathed out with relief. I had not dreamt everything.

'Listen,' I dissembled. 'I can't sleep here.'

The receptionist remained silent.

'Is there another room I could move to?'

'We can arrange one for you tomorrow,' he replied.

'NOW!' I said, raising my voice. 'I want to move *now*.'

'Now? It's three-thirty in the morning, *senhor*.'

'NOW! I want to move *now*,' I insisted.

I heard him shuffling some papers.

'There is one room three floors down,' he said. 'It's a twin, whereas now you have a double bed.'

'It will do fine,' I said instantly.

And so it came to pass that at 3.30 in the morning I moved to a room which was surprisingly bigger and better than the first, having exhausted the patience of the receptionist who helped me pack helter-skelter and carry my stuff. Don't shout, I gave him a decent tip.

No one knows my new room number now.

I went on to sleep like a log.

Mèje

As João Trevisan, a Brazilian gay activist, writes in his book *Perverts in Paradise*, only women, because of their sex, are suitable to deal with the deities. It may be the nourishing Mother Earth nature of the feminine, for the divine in candomblé is downright physical: *orixás* eat and have special alimentary preferences, instantiate themselves corporeally after being summoned carefully by the musicians – the rhythmic patterns I heard at the feast of Ogum were as carefully and strictly memorised note for note as a Bach music score, else the gods would not recognise them – and have palpable human qualities, like the Greek and Roman gods with their jealousies, adulteries and tribulations. It was thus considered 'unmanly', if not blasphemous, for males to function as priests, and candomblé has an ecclesiastical order to match the Vatican's. Unlike the Catholic Church, though, tradition was relaxed to admit men in the priesthood – what a fabulous counterpoint to the Christian debate on the ordination of women – though the central precept of the supremacy of femininity remained the cornerstone of candomblé doctrine. This laxity was the result of a syncretism not with Christianity but with native beliefs: the *caboclos* and *pretos velhos*, the ancestors and forest spirits of the Tupi and Tapuia were also introduced into the worship, like saints were in Christianity and Islam. Except that the native Amerindians' medicine men, the *pagés*, were homosexual or bisexual because of their 'feminine', ergo mystical, qualities. This is how Brazilian Oxumarê turned androgynous – to refuse homosexuals in candomblé was to refuse the god himself.

And they're not only welcome – they're revered.

*****

All those days in Salvador and I hadn't left the central area, so my headache, my Solpadeines and I decided to walk several miles down the beach to Barra and relax after last night's tension. The gaze of the personnel at Hotel Palace followed me around with disquiet. My nocturnal shenanigans, which seemed so silly in the light of day, must have made the office rounds.

After the dilapidation, dereliction and desuetude of the old district, it was a relief to walk in the modern, refined streets of Barra and its strikingly parvenu shopping centre. Barra Beach, coming after the sandy wonders of Fortaleza, Recife and Maceió, was several strokes below par, but watching the surf that sunny afternoon was exactly what I wanted to do. Perhaps I should leave that compromised Hotel Palace and move to Barra for the rest of my stay in Salvador.

I lay down, closed my eyes and tried to relax the headache away.

I woke up, having dozed off for a few hours, a no-no in my health ledger and highly out of character. Thankfully, I was wearing a baseball cap which protected me from sunstroke. I had slept badly overnight, so I suppose the nap was understandable – but it still did my headache no good.

If this persists, I'll have to go to a farmácia.

....

Things I Like About Brazil #6: The Farmácias

They are not just chemists or drugstores. These are places open 24 hours a day where you can buy aspirins, insecticides, sun protection creams, aphrodisiac ampoules and sanitary towels (not, I should advertise, that I have ever needed one); where you can be sure to find laxatives, antiemetics and antidepressants, vitamin C and toilet paper, steroid creams and antimycotics, cortisone pills and antihistamines; where medical prescriptions are considered red tape and the pharmacist is nurse and doctor ('Do you want the amoxycyllin in pills of 100 or 500mg? Will thirty do?') and where in smaller towns you can still find scales for the microsale of salts from magnesium oxide to antimony potassium tartrate.

They are a hypochondriac's paradise, and I love them.

....

I had a coffee (*com leite frio* – something which perplexes Brazilians) in one of the waterfront cafés, in full sight of the Farol de Barra, the most famous sight in Salvador, theme of a thousand postcards. It is really called the Fort of Santo Antônio de Barra and was constructed in the mid-1580s, though it was unable to repel the Dutch 40 years later. When the Portuguese returned, they started building an estimated 450 fortifications on the coast. As I walked vacant and sun-dazed to the Farol de Barra, now containing the Nautical Museum of Bahia, I noticed a couple of Baianas selling food opposite the building. One of them looked at me directly as I passed. I recognised her immediately with alarm.

It was Dona Tania.

So this is what she does when she's not answering the calls of the gods. She's a plain acarajé *lady.*

I entered the Nautical Museum to collect my thoughts. I went past the shipping exhibits on mental automatic pilot until I found myself on the inner, elevated bailey with its old cannons, crenels, watchman towers and wonderful bay views. The sun was going down, but idyllic was not my disposition. I looked towards the front of the fort. I could only distinguish the silhouettes of the Baianas; Dona Tania was still there.

Once you enter candomblé you never leave it, Nelson had said.

I despaired. He might be right. Did I stay a tad too long in the *terreiro* and witness something I shouldn't have? Was I hexed? Is there an offering to Exú on some street corner with candles and my name on it? They have even followed me to Barra. Perhaps I should leave Salvador. If I could only enter Dona Tania's head, I would persuade her that it was Nelson who was responsible for yesterday's mix-up. I wanted an interview, not a consultation. It was he who had interfered and wasted everyone's time, part ripping me off, part befriending me, part manipulating me. If Dona Tania was angry at someone it should be *him*. If Dona Tania was so powerful, she should be able to read my thoughts and realise that I am sensitive to her religion and what it stands for, considerate to the memory of her ancestors and their fate – so why hound *me*?

It's unfair Dona Tania – it's unjust!

I left the museum furtively and walked up towards Vitória, avoiding the women. Then I stopped. Surely running away was not the solution. Better talk to Dona Tania face to face; ask her if I'm being followed; convey to her verbally what I'd been thinking inside the Farol. Agitated and flushed, I crossed the road just before the Forte de Santa Maria and approached the Baianas from behind.

'*Com licença,*' I said to Dona Tania as she turned her head.

I gasped. I couldn't have been more shocked had I been whacked with Iansã's featherduster.

This was not Dona Tania.

'*Acarajé?*' she asked.

I stood there even more shocked than when I saw her. I mean when I thought I'd seen her. Had I seen her? Well, not her as in 'her', but 'her' as in Dona Tania.

I recovered my verbal abilities enough to ask for the bus stop. She pointed at a spot a few yards away. What a jerk I must have seemed ...

Or better put: what a jerk I was. How could Dona Tania even be selling anything? I'd been told she lived from charity alone. I'd made a mistake. All this fucking mumbo-jumbo, all this superstition coming from within, all this make-believe: changing rooms in the middle of the night, imagining noises, wanting to leave town, devising supernatural scenarios, conjuring up visions – John, you're such a receptive, credulous headcase.

It was when I stepped on the bus that I realised my splitting headache had gone.

*****

The bus took me to the Praça da Sé. I walked by the Elevador Lacerda to watch the sunset and instinctively took the lift down. It's so cheap, only five centavos, and the gravitational pull as you arrive moves your guts in that special, nauseating way I enjoy.

I looked at my watch. It was about 5 p.m. Any monument still open to take my mind off things?

A bus came, heading towards Bonfim. I hopped on impulsively to visit the famous Senhor do Bonfim, a church that has been identified with Oxalá/Jesus for centuries, a common place of worship for candomblé initiates and Catholics alike, a church whose steps are ritually washed by believers during one of Salvador's most famous festivals, the Lavagem do Bonfim, an extraordinary church where miracles are an everyday expectation.

I should have known that it would be far away from the fact that the church is never shown on the maps of central Salvador, but I'd never have guessed how far. In Salvador's traffic, it took me one whole hour to get there and by the time I reached the square in front, night had fallen and the church's edges were accentuated by illuminations. It was time for Vespers and the Praça was teeming with relic vendors; it's so easy to fulfil your wishes here – buy a multicoloured ribbon, a '*Lembrança do*

Bonfim', tie it around your wrist and make a wish. When it falls off, your wish will be granted.

I walked into the church along with many believers; amputees crawled up the steps unaided; old black women in those familiar white robes, straight out of some *terreiro*, kneeled and prayed, rosaries in hand; young and old responded to the Catholic priest who conducted the ceremony for the packed congregation. There were pictures hanging in the annexe; pictures of people with ill-health who had believed and hoped for a miracle; there were scores of replica hands, heads, legs and arms next to the obligatory donation boxes for God, some god, to cure. It's odd looking at churches as architectural gems, admiring the gold and silver and works of art and not experiencing their *raison d'être*: liturgy and collective prayer, the communal sorting out of 'Who am I?'

So who *am* I?

I know I am the sum of my experiences, the behaviour of my parents and the lottery of my genes. But I don't know the Real Me, because I live within my Gestalt. The only way I can answer the question is to look at myself from the non-transparent face of a double mirror. And in the modern global village, disentangling the knots is more difficult than ever.

However, there is one knot somewhere I know not, that's been untied.

We in the West took a wrong turn long ago, after the words were uttered: eat my bread for it is my flesh; drink the wine for it is my blood. We took a wrong turn, for we *abstracted*. That has been our problem ever since – living in our heads, observing, but not seeing. And when we tried to picture God again, it was already too late: we'd lost the plot, for we had trekked too far up the ersatz path. God is not a wise old man sitting on a cloud sticking out his index finger to a naked Adam – and oh, how skin colour matters – as Michelangelo would have us believe; God is not a jealous entity barking down commands from Mount Sinai to a chosen race – and oh, how race matters; God certainly does not wear a turban and decree that a woman is half a man's worth – and oh, how gender matters. If God exists, She is mysterious indeed, but She's around us, and I'd like to meet Her.

Well, maybe I have.

Chapter 7

The Children of Oxumarê (Bahia)

In a 1976 study by the National Institute of Geography and Statistics, Brazilians used 134 terms to describe their pigmentation. They described themselves as *alva, alva-escura, aliveira, alvarinta, jambote, alvinha, cor-de-rosa, cor-de-leite, clara* or *clarinha, rosa, rosada, saraíba, pálida, pouco clara, ruíva, branca* and oh, how many permutations on that: *branca-avermelhada, meio-branca, branca-morena, branca-queimada, branca-sardenta, branquiça, branquinha, branca-suja, bem-branca* – and those are just some of the white ones.

This is the chapter about colour.

....
The Words You'll Need
axé = ancient candomblé term surprisingly similar to the Star Wars 'May the force be with you', which is the best translation. Also, a Bahian musical style.
fazenda = agrifactory – equivalent to the Spanish hacienda
fazendeiro = owner of above fazenda
ginecologista = gynaecologist (as if you couldn't guess!)
Mineiro = inhabitant of Minas Gerais
moqueca = Bahian fish stew
Nossa Senhora da Pegação = One of my Brazilian mannerisms. When something odd happens I cross myself and say 'Nossa Senhora da Pegação' as in 'Oh, Our Lady of Cruising': a pun on 'Nossa Senhora da Conceição', 'Our Lady of Conception', a common name for the Madonna.
pardo = of mixed race
perigoso = dangerous
pesce (Italian) = fish
pollo (Italian) = chicken
porteño (Spanish) = born in Buenos Aires
....

– 28 –

Peter pulled me over to one side of the schooner.

'Let's keep away from the Germans,' he said with an acidic expression.

I looked at him in surprise. 'But you *are* German,' I said.

'Exactly,' Peter answered. 'I know what they're like.'

Peter was in his late fifties, sunburnt-white (#25, *branco-pálido*), but his athletic build cut many years off his age. I bet it helped that his wife, curvy, Turkish-born Jasmin was a quarter of a century younger. They had befriended me as soon as I stepped on the Bahia Tours leisure boat for a day in the Bay of All Saints. They seemed well adjusted and entertaining – until this comment.

'Let's stay here, shall we?' Peter pleaded.

My agreement was rewarded with a welcome can of beer. The day was scorching, and the light was at its brightest as we anchored off the first and strangest island of the bay: the Ilha dos Frades. This island is as real a step into the past as one can experience in Bahia and she has her fair share of timewarps. One hour out from the state capital and you have a fishing village with inhabitants who live as they did one hundred years ago, inside wooden huts next to their domestic animals (*There's a pig! There's a dog!*) without running water or electricity; there is only a small generator which switches off at 10 p.m. This would be a gimmick, if there was some *pensão* or other, but there isn't. Any tourist infrastructure is reduced to the few beach waiters who serve drinks, cook fish and try to sell shells and coral to the few interested foreigners.

Peter pointed disapprovingly with his beer can at the Germans who were forming a queue by the shell hut.

'They will not be able to import them into Europe,' he said. 'I tried to bring in some from Zanzibar once. Everything is protected now.'

Peter was alternating between merry and morose. I took a dip to clear my head.

'Jasmin is my second wife,' he said to me unprompted as he bought us more drinks. 'Married her eight years ago.'

We all took a sip while the sentence filtered through.

'My first wife died in eighty-nine,' said Peter. 'I had a son, thirteen at the time.'

He looked at me and embraced Jasmin.

'Met her in Istanbul and she gave me new life,' he added, squeezing her hand.

I became increasingly embarrassed, so I asked them about Ondina where they were staying.

'Well, I was lying on the beach at Ondina …' started Jasmin.

'All pebbles, no sand,' interrupted Peter.

'… and this woman started talking to me. So what? I thought, but then she asked me to put oil on her back.'

No harm in that.

Jasmin agreed. 'I didn't see any problem either. But then she asked me out for dinner.'

Where was Peter?

'Back in the bar under the shade.'

'Brazilians are like that,' I said. 'I give them the benefit of the doubt. If you don't, you won't make friends.'

Peter and Jasmin looked at me blankly.

'We expect the worst because that's what we're used to in Europe,' I said. 'But this is a different, more relaxed culture – believe me, I've been analysing it for weeks now.'

Peter spoke hollowly: 'Good luck to you. I hope you never see the worst people are capable of.'

....

Logbook from the British Warship *Fawn*, February 1841

The living, the dying and the dead huddled together in one mass. Some unfortunates in the most disgusting state of smallpox, distressingly ill with opthalmia, a few perfectly blind, others living skeletons, with difficulty crawled from below unable to bear the weight of their miserable bodies. Mothers with young infants hanging at their breasts unable to give them a drop of nourishment. How they had brought them thus far appeared astonishing. All were perfectly naked. Their limbs were excoriated from lying on the hard plank for so long a period. On going below, the stench was insupportable. How beings could breathe such an atmosphere and live appeared incredible. Several were under the soughing which was called the deck, dying – one dead.

– Entry after the seizure of a slave ship bound for Brazil.

....

The main island on the Bay of All Saints is Itaparica (from the Tupi *Ytá- parica* – a wall of stones, an allusion to the reefs surrounding the island). Our beach stretched as far as the eye could see, the Ponta de Areia, Sandy Point to you, and never has a place been more aptly named. I was by now immune to the sight of golden, tranquil beaches, but the sheer length of the Itaparican coastline vanishing far into the horizon marked it as Division One in my book. There were hotels, there were yachts and there were locals selling crafts which meant that a chicken-wire fence had been erected to 'protect' the tourists inside the hotel gardens from the beggars outside. Half-naked, barefoot street kids were weighing their bodies inwards on the wire, watching us eat from our hotel's princely buffet under large, thatched, shady umbrellas. It felt like South Africa.

I was squeezed among a party of Italian tourists who followed the exact same routine: first they would all congregate in front of a dish. Then one of them would taste it.

'*Pesce*,' he would announce to the crowd.

'Ahhhhhhhh,' they'd all murmur in unison and then put some on their plates.

This was taking ages, so I threw buffet protocol out of the window and jumped the queue to reach a stew. I put some on my plate and noticed that all the Italians were looking at me. Embarrassed by my lack of manners, I grinned an apology. But no, this was not a reproachful look; it was an enquiring look. I tasted some of the stew.

'*Pollo*,' I proclaimed.

'Ahhhhh,' they all murmured in unison and surrounded the pot.

The commotion outside attracted our attention.

Oh. Capoeira. At last.

Capoeira is a unique and little-known Brazilian martial art practised by the slaves in the plantations – some claim that it actually flourished in Palmares. It is as spectacular and dramatic in its execution as anything that Far Eastern minds and bodies have produced, and it is Zen-like in its master-pupil obedience, relationship and memorisation of standard canons. There are several 'academies' and two styles: traditional Angolan and modern *regional*. Disciples have to pass an initiation ceremony, be baptised with a capoeira nom-de-guerre and train regularly. There are exhibitions where the practitioners perform their basic *gingas* and strikes, *bênção* high kicks, *pião* headspins, *recuo* retreat moves with one hand on the ground, squat *cocorinhas*, and *meia-lua* spin-kicks for the benefit of paying tourists. Capoeira is accompanied by the music of the *berimbau*, a long, stringed bow, the *vêrga*, terminating in a gourd for resonance. It has a single string plucked by a coin, the *dobrão*. Its rhythms, the *avisos*, *cavalarias* and *barravents*, are steadied by the rattle of the *caxixí*, a tambourine and the scratching of the ribbed bamboo scraper, the *reco-reco*. Imagine, if you can, break-dancing to the sound of a stringed didgeridoo on maracas and you're halfway there.

As I admired the sweating, muscular black bodies executing their athletic handstands and high kicks one-to-one, comrade-to-comrade, it struck me how homoerotic it all appeared: a choreographed, teasing, male pas-de-deux with no contact, narcissistic shadow-boxing with an underlying code only decipherable for the ones 'in the know', ritualised foreplay to release the hormonal tension of a fraternity with few females.

I wondered what the initiation entails.

*****

On the way back, we could not get enough of the Salvador skyline, spread on a gentle parabola as it sloped towards the sea on a pink sunset background. It felt like, it felt like …

'Istanbul,' I murmured. 'This feels like Istanbul, coming in from the Sea of Marmara. The shape is exactly right, the bay is about the right size, the orientation, the length …'

Jasmin sat up from the shade. Her rosy complexion (#8, *alvinha*) suffered from the sun. 'Yes,' she agreed. 'A Christian Istanbul with churches sticking out instead of mosques.'

Indeed, if Buenos Aires is the Paris of South America with its wide boulevards and Art Nouveau ambience, then Salvador is its Istanbul: the chaotic, sweaty seat of a theocratic empire in the East. Cuzco could play the role of Rome: the seat of an older empire, its religion replaced by Christian beliefs, its ancient monuments providing the foundation of new architectural masterpieces.

Peter spoke wistfully.

'When we met,' he said, talking to no one in particular, 'everyone was against it, even my son. I don't know if it was more difficult for me or for Jasmin. She followed me to Germany and had to put up with such hostility. She spoke no German, but she learned – she learned.'

Peter was now quite drunk.

'Do you know how much trouble I've had because of Jasmin?' he continued.

This was too much.

'Peter,' I said to him, 'I'm sure that whatever you've done has been for the best. You don't have to justify your life to me.'

'I don't?'

'No.'

He paused and smiled.

'Ah,' he sighed. 'That's what I like about the British.'

....

Things I Don't Like About Brazil #7: Race Epithets

The various racial admixtures are described as crioulos, cabras, capangas, caboclos, mulattos, pardos, sararás, muleques, pardovascos, mamelucos, mestiços, cafusos, caborés, curibocas *and* mazombos – *and those are just the words I know.*

....

– 29 –

It was Friday and hard to find a seat in Conexão Arco-Iris (the Rainbow Connection) which lies in the Beco dos Artistas, a small alley by the side of Campo Grande. This is the 'alternative' corner in the centre of Salvador with 'GLS bars and restaurants' as the *City Guide* brands them, the critical keyword being 'GLS', denoting gays, lesbians and – an odd word this – 'sympathisers'. As I sipped my Antártica slowly, I found myself under the intense gaze of a dark, corpulent guy in front of me. His gaunt, pale friend was talking to him drunkenly, but instead he was half nodding back, half staring at me with a combination of curiosity and pure unadulterated pick-up intention.

'Hi,' he introduced himself, revealing a wide friendly smile, 'I am Márcio, and my friend here is Jorge.'

My mother would approve: Márcio (#62, *escurinho*, semi-dark) was an accountant in a bank, and Jorge (#28, *branco-sujo*, dirty white) was a solicitor, both Bahians to the core, despite the stark difference in colouration. Jorge started talking in a language I could not comprehend.

'*Prsh ts dzheang*,' he murmured.

I tried to listen in. Jorge was sounding more nasal than is normal for a Brazilian. '*Jãom bãolho zhãom sãog*,' he said.

'I can't understand you,' I replied.

Márcio shook his head.

'Oh, he does that when he's drunk. He speaks his own language. I can't follow him so I nod every now and again.'

I see.

'Any GLS club to go to tonight?' I asked. 'I read Holmes is supposed to be good.'

Márcio made a grand dismissive gesture.

'*Perigoso*,' he said. 'You'll be robbed *inside* the club not outside. The best clubs in Salvador are Mix-Ozone and the Off Club in Barra.'

'I went to Off Club last night,' I said. 'I walked into the dance area and suddenly they were all facing me and clapping. It took me a few seconds to realise that the door I opened was next to the stage and they were clapping at the group who had just finished a song.'

'*Btsh she kñzh?*' asked Jorge.

'Who was playing?' Márcio seemed to translate.

'Margareth Menezes. She was really good.'

I had to recount my whole life and my whole trip to Márcio in half an hour. He heard about Isaías with rapt attention.

'I have actually been to Limoeiro,' he said. 'My job in the bank had me travelling all around Pernambuco.'

'Pernambuco,' said Jorge.

'He's alive,' I said.

Márcio hit him with a sideways glance.

'Hmmm,' he pouted dubiously.

'Is he your boyfriend?'

Márcio chuckled.

'He's been one of my best friends for five years now. I helped him come out. Though Jorge is a *Gillette*.'

'*Gillette?* Like the razor?'

Márcio winked.

'Bisexual. You know, the blade cuts both ways.'

Oh.

'He's got a wife and two kids.'

'No! So young.'

'He married young because his parents wanted him to. When I met him – here, it was here – Jorge was in a sorry state. I took him out to gay clubs, and introduced him to the love of his life.'

'So where is the love of his life now?'

Márcio grimaced sourly.

'When they split there were tears and dramas. Jorge saw him with another guy – after they had finished – and pulled him away vigorously, saying things like *"You are mine. Always mine"*.' He tut-tutted. 'Created quite a stir in the disco.'

'And his wife?'

Márcio made one of the sweeping gestures he was fond of.

'She's "understanding". Which is more than his brothers were when they found out. They blamed *me*! There was a big fracas when they saw him once in the queue for Ozone.'

'Ozone,' said Jorge.

'He's coming round,' said Márcio. 'Shall we all go there in his car?'

'You mean he'll *drive*?'

Márcio made a dismissive 'pah' with his hand.

'He'll be OK behind the wheel. All alcohol evaporates when he gets into the car,' and he raised his palm, *'pouf* – like that.'

*****

Jorge was circling the mega-square of Campo Grande trying to find the correct exit; it was obvious that the alcohol had not gone *pouf* in the air, but was still puffing up his veins. Márcio, completely oblivious, had twisted his body to talk to me in the back seat about the *Carnaval* in Salvador.

'Rio's is for show. Olinda's is smaller. Rio's got the Sambódromo, but in Salvador the streets from Ondina to Barra all the way to the Praça da Sé are full of *blocos* and *trios elétricos*. Gringos go to Rio, but Brazilians come here.'

The *blocos* are the equivalent of the samba schools in Rio and the *maracatu* groups of Recife. They accept associates and sometimes act like mutual friendly societies amid the lack of social care in the poverty of Salvador. The number of famous bands playing in the Salvador *Carnaval* looks like a *Who's Who* of Brazilian music: there is a *trio elétrico* with Olodum and its 6,000 faithful associates; Crocodilo with the queen of *axé* Daniela Mercury; the traditional Ilê Aiyé, the preferred *bloco* of Caetano Veloso and Gilberto Gil. Then there are the society *blocos*: the reggae of Muzenza with twelve *Carnaval* championships behind it; the all-female and feminist Filhas de Oxum under the aegis of actress Zezé Mota which offers courses and seminars for women; As Muquiranas, the *bloco* whose history goes back to the mid-1960s and is composed of 2,000 heterosexual men proudly parading in outrageous drag – and so on. There are six *blocos* composed entirely of children, with an Olodum spin-off for the kids. This is a huge festival attracting half a million tourists with a significant infrastructure: deployment of 1,000 chemical toilets, 15,000 patrolling police with 50-odd observation posts, twelve tourist information offices and ten 24-hour medical emergency centres.

'Next time you'll have to come to Salvador during *Carnaval*,' said Márcio, 'and you'll stay with *me*.'

I smiled. He hardly knew me.

'OK?' said Márcio. 'Sure?'

Sure.

Márcio's attention turned to Jorge. 'Are we still in Campo Grande?' he asked. 'Turn off HERE!'

I closed my eyes until we reached the club. We had arrived in time to see the show – participatory drag. We all ducked when Madam Silvetty Montilla asked for volunteers to come on stage. Jorge stood tall, lanky, pissed and not quite there, so she picked him along with two other unlucky guys for a dancing contest. When the drag queen interviewed them, Jorge was slurring his words again.

'Ah,' said the drag queen. 'Mineiro.'

So there was Jorge, now a figure of fun from Minas Gerais. Human nature being what it is, in Bahia they need the Mineiros to poke fun at; in the southern states of Brazil they poke fun at Bahians, like the English need the Irish and the French need the Belgians. When the sensual rhythms of Bahian music came on and the three were asked to dance, Jorge's lack of co-ordination with *afoxé* played well with the stereotype. When he descended from the stage with a silly grin on his face, Márcio told him in a gentle voice, which, however, accepted no dissent, that it was time to go, for he had disgraced himself.

'Tomorrow you are coming to my place for lunch,' he said to me as we exchanged phone numbers.

How could I resist?

– 30 –

Márcio met me in the small square at Stiep (pronounced 'es-cheapy') where he lived: lower middle-class suburbia with high, faceless apartment blocks and no signs of life except for a few kids kicking a ball. But, unlike the township grotesqueness of Federação, Stiep was stolidly dowdy and reassuringly uninviting.

'Hmmm,' nodded Márcio as we walked towards his apartment. 'I wouldn't say that. See that bar?'

I looked at a drab bungalow by the bus stop.

'It doesn't look too heavy,' I said.

'It isn't,' replied Márcio. 'But one night Jorge and I were drinking inside. Jorge decided to go to the toilet. While I was waiting for him, a robber arrived with a gun. It was just me and the barman. He took all our money while Jorge was having a piss. Can you believe it?'

'*Nossa Senhora da Pegação,*' I exclaimed. 'Were you hurt?'

Márcio made another grand dismissive gesture.

'No, no, no. You don't understand. It wasn't *scary*. I wasn't *afraid*. The guy wasn't going to *shoot* us. He was very polite and apologised as he left. It was like being pickpocketed. But can you believe it – Jorge was in the toilet, and when he came back the robber had gone. He found us both cursing.'

'Did the barman ask him to pay the bill?' I asked.

Márcio looked at me sideways as he opened the door: that was a very European comment to have made.

He lived in a two-bedroom ground-floor flat with surrealist paintings dominating the walls. A guy in shorts and flip-flops was lying on the sofa reading.

'This is Paulo, this is John, my friend from London,' he introduced us.

Paulo looked morose; his greeting was forced. Márcio grabbed me by the arm and pulled me into the kitchen.

'Your flatmate?' I asked.

Márcio shook his head and lowered his voice.

'No, just a friend. I asked him around for lunch. He's a bit down.'

'Problems with men?' I ventured.

'Is there another kind?' gesticulated Márcio. 'He just finished with his boyfriend. He caught him with someone else.'

'What? *In flagrante*?' I asked, surprised.

'No, no,' replied Márcio. 'In the street. But the other guy turned out to be his long-term boyfriend. Men are *such* shits.'

I thought of Vicente and Ab in Fortaleza. 'There's always a reason,' I said carefully. 'How long did Paulo know him?'

'Three weeks. I know, I know. Paulo is so emotional. But when I saw his man, I immediately told him. "There's something about Ricky I don't like, Paulo." And,' he added with aplomb, 'I was *right*!'

Paulo entered the kitchen, and we both smiled on cue. He made for the fridge to take out a beer.

'What's for dinner?' I asked. 'Bahian food?'

'Well,' said Márcio. 'I thought of you and I prepared beef Stroganoff with Greek rice.'

I will never know why Brazilians call rice with sultanas 'Greek'. As someone born in Athens, I can't really match the two.

'Can I help?'

'No,' said Márcio, horrified. 'You are a *guest*. Put on a CD if you like.'

I put on an old Daniela Mercury CD to create the right ambience, occasionally peeping at Paulo who had shrunk into the sofa. Márcio did eventually need our help – or in truth Paulo's since I wasn't allowed to approach the kitchen – because the phone rang while he was cooking.

When the food arrived, I noticed a shadow on Márcio's jovial, chubby face.

'The phone call upset you?' I asked. Was I impertinent? I don't know. I felt as if I could ask Márcio anything I wanted.

He nodded gravely.

'An old flame from Recife. Aleixo. I've known him for fifteen years. We were in love when I was seventeen.'

'Oh,' I said. 'How nice you had a boyfriend that young.'

Márcio looked at me strangely.

'I had a boyfriend when I was *fourteen*,' he corrected me.

Paulo's seriousness broke with mute laughter at my shock.

'So this friend of mine of fifteen years was not my first boyfriend. But,' he lowered his eyes, 'he *was* the love of my life.'

Márcio's smiley face was clouded once more.

'Unfortunately, the distance came between us. So I put an end to it. However, before I left him, I found him another boyfriend. I introduced him to this guy and asked him to look after Aleixo – my *best* friend.'

There seems to be a queue of best friends.

Paulo had finished his food by now and was listening perkily. There's nothing like someone else's sorrows to drown your own.

'And you know what?' asked Márcio.

'What?'

'This guy and Aleixo – they are still together.'

'Well done.'

'Anyway, Aleixo is coming next week. We'll be flying together to Morro de São Paulo.'

'Long time since you've seen him?'

'Yes. But it's not that. He left a message yesterday in which he insinuated that he may still be attached to the past.'

Paulo and I were listening.

'He even suggested that *we sleep in the same bed*!'

'NO!' we said in unison.

'YES!' declared Márcio half triumphantly. 'And,' Márcio rotated his hand to denote so-so, 'he almost repeated it on the phone just now. I don't want to play *Katia Cega* under the sheets.'

I looked at Márcio, bewildered.

'Katia Cega – the Blind Katia – was this blind Brazilian singer. You can imagine her groping in the dark, can't you?'

He turned back pensively to his food.

'You should have said no,' I ventured.

Márcio swallowed quickly.

'Well, I was cooking and you were both here, and I couldn't have a long discussion. But, yes, I'll tell him.'

'*Before* he comes,' Paulo added.

Márcio and I exchanged furtive glances. Paulo had spoken.

*****

Aeroclube in Jardim d'Alá is another of those shopping-mall-cum-entertainment-multiplexes so beloved by New World cities with acres of suburban space to spare. City dwellers all over South America have wanted to show me the latest 'Shopping' as if this would notch them up in my sophistication notebook.

We sat in a bar and watched a big-screen video of Maria Bethânia, a popular singer, live.

'Female singers. They're all lesbians,' Márcio whispered conspiratorially.

I looked at him.

'And Caetano Veloso, her brother?'

'*Gillette*,' Márcio replied. 'They're all gay, lesbian or bisexual.'

'I presume you've been following their sexual predilections from the age of fourteen,' I said.

Márcio didn't understand.

'When you lost your virginity.'

Márcio gave me one of his oblique glances.

'Who said that? I said I had a boyfriend at fourteen. I didn't say I lost my virginity at fourteen,' he corrected me. 'It was much earlier –'

That's more than I want to know, thank you!

Paulo was in hysterics at my expression. Márcio turned around and winked at me.

'See?' he said thrilled. 'He's forgotten.'

It had not crossed my mind until I saw the twinkle in Márcio's eyes that much of the conversation that afternoon was deliberately aimed at lifting Paulo's spirits.

I wonder now how much of it was true.

The rainy season seemed to have started in Salvador that Sunday. It was only a week after Nelson had approached me outside São Pedro, but so much had happened I felt I had spent months in Hotel Palace and seen the seasons come and go. When the low hangs over Salvador, it hangs pretty comprehensively; the rain drowns everything for days and that includes the sun itself. I didn't care though – I had found new friends, and there were all these museums to visit.

Unsurprisingly, all the interesting ones have to do with African culture, first and foremost being the Afro-Brazilian Museum standing on the site of the first medical school in Brazil. There is at least one modern art treasure in the museum: the Carybé panels. Argentinian-born – *porteño*, in fact – Carybé (Hector Julio Partide Bernabó) lived in Rio from 1920, but visited Bahia as a journalist in 1938. He fell in love with Salvador and its candomblé culture and by 1950 he had turned native, ending up as the president of one of its most eminent *terreiros*, Ilê Axé Opô Afonjá. His work consists mostly of paintings of Bahian scenes, but he's more famous for the large panels decorating the Latin American Memorial in São Paulo and the remarkable set of huge carved wooden panels devoted to *orixás* in the Afro-Brazilian Museum of Salvador. Perhaps as a tribute these *orixás* conveyed upon him the ultimate accolade: they called him to their otherworld during a candomblé celebration, where he died midway through of a heart attack.

But the Afro-Brazilian Museum really is about the slave trade. And as the museum points out, the rulers of African nations like Angola and Dahomey, now Benin – its twelve glorious kings depicted in a large tapestry – were a vital part of this trade. Ultimately it was through the buying and selling of human beings that Africa, from Zanzibar to the Gulf of Guinea, was brought into the global capitalist trading structure of the fifteenth century. The Arabs (let's not forget who started it), the Portuguese, the Dutch, and the British all had a go in turn at this lucrative business that ended not because reason, sentiment or morality got the better of governments, but when New World exploitation economies started favouring paid labour. The nineteenth-century proletariat could be sacked and got rid of, rather than slave labour which had to be fed and kept alive even during times of economic recession. Put bluntly, seasonal paid labour was more cost-efficient than keeping slaves all year round, and that was the argument that eventually clinched it. Any remorseful window-dressing disappears when one considers how the slaves were thrown out cruelly in the streets after emancipation.

*****

I met up with Márcio late Sunday afternoon in Red-Blue, an outdoor gay club with an open-air dance area. We retired under a covering because the rain had been stop-go all day. Márcio had promised me more of his friends, and he had kept his word. He waved one over and turned to me, making an obscene gesture with his arm. It turned out he was describing his friend's occupation.

'*O ginecologista,*' he explained.

'Interesting,' I said. 'So many gay men I know are gynaecologists.'

Márcio nodded.

'I've never understood why,' he said.

'It must be the husbands who demand it,' I ventured.

His friend (#42 *castanho*, maroon) sat next to me, and I went on auto describing myself.

'You were born in Greece?' he asked. 'How interesting. It must be like Brazil.'

'Well –' I started.

'And the language must be like Portuguese.'

'Well –'

'Portuguese comes from Greek!'

'Not quite,' I managed to interject. 'It comes from Latin.'

The gynaecologist looked at me as if I were committing an offence.

'No,' he said, 'it comes from Greek.'

It's rude to question a doctor's opinion in Brazil. In fact, it's rude to question anyone's opinion. What matters is not accuracy, but keeping the consensus of the moment. But I didn't know that then.

'No, believe me,' I said, 'I speak both Greek and Portuguese. It's from Latin.'

The gynaecologist cut the Gordian knot by ordering caipirinhas. Thankfully, two more friends of Márcio's arrived.

'This is Ari,' said Márcio, 'and this is Graciliano.'

Ari was tall and handsome with the complexion and build of a Berber Arab (#45 *chocolate*). He was an economics student and his was the best English I'd heard since Dora's in Fortaleza. Graciliano's equally fine complexion was no darker than an Italian's (#4, *alvo escuro*). Ah, I was so pleased: here was Brazil's famous colour mix that had first stirred my imagination as a blueprint for racial integration, the more impressive for the natural colour-blindness of its participants. And yet I thought of Nelson and his family. For all the hue differences there was no one patently African-featured around this table. Where did *they* fit in?

'So are you together today, you two?' asked Márcio when Graciliano left our table.

'We are,' said Ari, and smiled.

Márcio whispered in my ear.

'They are boyfriends but they break up all the time. Even I can't even keep up with the state of their relationship. It's like a yo-yo.'

The gynaecologist turned to me.

'If you say something in Greek, I'm sure I can understand it,' he said.

I looked at Ari with a 'save me' look. He obliged since he wanted to practise his English and asked me about my trip. I should produce a FAQ and keep a copy in my pocket.

'So, what's the best place in Brazil, then?'

That should also be on the FAQ. As the question crops up so often, I will need the next chapter to answer it.

Suddenly Ari focused into the distance, stood up and ran off.

Márcio knew that expression.

'There it goes,' he said.

I didn't understand.

He pointed at Ari who was now arguing with Graciliano. 'There it goes.'

I shrugged my shoulders. 'Where is Jorge today?'

'With his family. He spends most weekends with his kids.'

I'd forgotten he had two kids.

'We'll see you tomorrow. Take you out for dinner.'

'I'm going to the Recôncavo tomorrow.'

'When you come back, I'll call you.'

Ari returned, moody, with more drinks. Márcio winked at me and asked him again: 'So, are you still together, you and Graciliano?'

'No,' replied Ari. 'He's cruising again.'

Graciliano was sitting alone at a table on the other side of the club.

Márcio gave me an I-told-you-so look. 'No wonder if you had a fight,' he said.

The rain started falling like a shower. We couldn't dance, there couldn't be a show, so we drank and chatted. Ari monopolised me.

'So what do you think of Bahian men?' he baited me.

'I don't know,' I replied. 'I haven't been with anyone yet.'

This surprised Ari.

'No?' he asked. 'Why not?'

'No one likes me,' I sighed.

Graciliano came to our table, half ignoring Ari, half stealing glances in his direction.

I felt someone's foot touch my thigh under the table. I turned and faced a smiling Ari.

Oh.

I quite fancied Ari.

I made my excuses and went to the toilet. As I waited in the queue, Ari came by and stood next to me, fixing me irresistibly with his gaze. We lasted just a few seconds before we drunkenly snogged.

I pulled back first. 'Listen,' I said, 'I don't want to come between you and Graciliano.'

'Graciliano and I are finished. *Finished.*'

'And how many times have you "finished"?'

'This one's for good. He's driving me crazy.'

I looked into Ari's eyes. There was clearly a game on, and I was part of it. But I was leaving Salvador altogether in three days. Should I care? Did I care? And why shouldn't I play the game, too?

'Shall I come to your hotel tonight?' Ari asked.

I looked at my watch. It was still early. The night was young. Márcio would be disappointed. But friendship is friendship and sex is sex, no?

I waved Márcio over.

'I know,' he said before I opened my mouth. 'I noticed.'

Really?

'You are such an open book, John,' he said with a grand flowering gesture. 'You are sorted now for the day. Go home. Enjoy the night. Enjoy Bahia!'

And with a wicked smile he added: 'About time, too!'

I thought of Paulo yesterday, and Jorge the day before: how Márcio created relationships and cared for his friends, all Márcio's children, looked after by their special, benevolent *orixá*.

Had I joined them, too?

'Yes, mother,' I retorted.

Márcio laughed loudly and pushed me away.

The bus drove slowly into the Recôncavo, the plush, green zone around the Bay of All Saints, primary settlement territory with homesteads more ancient than most towns in North America; it moved slowly because the early morning mist enveloped us: more of a strange, warm jungle cocoon than a cold, icy Northern European shroud. This was a setting more appropriate for a Wes Craven movie than a tropical travelogue.

The first town out of the fog was Santo Amaro, with its muddy streets, broken fences, leaning walls and abandoned houses overgrown with grass or steeped in moss. It really is a walk-in, walk-out town without a saving grace but one. It is the birthplace of two of Brazil's most popular singers: Caetano Veloso and Maria Bethânia. I am marginally more familiar with the latter – Joni Mitchell-like in her jazzy, eclectic singer-songwriter choice of material – than with Brazil's greatest star. The point is that Caetano Veloso was far too big, famous and respected by the time I started delving into the country's music, and I am naturally suspicious of someone whose lyrics are being studied at university, so I've missed out. The consensus is that Caetano Veloso is Brazil's Bob Dylan and John Lennon combined. He certainly stems from the same protest era and ethos, with the addition of a real live junta breathing down his neck – along with other Brazilians, he came to London in 1968 in preventative exile. The comparisons with Dylan are uncanny: Veloso was booed off stage for using electric guitars in the 2nd Festival of Brazilian Popular Music in 1968 just like Bob Dylan alienated his acoustic folk fans using guitars in the Newport Festival in 1965. And as a dozen folk-rock groups sprang from Dylan's electric cradle – from The Band to Crosby, Stills, Nash and Young – Veloso also spawned a style of music called Tropicalismo: a blend of native rhythms and Western sound which has sadly metamorphosed into the tranquilliser sounds of current MPB: *Música Popular Brasileira*, the country's Adult-Oriented Rock. It is against this anodyne establishment that mangue-beat sprouted in the 1990s but we've had enough of *that*.

It was not Santo Amaro that was my final destination: it was Cachoeira, Brazil's most African state's most African town, with its secretive cults and *terreiros*, the faded splendour of forsaken churches, and the charm of its zigzag-roofed houses. This is a town that was the capital of Bahia during the Dutch occupation and during the insurrection against the Portuguese in 1822; a thriving river port, which declined when land transport via the newly constructed tarmac roads started developing. The Paraguaçu River splits the town from the smaller, less absorbing São Felix over an old railroad iron bridge, which also serves as a car highway with a side footpath for pedestrians, only wide enough for one person: it would have been declared highly perilous where I come from due to missing planks, gaping holes and slippery surfaces. I thought it was a real adventure crossing it, until the pushbike behind me overtook me at one of the hazardous spots by circus-balancing along a single rail. Is life cheaper in the Recôncavo, are we in the West too stuffy with our rules and regulations, or is it that the poor in Brazil can't afford to sue their town council if they trip on the proverbial paving stone?

The old rail terminus in Cachoeira is an impressive warehouse-like building, rotting from the outside in. I went inside and my first reaction was to check the soles of my shoes, as I noticed a toddler, wearing just a small vest, having a dump. Further in, the air was warm, sweet and fetid. My eyes became used to the darkness and started discerning movement. Silhouettes embossed themselves through motion, black against pitch black like troglodytes from a forgotten era. They were all small; they were all children. I retreated back to the entrance, squeezing my camera tightly against my chest. One of the shadows, ragged and runny-nosed, crossed the semi-lit path in front of me to the toddler, who stood up, wiped himself with his hand and scrubbed it off against a railing. The older boy took him by the hand – yes, the other one – and walked him past me to the river by the bridge. His eyes crossed mine for an instant, and in them I saw no enmity, no will to beg, no envy and certainly no anger: just a flash of pure, plain curiosity; for despite the older boy's streetwise composure, he was a child first and foremost. I could have handled hostility better.

It was while I ambled along the cobbled streets up to the impossibly steep *ladeira* of Nossa Senhora de Conceição do Monte, past the rectangular one-floor terraced houses with the signature zigzag roofs, some yellow, some pale blue, some pink, typically with two windows on one side of the door, that I was reminded that this was the second most important town in Bahia in times past. This is where, in the early part of the eighteenth century, the Frenchman Pyrard de Laval praised the colonial *Casas Grandes* – such *'fine and noble dwellings'* – in one of which he was entertained lavishly. The landowner, whose francified name we are given as Mangue La Bote, had dinner accompanied by a 30-piece slave orchestra for he was worth, we are told, 300,000 crowns in land, sugar and slaves. That makes Senhor La Bote one of the hundred-odd Bahian manor lords who pioneered a new world order: private capital, moving on to new lands, exploiting the resources through enforced labour – and settling there permanently.

Cachoeira was no corsair's cove, no here today, gone tomorrow gold-rusher's hovel: it was the permanent extension of the Motherland's economic tentacles to jungles unknown, populated by people who had to be subdued. There were no natural resources but land – no gold or silver which kept the Spanish eyes glinting in Hispanoamerica: the sugar cane had to be planted and farmed. A few hundred families could hardly tame the difficult environment, let alone mass-produce such a difficult crop; the only way the system could succeed was by utilising slave labour on an industrial scale. Each landowner had an immediate licence to import 120 slaves and the numbers escalated from hundreds to tens of thousands of toiling hands. Slavery was a necessary condition for colonialism, which was why Pope Nicholas V and a succession of popes after him not only accepted, but *defended* the status quo of masters and slaves as a natural state of society: and if any Biblical quotes were needed, well, the Good Book could provide plenty.

I sat down in the small park near the river. The sun had come out and Cachoeira was a boiling cauldron. People were asleep around me; on a bench, under the shadow of a tree or even, in the case of a street child, on a tree branch itself. When they were not asleep, they were lying lazily on a roof, perching out of a window, squatting against a wall, curling up by the side of the road, for the Bahian sun is hot, dangerous, adversarial. And yet under its full glare, a teenage couple of the Gegê nation was holding hands without care. The boy was declaring his love to her, reading a poem from a white sheet of paper in a loud, crisp voice which had hardly broken yet. I was just opposite, but to them I was invisible.

A cock crowing continuously in a side street gave me an excuse to leave and walk towards the unusual noise. A middle-aged man in shorts and broken sandals was sitting in the shade, leaning against the peeling paint of a wall. He was throwing a black-plumed, crestless, lapless and tailless cock in the air, catching it as its legs touched the ground before it could flee away and before it could hurt him with its spurs.

'I'm training him,' he answered my unspoken question.

'Training him?'

'For a fight,' he said. 'He's my prize champion.'

The cock looked at me, and an evil look it was, as he started sharpening his claws.

'When will it take place?'

'In a fortnight. And he'll win – won't you?' he asked the cock, throwing him in the air again. 'You must win, you hear me?'

And then he, too, forgot about me as he continued his champion cock Masterclass.

*****

Most of the churches in Cachoeira were closed except the Igreja de Nossa Senhora do Rosario, which had been meticulously renovated. As I entered, its three small rotund and merry matrons fussed over me like the three fairies in the Cinderella cartoon movie.

'You want to turn the light on,' said the First One to the Second – who smiled and obliged.

'Look around you,' prompted the Third cheerfully.

The walls, covered with 16-foot-high blue *azulejos*, were spectacular. I took out my camera.

'No, you can't take a picture,' said the First. 'No flash.'

'Show him the Treasury,' said Number Three.

Number Two took me by the hand to the room next door.

'You want to open the curtains,' said the First One to the Second.

The light through the curtains illuminated a beautifully adorned room with thick wooden floors, painted ceilings and cornices.

'Beautiful, isn't it?' smiled Number Three.

'It's beautiful,' agreed the First One.

I nodded as the past glories of Cachoeira glittered in front of my eyes. This room, laden with glitz and riches, wouldn't look out of place in Versailles.

I looked at the three fairy women giggling in front of me. Could they be …

'Are you members of the Sisterhood of Good Death?' I asked naively.

They stopped giggling.

'No,' they all said at once. 'The Sisterhood is *African*.'

Of course. My three fairies were light-skinned (#51 *cor-de-canela*, cinnamon-coloured). The Sisters in their church, the Igreja de Ajuda, an unassuming, locked edifice, are ebony black.

The Sisterhood of Good Death – *A Irmandade da Boa Morte* – is what

Cachoeira is famous for at the dawn of the twenty-first century, because the Sisterhood, as old as independent Brazil itself, is responsible for one of the best examples of Afro-Catholic religiosity in the New World. If that was not enough, it is composed solely of black women over 40 years old.

When the rollercoaster of emancipation started spinning in the early nineteenth century, fraternities of freed blacks of every African nation started forming to help each other materially in the manner of twentieth-century co-operatives. The Sisterhood, openly supporting the abolition of slavery and attempting to buy off members of its kin, was ahead of its time as it cut through race, gender, age and politics. The original reason for its formation around 1820 in Salvador (it moved to Cachoeira in 1823 along with many freed slaves who worked in the new tobacco industry) was humble: to procure funds so that its elderly members could have a decent burial, for in the Bahia of times past it was not exactly unknown for black corpses to be dumped unceremoniously in the bay. *The Society of Decent Burial* would be a better translation.

As in candomblé there is an internal hierarchy: although the oldest becomes the unelected Perpetual Judge, members (whose apprenticeship lasts three years) vote using a grain of corn for yes and a bean for no, to elect a rotating presidency of four administrative positions: the Attorney General, the Provider, the Treasurer and the Secretary. Their task is to organise the celebration of the Assumption of the Virgin on 15 August with a festival as sumptuous as it is shrouded in mystery. It is only during that festival that the Sisters appear in public, dressed in white turbans and red and black satins over their white crinolines.

Many rituals of the Sisterhood are highly secret, but the public face of the festivities has been subject to much documentary ethnological research: on the Friday before 15 August they have a ceremonious White Dinner of fish and seafood, where no palm oil is used – echoes of Catholic fasting. On the Saturday, the burial of the Virgin takes place in a grand procession punctuated by wails and tears of grief from the Sisters dressed in black. But on the Sunday – the Easter paradigm is hard to shake – the Assumption of the Virgin is celebrated with a thrilling pageant and a parade with the Sisters in full regalia dancing *samba da roda* – a form of samba in a circle. As in Rio's *Carnaval*, the festivities continue until Tuesday, assuming a more covert candomblé character with offerings to Oxalá and ceremonies for the souls of dead members. Despite having put Cachoeira firmly on the tourist map, the Sisters – to their credit –

have complained bitterly about the commercialisation of their festival, especially since the sombre mood of the burial of the Virgin on Saturday night is spoiled by music concerts and general merrymaking. They know from their past that there may be a time for dancing, but only once the time for crying is over.

The voyeuristic Hollywood image of slavery is of lithe black bodies in chains being whipped. The mundane reality was much more horrific than that because of its routine nature. You can only fully comprehend the prevailing attitude and its excesses if you understand that slaves were considered cattle. The master's concubinistic forays with female slaves which resulted in offspring were justified as attempts to increase the herd. (I wouldn't be terribly surprised if zoophilia in ancient societies did not stem from the naive belief that cows or sheep impregnated by their owner would actually conceive). Rape was simply an increase of capital with the pleasurable studding extras that the work entailed. For this task of course, looks came at a premium.

....

For sale: a female slave at an incredibly low price for the present time; the said slave has no vice whatever and is a confectioner by trade; the only thing against her is an unpleasant figure and it is for this reason that she is being sold; inquire in the city of Olinda at the second house above the embankment or in Recife, Rua do Crespo D.3
– Diário de Pernambuco, 23 September 1830

For sale: Catarina of the Benguella tribe, tall, heavy set, upstanding breasts, broad face, thick lips, prominent teeth, very black, pretty figure.
– Diário de Pernambuco, 9 October, 1828

....

Slaves who worked in the fields lived on average for seven years and their lot was only marginally better than in the American South. The Catholic Church insisted that they marry before any intra-slave sex took place (it was also useful to have married slave girls giving birth even if they had conceived from their master) and there were often many black and mulatto children, *negrinhos*, who roamed freely around the house befriending their master's legitimate offspring. Dom Pedro II himself took with him only a small circle of ten people when he travelled to Europe incognito in 1871; amongst them was his black childhood friend and servant Rafael, whose later duties were restricted to shoe-shining.

Rafael was an exception; as a rule on reaching adulthood slaves were sold as far away as possible from the family *fazenda* to break up friendships, family and village ties. And if they were young virgin girls they were in for a shock: they could be sold to syphilitic patients to provide them with a cure (this all-powerful myth has now mutated into a 'cure' for Aids in some African societies). The effects of this practice continued far into the future; so much so that the writer Gilberto Freyre quotes sources that show that by the 1920s 50 per cent of cases in the Rio's pauper hospital were syphilitic. The slave girls passed on the disease not only to their kids and lovers, but also through breastfeeding, in an act of ironic divine punishment, back to the children of the *Casas Grandes* where they acted as milchcows for the master's brood.

Beatings came as extras: the original whipping post still exists in places as distant as Natal in Rio Grande do Norte and Mariana in Minas Gerais. The wearing of large, rough iron collars was such an everyday event it features in casual drawings by Debret, better known for his Brazilian court portraits. Another commonplace accoutrement was the Flanders mask, a face restraint, made famous by Dumas' *The Man in the Iron Mask*; this was regularly worn by slaves working in mines in case they ingested any precious metals. Shackles and stocks are described by Thomas Ewbank in his 1850s Brazil travelogue: '[the shackles] *were the heaviest and cruellest instruments of torture* – [they were used] *for binding the ankles and wrists close together and consequently doubling the bodies of the victims into the most painful unnatural positions.*' They may not have the photogenic celluloid quality of whipping, but as anyone who has suffered from office backache due to bad posture can attest, they were excruciatingly and debilitatingly agonising.

But I bet you haven't thought of the most hair-raising aspect of slavery: forget the torture, the feeling of hopelessness and the raging sense of injustice. How, if you were a slave, the property of your master, could you get your own back? One way would be to attempt to kill him, and the newspapers of nineteenth-century Brazil were full of such stories. But sometimes your options were limited – the answer, glacial in its chilliness, is simple.

You destroy his property.

.. … .. .. … .. … .. … .. … .. … .. … .. … .. … .. … .. … .. … .. … .. … .. … .. … ..

Porto Feliz: In the month of September [1874] *in the* fazenda *of Francisco Aguiar e Silva, the* pardo *Salvador and his wife named Romana, both slaves in the said* fazenda, *committed suicide by jumping from a depot. The appropriate authority proceeded with a preliminary investigation, but from its findings nothing could explain the motives responsible for such an act of despair.*

Piraricaba: on the 18th of the month [November 1884] *around 8 a.m. in the morning at Pau-Queimado, the slave-woman Tertuliana, belonging to the fazendeiro José Vieira de Morias, killed her three sons, all minors: Pedro, 6 years old, Marinho, 26 months old and Benedito, 8 months old.*
– Reports of the Chief of Police of the state of São Paulo, from Gilberto Freyre's *The Masters and The Slaves.*

....

Psychologists have delved into the sadomasochistic nature of the master-slave relationship (the terms of which are still used in specialised S&M adverts the world over) and it may take a thesis to analyse their effect on post-colonial society. But it is hard to conceive the soul of modern Brazil – one ought to say of the Americas – without sitting back and pondering the effects of such a demeaning institution. Its influence was in the language even in the form of polite address: whereas a European aristocrat might sign his letters respectfully with 'Your obedient slave', a Brazilian would sign as '*seu negrinho*' – your Negro boy. Its influence still exists in the violent sadism of the crimes: remnants of centuries of mutual hate, bitterness and inequality. It lives on in the famously lax attitudes to sex: after all, the black and mulatto girls were there for the taking, were they not? It surfaces in the paternalistic attitude towards native Indians: they were considered and treated like minors, their interest safeguarded by the unelected employees of the State Indian Protection Service who would decide their fate on their behalf for decades. It is inherent in the bossy attitude of the bureaucrats: you are expected to obey, humble yourself in front of the display of authority and be grateful for their time. Finally, it is perpetuated in the intimidatory vigilantism of the police: prisoners are scum with no rights and street kids are vermin to be exterminated.

– 33 –

I spent my last day with Ari and his mobile phone, for they come together and they are inseparable. For good measure he called Graciliano twice: 'I am calling him about a job I found for him,' he said sheepishly. It was nice of him to show such concern for my feelings, but I was leaving next day, and I was hoping that their temporary split would soon heal up. Because I liked Ari. I liked him a lot. He was gentle, relaxed, softly spoken and his English was an oasis of escape amongst the enforced nasality of Brazilian Portuguese. We immediately developed an empathy which normally grows months into a relationship. This was more a friend to pour your heart out to than a lover to antagonise.

We walked around the old town, checking out the odd sight I had missed – and you might say the oversized cathedral and the ornate governor's palace were rather important to have been left out; we went up and down various *elevadores*, including the lesser-known funicular behind the Praça da Sé, and sat in the restaurant above the Mercado Modelo which specialised in roast meats.

Ari was comfortably middle class: his father was in the construction industry, his mother was a history teacher. He was finishing economics at uni – and English, which he wanted to practise with me, was one of his exam subjects. Unlike Márcio, though, Ari was not open about his homosexuality.

I could imagine Graciliano being camp. Was that a problem?

Ari nodded.

'He is out, and he is very open. Once in a fiesta he was hanging out with the drag queens. I had asked him not to, as I feel uncomfortable.'

Difficult relationship.

'Another time he was reading a gay magazine openly in the kiosk. I left him there and then.'

'That's not a reason to get angry.'

Ari shook his head.

'I know,' he agreed, 'but – but I believe that sometimes he does that to annoy me. We've been fighting constantly. We nearly came to blows one day because I asked him to turn down the air conditioning.'

His handsome features winced.

'You know,' I said, 'from experience I have found out that love stories with happy endings are so popular because they are rare in real life. You don't necessarily marry the one you love; you marry the one you get on with.'

He continued eating quietly.

'Can I come to see you in London sometime?' he asked timidly between mouthfuls of baby beef.

'Of course,' I said and meant it.

'Can I stay with you?'

I thought of Peter and Jasmin. How could I spell it out?

'You realise that you will encounter – ahem, some *racist* behaviour, don't you?'

His eyes registered incomprehension.

'Oh, Britain is much, much better than many countries in Europe in terms of race,' I said, 'and London is international and multicultural enough for someone to fit in without much ado, but let's say there are countries with a better racial record.'

'You mean we wouldn't be able to sit down here together, talking?'

I waved an exaggerated no. 'Of course we would. Not even in modern South Africa does such segregation exist. But there isn't much mixing as such either. You don't get many cross-colour friendships or relationships; the racism is more insidious, because it's hidden within politically correct language. As long as you say the approved things you're in the clear and your behaviour, which is far more important, is hardly examined.'

Ari appeared downcast.

'Don't let me put you off,' I said. 'Just that you won't have experienced in Bahia some looks you are likely to get in Europe.'

Then Ari produced the bolt that illuminated the whole structure of colour in Brazil in a flash. It was a soft and shy bolt, spoken sweetly.

'People have told me that I don't look that black,' Ari said coyly and hopefully. 'People say that I can be mistaken for an Arab.'

Oh, modern Brazil, the place which has inspired studies in colour-blindness from North American sociology departments; the place that produced Pelé, the best-paid athlete in the 1960s, black or white; the place which I had always taken as a counterbalance to the madness of South African apartheid. I could see now why Nelson and his candomblé friends did not mix with the crowd in Red-Blue; why they put up chicken-wire fences in the Ponta de Areia; why there could be no real friendship between the *terreiro* devotees and a white tourist; I could understand the surprise of my three Cinderella fairies in Cachoeira: how could we be mistaken for Sisters? I could understand the 134 variations in colour hues, nay, the whole bloody social structure which is as racist as any – with a twist: in the West, a drop of black blood makes you black; in Brazil, a drop of white blood makes you white. There it is, as simple as that. Why? Because the sheer number of Portuguese progeny of mixed blood was the secret weapon the Portuguese introduced to colonise the country.

A ruling class always forms an alliance with another to defend its control over the means of production. In the Middle Ages it was the clergy. In South Africa the Coloured Malay and Indian population was used as a buffer. In the capitalist West, the middle class has been persuaded that it, too, can rise materially and socially to the top. The white Brazilian colonialists needed to take in the people of mixed race and colour who defined themselves as 'we-are-not-African' and co-opt them as white. But that in turn makes the smallest shade of your skin colour important. Racism exists in Brazil, but in a mutated form: in the West we see blacks and whites working side by side and mixed race circles in bars and clubs astonish us; but the Brazilians don't see it that way, for they have refined and redefined colour characteristics to a degree we are oblivious of.

Still, I bow my head. Subtle its racism may be, but Brazilian society lies a step forward from the sharp dividing lines in our Western thinking, since ultimately, it is more inclusive, more *colour-full* if you like, and dwarfs our excesses in the West. So yes, I approve of the mix as before, but I do it now in the full knowledge that it, too, deep down below is governed by the same human curses of prejudice and exclusion; it is only through such awareness that ultimately change can take effect.

I held Ari's hand and smiled.

'Ari,' I reassured him, 'if you come to London they'll adore you, 'cos you're a lovely guy.'

He beamed.

*****

Once more it was Tuesday and the echoes of drums were resounding in Pelourinho, although the rainy drip-drip weather had thinned the crowds. Ari, Márcio and I had a meal at Uauá, one of the best restaurants in the area, feasting on *bobó de camarão* and various *moquecas*. The atmosphere was subdued, for Márcio was.

'Aleixo on your mind?' I asked.

He nodded.

'Called me again and left a message which sounded like a declaration of love.'

'You must clear up the situation from the start.'

Márcio sighed.

'Once, of course, you are clear yourself about what you want.'

Márcio sighed again: 'Why do we always argue with our lovers?'

I looked at Ari who was quiet. 'I hope he's listening,' I said.

Márcio made a sweeping gesture in Ari's direction.

'*O truque da galinha*,' he said.

'The "chicken trick"? What's the "chicken trick"?' I asked.

'Have you seen how chickens stay immobile, but their eyes follow you around? They sit still, but they look and listen and take everything in.'

Ari smiled.

'What time are you leaving for Ilhéus tomorrow?' he asked.

'Very early in the morning. I need a taxi at about five for the airport.'

Márcio took a folded and stapled piece of paper from his pocket.

'Take this,' he said. 'Promise to open it when you are on the plane.'

I was taken aback.

'*Promise!*' Márcio cried and in his eyes I thought I saw the faint glimpse of unrequited love.

'Yes, mother,' I uttered mockingly, distinct quavers in my voice.

Things I Like About Brazil #7: The Bahians

I kept my promise to Márcio, and after the plane took off I pulled out the staple that was holding his note together. I read through the lyrics from Milton Nascimento's 'Encontros e Despedidas' ('Meetings and Farewells'), which Márcio had chosen especially for me. At the end he had typed his own few sentences:

'Mother will always be here in Salvador to receive you with open arms. I can't go on typing more, because I have become too emotional, but like the tear running down my cheek, it is with the most sincere and deepest sentiments that I wish you John all the happiness in the world.

Greetings to all your friends in London. Smile! You will come again to Bahia!

Your friend for ever,

Márcio

Salvador – Bahia – Brazil'

AXÉ!

Chapter 8

Rich Town, Black Gold, Little Cripple, Filthy Beggar (Ouro Preto, Belo Horizonte)

A promised fulfilled: in order to answer Ari's question: 'What's the best place in Brazil?' I have to resort to my first trip to the country once more.

This is a chapter about ghosts and inflation.

....

The Words You'll Need

aqui jaz = 'here lies'
as cidades históricas = *the historical cities*
bandeira = *flag. It also denotes an expedition into the interior of Brazil by*
    bandeirantes: explorers and Indian slavers who were 'carrying the flag'.
chafariz = *public water fountain*
rodoviária = *bus station*
roteiro histórico = *historical route*
Scheisse = *You should know that! German for shit!*

....

– 34 –

I am a cartophile; I love maps. Apart from my world atlases, I keep local maps in alphabetical order in an old paper filing folder. And I have more maps of Belo Horizonte than of any other city. I have maps from three different travel guides, maps from history books, maps given free by hotels and maps that come with the state tourism brochures. I have so many maps of BH (only Westerners call it Belo: locals use its initials, *Be Agá* in Portuguese), and I still manage to get lost in the place.

Originally I blamed it on that early edition of a travel guide which shall remain nameless. It had printed the *mirror image* of the central town section by mistake in the way newspapers sometimes print photos and make you look out of the window to check if cars in England still drive on the left or if, as the picture shows, they changed the system while you had a catnap on the couch. You can imagine the havoc such a misprint can cause to a new arrival. After hours of exhibiting the spatial awareness of a pair of windscreen wipers, which included an animated visit to the tourist office ('You have built the town wrong!'), the penny finally dropped. But even with correct maps – and my collection now looks like overcompensation – I still managed to get lost. BH, Brazil's first planned city more than 100 years ago, does not just have a grid that crosses at right angles; occasionally a diagonal street comes through, resulting in a six-way crossing, which makes following a straight line quite a challenge: oops, once more I have moved to another Avenida. What fun.

BH and I didn't start on the best of terms. It didn't help that BH, with its rapid post-World War Two industrialisation, is an ugly modern city, its original features dynamited by developers. One of the nicer Art Deco buildings, the old market, Feira de Amostras Permanentes, was demolished in 1970 and the *rodoviária* – which I would get to know very well – built in its place.

With my backpack on my stiff shoulders and a late flight from Manaus behind me, I chose to walk the small distance from that very same *rodoviária* to the oddly named Hotel Ambassy (with an 'A') which sounds grand, but ain't. It's at a rickety-rackety junction, ear-splitting with noise and brimming with danger, since the area around the *rodoviária* until at least the Praça Sete is one of the most crime-ridden in BH with pimps, whores and drug-dealers monopolising not only the night hours, but also the daytime as well. Who cares? I thought. I was only in BH in order to return to the *rodoviária* next morning to visit *as cidades históricas* of Minas Gerais.

*****

There was a particular town with a cult reputation: one that had witnessed the first gold rush of modern times and was the first to be declared a Unesco heritage site by Brazil. It is the *whole* town, laden with baroque interiors and rococo façades, that is a monument in the manner of Venice or Kyoto. It is also a town that became the revered pivot of Brazilian independence and where for the first time on American soil a colony surpassed the art – in poetry, sculpture and architecture – of the European mother country.

I knew that this town was crowned by the very distinctive peak of Itacolomi, a mountain everyone seemed to be searching for in the late seventeenth century. One group of Paulista *bandeirantes* explored the area between Salvador, Rio and São Paulo for seven difficult years under Fernão Dias, who died on the banks of the Rio das Velhas. As his tearful son Garcia Fernandes took his remains back to the town, the rest of his *bandeira* under the Spaniard Manuel Borba Gato encountered a royal party. Borba Gato was unusually adverse to relinquishing command: in October 1681, after an affray, he murdered the royal representative and disappeared into the Mata Atlântica.

The inhabitants of São Paulo couldn't make head or tail of such odd behaviour, for Borba Gato had condemned himself to death, be it on the gallows or in the jungle. But Garcia Fernandes held the key to the motive: his father's group had accomplished the dream of the Portuguese ever since Brazil had been discovered. Green with envy at the Spanish crown's acquisition of the Aztec and Inca gold treasures, begrudging the subsequent discovery of the silver mines at Potosí, the Portuguese had been impeded in their search for treasure for two centuries by Brazil's unhealthy climate, inhospitable jungles and hostile natives. The word was out: Borba Gato had killed the royal envoy because the expedition had found gold. The New World's first gold rush had started aptly, with a bloody murder.

Unfortunately Garcia Fernandes couldn't scout his way back and for the next 17 years the Paulistas made various explorations into their north-eastern interior until a dark mulatto brought back some strange black pebbles. When he had them examined properly, the tests revealed rich gold ore under a thin film of black oxide. The news spread like a jungle hyperblaze: this black gold had been panned by the banks of a river under a peak which split into two: the smaller appeared like a boy, the Boy Rock, *Itacurumim* in Tupi, or as it is now known, Itacolomi.

The race became more feverish.

On the evening of the Feast of St John, 23 June 1698, a party led by the Paulista Antônio Dias de Oliveira made their camp at the bottom of a valley covered in freezing fog. That June night was chilly in the extreme, and the fires of the *bandeirantes* could barely keep them alive. The next day, however, brought the sun out, which broke the fog and warmed their hearts as it revealed to them in all their astonishment that they had camped below the shadow of the Boy Rock.

The discovery of gold in Brazil was to change the course not only of the country's history, shifting irrevocably as it did the economic and political centre of gravity away from the Nordeste (the capital moved from Salvador to Rio, the main gold-shipping port, in 1753), but also the global balance of power. For the gold in the region that became known by the coldly efficient name of Minas Gerais (General Mines – imagine Michigan being called General Motors) ended up in England, paying for the new mass-produced goods from its novel northern factories.

In the eighteenth century an estimated 80 per cent of gold circulating in Europe came from Brazil, leaving words like *joannes* – gold coins stamped with Portugal's Dom João V's portrait – still in English dictionaries. But the only thing that changed in Portugal, content to export olive oil, port wine and gold to England, were the court caparisons. In the permanent shadow of Spain, the Portuguese ruling house of Bragança allied themselves with England by marrying off Catherine of Bragança to Charles II. With the Treaty of Methuen in 1703 they attached themselves even closer to this new rising naval power: exports of capital from Portugal were freed, and they found their way into England's new banking institutions which lent them to those northern workshops. Later Dom João VI decreed that English products throughout the Portuguese Empire would attract only 15 per cent tax. Even Portugal's own were taxed more expensively at 16 per cent while the rest of the world's goods were on a prohibitive 24 per cent. No wonder a certain Reverend Walsh who visited Minas Gerais in the early nineteenth century found there '*Manchester cottons, Yorkshire woollens, Nottingham stockings, London hats and Sheffield cutlery.*' Brazil's gold bankrolled England's Industrial Revolution.

Eventually certain urban nuclei were formed: in Nossa Senhora do Carmo, which became known as Mariana; in the Vila Real de Nossa Senhora de Conceição de Sabará; in Rio das Mortes, Death River, which unsurprisingly changed its name to São João d'El Rei (please note the correct spelling of this grossly misspelt town). The settlement under Itacolomi was rightly baptised Vila Rica (Rich Town) and ended up as the capital of the new province of Minas Gerais. There Antônio Dias left his name to the parish which overlooks the peak he accidentally rediscovered. It joined the parish on the other side of the hill of Santa Quitéria, which was called after Vila Rica's mineral: Ouro Preto – Black Gold.

And that is the name that persisted over time.

....

Things I Like About Brazil #8: Ghosts

Indian myths may be alive in the Amazon and African Gods may stroll in the streets of Salvador, but Brazil – white Brazil – has its own ghosts. In Minas Gerais they're a white man's ghosts and they talk of greed, poverty and revenge.

For what are ghosts but tales which capture the imagination – for good or for bad – and live in our minds forever? Ghosts aren't physical but they sure have presence, for they live as long as a memory is told and retold.

One of them belongs to me.

....

– 35 –

The bus to Ouro Preto stops high above the city next to the tourist office. I remember vividly the thrill of seeing the twisted peak of Itacolomi for the first time; I could imagine Antônio Dias letting out a winner's cry. Then the town caught my eye and held it wide open: this was not the stereotypical Brazilian landscape I had come to expect; no beaches, no jungle, no concrete and corrugated-iron buildings, but gentle rolling hills and two-storey colonial houses with fuchsia-red pantiles on the roofs. Your first baroque Brazilian town is special for its surpassing of expectations as you are bombarded with architectural splendour of the highest calibre. After the wilderness of the Amazon and the shabbiness of Belo Horizonte, I stepped out of the bus onto Ouro Preto's narrow, roughly cobbled streets and felt as if I had walked right into a frameless Renaissance painting: I could be in eighteenth-century Florence or Sienna. There may be other great panorama points in Brazil gazing down on man-made magnificence or supreme natural beauty, but that initial, mouth-watering moment of surprised shock still brings me out in goose pimples.

The tourist office sold me another map and tried very hard to flog me a human guide as well. I would have none of it as I zigzagged my way to the central square, every step a new picture and every house posterworthy: two storeys, large wooden door, square windows, painted windowsills. Indeed, there was a beautifully photographed poster on sale: 'Balconies of Ouro Preto and Mariana'. It could have been titled 'Meetings with Remarkable Windows': first-floor French arched doors leading to narrow balconets with lanterns hanging on the sides, flowerbeds sprouting irregularly; railings ranging from simple horizontal beams to arabesques on sculpted soapstone; rectangular glass panes contrasting with elaborate shouldered arches and complex skewed fanlight designs; ceramic red, blue mauve, yellowish brown, sand pink, ink-blue coloured grilles framed in glowing white. The secret of the beauty of Ouro Preto is its homogeneity: streets of terraced two-floor houses, all in the same style, and yet each one unique in character.

I took up residence in the Hotel Pilão, which faced the main square – an old colonial mansion with creaking wooden floors and ceilings tall enough to accommodate a training trampoline gymnast. As I walked out, my eye fell on the price list. This was not the figure I had been told – had I heard correctly?

'250,000 cruzeiros for a single room? I thought it was 150,000,' I asked timidly.

'Yes, it is 150,000,' replied the woman receptionist wearily. 'It's such a pain rewriting the rates, we have put the list up to last a month. In the meantime we pretend we give discounts.' This was the time of spiralling inflation when the currency was the cruzeiro – so hard to come to terms with this mess even as a tourist. I grimaced empathetically and walked out into the wide space of Praça Tiradentes.

Something wasn't quite right, but I couldn't put my finger on it.

On my left stood the old town hall; on my right the winding stairs of the old governor's palace, now the School of Mines; in the centre, a tall memorial to Tiradentes, the Brazilian Independence hero; next to me stores selling precious stones, minerals and soapstone sculptures; opposite me restaurants, bars and taxis.

Something isn't quite right.

Only when I started walking down the side of the governor's palace, armed with my map of the *roteiro histórico* for the arduous trek east to the chapel of Padre Faria did it dawn on me that, unlike every other town in Latin America, there was no church in the main plaza.

The gold rush found the Portuguese crown unprepared but able to benefit from the Spanish plundering experiences of earlier centuries. It thus acted quickly to establish its authority to collect taxes. Dom João V, who was on the throne for almost half a century, acted decisively: there would be no foreigners in the region – and no troublesome Jesuits. Foreigners were only allowed to enter in the early 1800s after the mines had been depleted and a small number of Jesuits were only granted entrance in 1745 to establish an educational college; but as they were expelled from Brazil fifteen years later, they never acquired the domineering influence they had in Bahia or Pernambuco.

Central square, administrative buildings, no church!

One cannot comprehend the development of Minas Gerais and the character of its inhabitants without pondering over its isolation from the outside world and freedom from the Jesuit ultra-conservative influence. It was the lay orders, led by the Third Order of São Francisco and the Third Order of Carmo who were the motivational force, competing in extravagance – the former included the mine owners and the latter the town grandees. The result was an explosion in artistry with minds freed from the bridles of proscription.

*****

The church of Santa Ifigênia, commanding a top spot on the Alto da Cruz, was a welcome stop on the way to Padre Faria's chapel, if only to catch my breath after the tortuous ascent. This is the part of town where the slaves lived. You can still tell from the uneven sharp cobble stones, the ever-darkening colour of the residents and the one- rather than two-storey houses on the eponymous street. No wonder, for Santa Ifigênia was the church built by the black slaves and class mobility is not exactly a phenomenon colonial societies are famous for. Legend goes further: it is supposed to be the church built by Chico Rei.

It is now we enter the realm of ghosts – and it will be hard to leave it, for in Minas Gerais they merge with the living as easily as they straddle the dead.

Chico Rei's legend is a mixture of historical fact and folk tale compiled by that great ethnographer Câmara Cascudo. Mineiros have no doubts, however, about its veracity. Maybe Chico Rei's story is so popular because, if not authentic, it is certainly one we'd all like to be true, so I'm not going to cast doubt on it any more. Its background is that of the changing conditions of the mine slave labour. As more African slaves were imported to work in the gold mines, the Mineiros – many of whom were new, Enlightenment-minded Portuguese arrivals – realised that they were dependent on the skills and wills of their workforce more than the sugar-cane landowners who could treat their slaves as cattle and expect the same response. Here, free paid labour with some private incentive proved more productive, especially as the years wore on and gold became scarcer. Slaves were allowed to work extra hours to buy themselves off; a relatively benign attitude came to prevail and a new consensus emerged, receptive to the new ideas imported by the sons of the scions of the community who were sent to study in Europe.

Chico Rei was an African king who was sold to the slavers along with his family and his whole tribe. His wife and all his sons but one died in the passage. The ex-king gained everyone's respect for he worked non-stop in his own time, on Sundays and festive days, and earned the money for his release. He married for a second time and started to rebuild his life, working in mines belonging to a Major Augusto. One day the Major fell ill and on his death-bed requested a visit by Chico Rei – an act unheard of in Vila Rica as blacks did not walk into white men's houses. It was there that Chico Rei's luck changed. The ailing Major, impressed by Chico Rei's virtues, offered to sell him the mine of Encardadeira.

Would *you* hesitate for long?

Chico Rei earned the fee for his son's release and together they both worked to buy off his faithful servants of old who subsequently worked with him to free members of his tribe. It was thus that the king without a people became king again among the freed black population of Vila Rica. On Epiphany, the day of the Three Kings, the populace of Ouro Preto celebrates his memory by dancing the *congado*, a dance in which a black king and queen are crowned every year. Chico Rei is said to have died from hepatitis in 1776, but then the legend vanishes, like Chico Rei's heirs and his mine of gold.

Well, not quite.

*****

A small street urchin followed me and two elderly Brazilian women as we entered the church.

'Santa Ifigênia was built between '42 and '49 …' he started.

The two women turned and tut-tutted.

'What century my boy? It sounds like 1942 and 1949. What century? You must say 1742 and 1749. Say it,' said one school-marmishly.

'The church was built between 1742 and 1749,' the kid repeated slowly, staring at the woman with apprehension.

'Good,' she said abruptly and left the boy confused.

Santa Ifigênia stands high on a hill and can't be missed from wherever you are in town, a two-finger salute from the slaves to their masters. The front is old-fashioned and austere, but inside it is full of *grisalha* murals, uncovered during recent restorations. They are subtle, monochrome scenes of everyday eighteenth-century living: couples in love and guitar-playing musicians decorate the walls, a reminder of the life-affirming African beliefs – no wonder they were covered up later. I can picture nineteenth-century prudes shouting '*profanity!*'

'The church is haunted,' said the boy behind us suddenly, causing one of the women to scream.

The school marm tut-tutted again.

'Every church in Ouro Preto is haunted, my boy,' she said, confronting the kid, eyebrows crossed.

This time, he didn't budge.

'When the church empties,' he said, 'the walls start to speak in old African languages.'

I looked around. The greyish images felt alive and creepy. The screamer woman seemed perturbed.

'How come *you* know if they speak when the church is empty?' asked the school marm.

The boy had the answer ready.

'You can hear the murmurs from outside,' he said.

The screamer crossed herself and dug in her purse for some notes.

'There,' she said and winked let's-go to her friend. 'Thanks for the information.'

The boy looked at the notes and smiled. Living with 2,500 per cent inflation has many day-to-day side effects which you only notice when you experience it. One of these is that you start upping your tips and your handouts to the beggars with notes of ever-increasing value. So unless you are a real cheapskate and you pitch in last week's accepted rate, the poor see their intake increasing, so they never look glum when they check out your donation, even though it will be worthless next week.

– 36 –

Mineiro cuisine is one of those unexpected joys which make travelling exciting. This is *bandeirante* expedition food, high in protein. The base is the *feijão tropeiro* – a mix of black beans, manioc, bacon and eggs accompanying a range of meats: *vaca atolada* – ox ribs in manioc sauce; *carne de panela* – stewed steak; *dobradinha* – a kind of tripe; *moela de frango* – chicken giblets; *rabada com agrião* – an oxtail stew; *costelinha con canjiquinha* – pork chops in ground corn sauce; *frango ao molho pardo* – chicken cooked in its own blood in the manner of the Pernambucan *cabidela*; *linguiça* –

primitive, fatty sausage. They are all served with a range of steamed or boiled vegetables like *couve*, finely cut salty kale; chayote, okra, pumpkin, cabbage and *jiló*, a cucumber-like bitter Brazilian green whose tang goes well with meat. The sweets are, as in all Brazil, very sweet indeed, and they tend to be transportable: stewed fruit; crystallised citrus rinds; *goiabada*, guava marmalade chunks; and *rapadura* – cane sugar in cubes. It sounds terribly unhealthy on the carbohydrate front, but it all stores well for those interminable days on horseback through the jungle. Not that *I* did any riding, of course, but the hills of Ouro Preto make you feel as tired as a carthorse.

I reached the House of the Auditor on the way to the Largo do São Francisco where I had to struggle with souvenir-sellers for dear life. This is where the poet Tomás Antônio Gonzaga lived; he had been appointed a kind of ombudsman – *ouvidor* – in Ouro Preto and at the age of 45 fell in love with 15-year-old Maria Dorotéia Joaquina de Seixas. I know it sounds like a dirty-old-man scenario with our twenty-first-century morals, but eighteenth-century population-expanding mentality had a simple motto: if you could menstruate, then you should be saddled with a man on the path to procreation. Maria Dorotéia was visiting the house of her aunt next door when she caught the eye of the poet who was struck by her beauty. He was in luck, for Maria Dorotéia must have been into Daddy types. Overcome with love, Gonzaga started composing stanzas for her, and to spare her blushes he invented a love nickname for her: Marília, and he was her Dirceu.

I passed Marília's bridge, another of Ouro Preto's delights and sat by the *chafariz*, the sculpted fountain; both bridge and fountain are works of art by themselves. Marília's house doesn't exist any more, and a school has been built in its place. But this is the real fountain where the two lovers used to meet in those cooing and wooing days of 1788. Marília's family was not exactly over the moon, for she had been born with a silver spoon in her mouth (almost literally so; a silver spoon appears in her inventory of possessions stored in the Registry of Ouro Preto). They had better plans for their daughter than marrying a civil servant – worse, a poet: how much dosh can *he* provide? We can presume the teenage girl stomped her feet and threatened to die in the tradition of lovelorn teenagers throughout history and had her way. The marriage was earmarked for 30 May 1789.

It never took place.

It is here that tragedy assumes *Casablanca*-like proportions, for

Gonzaga's and Marília's lives were brutally caught up in one of those political maelstroms which, in the words of the cliché, really was bigger than both of them. It is the 1789 Conspiracy of Vila Rica which defines Brazilian patriotic sensitivities to this day – the first independence movement in Latin American history: the Inconfidência Mineira.

Secret societies were the rage in Europe at the time: from the hedonistic Hellfire Club in London with its famous orgies, to the nationalistic Friendly Society in Vienna which would become the fulcrum for Balkan independence. Gonzaga belonged to such a society with the independence of Brazil as its central cause. It was inspired by North American and French Enlightenment ideals: of Man as Responsible Citizen, of no Taxation without Representation and of Reason as the Measure of all things. Apart from the unfair taxation as the gold diminished – the tax was imposed on assumed, not actual, extraction – it did not pass unnoticed in Brazil that although the colony accounted for 60 per cent of Portugal's exports, it could not trade independently with other countries but only through the motherland; it was not allowed printing presses; it could not establish schools of higher learning; and it could not build its own industries.

This secret society had penetrated the cream of intellectuals of Vila Rica – among them another poet, magistrate Claudio Manuel da Costa; a second lieutenant, Joaquim José da Silva Xavier, who was known as Tiradentes (Tooth-puller), as he had a knack for dentistry; and José Joaquim de Maia who had been corresponding with Thomas Jefferson. The latter had replied with a cryptic remark: a revolution in Brazil *'would not be uninteresting to the United States'*, probably the first-ever indication of a long list of US interference to come.

A secret society, by definition, can only be betrayed from within. The Judas of Brazilian nationalists is Colonel Joaquim Silvério dos Reis who did rather well out of it: apart from the obligatory medal, he got a life pension and had his debts written off. By design or by accident, the authorities stepped in one week before Marília's marriage and arrested Gonzaga along with the other principal conspirators. They were put on trial and condemned to death, but their sentences were commuted by the Portuguese queen Maria the Mad. Tiradentes, who claimed to be the leader, was unrepentant in his principles and was the only one to be executed. It has not escaped the historians' attention that he was the only one not of noble birth and without any friends in high places. Indeed, his claims now cling strange: a lowly second lieutenant, a *dentist*, leader of the town aristos? The most likely leader was da Costa, who was conveniently 'suicided' so that his family would not have their fortune sequestered or considered infamous until the fifth generation. Whatever – it was Tiradentes who took the rap. He was hanged and then quartered; his head was placed in the main square of Vila Rica where his monument now stands; and he became the symbol of Brazilian independence, with plazas and streets named after him in every town. The anniversary of his execution, 21 April, is a national holiday, fully eclipsing the day after, 22 April, the day Cabral 'discovered' South America.

The remains of Tiradentes, as of all fifteen original conspirators including Gonzaga's, are buried in a mausoleum on the first floor of the old Ouro Preto town hall, now the Museu da Inconfidência. This rises nobly on the south side of the square, focusing the eye on its central clocktower and its soapstone statues of the four cardinal virtues: Prudence, Justice, Temperance and Fortitude. As it used to be a gaol as well, it has double bars on windows set in five-foot-thick walls and solid wooden doors. There is a portrait of Dona Maria, the mad queen, in what looks like a 1960s beehive hairdo and, yes, she looks positively loopy. The museum, with a steep entrance fee, inflation or no inflation, also contains Tiradentes' English watch, a piece of his noose, a photocopy of his sentence of execution and a warrant for '*the continuation of the interrogation of Tomás Antônio Gonzaga*'. This is the closest to a Brazilian Pantheon as can be, though I still can't bring myself to swallow the fact that a whole country worships a dentist. The profession either conjures up giggles as I think of Steve Martin's performance in *The Little Shop of Horrors* or evokes painful images of drills, scrapers and jaw injections with needles that would frighten charging bulls. It just doesn't do it for me.

Marília's tearful fate does.

Instead of being executed, Gonzaga was exiled to Mozambique. Marília tried desperately to join him, but she never met him again. Gonzaga fell critically ill upon arrival and was nursed back to health by another woman, Juliana de Souza Mascarenhas whom he eventually married upon his convalescence.

Marília didn't marry. She remained a spinster until the grand old age of 86 – proving that the Mineiro diet is not that unhealthy. She adopted and raised a boy, Anacleto, a love child of her sister's conceived out of wedlock. To her death, she remained a virgin, withering faithfully to the memory of her youth. But unloved she was not. Gonzaga's stanzas became the most popular love poem in the Portuguese language, 'Marília de Dirceu'. No less than sixty different editions exist of this widely translated epic, first published in 1792 in Lisbon. Marília remained true not only to Gonzaga, but also to the whole image that had been created around her, a Greta Garbo before her time, and that's why the fascination remains. Dom Pedro II, the Emperor of Brazil, visited her house 28 years after her death. '*I went to see the house of Marília where a chair and the clothes hanger are preserved in the alcove where she slept. They have cut down the pine trees at the bottom of the little orchard,*' he noted in his diary.

She was buried in her parish church of Nossa Senhora da Conceição; in a typical streak of Brazilian romantic compassion, her remains were later moved to the Museu da Inconfidência, where she lies close to her beloved Tomás Gonzaga in death, as she could not in life.

*****

Dusk was falling. Maybe I can fit it in.

I got up from Marília's fountain, crossed the street and turned right before the Largo Antônio Dias. There, past another small bridge, is the haunted mine of Chico Rei. In 1946 ground subsidence revealed a sealed mine in the area where the Encardadeira mine might have been – you sort out the fact from the fiction since this is Ouro Preto and I'm already overwhelmed.

In order to reach the mine I had to duck under the wide-leafed plants of someone's garden and cross to the yard of a private house where an unmanned reception desk awaited me.

'Anyone here?'

Talk about haunted.

'Anyone here?'

I walked past the desk – the ticket office? – into a patio. A small white statuette of a minstrel, which I assumed depicted Chico Rei, stood next to a modest cave opening.

'Hello?' I shouted again. No answer.

A sparse set of light bulbs illuminated the main gallery. I decided to go it alone. I walked in and cold air surrounded me, chilling my skin as my own sweat turned frosty on my T-shirt. After about 30 feet – *ouch!* – I bumped my head and caused a minor subsidence. I remembered how it was discovered. The ground had given in.

Did someone die here? Is that why it's haunted?

This was an old mine, indeed. The supports seemed more and more primitive the deeper I entered, and the ceiling ever lower. Five minutes in, I walked squatting.

A spotlight on the wall pointed at a seam. I checked. Can't be gold, of course, it would have been mined out already. Maybe fool's gold.

The air became warmer. I looked to my right – there was an arch leading to another gallery. Where does the warm air come from? I went in carefully. Pure Dark. Can I get up and rest my legs? I can. Can I stretch them? I can.

I had better not stray from the light in case there's a hidden shaft.

After a few minutes in that dark side-gallery, I heard the murmurs.

At first I thought it was the sound of water nearby, an underwater brook, or seepage, but then I distinguished the timbre of individual voices.

The mine is closing. A party is returning from a guided walk. Wait here and join them.

And what if I frighten them and cause an accident?

John, don't be silly.

So why aren't the voices getting any closer?

I said, don't be silly!

I left my Pure Dark chamber and walked into the narrow illuminated main gallery.

The voices had stopped.

Mines are full of vertical ventilation shafts propagating sound from the most improbable places.

I know that, but I'm splitting anyway.

*****

That night I had strange dreams. Dreams that woke me up at night in time to hear the floorboards creaking and the window grilles rattling in the slightest whiff of wind.

– 37 –

Forget the history of murder and betrayal of Ouro Preto's foundation, the tales of Chico Rei and Tiradentes or the tortuous passion of Marília de Dircéu. There is one thing Ouro Preto is famed for: its baroque and rococo. Hovering over them is the first American-born genius whose personal tale of even greater suffering and glory reigns supreme in Minas

Gerais: Aleijadinho. Like Bernini, not only was Aleijadinho a sculptor, but he was also a great architect who advanced the baroque he inherited into a graceful rococo.

My first glimpse of Aleijadinho's work was the wooden sculptures in the Museu da Inconfidência, and like every visitor before me, I was a convert: you immediately know that here was a grand master at play. The cedar statues are not lifelike – though many, like the statue of St George complete with spear, are lifesize – but they are highly individualistic in style: almond-eyed, hair obsessively undulated, clothing sharply pleated and expressions out of the Eastern book of spiritual countenance rather than the optically accurate canon of Western Renaissance. If there can be a comparison, it is with another unique stylist: Aleijadinho's sculptures are El Greco paintings come to life.

My baroque pilgrimage started from the western Ouro Preto parish and Nossa Senhora do Rosario dos Pretos. In the Catholic Church of times past, there was a kind of saint's apartheid operating. Nossa Senhora do Rosario was the Madonna of the Blacks, accompanied by a set of African-born saints: Santo Elisbão, Santo Benedito, Santo Antônio do Noto and our familiar Santa Ifigênia. The latter was a slaves' church; this was more of a multicultural one. A book on display informs us of the fraternity's orders of 1715: Article 1 states that *'Every person black or white of both sexes, free or captive, of whatever nation who wants to become brother may come to the fraternity's registry to apply.'* Article 2 reminds us that this is a black church, however: *'There shall be elected a King and Queen, both black, of any nation, and they will help and be present in festivities.'* The educational superiority of whites at the time is alluded to in Article 3: *'There shall be elected two judges, one male and one female, both black, freed or slave, a secretary and a treasurer, both white and a black proctor to administer the fraternity.'* In tune with such liberated thinking, the exterior of the church consists of a radical elliptic front, like a male athlete proudly puffing out his chest and tucking back his shoulders. It faces a courtyard of the best-looking and best-preserved complex of colonial houses in Ouro Preto. Had Nossa Senhora do Rosario been situated anywhere else but in this feast of baroque art that is Ouro Preto, it would have been the top attraction.

The walk down the Rua Antônio de Albuquerque past the simple chapel of Bonfim, where the last rites for those about to be hanged were administered, took me to the Matriz do Pilar, a church saturated with precious metals: a full 68 stone of gold and 63 stone of silver were used to decorate the interior. From the Bohemian crystal chandeliers to the eight silver angels, this is exhibitionist, extravagant baroque; when the Matriz do Pilar was started in 1733, the riches of Vila Rica seemed inexhaustible. The town historiographer Lúcia Machado de Almeida felt that *'there is a real orgy of the baroque, a touch of the profane that hinders devotion, suggesting a ballroom where minuets are heard, rather than litanies.'* Normally I walk into a church and take off my sunglasses; in the Matriz do Pilar I almost had to do the opposite.

Gothic was the style of the Catholic Church administrative: unquestioned, ultimate arbiter, superior to secular rule; baroque was the style of the Church in conflict against the new Protestant minimalism, overvenerating the Madonna, displaying its opulence to overwhelm through ornamentation; rococo was the Church triumphant, a pious paean like the newly emerging requiem music. Rococo did not really take root in Spain, but somehow it did in Portugal and found its peak in Brazil's colonial mining towns. It was the gold rush that brought the best Portuguese artists to Minas. Aleijadinho's father Manuel Francisco Lisboa was an architect and sculptor in his own right, and he was a major team leader of the Matriz do Pilar decorators.

I walked out to face a party of young German tourists. They were sitting in the yard, dejected. One of them – tall, chestnut-haired and cute – was close to tears.

'*Scheisse*,' I heard him say shaking his head.

Another – short, chestnut-haired and cute – looked at him and then, shaking his head, at me.

He was Berndt. The tall, distressed one was Thorsten. They were from the former East Germany (West Germans are called names like Michael, Nick and Andy. It's the East Germans who are called Siegfried, Dietmar and Wilhelm) and in Eastern European fashion, they were wearing well-worn denim clothes. They were all students at Leipzig University and had taken advantage of the German reunification – only a few years old then – and the good conversion rate to blow their savings on a trip to Brazil to satisfy their chronically suppressed wanderlust.

What did they think of Ouro Preto?

'It's fantastic so far,' said Berndt, 'except that' – he pointed at Thorsten – 'he can't get into the churches.'

Thorsten looked at me with his hurt, puppy-brown eyes and broke my heart.

'Why?' I asked.

'He's got shorts on.'

I had noticed. He was wearing tight jean shorts, showing off a pair of long, muscular, hairless legs.

'They won't let me into the church,' he moaned.

'No.' I refused to believe it.

They all nodded 'yes' gravely.

'They're *that* religious?' I repeated, shocked.

They nodded 'yes' in a replay of the previous scene.

I turned to Thorsten: 'You haven't got any long trousers?'

'He left them in Rio,' said Berndt. 'We only came to spend one night here.'

I despaired. 'Oh, no, you are missing – you are missing … all the gold …'

'I know! They haven't stopped telling me.' Thorsten sounded fed up.

I pointed at the impossibly steep climb to Nossa Senhora do Carmo.

'Let's try that church,' I proposed.

*****

Aleijadinho has become such a legend that despite ample historical record (like his signatures on his invoices) there has been controversy even regarding his very existence – surely the highest accolade for a man who would be myth. One of the unknowns is his birth date: either 1730 (going by a possibly wrong birth certificate) or 1738 (which most modern historians accept), counting back from the age on his death certificate in 1814. Whatever – he was born Antônio Francisco Lisboa of mixed race, his mother a slave, although his father, Manuel Francisco Lisboa, freed him at birth. Aleijadinho remained unmarried, but there is a record of a son of his with a concubine. We have no idea what became of his offspring. He learned his trade from his father who put his stamp on the architectural harmony of Ouro Preto, being the architect of Santa Ifigênia, the Matriz of Antônio Dias and, as we saw, he had a hand in the Matriz do Pilar. Aleijadinho's father became such a respected – read rich – figure in the town that he was elected a member of the fraternity of the exclusive Third Order of Carmo.

The Carmelite church stands high on the side of the Museu da Inconfidência. Aleijadinho's father started it, but he died soon after and his son, only 28, continued and produced his first exemplary monument. The early two-tiered physiognomy of the façade became Aleijadinho's trademark. The door, an upper central fanlight and its two lateral, subordinate windows are embossed under curved transoms with makeshift heraldic crests in floating, delicate soapstone reliefs and flanked by triumphant cherubic angels – individual elements being subordinate to the overall theme deciphered only by the onlooker. Inside, the church has six side altars with Aleijadinho-supervised or Aleijadinho-made dramatic sculptures. Blue *azulejos* add the final, tessellated touch in a harmonious interplay of diversity with the paintings of Brazil's master of frescos, Manuel da Costa Ataíde.

Again, Thorsten couldn't get in. We tried to describe it, but with our sparkling overawed eyes we only made it worse. Ahem – drink anyone?

'I don't want to sit down anywhere,' said Berndt, the more bubbly, talkative one. 'Can't we find a Coke machine or something?'

I looked at him surprised.

'Have you seen many drink-dispensers in Brazil?' I asked.

'Well,' Berndt answered, 'we haven't exactly been looking.'

'There are no vending machines in Brazil,' I said. 'Inflation.'

They looked at me, not comprehending.

'Inflation!' I repeated. 'Prices change every day. How can you run coin-operated machines in such an environment? Especially if there are no coins?'

My small speech silenced them. Thorsten scratched his head, got up and innocently bent over for a stretch. I checked. He wasn't wearing any underwear.

I had an idea.

I was *so* bad when I was younger.

– 38 –

In 1777 there is an insignificant entry in the annals of the church of Mercês e Perdões on whose construction Antônio Francisco Lisboa was working. There is a charge of 1/2 *oitavo* for two black slaves whose task was to transport Aleijadinho. It's our first indication that his illness had struck.

There has been a mountain of paper speculation regarding what debilitating misfortune hit Aleijadinho at the age of 39. Was it a venereal disease? Was it deformative neural rheumatism that made him scream with pain? Imagine: a master sculptor begging his slaves to amputate his malignant fingers with a chisel. Was it leprosy that turned first his legs and then his hands into stumps? But if so, how come he was not shunned by the townsfolk and was eventually buried inside a church? Was it porphyria as a recent exhumation – inconclusively – suggests? Was it a Faustian pact with the Devil, a romantic tale created by Saint-Hilaire after his trip in Minas: did Antônio Francisco Lisboa drink an elixir to enhance his senses and reach even greater heights of artistry – a strategy that backfired, turning him into *Aleijadinho* – the 'little cripple', the name he bequeathed to history?

*****

The receptionist gave me the key to my room and looked questioningly at Thorsten. Had it been night-time, she'd have said something stroppy. This is a city of the faithful, after all.

I walked up to my room, heart beating faster and faster; Thorsten followed me, his head bumping on the top of the staircase.

'It's really nice of you, John,' he said. 'Even if it doesn't work, I really appreciate it.'

'Oh, don't mention it,' I said, trying to hide my excitement.

'No, I really appreciate it,' he repeated.

I opened my door and went straight to my large wooden closet, probably stemming from the time of Saint-Hilaire.

'Wow,' said Thorsten, sitting on my bed. 'It's huge.'

I turned around. 'What's huge?'

'Your room.'

My brain was otherwise engaged. 'My room? Yes, it is.'

I opened my closet and took out a pair of blue jeans.

'There,' I said and threw them on the bed, 'try them on.'

I stood next to the window, pretending to look out, my peripheral vision catching sight of Thorsten struggling to slip out of his tight shorts. When I turned around he was facing me, naked from the waist down, my jeans still around his ankles.

'Sorry,' I said a bit too readily.

Thorsten froze for a split second as my unspoken question travelled through the ether and vanished in his expressionless stare, but he went on to pull up my jeans rapidly. They fitted.

'YES!' he said, waving his shorts in the air.

My only reward was a sexy grin.

*****

Thorsten ran off to check out the churches he had missed, leaving the Germans and myself to stroll down the Largo do São Francisco. This might be the best-looking square in Ouro Preto – if this sloping, irregular clearing could be called 'square' – had it not been for the permanent local craft market of gem-sellers, street-painters and soapstone carvers.

It was during the construction of the church of São Francisco that Aleijadinho fell ill, yet it is his ecclesiastical masterpiece. He composed the ornamental portal, the high altar, the chancel retable, the six side altars and their statues, the soapstone pulpits, even the elaborate baptismal font in the vestry, depicting a blind human figure. This is one of his best works, cruelly hidden in the back of a church, its existence only known to a few. Perhaps it is the very inaccessibility of Aleijadinho's works that makes him a cult figure: you have to travel far to get to admire them. The exterior is pure perfection, from Aleijadinho's own hand without any contribution from pupils; the portal decoration blends with a medal in place of the fanlight above a complex composition of St Francis receiving the stigmata on a mountain – a typical, sumptuous baroque chorus of shapes and figures: metaphysical, idealised, dramatic. The whole façade is flanked by two circular belfries which end in sharp spires.

Inside, the white and gold of the altars contrasts with the red ceiling, Ataíde's best work depicting a half-caste Madonna surrounded by mulatto angels. His chancel paintings depict the life of Abraham – and I could not help but smile noticing the oh, so Mineiro cutlet on the table of Abraham's supper. But it is part of the miracle: artists cut off from Europe by geography, as well as administrative laws, created their own vision. European rococo ended up draining the audience like an interminable heavy metal guitar solo; the Minas artists remained the master bluesmen who never lost sight of the maxim that craft is subservient to art. As Germain Bazin, a curator of the Louvre and expert in Mineiro art wrote with characteristic French syntax: *'the works of genius of Aleijadinho enliven with lyrical breath and reviving energy, Baroque art, which in Europe, by then, had been thoroughly exhausted through formalism and virtuosity.'*

*****

We caught up with Thorsten later. Wide-eyed and hopping-happy, he insisted on buying me a beer. We sat in a *lanchonete* for drinks, which turned naturally into dinner. No one can exhaust Ouro Preto in a few days in the same way no one can consume a royal banquet in one sitting.

We were all suffering from the Stendhal syndrome, normally experienced in Rome and Florence: running confused by sensual overload.

The first time we saw prices was when we got the bill – the menu simply listed the dishes. As prices changed constantly, they became obsolete as soon as they were typed. The meal was cheap. Very cheap! We were ready to leave when the waiter arrived with one of those large, unwieldy, noisy calculating machines with a print roll and large buttons.

'It's wrong, it's wrong,' the waiter kept saying, pointing at the calculating machine. 'It's one million more.'

It is not often you part with an extra million, even if it is cruzeiros. I checked the total from the printout – that's what we had paid and had left a tip on top. What was his problem?

'Add it yourself,' he said.

'Manually?' I asked him in surprise.

'He's right,' exclaimed Berndt.

I did the sum, checked the calculator total and fell back on my chair. The machine had overflowed and had truncated the sum to six digits, leaving out the million. Inflation had finally caught up with it.

'Why not ignore the last three digits, perform your addition and add them later?' I asked the proprietor.

He smiled one of those gringo-doesn't-understand smiles.

'We correct the prices every day,' he said. 'We use all five digits.'

Ah, that curse, indexation.

Things I Don't Like About Brazil #8: Indexation

This has been the deep cause of Brazilian inflation, which at the time of my trip to Manaus and Minas was running to 2,567 per cent per annum. Wages, pensions and absolutely everything under the sun had to catch up with rising prices by law. Hundreds of items of indexation run into complex pieces of legislation and have been the cause of institutional inflation for decades. There are many vested interests: from political capital, since the poor see indexation of the minimum wage as the litmus test of a government's commitment towards social justice, to self-preservation, as pensioned military officers want to keep their purchasing power intact. Extreme freezing measures (such as President Collor's) were tried from time to time, but indexation eventually destroyed any short-term benefits.

During the two-hour trip between Ouro Preto and Congonhas I had ample time to ponder over the morning's events. I had woken up early to catch the local bus to Mariana with the Germans. I remembered their distress: they had expected a small town, easy to stroll around, quickly explored in a short time. Instead, we had arrived at another Ouro Preto. Mariana has the same style of architectural harmony, the same eighteenth-century air and a similar abundance of sights, only with fewer tourists and more easy-going folk: Thorsten's shorts hardly caused a stir. It could have been, of course, because there was no one around.

This was the first settlement in the area and the first capital of Minas; its first bishop, Manuel da Cruz, arrived from Maranhão in 1748, crossing 2,500 miles in the interior. It took him 14 months; it is a miracle he survived. He did well to reach Mariana, for his cathedral, Nossa Senhora de Assunção, is the third most richly decorated church in Brazil – after São Francisco in Salvador and Matriz do Pilar in Ouro Preto – and possibly the best of all three in terms of aesthetic synthesis. The funny thing is that its exterior is old-fashioned: colonnaded, rectangular, stolid; nothing prepares you for the gilded splendour of the dark interior with not one, but three exquisite naves. It was there I said goodbye to the Germans. I wouldn't follow them, run off and peek inside the churches just to say I'd ticked them off: I had time.

My bus stopped. Time to change for Congonhas …

I had met the Germans again, running frantically in the distance, as I arrived in the main square which has a complex of buildings surpassing anything else in the rest of Mariana: a town hall in the style of the Ouro Preto School of Mines and two churches by the two main lay fraternities, São Francisco and Nossa Senhora do Carmo vying gracefully and coquettishly. *'Mirror, mirror on the wall, who's the prettiest of them all?'* The church of São Francisco in Mariana boasts a monumental portal by Aleijadinho's atelier, while the one on the Carmelite church tries to imitate his style but ends up like a mockery, with a set of perfectly symmetrical, podgy angels – whereas it is the slight asymmetry in the design that provides the baroque delights. It is only the round, pointed belfry towers that save the Carmelite ensemble.

Whatever the merits or not of the edifices in the square of Mariana, there is only one focus: this is a city with an original *pelourinho*. There it is, the monumental stony pole complete with slave shackles and with the image of blind justice, watched over by the solemn and unfeeling eyes of the four church windows. Mariana's cathedral overlooks the slave market; its two main churches the place of castigation of slaves. Bishop Manuel da Cruz did not see anything untoward in this – like all good Catholics he accepted the institution as a natural state of being. This has been a no-go area for the Vatican since later popes condemned the slave trade but accepted that slaves could exist in tied servitude – 'the curse of Ham'. As late as 1866 the Holy Office issued a statement in response to Abraham Lincoln's emancipation declaration countering that slaves could be bought and sold legitimately as it was in tune with natural law. Only after the abolition of slavery in Brazil in 1888 did Pope Leo XIII issue the encyclical '*In Plurimis*' welcoming the measure while providing a selective history of the Catholic Church's stance through the centuries. That encyclical falls flat on its face in Mariana's main square.

The bus started manoeuvring into the small *rodoviária*.

At last. Congonhas do Campo. Yet another Unesco cultural site in Minas Gerais, and undoubtedly the most spectacular.

*****

Whatever Aleijadinho's disease, its results were grim. His teeth rotted away and fell out. His lips retracted; his lower jaw dropped and gave him a sinister expression of ferocity. His hands ended up resembling stumps. He gradually lost his sight until he turned completely blind. He couldn't walk and was transported by his slaves: Maurício, Agostinho and Januário. He started wearing a blue cape from head to toe, special shoes on what remained of his feet and a brown broad-brimmed hat to hide his face. He became irascible, short-tempered and self-conscious about his ugliness. And throughout all this, pain, constant pain – for 38 long years. Even earlier, he is on record complaining that the Carmelites paid him with counterfeit gold; his advancing disability probably rendered him subject to exploitation. His family abandoned him except for his niece, who nursed him during the last, terrible, bedridden years of his life which he spent in abject poverty.

There ends his life, but here starts the legend, for he continued to work – in Sabará, São João d'El Rei, Ouro Preto. The myth of a handless master sculptor was created by European traveller-explorers starting with Saint-Hilaire. Because it was half blind, in constant pain, with mallet and chisel tied on his wrists that Aleijadinho produced his breath-taking *Gesamtkunstwerk* of Bom Jesus de Matosinhos in Congonhas. His story is either a triumph of the indomitability of the human spirit or proof that Faustian pacts do, after all, exist.

The first thing that strikes you about the church and sanctuary of Bom Jesus de Matosinhos is the setting, which has inspired travellers for centuries including the poet Oswald de Andrade, who called the complex: '*a Bible of soapstone bathed in Minas gold*'. The basilica stands on a hill, representing Calvary, with just the blue sky as a backdrop, flanked by tall, thin palm trees, their green tufts crowning the composition below. Six chapels containing no less than sixty-six magnificent life-sized polychromatic cedar sculptures by Aleijadinho, representing Jesus's martyrdom, crook their way to the main porch. But these – astounding as they may be – are still just the hors d'oevres.

In the church courtyard, over three levels, stands what has been boldly described as the best baroque ensemble of statues in the whole world. This is Aleijadinho's *piéce de résistance*: twelve Old Testament prophets carved in weathered grey soapstone, positioned carefully and symmetrically to each other in what Bazin described as choreography akin to an act of ballet. At the entrance level, a thick-bearded, hooded Isaiah points forcefully at his scroll of prophesies next to proud Jeremiah demanding respect and veneration. Higher up a regal Baruch (a surprise choice from the Apocrypha); Ezekiel, wise and graceful; a gallant Daniel on a dragon-like lion, which betrays the sculptor's sources: more T'ang Chinese than African Kalahari. The pathos reaches its apotheosis on the third level: Joel, questioning, apocalyptic, severe; Jonas looking inquiringly to Heaven, his figure carved boldly from a single monolith, with a creature at his feet, more of a sea monster than a whale; Hosea, inscrutable, reflective, with a deformed right hand hidden by perspective from the viewer as the prophet is placed on the far left ...

Deformed?

The crowning achievement of the ugly little cripple, who started half-blind on this monumental work at the age of 69 and went on to toil for a decade, is that his illness is moulded in with his prophets. They are anatomically wrong, or in some cases positively malformed, but it is these imperfections that create the overall grandeur of pathos, wisdom and agony. While Europe was disappearing up its arse in rationalist verisimilitude, the message from a small village, difficult to get to and almost forgotten by the world at large, is that it is the unspoken passion and emotion in art that moves us rather than arrogant scholasticism. Hovering above Aleijadinho's prophets is the spirit of the master, speaking allegorically about his own plight through the alembic of his art: '*Here I am, a life slowly strangled by disease and steeped in anguish, but there is my legacy which has the power to make you feel my pain.*'

I looked over my shoulder. Who says that statues cannot talk?

*****

My own haunting came later that night.

I returned to Belo Horizonte and the Hotel Ambassy – with an 'A' – needing to change money. This was such a hassle; it involved wading through a mass of paupers outside the bank who were trying to beg any last remnants of change off you; shady characters who were opportunistically preying upon your distraction; young men whose employment involved waiting permanently in queues. In such an environment tourists cause a big commotion and draw unwanted attention as the news of their arrival spreads rapidly to the nearest *favela*. The woman employee, thin, bespectacled, stereotypically annoying, looked at me with barely disguised contempt: the dirty young gringo was flashing his money about – who does he think he is?

'Wait there.' She pointed at a chair as she disappeared with my 100-dollar bill.

I waited for so long, I started worrying about a frame up. What if she returned with counterfeit money and a policeman? There were enough armed guards around to start a revolution with more success than the Inconfidência Mineira. After half an hour, I went to another till to enquire. Was the lady faxing the Federal Reserve to check the serial number? The yawning employee ignored me. I sat down, determined to win the war of attrition.

When the woman returned after fifteen more minutes, she was glum, as if disappointed I was going to get away with it. I wonder what tests my 100-dollar bill had been subjected to. She gave me my two million plus in four freshly printed 500,000-cruzeiro bills.

I refused them.

'I want fifty- and twenty-thousand bills,' I said. 'No one will change those. They're unusable.'

'We don't have any change,' she said curtly.

The blood went to my head.

'You have no change? What is this – a grocery store? You have no change? You are a *bank* for chrissake. MAKE SOME!'

'*Mal-educado*,' spat the woman and turned her back on me.

I walked up to her.

'Listen!' I shouted. 'You are not doing me a favour! I am the client. I demand my change in lower bills.'

Confrontation with authority is not something that comes naturally to a Brazilian. Everyone stopped and stared. One of the armed guards came closer. He asked me what was happening.

I explained.

'I gave her $100 and she paid me back in 500,000 notes,' I complained. 'Look! What am I going to do with these? Do *you* have any change?'

I presume the guard understood my plight, because he didn't intervene further. I changed tack. She had signed some papers in triplicate.

'I want my money back.'

She was doubly cross now.

'You can't have your money back,' she said. 'The transaction is complete.'

'It's not complete if I'm not happy,' I pounced. 'I want change or my money back.'

She was stuck now. Signatures had been procured.

'I want to speak to the manager! I want my money back!'

She stood up.

'Give me the money,' she ordered me.

That's it! I won.

I gave her my cruzeiros. She opened a drawer, took out a bundle of 50,000-cruzeiro notes, counted it and then casually threw the money at my feet, contemptuously, as if giving alms to a beggar.

That was the only time in my life I wanted to hit a woman.

Composing myself under the watchful eye of the armed guards, I picked it all up and left with only a '*mal-educada você*'.

With delayed shock, I stormed blindly through the crowds of Afonso Pena and yelled at the receptionist in Hotel Ambassy ('Why the *hell* do you spell it with an *A*?'), cursing the woman and the bank, the hotel and the noise, this crazy country and its inflation. I stayed in bed, convulsed from the humiliation for hours. I tried listening to my Walkman without effect. I tried to sleep and calm down in vain. By then it was dark, and my stomach was rumbling.

I walked out into the uninviting, dark and unseasonably chilly streets of Belo Horizonte. The town earned a reputation for good and healthy weather in the 1920s and attracted the sick and infirm from all over the country. Looking around they were still here, at the end of the century, living ghosts, shadowy figures standing around small bonfires, an army of destitutes silently lamenting their fate. This was raw urban poverty on a mammoth scale. I made my way back to the bus station and its fast-food outlets. I bought my pies, drinks and sandwiches and ate them on the spot. Munching in the street attracts the hungry.

Is it just the inflation or has this country's whole social fabric gone to the dogs?

My chest was still aching from suppressed rage. I took a left out of the station. Rubbish. Mountains of smelly rubbish. Filth. I took another turning towards what seemed to be a shopping mall. Deserted. Better the light of the bonfires. This could be hazardous. Darkness everywhere.

Where am I?

I looked up. Rua Curitiba. Where's that?

I still had a can of Coke. I tried to pull the ring. It broke in my hand.

Damn! Does nothing work in this country?

I passed by a huge pile of rubbish. I hurled the can, aiming at its middle.

THAT'S FOR BRAZIL!

I heard a noise behind me as I walked away; I turned my head.

And then I froze as the rubbish slowly rose and talked to me.

– **40** –

I returned to Belo Horizonte eight years later during my most recent trip to Brazil. This time I had more money, so I stayed as far from the dreaded *rodoviária* as I could: I got a good weekend deal in a hotel in upmarket Savassi with its illuminated restaurants, clubs and late-night bars. From my eleventh-floor window I could gaze upon the exceptional horizon that gives the town its name. Encircled by the dented peaks of the Serra do Curral, Belo Horizonte has the air of a tropical Denver.

Savassi with its high-rise luxury apartment blocks (attached garages for every resident) is plush, rich and self-assured, and attracts the young who party in its bars and clubs. The choice was staggering: there was a piano bar, straight out of a 1940s movie; a reggae bar decorated Jamaican-style with hammocks to lean back on; a cocktail bar where shelves and shelves of books vied for the attention of the Belohorizontino youth; a three-floor mansion on top of a hill converted into a restaurant with the clientele absorbed in board games; a video bar serving a range of margaritas. The extravagance of the gay club, Mix-Excess – mentioned with pride in the state tourist brochure – put anything in Rio or São Paulo to shame: I counted 30 multi-point lasers on three megalights revolving around the dance floor, straight out of *Saturday Night Fever*. So diss not Belo Horizonte: we have to thank it for becoming the new capital of Minas, drawing the developers and so keeping Ouro Preto pristine.

Once more I needed to change money, and I walked into a bank in Rua Sergipe. This time I didn't need to fret too much. Someone overheard me inside the office and offered to change the money on the spot. Eight years earlier this would have been a perilous transaction; in this new Brazil it was routine. For inflation *did* come under control in the mid-1990s with Finance Minister Fernando Henrique Cardoso's – later President FHC – Real Plan, which, much like the euro programme, introduced a new currency, the real, by working gradually in order to change people's perceptions rather than bludgeon them into submission at once. But then Brazil tied its currency to the dollar at a 1:1 rate, which became unsustainable. Jeez, Brazil, for a few years, became *expensive*.

Still, some things never change: in spite of my maps it took me two days to locate the Praça da República where many of the old Art Deco buildings of Belo Horizonte still remain, as well as a typically brash and unusual construction by Oscar Niemeyer. There were beggars and street kids lazing about, but the crumbs that filtered down to them from Brazil's industrial advances in the years since I'd been there had turned them less hostile and threatening, for unemployment is down, way down. There are jobs coming into Minas, the second most industrialised state in Brazil after São Paulo: Volkswagen, Fiat and Mercedes, Nippon Corporation's Usiminas steel works, state-controlled industries like the electricity company CEMIG, arms industries, mineral companies extracting zinc, bauxite, phosphates, diamonds, precious gems and, still, gold.

Hotel Ambassy – with an 'A' – still existed and looked outwardly less grim, although the noise level outside had increased; the sidestreets were still full of cheap restaurants, kiosks with porn magazines, and low-grade streetlife; in the *rodoviária* Passaro Verde was still the line for buses to Ouro Preto and Mariana, leaving every half an hour.

Every half an hour ...

On the spur of the moment, I bought a ticket for early next morning. I'd spend another day in my favourite city in all of Brazil.

*****

When I saw the peak of Itacolomi and the town of Ouro Preto spread below it, I stepped out and back into my own dream-like déjà vu. I sniffed the crisp mountain air, looked wistfully down below and felt those goose pimples again. The city map in the tourist office was more expensive at three reais, but the offer of a guide sounded all too familiar. This time, I did take the bus signposted 'Padre Faria', which ran down and up the narrow stony streets like a rollercoaster. Praça Tiradentes was full of people and buses; tourism was now internal as Brazilians with more money in their pockets started discovering their own country. Hotel Pilão was still there; the restaurants on the Praça were still serving; the bars on the Rua Direita where I had drunk with the Germans were all there, heaving with clients. I walked to the side of Nossa Senhora do Carmo. A bunch of backpackers were chatting, sitting on the stairs. A girl wearing shorts was taking photographs of the floating, delicate portal relief with a long zoom lens. Had they let her in? I mused, before I entered. Dear God, what opulence. Even though I knew what to expect, the multiple focal points still had the power to amaze.

Nossa Senhora do Rosario, further out and a little less in reach of the tourist buses, was much more serene, and the houses with the balconies and their freshly painted window grilles brought back the picture of my own, quiet Ouro Preto. A kiosk was advertising the very same poster of Ouro Preto balconies, ever the bestseller. I walked down to the Matriz do Pilar with its 68 stone of gold and came out heavy-headed. I walked up the steep hill of Santa Quitéria up to Praça Tiradentes – and oh, Goddess, did I ever come this way before? Was I fitter, chirpier, abler in body? How did Aleijadinho's slaves carry their master up this slope? They must have been fitter than mules.

I took a look at the Largo São Francisco with a density of ten crafts artists per square inch mobbed by a thick crowd of souvenir hunters – one always wants to recollect Ouro Preto. I took refuge inside the church. Scaffolding reached Ataíde's grand ceiling set for restoration and the six statues on the three lateral altars had disappeared. Well, I had seen them last time. Wait! Does that count? Should I not care because I'd seen them before although I can't remember them exactly?

I crossed the square quickly and entered Tomás Gonzaga's house, the House of the Auditor. Students from the School of Mines were manning the till, like in every museum in town – a nice little earner during holidays. The students are spread in fraternity houses called 'Repúblicas'. Nacão Zumbi music stormed loudly out of the windows of one such

República: '*Uma praiera*,' shouted Chico Science referring to one of the Recife uprisings. '*Uma praiera*.'

Why am I waiting for something to happen? Nothing ever does.

On Marília's fountain some sweet soul had placed a red rose, and remarkably it was still there, a few day's withering not having affected its appeal. Since I last stood here, I had found out that she is not lying next to her beloved Gonzaga; he's still buried in Mozambique – it is his nephew's remains that had been moved into the museum tomb instead.

Too much knowledge is a bad thing.

I walked into the church of Nossa Senhora da Conceição, the main parish church of Antônio Dias. Its exterior is lovely, painted in a vivid, rosy red with its outline touched up in white, giving it a two-dimensional fairytale feel. This is an older church, built by Aleijadinho's father. There are no less than eight lateral altars including superb polychromatic depictions of St John the Baptist, São Gonçalo, São Miguel das Almas and São José. I walked around, ignoring the congregation of tourists in front of the altar of Boa Morte. What a choice of statues to flank the retable: St Nepomuk of Bohemia, patron of confessors, and St Barbara, patron of artillery. The noise behind me subsided. The tourist party had left. I walked to the spot where they had been standing. There was something I'd missed last time. Down in front of me, panels covered the church floor. I read one inscription: '*Aqui jaz A. Fo. Lisboa o Aleijadinho 1738–1814.*' I wanted to remain respectfully quiet for a few minutes but the noise of more visitors disturbed my thoughts.

Outside the sun was setting rapidly. I looked at my watch. Could I fit in anything else? I always leave Chico Rei's mine for last.

It was easier to find the mine this time, as it was signposted and clearly marked on the maps; yet I still felt I was trespassing in a private garden. An ancient African-Brazilian woman, short, squint and slow-responding, let me in with a nod, since, amazingly, I was again there fifteen minutes before it closed. I walked into the garden; there was a small pie and beer bar on my left where two waiters were washing the dishes. The white statue of Chico Rei at the entrance had been painted over gaudily. The mine loomed open in front of me. I made a move to enter.

The silence was broken by a furious bark. A black dog, as big as a sheep, was baying at me from behind a chicken-wire fence. I instinctively pulled back. The dog became nastier and started lunging against the wire like mad. Behind me the two waiters stopped their work and came over to watch. Would the fence hold? I checked whether I was safe – it seemed so, although the dog's bark became more intense and its jumping more frantic. The old woman behind the counter rose and stood by, still.

What had I done?

The dog's maniacal leaping came to a stop when a topless, sweaty young black man emerged from behind it and grabbed its leash. The dog immediately calmed down, buried its head between the man's legs and starting wagging its tail. An uneasiness overcame me. The waiters behind me were standing immobile, rooted to the spot. The dog handler caught my eye; his stare was hostile like the dog he had just tamed. The old African woman moved away from the door.

She pointed at the exit.

*****

The bus to Belo Horizonte stopped, and the resulting commotion woke me up. What? I had fallen asleep on my seat? There's always a first time for everything.

I stepped out dozily, several maps of the town in hand. I went straight to a coffee shop and had a double espresso, which I gulped down like cough medicine. I looked at my watch. The night was still young. Club Mix-Excess would not be getting busy for a good few hours yet.

John, will you do it?

I walked out of the Belo Horizonte *rodoviária* for the last time and took a left. It was dark. I checked my map. So much has changed and so much has remained the same. It must be here.

Rua Curitiba.

Why am I waiting for something to happen? Nothing ever does.

I was wrong.

I saw a cockier, younger and more handsome version of myself – hey, I didn't look as bad as I thought at the time – walk amongst the piles of rubbish in a rage. I saw him walk in what would be called pique had it remained with no consequences. He flung an unopened can of Coke onto a mountain of rubbish.

I heard a cry of pain.

A shadow, who had been sleeping under the slimy cardboard and the rotting fruit, rose and held the can out accusingly.

'Why me?' he asked. 'Why me?'

I could see the silhouette more clearly than I could see my old self who I knew was frozen with fear. It was a filthy beggar, trousers torn, his shirt hanging by a thread. His long hair was stringed in knots that might once have been dreadlocks. He was ugly. He was unshaven and his curly beard made him look menacing. Part of his right hand was wrapped up in bandages that must once have been white. They covered a circle of dried blood that had seeped through, like the fresh blood that was now gushing down his face.

I watched myself run away, half frightened, half guilty, trying to dismiss and forget the whole incident. But the truth is, I have never been able to erase it from my mind.

The squalid shadow turned to me here and now. He looked at me and at the can he was holding and let it drop without a sound on the mouldy cardboard below. He stood there for a minute and then shrugged his shoulders and slowly walked away, taking with him the decomposing refuse mounds, the pestilential smell and the naked street children begging for worthless notes, as the city's darkness lit by bonfires turned into the brightness of the electric lights under which I was now standing – for this was not a malodorous sidestreet in a town ravaged by galloping inflation any more, but a tidy alleyway in a booming state capital, shaking off the nightmare by exorcising its ghosts.

Chapter 9

No Clove, and Certainly No Cinnamon (Ilhéus)

I don't know what I expected of Ilhéus; perhaps a stroll around the place names that roll from Amado's novels; maybe a visit to the master's childhood home so that the vibes could permeate my mind and bless it with inspiration.

But then, true adventure presumes an uncertain outcome.

....

The Words You'll Need

camisinha = *condom (I touch upon these, if I may use the expression)*
cataplana = *Portuguese flat pan used in Bahian cooking*
ecoparque = *eco park*
farofa = *side dish of dry, fried manioc flour*
kinkajou = *a local forest mammal that wraps its tail around a branch and hangs upside down. The word is of Algonquian origin.*
passarela na copa das árvores = *canopy walkway*
sertaneja = *from the interior of Brazil*
tempero baiano = *a mix of condiments to spice up Bahian cuisine, playing the role of garam masala in Indian dishes.*

....

– 41 –

Ilhéus was shutting down shop when I arrived from Salvador in early April. The restaurants facing Pontal had drawn their curtains and the crafts market in front of Praça Dom Eduardo was running out of stalls. The town beaches – which I can never imagine to be clean like Maceió's, popular like Rio's or majestic like Fortaleza's – were home to a few downtrodden surfers; I bet they wished they were somewhere other than the Cocoa Coast. I just *had* to put that tongue-twister in: *Cocoa Coast*. That's how Ilhéus markets itself nowadays – they should change their image consultants forthwith, since Ilhéus has no beaches to speak of. And yet, despite my fears of being stuck in a 1920s backwater for the sake of Jorge Amado, it's pretty and fetching in a subtle, non-invasive way.

Excuse me. Did I say non-invasive? Whatever possessed me? The famous character from *Gabriela, Clove and Cinnamon* – Amado's *sertaneja* beauty with the wide heart and even wider leg span – is as conspicuous as a politician kissing babies during an election campaign. There are Gabriela fashions, Gabriela beauty contests, Gabriela foodstuffs and liqueurs, a Gabriela lottery, Gabriela T-shirts, even a Gabriela petrol station (free showers offered). Let's not beat about the bush. Ilhéus is famous as the setting of Brazilian literature's best internationally known novel and as Jorge Amado's hometown. The inhabitants know it, which is why Vesúvio, Nacib's bar in the book, was having a blue paint-over and inner modernisng facelift. The whole town had a regenerative feel: streets were being asphalted, choking down the Guarani marketplace where all roads seemed to be converging; the Cocoa Museum was shut for refurbishment; the church of São Jorge appeared to be permanently locked and – and I was the only tourist in town.

....

The Languor of Ofenísia

Ofenísia took out her mother's shawl, an old heirloom, which as heirlooms go had seen better days, laid it on the grassy ground and sat herself on top of it expectantly. Heirlooms are fine if they are rings and bracelets made out of gold and silver and diamonds, for they look unseemly on the older generation, but when they are garments made in Olivença by Dona Quinquina, God bless her soul, in her younger, less skilful days they become like their original owners: wrinkled, torn and scraggy. At least this heirloom could be put to good use, if Ramiro decided to act like a man – at last – and not like a teenage mummy's boy. Mind you, if you had met Dona Armanda and heard her bloodcurdling scream, midway between the cadences of a ululating howler monkey and the cry of a mating sow, you might have felt some sympathy for both her offspring. The older son, Jacinto, had been swallowed whole by that devil of a town Salvador, and the younger one, Ramiro, was the biggest wimp between Malhado and Canavieiras.

Ofenísia sighed, for she felt more than sympathy for the timid young Ramiro, obligingly at her beck and call 24 hours a day, seven days a week, sometimes even skipping the morning vestibular *courses like today. She wondered what she'd have to do to get him to snog her at last. The only time they had kissed was at Malvina's birthday party after he had drunk two glasses of caipirinha and even then he had hardly used his tongue. That was a whole three weeks ago and since then Ramiro had all but disappeared. Malvina, her best friend, was excited and kept asking her what happened next – she wanted to know dates, places and details, but Ofenísia was so embarrassed she could provide none, she'd hung up on Malvina last weekend. Now that Ofenísia thought about it, she would call and make up. Perhaps Malvina might help her if she learned the truth. She might procure from her aunt Dona Glória one of those love potions one hears about so often. Perhaps Malvina had used such tricks herself, for how else could she have trapped Aristóteles, whose father was an estate agent and had the biggest yacht in Ilhéus, moored prominently in the Iate Clube at the end of the Rua do Barão de Rio Branco?*

Footsteps interrupted her thoughts. The figure of Ramiro, his wire-rimmed glasses sitting queerly on the small protuberance that passed as a nose on his inoffensive, caramel-coloured face, appeared from behind the big statue of Christ the Redeemer and walked towards her in his Nike sportswear. Ofenísia waved at him with relief and pointed at the empty space on the shawl next to her. Ramiro took his time sitting down, murmuring things like: 'This looks expensive Ofé, do you think it will get dirty?'

You get dirty, thought Ofenísia as she replied: 'No, don't worry Ramiro, it is so old it's hardly worth it.'

He sat down and they both looked out in silence towards Pontal, pretty and calm in the distance – not close enough to show up the details of the piles of muddy rubbish, worn streets and cracked houses, but not far enough either for its characteristic, cutesy little beachfront to merge indistinguishably with the background.

Ofenísia sighed again. This was so romantic. She peeked sideways at Ramiro and – now, this was heaven-sent, she must remember to light a candle to São Jorge –caught him stealing a glance at her. He looked away. But Ofenísia, emboldened by the sudden breathlessness in her chest and the fire smouldering in her loins, continued to look and look and did not turn away until his eyes were fished towards her by the nets of her insistence.

'About the party,' she heard Ramiro say.

Ofenísia's heart stopped. She closed her eyes. At last!

'I wanted to say how sorry I am,' he continued. 'I never drink, and I downed all this cachaça. I didn't know what I was doing.'

What?

'I, I told my mother afterwards, and she was very disappointed with me. She said that I should apologise to you. So …'

Ofenísia had heard enough. She turned over and brought her face closer and closer to his until Ramiro's head leaned back so much he fell over. She immediately jumped on top of him, kissed him voraciously in the mouth and this time she made sure her tongue was properly ensconced in his palate. And guess what? She felt his body stiffen in all the right places.

....

That first afternoon in Ilhéus I walked around the Avenida Dois de Julho, which wraps itself around the city's southern tip offering glimpses of the harbour and its distinctive long twin warehouses, the Ponte Lomanto Jr, and eventually Pontal. It is there that the strange geography of Ilhéus is revealed, for the town was built on a large, alluvial island at the confluence of the Rio Almada, the Rio Itacanpeira, the Rio Fundão, the Rio Cachoeira and the Rio Santana. However Recife it ain't, because Ilhéus and its surroundings are hillier, sturdier and less man-made than the capital of Pernambuco. There is also a sense of small-townness about it, which is strange given the fact that it's the most important commercial centre in the south of Bahia; maybe it is because its heart is clear, distinct and well-preserved, maybe it is because of its winding nature, which gives you glimpses of the city from different angles, or maybe it is because it has a mentality steeped in the 1950s, all probity disguised as coquettishness.

The Christ the Redeemer statue at the curve of the Avenida Dois de Julho was disappointing; life-size and crude, miles away (literally, I suppose) from its namesake on the Corcovado. Still, the view across the sandbank to Pontal was eye-catching. I took out my camera with the 200-mm zoom lens. Hey, is that the most famous sandbank in the world? But wasn't it dredged? What happened at the end of *Gabriela*? I forgot.

I noticed a movement in the grass below. Suddenly two teenage bodies emerged. The guy wore wire-rimmed glasses and was quite handsome in his Nike sportswear. The girl, who although could be called pretty was already on the way to being a fat, bossy matron, seemed very upset at the clumsiness of her boyfriend who had torn the middle of – was that a tablecloth spread on the ground? The boy looked dejected and ashamed. The girl was staring at me with murderous hostility and a look that cried out 'sex fiend!'

I followed her gaze, which was fixed on my camera.

Oh.

I walked away towards the Centro Histórico, not looking back. I think I messed up over there.

– **42** –

Clouds loomed menacingly in the distance.

'Will it rain?' I asked my driver.

He looked at the sky and shrugged his shoulders.

'Well, it is the rainy season,' he replied with a squeaky voice like chalk grazing a blackboard. He might have added to remind me: 'And we *are* going to a rainforest after all,' but he didn't, for he was glad to have a tourist, any tourist, out of season.

Brazil is famous for its rainforest in the Amazon Basin, which has attracted all the media attention. But not many have cared about its other huge ecosystem along the Atlantic seafront. When Cabral arrived and later, when the Portuguese carved the land up in 'captaincies' for their various aristocrat capitalists, the coast of Brazil was covered by the Mata Atlântica, the Atlantic rainforest. It's a perfect reminder of what can happen to the Amazon, as very little remains of it, and what remains is kept, museum-like, in ecological reserves. We were heading towards the *ecoparque* of Una, one of the few pockets of virgin rainforest in Bahia.

Here, amongst the hilly, unpassable terrain, the sixteenth-century Ilhéus settlers had to deal with a tribe of Tupiniquín who revolted in the late 1550s and destroyed the sugar plantations. They in turn faced the governor of Brazil, Mem de Sá, who had decimated the Tupinambá of northern Bahia. His campaign against the Tupiniquín of Ilhéus was lethal. He ambushed them in the woods in the dead of night, slaughtering men, women and children as they were asleep. He chased them into the sea where he sent his Tupinambá allies, their mortal enemies, to swim after the Tupiniquín and kill them – off today's beautiful beach of Cururupe – turning the ocean surf the colour of blood. This was one of the crowning achievements of the Iron Governor: after a thanksgiving ceremony in Ilhéus, he was honorifically carried on the shoulders of the colonists.

But within 30 years of the Tupiniquín defeat, the Gê-speaking Aimoré completely obliterated the captaincy of Ilhéus. 'Aimoré' is a derogatory Tupi word meaning 'monkeys' (and as monkeys steal things, this eventually came to mean 'thieves'). The Aimoré called each other many tribal names such as Carirí or, around Ilhéus, Camacán. In the nineteenth century, they came to be known as the dreaded Botocudos, from the decorative disks they inserted into their lower lips. Whatever their name, these natives who migrated from the interior were taller and more ferocious than the coastal Indians, crawling on the ground from the dense trees to attack isolated workers in the forest clearings. They were fierce cannibals who ate human meat as wild game. So feared were the Aimoré that the Portuguese crown resettled over 2,000 friendly Potiguar as a buffer. Despite all this, the colonists of southern Bahia fled their farms and barricaded themselves in the few coastal towns like Ilhéus; they had finally met their killer match. The Aimoré would keep the upper hand until some ostensibly unrelated events unfolded further away, in France. A short, ambitious general-cum-emperor in far-flung Europe would seal their fate, although he had no idea of the wave of consequences his battle victories would unleash.

When Napoleon invaded Portugal in November 1807, prompting Wellington's Peninsular Wars, Britain provided a naval convoy to take the Portuguese Court to Brazil. And what a Court that was: Queen Maria was certifiably mad, and the country was being ruled by her son, Dom João, later João VI. His Spanish wife Carlota Joaquina (married at ten, deflowered at fourteen) was epileptic and her marriage was a sham; both she and the King looked to men for sexual pleasure: Dom João is #62 in the list of famous Brazilian homosexuals of the Groupo Gay da Bahia. Of course he would hardly call himself Brazilian as he had never set foot in that backward colony of his until forced to by circumstances.

Once in Bahia in January 1808 after a stormy trip, which had played havoc with their alimentary systems, the royal family were shocked by the grubbiness and uncouthness of the locals; nevertheless, they took over the best mansions in Salvador and later Rio without paying a cent. They were planning a long sojourn; Napoleon seemed undefeatable, so they started founding universities (the medical school in Salvador) and a state bank (Banco do Brasil), dished out titles and medals to the rich landowners, and, most importantly, allowed direct trade to third countries. Another enduring legacy of the first European court on American soil was the annihilation of hostile Indians such as the Aimoré. A decree by Dom João declaring full-scale war was nothing less than state-sponsored genocide, a precursor of what would happen to the Plains Indians of North America and the tribes of Patagonia and the Amazon. By then, the primitive ways of the Aimoré had started lagging behind European killing technology and they were doomed.

My driver stopped my rambling thoughts by turning sharply right. 'The *ecoparque*,' he announced as he parked under a makeshift awning.

What's this?

In front of us, a white-haired, sunburnt American in his sixties was facing a Brazilian TV crew complete with boom mike, camera, director and presenter. They were from an environmental protection organisation based in São Paulo. And the elderly American?

'Hi, I'm Ian – Ian Green,' he said to me in that confident, genial American way. 'I represent Anheuser-Busch and, oh boy, I'm so excited.'

Anheuser-Busch?

'Budweiser,' he said. 'We are the company behind Budweiser. Have you heard of that?' he asked in all sincerity.

Erm … yes.

'This is so exciting,' he repeated.

What was exciting? What was he doing there?

'Mr Green, we are starting,' said the director.

'Oh boy,' said Ian and took his seat. Americans are such naturals in front of TV cameras, as if they've been taking lessons in Media Communications since kindergarten. It's *those* genes that made America.

'I come from St Louis, Missouri,' started Ian in response to a question, 'and I work for Anheuser-Busch. We at Anheuser-Busch care a lot about environmental issues, and, in particular, the disappearing rainforest. We have a dedicated Ecology Department, where I work, and we turned our attention here when we discovered that the Atlantic rainforest had shrunk to about eight per cent of its former size. One of the pockets of the rainforest is here, in Una.'

A hotel bus with Brazilian tourists stopped behind us.

'When I arrived here with my team in 1997, my grasp of the Portuguese language was nil. I would hold a tool and ask its name. I made a list of words and expressions I needed. "What's this?", "Dig here", "Get inside the truck". Phrases like that. When we arrived we had to face the rains, so we built a portable bridge made out of lumber to move our truck. Whenever there was an unpassable part, we unfolded the bridge, forded the path, then folded the bridge back on to our truck and continued.'

The *ecoparque* bus arrived.

'We brought battery-operated tools, surveyed the ground, gave lectures and started the project. I was the manager until the local Bahians were able to finish the project themselves, but this was the highlight of my working life.'

'Have you seen the finished work?' asked the presenter.

Ian grinned cheerfully.

'No, I haven't. I've only seen the plans and built the first foundations. And oh boy, I'm so excited. Today, I'll see the end result for the first time.'

'What is he talking about?' I asked my driver.

'In the *ecoparque* you will walk on a canopy walkway,' he explained. 'It's the main attraction.'

I looked at Ian.

'And this guy built it?' I asked.

'It looks that way,' my driver confirmed.

....

The Loneliness of Glória

Dona Glória sat down and looked at the big clock on the wall. It was nearly time for lunch, but was she hungry? No, she was alone in the house on União Hill and had been since four o'clock yesterday, when her brother-in-law Amâncio had popped in to ask her if she wanted anything brought back from the ecoparque.

Ah, Amâncio knew how difficult it was for her to obtain some of her herbs. There was a time when she could roam in the forest and pick them as she wanted: freshly sprouted, in bloom, next to a brook, in the shade of a tree – for even the location, the time of year, the time of day and the age of the plant was important. But back then you could go to Arataca and be surrounded by virgin forest. Now there was only a tiny reserve, which was fenced off to keep the folk out. She let out a small cry lamenting the passing of the forest. Why, even when the generals moved in back in the sixties, there had been thick forest from Buerarema to Santa Luzia, and Chico, the barber, had claimed that he had once been chased by a jaguar, although hardly anyone believed him. Who had ever heard of a jaguar hunting in daylight? Everyone had agreed that the marks were those of a lion-monkey.

In the absence of other distractions, she played back last night's scene in her mind's eye one more time.

'Amâncio,' she had said, 'don't bother. If they catch you, you won't work there again.'

'Dona Glória,' he had replied in that squeaky voice of his – such a big man and a voice like chalk grazing the blackboard – 'Dona Glória, they'll never search me and they can't check me. The tourists go on the trail to that new canopy bridge, and the drivers are left behind to wander alone.'

Dona Glória had taken her thick glasses off; she always did that when she thought deeply, because it's easier to concentrate when you can retire from the images of this world and contemplate the world of the orixás. *The bitter truth was that she was running low on her plants. She had long accepted that she had to buy the ritualistic ones from Salvador at an inflated price:* cana-de-macaco, *Ogum's special, required for the new initiates; powdered* canjerana *to fight the negative waves in ceremonies;* sangue-de-dragão *for ablutions of the head; white* flor-de-São José *for Oxalá;* catinga-de-mulata *for Obá;* mãe-boa *and* orriri *for Oxum. No, what she was craving were the medicinal herbs which she now needed for herself:* erva-de-Santa-Maria *for her bronchitis;* jabuticaba *for her asthma;* japecanga *for her rheumatism and* dormideira-sensitiva *to make her sleep. Ever since her beloved Josué had passed away five years ago, Dona Glória's bed was cold and her sleep disturbed. Perhaps she could have saved him, had the doctor diagnosed him correctly: she gave him* ivitinga *for ulcers, whereas he had needed* tanchagem *for angina. Now that she thought about it, she was running low on those, too. This was impossible, she must take count and check.*

'Come over tonight, and I'll give you a list,' she had replied.

She was indebted to Amâncio, although the herbal fumes of calêndula *she had prescribed many years ago certainly helped her sister's heavy periods. Who was more grateful was hard to judge: her sister or Amâncio himself, who had had to endure his wife's nerves when that time of the month arrived.*

Dona Glória gazed at the ocean below; this was another uninterrupted reverie, one of a string of uninterrupted, lonely reveries, day-in, day-out, month-in, month-out.

She heard a knock. Who could that be?

'It's me Dona Glória. It's Ofenísia,' a voice shouted below the balcony.

Ofenísia? The friend of her niece Malvina? Shouldn't she be at school? O, no, she finished last year. Or was it the year before last?

Long before Ofenísia asked for the favour, Dona Glória had guessed and had decided on the price, for there aren't many things young girls request from older women dabbling in herbal potions. When Ofenísia stopped, embarrassed and out of breath, Dona Glória spoke gravely: 'Your wish shall be granted Ofé, but first we have some business in the cemetery tomorrow.'

....

– 43 –

Linde was another good gringo – this time from Germany. Tall, thin and attractive in her jungle gear, she directed the proceedings with authority: a biologist, adventure backpacker and safari guide in one.

'This is not the Una Reserve,' she informed us in faultless Portuguese. 'This is the Una Ecoparque. Only scientists are allowed in the reserve. There are several animals that only exist in this region and are endangered.'

She stood in front of a tableau of pictures.

'This is the most famous of all,' she pointed, 'the golden-headed tamarin monkey, more commonly known as lion-monkey – *mico-leão-capa-dourada*. It is a beautiful creature, with a very distinctive golden mane, the symbol of the biodiversity of the Mata Atlântica. But we also have the yellow-breasted capuchin monkey, the maned sloth and the thin-spined porcupine, the rarest of all American porcupines. There are also margays or Brazilian jungle cats, *gatos-de-mato*, several rare frogs and tree-hoppers. Any questions?'

None.

'You have heard about the Amazon, you have heard about the Pantanal. But the biodiversity of the rainforest in southern Bahia – the number of species per hectare – is astonishing. Southern Bahia holds the world record: 456 species per hectare.'

This means nothing to the local landowners. During the 1980s, half of the population of the golden-headed tamarin monkeys was exported for pets, and two-thirds did not survive the trip. As the rainforest shrinks, and as a family of half-a-dozen individuals requires about 40 hectares to live in, the population necessarily drops. The capuchins exhibit great curiosity and are considered highly intelligent, although I'm told that unlike other monkeys they don't recognise themselves in the mirror, but we'll pass on that. By the way, they raise their eyebrows when they want sex: I will never watch a Joan Crawford film with the same concentration again.

'What is the most common animal here?' asked one of the Brazilians from the Transamérica Hotel in Una – which doesn't mean 'one' in Portuguese (this would be 'Uma') but 'dark' in Tupi; the forest of Una is the 'dark forest'.

Linde waved as one of the drivers passed around a bottle.

'The mosquito,' she replied. 'That's why we're giving you free protective lotion.'

While I plastered mine on, I saw my driver pick some twigs from a tiny bush and tie them clandestinely in a bundle.

Was that allowed? – but as we had started marching on the trail, there was something else I wanted to ask instead: 'Are there any jaguars here?'

'Yes, there are,' Linde replied. 'But they are nocturnal, and they don't normally attack if outnumbered.'

There were about a dozen of us marching in single file behind her lofty, commanding figure.

'This means that in a convoy the last one is the one most in danger,' she added. 'If a jaguar attacks, it attacks the laggard.'

We all turned around. I was the one-before-last. Ian was huffing and puffing several yards behind. He looked up and saw us stopped, our faces turned in his direction.

'What?' he asked.

We all turned our faces away and continued walking.

'What?' he repeated. He looked at me. 'What?'

'Nothing important,' I replied in case he speeded up and overtook me.

'Biodiversity,' Linde went on, as she sapped a rubber tree and collected the white fluid to show us the process. 'Biodiversity. Nature has been there: from the cloves that cure toothache to aspirin and quinine, Nature has provided us with a big laboratory which we are only now learning how to study. Look at this old *pau-copaiba* tree which produces excellent anti-inflammatory oil. Look at this natural rubber.'

I touched the sap. She shook her head.

'It's going to stink now,' she said.

I smelled my fingers with a sense of déjà vu.

Didn't I do the same thing in the Amazon?

I must have spoken loudly, because Linde turned around with curiosity.

'The Amazon? You've been to the Amazon? Was it interesting?'

I shrugged my shoulders. 'Rainforests aren't. You don't really see any animals.'

She smiled, like a biologist would. 'There are so many species around you – so many,' she said, 'full of interesting stories.'

She pointed at a line of leaf-cutter ants. 'Take these ants for instance. Do you know what they're doing?'

'They are carrying leaves to their nest.'

'And why are they carrying leaves to their nest?' asked Linde.

'To eat them?'

She shook her head.

'No, they don't eat them. They breed a kind of underground fungus which feeds on these leaves, and they don't even eat the fungus. They eat the *fruit* of the fungus. Believe it or not, they are farmers, just like us.'

She pointed at their anthill.

'You only see a third of it. The other two-thirds are below ground, extending into the earth. There is a whole farm underneath, and the farm feeds not only the ants and the fungus, but many more species who in turn feed more species, all forming an intricate, delicate ecosystem. And what do we humans do? We are irreversibly destroying their habitat, and we lose the genetic information Nature has struggled to create for billions of years.'

It was the Indians with their nomadic lifestyle and their small cultivated gardens here and there who contributed to the spread of species in the Mata Atlântica to achieve those 456 species per hectare. The dreaded Aimoré, themselves extinct, played their part in producing what we, the civilised, are busy extinguishing.

Linde stopped and showed us a plant with wide leaves.

'This is called *tiririca*,' she said. 'Rub against it.'

I rubbed my T-shirt against the plant. One of its long leaves fell off and attached itself to my sleeve.

'Natural velcro,' she pronounced triumphantly and turned the leaf over.

Its underside was sharp and rough like sandpaper.

'It *is* like sandpaper,' she explained. 'It's aluminium silicate. The leaves are hollow, stacked as if in concentric tubes, and stick out. The silicate makes them uneatable and, as animals rub off the leaves, they take them along on their fur and shake them off elsewhere. It will be no surprise to learn that this is how *tiririca* multiplies: by auto-cloning itself. It's an ancient plant, a grass, preceding all the later ecologically advanced plants with flowers and pollen and what-have-you. It has survived much longer than we have as a species.'

Linde stopped in front of a nest built on a tree.

'Ants like humidity, so they build their hills in the soil,' she announced. 'Termites like it dry, so they nest on trees.'

She waited for us to congregate around.

'Termites may be a disaster in São Paulo, but in the rainforest they are the refuse collection service. They rid the forest of all dead wood. Keep it clean.'

What looked like a wasp flew out of a small hose-like protrusion at the top. We stepped back.

'A wasps' nest,' a kid cried.

'It's not a wasp,' Linde explained. 'It's the *abelha-sem-terra*, the homeless bee. It can't build its own nest and has to invade others'.'

And what about the termites inside?

Linde pointed at a few termites leaving the nest from the opposite side of the bee entrance. 'They are still there. They are engaged in a permanent territorial war. I know for a fact that it's been going on for two of the three years I've been here.'

Wow! Like Starship Troopers: *a fight to the death between two species.*

'I would have thought the bees would win hands down,' I commented.

'These termites have a natural antibiotic which fights off bee venom,' she said. 'Nature has again been there first.'

You had to hand it to Linde: she knew her stuff.

She stopped when we reached the canopy walkway.

'Before we climb up,' she said, 'just observe the leaves around you on the bottom of the rainforest.'

We looked around.

'They are big, aren't they?'

They were huge.

'In the jungle, the plants have to fight for two things: sun and water. They need to pick out the sun and to collect water. Some plants invest in height, and their canopy is composed of small leaves, since the sun up there is strong and plentiful. The ones on the ground invest in leaf width because in the forest the rain will fall over a long period of time and will drip slowly from the leaves above to the leaves below. The function rainforests perform for our planet is that of storage tanks: storage tanks of fresh water. You destroy the rainforest, you bring in the desert and the drought, as Brazil itself has discovered in the Nordeste.'

'What about the oxygen?' someone asked.

'Rainforests do not contribute to the oxygen supply,' Linde replied. 'Most oxygen produced during the day is consumed during the night. What generates oxygen is swamps: mangrove swamps. These are the major oxygen-producers on our planet – its lungs.'

She paused. 'No, the destruction of the rainforests will bring desertification and the annihilation of our water supplies. The biggest problem of the twenty-first century will be water. In twenty-five years' time drinkable water will be a very precious commodity. In fifty years' time, we will see wars. And do you know how you can save the planet?'

'How?'

'Eat chocolate.'

What?

'Eat more chocolate. Cocoa trees need the shade and the wetness of the rainforest. The Mata Atlântica survived for as long as profits could be made from the cocoa plantations. It was afterwards when the price of cocoa collapsed that the farmers started logging.'

The thought of eating chocolate for our planet brought tears to my eyes. Protest has never been so enjoyable.

I heard Ian yell behind me.

'Oh, boy!'

I turned, licking my lips. *A jaguar?* No. We had reached the entrance to the *passarela na copa das árvores* Ian had built – Ian with Anheuser-Busch, he would have corrected me.

He ran to the front next to Linde, his sixty years shrunk to sixteen.

'So, there it is,' he said.

The walkway starts on a small hilltop – you don't have to climb a tree to enter; and it hovers 65 to 80 feet over the jungle floor for a good hundred yards. In the entrance there is a small wooden rest cabin.

'That's when I left,' said Ian proudly. 'After we finished this cabin. Built with a local palm tree.'

'*Piassava*,' popped in Linde.

'Yes, *piassava*,' he said. 'Very sturdy. I remember putting down the foundations.'

He ran over to it, and a family of bats flew out from below.

'We had to dig those holes at the side by hand,' he pointed excitedly. 'And they had to be deep enough for stability. In the US we'd have automatic nailers, pneumatic drills, motorised diggers – here we only had machetes.'

He was gesticulating like a South American.

'I tell you what,' Ian continued. 'They say Bahians are lazy. Gee – believe you me, they're not. The Bahians love to work. They lack knowledge and infrastructure – but you show them how something is done, and they never say "That's too much for me", no sir. These guys can do wonders with their machetes. They dug these holes in thirty minutes.'

He pointed at the walkway supports.

'Those poles – those 36-foot poles. I had no idea how we could raise them; in the States we would simply order a helicopter. We ended up using heavy three-in-one pulleys. Twelve people started pulling like a crane and one had to go down and risk his life while he guided the tip into the hole by hand.'

He breathed in proudly. 'I've done many things in my life, but this tops it all.'

'Go ahead,' we offered. 'You go first.'

'No,' he replied. 'I want to stay behind a little.'

The walk from tree to tree on this aerial bridge was fun; the rainforest lay below us, its leaves thick and impenetrable like a deep green marsh. The top branches were full of small yellow, red and green leaves and …

'Bromeliads,' said Linde, following my gaze. 'There are twelve species of bromeliads just on the canopy. Birds bring the seeds, which sprout wherever they can.

'I've only seen them on the floor,' I replied.

'They are actually a canopy plant,' said Linde. 'They can grow anywhere – in the poorest of soils like their relative, the pineapple, as long as there's a lot of rain. The reason they can is because their leaves are bunched up at the stem, storing water and mud and dead leaves: an organic soup that provides nutrients to them and many other species. Look.'

I looked down and saw a giant web with many small spiders crawling over.

'Social spiders,' said Linde. 'Normally spiders are solitary, and they're cannibals. But this species builds a huge web together and lives socially like ants.'

She gave me a sideways glance.

'Do you think that rainforests are more interesting now?'

'Fascinating,' I agreed.

Ian stopped in the middle of the canopy walkway and looked up and down. He took another step and looked left, and then right and then behind, like Tweety checking for Sylvester.

'Do you like your job?' I asked Linde.

She was still looking at Ian who was enjoying every inch of the walkway like a Gucci model on a catwalk.

'I wouldn't do anything else. My work is my life, and I enjoy it.'

'You don't miss Germany?'

'Europe!' she scoffed. 'We have forgotten how to live. We are spoiled.'

Ian wasn't walking; he was dancing in slow motion.

'Stuck in our offices. Playing with our computers. Dehumanising ourselves with factory farming. Bleeding our planet to death. All for the sake of comfort. Now with the advent of the Internet we are even losing the power to communicate face to face, to socialise. We have lost touch with reality.'

'What is reality?' I asked.

'Reality,' she said, 'is hard *physical* work.'

We reached the end of the walkway all too quickly.

There's not much left to triumph over in the West anymore.

A Brazilian came up to us.

'All this without the help of the Brazilian government?' he asked.

'Entirely private capital,' said Linde.

I remembered something I'd read at the entrance.

Anheuser-Busch. Hotel Transamerica.

'Who built this again?' I asked.

'A consortium called Conservation International.'

'Who are they?'

'Anheuser-Busch, Hotels Transamérica and US-AID.'

'There is a Hotel Transamerica in Una,' I said. 'These people ...'
It all clicked. I spoke slowly, intoning every word.
'These – people – have – come – from – Hotel – Transamerica – on – a – visit – to – a – canopy – walkway – the – hotel – has – built.'
I turned to Linde.
'Do you use the walkway for scientific purposes?'
'Oh, no,' said Linde, 'but there are plans to.'
'So – so this is all a *tourist attraction!*'
'It's mostly for tourists, yes.'
I felt betrayed.
Ian's great achievement was a frigging gimmick.

··

The Secret of Malvina

Malvina put the phone down tired. She had been talking for a good hour or so, and she had been constantly on her guard so as not to upset Ofenísia like she had last weekend. Since then, the twice-daily phone calls had stopped. She missed Ofé because they spent weekends lying on the beach in the Jardim Atlântico and, without Ofé, Malvina's parents refused to let her out on her own.

'Not as long as you live under my roof!' her father had said.

'But Daddy, Aristóteles and his gang will be there.'

'And he likes you because you are unavailable. If you were a little trollop, he wouldn't even look at you with all his father's money.'

That was always his argument: that Aristóteles would lose interest in her if her morals were looser. It was a winning argument because Malvina could not divulge – to her father of all people – that she had had sex with her boyfriend – although, ah, forget it ...

She started preparing the moqueca. *The fish was almost ready. Two juicy kilos of fresh, top-notch Atlantic sea-bream. She arranged it in the saucepan and juiced the zest of four limes over it. She had to let it marinate for at least half an hour.*

She finely chopped several sprigs of coriander and onion while she waited. Aristóteles would be coming over any time now with his friend Tuísca to have dinner. She looked at the two glasses in front of her. This was going to be tricky. She could not afford to make a mistake. Damn Tuísca!

It was good to talk to Ofé again. So Ramiro had finally been conquered and her friend was on cloud nine.

She chopped the tomatoes and the pepper, then she added a little bit of tempero baiano. *She checked the fish. Ten minutes more.*

Ofenísia had told her everything: how she had lured Ramiro to the statue of Christ, how they had lain on her mother's shawl and how that gringo had started taking pictures when she found herself on top of him like a kinkajou *in heat. Ramiro had been so shaken, he had torn a hole the size of Ofenísia's cleavage in the shawl.*

She laughed on her own when she imagined the scene.

But Ofenísia had gone on and told her how they quickly ended up in her room with the narrow bed and the Daniela Mercury posters on the wall; and how she felt during that tingling, scary, pleasurable moment when she walked through the threshold of womanhood to the subsequent worry of conception. Malvina had already known before she heard from Ofenísia that she had visited Glória for those herbs girls procure when their relationship with a boy goes beyond the purely platonic. Ofenísia still had to perform a sacrifice to Oxum later today in the cemetery.

The fish was ready. She poured the rest of the ingredients on top and put them all over a low fire. Another ten minutes.

Ofenísia had told her everything, like a best friend should.

And yet she, Malvina, had kept concealed the most important part of her relationship with Aristóteles.

She nearly forgot. The boys would be here any time now.

Malvina climbed onto a chair to reach that special bottle of dark rum she had been hiding – she could not afford to buy many herself, and her father was fond of white rum.

But white rum would not do.

She poured the liquor into the two glasses. She would offer Aristóteles the larger amount so that she could tell which was which.

She opened the cellar door and looked at herself in the mirror as she passed. Although thin, pretty and bronzed, she could still do with a few centimetres around her bosom. Ofenísia might be on the fat side, but she had breasts to nest the entire termite population of the ecoparque.

Malvina walked down into the cool cellar – she could hardly use the fridge, could she? – and from a dusty corner she picked up the small vial she had filled this morning: a vial full of a dark red fluid.

When she returned to the kitchen, the moqueca *had cooked in the big earthenware pot. She added a generous dose of palm oil for flavour. Then she opened the vial and added a few drops of her own menstrual blood to the glass containing Aristóteles's rum, before she was unexpectedly confronted by Gabriela.*

··

Things I Like About Brazil #9: Bahian Cuisine

Where do I start for someone who likes spicy food? The piquant sauce in the bean-fried acarajé? *The scent of palm oil that floats in the fish stews? The Louisiana flavour of the okra-based* caruru? *Or the subtle coconut taste of the* bobó de *camarão? Bahian cuisine is a mixture of a mixture: not just African, but polyethnic African mixed with Portuguese and local Indian cooking. Feed me hot fresh fish with lime and coriander in a deep-pan* cataplana *with the aromatic palm oil that constitutes a* moqueca *and I'll be your sex slave for eternity.*

....

– 44 –

The most impressive construct in Ilhéus is not a church – the centrally located church of São Sebastião is far too recent to attract the eye. It is not the *fin de siècle* Palace of Paranaguá, built on the foundations of an old Jesuit College which serves as the town hall, neo-classical, austere and restricted in the confines of the Praça Seabra; not even the eccentric statue of Sappho in the square outside saves it. As for the Amado locations: Nacib's bar had its twin floors demolished and the result is a hangar-like *Bierkeller*; and the Bataclã nightclub is not nearly as chic as its namesake, the Parisian Bataclan in Boulevard Voltaire. Amado's patrimonial house, which has become Casa de Cultura Jorge Amado, is an unassuming colonial mansion with a grand central staircase, period floors and not much more. Yes, it's full of the author's memorabilia – including some sculptures, pictures, posters and videos, but it loses out to the grander Casa Amado in Salvador's Pelourinho. This is where the author spent his youth; where he first put pen to paper and wrote his first novel, *País do Carnaval*, but there's no redeeming household touch, no sofa, bed or even chamber pot to liven up the place.

No, by far the most striking and distinctive building in the whole of Ilhéus is a school.

I had noticed it on my first day, as I was walking down the sloping circuit of the Avenida Dois de Julho. It stood opposite, on the Alto da Piedade, its neo-gothic spires dominating the landscape, sharp as if drawn like a film backdrop, clean and shiny as if it had been built yesterday. It is the old convent of Nossa Senhora da Piedade, which now houses a Catholic school run by Ursuline nuns.

I stood in front of it, gasping for air. The hill was steep, and my legs had run out of steam. I had decided to go for the view at sunset. The porter let me in after I gave him a tip. I didn't quite understand how the school was open at that advanced hour, but didn't complain, as the views towards the old city centre, the ocean and the river mouth compensated for the exertion. It was a large complex, also housing a chapel and a museum of sacred art; it was the work of a French nun, Mother Thaís, who founded the convent back in 1916. Nuns seem to go a long way in Brazil; this one had the whole street named after her.

It was getting dark. I started walking slowly in the direction of my hotel. I passed the open space of a cemetery built at the edge of a cliff; I could not resist a final sunset snap, so I jumped the low colonnade wall. To my surprise, I wasn't alone. A boy was playing leapfrog with the crosses, and two human forms, both dressed in white, were tending a grave: an old mulatto woman, thin as they come and a fat young girl who looked familiar. The young girl raised her head and saw me holding my camera. She was kneeling, while lit white candles and plates of food were scattered around her. I had seen that look before. Was she the one ...?

I knew at once what was in store.

'Be careful gringo. This is a dangerous area after dark,' shouted the old woman.

Was that a threat?

I looked around. The kid had stopped playing and was watching me with curiosity. I smiled, bowed respectfully, turned around and left.

Perhaps I can make a story out of this.

*****

My stomach started rumbling. There was one place I had to go for dinner. I had seen it by the seaside: Os Velhos Marineiros, straight out of a Jorge Amado book title.

That man again.

I've complained before that the greatest Brazilian storyteller was never granted the Nobel Prize – unlike his two friends of old, Pablo Neruda and Miguel Ángel Asturias. The trio emerged as the continent's left-wing propagandists who had joined the Communist Party and suffered as a result. Amado was born in 1912 in the *fazenda* Auricídia in the district of Ferradas in Itabuna, son of *coronel* João Amado de Faria and Eulália Leal Amado, the oldest of several children, but the family moved to Ilhéus in January 1914. In 1922 he went to Salvador, where a Jesuit College teacher spotted his literary talent and introduced him to the Portuguese classics. He became a journalist on several papers until he moved to a small *pensão* in Rio off the Avenida Copacabana. There, in 1931, he enrolled in the Law School to satisfy his father, but simultaneously published *O País do*

Carnaval with a small publishing house. In Rio he networked and shared apartments with many big names in Brazilian literature.

In 1934 he joined the Communist Party and was soon forced into exile; *Cacau*, his story of bad landowners and good cocoa workers was first published in Argentina. He returned clandestinely to Brazil, but was arrested in Manaus and spent two months in jail, while his books were publicly burnt in Salvador. Eventually he fled the country again. His early novels are seeped in the socialist realism so beloved – some would say dictated – by the Stalinist Communist Party. His books were banned in the country of his birth, and even those that were published were brushed over by the government censor: there is a passage in *Suor* where one of the characters says: '*This appears like a subversive party cell*' instead of '*This appears like a Communist Party cell*', which is what Amado wrote originally. (His novels had changed so much that Amado spent many of his later years – he died in August 2001 – revising his books against his manuscripts to restore the original text for eventual re-publication: the Author's Cut.) He was so loyal and disciplined, he was put forward by the party as a candidate for the post-Vargas Constitutional Assembly in 1946 – and elected. His crowning achievement as a Communist Party member must surely be his winning of the Stalin Peace Prize in 1951.

Then Stalin died. Krushschev told the world about the tyranny, the secret police, the show trials, the gulags and Jorge Amado, in his own words, became sick of being told what to think. He abandoned the party, but not his political philosophy: '*The socialist countries gained freedom indeed, but their people did not have the material capacity to enjoy that freedom.*' And something remarkable happened when that author with a talent for drawing multi-dimensional portraits of Bahian society threw away the restraining chains of discipline and wrote from the heart and head for the first time, for the heart had room for the whole world and the head had wisened up from disillusion.

Amado published *Gabriela, Clove and Cinnamon* in 1958, his first work after he left the Party. Twenty thousand copies were sold in a fortnight. By 1962 there had been 20 editions, a dozen translations and 160,000 copies sold in Brazil alone. It is the best-known Brazilian novel ever, was turned into a film with Sonia Braga in the lead, and gained Amado international recognition and fame. Why? Not just because it is a novel steeped in optimism, but also – as if to shake off the cardboard characterisation of his early revolutionary work – because it is a novel in which no character is fully good or fully evil, for flaws and redemption are twin aspects of the human character, and Amado loves all of them like a benign Almighty. And the sweep of his vision was grand: no less than 250 characters – some of them silent or passing – are mentioned in the novel, whereas the protagonist, Gabriela, doesn't appear until a quarter of the way through. What the novel is about is even grander: the breakdown of the old patriarchal morality whose destruction is brought about by Gabriela's twin weapons: *clove*, which represents her scent, for she is the most beautiful woman in Ilhéus, and *cinnamon*, which represents her culinary ability, her *métier*, for she's the best cook in town. Coinciding as it did with the rise of women power after the mass production of contraceptive pills and the fight for legalisation of abortions, *Gabriela* looks now like a feminist novel that captured the Zeitgeist. The transformation of the morality of Ilhéus, Brazil and the world as such came about not because of the Nazi defeat, the Cold War, the demise of Imperialism or the student revolutions – it came about whenever women refused to play ball and took their lives into their own hands. It is no coincidence that the four parts of *Gabriela* are called 'The Languor of Ofenísia', 'The Loneliness of Glória', 'The Secret of Malvina' and 'The Moonlight of Gabriela'.

I'll bring that last one up to date.

Gabriela 50 Years On

'You what?' shouted Gabriela.

Ofenísia cringed, for the outburst was directed at her.

'You what?'

Malvina looked sheepishly at her elder sister.

Gabriela's beautiful features were distorted. Her smooth olive skin was tempered by wrinkles of irritation; her hazel almond eyes had become two black horizontal slits peering down with contempt; and her rich, red lips were pouting in anger.

'You what?' she repeated.

It had been confession time amongst the trio, and Gabriela was incandescent with rage. She walked up to her cupboard, opened the drawer, took out something and threw it in the face of Ofenísia.

'Use that!' she shouted. 'Haven't you heard the news? The Middle Ages are over.'

Ofenísia looked at the green packaged condom in front of her. So that's what they looked like. Not that she understood any better how to use it.

'This is the only way Ofé,' said Gabriela. 'The only way. Learn before it's too late.'

'But Dona Glória is an expert,' Ofenísia mumbled. 'My mother, my aunts …'

Gabriela nearly hit her.

'How many kids does your aunt Jerusa have?'

Ofenísia shrugged her shoulders.

'Three.'

'And what's the age difference between the last two?'

Ofenísia felt strangely out-debated.

'Fifteen years.'

'Right. Fifteen years. Your cousin Miquelina is in her thirties and Lalú is your age. Do you think that Lalú was planned? Does that look as if Dona Glória succeeded?'

Ofenísia looked at Malvina for encouragement.

'But Malvina here swears …'

Gabriela turned sharply to Malvina.

'Tell her! Tell her now!' she screamed with a voice several decibels above unseemly.

Malvina looked at Ofenísia.

'We haven't really done it,' she said slowly.

Ofenísia jumped up. 'But you said …'

'I said we've had sex! We've had sex many times. But, but I haven't let him … you know.'

'That does it,' shouted Ofenísia and got up. 'I'm going.'

Gabriela pushed her down.

'No. I haven't finished.'

She turned to Malvina who squirmed in her seat uncomfortably.

'Have you ever heard of Aids?'

Malvina looked up.

'What does that have to do with the potion?'

Gabriela squatted in front of her and put her hands on Malvina's thighs.

'Listen little sister,' she said calmly but resolutely. 'Sex is fun. Sex is fantastic. But sex nowadays can be dangerous. It can be dangerous because there is a deadly disease out there which is transmitted by a virus. That virus lives in the blood and semen. By giving your disgusting potion to Aristóteles, you help spread the virus.'

'It's a gay disease,' Malvina replied. 'And I am a virgin – how can I have it?'

Ofenísia sprang up again. 'That's why you wanted to know all the details. Because you haven't done it.'

She fell back on her chair: 'What a fool I've been – what a fool,' she kept repeating.

Gabriela stood up and leaned against the window to calm herself down. The ocean was turbulent. The tide was coming in. She looked up. It might rain tonight.

'One,' she said. 'Aids is not a gay disease. It used to be – back in the eighties, in São Paulo. But it isn't any more. Two: Yes, Malvina you probably don't have Aids, although if you had any other type of sex – I don't want to know,' she interrupted with her gestures a distraught Malvina, 'you still might catch the virus. If you don't fuck Aristóteles, how do you know he doesn't fuck someone else?'

Malvina stood up with a jolt. 'He wouldn't. I know him!'

Gabriela laughed. 'Men. You think you know men. Hell, their fathers encourage them to lose their virginity in a brothel so that they can pretend they have done their duty and wash their hands of the rest of their upbringing! Everyone in that surfer lot go to prostitutes. Can you vouch that no one has caught anything?'

The two girls were silent. Malvina fell back lifelessly on the sofa. Gabriela's tone turned soft.

'Prevention is a state of mind,' she said slowly. 'You don't let blood be exchanged. If you don't know for sure, you assume that the virus is present. You don't give Aristóteles any potions. You use condoms.'

Ofenísia felt her eyes water. She saw that Malvina was weeping.

'Not only do you use condoms, but you force your men to buy them and wear them. They won't like it; they will insist they dislike the feeling. But remember one thing: your life – and their life, because men have two brains, one up here and one down there – is in your hands. If you love them, you'll protect them.'

Ofenísia's sight had blurred from the tears. Something somewhere had gone astray. Out of the corner of her eye she observed Malvina who was lifting her face. Their eyes met. It felt comfortable.

Gabriela picked up on the vibes and held both the girls' hands.

'Ofenísia?' she asked.

Ofenísia nodded.

'No more Dona Glória? No more sacrifices to Oxum?'

'No,' she whispered.

Gabriela turned to Malvina.

'No more blood potions?' she asked.

Malvina didn't answer.

'No more blood potions?' she repeated.

Malvina's gaze upwards was desperate.

'The blood binds him to me,' she said. 'It's a spell. Without the spell …'

'Malvina,' said Gabriela, 'he loves you with or without the spell.'

Malvina looked at her friends. Could it be true?

Gabriela guessed her thoughts.

'You'll never find out until you give up,' she said.

Malvina's eyes met Ofenísia's. She squeezed Gabriela's hand.

As if rehearsing for a threnody, they all fell into each other's arms in an exculpatory embrace. It seemed ages before Gabriela stood up and cleared her throat.

'I have to go to the restaurant,' she said. 'Anyone for karaoke?'

Before either of the two could answer, she continued, 'I feel like a duet tonight.'

....

Things I Don't Like About Brazil #9: Aids

By the year 2000 there had been 163,355 cases in Brazil, the majority in the São Paulo–Rio south-western axis with more than 80 per cent of the victims between the ages of 20–45. (However, it's worth putting this number in perspective: there were 187,990 cases of malaria in Brazil in 1999 alone, and at its peak, the dengue fever epidemic of 1992 reached 3.3 million cases.) Aids is now the fourth largest cause of death within the 20 and 45 age group in Brazil. About a quarter of the infected are women, and their numbers are on the increase as the original homosexual focus decreases. In Brazil, as in places like South Africa, the disease has caught a hold amongst the heterosexual population. Amongst men, the confirmed transmission method is firstly heterosexual and then homosexual, followed by intravenous use of drugs. Amongst the women, heterosexual transmission accounts for more than half of the cases. So, remember to bring camisinhas next time you find yourself in Brazil, OK?

....

If location, location, location is the secret of a successful establishment, the restaurant Os Velhos Marineiros has won the lottery; no, it doesn't occupy a particularly scenic spot, but one of convenience. It's on and off the beach; close to the centre but not too far; large enough to have the numbers but small enough to have a good atmosphere. Like most places in the Nordeste, it's outdoors, but thankfully protected by thatch against the downpour that started as soon as I arrived.

When I sat down, I froze. Tonight was 'videoke' night. Oh, the spread of the Japanese curse; Latin America has been highly prone to its influence: stand up there, open your mouth, shake your booty, and you are a star for the night. Thankfully, there were only about seven or eight full tables on this Thursday night; and as far as entertainment goes, it was educational. In Brazilian videoke, they show the original videos on a back screen, and as the lyrics appear simultaneously, the whole set-up proved instructive for my Portuguese, so I sat it out. I recommend it for learning any language in more depth. Many a Brazilian youngster can mouth '*I will always love you; Scaramouche, Scaramouche do the fandango; Billy*

Jean is not my lover,' from listening to pop songs. They might be mouthing nonsense, but at least it's nonsense in English. In the same vein, Kerosene Jacaré might not be poetry of Camões quality, but every little phrase helps.

The waitress took a shine to me.

'Where are you from?' she asked as she took my order. She was very pretty, in her early twenties, with shoulder-length black hair and smooth copper skin; she wore her waitress uniform with sensuality.

'I'm from Athens via London,' I said, ordering a *moqueca de camarão*.

'Oh!' she exclaimed. 'What are you doing here?'

'Passing through. I've been travelling in Bahia for a few weeks. I'm off tomorrow.'

'Where to?'

'The south. Curitiba.'

Her wide almond eyes sparkled with admiration.

'What's your name?'

'I'm John,' I said. 'And yours?'

She giggled

'Gabriela.'

I raised my eyebrows.

'Like …'

'Yes. Like the book. There are many of us in Ilhéus named after characters in the book. My sister there' – she pointed at a girl sitting at a table amongst a gang of surfers – 'is called Malvina.'

I made a mock sniffing noise.

'No aroma of clove,'

She laughed.

'And certainly no cinnamon. I don't like the taste. I don't like sweets.'

'No clove, no cinnamon,' I said. *'As if you can find them anyway now with the disappearing rainforest.'*

She laughed again.

'You get them in the market,' she jested. 'I take it you've been to the ecoparque *then?'*

I had.

'What did you think of our passarela na copa das árvores?'

I grinned in disappointment.

'A gimmick,' I said. 'A mockery.'

'Why?'

'It's just for the tourists. It serves no purpose. People make so much out of it, as if it were a big achievement.'

Gabriela brought me several large Brahmas and my moqueca, *which could lead one to a spiritual experience, like the sourpuss Danes in* Babette's Feast: *fresh king prawns, thick tomato sauce, orange-yellow palm oil and divine-smelling warm* farofa. *My skin positively glowed. Good food, a beautiful girl called Gabriela, and I am in Ilhéus. What's missing to make the Amado story complete?*

Gabriela stood up with her sister Malvina; they sang a song together: a song about boys and girls and love, their cheeks aglow as their bodies shook to the rhythm. We clapped along throughout.

Gabriela stayed on the stage. She looked at me and sang a song – in English. It was one of the few Caetano Veloso songs I knew: 'London, London'.

I nearly hid my face in the cataplana *from embarrassment. When she finished, she acknowledged the prolonged applause and came up to my table.*

'How did you learn English?'

'I study tourism. Finishing soon,' she replied.

'You have a good voice. You should become a singer.'

'No,' she said. 'I want to be better than that.'

*****

By midnight everyone had had a go at the mike, bar me, and everyone had eventually gone home to sleep. Gabriela brought me my bill and I left her a large tip.

'That passarela …' *she started as I was leaving.*

'What about it?'

'I know someone who helped build it. It was difficult. You shouldn't laugh about it.'

'I'm sure it was difficult to build, but what purpose does it serve?'

'It brings in tourists.'

'So?'

'So,' she said with seriousness, 'fewer trees get logged. The idea behind it was to show the landlords surrounding the area that it is to their advantage to keep the forest pristine, because there is money to be made out of eco-tourism. It may not seem much to you, but the farmers in this area would chop down the trees and make money and space for their farms. And if the government doesn't like it, then the farmers burn the forest. But if we can attract enough tourists, and they can make money another way, then the forest is safe. And the forest is our blood.'

She was right, of course. I checked out the ecoparque's *website later. The most difficult part of saving the Mata Atlântica has been to change the mentality of the farmers in the region who used to see it as a commodity to be exchanged, not as an inherited heirloom for the next generation. As the site says diplomatically: 'By studying the options available to landowners in Southern Bahia, we were able to formulate a conservation strategy in tune with the prevailing economic, political, and social realities.'*

It is only when the locals start seeing that they can make money out of their heritage that they may change their attitude towards it. Gabriela was right and I was wrong. The canopy walkway was not an eco-gimmick; it was not a Disney rollercoaster ride; it was a noble construction, a lifebuoy for the golden-faced lion tamarin and all the other unique rainforest species.

'If you want to save the rainforest, tell your friends to come here and visit us,' Gabriela said as I departed.

'And eat chocolate,' I added.

She laughed.

'And eat more chocolate,' she agreed.

Chapter 10

The Animal at the End of the Alphabet (Mato Grosso)

When I was a child I was given a globe. I could not make much of Europe with all the names compacted over the country maps. I liked the large countries in Asia and America, where my tiny index finger could follow their contours easily. I spent hours looking at Brazil and Argentina with their large landmass and wondered whether Chile was a practical joke. I read the names of the places: Tierra del Fuego, Amazonia, Patagonia, Atacama. But there, right in the middle of the continent was a large green mass with the name Mato Grosso.

'What does "Mato Grosso" mean?' I asked my father.

He was busy. 'Ask your uncle,' he said. 'He speaks Spanish.'

I turned to my uncle.

'This is Portuguese,' he informed me wisely. 'I think it means "thick forest" or something. It's wild and uncivilised and no one ever goes there.'

I looked at the scary, untamed, remote place with awe.

No one ever goes there.

··

The Words You'll Need

cachoeira = *small waterfall*
cerrado = *scrub vegetation in Central Brazil akin to African savannah*
cuidado = *careful*
fechado = *closed*
lago azul = *blue lake*
rodoviária = *if you have forgotten – and how could you? – it's the bus station*

··

– 45 –

There was no direct flight from Ilhéus to Curitiba so I had to change in São Paulo's smaller urban airport of Congonhas, which, unlike its Minas Gerais namesake, is certainly no Unesco site, although at some point I expect some out-of-the-way, inhospitable early twentieth-century airfield to be declared patrimony of mankind; I have certainly visited some shaky ones in South America which could fool you. The only thing one can do in Congonhas, which does not offer the 'shopping-completes-me' experience of Guarulhos International, is eat. Rio Sul offer free sandwiches inside their gate. They probably rely on pure embarrassment to stop you devouring the lot – but no-shame cases like me make marketing managers fear for their jobs.

Gorged with Rio Sul's food and drinks I started ruminating. Last time I was here, I was flying to Campo Grande with Air Pantanal. I was beginning my second and shortest visit to Brazil, which saw me in the country for only two weeks, crossing as I did the Bolivian border to the Andean republics.

You know the soft music and ripply picture they use in the movies when a flashback is due? Imagine one now.

It's going to last two chapters.

*****

Air Pantanal was good, efficient and very, very expensive. Air travel in Brazil was downright extortionate when the real, the new currency that killed off the great inflation, was pegged at 1:1 to the dollar. My short internal flight took off from a rainy São Paulo at 15 °C and landed at Campo Grande, basking at a super 35 °C, one and a half hours away. Since I would be leaving next day by bus, I stayed opposite the *rodoviária*, a colossal complex containing shops, restaurants, hairdressers and even a porn movie theatre; in short, everything the Mato Grosso cowboys would wish for – and there were a lot of them at large, open-eyed like babies in a nudist camp, bent legs limping with difficulty off-saddle, senses overpowered by the unceasing movement. If you live in the *cerrado* and your defences are wired to respond to every whoosh of wind and every shuffle of the bush, then the locomotion in the bus station must zonk you out like Crocodile Dundee gone to town. At least, as the Lonely Planet guide says, with the porn theatre and all, they hardly need to leave the *rodoviária*. Some of them perhaps never do, wandering aimlessly in the maze of shops – I got lost twice myself. Perhaps I should check out that porn cinema later.

Campo Grande has been the capital of the state of Mato Grosso do Sul since 1979 – the state itself having been created in 1977 – as I was reminded by a competition form on my bedside table. It was open to all visitors for the best travel story about the state with first prize a return trip to meet the governor. I finished mine too late – on purpose. Mato Grosso do Sul has the sixth highest murder rate in Brazil: guns, drink and macho cowboy clashes are the lethal cocktail in Campo Grande, which for the setting and the attitude could be the backdrop for a spaghetti Western. Old men, faces like collapsed lungs – on second thoughts, those wrinkles might be knife scars – were playing chess in the landscaped squares under gigantic jaguar murals; squatting peasants were plying herbs and fruit on the pavement; sleepy office workers stole a quick siesta under the blossoming, hardy *ipé* trees while busy horsemen galloped down dusty side alleys.

In case you needed reminding, this is a town built around cattle, predominantly the rearing of the white humpback zebu, which originated in Asia. Chickens, cows, sheep, goats and pigs were non-existent in the New World; the first bovines were introduced back in 1530 from the Cape Verde Islands. Zebus were introduced in Bahia in 1813 because the European breeds couldn't withstand the tropical climate and diseases, as they could in the pampas of the south. Nowadays Brazil is the biggest commercial zebu centre in the world (since in India they are sacred) and with 155 million in the land, it numbers almost as many zebu as it does people. Although Uberaba in Minas Gerais boasts a zebu museum and calls itself the zebu capital of the world, on Brazil's 500th year the Mato Grosso do Sul cattle population overtook the number held in Minas. They are not in competition, however; the Minas breeds are milk-producers, whereas the Mato Grosso ones are cross-bred with European cows for their meat.

And that's how exciting my town was.

I *had* to do something in Campo Grande apart from buying a ticket to leave the place, so powered by sugar-cane juice squeezed sweet, green and brackish on the spot, I discovered the most intriguing place in town: the Dom Bosco Museum created by the Salesian fathers back in 1950. 'Dom Bosco' is a label as prominent in the centre-west of Brazil as the Potiguar brand is in Fortaleza. You can find colleges, churches, sports fields and museums attributed to Dom Bosco, who was born in 1815 in Italy near the town of Castelnuovo. I am not one to praise Catholic priests, but the Venerable Bosco (beatified in 1903) was a truly remarkable man, if only because he fought prejudice within and without the Church. He initiated the whole movement of the Salesian Order, which has been very active in Brazil since the late nineteenth century.

The whole point of the order was the shelter and education of poor street children in the big industrial towns who, at the time, were considered vermin – echoes of 1980s Brazil. Dom Bosco's early efforts were torpedoed by the lay and ecclesiastical authorities alike: they even tried to certify him insane and send him to an asylum. He was against punishment as a means of discipline and encouraged play and sport as a positive influence on the spirit. His approach appears all the more enlightened when we consider that at the same time English public schools exalted the merits of the birch. You can still walk around Brazilian towns, bump into a Salesian school and see the priests kicking a football around with their pupils. OK, they may screw them for life with dogma, but at least their screwed-up future won't be a hungry one.

Back to the museum, which has a large and varied collection of minerals, Palaeolithic fossils, shells, insects and a full taxidermic selection of the birds and mammals of the Mato Grosso, including one of those huge anacondas you only see in Hollywood movies starring Jon Voight. There are 5,000-odd exhibits on the life of the Xavante, the Bororó and the Carajá explained in painstaking detail. For me the high point, which alone is worth the admission, is the section with the stuffed mutant monsters: wow, a lamb with two heads and a chicken with four legs – Kentucky Fried would *kill* for a DNA sample; its feet were facing opposite directions, so that the chicken would have to go forward with one pair and backwards with the other to move at all. Some of the samples are so teratogenic, I'm surprised they lived long enough to get stuffed. Fans of *Eraserhead*, the movie: obligatory pilgrimage alert!

There's always one surprise in some nook or corner of every city: this one was the Casa do Artesão where the ceramic work of the Kadiwéu Indians is displayed. Mato Grosso was the territory of the Gê-speaking Guaikuru and Guaná. Their only twenty-first-century descendants are the Kadiwéu and Terena tribes respectively. The asymmetric, abstract, brightly coloured decorative pottery of the Kadiwéu is some of the best in South America with pigments based solely on charcoal, the *jenipapú* dye and coloured earth. Yet before they became potters, the Guaikuru were the most feared of the tribes in Mato Grosso, and one with the weirdest customs.

By the time the Paulista *bandeirantes* reached the Mato Grosso, the Guaikuru had adopted and bred missionary horses and, like the North American Plains Indians, had become highly skilled horsemen. '*They use neither saddles nor stirrups in their horses. They ride bareback and mount them in a single leap. Even when they are walking or playing, one can see the suppleness of their bodies. They run after the horses to catch them or tie them with almost as much agility as the beasts themselves. They use no lassoes or lariats to catch them or corrals to subdue them,'* wrote the explorer Ricardo Franco de Almeida Serra back in the 1790s. The Guaikuru were arrogant and disdainful of other tribes and that included the whites whom they defeated time and time again. Their horsemanship – they charged violently into battle hanging off the flanks of their horses, holding their manes – allowed them to beat other tribes and enslave the docile, farming Guaná, who toiled for their masters and in turn received protection. The Guaná lived their whole lives in submission to the Guaikuru, but it was an easy life: there were no class distinctions between the conquerors and the conquered and they all ate communally.

The Guaikuru resisted conversion and remained masters of the Mato Grosso until the nineteenth century. They were pale, muscular and handsome, and inspired a painting by Debret who showed them valiantly galloping into battle. One could venture the designation 'Empire' for their sphere of influence if they were a bit more together. They tended their horses, bossed around the Guaná, went to war for their chiefs only if they felt like it, and they had sex, sex and more sex in drunken promiscuous feasts. In fact, they had so much sex that their women enraged the missionaries by practising abortion and infanticide – so much for inbred maternal instinct. Almeida Serra reports that *'when the women feel themselves pregnant they immediately abort the foetus with violent little injuries which they practise once or twice a year. This operation makes them look older than they are. It normally leaves them sterile from the age of thirty onwards, which is when they would like to rear children and conceive – something which they rarely succeed in doing.'* The women explained themselves thus to him: *'When we give birth at the end of a pregnancy, it mutilates, deforms and ages us. You men do not want us in that state. Besides, there is nothing more tedious for us than to raise children and take them on our various journeys during which we are often short of food. This is why we decide to arrange an abortion as soon as we feel pregnant for our foetus is smaller then and emerges more easily.'* The solution to the procreation problem was typically bellicose: they raided other tribes, killed the men and stole the children.

As if this wasn't enough, they practised self-scarification to show bravery – in the manner of Richard Harris in *A Man Called Horse* – and they did it publicly for white audiences in Brazil and Paraguay as far as

Asuncion. They skewered the skin on their legs and thighs, every other inch from the wrist to the shoulder, and from the ankle to the loin. They punctured their tongues, letting them bleed into their hands, which they then smeared on their bodies and – take a deep breath – they pierced their genitals and let the blood fall into a hole in the ground which they had dug themselves.

Frankly, after all these customs, it's a wonder any survived to the twenty-first century to produce pottery at all.

*****

At night I waited until it was dark to visit the porn cinema. An old woman was shutting down the box-office grilles.

'*FECHADO!*' she barked at me.

I looked in panic at my watch.

'But ... but it's only nine o'clock,' I managed to utter.

Her reply was a louder than usual clang which I took to mean: 'Don't *you* have cows to milk tomorrow, pervert?'

– 46 –

When the Cruzeiro do Sul bus left town and moved into the red earth of the *cerrado* around Campo Grande, I settled into a comfortable groove. I was going to Bolivia via an arc diversion south to Bonito, close to the Paraguayan border, a rare four-star destination in the *Guia Quatro Rodas*, the equivalent of our *Michelin Guide*.

....

Things I Like About Brazil #10: Guia Quatro Rodas

This is a cross between a map, a Michelin Guide *and a Brazilian Lonely Planet travel book. I own one that contains street maps of all the state capitals and lists almost every single restaurant and hotel of note in all but the smallest Brazilian communities. It comes with a supplement that suggests itineraries with sights rated with stars. Only Rio, Salvador, Petrópolis, Ouro Preto, Olinda, Bonito and Jericoacoara get four; many of the fabulous destinations you read about are considered just three-star by the Brazilians, including Manaus, the Pantanal and Iguaçu.*

....

Paulo, a vet – and Charles Bronson lookalike circa *Death Wish 2* – was sitting next to me; a zebu specialist of 20 years, he was working for the Brazilian Association of Zebu Breeders. He talked incessantly about his life's work, which revolved around *zebuinocultura*, and mad cows.

'You fed them *meat*?' he said disbelievingly as if I had given the order personally.

'I'm a computer programmer,' I complained. 'I *consume* burgers; I don't make them! I'm a potential victim! As far as I know there may be little prions strangling my brain cells as we speak.'

'Mad cow disease could never happen in Brazil,' he said, 'not only because the cattle are reared organically, but also because we breed them in such a way that the animal fights off infections. In fact, we have gone for healthy rather than juicy animals.'

He looked at me carefully and realised I had tasted zebu. I had certainly worn my mandibles on a steak last night.

'We are working on succulence right now,' he added sheepishly. 'Look, there's our latest breed.'

We were passing a field full of animals who were a cross between a zebu and a European cow, which apparently tastes like European beef but is as strong as a zebu. I'll give it the benefit of the doubt. Paulo pointed out the different subspecies, presuming I was interested. 'There's Nelore, Sindi, Gir from India. In Brazil we developed two new races: Tabapuã and Indubrasil.'

So what was Paulo doing in Bonito?

'I will be busy for the next three weeks visiting the *fazendas*,' he answered. 'This is the season to castrate cows.'

Pardon, did he mean steers?

'No, cows.'

As my mind was spinning trying to work out the mechanics, Paulo took out a set of photos which he always had at hand to show how it was done. I looked at them with grim fascination, seeing how he put his Edward Scissorhands-like pliers into a cow's vulva, how he inserted his whole arm up to the shoulder inside the poor animal and cut off her ovaries. He then sewed up the hole. The entire operation took 6 or 7 minutes, and he did about ten cows an hour, which at $7 per op comes to $70 an hour.

'Of course,' he added, 'I only do it for a few weeks at a time during spring. That's why I'm going to Bonito. I'll visit various *fazendas* nearby, many of them small, but some of them vast. There is one that contains more than 50,000 animals and has a small rainforest right through it.'

Fifty thousand times $7 a snip ...

'How come you don't have your own car?' I asked.

He looked down, embarrassed.

'I had an accident six months ago,' he said. 'I – *ahem* – hit a zebu. The car was a write-off.'

Perhaps it was an act of nelore revenge on a suicide mission.

'But why castrate a female zebu?'

'Because when they stop ovulating we feed them with hormones, natural of course, and they develop muscle like a steer. More weight means the cows demand higher prices since they have more meat. Look!'

He showed me the picture of a castrated beefy cow. She looked like a transvestite steer: male in all but her mammaries. She gave new meaning to the words 'bull dyke'.

I stared out of the window.

We were passing an Arcadian-idyllic pastoral scene with scattered zebus munching grass and others resting under trees as far as the eye could see. Zebus like shade; their grazing grounds need a combination of grass and trees. Zebu-breeding does not disrupt the ecology, so they are much more eco-friendly than cows. Now that's a thought for Burger King.

*****

Beyond Anastácio/Aquidana, twin towns situated on either side of Rio Aquidana that live mainly off angling, with every second shop selling live bait, there was a nasty surprise: 60 miles of dirt road, which occasionally looked positively shelled as massive holes created an impression of the Somme, 1917. There we entered the Thick Forest at last, and as the dusk settled in, the bus lights went off. I turned on the spotlight above me and was immediately attacked by a cricket – at least I hope it was a cricket – the size of a medium rodent. Paulo doughtily picked it up and threw it out while I was *hors de combat* with nausea.

> *In thy eye that shall appear*
> *When thou wak'st, it is thy dear.*
> *Wake when some vile thing is near.*

'They aim at the light and either hit the windows and go *splat!*' he said, 'or they land on your lap.' I heard a scream behind me. I turned back with perverse fascination. A black beetle-cum-cockroach immediately jumped into the aisle and disappeared under the feet of panicking Indian families, provoking shouts of 'Lights off!' by their offspring shoehorned in the back row.

John, close your eyes and dream away the time.

Oh dear, I'm descending into lyrical bathos.

With the forest closing on us, the night's swift dragons appeared thicker and more tangible over a moonless skyscape, chaperoned by a multitude of stars whose fey lights were randomly strewn on the astral sphere flickering after their own symphonic music.

John, stop it!

I looked out into imagined contours of trees and bushes where now and again the green eyes of some unidentified nocturnal animal gleamed for a second.

> *And I serve the Fairy Queen,*
> *To dew her orbs upon the green.*
> *The cowslips tall her pensioners be;*
> *In their gold coats spots you see;*

Small sparks with a half-life of a few effulgent seconds lit the woods and led the *pas de deux* from *The Dance of the Sugar Plum Fairy*. The stars came out from their celestial planes and began pirouetting on luminous strings held by an invisible hand to the tune of an inaudible march.

'Fireflies!' I whispered. 'So many of them. So many at once.'

> *Those be rubies, fairy favours,*
> *In those freckles live their savours!*

Spirits of another sort, I reminded myself before I let Titania and Oberon weave their cocoons over me.

> *And pluck the wings from painted butterflies,*
> *To fan the moonbeams from his sleeping eyes.*

Spirits of another sort, indeed. We were entering a battlefield.

*****

In 1865, when the concept of the Third World did not exist, Paraguay was a model country in any type of world you'd care to mention. It had conquered illiteracy as far back as 1840, about thirty years after independence from Spain. It had nationalised large, unproductive estates and employed the poor landless peasants to work them. It was self-sufficient, so it did not care to trade much with Great Britain, which meant it had an independent foreign policy. It did not have any external debt and was free of the yoke of European powers. Its highly spiritual and musically talented Guarani population was heavily into opera and classical music. It was a poke in the eye of the imperialist powers who were keen to proclaim European cultural and business superiority. Here was a successful country with a population of 800,000 (Brazil's population was still only eight million) and a disciplined army of 80,000 men.

Within five years three-quarters of its men would die. Its territory would be divided between Brazil and Argentina in the bloodiest conflict South America has known – a war fought with British capital by proxy in the Paraguayan Chaco, the hills of Rio Grande do Sul and the jungles of Mato Grosso. The Paraguayan War pitted the small republic against Uruguay, Argentina and Brazil. These four countries now form Mercosur, the free trade agreement bloc; as in the EU, their ruling classes realised that wars are fought for economic reasons under national colours. Capital is now transnational and does not need dead bodies – it needs consumers for sports shoes and fizzy drinks.

– 47 –

Although Bonito is just one long street, the *rodoviária* – a Brazilian trick this – was still a long way out. I said goodbye to Paulo, who had so entertained me during the trip, and made my way in the darkness to the Hotel Canaan, a name most apt the way I was feeling. Hotel Canaan was next to a travel agency, and I left a message at reception for them to include me in whatever tour was being organised for the following day.

Next morning, in the breakfast room, the secret of my arrival had leaked out: the owner of the hotel, his matronly wife, eldest son and heir and all the staff had turned out en masse to greet the gringo.

How did I find out about the hotel, asked the owner.

I showed him the pages from my guidebook. ('Look Maria, we're in a guide!')

Did I like Brazil?

Oh yes – this was my second trip.

And was I diabetic?

I looked at my cup. I had asked for coffee without sugar again.

'It's *unhealthy*,' I said. 'Sugar is unhealthy. And so is smoking.'

The hotel owner smiled condescendingly, put four spoonfuls of sugar in his coffee and took a long puff on his cigar. In the Mato Grosso if they have survived puberty they feel immortal.

'The agency has booked you for a day-trip to to a *fazenda*, Água Viva, near Rio Peixe,' he informed me, as he inspected me minutely while I was decadently deseeding the watermelon: real cowboys spit out the pips.

The 20 miles north of Bonito to the *fazenda* Água Viva took us two hours by car: the roads were that bad. The welcome committee consisted of a tame, playful toucan whose big act was to drink water from a plastic bottle by itself. After we greeted the toucan, we greeted the *fazendeiro*, who shook hands cordially with each one of us – and he stayed on to greet two more busloads of students who arrived later. They included a stag party en route to Ponta-Pora, a city divided between Paraguay and Brazil, with casinos and general smut on the Paraguayan side. The *fazenda* would eventually have to provide a buffet for over a hundred people. The queue for the roast zebu alone would be half an hour long. This was a big day in Água Viva. Had the owners lived here for a long time?

Since the Paraguayan War.

*****

Nations are damned by their geography to follow a certain realpolitik, which remains immutable throughout their history – because geography doesn't. Brazil's foreign policy has been to safeguard its two main river systems: the Amazon and the Plata, which is composed of the Paraná, Paraguay and Uruguay tributaries. Until the advent of the aeroplane, it was easier to reach Corumbá and Cuiabá by riverboat than through the jungle. So, when Paraguay threatened to cut off their lifeline, trying to dominate the southern river system, Brazil caught fire.

*****

Bonito is one of the few places in Brazil where you can bathe in a river or a lake without fear of piranhas, crocodilians, constrictor reptiles, leeches or deadly snails that cause schistosomiasis; the various lagoons and waterfalls are the trademark of the region. On the first sight of a *cachoeira* with its crystal clear water, I jumped in. We would eventually swim in no less than five different lagoons.

Did I say swim? We paddled amongst fish that came up fearlessly to our goggles and *pah-pahed* in that stupid mute way fish do. There were *dourados*, a golden-yellow fish as big as a salmon, striped *surubim* and spotty *pintados*, both kinds of catfish. The *fazendeiro*-appointed guide collected more fish by throwing corn in the water. They surrounded us, and we could literally stroke them. It was eerie. Are the fish dumb or do I have to quote poetry again?

Our guide took us up a slippery passage and reached a water hole in the rock about 30 feet above the most transparent emerald water I'd ever seen. There we were offered the option: to either jump into the water and swim underneath the rocks to the waterfall outside or retreat in disgrace.

'I have a camera,' I muttered.

'I will collect all cameras and return them to you later,' answered the guide, barely concealing a grin.

The groom-to-be jumped first, as he obviously had little to lose, and his mates followed. In Brazilian eyes at that moment I represented not only Great Britain, but Europe, Gringodom and civilisation in the Graeco-Judeo-Christian tradition as we know it. So I handed my camera to the guide, closed my eyes, pinched my nose and jumped in.

I did not die.

Then off to the Tarzan jump: you hold on to a pulley which slides on a rope across the banks of a lake – and halfway over you let go and drop in. We queued for this for a long time, but it was worth it. The adults got one try and the school kids three, but as I was a special guest, I elbowed my way forward again. We returned to the *fazenda* for lunch. The four-foot-high termite mounds around us had been stripped of the insects and were used as natural ovens. Hammocks were hung for sleepy bodies to sway in silence; the sun was blazing, the beer was cold and the stag party guys were buying me drinks like I was their best friend they hadn't seen in years. Do you know what it feels like to be in the middle of a hundred happy people? It feels like a rave with no beats.

....

Things I Don't Like About Brazil #10: The Drivers

There were two times when I faced real danger in Brazil, and they both had to do with traffic incidents. There were numerous occasions in the country whose national sporting hero is Ayrton Senna – not Pelé – where I closed my eyes and waited for the worst: trying to steady myself on Rio's buses while the driver sped through Avenida Copacabana as if in control of a hydrofoil; in a São Paolo taxi with a semi-blind driver ('I can't see at night even with glasses.' 'You aren't wearing any glasses.' 'I told you, it makes no difference.') who ignored every red light from the Jardins to Ibirapuera; in Belo Horizonte when in order to reach the Tancredo Neves Airport in time we took a shortcut through a town with speed humps, which we consistently ignored, risking our suspension at best and spine whiplash at worst; in Brasília where the G-forces on those sharp futuristic Niemeyer axial roads nearly threw me out of the open bus door; in the hills of Rio Grande do Sul where bumper-to-bumper car distances seem to be fixed by natural law, fog or no fog; in the town buses of Salvador, whose drivers expect you to jump off while they are still moving, and where I almost twisted my ankle performing such a dangerous manoeuvre.

Mirrors? Indicators? Lights? All pansy accessories imposed by law, and therefore to be avoided at any cost. Speed limits? Dictatorial decrees which every citizen has a duty to ignore. Other drivers? Competitors who must be beaten in the spirit of Ayrton Senna. Brazilians drive drunk, drive fast and even drive asleep. There are only two nationalities in my book who drive worse: the Argentinians (who also don't pay their fines) and, bless them, the French.

....

So here it comes.

On the way out of the *fazenda* we had to open and shut three cattle gates. My driver, sated, sleepy and solar-blinded, was driving fast. I was sitting in the front with him, with two girls asleep in the back. I closed my eyes, but opened them in time to see us about to ram a log gate.

'*CUIDADO!*' I shouted suddenly, as we skidded into the bushes, scattering the frightened cattle, scratching our chassis and denting our bumper. Yes, we provided the year's entertainment for the incredulous zebus grazing nearby: 'They didn't see *that* coming, and they call themselves superior? Superior – my floppy ears!' I didn't know what to reply to them, really.

We drove super-cautiously after that, so every car, including the school coaches, overtook us and made a big thing about it. But remember –

these were dirt roads. When we arrived in Bonito we were so begrimed from the dust of the vehicles in front we were worthy of exhibition in the Museum Dom Bosco as muddy fossils from the Pleistocene.

*****

The leader of Paraguay in the 1860s was Solano López, a dictator steeped in persecution paranoia and a demagogue who was proud of his Guarani Indian blood mixed on one side with the savage Guaikuru. He had travelled to Europe where he had met and brought back from Paris Elisa Lynch, an Irish beauty from Cork who had fled the potato famine to France. Although Lynch was pretty, intelligent, loyal and had borne him five children, she was still unwed because López had dreams of allying himself with European royalty in marriage.

By 1865 Brazil had once more intervened in Uruguay – a buffer state encouraged to independence by Great Britain in order to separate Brazil and Argentina in La Plata and internationalise the estuary – and was engaged in war with Argentina. It was at that moment López struck by capturing the riverboat *Marquês de Olinda* heading for Cuiabá. He then invaded Mato Grosso here, near Bonito, and marched through the Argentinian panhandle of Missiones to attack Rio Grande do Sul. This latter incursion was fatal for the dictator, because yesterday's three combatant countries turned against him, forming the Triple Alliance. Crucially, Great Britain, who wanted to keep the Plata system free for trade, gave the Alliance unlimited credit. Like the Great War in Europe in 1914, it should have been over in three months.

It lasted for five whole years, as the Guarani chose to die rather than surrender, with children as young as ten taking up arms. More than a century later, it is still the bloodiest conflict ever to have emerged in the Americas, as López brought his mistress, his family and his country down with him in an act worthy of a Wagnerian *Götterdämmerung*. There were battles to uphold any military historian's interest: Laguna, Brazil's Dunkirk; Riachuelo, the riverine equivalent of the Battle of Midway; Umaitá, a horrific combination of Normandy and a tropical Stalingrad. The war brought to the world barbed wire, the first torpedo – launched by Paraguayan boats to utilise the flow of the river – and the first armoured vehicle: a locomotive, which, although limited in function, was a precursor of the tank. It created heroes whose names can be seen in streets and squares all over Brazil: General Osório and the Duque de

Caxias. But it also shook the Army from its blind obedience to the landed aristocracy and its interests: Brazil's National Guard was needed to maintain order in the interior because the landowners were afraid that without its protection a slave revolt might erupt. So the foot-soldier volunteers who won the war were black slaves sent by the oligarchy instead of their sons, with the promise of emancipation should they come back alive; the cannon fodder were poor *sertanejos* from Pernambuco and Bahia who felt deeply for the glory of their country. How could soldiers who had fought shoulder-to-shoulder with their black and mulatto brothers return to hunt their runaway cousins to be punished on the whipping post? Who had the interests of Brazil at heart? Those who made money out of its land, or those who shed their blood to defend it?

No, oh no, there was only one institution that would uphold the integrity and honour of the country: the Army would never be fooled again. From then on, the generals would take up the saviour's mantle: sometimes in modernising colours, sometimes in totalitarian, illiberal shades of red and black; sometimes nudging gently behind the scenes, sometimes assuming power overtly – but always, ever always, *in charge*.

– 48 –

I woke up at the crack of dawn – and what a crack it was: the heavens had opened their bladders for a torrential micturition upon us mortals and, matching the car park, my heart was flooded with thoughts of '*Dammit, wrong season*'. I went back to sleep, where I wouldn't worry.

A phone call from the travel agency woke me up.

'Would you like to join two guys who are going to the Gruta do Lago Azul?'

I looked out. The rain had stopped.

'OK,' I said. I dressed quickly and slouched on a sofa at reception.

'You were supposed to have eaten your breakfast by nine,' the matron told me off.

I looked at my watch. It was half-past ten. 'Erm, that's OK,' I replied dizzily.

'But the staff are waiting for you in the dining room.'

'That's OK,' I repeated. 'I'm being picked up in a few minutes.'

'The staff won't go home until you've had your breakfast!' she said in a voice that had never accepted dissent.

That made me feel guilty, so I had a quick coffee. The Indian waiters stared at me while I drank it neat with no sugar. I suppose to them this was masochism as entertaining as a Guaikuru piercing ceremony.

When I finished I met Zé & Zé, an odd couple in their mid-fifties: a short, talkative, lively one, and a tall, silent, grumpy one. They had a few days off and drove in one go for more than six hundred miles from São Paulo to come to Bonito to fish ('Away from our wives').

'All alone Zé,' said Little Zé, the Jack Lemmon of the two. 'He's come here all alone. Going off to Bolivia after that. Amazing.'

'I've never been to Bolivia,' said Big Zé, a grumpy Walter Matthau. 'I've been to Paraguay.'

'That was the time when we went to Iguaçu,' explained Little Zé.

'With our wives,' said Big Zé, his face in a snarl.

'They bought the whole Ciudad del Este,' said Little Zé.

'All crap stuff,' scoffed Big Zé.

'But cheap crap stuff,' continued Little Zé, involuntarily providing a slight clue about the interdependence of the Mercosur economies. 'The car was so loaded we had to drive back to São Paulo with ceiling fans between our legs. Have you been to Iguaçu?'

I nodded yes, during my first trip to Brazil. And to the Ciudad del Este, a Guarani bazaar town across the Rio Paraná. 'But I didn't buy anything,' I added.

Little Zé's eyes opened wide as he turned to Big Zé.

'He didn't buy anything, Zé! Did you hear that?'

And then admiringly to me: 'Amazing.'

*****

The Grotto of the Blue Lake is Bonito's famous sight. It was only discovered in 1923 by the Terena Indians and is the most spectacular of the 500-odd caves in the area. After a hair-raising, precipitous 300-foot descent, the floor evened out and we encountered the brilliant underground Lago Azul.

Our guide explained: 'The colour is blue because it contains rare, photosensitive algae. In fact the ecosystem' – which, I found out later, also contains an albino shrimp – 'is so fragile, you should not even touch the lake with your hands. Grease might kill those organisms.'

I'd heard this was not the only underground lake in the region.

'The other underground lake at Nossa Senhora Aparecida is closed, because excessive tourism caused irreversible rock collapse.'

And this one?

'This one's safe. It's the largest and the passage down is wide.'

We all posed for pictures by the lakeside.

'An expedition in the early nineties found some prehistoric vases and the remains of a sabre-toothed tiger and a giant sloth from ten million years ago.'

Out of the corner of my eye, I spotted a schoolgirl who wanted to frame the stalactites, the lake and all of us together. She was leaning so far forward that –

SPLASH!

We watched with dread as the compact camera disappeared into the lake. Poor delicate algae rest in peace; I'm glad I caught the *lago* while it was still *azul*.

The girl glanced at the guide, expecting to be handcuffed and whipped on the local *pelourinho*. We held our breath. The guide turned to us and cleared his throat.

'The Lago Azul is ninety metres deep,' he continued.

We all breathed out, relieved.

*****

'Do you like fishing, John?' asked Little Zé.

I told them that my only attempt at fishing piranha in the Amazon came to a grand null.

'We have some very different fish here in the Mato Grosso,' said Little Zé.

'I know, I swam with them in the Rio Peixe yesterday,' I said.

'The best way to learn about fish is to try and catch them,' said Little Zé.

'No,' said Big Zé. 'The best way to learn about fish is to *eat* them.'

According to that, I'm now an expert.

The largest fish in the waters of the Paraguay is the *jaú* – a 3-foot-long catfish, although if I believe Zé & Zé, we are dealing with a medium-sized dolphin. In the taste stakes, it's in competition with the *dourado*, a salmon-like species. This is the one I swam with in Bonito's lagoons for it is only there, where it is protected, that you can approach and even touch its golden-orange scales. The *pintado* is another 3-foot-long catfish, but much more graceful and photogenic than the *jaú*: it is olive-green with a white belly and has black dots and white-tipped stripes on its skin, hence its name, the 'painted' fish. Gourmets go for the nocturnal slippery red and yellow *jurupoca*, which is covered in a slimy mucous – now that is a fish I would like to catch, because I'm told that, when captured, it emits a deep, pathetic howl from its gills as it attempts to breathe outside the water. The *piraputanga* is another oddity. In Bonito you can actually see it swimming below tree branches where monkeys eat berries, waiting for fruit to drop off – which they immediately devour. Call me pedantic, but that would mean not only that the *piraputanga* can see outside the water and that they have a concept of a greedy, clumsy monkey, but also that they can calculate air-water refraction indices and accurately estimate where the berries will fall. If anything can freak me out more than a roaring fish, it's a smart, academic snapper. The *piraputanga* is so clever it actually participates during a piranha attack on some animal or other and manages to escape not only intact, but also full as well.

Ah, the voracious piranha! Might as well talk about it now. It has a terrible reputation, which is thoroughly deserved: a shoal can devour a small animal in less than two minutes. As someone who has a full-blown stuffed specimen on his mantelpiece, I feel uniquely qualified to comment. Visitors are grossed out by its dentition and its fearsome demeanour, enhanced by two evil yellow false eyes. Mine is a red piranha which means it's mackerel-yellow except the belly, which appears crimson, pushing the right buttons for subliminal recollections of blood. But it's the *teeth* that scare. They are bared upwards from the protruding lower jaw like a bulldog's and they are long, sharp and grotesque, out of proportion to its short, flat, square body, not much bigger than a hand. Like the shark, it inspires primitive gut reactions of being eaten alive in an environment we are not in control of. But is such fear justified?

The piranha is one of the most common fishes in the rivers of South America – yet reported attacks on people are very rare. Like sharks, they need to smell blood to get in a feeding frenzy, and then they are highly territorial: if you don't swim in a piranha area – and all the locals know where these are – you only have the rest of the nasties in the water to fear. Even then, you can still swim in an infested area if you do a gentle breast-stroke that doesn't violently agitate the surface like, say, crawl. As a rule, piranhas avoid shallow stretches or where there are crocodiles and, since most South American *jacaré* avoid man or large mammals, you are more than safe with them. The piranha are more likely to bite your thumb as you take them off the fishing hook.

The piranha, though, is not the only carnivorous piscean predator of Brazil – it's just the most famous. The *traíra*, with teeth as sharp and big as a small canine, is equally fierce, but it hunts alone, like a lamprey, hidden within the vegetation. And it is the *traíra* that wins the JohnM yummy prize for Best Meal Accompanied with Chips.

After dinner the two Zés and I drank a few Antárticas.

'Those roads!' I lamented. 'Bonito is one of the great tourist places in Brazil and still they haven't fixed them.'

'Corruption,' barked Big Zé.

'The military,' replied Little Zé. 'They came in to fight corruption in 1964 and when they left it was worse.'

'If it's not São Paulo, Rio or Minas it doesn't count,' continued Big Zé.

'I mean, Chile had Pinochet, and he was far, far worse than our generals, but at least he didn't steal so much,' chipped in Little Zé, following his own thread.

'And that Collor, the scoundrel, just stole and stole,' said Big Zé.

'What I can't understand,' I said, 'is how a country with so much corruption, unable to tarmac the road to one of its leading resorts, can peg its currency to the dollar at one to one. Last time I was here, there was terrible inflation and the country was cheap. Now, I'm looking forward to entering Bolivia. I've overshot my budget.'

Zé & Zé looked at me silently.

'When did you last change money?' asked Little Zé.

'A week ago in São Paulo. Here I've been paying by credit card. Why?'

'It's not one to one any more,' said Big Zé triumphantly.

Really?

'There is a crisis in South-East Asia, and there is turmoil all over the world's stock exchanges,' continued Big Zé.

Really?

'São Paulo Exchange has crashed and interest rates have gone up to forty per cent,' Big Zé was radiant as he bellowed the bad news.

Really?

'Which means the currency has been hit. No business can withstand such high interest rates.'

I imagined the TV talking heads in London reporting crashes with graphs and curves, providing ponderous explanations and predicting chaos and panic. Here, in the middle of the Mato Grosso, one could get a proper perspective: financial markets are not real. Trees are real.

That was the end of the big Real Plan and it happened while I was in Bonito. Within four years, when I returned for the Rio *Carnaval*, the currency had lost 50 per cent of its value. Nevertheless, this market-determined rate seemed to reflect Brazil's true economic status – it only affected its growth short-term and, most importantly, inflation did not defy gravity again.

– 49 –

Although Brazil won the Paraguayan War – and it was Brazil that had borne the brunt – it was a Pyrrhic victory. Slavocracy and Empire had been fatally wounded. The Army had begun to flex its muscle. Abroad, its image had been tarnished with details of atrocities. But more importantly, it had shattered its self-image. This was no European empire in the tropics administered by superior white men ruling over darker-skinned inferiors; no Australia, South Africa or even India: instead it had become something that historians did not yet have a reference for. What it was, Brazilians would have to figure out themselves, starting there and then.

The Guaná vigorously defended their territory near Miranda in guerrilla groups against the invading troops; this gave them a moral right to their land that even the hooves of encroaching cattle herds could not wipe out completely: many soldiers decamped in the Mato Grosso to stay and populate those boundary lands after an official westward settlement policy was instated for obvious defensive reasons. The Guaikuru protected fleeing soldiers from that first wave of invasion, and most notably escorted a party on their horses hundreds of miles upstream to Cuiabá. Soon they started raiding Guarani Paraguayans across the frontier themselves, which endeared them to Rio's chattering classes. John Hemming reports that even Dom Pedro himself asked about the welfare of the Guaikuru and '*when informed that they were suffering the usual privations from* fazendeiros *he granted them the land they still possess on the Serra da Bodoquena.*'

In fact that road to the Serra da Bodoquena looked as if it had been dug by the Guaná on assignment for the Guaikuru and never maintained since. The storm had reduced it further to a grand puddle, a reminder of why the riverboat has always been the preferred transport in the region. The rainy season can still cut off communities in the Mato Grosso, including Bonito itself. From Miranda onwards, a town on the river of the same name, we joined the highway at last. It is here that the road enters the Pantanal proper: 60-odd miles of flowering water lilies, *aguapé*, adorning the route. Swamps enclose both sides of the road with the creeping jungle trying to reclaim its paved parts.

I have seen many shake their heads when I rave about the Pantanal, the largest swampland of the planet – understandably, because swamps have had bad press; in Europe they were the fetid, unsanitary prime breeding grounds for mosquitoes, and their drainage went hand-in-hand with the eradication of contagious, insect-borne diseases. The Pantanal has its fair share of ticks, sandflies and mosquitoes and suffers from *falciparum* malaria, it's true, but the waters are not dirty and stagnant: there is a constant flow between lagoons, small lakes and streams, which keeps the area much cleaner-looking than your average European waterway. Furthermore, its great asset is the accessibility of animal life. Unlike its more famous cousin, the Amazon, the Pantanal has no thick, impenetrable rainforest for the fauna to hide in. There are reeds, bushes and woods, but they are not as dense and dark as the Amazon; it's a wetter version of the pellucid South African game reserves.

The Brazilians themselves were unacquainted with the beauty of the area until a popular telenovela in 1990, imaginatively called *Pantanal*, photographed it spectacularly and transmitted its pell-mell, yet demulcent elegance. It was set in the Fazenda Rio Negro, which is doing good business now, situated at the edge of the Pantanal. The *fazenda* is owned by the famous old Portuguese aristocratic Rondon family, who bred one of the great names in Brazilian exploration: that of Cândido Rondon, upon whom the title of Marshall was bestowed a few years before he died. He is better known abroad as the Brazilian who accompanied Theodore Roosevelt on his Amazon trip of 1913/14, but in Brazil he is famous as the man who spread the telegraph line to the borders of the Mato Grosso, came into contact with newly discovered tribes such as the hostile Nambikwara, and became a champion of native Indian rights in Brazil as head of its first Indian Protection Service back in 1910. When Rondon's telegraph line reached Miranda, he came into contact with the Terena Indians who were being threatened to extinction by the sprouting cattle ranches. He gathered them together, offered them protection and was instrumental in obtaining guarantees for enough land so that they could continue to live in their traditional ways. They owe him their survival, no less than the Schindler's list descendants in Israel owe Oscar Schindler theirs.

*****

We crossed the Rio Paraguay by ferry at Porto Esperança, one of the widest areas of the river: the crossing took about half an hour. I bought three *esfihas* (meat pies) from the bar, quaffed beer to last me for the night and took pictures of the noisy children dipping in and out of the water next to huts built on stilts to withstand flooding. On the north side of the Pantanal is the geodesic centre of South America; this is as far from the ocean as it gets, and you can still reach it by boat.

Hey!

I forgot the whys and wherefores, and my body shot upwards like a Guaikuru lance. That was a *jacaré* by the roadside; and that beautiful white bird with the black head and red spot on its neck, spanning its wings, was a *jabiru* stork with its tell-tale Anglepoise-lamp silhouette.

Where am I?

I looked at my map and traced the contours with my index finger – ah, lost somewhere in that green mass called Mato Grosso. But oh, no, this was home. Anywhere here is home. If you don't care where you are, you ain't lost.

I watched the *jabiru* stork fly away serenely.

To urbanised Westerners, gadget-crazy and isolated from the natural world, any contact with Nature, however feeble, sends them into paroxysms of superlatives. *'If there is a Garden of Eden, it can't be far away from here,'* said Amerigo, and that was 500 years ago. Centuries later, there's some godliness still left, which affects everyone who comes into contact with it. From the silly tourist who pathetically quotes *A Midsummer Night's Dream* as he first enters the forest, to explorers like Rondon who built their lives around this physical world rather than chase digits on paper; from the silent fishermen on the Rio Miranda to the rowdy stag parties who swim Bonito's lagoons and talk to the fish eyeball to eyeball; from the cinematographers who so lovingly portray its beauty in telenovelas, to the haughty Guaikuru: we all come from that place where no one ever goes, and, like adopted teenagers looking for their natural parents, we all crave to return to it.

If only we could find the key.

Chapter 11

The Macaw and the Anteater (Pantanal)

A long time ago people lived without fire.

A jaguar was strolling in the jungle and found a boy stealing a macaw's baby hatchlings perched on a ledge. He growled at the boy and paced patiently underneath. The Xavante boy started throwing the baby macaws to the jaguar to placate him.

With the stomach full, the jaguar's attention turned to the boy.

'How did you get up there?' he asked.

The boy showed him a log which he had used to climb up but had subsequently fallen off. The jaguar realised that the boy was stranded and moved the log back in place.

'Water,' asked the boy, half-dead when he came down; he was weak and thirsty.

The jaguar carried the boy to a stream where he let him drink and then to his house to nourish him with some food. The jaguar's wife was cooking wild pig meat.

The boy looked at the burning embers.

This was the first time a Xavante had seen fire.

....

The Words You'll Need

armazém = *bulk grocery store*
assado = *roast*
bravo = *a false friend this: fierce, wild – not brave*
caldo = *stew*
cogumelos = *mushrooms*
cojones (Spanish) = *balls*
cruceño (Spanish) = *inhabitant of Santa Cruz, Bolivia*
lagartixa = *lizard*
ordem e progresso = *order and progress*
paceño (Spanish) = *inhabitant of La Paz, Bolivia*
patriotaki (Greek) = *means 'compatriot', used in the sense of 'homeboy'*
tênis = *sneakers/trainers when referring to clothing*

....

Corumbá is not only the ultimate frontier town on the Paraguay River, facing Bolivia at the edge of the Brazilian Pantanal. It has created a meaning as a word in its own right: it is a Timbuktu without the exoticism. The *Novo Aurélio* dictionary defines the word as 'distant and forsaken'; a well-known novel *Os Corumbás* by Amando Fontes, school material in Brazil, has been aptly translated into English as *The Forgotten*. Yet this was South America's largest riverport in the early nineteenth century, where gold was transported from the auriferous veins of Cuiabá. The grand, empty mansions by the river stand as a jerky reminder of the cruelty of economic cycles. Today Corumbá is a town with a large military presence, whose population dabbles in contraband and border smuggling with a police force to match.

Corumbá alerted me to its status when a taxi driver ripped me off upon arrival: ten reais with no meter to drive me from the bus station to Hotel Alfa, only eight blocks away; I gave him half that and sent him to hell. At Hotel Alfa, the price was 20 reais for a dirty, airless and windowless, well, *cell*. With Manaus cockroach memories still resonant, I escaped next door to Hotel Premier. Full. Next door, the Hotel Santa Monica: full. Exactly *how* forgotten was this place?

As the Santa Monica porter explained, that October weekend was a big one for the town; it was hosting an annual fishing competition and all cheap-to-medium hotels were full. It was 9 p.m. in a new town, Corumbá was getting deserted, and this was not the time to go checking out the wild side with my backpack. On the porter's recommendation, I walked to the Hotel International and blew my budget on a huge room with a minibar, laundry facilities, a TV and very importantly, air-con. But I didn't stay long to enjoy it: I dashed out immediately to Gil's Tours on Rua Delamar, a street saturated with the rancid smell of cheapo hostels. It brought a whiff of longing: maybe I should have looked around here.

The tour offices were closed when I arrived. *Damn!*

A woman's shadow accosted me. That's what I needed now – to be propositioned.

'Are you looking for Gil's Tours?' she asked in English.

That startled me. 'I am, actually.'

'I was looking at you. I thought you were a backpacker, but you are wearing the wrong shoes, and I was confused.'

I glanced at my feet. She was expecting trainers, but I was wearing my black Doc Martens. More so in Spanish America than Brazil, black leather shoes rather than *tênis* will let you into any club or restaurant at night.

'Well, I'm John, and I'm not a backpacker,' I jested. 'Too old for that. I call myself a traveller. It's grander.'

'I'm Claudia. I work for Gil's Tours,' she said. 'I just locked up the office, but I'll open it for you if you want.'

Bingo!

'We have recommendations in various languages,' said Claudia, once inside.

I thumbed through albums of pictures of young, smiling people swimming with crocodiles; pictures of young, smiling people on hammocks. They could have been stills from an R.E.M video.

'Let me explain,' she said. 'We have a permanent camp in the jungle, and every day a truck drives to the camp with new guests and provisions. There are two guests going tomorrow. The standard package is three days, two nights for $90, treks, accommodation and three meals a day included. Each day afterwards is $10.'

'I'm convinced,' I declared quickly as I needed dinner. Three days would be enough: I paid and signed the forms.

When Claudia read my surname and found out my origin, she jumped.

'We don't have a recommendation in Greek,' she said. 'Will you write one for us?'

'Can it wait until after the tour?' I suggested politely.

'Of course, of course. We have a Greek friend,' she said. 'Stavros, the manager of Hotel Paris. He'll be thrilled to meet you.'

'OK, fine, cool,' I said.

'We'll pick you up at your hotel. Which one is it?'

'Hotel International.'

Her eyes widened. 'You are staying at Hotel International?' she asked me with disbelief.

'I couldn't find a room,' I said sheepishly. 'The fishing festival.'

'Hotel Paris has rooms,' she informed me. 'It always does.'

*****

Next morning, at 7.00 sharp, I jumped onto the back of the truck, and we were off to Hotel Paris. There I met Katje, a Swiss German personnel consultant from Basle, who had been travelling alone since Guatemala. She looked like … looked like …

'Has anyone told you, you look like Sigourney Weaver?' I asked her.

She laughed: 'Before this trip no one had told me that, but since I started, you are the third so far.'

'Maybe travelling solo has brought out a new, strong-willed dimension in your character,' I ventured, 'like Sigourney blasting the aliens.'

Katje decided to chortle, so I was safe.

My other companion was Froude, a Norwegian electrician from Trondheim. He was typically Viking-looking: tall, trim, blond, blue-eyed. He was on a trip-around-the-world-but-not-quite.

'What do you mean?'

'My ticket takes me from Europe to South America and then to Africa, but then I return to Norway so I never quite circle the globe,' he said somewhat despondently.

'More like an ellipse-round-the-world,' I said.

'You got it.'

Well, still in the great conics category.

'Are you two together?' I asked.

They looked embarrassed. Oh, I'd hit on something there.

'No, we met yesterday,' said Katje. 'We both arrived by plane from Santa Cruz. Claudia was hanging around at the airport touting for clients.'

Claudia emerged from behind reception with a short and shifty-eyed guy.

'There he is,' she pointed at me. 'John, meet Stavros.'

Stavros was stereotypically swarthy and moustachioed.

'*Patriotaki!*' he cried in Greek. I shook his hand, taking a step back, which he ignored as he pulled me forward and embraced me forcefully. 'Why did you not sleep here yesterday?'

'Arrived too late.'

Stavros was up in arms. Where was my luggage? I was not to return to the Hotel International.

'I'll have your stuff picked up and store it here.'

'No way,' I said. 'You don't even know what it looks like. The hotel won't give it to you.'

'If you give me a letter …'

'*Stavros,*' I said. 'Enough!'

'OK, OK. I expect you to return here, where I can cook you some moussaka.'

The question was scalding my tongue. What was he doing in Corumbá?

He cocked his body upwards with pride.

'Do you know of the Koskotas case?' he asked me.

He was referring to the Bank of Crete corruption scandal which brought down the Papandreou government in the early 1990s and led to the Greek prime minister's arrest and subsequent trial (he was acquitted).

'Well,' he winked at me. 'I slipped away before they could deliver the warrant.'

'You were involved?'

'Brazil does not have extradition treaties with many countries,' he winked again.

I thought of Ronnie Biggs.

'But – but, *here?*'

'I've been in Corumbá three years now. I like it here; it's my kinda town, full of swindlers,' he said. 'Can you lend me two dollars for cigarettes?'

– 51 –

We drove onto the Estrada Parque, the road that runs 75 miles into the Pantanal from Miranda; until the 1980s it was still the only way to reach Corumbá. This is the original passage opened by Rondon, and with no less than 87 wooden bridges over ponds and brooks it is extremely picturesque. For many tourists this is their only excursion into the Pantanal, and for a day-trip it's quite exciting. As if we needed reminding, 20 minutes into the Estrada the truck pulled up sharply by the road.

'*SUCURI!*' cried the driver.

'ANACONDA!' exclaimed Froude in quasi-unison, providing us with a spontaneous translation.

Our long-haired hippy guide jumped out and ran after the serpent, which tried to get away as fast as it could wriggle. He grabbed it by the tail and pulled it back as it was stretching to escape. It was a yellow anaconda, tiny at under 7 feet long.

'Photos?' he asked, offering Froude the snake.

Oh.

When my derring-do turn came, the snake started writhing around my neck.

'Don't hold it so hard, you'll choke it,' said the guide.

I had assumed you were supposed to grip it hard and wrestle it, but no, holding the anaconda's head and tail gently is all you need to do. The snake surrendered, frightened, and its prehensile, powerful body lay on my shoulders in defeat. What surprised me even more was its touch. I had expected something wet, cold and slimy, but the snake was warm and dry, like me.

'It was standing in the sun,' offered our guide as an explanation.

After a while we stopped to watch an otters' nest with binoculars. The giant otter can weigh up to five and a half stone, and reaches up to 4.5 feet in length, the size of a small, aggressive teenager with sharp teeth. The nest we were observing from a safe distance consisted of five adults swimming on their backs and diving around a strangler fig-tree wrapped around an *acuri* palm like the body of an anaconda.

Like the piranha, tales about the anaconda are exaggerated: firstly its length can only reach about 25 or 30 feet (which is still bloody long!) No, it cannot swallow a cow. It mainly feeds on aquatic birds and mammals, fish and other serpents. The big spectacle in the Pantanal is a struggle between a crocodile and an anaconda. They are evenly matched, and the outcome depends on whether or not the crocodile can snap the anaconda's back quickly with its strong, powerful jaws.

Froude spotted our first crocodile. The correct name is cayman, a crocodilian by order, with the species name *caiman crocodilus yacare*, or *jacaré* in Brazilian Portuguese. They are so common in the Pantanal – all 32 million of them – we became immune to their presence after a while. These caymans, especially the spectacled ones, which have a yellow circle around their eyes, are beautiful animals that can reach 8 feet in length and, unlike their African cousins, they are harmless.

Which species were the most dangerous then?

'The *ariranha* – the giant otter,' said our guide. 'It can rip you apart with its claws, if you but approach its nest. The giant macaw, *arara*, whose beak can crack a skull, and the peccary – the wild pig – which gores you if you're not quick enough to climb up a tree.'

'The way to stop a charging peccary,' said Katje, 'is to run towards a river, grab its head, dip it in the water, and hold it there.'

We all looked at her in astonishment.

'You cannot be serious,' I said in my best John McEnroe arguing voice. 'Grab its head and hold it under water? What are we dealing with? A kitten?'

'I didn't say it was easy,' Katje replied.

We were about to continue quibbling, but the driver stopped.

'BAMBI!' he shouted and pointed at a marsh deer, *veado*. Deer are an endangered species in the Pantanal – they catch diseases from cattle and are dying off.

'Note that he didn't shout *veado*,' said the guide, laughing. Some of us got the joke: *veado* is also Brazilian slang for a homosexual.

The funny thing is that there was a town called Veado in the state of Espirito Santo. No surprise then that the population decided to change the name to Siqueira Campos after the Brazilian lieutenant hero of the Copacabana Fort rebellion. But that's where the problem started. To make sure a letter reached its destination, the senders wrote on the address: 'Siqueira Campos – ex Veado' akin to someone posting an envelope addressed to, say, 'Winston Churchill, ex-faggot.' The authorities took a dim view of this so they renamed it again – to Guaçui, the Tupi term for the marsh deer, which should be suitably obscure.

....

Months passed and the boy fattened up.

'Are you tired of being here?' asked the jaguar.

'Yes,' said the boy. 'I want to go.'

The jaguar cooked some wild pig meat to take with him.

'When you go away you will lie about me,' said the jaguar. 'If they ask you about the cooked meat, you will say I used a hot flat rock. Because if you tell them about the fire, I will become man's enemy.'

Then the jaguar painted up the boy to make him look impressive and wove a large basket for him to carry his food.

But the boy put a spent charcoal back into the basket as he left.

....

Any description of the Pantanal cannot be complete without reference to the birdlife, which in itself is worth a chapter, for this is a birdwatcher's Elysium. The omnipresent *jabiru* stork, 8 feet of wingspan, resplendent in a white body, black neck and with a red spot on its collar, has become the symbol of the region. You can see them wading in pairs, for they mate for life despite their habit of cooling their legs by urinating down their sides; if you can stand that in your partner, it must be love.

There are numerous rheas, relatives of the Australian emu and the African ostrich, one of the three bird species that can't fly in South America – the others being the penguin and the propeller duck, which you can encounter in Patagonia. The rhea can reach an astonishing 37 miles an hour when running and is the bird upon which the Warner Brothers cartoon character of Road Runner ('Beep-Beep!') was based – the one who wreaks havoc upon the coyote. When you next laugh with

Road Runner, consider that it is the most ancient bird on the American continent; fossils have been found dated to 55 million years ago. There are kingfishers of various colours, green lovebird budgies (*caturrittas*), which not only pair for life but seem to constantly hug each other even in mid-flight, macaws, the red-and-green and blue-and-yellow varieties being the most common, woodpeckers, white egrets threatened with extinction, hunted as they are for their plumage, and finally a strange gallinaceous bird with a white head and large red legs: the *anhuma*. This last one is popularly called the 'police of the Pantanal', because it starts crowing when it sees danger, informing the rest of the animals in the vicinity. We kept hearing their squawks before we detected them; they were snitching on us.

'*Caracará*.' Our guide pointed at the red-headed falcon-like raptor walking awkwardly at the edge of the road. 'It's looking for animals that have been run over.'

This is a special bird of prey: the *caracará* is revered by the Guaikuru; in their legends they consider it as their common ancestor. It is from the *caracará*'s eggs that the first humans hatched in the jungle. If you consider this far-fetched, another tribe of the Northern Pantanal, the Paiaguá, thought they were descended from the *pacu* fish. Common theology amongst the Indian tribes of the centre of Brazil rejects the species uniqueness we aspire to in the West; instead there is a recognition that humans are only one of the animals hunting and being hunted – with a difference: a benign forest spirit has acceded to the ascendancy of Man and granted him the right of dominion over the forest world. We are only here as first among equals – and that is a concession.

*****

After almost four hours' drive we reached our lakeside camp. We met up with the staff: the cook who also hunted for food, the boss who was the famous (according to the Brazil Bradt guide) Johnny Indiano and his German girlfriend Sabine, the real leader of the camp. There was Fernão, an older local guide with plenty of hair but very few teeth, and César, a 22-year-old jack of all trades. Johnny, Fernão and César were all native Terena; none had been outside Mato Grosso in their lives.

Most of the other guests were leaving. The ones who were staying were an Italian and a Welsh couple on their way to Bonito. They had been travelling since the beginning of the year in South America and were only shaving Brazil, so to speak, at the Pantanal.

'We have to be in Asuncion for a wedding,' the Welsh guy said to me. 'One of our friends is marrying a Paraguayan girl.'

A Celtic-Guarani cross-breeding – good gene combination. Will milk or bulk predominate?

John, you're still under Paulo's zebu spell.

But it is those exchanges of genes that have progressed our species – not?

You shouldn't talk like that about people!

Why?

Because we're different, that's why.

Or so we'd like to think.

I forgot dark, handsome, broody Alfredo, a Catalan from Valencia ('Don't ever call me Spanish!') already in his sixth day in the camp.

'Where else would I find a place to live for ten dollars a day?'

'Don't you get bored?' I asked. 'How long do you have on holiday?'

He shook his head. 'Who wants to return to Spain?'

'Don't you have to work?'

He looked up.

'Who wants to work?'

I stopped short before I asked him if he had a girlfriend.

As Froude was planning on leaving next day, Johnny tried to arrange for me and him to share a one-man tent; we looked inside, at each other and both said 'No way!' Froude was good-looking, and we had kind of clicked, but the only way two big guys like us could share that tent is if we passed the night permanently entangled in coitus, which by necessity would have to be *uninterruptus*. So I ended up with the leaky tent and a mosquito net with a gaping hole, which, I suppose, makes it an ex-mosquito net. Or is it a mosquito ex-net? Forget it – I changed and dived in the lake with Froude, Katje and Sabine.

My eye intercepted a ripple below the *aguapé* on my left. I saw a cayman hiding below the foliage, his yellow-spectacled eyes focused on mine.

'*Jacaré!*' I exclaimed. 'There are *jacaré* in the lake.'

'Pfff, they won't harm us,' said Sabine dismissively. 'Look.'

She swam swiftly towards the crocodile which immediately disappeared below the water.

'See? They don't attack humans. They're afraid.'

The Pantanal caymans only eat fish and small animals and are terrified of humans with good reason. In the 1980s an estimated 5 million were killed for their skin, which was exported to the West. In 1991 a co-operative of crocodile farmers was created in Cáceres with a farming capacity of 100,000 reptiles per annum. The fact that the skin of animals bred in captivity is superior to that of those in the wild because of the healthier environment seems to have halted the illegal hunting and created the present cayman population explosion.

A bell sounded. Lunch was ready. Food at the camp was good but basic as the pattern repeated itself over the three days: a buffet of veg, tough meat, coffee, rice, beans and fruit. We also fed the crocodiles – our pets – with piranhas caught during the day. Froude was delighted with how timid the crocodiles were and his favourite pastime was to run at the ones lying on the beach and scare them into diving. Only once did he come across a large crocodile who seemed unafraid, so he threw a stick at him. The roar of disapproval from the rest of us was so loud, he stopped his sport at once.

By mid-afternoon the howler monkeys on the opposite bank of the lake started living up to their name. I should insert here gratuitously that by the third day, I'd won first prize in the howler monkey imitation contest. I'm really proud of that. But back to now and our camp saying: *'When the howler monkeys howl, it's going to piss down with rain.'*

A storm reached us within minutes; very abrupt, very thundery and very hard. It was pouring out of the sky in buckets, and the camp was quickly in danger of flooding. My tent was on the border of our terraced shelter concocted out of palm fronds. We started desperately digging a moat. After a frantic twenty minutes the storm stopped as suddenly as it had started, and the sun came out even more scorching than before. Half an hour later the earth was dry again.

After the shock thunderstorm, we deserved a fiesta. César, Froude, Katje and I would take a boat and trek to the nearest off-licence, an hour away at the next *fazenda* along. I had a secret agenda: I wanted to use the toilet. The camp lavatory was an outhouse some 50 feet further out where you had to squat over a hole drilled in a wooden floor. If you looked down what can only be termed a shithole, you saw a wriggling mass of brown maggots in a feeding frenzy: hey, we could have provided live bait for the whole of Mato Grosso during the fishing season. Eco-tourism nowadays tends to signify 'We have no facilities' but none can be as disgusting as the view down our khazi in the Pantanal; it was worse than the muddy piss-pond outside the men's loos at the Reading Festival.

So I squirted my stuff in the forest, much to the chagrin of Sabine who kept fulminating: 'Use the toilets provided, and don't soil the surrounding area. We don't want to be surrounded by shit!'

Oh, shut your face, then …

………………………………………………………………………………………………

When the boy returned to his village, he found his family had all shaved their heads in mourning because they thought he was dead. When he arrived, they all wailed for him and he distributed the wild pig meat to everyone.

They all marvelled at the cooking.

'How was this meat cooked?' a relative asked.

'On a hot flat rock,' said the boy.

At that point one of his relatives saw the piece of charcoal that the boy had placed in the head of the cooked wild pig.

'So what is this?' asked the relative.

The boy knew that he had to tell the truth. He named the black rock 'charcoal'.

And he named the jaguar's precious secret 'fire'.

………………………………………………………………………………………………

When we arrived at the *fazenda*'s *armazém* we were sweaty, thirsty and tired, so we ordered beers at once. Froude and César only had eyes for Katje. I observed with much interest our species' male sexual response: how both took turns to refill her glass; how they were in competition to laugh first at her jokes; how they quivered if she but tilted her head in their direction; how they sophomorically sucked in their stomachs, laddishly stretched their legs and vainly protruded their chests. This was male courting any *jabiru* stork would empathise with.

César brought back two bottles of cachaça. By my calculations we had money for three.

'I paid for one, Katje for one and the Italians paid for one,' I said resolutely. 'Three bottles minimum.'

César made a sour face but bought another one without any complaints. Froude was quick to upbraid his rival. 'He's keeping the money for himself.'

'César's dizzy,' Katje defended him. 'He can't take the alcohol.'

'I think he can, very well, and that may be the problem,' I commented, as we got up to leave.

Half an hour into our walk back, César froze and pointed at the tracks of an animal.

'Shh,' he said, hushing us with his finger. 'There.'

A group of black peccaries was grazing to our left at ten o'clock. César showed us a scar on his calf.

'*Queixada*,' he said.

There are two kinds of peccaries in the Pantanal: the smaller, obsessively self-cleansing *cateto* and the bigger, menacing, black *queixada* with its sharp tusks and a temper resembling that of European wild boars. César warned us: if they charged, which well they might as they had babies, make a run for the thicket of trees about half a mile away. We moved as unthreateningly as we could, looking back in case the pigs decided to go for it. Ten minutes of tense silence passed before we reached safety in the woods. It was with the utmost pleasure that, when we returned to the camp, we found that the cook had been hunting and was hanging the meat – tomorrow we would have peccary *assado*. It was reassuring to show those bastards who was king of the jungle: our cook.

We ate dinner under gas lamps, while César and Fernão prepared pineapple caipirinha. They were taking their time.

'Check they haven't gulped it all,' said Froude suspiciously.

I stood up and nearly stepped on a giant brown bullfrog who was roaming around the site.

'CAREFUL!' shouted Sabine. 'That's a *sapo-cururu*. If he gets upset or afraid, he squirts poison at you from those glands on his head. Don't even go near him.'

I looked down at the bullfrog respectfully. I gave him a wide berth and bumped into César instead. He offered Katje a glass of caipirinha, and asked her for a walk by the lake; he could speak some English so conversation was possible. Froude and I retired to the hammocks. His attention was concentrated on the great dark void that had swallowed Katje and César. He remained impervious to my attempts to spark up a conversation. He got animated when they returned: they appeared flushed. Katje came straight to me.

'What is "maybe" in Portuguese?'

'*Talvez*,' I replied.

She turned around to César. '*Talvez*,' she said.

Froude and I exchanged looks.

'Sorry mate,' I said to him when she left. 'I thought you were in there with a chance.'

Froude stretched himself on the hammock and let his legs drop either side. 'She's very pretty. And she's so not-girlie.'

'You're leaving tomorrow. Katje is staying on. Forget her,' I said.

He kept staring at Katje's slender silhouette.

The entertainment was my idea: karaoke where each one of us would sing their national anthem. I sang *God Save the Queen* to start us off. The Italians sang theirs, which properly belongs to an overture by Rossini. Froude gave a boisterous rendition of the Norwegian national anthem. He had to be stopped after the third stanza lest he scare the howler monkeys ('But I haven't finished yet!' 'Oh, well, the tune doesn't change anyway.'). Katje didn't sing ('I don't know the words,' she insisted). The Brazilians did an acapella version of their own anthem. Alfredo the Catalan?

'I find anthems too nationalistic and fascist,' he said, and that was it.

'Will Frau Kommandant sing *Deutschland Über Alles*?' I whispered to Froude. Sabine remained stumm.

The winners were, by unanimous vote, the Welsh. But then again they sing for breakfast, lunch and dinner; it ain't fair.

....

Things I Like About Brazil #11: The Flag

I still rack my brain as to why people who like their free time and relaxation so much have opted to design what must be the most laborious flag to get right throughout the five continents. Yes, it's a green background, a yellow rhombus and a blue coffee bean, but that's just for starters. An elliptic band runs through the coffee bean proclaiming 'ORDEM E PROGRESSO', a nineteenth-century positivist slogan, so unlike in other countries illiterates or primary school kids can't draw it.

Then there is the matter of the stars. Unlike the US of A they are not formalised on the left-hand side, however many they are: they appear in their correct constellations inside the coffee bean. The lone one on the top above the G of Progresso is Spica (Alpha Virgo) which symbolises Pará. In the bottom half you get Scorpio for the Nordeste – with Piauí the Alpha star, Ceará the Epsilon and so on. Once you're done with Scorpio, you'll have to repeat the exercise for the Southern Cross: São Paulo is the Alpha star and Rio de Janeiro the Beta, Minas the Gamma and Bahia the Delta – even in the flag the big states ensured that their pecking order was immortalised by relative astral luminance. Then we have the aptly named Southern Triangle (Paraná, Santa Catarina and Rio Grande do Sul) and for good measure Canis Major and the Hydra, too.

You have to draw no less than five constellations inside half a coffee bean to get the flag right: only miniaturists with an astronomical bent need apply. Which is why I love the flag. It's so fastidious, it almost makes me want to be a teacher in a Brazilian school just to see the pupils sweat out the assignment on 19 November – Flag Day.

....

Any night walks?

'We stopped doing night walks to watch jaguars,' said Johnny, 'because people from the *fazenda* are sometimes hunting at the same time.'

Did they shoot at the walkers?

'You bet. But it was OK. They're bad shots.'

After everyone went to sleep, Froude, Katje, my adrenaline and I went to sit on a bench by the lake and stare at the Milky Way. Katje was drunkenly flirting with both of us while we were being eaten alive by mosquitoes and sandflies, as all insects in the Pantanal were totally immune to my 100 per cent DEET solution. I left Katje and Froude scratching romantically under the shooting stars, as I retired to my tent, picked a huge tick from my pubes and went to sleep.

– 52 –

At six in the morning we went for a walk with Johnny Indiano. We rowed across the lake to observe the howler monkeys. There was a large family with a female carrying a baby on her back and an aggressive black male who tried to defend his territory. I don't know if you are familiar with the manner of his defending: he throws his shit at you – highly effective. I will try this in London against Jehovah's Witnesses.

Johnny had located a *coati mundi*. This is no more than a male coati (an animal like a racoon) which prefers to live solo – not all animals go for family values. It is still unknown what drives some males to leave the group and go it alone – for decades it was thought to be a different species. It was in trying to imitate the coati's black-ringed tail that Indian body colouring started, and the verb 'to paint' in Tupi is indeed *coatiá*. Ah, look – an armadillo.

Breakfast and another walk, with César this time. We soon encountered what became our favourite animal: the anteater (*tamanduá*). No, not the giant kind with the elongated snout, the stuff of most nature documentaries. This one was the four-fingered anteater, no more than a foot long.

'Look,' said César and pretended to grab him.

The little anteater had been cornered against a tree trunk, so he stood on his hind legs and raised his front arms.

'What is he doing?' I asked.

'He's trying to scare us,' said César. 'He's trying to make us go away.'

We fell back laughing. This was as scary as Bela Lugosi's double hiding behind his cape in *Plan B From Outer Space*.

....

'The jaguar who saved me forbade me from speaking about fire!' cried the boy. 'He said if I told anyone he would become everyone's enemy. He would never be at peace with man.'

But the secret was out.

The Xavante called a meeting in the middle of the village. They talked to each other about charcoal and fire. They decided to steal the fire. For this they needed a good runner.

A Xavante turned into a tapir. 'I'll run like a tapir,' he called out and ran around: PUTU, PUTU, PUTU.

They all laughed. 'You sure run fast,' they said. 'But you make such a racket!'

....

By midday we had conveniently reached a stream. I swam in it for a while as the César-Katje-Froude love triangle sunbathed on a sand island.

BANG!

César immediately ran towards the direction of the shot. We were a bit unnerved. Who was firing at us? I remembered Johnny's words at dinner yesterday. Didn't the *fazendeiros* like backpackers? César came back, shaking his head; he couldn't figure out what it was, so we decided to leave at once. The mystery wasn't solved until we went to where we'd left our clothes and Froude picked up his trousers. His lighter had exploded from the heat.

'Wow,' he murmured. 'What if this had happened while it was in my pocket?'

We winced.

'Now I have a hole in my pocket,' he said with childlike affectation as he turned to Katje. 'Will you carry my cigarettes, please?'

Oh, the tricks of the trade ...

When we arrived for lunch we noticed a poster on our water tank: 'This water is for drinking only! Do not use for other purposes.'

Any reason this was up?

Sabine exploded: 'This water is precious and *you people* use it for washing your face and brushing your teeth in the morning! You must do that in the lake!'

This was contrary to the health advice I had received, so I clicked my heels, shouted '*Jawohl, Frau Kommandant,*' retired to my tent, took a roll of toilet paper and waltzed merrily towards the trees close to Johnny and Sabine's tent.

*****

Over lunch we discussed our plans. The Italians and the Welsh were leaving. Alfredo would be staying. Froude, disappointed, was in two minds: should he leave today, as planned? I pushed things along by chatting to Katje within his earshot.

'So, has César made a pass at you yet?'

'A bit obvious, isn't he? But I'm immune to his charms.'

'What about last night when you told him *"talvez"*?' I winked.

She looked stunned. 'Is *that* what you thought?'

I nodded yes. 'And not just me,' I added and tilted my head in Froude's direction.

'Oh,' she said and went quiet.

'You're giving the wrong signals there, Katje.'

Out of the corner of my eye, I saw Froude wink at me.

My middle name is Cupid.

Froude stayed, and Katje started spending more time with him. They started radiating a warm glow together; their auras excluded everyone in the camp, including me. They touched each other without pretences: Froude lay his chin on Katje's shoulder to observe a bird; she tickled his sides to make him move out of the way. His chest heaved as he called her name; she looked languidly at him whenever he spoke; they nestled in each other's arms on a hammock, legs entwined like creepers on tree trunks.

'Look at them,' mused Alfredo. 'What a place to meet your girl.'

As if to underline his words, two green budgies fluttered through the branches. The mating season had arrived in the Pantanal. I turned my gaze to the crocodiles.

'There are certainly many serpents here,' I quipped. 'Has she given him the apple yet?'

*****

The truck came three hours late. Anyone new? A rarity: a Japanese girl travelling alone. She worked as a volunteer kindergarten teacher in Santa Cruz and had popped over to Brazil for five days. She is mostly a silent character in our story as she was in real life – but her only contribution was decisive for this chapter.

'I'll be off to Santa Cruz next,' I said to her, trying to make small talk. 'Any tips?'

She thought long, probably to master the grammar.

'The Central Plaza,' she said. 'And the zoo. Oh yes, the zoo. One of the best in South America.'

The *zoo*? What a strange suggestion to make in the Pantanal. I was getting ready to argue, but Froude and Katje approached me.

'Do you want to hitch a ride up to the *fazenda* to have a few beers?' they asked.

'I'm always game.'

'BRING SOME CACHAÇA!' shouted Sabine.

I thought that was a bit rich.

'We bought two bottles yesterday,' I said.

'No,' she said. 'I bought two bottles yesterday, and the Italians bought the other one. Three bottles.'

Froude, Katje and I looked at each other. César had been given the money for five bottles, but had bought only three – and would have only bought two if I had not insisted. He wasn't around, so we said nothing.

Remembering Avelinho from the Amazon, I brought up the subject of hallucinogenics as gently as I could. Were there any such plants about?

'*Cogumelos*,' Johnny said. 'You make tea and you fly.'

We would bring cachaça, if he would find us some *cogumelos*.

*****

In the absence of César, it was Fernão who escorted us to the *fazenda*. He was only 45, but considered a pensioner in the Pantanal; his wrinkled, toothless expression added a decade more to his appearance. He was divorced with kids and was living alone in Corumbá.

'I thought you lived in the camp,' I said, offering him a beer.

'When I'm working. When I'm not, I return home with the truck.'

'Do you earn a lot?'

'I have no expenses. Most of my wages go to my wife for maintenance.'

Fernão was dreaming of finding a rich Western woman who would take him away.

'I'm waiting for another wife,' he sighed. 'A rich, pretty, young tourist – preferably American.'

Katje's elbow nudged me. 'For your information, he made a pass at me more direct than César,' she said to me *sotto voce*. 'He's in for a long wait if he's after a backpacker.'

I looked at our stud who had more lines on his face than an Andes ordnance survey map.

'He'll have to get some teeth in first as well,' I added.

Bitching stopped as we saw César approaching. He sat with us, and we bought him a beer. He drank, staring anxiously at Katje who studiously avoided his eyes.

'You buy the cachaça, I buy the limes,' César said. 'We make proper caipirinha.'

I bought another bottle with Froude – at $7 per bottle they weren't that cheap – and waited for César. He came back empty-handed: 'I couldn't find any limes.'

'You must be joking,' I said. 'They have many in the *armazém*. I saw them.'

'Then give me two reais to buy a few.'

I gritted my teeth.

'César,' I said, raising my voice, 'yesterday we paid for bottles you didn't buy. We treated you beers here. We paid for one more cachaça now. No more. *You* get the limes!'

César marched off in a pique.

Fernão was splitting himself.

'Ha, ha, ha, how funny, the way you said it. *You* get the limes!'

. . . .

Another Xavante turned into a deer.

'I'll run like the deer,' he said. And he ran fast like a large deer.

The Xavante laughed and imitated his manner of running.

'Hey, you sure run fast. But you take big, awkward steps.'

Another turned into the small jungle deer.

'I am going as the small jungle deer,' he said and ran around.

The Xavante laughed again.

'Hey, you sure run fast,' they said. 'But you run with your neck way down to the ground!'

Another turned into the plains deer and sprinted away.

The Xavante also made fun of him.
'Hey, you sure run fast,' they said. 'Pity you bobble your arse up in the air a lot.'
This is how the Xavante named the animals.

....

Johnny didn't have any *cogumelos* when I returned.

'I was thinking of collecting them tomorrow,' he said.

'But I'm leaving tomorrow.'

'Do you know how nice it is to be stoned during the day?'

Cue that howler monkey imitation contest while we waited for the drinks. Fernão was dragging his feet on the caipirinha front and kept disappearing behind the bushes.

'Fernão, give me the bottle. I'll mix it myself,' I said.

'Later.'

'What do you mean, later? I paid for it, I want it now.'

The bottle, when it came, was half empty. Sabine's Teutonic sense of fair play was punctured.

'Fernão!' she shouted. 'This was John's bottle.'

All hell let loose. Angry as I was, I told Sabine about César's scam: how he had collected money for five bottles but bought only three. César was summoned. Sabine asked how much we paid for the bottles. We had also been overcharged. At last, Sabine had a pivot for her anger and frustration; she turned to César and Fernão.

'All this will be docked out of your wages,' she barked, revealing more about Brazilian labour practices than a handful of ILO declarations.

When things calmed down I made a carafe of Guaraná caipirinha which I offered as a vulnerary potion to everyone in the camp, including Fernão – who accepted – and César – who did not. By then he had realised he was losing Katje and was doubly stroppy.

A noise up in the canopy made us all look up. Torches shone on a howler monkey. Was he? Yes, he was. Wounded, that is. You could see the blood.

'It's him again,' said Johnny. 'He's from across the lake and keeps fighting with the other dominant male. He loses every time and comes here for safety.'

The howler monkey was not the only invader. An army of tiny sandflies which bit like vampire bats had descended upon the camp. It was hot, but we couldn't sit on the bench by the lake because a huge crocodile was cooling itself underneath it. Froude tried to scare it, but it wouldn't budge. I know they were harmless, but still, sitting on a bench nonchalantly with a frigging big croc below is not conducive to relaxation.

The mood in the camp was subdued. The Italians and the Welsh had gone, Froude and Katje were into each other in a corner, Sabine was fuming, Fernão was snoring, César had retired to his tent and the Japanese girl was a quasi-mute character, so that left only me and Alfredo to try and make some bonfire conversation. We didn't know what to talk about, so we had an argument about cultural imperialism, as one does.

Alfredo's thrust was that we are all brainwashed by the media and that we are all losing our cultural identity to the multinationals of this world.

'People are smart, Alfredo, and only patronising do-gooders assume otherwise. You look at the US and condemn McDonald's and Coca-Cola, conveniently forgetting the inroads of pizza and karaoke.'

My line was that if there is something universally appealing in a foreign approach, then why not adopt it? Cross-cultural influences have in general been benign. Think of Arab algebra, Greek philosophy and Chinese porcelain. American blue jeans are popular even in the jungle because they're practical and sexy.

'It's all advertising. We are always swayed by advertising.'

'Are we? Has Michael Jackson's disco wiped out the samba, the flamenco or the fado?'

'We need to preserve each individual culture.'

'Does every culture need to be preserved? What, then – should we not have abolished slavery, cannibalism or defeated the Nazis?'

I saw Alfredo move his mouth in protest. I continued: 'Ah, but once you admit that some cultures are worth preserving but not others, then you can't pick and choose – who's going to decide? The most we can hope for is to try and find ways to allow more primitive cultures a soft landing in their encounter with our advanced technological world. We cannot undo history.'

'It's immoral to force Indians to accept our culture.'

'I agree it is immoral to rob Indians of their land or to try to "civilise" them by forcing them to speak Spanish or Portuguese. I agree it is immoral to leave them unaided, drifting between their world and ours. But should we abandon them? Exempt them from the progress of technology for eco-tourism's sake and keep them in the zoo for the benefit of sociologists? What's the morality in that?'

'This is a fascist acculturation argument.'

'The Uros Indians on Lake Titicaca use modern boats that don't leak that much. We would all prefer to take pictures of their traditional reed boats, but what do *they* want? Surely we want them to have better health, live longer, enjoy some of the fruits of our modern civilisation – but shall we patronisingly choose what is best for them from our world and what is not?'

'Look at us in Spain – the Catalans, the Basques.'

'Alfredo, we are not talking about the right of peoples to self-determination. We are talking about cultural imperialism.'

'You accept it exists then.'

'The culture of the victorious always takes root,' I replied. 'It's an unfortunate fact of life.'

'So if a culture is pushing us in one direction,' said Alfredo, 'we have a right to push back. I want to push society in one direction, through activism.'

'What kind of activism?'

'Direct action.'

'Like Greenpeace?'

'More than that,' he said and gave me a piercing, fanatical look. 'Else we are all going to disappear into greyness.'

'I don't see greyness. I see Japanese karaoke, American baseball caps, Thai food, Italian pizzas.'

'We need to protect our culture.'

I thought of Friedrich Dürrenmatt, the Swiss author, who asks in his *Romulus the Great*: '*Is culture something that needs to be defended?*'

'Leave this to the people themselves,' I said. 'Let them live and let them choose.'

'Is everyone able to make this judgement? The Xavante? The Yanomani?'

First we kill them, then we're sorry.

'So who's making the decision on their behalf that they should not receive health, comforts, education?' I asked.

'Pah! Education. Eve's apple. Don't you think people are better off not knowing what they miss?'

'So you admit that they miss something worth having.'

Alfredo did not want to talk to me any more. He got up from his log and walked slowly to his tent.

It was 6 a.m. and another hung-over trek. Sabine wanted to photograph a blue-and-yellow macaw nest where chicks had just hatched. Macaws count among the most magnificent of birds: dazzlingly coloured plumage, marigold eyes, 3-foot-long wings flapping, bright, mighty beaks crowing hoarsely. When they started hovering menacingly over Sabine, who had climbed a tree nearby, it was time to split.

'*Arara, caracará,*' I said to Johnny. 'The Tupi sure liked syllable repetition.'

'Repetition denotes largeness,' he replied. 'An *ara* is a small parrot. An *arara* is a big parrot – a macaw.'

'Cool birds,' I whispered to Katje. 'They pissed Sabine off.'

'Not too difficult,' she replied. Her eyes caught Sabine's sour gaze, and she shut up like a girl caught in the act of talking in class by her schoolteacher. Oh, how we had regressed …

I convinced Sabine that *cogumelo* tea would make a nice beverage for her nerves, so off we went in search of magic mushrooms of the Brazilian kind. They live around cowpats, so we had to go to a zebu grazing field and examine their droppings. The things we do for kicks.

A gentle rustling of leaves revealed a large rat which turned out to be an *agouti*, a diurnal rodent, which lives on land and looks like a large short-tailed squirrel on steroids. It's a remarkable animal. It's only a couple of feet long, but it can gallop as fast as a rabbit and jump vertically up to four times its height. It eats fruit and seeds and sometimes it buries them in the soil like a squirrel, contributing to the spread of species that comprise its diet. This one was feeding on what appeared to be a date, standing upright on its hind legs always aware and wary of our presence.

'There's a wild bee nest,' said Johnny. 'Be careful. Move slowly.'

Too late. I looked down at my left calf where I was being, erm … *penetrated*. Excruciating pain. I looked at my right arm. Shit. Another one.

'Don't move,' said Johnny.

He tried to shoo the bee away. A second sting. More excruciating pain. The bees were stuck on me, unable to withdraw. I ran with everyone else. I swatted the bees and removed the stings. I was in agony.

Johnny looked at me. 'Do you know what you have to do?'

I knew. I needed a weak basic solution: ammonia, as can be found in piss. I urinated on my leg and inner arm as the rest of the group looked discreetly away.

'Are you allergic?' asked Sabine.

'I don't know, I've never been stung before.'

'We'll soon find out,' she said. 'Anaphylactic shock kills you within an hour.'

Now you know and I know that since I am writing this, I survived. But at the time, I didn't. Would I die in the next hour? Yet the enormity of the pain was such that it took my mind off morbid thoughts: death might be around the corner, but I could only think of my immediate misery.

After that we just *had* to find *cogumelos*. We reached a zebu grazing ground and started checking the pats. I must have come too close, because the animals started marching in formation: at first a lone zebu approached a second from behind, and then they both turned around with their horns low. They then both swirled, approached a third zebu and all three synchronised themselves to turn once more, a bit closer this time, with three sets of horns pointed at me simultaneously. I was watching the strange ballet with fascination, but when the number reached half a dozen, I pointed them out to Johnny.

'Oh,' he said. 'They're preparing to attack us.'

He lunged at them, screaming and waving his hands wildly over his head. The zebus took flight in six different directions and the whole flock disappeared with them. I looked on in amazement. Johnny turned to me: 'Thankfully, they're easy to scare.'

We scoured the pats, but didn't locate any *cogumelos*. What we did find was a mudhole with fresh peccary tracks. They had been there recently, rolling in the dirt; we withdrew back to a copse of tall, flowering *cambará* trees for safety. Good news is that we did find *cogumelos* there; the bad news is that they were just sprouting.

'They appear after a big rain. We had that storm two days ago; I would have thought they would be much larger than this,' said Johnny. 'We'll pick them tomorrow. Will you be here tomorrow?'

'Not me,' said Froude.

Nor me. I looked at Katje.

'It won't be the same without you two,' she said. 'I'll be leaving today with you.'

Froude beamed and so did I.

Bzzzz!

The buzzing scared me at first – my stings were still aching – before I noticed the tiny red-beaked hummingbirds above us, sounding like an army of bumble-bees.

'*Beija-flor*,' said Johnny to no one in particular.

We call them hummingbirds; the Brazilians call them 'flower-kissers'. Cultures differ in basic postulates of thought: the Inuit have 17 words for snow; the Tuareg 11 words for sand and Americans 94 expressions for shades of lipstick, for it is what matters to each culture that is analysed and classified. And what's more, one's view of the world is embedded in one's language as my hovering *beija-flor* manifests, an irritating hum to some, a gentle flower-kisser to others. Sand is sometimes not just sand and snow is not always snow, for human cultures recognise different things differently, and the question really is why does ours deem lipstick so important?

Maybe it's our creation myths.

....

A rhea appeared. Now the rhea runs very fast. 'I am the rhea, and I run faster than any other animal,' he said.

When he stopped, the Xavante were ready.

'You sure run fast. But you run with your wings extended way out, so funny.'

A paca appeared. Now the paca runs very fast. 'I am the paca and I run fast.'

When he stopped the Xavante knew what to say.

'You sure run fast. But you won't leave the bank of the river!'

And this is how they made fun of all the creatures.

....

During the ride back to Corumbá we completed our nature watch by observing a family of capybaras – the largest rodents alive, as large as a brown, furry pig. Tailless and semi-aquatic, they adopt the role of the hippo in South America: fertilising the waters. Like African antelopes, their safety lies in numbers – a large herd (or is it pod?) can reach up to 40 individuals, all sniffing and listening for danger. The capybaras took refuge in the bush when they saw our truck, but the birds were undisturbed by our presence: *jacanã* waders, which have perfected walking on water with their specialised toes and heels, a wood ibis eating a small snake, several cormorants and a large stork, *tabuiaiá*, a close cousin of our common European species.

Fernão was travelling with us as he had two days off; he didn't have anything to eat for dinner, so we stopped before the Paraguay River to catch some food for him. The truck driver fished for small fish with maggots – we did not discuss their provenance – and the fish were cut in turn for Fernão's piranha bait. I can understand why the area is an angler's paradise: we didn't have to wait more than five minutes before the fishing line jerked. In about half an hour he'd caught four large red piranhas; Fernão could easily cook a *caldo*. He invited us home with him, but we declined.

Back in Corumbá the spectre of Stavros returned to haunt me. I was tired, I was dirty and a room at Hotel International, where I could avoid him, seemed a small price to pay. Once there, I washed myself meticulously. I cleaned the dirt from my nails. I checked my battle scars from the Pantanal: I removed more ticks from my crotch, I tended the swollen bee stings and noticed for the first time that a scratch on my ankle had ulcerated. I bought a dexametazone cream fortified by neomycin from a pharmacy and applied it carefully along with an antiseptic. The scratch was to fester for seven more days, until I reached the altiplano where the combined effects of the cold and the lower pressure killed off whatever was causing the infection.

I wanted to travel to Santa Cruz by train – called with gusto the 'Train of Death' – so I started asking around for information. I would have to cross the river to Bolivia just to find out prices and timetables. No one seemed to know anything except that the journey took a long and unpredictable period of time – 18 hours minimum – and that I would have to keep my wits about me and not fall asleep: I would be sharing with *contrabandistas*. 'Take the one-hour fifty-dollar flight to Santa Cruz,' was what everyone said; that was what Katje and Froude had done.

I missed them already. On the way to the deserted Corumbá train station, I spotted a large lizard on the overgrown tracks. I wanted to point at it and shout '*lagartixa*' to my friends, as we did in the jungle – but they weren't around. We had only been together for three days, but it felt like a packed three months.

If you ever read this, Katje or Froude, get in touch.

···

The animals approached the jaguar's house. He was fast asleep. He was snoring. It is because they remember the jaguar's growl that people snore nowadays.

The tapir went first. He snuck up on the jaguar, picked up a large piece of firewood and started running.

But he made a lot of noise and woke up the jaguar.

Then the tapir handed the fire to the large deer lying in wait. The large deer ran fast to the small deer and passed the firewood to him. The small deer ran fast and carried the firewood to the plains deer who ran to the rhea who ran all the way to the river as the jaguar was getting tired.

The rhea passed the firewood to the paca who was lying in wait by the river. The paca ran fast and almost fell into the river, but the Xavante were there and retrieved it in time.

....

– 54 –

On my final day in Corumbá the thermometer shot to 43 °C in the shade with humidity hovering above 80 per cent. There is a local saying: 'People who die in Corumbá go to Heaven, for they have already experienced Hell.'

I was woken up at 11 a.m. by a phone call. It was Stavros.

'Hi, *patriotaki*,' he said in Greek (which threw me a bit as I was still dozy). 'Why are you there? You should have come here! I was waiting.' He went on babbling like Zé & Zé about how the tiger economies were collapsing in East Asia and that there was a global stock-exchange meltdown with the real being badly hit. I fell half asleep until –

'Ten dollars.'

'What? Can you repeat that?'

'Are you still asleep *patriotaki*? I have to pick up some money, but they are sending it to a Bolivian bank so I have to cross to Puerto Suarez. I don't have money for the fare. Can you lend me ten dollars?'

'No.'

I offered no explanation or excuse. There was a pause.

'Did you say no?'

'I said no.'

'Oh.' There was another pause. 'See you later then.'

'Yeah, see you later.'

Good riddance.

*****

'The plane leaves at six,' the agent said.

I looked at my ticket. 'But it says five.'

'It's Bolivian time. They are one hour behind.'

'But we are in Brazil.'

'Yes, but Aerosur, the airline, is Bolivian.'

I see.

'It also says, Puerto Suarez to Santa Cruz.'

'It's Corumbá, really. Puerto Suarez Airport is temporarily closed, and all flights fly from Corumbá.'

So I bought a plane ticket for a flight from Corumbá to Santa Cruz at 18.00 that said: 'Puerto Suarez–Santa Cruz 17.00.' There was nothing correct about it except the destination.

*****

I sat alone in the restaurant for dinner. I breathed out deeply and looked at the night sky. Even in the middle of the city there was hardly any light pollution.

While I was eating, a moto-taxi stopped next to me. A *what*? Sorry, I haven't described Corumbá's unique mode of transport: scooter-taxis which cost one real to take you anywhere in town. You ride pillion, hold the driver tight and away you go. Who was that removing his helmet to greet me?

'Hi, *patriotaki*,' said Stavros. 'Stay here; I'll be back in a minute and give you the two dollars I owe you. We can have a final beer together.'

That was the last I saw of him.

*****

The plane to Santa Cruz was leaving at 18:00. At 16:30 I checked in with Aerosur, handed over my luggage and received my boarding pass. The last thing missing was … ahem –

Where *was* Immigration?

'At the main bus terminal in town,' said the policeman manning a booth.

'So why does the sign in that office say "Immigration"?' I pointed out.

'Oh, it's an old sign. The office has been closed for some time, because Corumbá Airport is used only for domestic flights.'

'But I'm flying to Santa Cruz. Surely that's in Bolivia?'

'Yes, but this flight is supposed to be leaving from Puerto Suarez in Bolivia at 17.00 – look at your ticket.'

'But Puerto Suarez Airport is closed, so I can't fly from there.'

'Exactly,' said the policeman and smiled happily, as if all was now clear.

*****

I needed an exit stamp from Brazil to enter Bolivia, so I jumped on a moto-taxi to the bus terminal. I looked at my watch: 17:00. The police Immigration office was closed, and there was a queue of about a dozen confused Bolivians outside. There was a sign, rubbing it in, saying that the office was open continuously from 8.00 to 18.00.

A taxi tout shouted: 'The police are not coming today; only the Polícia Federal in the centre of town is open.'

I only had two reais left; enough for two rides. I flagged down a moto-taxi to the Polícia Federal in town. I rushed to the policeman in the reception: 'Do you give exit visas here?'

'No,' he replied. 'In the bus terminal. The officer responsible just left to open the office there.'

I looked at my watch. 17.30. I had only one real left and half an hour to catch my plane.

There must be a *jeitinho*.

....

Things I Don't Like About Brazil #11: *Jeitinho*

This translates roughly as 'a way', like 'Can't we manage a way out of this?' You refer to it in Brazil to circumvent bureaucracy, inefficiency or simply a law you think is unfair. It is normally accompanied by a discreet – or not so discreet – offer of a bribe to expedite matters. There is a jeitinho *for Immigration, for extending your Air Pass beyond 21 days, for finding a seat in a packed plane, even for obtaining a ticket to a sold-out Maracanã football derby.*

....

Still at Polícia Federal in town, I played the downtrodden, hopelessly lost gringo. I explained that I'd travelled from the airport to the bus station to the police building and that I had no money left to return to the bus station. I opened my wallet – the policeman's eyes shone – but I showed him my one real, my boarding ticket and explained that in 30 minutes my plane would leave with all my belongings.

'Do you have any dollars?' the policeman asked me openly. I had 100-dollar bills stashed in my money belt, but I showed him my travellers cheques. No good to him.

'Oh please, give me a stamp …' I moaned with desperation.

The policeman took pity on me, opened a drawer, took out a stamp, stamped my passport and took the immigration slip, which a tourist has to carry with him all the time in Brazil. The whole operation took five seconds.

'Don't tell anyone about this,' he added.

Tough.

With my last real, I jumped on the waiting moto-taxi and arrived at the airport with only fifteen minutes to spare.

....

The crested curassows saw the coals that had dropped off on the way and carried them under their beaks. This is why they have a red patch under their chin.

A lot of coals had fallen. The curassows carried the coals to the tribe who carried off the firewood and distributed them to all the people in the forest.

And now people can warm themselves with fire.

At first fire belonged to the jaguar. That was a long time ago. But then the Xavante and the animals carried off the fire from the jaguar who became the enemy of Man.

Yes, it was from the jaguar that man learned how to make fire.

And this is how it was.

[This is an abridged version of a Xavante creation myth compiled by Alec Harrison.]

....

This chapter has to end in Bolivia.

Santa Cruz de la Sierra is not a city we normally associate with the birthplace of *El Condor Pasa*. There are no Quechua or Aymara Andean natives – there are Amazonian Beni. It is not on the altiplano – it's in the jungle. As recently as the 1970s it was a backwater of 30,000, where you could drive a horse and cart around the main plaza; now its highways rival La Paz with a vengeance. Santa Cruz is a boomtown with *cojones*: 1.5 million inhabitants, temperate climate, karaoke bars, late night discos and a large foreign contingent. Many of them are Brazilians, since Santa Cruz has become the natural urban magnet of the central jungle lowlands in South America, its geographical position transcending political frontiers.

Many factors have contributed to the spectacular growth of Santa Cruz. There is commerce: the city stands at the crossroads of the vast centre of the South American continent and handles the freight of the busy Arica–La Paz Andes pass, which includes much of the trade between Brazil and Japan. There is agriculture: Santa Cruz grows food for the rainforest hinterland. On top of that there are natural gas fields nearby, which has led to foreign investment and an influx of gringo workers who want their clubs, their bars and their prostitutes. But the greatest invisible trade involves Bolivia's biggest crop: coca. Colombia, by nature of its geography, serves the US almost directly – might as well build a cocaine pipeline to the North American nostril. Bolivia, however, has no access to either the Atlantic or the Pacific ocean, and the Pacific routes to Chile via Arica and Antofagasta are narrow corridors and thus easily policed. Bolivia's drug traffickers need Brazil's Atlantic ports or the Paraguay River; they need Santa Cruz, which has become the main dispersal centre of drug trafficking from all over Bolivia, especially the Yungas valleys around La Paz. This means that Santa Cruz leans more towards Brasília than La Paz; and yes, this seemed a Spanish-speaking Brazil, its *cruceño* inhabitants more fun-loving and outgoing than the moody and sombre highland *paceños*.

'Go to the zoo,' the Japanese girl had said. 'It's one of the best in South America.'

It is, if zoos are your sort of thing. By now I could tell the difference between macaws, parakeets, parrots and curassows, owls and harpy eagles, agoutis and capybaras. The zoo was also home to some very rare species: the yellow monkey, the crested *caracará* and the lesser-billed curassow amongst them; it's also the only place you'll see jaguars or approach peccaries with no fear of being gored.

On the way to the pumas, a group of kindergarten kids ran around unrestrained. One little girl jumped into a puddle in front of me, soiling my newly washed trousers with mud.

Rats! Agoutis!

Dirty and furious, I walked to the big cats' enclosure. They were asleep. Next door the peccaries were lying immobile in their mudholes.

I know exactly how you feel.

In fact I did.

Did I?

I had observed *jabiru* storks at their splendid best, so I was shocked to see that the colourful plumage of the captured animals had faded, their feathers had shrivelled and their long beaks sported fungal growths. And what was that noise? I stood outside the red and green macaw's pen and heard them ululating. Now I *know* the cry of macaws in their natural habitat – and that red and green individual screaming its head off was not a happy bird.

The macaw stopped and looked at me. A discharge was running from its left eye. I know exactly how you feel, mate.

Did I think that?

For a few seconds we stared at each other before the macaw resumed its piercing shrieks. I was to learn later that macaws are one of the species that have serious psychological problems in captivity.

I entered the walk-in aviary. After my favourite bird, my favourite animal: a small anteater was roaming loose, his tongue sweeping the ground for ants.

I'll stand in his way to see him try and scare me.

The little anteater came up to my feet undaunted by my presence. He did not stand on his hind legs nor open his arms wide. He simply ignored me and passed me by.

He's forgotten how he should behave.

Whether or not the indigenous people of South America have a word for philosophy or not, they certainly have a world view that involves Man evolving in tune with the rest of the animal world. The jaguar was the guardian of fire in one of the Xavante's celebrated myths and Man stole it with the help of tapirs, deers and rheas. Their answer to the big question 'Why are we here?' is simple and direct: we are first among equals, the gatekeepers of the garden. Because yes, we are still in the Garden of Eden, but we are too greedy consuming its fruit to realise it.

I stood in the aviary, my eyes fixed on the small, dirty, furry bundle licking away at the ground, my ears still reverberating with the macaw's squawk over the incessant twitter around me. For a fleeting moment, I felt the enormity of their predicament, and, then, as I empathised with their plight, I felt more human than ever.

This gatekeeper wants to unlock the door.

No, by granting the Indians territories in the Xingu, the Tocantins and the Tapajós we are not putting them in a zoo for we are not curbing their liberty or curtailing their rights. Instead we are letting them maintain their culture, for cultures are only nourished in freedom. What surprises missionaries and bureaucrats constantly is why so many Indians turn their backs on ours. It was in Santa Cruz I finally understood what the Indians perceived long ago: that embracing our culture means entering the zoo – for it is us, in London, Tokyo, New York or São Paulo who are living in cages, having lost the thread and the keys to the meaning of our existence, our fate either that of the traumatised dropout or the alienated behavioural cripple – the fate of the macaw or the anteater.

Some choice.

Chapter 12

Model Traffic (The Most Wonderful State of Paraná)

It all went pear-shaped in Curitiba.

....

The Words You'll Need

borboleta = *butterfly*

Falo. Um pouco = *I speak. A little.*

figa = *a Brazilian good-luck charm: a fist with the thumb protruding slightly
between the second and third finger*

Litorina = *coastal*

não falo português = *'I don't speak Portuguese'* – *probably the single most useful
phrase for a tourist, even if he or she does speak Portuguese, as you will see in
this chapter*

pirão de peixe = *a kind of fish chowder*

puta = *although literally it means 'whore', the casual use in everyday speech
makes it more akin to the way we use 'bitch'*

você é muito simpático = *you are very nice*

....

– 55 –

Forget about my extended flashback: I'm back en route from Congonhas
to Curitiba, the capital of Paraná, a state two-thirds the size of Italy. (If
you think that's a lot of Belgiums, Minas Gerais is twice the size of
Great Britain.) Paraná boasts one of the world's most famous natural
sights, the Falls of Iguaçu; one of the world's most scenic railway journeys
from Curitiba to the port of Paranaguá; and one of Brazil's best-kept
secrets: Vila Velha, a park of natural stone formations eroded by sand
and wind.

If you search the Internet for 'Curitiba traffic' you'll find scores of
papers in environmental and planning journals heaping praise on the
city's unique achievement. Curitiba numbered 150,000 people in 1950
and has grown ten times since to a million and a half, but as the city grew,
commuting times *decreased*, because instead of going mental like São
Paulo (or Mexico City or Los Angeles, for that matter), Curitiba created
a harmonious urban ambience which, considering this is Brazil, makes

the feat infinitely more impressive. Delegations from Canada, France and the United States have come to study the miracle: 17 parks, 590 square feet of greenery per inhabitant (São Paulo: 54), 1.5 million trees planted in the last 30 years, 56 miles of bike paths and 1,100 buses integrated in a network, carrying around 70 per cent of the city's inhabitants. All buses are privatised with the municipal authorities and operators sharing the profits. Model traffic, indeed.

And this is only half of it.

Curitiba recycles two-thirds of its waste with incentives for the poor to deliver their rubbish in exchange for food or bus coupons, a policy which has made even the city's *favelas* spotless. Two different types of truck pick up organic and inorganic rubbish separately. Recycling plants employ more than 100 handicapped or alcoholic workers to sort the refuse in a process estimated to save 1,200 trees a day. The mayor's own offices are made out of logs from recycled telephone poles. Styrofoam discarded by fast-food joints is shredded and recycled to provide blankets for the homeless. The flood problems of the town have been solved by redirecting the waters to irrigate the city's parks. An abandoned quarry has been turned into a rock concert arena. The central shopping street, Rua das Flores, became Brazil's first pedestrian-only area where street children are paid to look after the flowers.

Jaime Lerner is the brains behind these imaginative policies: an architect whose designs followed the growth of the city; a technocrat who was appointed mayor at the age of 33 during the junta years and who later became a multiply-elected governor whose approval ratings regularly top 90 per cent. He's brought Curitiba foreign investment, industry and nationwide, if not worldwide, envy.

Are we dealing with an urban paradise? What can this city be like? Can it really be Brazil?

Oh yes, it can.

*****

As my plane taxied along, I shot up from my seat to pick up the overhead luggage – and then sat down promptly again, as no one else moved. The plane jerked forward and stopped. It was then that people stood up to get off and enter the supermodern marble airport of Afonso Pena. After the inchoate confusion that is Bahia, the passenger discipline was as disorientating as my tiresome twin-leg long flight.

Suits! Look – Brazilians in suits! And everyone wears shoes!

Like in Recife, I was advised by the airport tourist office to check in to a central business hotel with special weekend rates. Like in Belo Horizonte, I was loaded with maps: a tourist map, a bus map, a walking map and a highway map of greater Curitiba annotated with information. I am wary of city tourist offices bearing maps for this may be the precursor of true boredom. In Rio they give you two fingers: you want the sites, *senhor*? Why do you need a map? Just look around you.

As the bus took me to the Centro, I spotted the big secret of the quick-moving traffic: the conductor sits outside the vehicle at every stop, inside large metal and glass tubular bus stations, which are elevated slightly (with a ramp for the disabled). You pay for your ticket there and when the bus arrives, it stops exactly by the station's rolling doors which allow people to embark and disembark swiftly. The buses are huge: double or triple carriages with a capacity of 300 each and several sets of wheels; profitable passenger juggernauts, running fast on the wide avenues of a newly planned town, religiously pursuing yellow lines painted on the street. These monsters are trams-without-rails.

Of course, Curitibanos have had one advantage over other urban areas. Their city has exploded recently, so they could afford to design it from scratch: those tubular bus stations were installed in 1992. Such mega-buses could not function in the narrow streets of London, the labyrinthine maze of Rome, the tricky bridges of Amsterdam or even the hills of San Francisco. But I could certainly see them in the wide Housemann boulevards of Paris or the limitless stretches of Los Angeles, if there was political goodwill. Newly built or not, look at what architects dreamt for Brasília: at least Curitiba feels less of a failed experiment and more like a real city. And what, you may ask, does a real city feel like? Now let's see: the walls have posters for a heavy metal thrash spree for alienated teenagers; at Bill's Bar there was a splatter metal festival with bands like Epilépsia, RatCide, SubFreak, Imperious Malevolence, Dying Embers, Doomsday Ceremony, Brain For Tea, Splatter Death Grind II, Os Vomitos and my favourite: Aaaaá.

How very 1980s.

In fact, there is a 1980s feel to the whole city: it's brash, young and loud, much like London City traders during that euphoric post-Big Bang period. A large number of tourist attractions were inaugurated in the 1990s, which means they were conceived in the previous decade: the Ukrainian Memorial (1995); the Opera House (1992); the Torre Mercés

(1991), a telecommunications tower with 360-degree views; the Open Environmental University (1992), a museum graced on its opening day by none other than Jacques Cousteau; and the Botanical Gardens (1991), whose beautiful glass greenhouse is rapidly becoming Curitiba's landmark.

I dismissed the careful enumeration of the sights in the tourist brochure as artificial creations for photo-opportunities. But after I visited a few – the Botanical Gardens and the stunning Tanguá Park (meriting two stars in the *Guia 4 Rodas* and absent from English travel guides) – I had become a convert. Curitibanos did not design a botanical garden for a garden's sake (even if the famous glasshouse is half empty); they went for the utilisation of empty space with architectural structures and landscapes of immaculate perfection. The Botanical Gardens have an in-built forest walk signposted and marked with floral and animal facts and figures. It has a pond with water lilies, aquatic plants and swans. Old ladies feed the ducks; students sit on benches and prepare for their lessons; couples hold hands, look into each other's eyes and profess their love as the sun disappears behind the distant downtown skyscape. In Tanguá Park a pink, semi-circular, turreted structure-cum-plaza (which would certainly look better in marble, but times must have been belt-tightening) oversees a green forested maze of cycle, boat and walking trails. It has been built for the Sunday family crowd who can picnic with thousands of others in the same grounds and never meet them, for the park spans a phenomenal 110 acres. In Maceió the blue sky is reflected in the emerald sea; in Curitiba's Tanguá Park it's reflected in the late afternoon haze of the greenery. I stood in the pink elevated plaza and looked down in disbelief as the woods unfolded as far as the eye could see; are there no nasty property developers in this town?

I bet it's boring at night.

– 56 –

Nick Havana's is a gay/mixed bar-restaurant as coolly European as any you could find in South America. Sophistication in a restaurant nowadays means moody acid jazz and imaginative salads described with lascivious praise. We don't have Greek salads any more, we have *gold sesame bun toasted under a light grill, with crumbly Bulgarian feta and dark kalamata olives tossed in a mixture of Modena balsamic vinegar and coriander olive oil, on a bed of crispy lettuce, bright red radicchio and tangy roquette.* Translate that into Portuguese and you can surmise correctly that my linguistic abilities were sorely tested by the menu; I ordered a hamburger and chips. At least I knew what I was getting.

Elsie, the waitress, was blonde, well built and looked more German than some Germans I know.

'Are you new in Curitiba?' she asked.

'Just arrived today,' I told her.

'Business?'

'No, I'm spending the weekend in Curitiba to check it out.'

She was impressed.

'You found *this* place quickly,' she winked.

'I couldn't find any other gay venues.'

She turned to the bar.

'Marcos!'

An affable Italian-looking barman approached my table.

'Meet ...'

'John,' I filled in.

She took a step back.

'You thought I was *Brazilian*?' I cried, excited.

'No,' said Elsie. 'No. No.'

That was one 'No' too many. I smirked.

'John is a tourist and wants to know about the gay clubs and bars in Curitiba.'

Marcos sat down and took out a pen.

'Elektra is the best,' he said.

Elsie agreed. 'As good as any in São Paulo.'

Marcos resumed his writing.

'Época on Fernando Moreira,' he said.

'Cats,' said Elsie.

'And CEDEX.'

Elsie started marking the places on my map.

'Where should I go after here?'

They looked at each other.

'Bar 21,' said Marcos. 'It's packed right now.'

....

Things I Like About Brazil #12: Unesco Heritage Sites

In order of date of inscription:

- *The town of Ouro Preto*
- *The town of Olinda*
- *The ruins of Sao Miguel das Missões*

- *The historic centre of Salvador*
- *The sanctuary of Bom Jesus in Congonhas*
- *Iguaçu National Park*
- *The city of Brasília*
- *The National Park of Serra da Capivara*
- *The historic centre of São Luis*
- *The historic centre of Diamantina*
- *The Mata Atlântica Reserves*
- *The Pantanal*
- *Jaú National Park, Amazonas*
- *Chapada dos Veadeiros and Emas National Park*
- *Archipelago of Fernando De Noronha*
- *The historic centre of the town of Goiás.*

....

Bar 21 was a loud, seedy, spit-and-sawdust bar of the kind you see lonely women in the movies walk into by accident, stopping the conversation buzz as if with a razor blade. Except that in this bar no harm could possibly befall them.

I ordered a caipirinha to continue my streak from Nick Havana's.

'We don't have any,' said the barman.

'What do you have then?'

'Beer.'

I looked around. This was a one-drink establishment. Everyone was holding large 600-ml Brahmas.

'I'll have a Brahma.'

When it came, I asked for a glass. The waiter grudgingly gave me a champagne glass with a long stem; I was taking up too much of his time and the place was busy, busy, busy. Frankly, even if I didn't look like a tenderfoot, my flute glass made sure I appeared as effete as Oscar Wilde seeking to compete in the Turkish oil-wrestling games in Edirne. Bar 21 was rough: R-U-F-F. *I'll just drink quietly and go.*

It was not to be. Someone came up to me and introduced himself just as I was gulping the last drop.

'Hi, I'm Glauber,' he said. 'And you?'

Glauber was in his early thirties, but far too wrinkled for his age, which made him look shifty and furtive. He was of Italian stock and had been working in coffee plantations all his life. Before I could refuse, he bought me another Brahma. I was getting very tired, but when someone offers you a drink in a new town, you accept.

Glauber kept looking at me.

'You are very sympathetic,' he tried in English.

I laughed.

'You mean *simpático*?'

'Yes.'

A false friend.

'*Simpático* means nice. Sympathetic is *compassivo*.'

'You are very *nice*,' he repeated.

'We'd better stick to Portuguese.'

'*Você é muito simpático*,' he repeated.

I felt like shit. I felt I looked like shit. What was up with him? I had to go to the toilet to look in the mirror. I divide mirrors into two types: good mirrors make me look good; bad mirrors make me look bad. Bar 21 had a very bad mirror. I returned as the room started spinning.

It's been ages since I've felt as drunk as this.

'I'm going home,' I said.

Was Glauber looking at me in an expectant way?

'Won't you finish your beer?'

'You finish it for me.'

'Let me walk you home.'

There was something of the night about Glauber.

And there might be something funny about the drink.

'No, thanks. Where are you going tomorrow? I owe you a beer.'

He mentioned the name of a club Elsie and Marcos seem to have missed.

I wonder why.

*****

By now you know where I went to on that first trip to Brazil: São Paulo by necessity, Rio by choice, Manaus for the Amazon, Ouro Preto and Minas Gerais for the art. There is one more place I visited, and you must surely have suspected its turn was coming.

Foz de Iguaçu is a town at the triple frontier of Paraguay, Argentina and Brazil. Imagine a large capital L. The eastern part, the 'interior' of the L is Brazil and Foz. The lower horizontal line of the L is the Iguaçu River which starts from the Serra do Mar, the coastal mountainous range, and falls into the furious Paraná River, which forms the vertical line of the L. South, below the Iguaçu, there lies Argentina and Puerto Iguazú;

in the west, beyond the Paraná, lies Paraguay and the Ciudad del Este. And on the bottom right, at the tip of the horizontal line of the L, shaped photogenically in a crowning crescent, lie the famous Iguaçu Falls.

I arrived in Foz at two in the afternoon. I quickly found lodgings, taking one of the cheap, sparse but large rooms of the Hotel Imperial before setting off for Hotel Cataratas. There are some hotels in the world that have become legends in themselves: the Dorchester in London; the Chelsea in New York; Mamounia in Marrakech; the Taj in Bombay; the Ritz in Paris; the Ruinas in Machu Picchu – but only the latter, positioned as it is next to the lost city of the Incas, can be compared with the setting of Foz's five-star establishment. The signs to 'Cataratas' direct you both to the falls and the hotel, where the sight of its car park raises your heartbeat to 'expectant'.

So here they are.

The waterfalls of the Iguaçu River are 2.5 miles wide and, depending on the season, comprise up to 275 different cascades where the water plunges down with explosive power. As far as the eye can see there is a never-ending set of cataracts; although none is nearly as high as the Victoria or Angel Falls, their combined grandeur is overpowering. Rainbows frame the hefty bursts of water with saints' halos; exotic birds soar above as if they too are gripped by the spectacle, hovering like the helicopters chartered by the richer type of tourist; lush vegetation punctuates the divisions of the individual falls, marking in the process the end of the tropics. Looking at this volume of water, it seems quite inconceivable that the falls should ever dry out, but they have: in 1934 and, more recently, in May and June 1978 over a period of 28 days when a particularly dry season caused apoplexy among hapless tourists. I was well prepared; I saw them in March at the end of the rainy season in full flood, so to speak, and the rainfall had been such that the total bulk flow was one of the biggest in living memory.

Now for the twist. The falls are not in Brazil. Brazil has the best views from the interior of the L, looking south-east; Brazilian Foz is the biggest and most easily accessible town; but the falls chiefly belong to Argentina. There's still a lot to do on the Brazilian side: a small path winds down to the river level – and oh, those are toucans flying overhead! I never expected birds so oddly shaped to be so gentle and gracious in the air – but no, they flatten their bodies aerodynamically behind their beak, like swimmers in the sky, displaying an unexpected athleticism. A coati family, cuddly and fearless, crossed my path, eliciting oohs and ahs from an elderly Argentinian couple. I turned carefully to avoid a giant spider's web overhanging the path from a branch; she'd caught an extra-large beetle, and she was spinning in a frenzy, cocooning her paralysed victim with dexterity. Even on this well-trodden path, the wildlife was astonishing. I sneezed. I thought only English catkins and pollens were deadly in the summer, but look – there are plenty of new orchids to be allergic to.

At the bottom of the falls, tourists were sunning themselves in benches by a café next to an elevator shaft that takes you up to the top; there were snacks and cold drinks – most welcome in the heat. But I and fifty or so backpackers, families and honeymooning couples just stood there and stared, mesmerised at the aquatic majesty before us and no one, but no one, dared utter a single word.

– 57 –

This is the reason I came to Curitiba in the first place.

The railway line through the Serra do Mar to the Atlantic Ocean is a small miracle of nineteenth-century engineering. It was finished in five years, from 1875 to 1880, and winds itself through some of the most forbidding terrain a railway has been asked to chug across. The newly privatised service that runs the modern tourist *Litorina* train has restored buildings en route and reinforced some of the bridge spans – and there are quite a few: the line runs over 65 miles, incorporating 13 tunnels, 37 bridges and 4 ridge viaducts as it descends 3,000 feet from the Paraná tablelands to the sea.

I sat myself by a window on the left where seats cost more, for this is where the views are most spectacular. A party of Swiss – they are so well informed, it's maddening – had block-booked that side and mine was the last window on the left, well, *left*. I glanced at the jealous backpackers on the right-hand side, one of whom ensconced himself next to me as soon as the train departed. *Cheapskate*.

The four-hour journey starts with a ride through a forest of araucaria pine, this being the more majestic Paraná pine, not the normal 'monkey puzzle' araucaria found in Chile, all horizontal branches with tufts of needles at the ends. That's what *Curitiba* means in Tupi: place of many pines, but sadly no more; around 80 per cent of the Brazilian araucaria forests have been cleared by short-sighted logging. Lake Caiguara is next (on the *right*? I want my money back), formed by the damming of the Ipiranga River, which powered the construction of the railway; soon after the train enters the Roça Nova tunnel, and you know you're in for a treat, for it seems you have boarded a funfair ghost train – the *Litorina* travels in darkness for 500 yards before it comes out on the other side. I notice my backpacker has monopolised the armrest. Next tunnel down I elbow him out forcefully.

This is what the trip is like: tunnel – peak – waterfall (the Bridal Veil) – tunnel – crevice view (the Devil's Peak) – tunnel – viaduct and we are on a natural balcony looking down on bromeliads that flower at the top of the pine trees. Spectacular? You bet.

The train stops for twenty minutes at the sanctuary of Nossa Senhora do Cadeado – a sixties' picnic-awning erected in the place of an old train service station – to observe the state park below the Marumbi mountain massif. The highest peak – 5,075 feet – is called Olympus, and I can see the logic behind the name. This is subtropical forest with a vaguely Mediterranean aspect: deep green horizon meshed with a cerulean sky and a calm distant sea.

When we returned to move off again, my annoying backpacker had sat in my window seat – but the Serra do Mar's warm sun, pine scent and unbroken tranquillity infused me with charity: I let him be and walked to the front next to the train driver. This was a view not to be missed: in front us the Ponte São João, a real-life, implausible 180-feet high *Cassandra Crossing* of a four-span bridge, followed by a sharp 90-degree turn to the left.

We're into the famous Tunnel Five.

When we emerge, we are at the edge of the Rochedinho Ridge, travelling slowly on the Carvalho Viaduct, suspended over the valley below, buoyant in mid-air like the souls of dozens of railway workers who died to complete this perilous stretch. I look at the driver and he smiles: for a few hairy minutes he stops being an earthbound locomotive operator and turns into a daring aeroplane pilot. I catch another glimpse of the scenery for a few long seconds, like a passenger on a slo-mo rollercoaster. Then it's Tunnel Number Four – and I breathe in. The thrill is over: short, sharp and unrepeatable, like all good thrills should be.

Mount Marumbi is followed by the picturesque station at Morretes, another eighteenth-century gold-mining town, a simple Mariana-divested-of-baroque. It's midday, and the town is having its siesta with people laid out asleep in shady corners, an experience so Mexican I look around for the sombreros. We have reached the coastal plateau where five rivers join to produce the Bay of Paranaguá. The Swiss leave and join a bus waiting for them outside. Their excursion will be taking them to Antonina and her beaches, while the rest of us are offered videos of the train ride in Portuguese, German, Spanish and English. I grin mischievously, spotting the missing language. They will be furious if they find out.

It takes ages to reach Paranaguá, a city as industrial as Belo Horizonte or São Paulo. Forget Recife and Salvador – this is the second most important Brazilian harbour after Santos, also doubling as a free port for landlocked Paraguay. Our train crosses busy city streets with no safety barriers. There's constant stop-go, hooting, start-ups and driver communication by walkie-talkie with the line controller. I'm waved back to the carriage as we pass slowly an interminable succession of goods containers.

I bet they're all full of drugs, I joke to myself.

Thankfully the *Litorina* stops at the more picturesque part of Paranaguá, only fifteen minutes' walk to the Rua da Praia and the seaside restaurants. Ferries were waiting to transfer tourists to the Ilha do Mel, an island so close it makes the landscape appear more like a river lagoon than a seaside bay. I was tired, so I had a quick *pirão de peixe* for lunch and then walked down the waterfront past the amateur fishermen, beyond the Mercado Municipal and crafts market to the inter-urban bus station. It was Saturday, and I had a sneaking suspicion I'd have a good time back in Curitiba.

I had no idea what a nightmare it would turn out to be.

*****

There isn't much to do in Foz at night and as next day I had to wake up early to trek on the Argentinian side, I had dinner at a self-service restaurant and retired early to my hotel where the noisy blades of the ceiling fan kept me awake.

Let's put on my radio Walkman. I'll try to sleep with music on, like I did when I was a kid.

'*¡DELICIOSAS HABURGUESAS!*' shouted the radio announcer.

An Argentinian station – what a wonderful Spanish accent. So clear, so manly, so, well, *commanding*. They all talk as if they're giving orders, don't they? And what are they playing? Men At Work. '*I come from a land down under …*'

VZOOP!

This is a language I'm only just beginning to learn. A Brazilian station. Erasure. *'Oh, L'amour.'* Expect the Brazilians to be camper than thou. I listen, humming to the end. Another Erasure single – 'Follow Me' and now another: *'Give a little respect, ohh, baby please ...'* I must have hit an Erasure retrospective.

VZOOP!

Another Brazilian station – this one is playing samba. Actually I'm looking for ...

VZOOP!

Oh, that first Argentinian station again. It's playing Vanilla Ice. He's finished now. This must be a local band. *'Noches de Verano.'* Is that the song or the band's name?

VZOOP!

What's this? Yes! This accent doesn't have the Argentinian *zh* sound – or the unfamiliar 'vos' verb declensions. It's Paraguayan! I am listening to a Paraguayan radio station!

And oh, how cute – it's playing military marches ...

– 58 –

I was already sloshed when I entered Elektra, and by the time I had drunk two caipirínhas, I was anyone's. I liked Elektra. Deep House, New York funk, interesting DJ, good crowd, small size, go-go boys and plenty of fag-haggery in an atmosphere which became more animated when my T-shirt started flashing. *'Legal!'* shouted a tall, European-looking guy who dragged me to the front to show me to his mates. *'Legal,'* they all repeated as we danced, the alcohol flooding my veins – and I can't remember more ...

... I resurfaced back to reality as I was walking up some stairs with the tall guy.

'This way, John,' he said. So he knew my name.

Where am I?

The music in my ears told me that I was still in Elektra. The light was dim up here. I noticed guys – and a few girls – watching porn videos on a TV opposite.

'What's your name again?' I asked my companion.

'Max – you forgot already?'

'Strange name,' I mumbled. Goddess, I was drunk.

'You've forgotten everything,' he said. 'It's from Massimiliano. It's Italian.'

We walked into a darker corner and canoodled. Around us silhouettes engaged in various degrees of covert or in certain cases quite, quite overt sex. A creepy, hot, stuffy silence permeated the room like an everlasting careful hush.

Swearing broke out to our left. A girl with a shrill laugh had voyeuristically walked too close to a pair in a state of semi-undress.

I felt Max's body shake.

'*Puta*,' he said. '*Puta*.'

I could see her now – short, rotund and pissed, she was walking around, a giggling siren of annoyance. I tried to ignore her, but couldn't as she eventually reached us.

I felt Max's body tense up.

'Ha, ha, ha,' she giggled as she came close and recognised me. 'Turn on your T-shirt! We need some light in here,' she joked. 'Ha, ha –'

The edge was razed off the laugh as Max grabbed her breasts.

'Come here,' he said, animated. 'You like it, don't you?'

'Max, leave her.'

'Don't you know it's dangerous to come into a dark room full of horny men?' he continued as he tried to take her blouse off. 'PUTA!'

She started screaming.

'MAX!'

'You come here – you play,' he continued, squeezing her breasts through her screams.

An enormous force dragged me forwards while the torchlight blinded me temporarily.

*****

Christoff, a lanky, blond, short-haired – one could say cropped-before-his-time – German student from Hanover, sat next to me on the inter-country bus which drives across the Bridge Tancredo Neves to the Argentinian *rodoviária* in Puerto Iguazú. I say 'student' loosely, for the last time he had studied anything was more than a year ago. He was your typical cool, streetwise backpacker whose enthusiastic bright eyes had the infectious charm of a brightly coloured painting on a white wall.

Christoff had criss-crossed Brazil, sleeping overnight on the reclining seats. He loved 36-hour journeys.

'I spend no money on hotels,' he said. 'I travelled from Rio all the way up the coast to Fortaleza down to Brasília and now Foz. So cheap.'

'I've only just arrived,' I said. 'I spent two days in São Paulo, and I'm off to Manaus next.'

'I'm going to Manaus, too,' said Christoff.

'Going up again?'

'My return ticket is from Caracas,' he replied.

I was impressed.

'One peso each,' the bus conductor said. 'Please have your passports ready.'

'Where did you like it best?' I continued.

He thought for a bit.

'Rio is fantastic, but you know another good city to visit? Fortaleza.' Christoff looked up dreamily.

'The beaches there are so sandy and deserted. I was swimming naked.'

He put his hand on my shoulder as naturally as if we had gone skinny-dipping together in Ceará.

'And the whole city dances crazy every night.'

Fortaleza. I wonder if I'll ever go there.

We arrived at the Argentinian Visitors Centre deep in the primeval fern-and-shrub forest that girdles Iguaçu River, the falls a constant roar in our ears. We started on the *circuito interior*, a small catwalk that takes you first to the twin falls of Dos Hermanas and then on to the Isla San Martín. The Brazilians have the panoramic end, but the paths on the Argentinian side have many vantage points as close to the cataracts as you can handle. The sheer mileage of the spectacle – here's one set of falls, now there's another – is phenomenal. As soon as we reached Dos Hermanas, Christoff gave me his camera, dropped his rucksack and ran to the path next to the wet and slippery rocks begging for a picture. *He's leaving all his things behind with a stranger*, I thought as I saw him slip and struggle to get as close as possible to the falls. The misty, drenched silhouette at the end of the focused lens bore no resemblance to Christoff, a German, or indeed an Earthling.

'They don't issue any protective clothing like at Niagara,' Christoff mused when he returned, dripping from head to toe.

'Macho culture,' I quipped back.

'No,' he said. 'They probably don't want to spoil your fun.'

He bent over to pick up a blue butterfly.

'Look,' he said, breaking his composed exterior with a sunny Colgate smile.

'*You* look.' I pointed around us where dozens and dozens of butterflies surrounded us fearlessly.

There are over 500 species of *borboletas* in the ecosystem of Foz. The most celebrated and ubiquitous is the shiny metallic-blue Cramer's Morpho, the male of which reaches five inches (we are – ahem – talking wingspan here) whereas the female has a warm yellow colouration with orange and black markings. But there are other beauties: the yellow-and black-striped Zebra, the Black Doris (surely the silliest-named *lepidopterum*), the bright yellow Giant Sulphur, the remarkable Blue Hairstreak whose long dainty tails emanate kite-like from the base of its violet hindwings, and the large six-inch Owl butterfly with brown-and-white running patterns and large owl-like eyes spotting its wings.

At the southernmost tip of the falls there is Puerto Canoas. By then we had given up trying to stay dry as the drizzle was all-pervasive; our main preoccupation was to keep our cameras protected. In Puerto Canoas, the extortionate sum of two pesos takes you by motorised boat to a catwalk by the crevice of the falls opposite the Garganta do Diablo – the Devil's Throat: 230 feet high and 500 feet wide. Christoff had to be prodded heavily to cough up, but how else could we reach the platform? Reluctantly he jumped in the boat and gasped, like the rest of us, at how earlier in the year the power of the waters had bent the platform metal with all the force of a Hiroshima H-bomb.

'Is it safe?' asked a young Australian couple in front of us.

The English-speaking guide of an American group – resplendent and conspicuous in their shiny wet Day-Glo raingear – reassured them.

'It's only during storms that the water can break the platform,' he said. 'It's calm today.'

The boat carefully approached the rim of the waterfall. I could feel the throb of the current underneath and hear the thunder, the constant thunder, of the water.

And then the engine went *put-put* and stopped.

I looked at the boat driver. The Australians screamed.

'*Shit!*' I heard our captain curse. 'We're stuck.'

We were drifting towards the Devil's Throat in a boat with a failed engine. I looked at Christoff who tensed up and squeezed my hand. Is this it? Shall I say my prayers? Perhaps a last snog, with anyone, *anyone* – maybe Christoff?

'HAHAHA!' roared the Argentinian captain and started the engine again. 'You thought we were dead, eh? HAHAHA! Everyone falls for it.'

Well, everyone individually and all collectively could have strangled our Argentinian there and then, but we all sat back politely, relaxed and pretended to laugh at his practical joke. I was especially relieved that I hadn't made a pass at Christoff – who had not lost his boyish backpacker insouciance for a minute, except for that momentary hand-grabbing which fuelled my fancy. My brain checked my nerve-endings. He had let go.

'Careful,' cried the captain, still sniggering like a fifteen-year-old as we stepped cautiously onto the platform. 'You don't want to fall in, do you?'

Indeed we didn't, for what we saw at the end of the catwalk, right at the edge of the precipice, was not just imposing and dramatic – it was frightful. The waters at the Devil's Throat dropped with such power that the spray – rough, frothy and violent – sprang 100 yards up in the air with a noise as deafening as a Harrier jet upon take-off. From above the white-on-blue stripes of the convection eddies alternated like a high-speed oscilloscopic sequence. And yet, in the midst of this triumphant and terrifying spectacle, dozens of swifts were dipping in and out of the spray, frolicking playfully, teasing the waters facetiously, crowned by the thickest close-up rainbow I have ever laid eyes on.

If interstellar visitors ever came to Earth, here is where I'd take them to marvel at our planet's wonders.

– 59 –

I re-emerged into consciousness.

'Where are we?' I asked Max, although it was obvious we were in a club, seedier and darker than Elektra. When Max replied, I looked around with renewed drunken interest. This was the mysterious club Glauber had mentioned, but Elsie and Carlos had left out. I could see why. It wasn't a matter of the music, which was much harder than Elektra, but the mixed crowd: there were many heterosexual couples tripping heavily, red eyes bulging and trainers reeking of advanced decomposition.

'I want to buy some cocaine,' said Max. 'Give me some money.'

What?

'Cocaine. I'm upset. I need a snort.'

My thoughts went over the happenings of the last half-hour. The girl's cries, her eviction and ours from the club – '*Don't ever come here again!*' – and my blind following of Max to what I thought was his apartment. Did we go to his apartment?

I looked at my watch. No, too early. We can't have had sex yet.

I'm getting an early hangover, and I haven't even gone to bed.

'It's ten reais a ball.'

I had hidden most of my money in my sock, so I checked my pockets and wallet – still there – and obediently took out 30 reais for Max. He grabbed the money and left. I walked behind him and saw him approach a dreadlocked black Rasta.

The transaction took less than a minute.

Max returned and winked at me to follow him to the Ladies, where we both entered a cubicle. He took out three red wrapped balls, each half an inch in size.

'Cocaine. I'll make a line,' he said to my incredulous ears.

'Is it so easy?' I asked.

'If you know where to look.'

'So cheap?'

'It's local.'

'From Brazil? You grow cocaine in Paraná?'

He stopped lining and looked up at me.

'No, stupid. From Paraguay.'

I still couldn't grasp it.

'Paraguay grows cocaine?'

Max shook his head and didn't answer. He picked up a ten-real note and made a small snorter. We split the balls. He gave me the third wrapper.

'You keep it,' he said, pulled me close and kissed me in the mouth, his hands all over my body.

....

Things I Don't Like About Brazil #12:
Another Kind Of Traffic

Bolivian cocaine is refined in the favelas of Rio and São Paulo, controlled by drug barons who rule by iron hand and where the only penalty – like in the old Inca Empire – is death. The gangs – the quadrilhas *– are encouraged to enlist in the army so that they can become experts in handling weapons; police raids regularly discover rifles, bazookas and hand grenades. That's how the favelas' samba schools can afford those extravagant Carnaval creations. It's their payback by the drug barons.*

There are two main corridors for Bolivian cocaine to enter Brazil: the federal road BR-364 from the Yungas to Manaus via Rondônia and Porto Velho, and the Pantanal route from Santa Cruz to Corumbá and from there to Campo Grande.

Now if I were a drug smuggler or money launderer, I would choose a place on a frontier with a high turnover of tourists, who provide so-called 'invisible' earnings and where border controls are minimal. So there is a third, indirect option: via Paraguay – down the eponymous river to Asuncion and then via Ponta Pora to Londrina or via Ciudad del Este into Foz de Iguaçu.

Hey, that's a tourist place and a half.

....

The music in the club seemed better and raunchier; the few lights brighter and more vivid. The treble see-sawed inside my brain and the bass choked my throat. I was on the dance floor, but I don't remember dancing. I don't remember where Max went. In fact, I remember hardly anything.

Except Glauber.

'Glauber?' I said. 'Here!'

His eyes were already fixed on me through a psychedelic haze.

'You're always drunk,' he said.

I giggled.

'I'm not drunk,' I said. 'I'm stoned.'

'What did you say?'

'My friend Max bought some cocaine.'

Glauber's mulatto features went pale.

'You know this is a crime?'

Huh?

His hand grabbed my arm tightly.

'Glauber,' I said, 'you're hurting me.'

'My friend here is a policeman,' he said.

What?

A thirtyish, heavily built bloke stepped forward. Glauber whispered something in his ear while still holding me by the arm, his grip tight as ever.

My alcohol levels dropped at once. The third wrapper was still in my pocket.

'Did you just buy drugs?' asked the policeman in Portuguese.

'Huh?' I said. '*Não falo português.*'

'He does,' said Glauber. 'He speaks perfect Portuguese.'

The policeman looked at me and repeated, 'Did you just buy drugs?'

I looked at him uncomprehendingly.

'He doesn't speak any Portuguese,' complained the policeman to Glauber.

Glauber shook me violently.

'Tell – him – you – speak – Portuguese,' he said slowly in English.

'*Falo. Um pouco,*' I pretended to obey.

The policeman made a go-away sign to Glauber. They started gesticulating and talking to each other rapidly.

Glauber had let go of my arm.

I quickly let the third wrapper roll down my back trouser leg to the floor.

The policeman spoke to me, and this time I really didn't understand what he was saying. I smiled and shrugged my shoulders.

Out of the corner of my eye, I saw Glauber point at the black Rasta who was leaning on the wall, merging with the surrounding darkness.

I stepped slowly onto the third red wrapper and twisted my foot on it.

The policeman approached the Rasta and asked him something. The Rasta turned round to scrutinise me and even though it was dark, I saw his eyes flash and slice me like salami.

Had he seen me with Max?

The Rasta shook his head. The policeman waved Glauber over, and from what I could gather, gave him a pasting. They disappeared into the darkness, and I never saw them again.

I breathed in, then I breathed out and looked at my shoes.

Licking my sole would surely draw attention …

*****

My recollection of the heat in Foz de Iguaçu is that it was the most infernal I have experienced in Brazil. Maybe it was the faulty ceiling fan, maybe it was the natural humidifier of the falls themselves, or maybe it was an early tropical intolerance of mine. Not even Corumbá four years later could compare with the vast outdoor parboiler Foz had turned into. Even so, I was determined to go to the infamous Ciudad del Este; I had just been to Argentina – now I could boast I'd been to Paraguay. I looked at my watch. I was meeting Christoff outside the Bridge of Friendship in half an hour.

The walk to the Bridge of Friendship across the Rio Paraná, which divides Paraguay from Brazil, passes through the lacklustre, untouristworthy north part of Foz and the barracks of the Brazilian 34th Battalion whose guards were all hand-picked hunks – and who were being highly unguarded in their behaviour. They were whistling at the girls, surreptitiously eyeing the boys, and I swear I caught them salivating at the smooth behinds of the horses dragging the passing carts. Any invader from across the river would think twice before letting himself be taken prisoner. Maybe that's why the Guaranis fought to the death in the Paraguayan War.

I sighted Christoff.

'There are no Customs,' he said, his well-ordered Middle European world upside-down. 'No Immigration. Nothing.'

I inspected the volume of loaded pedestrians, motorised cars and horse-drawn carts stacked to the brim.

This was a smugglers' paradise.

There was a sort of shack on the Paraguayan side manned by short and mean-looking soldiers brandishing automatic weapons but still dressed in what looked like garb dating from the Paraguayan War. Christoff and I applied there with our passports and were given short shrift; if we returned to Brazil the same day we would need no stamps.

'But when we come back, how will they know that we haven't spent, say, a fortnight outside the country?' Christoff wondered.

'They must have photographic memories,' I snapped. 'Now let's go!'

Ten minutes later I heard him speak behind me.

'I don't think they looked at us long enough to keep us in their memories,' he said. 'Maybe we should return to remind them.'

Sometimes I forgot Christoff was German.

'Christoff, I was joking. These soldiers don't care. They probably pick up travellers randomly and demand bribes to let them through and that's it.'

'What if they pick on us on the way back?'

I shrugged my shoulders. 'We'll deal with it if and when.'

We slowly entered the city, although this was a misnomer. This was a large bazaar, a compilation of corrugated-iron market stalls full of cheap goods of highly dubious provenance; I nominate it a Unesco cultural monument to retail therapy.

'Where do these people sleep?' wondered Christoff.

Indeed. We could see no houses, few restaurants or cafés, no hotels. There were shops, shoppers, cars, buses and taxis (for those unable to carry their shopping), everyone in a hurry. The natives must sleep on top of their wares.

A Mona Lisa looked down on us from the middle of the street. Was there an art exhibition in this town? No, Mona Lisa was a department store which knew how to attract attention using cultural incongruity. The streets were indistinguishable in the way only an amorphous shopping mall can be, with crowds hissing and flowing in a human traffic version of the famous spectacle of nature next door. We were swamped by the usual universal logos: Kent cigarettes, Coca-Cola, Heineken beer. There's Kyos, a shop selling and recharging batteries of all sorts; Casa Mandala, a psychedelic headshop next to an off-licence with cheap suspect Ballantine's whisky; leather goods from soft shammy brown leather to strong hide good enough for suitcases; fans, fans and more electric fans – to date, a Guarani market still brings an image of rotating blades to my mind; Casa Argento, a cheap silversmith's, its neglected window products covered with a dark oxide coating; fans and more fans; Casa Liliana, Casa Fatima and Casa 5★★★★ for comprehension in all languages; Casa Robert offering sunglasses; Casa Julia, 'Eletrónicos em Geral'; Casa Sol with male clothing, Casa Fenix with female clothing; Casa Riba Star with Casio organs and calculators; films, handbags, prints, stamps, vinyl records, CDs, Walkmans and cassettes, Indian artefacts, cheap plastic dolls and fans, fans, fans. A young woman stood in the middle of the road with ten suit carriers – had she bought them or was she selling them? A family was using a wheelbarrow to carry a large box containing a television – with the obligatory electric fan on top.

'This is horrible,' whispered Christoff. 'What's that science fiction series on TV? We've entered *The Twilight Zone*.'

Ciudad del Este is much more: it is supposed to be the third-largest black market in the world after Hong Kong and Miami with a turnover larger than Paraguay's own GDP. Bolivian cocaine is imported and exported routinely via hundreds of James Bond-style smuggler landing strips in the jungle. Latin American insurance companies have permanent agents to trace stolen luxury automobiles offered for sale in the town. As for the money-laundering services taking place in its vast network of banks and *cambios*: their turnover is larger than the gross national product of a medium European country like Hungary.

We sat down at a *lanchonete* to eat a greasy hamburger and chips. Food in Ciudad del Este is an ordeal by fork. Paraguay is not famed for its culinary delights, with good reason I'm afraid.

A well-groomed kid in a red top, not older than twelve, popped up from behind a table: 'You want Rolex watches?' he said.

'I don't want any.'

'You want Chanel Number Five for your girlfriend?'

'I'm not interested.'

'A Canon camera? Very cheap.'

'No.'

'You want *cocaína*?'

Christoff and I looked at each other, and I could sense we were both constructing scenarios involving illegal transactions, Paraguayan soldier guards acquiring a sudden photographic memory and large hard currency amounts of blackmail money.

'GO AWAY!'

'You want pictures?' the kid persisted. 'A dollar for him.'

Out of the throng emerged a large Guarani Indian with a face like Mount Rushmore halfway through the carving of the giant presidential sculptures. He was wearing a tight red, white and blue T-shirt over his belly, oversized jeans and moccasins and was holding feathered purses, Bolivian flutes and knitted shoulder bags. He was a dream of a picture, and we gladly paid our one dollar. The Indian posed unsmiling – not unlike Mona Lisa – and looked to his right. Hmm, I could get a better picture than that!

'Can you ask him to look over here and smile?' I asked the kid.

'If you want him to smile, it will cost you another dollar,' he answered. *Now that's the spirit.*

*****

When the club closed at six o'clock I was still buzzing. There must be an afterparty somewhere. Had all that happened in the club or was it a product of my imagination?

If I could only find Max.

Lo and behold, there he was, dapper, tall and, in the soft dawn light, moodily beautiful. I noticed for the first time a scar next to his eyebrow which enhanced rather than diminished his features by providing a focal counterpoint. He was standing outside with a party of friends as if waiting for someone. Was it me?

I tried to hug him.

He withdrew.

'What's wrong?' I asked.

'Nothing.'

I tried to hug him again.

He shooed me away.

'Where do we go now?'

The other guys laughed.

'The gringo wants more,' one of them said.

'Is there an afterparty?' I asked.

'My home,' said Max.

'Let's go then,' I said, remembering the scene in the toilets.

'I'm going alone.'

I stood back. The other guys suddenly went quiet.

I don't like this silence.

I tried to look into Max's eyes. He avoided mine.

I turned on my flashing T-shirt.

'Remember?' I tried to joke.

'You told someone that I take drugs,' he said, turning his head abruptly, his chin not far from mine.

'No, I didn't.'

His posse remained immobile.

This silence.

'You told someone I take drugs,' he said again. 'I don't take drugs.'

'Oh, *c'mon*, Max,' I said and tried to embrace him.

Like a shot he pulled away and pushed me to the ground.

And then they were upon me.

*****

Back in Foz it's nine at night and I am sprinkling manioc flour on my rice and beans, sitting next to Christoff for our last meal together. Tomorrow I'm returning to São Paulo for a weekend before I take the plane to Manaus. Christoff has a bus ticket on the Transamazônica.

'You're just a tourist,' he mocks me. 'I look at places and cities on the map, and I sit there wondering what they're like.'

'You're wrong,' I tell him. 'That's what I do, too. But I find that most of them are alike.'

'No, they're not. Each one has its own atmosphere. And from each one you take your own unique memories.'

I look at him with a mixture of tenderness and admiration.

'Have you always been a philosopher?' I muse.

Christoff doesn't answer. He munches his food, the small light in the self-service restaurant shining on his smooth forehead turning him paler than he already is, for despite his voyages in Brazil he has acquired no proper tan.

'We should meet in Manaus. We'll both be there next weekend, won't we?'

For the first time he studies me carefully, then smiles.

'OK,' he agrees. 'Where?'

I think.

'Manaus has a famous opera house. In front of the opera house, say eight in the evening next Saturday night?'

'OK,' he says simply and continues eating.

'I'll be there,' I say.

'Me too.'

We sit there without talking, and I drink my beer while he sips his Coke, for Christoff doesn't touch alcohol. Traveller friendships are formed on an instinctive basis, are intense, and they live with you forever.

When I catch his eye again, he is staring at me. He pulls out a pendant from around his neck that I hadn't seen him wear before.

'Take it,' he says. 'It's a present.'

'I can't,' I say quickly.

'It cost me nothing,' he says with no expression in his voice. 'I bought it here in Foz. I want you to have it.'

I am moved. This is a special present coming from a character as frugal as Christoff. I examine it carefully. It's a small wooden fist with the thumb protruding slightly between the second and third finger. Was that an obscene gesture?

'What is it?' I ask.

'It's a *figa*. A Brazilian good-luck charm. You need it.'

'Why do I need it?'

'Because you travel alone. It's dangerous travelling alone in Brazil.'

'You also travel alone,' I counter.

He had the answer ready.

'Yes,' he replies. 'But it's you who needs the lucky charm, because you trust people too much.'

I never met him in Manaus.

*****

In Nick Havana's Elsie and Carlos were listening raptly.

'So I fell to the ground. There were four of them, and they started kicking me and tried to steal my wallet. They tore up my T-shirt but somehow I managed to stand up. I don't know how I managed to salvage my watch – the strap was only partly broken. I lost my wallet but there was hardly anything in it – my money was hidden in my sock. I got up very quickly and ran away. They didn't follow me. I saw a taxi coming on the other side of the avenue, and I got in.'

I remembered waving at them and mouthing 'Why?' before I got in the taxi, as they looked at me immobile and unwilling to move. 'I don't reckon they wanted a fight. It was all opportunistic.'

I sipped my glass of Chilean Merlot and tucked into my Cuban salad (lettuce, rocket, alfalfa and bacon). I didn't tell Elsie and Carlos that I'd cried afterwards, more a release of adrenaline than an expression of sorrow. I still had a bloody lip and a few bruises on my thighs where they'd kicked me.

'The taxi driver told me I should go to the police. I said no. Exactly what would my story be?'

'Glauber – he was obviously planning something with the so-called policeman. He was never a policeman,' said Elsie. 'You were very lucky to escape both times.'

'And with your watch – and your money,' added Carlos.

I had the strap fixed in a jeweller's that morning. He did it for free when he heard my story. But the flashing T-shirt was a goner.

'So, I can't return to Curitiba,' I finished with a sigh. 'I'm afraid of meeting Glauber in Bar 21. I'm banned from Elektra. I'm scared of meeting Max in another club. Me and this town are finished.'

Carlos looked at Elsie, winked at her and filled my glass with red wine.

'On the house,' he said. 'We do hope you come back.'

Elsie kissed me. 'Have a great time in Florianópolis. And be careful. Don't trust people. Trust your instinct.'

No, *no*. I wish I could agree with Elsie. You have to trust people even if they let you down – because if I didn't trust people, I wouldn't have any tales to tell.

'When my instinct is not drowned by alcohol,' I said.

Their friendly faces cheered me up: 'Well, you will always be welcome at Nick Havana's.'

And that is my last, special memory of Curitiba, model city, and its oh, so model, *traffic*.

Chapter 13

The Boys from Brazil
(Florianópolis, Petrópolis)

The Boys from Brazil is a 1978 Hollywood production based on an Ira Levin bestseller. It concerns a secret plot to clone the dead Adolf Hitler, masterminded by Gregory Peck's villain who is none other than the Nazi Angel of Death, Dr Josef Mengele; we are supposed to swallow the implausible scenario that he was alive and well and plotting in Brazil. Laurence Olivier gives a great hammy performance in a thriller with moments of high camp, peppered by streaks of intense violence and punctuated by a good original score which lost the Oscar to the music from *Midnight Express*. The title has entered English usage denoting South America's fictitious neo-Nazi sympathisers in Chile, Brazil and Argentina, whereas the movie and its preposterous plot is forgotten.

Except that we now know that when the book was written and the film was shot, Dr Josef Mengele was indeed alive and well, leading an uneventful existence in São Paulo.

....

The Words You'll Need
*Auslandsorganisationen (German) = Foreign (affiliate) organisations of the
  Nazi Party*
Cortes = Portuguese parliament
irmãos = brothers
Kreise (German) = circles, in this context, districts
mais um? = one more?
queijo = cheese
você é de Curitiba? = are you from Curitiba?

....

– 60 –

My Caterinense bus to Florianópolis was a two-storey modern monster with TV up front and toilet at the back; reclining seats let me put my feet up. I still recall my surprise at the noiselessness of the engine, the functioning air conditioning, the comfort combined with punctuality and the American-style have-a-nice-day service. Where were the screaming children? They were sitting obediently playing with their Gameboys. Where were the loud chatting couples? There, reading newspapers and magazines. Where was the pandemonium occasioned when storing your luggage under the bus? I checked mine in at the Caterinense counter with a brunette who flirted with me. I glanced at my coupon. I wasn't *flying* to Florianópolis, was I? No, John, this is a bus station, but Caterinense is a Santa Catarina company, and there are many German-Brazilians there.

To reach the said state of Santa Catarina we had to descend from Curitiba to Joinville, edged in by the pines of the Mata Atlântica and by three-lorry-long logging juggernauts whose motorway antics, such as overtaking each other on blind curves, reminded me that, refined behaviour aside, this is South America after all. If anything, as one approaches Argentina, the drivers become more erratic, not less.

Things I Don't Like About Brazil #13: Motels

I think it's the hypocrisy behind the concept which makes me scoff at this uniquely Brazilian institution. Motels are not hotels based around the car as in the United States; they are hotels for couples who go there to shag. There are cheap motels, which rent rooms by the hour, expensive motels, which offer special breakfasts and luxury motels, which offer bridal suites, en-suite jacuzzis and porn video channels.

My friends in Brazil see nothing untoward; they make use of them all the time. Because for casual sex, especially if it involves a prostitute, they're safer; they're not going to ask any questions or demand ID cards. But it is exactly this institutionalisation of one-night stands by businessmen cheating on their wives that annoys me. Gay saunas and darkrooms provide a sheltered space for men whose sexuality might otherwise lead them to seek satisfaction outdoors and compromise their safety, but motels thrive on adultery, prostitution and maintaining one's 'good name'. Ultimately, men – almost always men – use motels because they don't want to be seen having sex with a prostitute, with someone other than their wife or girlfriend or with other men, thus keeping alive the flame of shame that caused them to be clandestine in the first place. So this is what I have against motels: they are either perpetuating the stigma attached to prostitution and homosexuality or facilitating the disintegration of trust.

Joinville is an embarrassment. Industrial and ugly with snooker halls and over-the-top motels: here's one shaped like a windmill (for S&M sessions?), another, comprising several individual log-cabins, advertises itself as 'Motel California' (for the discerning ageing hippie?) and a whale-shaped motel (catering for the Moby Dick-sized punter?)

The further we go into Santa Catarina, whose coastline we begin to hug after Barra Velha, the more I notice the names – Bar Schmitt, Fazenda Breitner, Hotel Fischer (offering cachaça and *queijo colonial*) – and the buildings: gone are the usual cement-and-corrugated iron or adobe-and-wattle swellings-rather-than-dwellings and in come Scandinavian log cabins and Swiss wooden-slatted chalets. As if to confirm the confusion, we pass a sign to Blumenau, the most German of Brazilian towns, which celebrates its own Oktoberfest – unlike the Bavarian original, this actually does occur in October.

Brazil started attracting European migrants for two reasons: the gradual abolition of slavery during a period of agricultural expansion, and a political desire to 'whiten' the country's population, an unspoken thesis which became quite outspoken in the early twentieth century. Its prime exponent was Oliveira Vianna who, in a series of books, professed the view that blacks were an inferior race that dragged Brazil downwards – only Aryanisation could help the country.

In the 1840s a group of Germans and Swiss first came to work in the coffee plantations of São Paulo and immediately rebelled at the conditions they were supposed to work under – so much so that some European states, notably Prussia, banned Brazilian agencies from advertising passages for prospective migrants. It would take many steps towards the eventual abolition of slavery for European immigration really to take off in Brazil. In the eleven years from 1872 to 1883 about 50,000 immigrants arrived; in 1888 alone, the year of the abolition, Brazil welcomed 132,000 new faces.

As the British and the French had their own colonies to choose from, it was left to the poor of the countries who had lost out on the initial carving up of the globe to immigrate to Brazil: East Europeans, Italians and, last but not least, Germans, who settled in the south. The Italians, who made up about 50 per cent of new arrivals, any Spanish who made the move and, of course, the steady wave of mainland Portuguese were acculturated easily. Not so the Germans, who formed the fourth largest immigrant group, for their language was very different, their customs Northern European and their demeanour more exclusive. They started building their own schools in their own towns and only learned sufficient Portuguese to communicate outside their sheltered enclaves, which under other circumstances might have been called ghettos. This isolationism, combined with the doctrine of Pan-Germanism in Europe, which fuelled Prussian expansion at the end of the nineteenth century and continued in Hitler's time, created mistrust between the German immigrants and the Portuguese establishment.

The creation of a Nazi Party in Santa Catarina didn't help much either ...

*****

When we reach Itajaí I notice that this is the same BR-101 motorway I rode on from Recife to Porto de Galinhas. It doesn't quite have the ring of a Route 66, but it more than compensates with the sights. I'd been on it from Natal to Pippa, and I hit it again near Cachoeira. It continues just off Ilhéus onwards to Vitória and Rio de Janeiro where it forms the highly scenic coastal route to Santos, passing Paratí, Angra dos Reis and Guarujá. It sort of disappears around São Paulo (doesn't everything?) into various state highways, to re-emerge in Joinville and continue uninterrupted to Rio Grande do Sul through the national park of Lagoa do Peixe where the perilous stretch between Bojuru and Tavares is nicknamed the 'Road of Hell'. The BR-101 stops at the bottom of the park peninsula opposite Rio Grande, the town which gave the southern state its name. It was at the turnoff to Brusque I spotted the highway name again, near a car showroom of the Irmãos Fischer, full of solid, commodious lorries. The Brusques seem to like their cars, well, *sturdy*.

As the afternoon progressed, the shadows became longer, the twittering birds emerged – along with the vultures – and the ghastly painted-by-numbers skyscrapers of Balneário Camboriú blotted the landscape ahead. This resort offers the best imitation of a Spanish Costa overbuilding in South America this side of Viña del Mar. It's a kind of Torremolinos-without-the-lager-louts, with the role of the British assumed by the ubiquitous Argentinians, Santa Catarina's main source of foreign exchange. It is not widely known that Florianópolis is the second most visited town in Brazil after Rio, but yes, it eclipses Manaus, Foz do Iguaçu, Olinda and Salvador; it makes Ouro Preto bite the dust and Fortaleza turn green with envy. And the only thing Florianópolis and Santa Catarina have to show for, is beaches.

At Itapema we hit one of those beaches with a thicket of villas sporting enough satellite dishes to intercept communications over the whole of Patagonia, before we ascend the mountains again. Santa Catarina is a small state of three Belgiums, full of mountains and coastline which make for an appealing combination like in Chile – especially now, as we drive through hydrangeas, wild banana trees and ivy creepers which frame beautifully the town of Porto Belo below. Why anyone would spend time in Balneário Camboriú when this gem of a peninsula is so close is for advertisers to ponder over. But tackiness rears its head even here. Forget those whale-and-windmill motels: here is a whole pizzeria within an old, rusting *aeroplane*. Excuse me. Do people crave for airline food and plastic cutlery on a Saturday night? Do they get to wear seatbelts, sit uncomfortably with the minimum of legroom and queue interminably for the tiny toilets? And how did the frigging plane get there?

Before I have time to solve such eternal questions, we turn a curve and I shut down my brain, for there's a panoramic view of Florianópolis that has the whole bus enthralled. The setting only Brazil can provide: a city split between the mainland shore and the hills of the island of Santa Catarina, less than two miles across a channel that divides the sea into a north and south 'bay'. The two city halves are joined by an old iron suspension bridge – now a spectacular state monument – and a more modern bridge below. Dusk in shades of blood orange has brought on the lights, which flicker in a sloping, subtropical San Francisco without the fog.

So many chapters into this, and I fall in love with a Brazilian town again.

– 61 –

If someone offered you a window seat in a time-machine to Brazil's 500-year-old historical past, where would you choose to land? At Monte Pascoal with Cabral and his men checking out the first contact between the Old World and the New? In Salvador watching a slave ship unload its human cargo? In Aleijadinho's atelier observing the master at work, trying to second-guess his disease?

Nah – I'd go for a laugh, attending moments of the Portuguese Court in Rio de Janeiro. Dom João, a plump, effeminate slob carrying chicken drumsticks in his pocket in case he needed a snack, his ugly-as-sin, scheming, autocratic wife Carlota Joaquina, and their two sons – acne-ridden Dom Pedro and cowboy-playboy Dom Miguel, extraordinary womanisers both. Mad Queen Maria died in exile in March 1816, but was not buried until the Court's return to Portugal in 1821. Of course, the royal funerary rites had to be observed back home: the queen had to lie in state for all to pay their respects. When they opened the coffin, which had suffered the heat of the tropics for all those years, the stench of decomposition was such that one of the princesses fainted. The ladies-in-waiting earned their keep as they had to reclothe the body in a black robe, gloves, shoes and stockings, while the nobles and the bishops had to line up and kiss her hand. I'd pay good money to watch that.

Dom João opened Brazil's ports to trade with Great Britain and caused a major boom on the London Stock Exchange where thousands of madcap schemes were launched. In the year 2000, when asked about the capital of Brazil, many Brits answered Buenos Aires, so imagine the extent of their ignorance two centuries back: they tried to sell ladies' corsets to the sweating mulattas, cast-iron fireplaces to the denizens of Rio and ice skates to the barefoot population of the Nordeste. But soon enough the British ships outnumbered the Portuguese in the ports by twenty to one, and Brazil entered the chessboard of Great Power machinations. Around it Spanish Latin America was ablaze as Napoleonic ideas spread. Perhaps it is fitting for a continent with operetta politics that Simon Bolívar, a Basque revolutionary with a Clintonesque libido, aided by the bastard son of an Irish settler (Bernardo O'Higgins) and an Argentinian hypochondriac (José de San Martín) should liberate the Spanish colonies, with the fearsome English seadog, Admiral Cochrane, playing the pantomime dame.

It was the very presence of the king in Brazil that avoided the bloodiness of the uprisings from Santiago to Caracas, for Brazil was no longer a colony: it had now become equal in status with the motherland. Even after the Duke of Wellington's successful Second Peninsular War, even after Waterloo, even after the newly assembled Cortes recalled him back to Lisbon, King João VI stayed in Rio, his only moves being from the Palace of São Cristóvão to the one on the Ilha do Governador. Some say he was sluggish and indecisive, some say he liked Brazil and his new subjects more than Portugal and its power games – and who can blame him? – but his actions always make sense with hindsight. He left Portugal when he should have done, he stayed in Brazil as long as he had to in order to avoid bloodshed, he returned to Portugal at the right time to save it from anarchy, and he left his 23-year-old heir Dom Pedro in Rio to take care of business in case independence *did* catch on. Dom

João remained to his death a rare figure of equanimity in an era seething with conspiracy, although he is loathed in Brazil for ransacking the Treasury upon his return to Portugal. He looked increasingly porcine towards the end of his life and, like Elvis, he died by food. His supposed last words were: *'This broth has killed me'*, giving rise to the usual speculation that he was poisoned. The last momentous act of his reign was to recognise the independence of Brazil. This happened so quickly and so relatively bloodlessly, it left everyone astounded, including the king, the Cortes and the London Foreign Office.

It was in the Lisbon post-Napoleonic Constitutional Assembly that the envy towards the rich ex-colony had exploded. The Rio notables were enraged when they found out that laws were being passed before the deputies from Brazil, now an ex-colony with equal status to Portugal, had taken their seats. And when they did, they were taunted and shouted down when they refused to accept that their courts of law should be moved to Lisbon and that they should lose their new commercial privileges. The question of sending troops to Brazil – which had none of its own – was raised. The Cortes talked of exiling Dom Pedro to England.

The first act of defiance by the young Prince was his public declaration on 9 February 1822 that he would not leave; an episode which has been labelled *'dia do fico'* – the day of *'I'm staying'*. *Fico – ficus*: for years I lived under the impression that those giddy Brazilians were celebrating a Day of the Fig or, judging from their dental-floss swimming suits, the Day of the Fig Leaf. It would be a nice idea.

In August 1822, Dom Pedro set off from Rio to São Paulo just as he found out that the Cortes in Lisbon had declared its intention to undertake 'the reconquest of Brazil'. The Paulistas welcomed him into their town with fireworks and cheers; Dom Pedro had to smile and gesture royally despite terrible diarrhoea – we all have our crosses to bear. He also checked out the mood in Santos, and on 7 September at the banks of the Ipiranga River, he received two letters from Rio. His secretary read them while Dom Pedro was 'crouching by' as historians put it, not explaining why he didn't read them himself, although they pointedly stress that he was still suffering from dysentery. The first missive was from the Cortes, which had sent an ultimatum – arrest Prime Minister José Bonifácio and return to Lisbon now. The other was a plea from the said José Bonifácio and Pedro's Habsburg wife, Empress Leopoldina (who is #94 on the list of famous gays and lesbians of the Grupo Gay da Bahia with at least one well-documented affair with English traveller Maria Graham). The letters asked him either to return to Portugal as a prisoner or stay free and proclaim independence. Dom Pedro rose, ripped up the letters and told his equerry: 'Inform my guard, I have decided upon the independence of Brazil.' It was 4.30 p.m. and a scene I would like to have witnessed with my time-machine, if only to ascertain what Dom Pedro's squatting involved and whether history would have been different had Imodium already been invented.

From then on, events progressed rapidly. The Portuguese garrisons in the Nordeste rebelled. The main resistance occurred in Salvador. There, General Luiz Madeira only surrendered when Admiral Cochrane, fresh from supporting the Spanish rebels, accepted Dom Pedro's invitation to head the new Brazilian Navy and blockaded Salvador. On 2 July – the famous *Dois de Julho* in Bahian history – the last Portuguese were driven out of Bahia. The further capitulation of Pernambuco and last of all Maranhão was a matter of months. All Portuguese property in Brazil was confiscated to force the Cortes into acceptance. Dom Pedro was crowned Emperor Pedro I on 1 December 1822: a constitutional monarch in the New World, at war with the country of his birth – and his father.

It was that dynastic succession that ensured Brazil's survival, because its future was not secure until the newly formed Holy Alliance of Great Powers agreed to its independence. The first country to recognise Brazil was James Monroe's United States, but the Holy Alliance was at odds. Bourbon France and Czarist Russia were for the *status quo ante*; Metternich's Austria saw a monarchy in South America as a counterpoise to all these new caudillo democracies; this left Great Britain with a carte blanche to mediate for Brazil's independence, finally obtaining a treaty on 29 August 1825, ratified on 9 November. Perhaps it was this ratification that was the last nail in the coffin of João VI – the only European monarch who had ever witnessed the vitality, vigour and promise of his transatlantic colonies and seen the child grow taller than the parent. The treaty recognised the independence of Brazil and, tagged at the end of other clauses, it arranged for the payment of reparations to Portugal – with money lent by London banks. Thus it was in debt to international bankers that Brazil was born and that has been its curse ever since; it has lived in debt for most of its history and in her 500th year she owed more to foreigners than all the African countries from the Sahara to Cape Town.

One of Dom Pedro's daughters from his first wife Leopoldina was Francisca Carolina who married the son of French King Louis Philippe in 1843. Dona Francisca's dowry was 25 square leagues of land. With the 1848 revolt and subsequent rule of Louis Napoleon, the Philippes fled to England and in order to survive sold their large plot to the Colonisation Society of Hamburg which sent 118 German and Swiss immigrants to found the city of Dona Francisca in 1851. Its name was soon changed to honour the title of Dona Francisca's husband: Prince de *Joinville*.

You thought I was drifting, eh?

*****

The receptionist at Hotel Faial on the beautifully named Rua Felipe Schmidt gave me a map of Florianópolis. I was buzzing after a short taxi ride from the bus station where I had successfully convinced the driver I was on business from Curitiba. *Hey, I can fool anyone!* I thought until I saw the city map with all the GLS spots of Florianópolis clearly marked. I was doubly impressed. Not only by the town tourist board, which had printed out a map specially for gays and lesbians, but also by my receptionist who had earned his tip.

Things I Like About Brazil #13: GLS Perspectives

The attitude towards gays and lesbians in new Brazil has progressed in leaps and bounds since the homophobia of the military regime. Rio Grande do Sul leads the way: the State High Court has made a series of remarkable decisions, some not even found in many European countries: forcing employers to apply the concept of 'dependent' to same-sex couples in health plans (1996); granting permission for male-to-female transsexuals to use their female identity in law (1998); transferring wholesale family law to same-sex couples for resolution of financial disputes (1999, reconfirmed for inheritance purposes in 2001); and treating same-sex couples the same as opposite-sex couples for the provision of pensions by state bodies (2000). In Bahia non-discrimination laws against homosexuals and laws recognising transsexual rights were passed in 1997. In Rio de Janeiro immigration rights for same-sex partners were conceded after a high profile case where the mother of the Brazilian partner of a gay couple offered to marry her son's lover to keep him in the country. São Paulo's Gay Pride has grown from a demonstration of a mere 5,000 people to a celebration of 150,000 in five years. The most homophobic state is still Pernambuco – the one with the oldest Portuguese influence, as strictly conservative socially as the mother country. Of course, no law can change the mentality of the man on the avenida or, more importantly, the abuse of existing laws by the Brazilian Military Police – but the pace of progress has been breathtaking.

....

The hippest place in town is 32, chosen by the Brazilian *Playboy* magazine as having one of the best selections of beers in the country. It's within the confines of the city's market, the Mercado Público, which is full of popular watering holes from the early evening on. For such a famous institution it's tiny. This place with fewer than ten two-person tables sells the most champagne in the whole of Brazil? I looked at the menu: Norwegian gravadlax, Scottish whisky, Chilean wine, Metaxa brandy, French *foie gras*, caviar, lobster, crab. I chose the oysters – the only live food I allow myself to digest – and a glass of Undurraga, a Chilean dry white wine. I expected half a dozen; I was served twelve. I expected them size AA like French farmed *ouitres*, and when they came they were deep-sea monstrous. The busy waiter picked up my empty wine glass.

'*Mais um?*'

Why not?

'*Você é de Curitiba?*'

Tanned and relaxed I surely didn't look like a gringo.

'No,' I said, 'from London.'

'Ah, London,' he said taking more interest in me. 'I'm originally from Italy.'

It's reassuring to note that long distance can be responsible for geographical confusion both ways: it's not just Europeans who view Latin America as a homogeneous whole.

'London is in England,' I smiled condescendingly. 'But I've been to –'

Was that a shot?

'Was that a shot?' asked the waiter, eyes wide.

We heard another shot. And another. They were from next door.

The waiter got up along with all of the bar's patrons.

'My wine!' I reminded him. I couldn't swallow those oysters dry.

The waiter had already run off.

So that's what shots sound like. Better stay here.

There was no one at the bar or behind the till. I walked over and refilled my glass with wine. I heard the ambulance arrive. I checked my watch. Fifteen minutes, a long time in a small town like this. The waiter returned gesticulating excitedly.

'Personal dispute,' he said. 'In the bar, Goiánio, next arcade along. One guy shot another over a woman.'

And I thought it was only in Rio and Salvador that I had to watch out ...

....

ENVY PROVOKES FIGHT AND LEAVES TWO WOUNDED

Because of a woman, two men caused a violent fight close to the capital's Mercado Público around 20.30 last night and both were shot. According to the Operations Centre of the Military Police, which called the Ambulance, Rodrigo Gonçalves, shot in the shoulder, neck and buttocks, is in the Intensive Care Unit of the Hospital Celso Ramos. Ademir João Coelho, 30, shot in the abdomen, received attention in the Emergency Surgery. Until late last night both patients were subjected to operations to remove the projectiles from their bodies.

A police spokesman said that Ademir, a bus driver, became jealous when he saw his ex-girlfriend with Rodrigo and gun in hand, appeared and shot his rival. Although wounded, Rodrigo was able to react. He removed the 22-calibre revolver from the hand of the aggressor and managed to shoot him in the abdomen. The weapon was apprehended by the police and handed over to the duty officer of the 1st Police Station for safekeeping.

– A Notícia, Santa Catarina local paper.

....

– 62 –

The onslaught of the beaches of Santa Catarina started next morning when I took a tour of the island with several Paulista tourists and one of these arrogant Cariocas who believe that splendour and elegance begins and ends in Rio.

We first headed to the bar Ponto da Vista for a panoramic view of the Lagoa de Conceição. I find the concept of an island with many beaches tolerable – but an island with many beaches *and* a large and lengthy inland lagoon perfectly reflecting the forested dunes which surround it, smacks of excessive goodwill by the Creator.

'We have two such lagoons,' said our guide. 'This is the developed one, with villas and nightlife. There is one further south, the Lagoa do Peri, which is still pristine.'

We did manage to get a glimpse of the smaller lagoon after we stopped at a promontory to admire the long curve of the beach at Armação, somnolently Bahian in its laziness, with one of the smaller islands, the Ilha do Campeche, figuring hazily in the distance.

'Any secluded beaches?' asked the Carioca.

'There is the Praia do Mole, with a nudist beach at Galheta,' replied the guide, 'but it's too accessible from the highway. If you really want complete solitude, then you have to walk the half-hour through the woods from this turn-off' – he showed us a side road – 'to Lagoinha do Leste. Some say this is the best beach in Brazil, better than Ceará's Jericoacoara, and it's so difficult to get to that it will stay that way for years to come.'

At Pántano do Sul the fishermen were dragging their nets in. The catch is so abundant in these South Atlantic waters that the whole village participates in the haul, rushing afterwards to pick up the fish that are flapping for dear life. You can pick up yours – although if you haven't helped, your action is frowned upon – and give it to a restaurant to grill straight away. I walked up close. Some fish were already cut in half.

'Sharks?' I asked a tranquil local who was mending his nets, ignoring the commotion. He looked so old, he had probably assisted Admiral Cochrane in person.

'No,' he said. 'Dolphins.'

'They don't get entangled in the nets?'

The old man frowned incomprehensibly.

'Why should they?' he replied.

John – small-scale fishing is ecologically sound.

*****

We started clocking the beaches. In my mind's eye they melted into a stretch of golden sand surrounding the island: Joaquina, the surfer's shore with waves to equal Recife's; Moçambique, at the edge of the modest but solid national park of São João do Rio Vermelho; Santinho, small and sweet with its beginners' surf school; Ingleses, calm, safe and gentle; Canasvieiras, with couples and their brood building small sandcastles; Jureré, with its villa follies, the nouveau riche wanting to outdo each other in extravagance. Just above the Praia do Forte on the north tip of the island stands São José da Ponta Grossa, one of the three formidable forts guarding the north bay of Santa Catarina – the other two being on the smaller islands in the bay. The imposing, walled fort of

São José, now restored and functioning as a museum, has a monumental view of the continent across the bay with ancient canons still facing the open sea. Although low on the scale of military command prestige, this large, charming complex of orange-plastered stone dwellings with green doors and window grilles – now home to a lacemaking enterprise – must have been one of the most agreeable garrisons to be posted to in the Portuguese Empire. The cobbled road surface, the sloping Mediterranean roofs, the confined beach below, the hot sun tempered by wind and the scent from the ocean could have been transplanted from Lagos or Sagres in the Algarve.

By Sambaquí the Carioca had to admit defeat.

'And all this is supposed to be inside a whole city?'

'Yes,' answered the guide, 'Florianópolis covers the whole island.'

'It's fantastic,' conceded the Carioca. 'Fantastic.'

He was right. Not since Ceará had I seen such open marine horizons marked by such unsullied seashore; and if you count liveliness and energy, the island city of Florianópolis can only be compared with Fortaleza. If you ever go to Brazil with a pair of swimming trunks, you want to head to one or the other – or both.

*****

I am sitting alone – for after the incidents at Curitiba I am still uneasy and have not yet emerged from my shell, like a tortoise who can still perceive the presence of a predator. I am sitting at a restaurant table facing Joaquina Beach, a vast expanse of quietly siffling sand, sealed by leafy hills in the south and greensward dunes in the west. I'm eating barbecued king prawns brushed with oil and garlic. The flag is red, the wind comes from the Nordeste, the cold marine waves are medium and the surfer boys from Brazil – who can be awfully middle-aged looking sometimes – are all dressed up in their black wetsuits, walking up and down holding their boards; some have pulled down the suit tops and are playing beach volleyball. Although the infrastructure in Joaquina is one of the best in South America, it's not the Maracanã of surf it wants to advertise itself as. The whole of the south Caterinense coast from Guarda do Embau to Farol de Santa Maria is windswept by mighty southerlies, and in Silveira the waves create the best pointbreak in Brazil; for you need a rocky underside to create a pointbreak in this land of sandy coasts and Salveira is blessed with what can only be described as – pun unintended – a rock bottom.

Unlike Fortaleza or Natal with their primitive dry, sandy tracts of seashore, there is a beach for everyone in Santa Catarina: surfers in Joaquina, nudists in Galheta, families on Ingleses, Argentinians in Canasvieiras, picnickers in Moçambique, beachcombers in Lagoinha, gourmands in Pántano do Sul, fat cats in Jureré, romantics in Naufragados, lake-lovers in Conceição. No wonder the *New York Times* once ranked Florianópolis seventh in a list of the world's most beautiful cities. There is a lack of observable poverty, a sense of order and tranquillity and, despite last night's *crime passionel*, a very Mediterranean outlook both in nature and in the inhabitants. I want to return to Florianópolis more than I want to return to any other Brazilian town. It feels like being abroad, abroad. Yet the unpleasant question rears its head, and I dare to pose it because someone somewhere is already thinking about it: is it all because Santa Catarina is more white and European than the rest of Brazil?

Ultimately, it is not colour that matters, but poverty and degradation. The southern states of Paraná, Santa Catarina and Rio Grande do Sul were blessed in that they did not suffer from the long scars of slavery, so for a start there is little historical guilt on the shoulders of the rich and fewer chips on the shoulders of the poor. The plantation owners of the rest of Brazil chucked their ex-slaves out when they didn't have to provide them with food and lodging anymore (of whatever abysmal standard), so the army of the poor started congregating in the large cities to beg and live in, creating the first marginal shanty towns. When Rio, Salvador, Recife, São Paulo and the Minas towns were rich and populous, Paraná and Santa Catarina were underdeveloped and split into rural, agricultural homesteads granted to recently arrived Europeans; so not only did they avoid the favelisation of the big cities, but they were also settled by immigrants imbued with values regarding the merits of education, democratic pluralism and the self-liberating dignity of labour. You see, the south appears to be the big white hope of Brazil's future not because it is white-skinned, but because it is unblemished by the cycle of hate and humiliation of the economic systems from the past.

But it has generated its own share of bad karma. Were these new immigrants liberal-minded towards the Tupi-speaking tribes of the coastline?

*****

I'm lying on Praia dos Ingleses, a small bay-in-the-bay, a lighthouse breaker on my right. The sand is much finer than Joaquina and, oh, the miracle, no wind. The bay is closed, safe, no currents and the sea is calm and warm like olive oil. There are no swimmers; two youths are washing their shoulders, their midi Bermudas showing bottom cleavage, for that's ultimately the point of wearing surf shorts. Fishing boats are moored on the beach, some being tarred, some mended, some simply stranded on the edge of the tide. The sun is setting spectacularly behind the hills. Every small sandbank undulates ever higher and higher until it eventually becomes a forested headland where, in some remote villages, some Indians still live, refusing to be exterminated.

The Kaingáng in Paraná and the Xokleng in Santa Catarina, both called *Coroados* by the Portuguese, stubbornly resisted the inroads of the German colonists. They were violent and warlike with bloody intertribal competitions, protected by impenetrable forests and, unusually for Brazil, mountainous terrain. They were immune to the material offerings of the Paulista *bandeirantes* and ferociously resisted the incursions of the Germans. The colonists formed a militia, the *bugreiros*, specifically to hunt, enslave and exterminate the Indians. The pattern of killing was to find Indian tracks, follow them to their reservation, wait overnight, surprise the tribe during their sleep, spare no men and abduct the women and children. The governor of Santa Catarina, João Coutinho, was all for imprisoning the natives as a *precautionary* measure because they scared off the European immigrants. The German consul in Santa Catarina proposed that *bugreiros* be hired and paid for by the state to kill and enslave the Indians, whom the locals called 'vermin'.

In 1910, an anthropological congress in Vienna was shaken by the paper of a young Czech, Vojtech Fric, who exposed the murders, rapes, enslavement and general atrocities against the Indians in Paraná and Santa Catarina, including the scandalous revelation that clothing impregnated with smallpox was distributed amongst the Xokleng and Kaingáng. The debate was acrimonious. Brazilian diplomats dismissed the accounts as exaggerations; Fric's motivation was questioned: he was Czech – was he anti-German? The illustrious members of the Vienna Congress could not accept that organised killing could ever be officially sanctioned by a so-called civilised state. They would be in for a shock a few decades later, and they wouldn't have to move very far from Vienna itself as the ideology of genocide rebounded terribly. Nazi doctrines did not appear in a vacuum, for in those heady days extermination of 'subhuman' races from American Indians to Australian Aborigines was practised in varying degrees worldwide. It was just a matter of time before they would be tried in Europe itself.

– 63 –

The rain turned into a tempest, the sea roared, the lights went out, the sea rose up in fury, the wind whistled: I mentally quoted Jorge Amado as I entered Club Mix to shelter from the dense drops of the hard-hitting storm. I ordered a caipirinha and sat next to an Aryan prototype – or perhaps mock-Aryan: he was light-skinned and leptorrhine but not-quite-blond, though his brown hair had blond fringes. If I had seen him under different circumstances, I might have made a move, but I was unsociable, still under my Curitiba downer cloud. As it happens, André, for that was his name, spoke to me first.

'Are you from Floripa?' was his opening line, employing the local abbreviation for Florianópolis.

Someone once thought I looked Finnish, which is the oddest guess I've had made regarding my provenance. This came a close second.

'Do I look German?' I asked.

He laughed.

'No, I didn't think so. Just to make conversation. You must be from Curitiba.'

'Further north,' I said, hoping he'd go away.

'São Paulo?'

'Further up.'

'Baiano?' André asked, apprehension in his voice.

Of course, everyone from São Paulo upwards comes from Bahia, that mysterious, amorphous territory bordering on Africa.

'No,' I said. 'I'm not Brazilian.'

'But you have Brazilian parents.'

I looked at André. When the Goddess in the sky allotted the brains, André was probably taking a leak. Perhaps he had some hidden qualities. I'm sure he tells a mean knock-knock joke.

'*Americano!*'

'No, British,' I said.

That freaked him out. He stared at me as if my eyeball had fallen out of its socket. Whatever you say about me, I certainly do not look English and everyone, but *everyone* has seen *A Room with a View*.

'Have you been upstairs?' he asked me some minutes of silence later.

'What's upstairs?'

'The dance floor.'

The dance floor?

Well, but for André I might have missed the second room: a dance floor with a stage where several youths were dancing, including a topless muscular guy with piercing dark eyes. The DJ was playing cheesy house mixed with funk – hey, the topless guy was taking his shoes off. And his socks!

A stripper?

'Sorry I took you for a Baiano,' André said behind me.

The guy was slowly taking off his trousers in rhythm.

'I'm not offended,' I replied.

André chuckled.

'You aren't offended because you're a gringo.'

I was ready to have this clarified when the stage hunk took off his trousers and started dancing only in his underwear. Something didn't feel quite right. For a start the crowd appeared oblivious.

'Is this guy the show?' I asked André.

'No,' he replied. 'He's here every Wednesday. He does it for fun.'

The hunk put his hands inside his underwear and moved his fingers around.

One eye on the stage, the other lizard-like on André, I asked that pending question.

'Why should I be offended?'

'Because down here "Baiano" means stupid.'

Sometimes I wish I could have a firing squad at my beck and call.

'Why? Because they're black?' I asked, annoyed.

André laughed through his nose.

'No. Because they're stupid.'

Back on stage the hunk bent over.

*****

The first Brazilian Nazi group was formed in the district of Bela Aliança near Itajaí on 20 January 1929. I am looking at the faded black and white picture and count 36 men and one woman. Many sport moustaches. A swastika flag is held by a curly-haired youth at the back. They are sitting on three benches, organised like a school party. Someone has written on the bottom: *Hitler-Ortsgruppe Bella Alliança Sta Catharina Brasilien 20.1.29.*

By 1933 the Nazi Party had divided Brazil into seven independent districts under a *Landsgruppenleiter.* Below him there stood seven *Kreisleiter* and finally the *Ortsgruppenleiter,* the local area group leaders. We don't know how many of the 262 million marks assigned to the AOs (*Auslandsorganisationen*) ended up in Brazil, but there is informed speculation that around 2,500 German schools in Paraná, Santa Catarina and Rio Grande do Sul were Nazified.

The *Kreisleiter* of Santa Catarina, based in Blumenau, was Otto Schinke who, although a Brazilian citizen born in Rio Grande do Sul, fought for the German Army in World War I. He had control not only of the schools, but also of the Protestant churches through the ecclesiastical *Evangelische Kirchengemeinde,* the youth organisations via the *Deutsch-Brasilianischer Jugendring,* which was affiliated to the Hitler Youth, and the workers through the German-Brazilian labour organisation *Deutsch Arbeiter Front.* The Nazi influence was not restricted to German-speaking Brazilians. Otto Schinke was also director of the State Retirement and Pensions Fund; another active Nazi, Jorge Büchle, was head of the Teachers' Association. In every town there was a Nazi-sponsored *Schutzverein,* a cultural club for German settlers who by 1937 had multiplied to one million.

These tight relations with the Fatherland caused hysteria in the Brazilian press, especially when a weighty tome published in Germany spoke of Santa Catarina and Rio Grande do Sul as overseas German colonies. Charles W. Domville-Fife comments in a Brazilian travelogue back in 1910:

The fear is expressed in responsible circles that the German colonists, maintaining as they do a strict reserve, building their own towns which are practically ruled by themselves, preserving the customs of their Fatherland and seldom marrying into Brazilian families may in time become dangerous. Many astute politicians and an important section of the Press declare that the ever-increasing thousands of Germans in Southern Brazil, keeping aloof from the natives of the land in which they live are a menace to the homogeneity of the Brazilian people and a real danger to the integrity of the country.

But what could a government do faced not only with the industry and order of the law-abiding German settlers, but also with the investment they brought in? The most spectacular example was the 1927 joint venture between a new enterprise and the Kondor Syndikat – a Berlin-based aeronautical concern that manufactured the aeroplanes which would later bomb Guernica. The new company was an airline to serve the cities of Porto Alegre, Pelotas and Rio Grande in the state of Rio Grande do Sul: the Viação Aérea Rio-Grandense, which went on to become the biggest airline in South America. We know it now from its original initials as simply Varig.

It was another populist dictator from Rio Grande do Sul who became the scourge of the Nazi Party: Getúlio Vargas, who created the totalitarian Estado Novo. He outlawed all political parties, but most importantly, he decreed in March 1938 that all foreign language schools would be absorbed into the state system – from then on, German children would be taught the Portuguese language and Brazilian history. In other words, by hook or by crook, foreign immigrants would be forced to integrate. Vargas' measures bore fruit quickly: various *Kreisleiter*, including Otto Schinke, were jailed, and the last *Landsgruppenleiter*, Hans Henning von Kossel, left hurriedly in May 1938 (though he returned in June with diplomatic immunity as cultural attaché in the German Embassy in Rio). As happens on such occasions, when the backlash came it was so strong that German identity only resurfaced again half a century later. It was only in 1984 that Blumenau citizens felt safe enough to celebrate their Oktoberfest. Vargas saw to it that the country became the remarkable homogeneous social and cultural entity we see today. He also indirectly saved the Brazilian Nazis from ignominy, because they did not officially exist by the time the Second World War broke out when Brazil threw herself on the side of the Allies. It is inconceivable that the vast majority of the settlers, separated by an ocean and without access to good communications, realised the eerie footnote they had signed when they celebrated Hitler's birthday year after year. It is equally inconceivable that their leaders and intelligentsia had no idea of the consequences of their doctrine of hate. For how else could Dr Mengele survive unmolested, so peacefully for so long?

When police invaded the house Mengele had shared with an illiterate Brazilian family, they found a bundle of letters. We now know he had been corresponding with his son in Germany for years; we also know that he lived in poverty and in a state of permanent depression. From an old retainer, we know that Mengele died in 1979 after suffering a stroke while swimming in the Atlantic and drowned before succour could be summoned. But we still don't know who helped him in Brazil. Maybe it was Albert Blume, a member of the Nazi Party who moved to Brazil in 1938 – supposedly a homosexual fleeing a homophobic regime. He lived in poverty and anonymity, but when he died in 1983 he left a hoard of gold (in luxury watches, rings, gold bars and gold teeth), prompting Brazil's commission for the investigation of Nazi war criminals to examine allegations that he was a spy and that his bank accounts had become a conduit for transferring Nazi money abroad. This is, in any case, what Brazil's chief rabbi believes.

Why am I digging all this up? Eichmann was, after all, arrested in Argentina, Klaus Barbie in Bolivia, and Chile's German colonists were very vocal in their support of the Reich. But it is the Boys from Brazil that have become one of the defining images of the country, for every criminal seems to want to escape with his loot and live in Rio. Apart from the real life criminals – Ronnie Biggs, who finally decided to die in the UK, and my own Stavros in Corumbá – there are numerous popular fictional references, such as Steve McQueen in *The Thomas Crown Affair*, John Cleese in *A Fish Called Wanda*, Alec Guinness in *The Lavender Hill Mob*, Gene Wilder and Zero Mostel in *The Producers* and Jean Paul Belmondo in *L'Homme de Rio*. It only takes a few cinematic allusions to create a popular image – fugitives are supposed to like Brazil because it appeals to the criminal mind as a vast country of lawlessness, of sun, sea and sexpots, a place where dangerously earned booty can buy off everyone and everything.

After all, the unexpressed question goes, if Nazi fugitives can hide there successfully, who couldn't?

*****

The rain is pounding on my windowpane. This April Santa Catarina weather is unsettled and un-Brazilian. There are some wonderful browser-friendly bookshops in Florianópolis, and I have replenished my stock to keep me company in bed during this bout of bad weather.

Now, there are people in Brazilian history I would like to have met rather than observe through my time-machine: the Prince of Nassau, Aleijadinho, Jorge Amado. But there is no one who fascinates me more than the Emperor who built his palace on Petrópolis, that leafy Brazilian Simla above Rio de Janeiro, Dom Pedro II.

His father, Dom Pedro I, first reigned in Brazil as a liberator, but soon his true repressive character shone through as he bumptiously pushed through an autocratic constitution. He faced rebellions from states, one of which he lost to history: Uruguay became independent and a semi-permanent *casus belli* between Brazil and Argentina until that epoch-shattering Paraguayan war. He had two wives and 15 children, including some from his mistresses, the most famous and startling being Domitila de Castro e Melo, the big love of his life whom he raised to the rank of Marquesa de Santos. Given his growing unpopularity in Brazil, when the throne of Portugal became the subject of contention, Pedro I abdicated and sailed for the mother country to ensure his first-born daughter's succession, pitting himself against his brother Miguel. Like his father, he left in Brazil his five-year-old son, also called Pedro – future Pedro II, the first South American monarch born in the continent since – well, since the Incas.

And the last.

I sat on my bed, read and remembered.

*****

It takes one hour to reach the Rio *rodoviária* from Ipanema – and the approach is scary. Beyond Praça Mauá the bus zigzags through residential areas so old and decrepit that they look as if they haven't had a coat of paint since the abdication of Dom Pedro I, with rubbish organically growing by itself on window-sills and what passes as pavements. My co-passengers were semi-naked, belching drunks, old women with lost, wandering eyes who might have escaped from one of Africa's periodic famines, and a posse of tattooed teenagers who never bothered to pass the conductor and pay the fare. I was constantly on my guard; selling my SLR camera in my backpack, itself huddling on the floor between my legs, could feed the whole bus for a month. Only Rio can be that grotesque and only Rio can have a *rodoviária* to match; the elevated highway around the old port would look great in a *French Connection* car chase. There are armed guards everywhere, with the posh destinations – Petrópolis, Teresópolis, Angra dos Reis or Parati – bundled together in a corner with a 'safe' area which you can enter by ticket only. When I boarded the bus to Petrópolis, three black youths followed suit, and I could feel the seated passengers hold their breath. The collective wind when they exhaled, as the youths took their seats politely, could have blown the Spanish Armada off course. At the other end, in Petrópolis, I had to pass through a metal detector – was this reassuring? So why did I find it even more alarming?

The approach to Petrópolis, a cool oasis 1,000 feet up the Serra da Mantiqueira, is via a slow, winding road sloping with a gradient just perfect for the gallop of the nineteenth-century carriages of the wealthy Cariocas, for this was their escape from the heat and the disease and the stench of the capital during the sweaty summer months. The town would look even better if it didn't have cesspools masquerading as canals: dainty red oriental bridges span these open sewers, bordered by pines fighting for ground with palm trees. My strongest memory was the sense of relief: one hour away from northern Rio and one's street-fear disappears. Here was a thriving low-rise nineteenth-century town, a reminder of what the centre of Rio – Rua Uruguay, Rua Carioca – might have been, had it not been left to rot away or been downright demolished. The avenue leading to the cathedral of São Pedro de Alcântara with its beautiful marble reliefs is strewn with stately homes, many of them palaces in their own right: I felt as if I was promenading in the Gardens district of New Orleans admiring the ante-bellum mansions. Further up is the Crystal Palace, all coloured crystal in the middle of an Oriental garden. When I walked in, chairs were being assembled in rows. I picked up a leaflet. There was a concert tomorrow. A concert? I suppose only bad sopranos need apply – good ones might literally bring the house down.

There are many things to do in Petrópolis, but the centre of attention is still the Emperor's Summer Palace, set amidst shaded public gardens with old-fashioned coaches parked outside for the tourists to experience the town as one was meant to: by horse-drawn carriage. The palace itself is another neo-classical edifice, lipstick rouge with white columns. It has none of the extravagance of Rio's other palaces; it is much more simple and measured and contemplative – like its most famous resident, Dom Pedro II. The building is kept in pristine condition and the parquet floors are a work of art in themselves, so much so that you are obliged to wear slippers over your shoes.

Dom Pedro II came to the throne by public demand in 1840 at the age of 14, four years earlier than the constitution anticipated, and reigned for just under fifty. He presided over the gradual erosion of slavery, the Paraguayan War – *his* war – the new technological advances and is as much a symbol of his era in Brazil as Queen Victoria is for Great Britain or Franz Josef for Austria. The Summer Palace is full of his portraits: as white as a Scandinavian prince, eyes piercing blue, with a long and fuzzy beard, he looks like a royal Friedrich Engels.

The Diplomats' Chamber lies open in front of me with a mirror from Rio's Lyric Theatre and French Louis-Philippe furniture: a Renaissance clock, mahogany consoles with bronze drawers, panels with tropical flora; the Dining Room is next with six simple wicker chairs contrasting strongly with Pedro I's Imperial crystal. The table sits on top of an Aubusson carpet, the first of many; paintings of old Rio abound on the walls.

Dom Pedro II was raised an orphan, and like Louis XIV knew nothing but royal life and the palace. Unlike his father he was more liberal – he freed his own slaves, for instance – and much more discreet about his extra-marital activities. He was a Freemason who kept the Catholic Church at bay: less than 100 years later, secret societies like those on which the Inconfidência Mineira was based, claimed the Emperor himself whose agnosticism made him enemies amongst the clergy. The Army was already at odds with the Court, seeing the imperial budget skyrocket by 70 per cent in the decade after the Paraguayan War while the military had to make do with an increase of 8 per cent during the same period. The political establishment had also changed. One year after the war, a Republican Party was formed in São Paulo with an anti-monarchist manifesto that ended with the words '*We are from America and we want to be Americans*', penned by Benjamin Constant, Quintino Bocaiúva and Rui Barbosa who have become immortalised in street names all over Brazil that any tourist will recognise. By 1880, only the might of the slave-and-land-owning elites supported the Emperor.

This is the Drawing Room with a large grandfather clock and two windows with floor-to-ceiling pink and white curtains; the piano room with a Chickering jacaranda piano belonging to Empress Teresa Cristina. There's an 1857 portrait of the royal family by Moreaux with Dom Pedro, the two princesses and the Empress. She is seated – mind you, if she were standing she wouldn't be much taller. Dom Pedro II knew her only by her flattering portrait, and when he met her at the juice-flowing age of 17 after they had married by proxy, the poor boy had the shock of his life. Mildly put, her court painter should have been convicted under the Trade Descriptions Act: she was very short, very fat, quite lame and in her later depictions a discerning eye can spot a small moustache.

Here is the Music Room; although we could be in any European stately home, this accent on music and dancing is a reminder that we have not yet left Brazil. There is a harp, strings and three pianos by John Broadway & Sons. I look at the ceilings – unadorned. In the Summer Palace, any sumptuousness arises from the contents, not the packaging, and the display of wealth is almost obscene. Surely those two lacquered Chinese fans and enamelled ivory binoculars could have fed half the population of Ceará during the famine of 1877 which so upset Dom Pedro II. He was said to have promised to sell the last precious stone from his crown to help feed the starving.

As I walked from the Golden Room with its gilded wood furniture into the Treasury, I realised that this is a corner of Brazil that will be forever Europe. This is probably how England was under the Plantagenets: a conqueror upper class standing on the shoulders of the defeated whose culture started to diverge from that of their masters. What was Brazil like in the nineteenth century? For that matter, what was the United States like? A land full of slaves filled with old certainties or a land full of hope and new desires? I doubt whether in 1850 São Paulo, Recife and Salvador were much different than Memphis, Montgomery or Baton Rouge or whether the Sioux and the Navajo were less belligerent than the Kaingáng or the Guaikuru – but at some point the countries diverged, and they diverged with a vengeance: Brazil looked to the past while the United States looked to the future.

The reason probably lies before me. I am looking at Dom Pedro II's crown, made by Carlos Marim in Rio in 1841. The famine in Ceará must have claimed its victims before the Emperor could sell the jewels, for there they all are: 639 diamonds, 77 pearls and 1,720 grams of gold capped with green velour, the same colour as His Majesty's velvet robe which he wore to open Rio's Assembly twice a year. It stands next to Dom Pedro's I golden crown and the sabre and staff used in his own 1822 coronation. Emperors and kings are not emperors and kings if they are not surrounded by pomp and circumstance to generate false respect. In a democracy power emanates from the people because so does respect itself.

Upstairs the sleeping quarters: first for Princesa Isabel who signed the Abolition of Slavery Bill in 1888 when her father was on a trip to Europe for health reasons – he suffered from diabetes. This was the death knell for the monarchy because as well as the Church and the disaffected Army, the old landocracy now felt betrayed and ganged up with them against the Crown. The Babies' Room follows, with cots hanging like hammocks. There follow the dressing quarters of the Emperor and the joint bedroom of the royal couple with more gilded bronze furniture and a display of sacred art objects. Next, the large State Reception room with a throne under a large, carved 'P 2 I' (Pedro II

Imperator); the room leads to a balcony through three large windows with a prime view of the gardens.

The abolition of the monarchy when it came was swift and, as happens in Brazil, bloodless. An army coup under Deodoro da Fonseca (woken up in the middle of the night to take charge) deposed the Emperor who was here, in Petrópolis, recuperating from the last ball he had given. He could only pack a few belongings as he was marched off unceremoniously within 48 hours.

Next to the Throne Room is Dom Pedro II's personal office. Dom Pedro was considerably geeky and went for all the latest inventions. His was the motivation and inspiration behind the Curitiba–Paranaguá Railway. He owned the very first telephone in the country (what was it? Dial 01 for the Emperor?). He spoke eight languages including Tupi-Guarani. He was an avid observer of the skies – there is his own telescope on another Aubusson carpet amongst more Louis-Philippe armchairs embossed with the imperial arms. Finally, there is an image of his hand made out of bronze. This hand held a piece of Brazilian earth as he sailed to the old continent accompanied by his family. He died of pneumonia within two years in a suite in the Hotel Bedford in Paris. Lying in his coffin, he was sprinkled with that handful of soil from Brazil. His remains returned to his beloved country for reburial in 1922 upon the centenary of the Proclamation of Independence. Those of his less popular father – memories are long in South America – had to wait for the 150th anniversary in 1972.

I step down the central staircase – and believe me it's tricky with these large slippers on – to an exhibition of more jewellery from the two Pedros and their wives: earrings, watches, tobacco containers, necklaces, Bahian bracelets, brooches, rings, reliquaries, crosses, even a pair of golden nail scissors. When you see such royal wealth in Europe, you sense its historical context; when you see it in Brazil, you feel the weight of the anachronism. L. T. Chen's *History of Political Thought* has a shattering passage: '*When an institution whose roots are not among the people is introduced from the top it is like plucking the flowers of a neighbour's garden to embellish the dying branches of one's own tree [...] the reconstruction of a nation's thought is not to be accomplished by the wholesale transplantation of the thoughts of another society: it must follow the natural development and must begin with the proper retention of elements of the old social heritage.*'

I walk out and look at Dom Pedro II's portrait again. Dom Pedro's eyes look sad. He always looked sad when he was serious – like Princess

Diana. I have never been a king, so I can never know how it feels to be hated, not for who you are, but for what you represent. How does it feel when you are banished from the land of your birth because what people see in you is a dark past full of dusty cobwebs? And yet, as your mother died when you were but a year old and your father left you when you were five, and you grew up with a people who expected you to fulfil your duty and you did whatever you could – how could it be your fault that what was progressive yesterday seems tyrannical today? You, after all, have always done your job, been the same, played the game according to the rules. Suddenly someone changes the rules and you can't play any more.

How does it feel?

Oh yes, I would like to have met Dom Pedro II, the linguist, the savant, the geek, who tried so hard to gain knowledge – but is it ever possible to become wise without suffering?

*****

The rain has now stopped and the lingering crimson sunset does justice to U2's 'Under a Blood Red Sky'.

I close my history book and my mind returns to the present. Kubitschek built Brasília with the slogan 'Fifty Years in Five!' – hey, I have given you one hundred in much less.

So when did Brazil become Brazil? I look at some old faded photos of Manaus and I see a white European elite in French bustles and crinolines and English tuxedos being tended by black servants in livery coats. I look at São Paulo's Avenida Paulista in 1910: a long, straight, tree-lined avenue with three-storey mansions placed hundreds of yards apart – like London's Regent Street stretched to infinity. I look at an evangelical church in Santa Catarina draped with the Nazi flag. I am in search of Brazilianness, and I can't even figure out when it started. At Independence with Dom Pedro I's proclamation? During the Paraguayan War with blacks, mulattos and whites fighting next to each other? When the monarchy collapsed? Or was it during the totalitarianism of the Estado Novo when Vargas forced all minorities to acculturate?

I know so much about Brazil, perhaps I should write all this down.

I know that there is a colour bar and that this is not the non-racist society images of Pelé kicking a ball have created the impression of. I know that the country still bears the scars and bad karma of centuries of slavery and the annihilation of the natives for the soil is still tainted with their blood and its ghosts are crying out for justice. I know that Africans, Indians, Portuguese and other European immigrants have equally shaped its mind and its manners. I know that the beauty beyond description – *saintly* beauty – of the country is the reason for its people's optimism, who keep holding on to some basic truths, *because* and not in spite of their misery.

Is it ever possible to become wise without suffering?

I know a lot, but I am missing too much besides. There are gaps in my understanding.

I'm really missing the twentieth century.

And some very important places.

SOUL

Chapter 14

The Eighth Deadly Sin (São Paulo)

It is forbidden under penalty of a fine to discriminate by virtue of race, sex, colour, origin, social circumstance, age, disability or illness non-contagious by social contact, of the access to the elevators of this building.

– Municipal Law 11.995 of 16/1/96, São Paulo

···

The Words You'll Need

bauru = *type of sandwich you find in São Paulo*
bicha = *exclamation – poof! queen!*
bunda = *arse*
caatinga = *the desert-style vegetation found in the sertão*
música = *means music and also a particular track*
ryokan = *traditional Japanese inn*
sertão = *the Brazilian north-eastern backlands, dry and arid like a savannah*

···

– 64 –

Coffee

It was in São Paulo that I had my first glimpse of Brazil back in 1993. Heavy-lidded after a long, delayed flight from London and untried in the ways of the country, I made the mistake of hiring a taxi which blew out two days' budget: the trip into town from Guarulhos International – almost dead on the Tropic of Capricorn – is quasi-interplanetary in duration. I remember looking with dread at the meter while wondering why all those people were jogging on the highway at seven in the morning. These Brazilians are crazy. Running on the hard shoulder? Won't they smell when they get to the office? Where are they going to change? And look: the landscape is full of tatterdemalion shacks over miles and miles of relentless uniformity. Even the air stinks. Hey, isn't it dangerous for those joggers over there?

Joggers who aren't wearing any shoes …

The twin jolt when it hit me was so memorable, I can trace my thoughts at the time with lucid alacrity: these people were running not for pleasure, but to get to work. I saw a sign on a hut: '*Vende-se esta*' ('For

Sale'). This smelly city of ragtag beggars was no transient settlement, but real estate valued in a free market. It may have been unsanitary, it may have been ramshackle, it may have been pathetic in its squalor, but permanent it was: people were born, people lived their lives, and, more often than not, died in the same *favela*.

That was my first lesson in Brazilian affairs.

The arrival in São Paulo is spine-tingling. Unlike Rio with its tropical vegetation and hilly landscape, São Paulo lies on a flat plateau, criss-crossed by motorways; skyscrapers crop up here and there in continuous yet segmented patches. If you are landing at the domestic airport of Congonhas, you look incredulously at the eye-level curtains on windows, where the Dona Flors of the city wash their dishes. In 1999 a TAM plane crashed into an apartment block, killing 100 people. But what is 100 people in São Paulo? How big is the metropolitan area? Is it the second or the third largest city in the world, three times the size of Los Angeles, a staggering one-twelfth the size of Belgium? Does it have 15, 17 or 20 million people? This is not a place to come for those who dislike crowds.

This is also the place that will forever remind me of François.

São Paulo did not shine like Salvador, Recife, Rio or Ouro Preto because the dispersal of talent into Minas Gerais, the south and the Mato Grosso kept the town population low as it became a staging post for conquest. Its industrious, live-wire population gave birth to the *bandeirantes* who explored the interior, discovered gold and diamonds, and subjugated the natives. Portugal discovered Brazil, but it is São Paulo that expanded the limits of Portuguese dominion in the centre and the south to an area almost equal to Australia. If today half of South America speaks Portuguese, it is mostly because of those early trailblazers.

São Paulo is the capital of a state the size of Britain and with the population of Spain; it provides between 30 and 40 per cent of the total GDP of Brazil. The annual budget of the city of São Paulo is the third largest in Brazil, behind those of the country as a whole and that of the state of São Paulo itself. The unionised workers in the blue-collar 'ABC' residential zone have a higher annual income than the average in the model city of Curitiba. Incredibly, because of its commercial links, São Paulo has the third-highest number of foreign visitors after Rio and Florianópolis. Business concerns in a radius of 100 miles around me form the engine of Brazil's defence industry, the fifth largest in the world, exporting – with no strings attached – to countries ranging from Iraq to China. An even more astonishing fact is that in the twenty-first century it is not Bahia or Pernambuco which is the greatest exporter of sugar cane, but São Paulo. It seems everything grows on the red earth of this plateau.

And yet, if it weren't for a world-shattering event in the colony of New England in the 1770s, São Paulo might have become another cousin of Curitiba and Florianópolis: a modest but sorted, low-key Brazilian town. But the Boston Tea Party changed the face of the world and the fate of Brazil: the American colonial rebels threw the English tea shipment into Boston harbour symbolically, but the truth was more substantial. The new, expanding, self-confident country of the US of A changed its source of imbibed caffeine for political reasons: from tea, the trade of which was controlled by Great Britain, to coffee which was not. Except that this crop could not be grown in North America. It flourished, however, in the rich, red earth of São Paulo.

This is the town that coffee built.

*****

Sir Richard Burton (no, not Liz Taylor's ex-husband but the great explorer, British imperialist, polymath and linguist, translator of both the *1001 Nights* and Camões' *Luisiads*), was the British consul in Santos and São Paulo between 1865 and 1868, during the Paraguayan War. He has left a description of his time in South America in his travelogue *The Highlands of Brazil*. He was surprised by the fertility of the land: '*I well remember at Hyderabad in Sind, that during the inundation of the Indus we could perceive in the morning that the maize had lengthened during the night and the same is the case with certain toadstools and fungi in Brazil.*'

A bisexual, who used to cruise with Rio's demi-monde in the Passeio Público until the snakes scared him off, Sir Richard married Isabel Arundell, who burned all his personal diaries when he died. At least she published a book of her own which is wonderfully bitchy. From her diaries and letters we learn that she hated Santos calling it '*the Wapping of Brazil*' and settled in São Paulo's Rua do Carmo. The Burtons' São Paulo was a noisy place of 25,000 souls, spread out even then – Greater São Paulo was three times as big – with a disproportionate traffic chaos. '*A number of carriages and tilburys are constantly in motion, conveying passengers about the city or the outskirts, causing a degree of activity one would otherwise hardly expect to find.*'

Few modern readers would not recognise the city even from Isabel's over-the-top descriptions: *'For those who are launched in Brazilian society it is a fast and immoral place without any chic or style. It is full of students and no one is religious or honest in money matters; and I should never be surprised if fire were rained down upon it as in a city of the Old Testament, for want of a just Brazilian. En revanche, it is very healthy, and only one month's journey to England. São Paulo itself is a pretty, white, straggling town on a hill and running down into a high tableland, which is well wooded and watered, and mountains all round in the distance. We are about three thousand feet above sea-level. It is a fine climate, too hot from nine till four in summer, but fairly cool all the other hours. No cockroaches, fleas, bugs and sand-flies, but only mosquitoes and jiggers. Out in the country there are snakes, monkeys, jaguars and wild cats, scorpion-centipedes and spiders but not in the town. Of course it is dull for those who have time to be dull and very expensive.'*

The Burtons, like all subsequent visitors to the city, kept complaining about the cost of living: *'The English here mislead one about expense. I am obliged to buy my own experience and I do not expect to shake down into my income for three or four months more. The English like to appear grand, saving all the while; and they like to show me off as their lady consul and make me run into expenses, while I want honestly to live within £700 a year and have as much comfort as that would allow us. It will only go as far as £300 in England [...] Only fancy the Brazilians are dreadfully shocked at me for working! They never do anything but live in rags, filth and discomfort at the back of their houses and have one show-room and one show-dress for strangers, eat feijão (black beans), and pretend they are spending the deuce and all.*

The eighth deadly sin here is to be poor, or worse, economical.'

No change there, Isabel.

*****

Like many São Paulo virgins, I stayed in the Centro off the Praça República. To me, this was something like Mexico City's Zócalo or Madrid's Puerta del Sol; I didn't know that the Centro – from Sé to Luz – is as dangerous as south Bogotá. But fear is in the mind and because I didn't realise all this, nothing happened to me. My room in the old-fashioned Hotel Amazonas was spacious with a four-poster bed and mahogany furniture and only a hint of cheapness in the worn-out armrests and the discolouration of the carpets. Inside the hotel time stood still and the decade was definitely the 1940s. Staff wore uniforms, were in awe of the gringo and did not speak but nodded even when addressed directly. When I tried exercising my newly learned BBC cassette

Portuguese with the cleaner, she hid in the bathroom in mute horror. A client who asks a maid for her name! This was a mixture of *Exú* insolence and lack of self-respect!

My greatest athletic feat in Brazil, surpassing future jungle walks or steep *ladeira* climbs, happened on my first full day: I walked from the Praça República to the Butantã Institute.

It says a lot about Sao Paulo that its biggest crowd-puller is a snake farm. Dating from 1901 when it was only a small *fazenda* using horses (regularly bitten I presume) to gather anti-serum, Butantã is a renowned world centre for antivenin research and production. Paulistas will cry with horror: what about MASP (Museu de Arte de São Paulo) with its special collection of Van Goghs, Gauguins and Goyas, Rafaels, Renoirs and Rembrandts? What about the basilica of São Bento with its ornate ceiling and the Jesuit Museum? What about the Ipiranga Casa do Grito devoted to that moment when Dom Pedro I proclaimed Brazil's Independence with its Versailles-like gardens and the royal mausoleum? Perhaps I should have visited the normal attractions; by the time I arrived on foot from the Praça República, the milking of the snakes had come and gone and dozing reptiles in their pits were singularly unexciting. After more than three hours' walk, the only snakebite I had in mind was of the cocktail kind.

Yet the trek was not without effect: this was a city larger than I could comprehend. It was also ugly with skyscrapers in distant hubs, connected with square cement boxes masquerading as houses, akin to those on the main street of a dusty one-horse town. On the road to Butantã anything to do with cars predominated: spare parts, showrooms and petrol stations where alcohol was on offer in pumps labelled with a large 'A'. Brazil made a bid to shake off its dependence on petrol and had an ambitious programme to convert car engines to run on alcohol. It made sense on paper: the explosion of petrol prices after the 1979 oil crisis led to the country defaulting on its debt in 1981. By the mid-1980s the vast majority of all newly assembled automobiles had engines that ran on alcohol distilled from that old faithful crop, sugar cane. But then oil prices stabilised and Collor's dismantling of state intervention killed the experiment off.

Distance and cars. Pollution. Heat. Why would anyone in their right mind want to live here? What was the attraction of this hideous-looking, foul-smelling, screechy-sounding, grime-tasting city?

*****

Coffee's grand journey around the world is evocatively described in Stewart Lee Allen's book *The Devil's Cup*. It started in Ethiopia where the natives ritually drank their local *Arabica* variety in ceremonies invoking the mythical Zar spirits. A tribe further down in Zaire, the Oromos, chewed on the beans, not unlike the Incas did with coca. Coffee remained an unknown African psychedelic drug until the Arab slavers brought a shipment to the port of Mocha in Yemen. There, around 1200 AD, an Islamic holy man decided to crush and brew the beans. His name was Umar al-Shadili and it was none other than a clued-up archangel who inspired him. In Islam much is made of alcohol as an intoxicant, but no mullah or imam had heard of coffee – so Arabs, and then Turks, became inveterate coffee drinkers. Portuguese sailors developed a taste for it, the French beau monde drank it as a *digestif,* English traders arrived and tried to make money out of it, and Kara Mustapha left sacks of it behind after the second Turkish siege of Vienna. In a repeat performance of its spread in the Islamic world, Reformation Europe embraced the drug not mentioned in the Bible. The Puritans even wrote odes in its honour:

> *When the sweet Poison of the Treacherous Grape*
> *Had acted on the world a general rape;*
> *Coffee arrives that grave and wholesome Liquor*
> *That heals the stomach and makes the genius quicker.*

By the 1660s Reformation London had a string of Ye Olde Coffee Shoppes, where patrons discussed politics and religion 'with reason propelled by caffeine rather than dulled by ale' as Allen shrewdly observes. Charles II was incensed and closed all coffee shops in 1675. The reaction was so strong, he unbanned them after eleven days. As the coffee drinkers who discussed controversial subjects did not want to be identified, the famous Turk's Head coffee house instituted something called a 'ballot box' for its debating customers – and modern democracy was born.

What stuck in the European capitalists' throats was that the infidel Turks should monopolise the trade of this dark, aromatic liquid. Their reactions varied. The English switched to tea, whose production they could control in India. The Dutch smuggled coffee to their high-altitude plantations in Java. And the French?

As Allen tells us, in 1720 Gabriel de Clieu sailed off from Dieppe to the French West Indies on a ship called the *Dromedaire*, with a precious cargo containing some coffee seedlings in a wooden box with a glass front sealed with wire. This was an epic journey: Berber pirates pursued them off Morocco; a Dutch spy on board was caught attempting to destroy the makeshift greenhouse; finally a dead calm prevailed and the ship was stuck motionless in the Caribbean. The crew rationed the water.

De Clieu's own share went to the coffee plants.

Fortunately for him, the crew and all future inhabitants of the lands from Nicaragua and Guatemala to Colombia and Brazil, the wind picked up soon and his gamble paid off. The *Dromedaire* finally reached Martinique, sealing the commercial fate of a continent. But nowhere, *nowhere* did the coffee tree flourish as much as on the red earth of the hilly São Paulo tablelands. The construction of a railway from São Paulo to the Atlantic, one of the main tasks overseen by Sir Richard Burton, catapulted the port of Santos to the biggest in South America purely because of the coffee shipments. And yet in 2001 coffee contributes only 6 per cent to São Paulo's own gross domestic product: industry provides 37 per cent and that modern keyword, services, a whopping 55 per cent.

The kid has grown up.

An economy based on coffee, which at times accounted for more than half of Brazil's exports, is dependent on fluctuating world prices. In the early 1900s what São Paulo wanted from central government was price stability. Like a premature version of Europe's Common Agricultural Policy, the central government of the First Republic pushed up prices by destroying coffee crops and compensating farmers. Minas Gerais and São Paulo between them fixed the presidency in a powerful axis (only challenged by Rio Grande do Sul, which allied itself with the military, most of whom either stemmed from or served in that border state). The two opposing blocks clashed after the 1929 stock exchange crash which affected the exporter states of Minas Gerais and São Paulo, throwing their alliance to the wind. Getúlio Vargas and his generals captured the presidency with a coup in 1930, shocking the Rio citizens by tying their horses to the statues of the Avenida Rio Branco.

The political landscape of Brazil has always been shaped by the struggle between the states and central government. Strong monarchy was followed by a weak First Republic where states imposed their own taxes and tariffs, arranged their own loans directly with foreign banks and kept their own armies. But the 1930s was the age of planes and tanks, of costly military equipment only federal government could afford, so state power decreased – except the militia of super-rich São Paulo.

Vargas was a control freak who wanted to put brakes on the richest state; it was inevitable that São Paulo would revolt. It happened in 1932 after Vargas imposed an out-of-state governor or, as he called him bluntly, *interventor*. Middle-class volunteers flooded to fight for the old style democracy of the elites; money and jewellery poured in (including more than 87,000 wedding rings) after the Gold for São Paulo initiative calling for all citizens to aid the cause. The result was a stand-off and the revolution fizzled out after Vargas blinked. He offered an amnesty and generous concessions to São Paulo which, proud and unbeaten, became the linchpin of his galloping industrialisation programme.

Many people wonder why it should be São Paulo out of all the cities in South America that would go stratospheric. Put simply: its citizens *earned* it. Unlike other Latin Americans or even the Germans, Italians and motherland Portuguese, the Paulistas at least fought their dictator.

*****

Walk the other way. No Butantã. Try the normal sights. I only have this one weekend in São Paulo, and I feel it's one weekend too long: this sprawl has no redeeming features.

The sheer number of people in the streets was staggering. Inefficiency creates employment for young men always on the go, carrying small briefcases, queuing up to procure stamps, signatures and other examples of unnecessary bureaucracy outside offices open 'Seg-Sex'. I wondered what tourists make of such signs: 'Segregated Sex'? I bet Portuguese speakers enjoy writing 'Mon-Fri' in that naughty shorthand way.

I crossed the viaduct of Santa Ifigênia, looking down on Anhangabaú to the cars streaming down to the Avenida Nove de Julho. On the motorway island a dog was barking psychotically at the vehicles passing by. I leaned forward and looked closer. It was tied on a leash, tied so high it had to stand erect on its hind legs. How long had the animal been like that? Who did it and why?

The cars kept flowing down Anhangabaú.

There is no way anyone can cross that busy highway.

And yet someone had to in order to tie the dog to that tree. It would go mad and die in great pain, permanently suspended, unable to rest on all fours. Perhaps I should call the police.

I asked a well-dressed elderly woman where the police station was. She looked me up and down with concern.

'You've been robbed?'

'No – it's the dog.' I pointed at the poor animal below.

She looked and shook her head. 'They're in Praça da Sé,' she informed me. 'But they won't shoot it with all these cars around. It's too dangerous.'

I see.

On the way to the Praça, I reached the small Jesuit College, now open as a museum. A miniature mock-up of the original São Paulo Jesuit settlement stood in the middle of the main chamber. It appeared to be on a hill. *I'm on a hill? How can one tell with all the skyscrapers around?* The bored guard showed me out to the patio. Oh – I *was* on a hill, unmistakably so, because this side sharply tailed off and nothing could be built upon it. Though, unlike the settlers of the sixteenth-century homestead, I did not look out upon a sylvan terrain of bushes and trees, or listen to the rolling waters of brooks and rivers. Instead I faced a forest of skyscrapers traversed by highways with the tumult of cars accelerating, downshifting gear and honking loudly in my ears.

The first European to settle in this area was Antônio Ramalho, one of the first *degredados* exiled to Brazil, where he turned native and kept a harem of Tupi women (they call that a punishment?). A party that took to the mountains beyond the heat of the coast when the first governor of the new captaincy of São Vicente arrived were surprised by his existence and scandalised by his lifestyle. Theirs was the first official settlement in Brazil, dated at 1532, much earlier than Olinda or Salvador, though it appears on maps as early as 1507. Ramalho, his progeny and the few cool-weather seekers built a small hamlet in Piratininga. The next big visitor was our famous Padre Anchieta, a Spanish Jesuit from the Canary Islands, who founded a settlement right here by the river Anhangabaú, now that high-speed dual carriageway. Padre Anchieta – a saint, after John Paul II beatified him in 1980 – was one of the most prolific men of the cloth in the New World. His enduring legacy was a composite grammar of all the languages on the coast of Brazil; at a stroke he invented the *língua geral*, a kind of Tupi/Guarani *Hochdeutsch* which could be understood by all tribes. On 25 January 1554 Padre Anchieta founded this very college I'm in, hopeful that the community would grow larger. Could he have ever foreseen it would turn out to be the twenty-first century's worst urban nightmare?

It is in the Praça da Sé under the gothic cathedral flanked by two columns of tall palm trees that the scene becomes worthy of a Bosch or a Breughel seen through the eyes of Freddie Kruger: a shocking relapse into primitive animaggression. This is the realm of a twilight zombie video by Michael Jackson. This is India without the cows. The crowds are drunk, drugged, dirty, unhealthily thin, unshaven, smelly, hustling, staring blankly on benches, surrounded by hordes of street children. There may be no predators around, but the whole life, the aspirations and consciousness of the wretched beings in the Praça da Sé are as far from mine as a jaguar's, their life perspective the same as that of a gerbil on a wheel. I gasped at the high-profile police presence, armed like occupying soldiers, manning a post in the centre of the square next to a series of makeshift toilet booths.

I'm scared.

I retire discreetly just inside a café. I see a sign for an Amazonian drink served as a *vitamina*. I squint. It says 'guaraná'. I've heard about it. A tonic.

'I'll have that,' I say to the girl behind the counter. I have to pay the cashier separately – a cashier who works isolated inside a bullet-proof booth.

A little boy enters the café begging. I swallow hard. This cannot be. A barefoot boy, not more than ten, dirt forming scars on his face – but unlike the Third World starving type, this is not a black- or brown-skinned kid: he's white, sugar-white and blond. I look on fascinated as the girl who served me gives the boy some water and a half-eaten *bauru* sandwich. Where is Dickens to recognise his Oliver Twist?

A loud noise from the square makes the crowd disappear and take cover in the surrounding side streets like deer that smell a predator. A policeman appears dragging a fat teenager who is crying and screaming.

'Please, please! PLEASE! NO! Oh, no!' he cries. 'NO!' – and the voice is breaking, sometimes a man's, sometimes a choir boy's.

The policeman turns and *fap!* hits him on the ribs with his long baton. I instinctively jump. The policeman thumps him again. *Fap!*

The teenager sobs with a high-pitched whine. The policeman drags him towards the toilets. Hey, these quick-assembly portacabins are no toilets.

They are portable interrogation booths.

The door slams shut behind the boy and the policeman, and with that the moans stop.

Soundproofed.

Little by little, the denizens of the Praça da Sé emerge from their lookouts and their shelters to resume their life on the square. The blond boy behind me smells my discomfort, manages to flash a smile and stretches his palm towards me.

Who cares about the dog now?

....

Things I Don't Like About Brazil #14: Police Impunity

Brazil provides a telling case study of how total impunity for human rights violations under military rule (1964–1985) has led to a culture of impunity for human rights violations being ingrained in police forces to the extent that it threatens the very rule of law. Under military rule torture, extrajudicial executions and 'disappearances' were committed against perceived political opponents by the security forces, and impunity was guaranteed through the military government's own 1979 Amnesty Law.

Under civilian rule these same human-rights violations are committed against perceived criminal suspects with almost universal impunity. The effects of impunity are taken one stage further, however. Instead of purportedly serving a so-called 'war against crime', the toleration of human rights violations has allowed police to torture and kill in pursuit of personal gain through extortion, and this has drawn police agents ever more deeply into criminal activities.

Tackling impunity in Brazil is important not only to preserve human rights, but also to bring police forces under the control of the elected authorities. The government needs to take determined action to agree, negotiate and implement concrete measures to tackle a situation that has escaped control.

– Amnesty International, *Crime Without Punishment: Impunity in Latin America*, AMR 01/008/1996

....

On my last night in São Paulo, I checked out an address in Alameda Franca, a gay/mixed bar-restaurant called Ritz. This time I took the metro and got off at MASP-Trianon in the middle of the Avenida Paulista. It was early evening, and when I reached the street level a deluge of neon hit my eyes. I looked to my left where slender skyscrapers reached to the sky and the flailing early evening sunlight had to compete with digital videoboards. I walked past a small park, looking at giant luxury apartment blocks sheltering behind high security railings, their premises patrolled by guards. This was a Saturday night and the streets were full of men in elegant Armani suits tipping uniformed bellboys outside the Sheraton, the Radisson, the Sofitel; women were ostentatiously sporting diamond rings, silver bracelets, pearl necklaces and golden brooches as they stepped out of their limousines in front of Italian, French and American restaurants with valets in attendance.

I had been in São Paulo all this time and, like the proverbial blind man who tries to figure out what an elephant looks like, I was fumbling on the city's backside. I had prepared myself for a Portuguese-speaking Mexico City, and I was slowly downgrading it to a concrete Calcutta, but I was not prepared for a Latin New York. The poor had vanished – or did they never venture here? Where were the police? Is this the same town, just a few stops down on the metro from the nefarious poverty of the Praça da Sé?

Is this the same country?

The answer is, of course, no, it isn't. The legacy of slavery and innate suspicion of the poor meant that there was no universal suffrage in Brazil until, wait for it, 1985. (And who got voted in first? Collor de Melo. Ah, the beauty of democracy.) When the illiterate masses were finally enfranchised, it was too late; the haves and the have nots were living in two different worlds: a whopping 25 per cent of Brazilians could not read or write. Empowerment by vote has reduced this to the still unacceptable 15 per cent. But the damage had been done. Brazil had and continues to have the worst distribution of income in the world. In the year 2000 the income of the richest 20 per cent of the population in the United Kingdom was 10 times as large as the income of the poorest 20 per cent. The ratio increases for more unequal societies. The ratio for France was 7; for the United States, 9. For Brazil it was a whopping 32. And nowhere is the contrast sharper than São Paulo.

I pulled out my map next to a streetlight: Cerqueira César.

I had discovered the Jardins.

– 65 –

Sex and Death

'Rua Pamplona,' I said to the taxi driver. 'Do you know where it is?'

He shook his head, perplexed.

'Near Rua Augusta,' I said, pointing at the map. 'You know Rua Augusta?'

He nodded.

Everyone knows where Rua Augusta is thanks to Rita Lee and Os Mutantes.

> *I climbed Rua Augusta at 120 km an hour*
> *Scattering away all the people from my path*
> *I turned round a curve on two tyres without a signal*
> *I stopped four inches away from the shop window.*

Os Mutantes – The Mutants – were a revolutionary Paulista sixties' group who, unlike their contemporaries Caetano Veloso and Gilberto Gil, truly transcended the confines of their home country: they became a cult group in Europe and the US, with fans as diverse as David Byrne and the late Kurt Cobain. There were three members: brothers Sérgio and Arnaldo Baptista, and long-haired, cool Rita Lee, a cross between Nico and Grace Slick. Arnaldo and Rita met at a high school band contest in São Paulo back in 1964 when they were both sixteen; they left their respective bands and started going out and gigging together. The trio was completed with Arnaldo's brother Sérgio, only 15 at the time but a pretty mean guitar player nevertheless.

The generals had stepped in again in 1964 and the military dictatorship's pseudo-parliamentarism would continue for another 21 years: longer than Margaret Thatcher's and John Major's governments and Tony Blair's first term combined. By 1967 when Os Mutantes, Gilberto Gil and Caetano Veloso were being booed by the left for introducing Yankee electric guitars into Brazilian popular music, the noose was getting tighter for the opponents of the regime; after all, Che Guevara was in the Bolivian jungle, right next door. The repression that followed led to the exile of Veloso and Gil in 1969, and can't be dissociated from Os Mutantes' output. The group stayed put inside the country and bravely fought convention in the way they resisted censorship. Between 1968 and 1972 they recorded five albums with songs that spanned the spectrum from the ethereal ('*Fuga no 11*') to proto-metal ('*A Hora e A Vez do Cabelo Nascer*'). The aforementioned '*Rua Augusta*' is in fact a mock rock'n'roll jive track sounding all the weirder in Portuguese.

Like Western sixties' groups, Os Mutantes experimented with drugs, but what was daring in San Francisco '67 was lethally challenging in São Paulo '69. '*Ando Meio Desligado*' ('A Bit Spaced Out'), their biggest hit, could have been recorded by The Doors fronted by Marianne Faithful. It owes its importance – commercial and artistic – to the audacity of its defiance: the regime did not accept non-conformity or a whiff of rebellion. And yet rebellious Os Mutantes were: Rita Lee using bug spray in place of the hi-hat in '*Le Premier Bonheur du Jour*', Sérgio's jerry-built voicebox (a precursor of Peter Frampton's vocoder), their forthright 'head' lyrics. Like Mineiro baroque, this is another example of isolationism creating unclassified, pioneering art. Their psychedelic experiments were not ahead of their time – they were most definitely *of* their time – but without free access to their Western contemporaries and their techniques, they were left to improvise and deconstruct.

I had nodded off. The driver shook me awake.

'Pamplona Palace,' he said.

'First time in Brazil?' asked the receptionist who demanded to be paid in cash, in advance.

'No, second. Second time in São Paulo, too,' I replied.

'Staying in São Paulo?'

'No, I'm off to Bonito and the Pantanal.'

If the past is another country, then the Brazil of 1997 bore little resemblance to that of four years earlier. Even the *favelas* by the highway had disappeared, not because their impoverished residents had risen in life, but because the police had demolished them for blotting the landscape. Fernando Henrique Cardoso had stopped the bleeding by inflation and turned the real into hard currency – well, until I reached Bonito at least. This time I took a bus into town and a taxi from there to Hotel Pamplona Palace, which at $40 in the most expensive city in South America was absolutely no palace, but location-wise perfect. OK, there was the occasional prostitute hanging out at night, the electrics from the shower seemed to have been put together by a twelve-year-old with a 'Learn Electricity For Juniors' set, and the door key was little more than a lever – but, *but* it was the only cheap hotel in the Jardins.

And I *so* wanted to live in the Jardins.

....

As capital of the State of the same name, São Paulo ranks as the second city of Brazil, and the third in the whole of South America. This is not merely a local reputation, but an acknowledged fact which should go far to combat the assertion that Brazilians cannot do what their neighbours have already done – build a city that even civilised Europe need not blush to own. One has only to walk through Tiradentes Avenue, with its rows of trees and its double carriage drive, flanked by palatial mansions to imagine oneself in Paris; or through Rua S. Bento or Rosario Square to receive suggestions of the great London thoroughfares. But approach the Tieté district – the 'East End' of São Paulo – and you will think yourself among the docks of Lisbon or Oporto […] Society in São Paulo is, therefore, about as cosmopolitan as any idealist could reasonably wish; but money rules as in all republican countries, and in the Whitechapel of São Paulo the scene changes. Here the throng of varying nationalities is even more confused, and although happiness seems to prevail in most quarters and there is work and airspace for all, it would be an untruth to say that the labourer enjoys more freedom or security or even as much as he does under the limited monarchy of Great and Greater Britain.

– Charles W. Domville-Fife painting an idyllic picture of São Paulo in 1910. By then, Sir Richard Burton's city had grown, with the immigration infusion of mostly Italian settlers, to over 200,000.

....

I slept off my jetlag and woke up hungry. I dressed up in anticipation.

Palmitos.

I left the hotel and walked slowly down Alameda Santos, the cool, unexpected October air appreciated by my warm, sleepy skin. I passed Siqueira Campos Park and tree-lined streets, counting towards Rebouças: Alameda Casa Branca, Peixoto, Rocha Azevedo, João Manuel – Rua Augusta. The cinema there advertised São Paulo's Mostra; its annual film festival had just started. Walk on: Alameda Haddock Lobo – which sounds like a Tintin character in Portuguese – Alameda Bela Cintra. I stopped at the best-value restaurant in Brazil: Bovinu's with its cheap all-you-can-eat buffet, which includes salads, cooked foods, *churrasco*-by-order and sweets from a trolley. Bovinu's is also quite inventive in serving palm hearts – *palmitos* – in various guises; not just pickled from the jar. You know what? I *love palmitos*. So, if the Puritans were inspired by coffee, then – then …

....

Things I Like About Brazil #14: *Palmitos*

Palm tree hearts
You take my breath away.
Nature's white artefacts
Demand my tongue to obey.

Long and slim,
Laid cool upon the plate.
Unfattening,
My waist does not dilate.

I pig out on a jarful
In sixes and in tens,
And always I marvel
Unlayering your stems.

For me you are the only veg
In Brazilian salad bars,
Sometimes I make a pledge
To shove you up the –
*   [but no, you're too soft].*

– My own 'Ode to *Palmitos*'

…..

The Ritz – established 1982, it declares proudly – was still there on Alameda Franca, and in the four years that had elapsed it had become more of a restaurant. Its wall was full of awards (Best Bar this year, Best Food another) and its atmosphere was not unlike the Village in London or Este in Barcelona. I asked for a beer and a glass. The waiter looked at me askance; I had been identified as a gringo. He shook his head and gave me a can wrapped in a napkin to keep it cool.

On the corner of Avenidas Itu and Consolação, there was much commotion outside Club Massivo, but it looked too much of a square crowd, so after a strong caipirinha in Bar Espanhola by the corner, I decided to check out Nostro Mundo, advertised as the first gay club in Brazil. And oh, was it old! Parts of it had not seen the sun since the seventies. Plastic chairs, a sound system I had last heard in East Germany just after the fall of the Berlin Wall (college-overused and crackling), an upstairs balcony in danger of terminal collapse, and a bar totally behind bullet-proof glass. This was less of a nineties' club and more of a twenties' Chicago speakeasy full of rough trade. There was a drag show at 1.30 a.m., so I stayed. My patience was rewarded with the oldest-looking, skinniest and ugliest female impersonator I had ever set eyes on, who looked a bit like Keith Richards, but a lot more diseased.

Yawn.

Walked home at 3 a.m. In Brazil. In São Paulo. At night. I'm tough. It's official.

As I passed the multiplex by Rua Augusta, I noticed the billboard for the main feature: a street kid in what seemed the *sertão* in the middle of a war. The film was called *Canudos*.

I scratched my head as I translated the title.

Straws? A war about straws?

I made a mental note to check my history.

*****

403

Canudos was a phenomenal event. It inspired not just one, but two literary masterpieces in the two main Latin American languages: Euclides da Cunha's turn-of-the-century *Os Sertões*, translated rather freely in English as *Rebellion in the Backlands*, and more recently Mario Vargas Llosa's – a Peruvian friend of Jorge Amado and another Nobel prize contender – *La Guerra del Fin del Mundo, The War at the End of the World*. What happened is mostly unknown outside the continent, but that does not diminish its significance. You know the feeling you get while reading about the indignity of slavery and the poverty and the injustice and how you wish the society that caused such misery got its come-uppance? Well, that's what happened in Canudos, where the cohesion of the newly formed secular Republic of Brazil faced its greatest test – ever – from an army of destitute, disparate, desperate settlers – the word *desperados* could not fit them better – in the parched, inhospitable backlands of the Bahian *sertão*. They were led by the controversial figure of Antônio Conselheiro ('The Counsellor'), a combination of mystic guru, guerrilla leader and fire-and-brimstone preacher in the grand tradition of the American West. A dammed lake now covers the site in Bahia where more than 20,000 people lost their lives and provided the world with an emotive new word not many people recognise as a by-product of the conflict.

Antônio Conselheiro was the closest to a Jesus figure there has been since the original was crucified. Born in Ceará, he lived in the backlands with his wife, quietly studying for a law career until he discovered she was having an affair. He wasn't exactly blasé about it and almost murdered her; but he got over it and went on to form another relationship and be blessed with a son. However, when his second wife also dumped him, he became unhinged and left everything behind, like Gautama Buddha, to live preaching from village to village. He built up his reputation in the 1870s and was offended by the positivism of the Republic after the abolition of the monarchy; in particular he was outraged by the new provision of civil marriage. In his mind God and the Emperor became one; the end of the century turned apocalyptic; the godless Republic was the Antichrist. He was eloquent and had enough moral gravitas to establish a regular crowd of devoted disciples and eventually a commune in a place called Canudos. It was an all-sharing religious community, self-sufficient and dry – for he abhorred alcohol. It was also crime-free; such was his authority and personal standing no one dared face the only punishment that existed: banishment. He might have ended up a weirdo cult leader Waco-style if it weren't for the abolition of slavery, which filled his ranks with the confused, the illiterate and the emancipated dispossessed. In the absence of social security he was the next best thing; the residents of Canudos shared everything. That was bad enough in the eyes of the elites, but when Antônio Conselheiro started blessing marriages and performing mass the Bahian Archbishop was incensed. The bona fide priests who were sent to the commune were chased away; a dispute about wood with a nearby village for the construction of a church turned into a riot.

The authorities decided to act.

If you don't know the story, you're in for a treat.

*****

Liberdade is the Japanese neighbourhood: a place of exotic red oriental shrine gates, katakana signs and lantern streetlights. This is the largest concentration of Japanese outside their homeland. During the twentieth century about 250,000 Japanese immigrated to Brazil and settled mostly in the state of São Paulo. Unlike European immigrants, their peculiar historic background has turned them into something of an oddity. Outwardly, they appear as Japanese as the Imperial Household staff after a week of sunbathing in Florida – it would take a lot of intermarriage, of which there is little, to change the Japanese physiognomy. Once they open their mouths, though, you are confronted with an uncharacteristic openness and typically Brazilian gregariousness, and you know that their hearts and minds have been fully assimilated. This is at its most prominent in the shock waves they cause in Japanese society when they return. Something in the air or the water of Brazil has turned them into temperamental misfits. The *dekasseguis*, as they are called (and nearly a century later, there are 200,000 Brazilians of Japanese extraction living in Japan) with their sunny devil-may-care attitude, have major difficulties integrating into the corseted country of their ancestors, and have ended up as second-class citizens, employed in the so-called 3K industries: *kitanai* (dirty), *kitsui* (arduous) or *kiken* (dangerous). But enough Japanese lessons for one chapter.

I watched, fascinated, outside a traditional *ryokan*, as a giant cockroach found itself in the middle of the road and ran in all directions at once. I could see it frantically trying to make for cover. South? No, there's that motorcycle coming. West? No, no, that's a bus. The cockroach stayed trapped on the road for about five minutes until it disappeared down a sewer grille to safety. Funny how Japanese restaurants attract such Brobdingnagian cockroaches. The biggest I've ever seen was in a small Kyoto diner. 'Don't look down, John. Just don't,' my travelling friends at the time said. I, of course, did so at once and saw the Hiroshima mutant. My scream alerted the Japanese chef, who appeared undisturbed with a pair of mighty tongs and with a Zen-like movement clipped the monster between my legs (no, no, the other one) and disappeared in the direction of the kitchen. So that's why chicken yakitori has that special bite. I wonder what happened to that dog four years ago. Perhaps it had been hung for tenderising.

Call me politically incorrect, but a thin, kimono-clad Japanese woman swearing in perfect Portuguese is an unsettling sight; a reminder that Brazil, and, most of all São Paulo, is a nation of immigrants: even Catholic Mass is celebrated in more than twenty languages. Open a São Paulo phone directory at random, start reading the names of the citizens fortunate enough to have a connection, and what do you read? Margarida Karakulov, Maura Karakida, Khatchig Karamekian, Cintia Karaoglan, Giuseppina Karapipperi, Luiz Karapurnale, Makiko Karasawa, Gabor Karasz, Elias Karbaga, Roman Karszerski. OK, I cheated and opened it at K, but you get the picture.

*****

The first expedition against Canudos involved 150 state militia under Lieutenant Pires Ferreira on 7 November 1896. His mission was to ask the villagers to submit to the authority of the local sheriff. The lieutenant was already thinking about his promotion when he left Juazeiro, the nearest town. But as he and his men marched through the *caatinga* under the hot sun, with all marked wells dry, all the *fazendas* abandoned and no tree to shade them during the long summer days, they became more and more concerned with sheer survival. When they reached Uauá on the 19th they had no time to rest their exhausted bodies when the Canudenses attacked with pitchforks, crossbows and shotguns next morning. Outnumbered, the militiamen panicked and only their superior weaponry saved them. The toll was 150 dead from the villagers and only 10 from the soldiers, but every single one of them was wounded. They fled.

The chief of the Bahian federal troops was beside himself. These were ex-slaves and cut-throats; they should be punished forthwith. A second expedition under Captain Febrônio de Brito with two Krupp canons, two machine guns, and 560 men left from Queimadas almost immediately on 25 November. From there they passed Monte Santo in December, where crucially they abandoned about a third of the munitions so that they could advance faster. Febrônio finally marched on Canudos on 17 January 1897. The delays had been costly: there were only two cows for the whole of the army; the troops could not be fed. The only solution was to try and capture Canudos quickly. So the soldiers rushed ahead, harried day and night by guerrilla attacks, which wasted their energy, and more importantly their ammunition. By the time they reached Canudos they were exhausted by thirst, hunger and lack of sleep. Engaged in hand-to-hand combat in a surprise attack by the Canudos villagers on a mountain pass, they were routed.

*****

Half of the 80-page *Hotel and Travel Guide* magazine you get from the tourist offices in São Paulo is aimed at the businessman: advertising the comforts of various hotels, offering VIP services and the renting of limousines or helicopters – the rich don't travel by car any more in this permanent gridlock of a city. The largest section is occupied by escort ads: GiGi's models (of 'all ages' the ad sinisterly proclaims); Sayuri Japanese escorts; Moulin Rouge lap dancing in Moema; Afrodite Relax for men in Santana; American Bar for men in Liberdade; Pizzeria Erótica in Vila Nova Conceição: eat your pizza and meet girls from paradise; Ravena's Roman sights for VIPs; Harem Night Club staffed by naked girls; Cocktail Nightclub with Sushi Erótico every Wednesday; Vagon – strip tease, topless go-go girls; Stop Night with Gaucha night on Tuesdays, Oriental Night on Wednesdays and Erotic Bingo on Saturdays; Eclipse Café for a quickie in Guarulhos. Then the sole traders: Sabrina, Daniella, Andress the *travesti*, Alina (19), who can bring her friends, Ana Paula (Hablo español), Bianca (black hair 1.82), Paula (discreet), Cibria Cortes (Speak English, Parlo Italiano), Denise from the South, Marcelle (university student for unforgettable moments), Juliana (only for you), Samantha (girl, doll and boy), Laura (Kama Sutra qualified) …

And they call gay men promiscuous.

I turned to the *Veja* gay section – imagine *Time* magazine with a gay section – where Massivo was Saturday's recommended *club-du-jour*. So that night I was back at the corner of Itu and Consolação where the

Massivo queue was, well, *massive*, as the doormen were playing Let's-Be-Studio-54. With Dutch courage, I wedged myself at the front (hell, if you are going to jump a queue, don't be too high-minded about it) by smiling at a couple as if we were lifelong friends.

Massivo was a cross between London's Trade and the Ministry of Sound: gay and straight, cool and naff at the same time. The beat was hard house, which was just making inroads into Brazil but the locals weren't quite up for it; 4/4@140bpm was too easy for them to dance to. Upstairs there was a long balcony where women and men entered and stripped off in that outrageous Latin way before they entered a cage. The same men who would snog the women downstairs, snogged the men in the dark cage. There were two women kissing in a corner, and a straight couple doing godknowswhat in *that* position. I paired off with the weirdest haircut in the place: brown goatee and short blond dreadlocks, but we struggled to find a space in the very crowded room. And out of nowhere, I was in a foursome: a topless woman grabbed me from behind and started biting my neck. Someone else – what sex I know not – started kissing her soon after. Hey, when in Brazil, do as the Romans do.

I left at 4.30 a.m. and walked home down Alameda Itu. In Brazil. In São Paulo. At night. Wasn't I tough?

Uh-oh.

Was this a silhouette behind a lamp-post? *Shit.* It was, after all, 4.30 a.m. in São Paulo. I've had it. There was definitely someone lurking, hiding from me. I could see his shadow. I mentally checked my money. About $50 left. Was this the standard muggable amount in this much improved Brazilian economy? I swallowed noiselessly.

John, you'll be fine.

I quickly stepped into the street and passed the pole. I had a quick look. There was a man there pretending to be urinating and staring at me suggestively. In fact, I could make out a hustler at every pole extending all the way to the Trianon. A car stopped some fifty yards further down and one of the guys jumped in. These people were not going to mug me. They wanted to have sex with me.

Phew! I can handle that.

Half a century after Amado's *Gabriela* dared bring to the fore the Brazilian love of pure, unadulterated sex for its own sake, a tourist doesn't have to look far. Sex finds you, for sex is how the natives conquered the *degredados*, the exterminators and the Jesuits. After the military's repression, sex is now an expanding industry producing porn movies for national and international consumption. Brazil has the exotic locations, the beautiful women and the cheap and willing labour. The Buttman series, the Scorpion series, the Concept Flux hardcore: here is an industry with studs like Fábio Scorpion being stopped and recognised in the *supermercado*. Porn Brazilian-style is different: the actors deep kiss a lot more; they touch and caress with primitive hedonism. But there is a twist: no big breast fixation like in US and European hardcore or the North American obsession with oral sex. Instead, there are bottoms aplenty: those call girls in the *Hotel and Travel Guide* do not advertise their bosoms – they pose back to the camera to display their smooth behinds with a torso half-twist to show their faces. Anal sex figures as the focal point of a heterosexual porn video. American and European sex actresses are not as willing to indulge in such antics as Brazilian ones, so the US businesses have moved in looking for new flesh and at $1,000 per sex scene, this is a lot of money for a pretty girl from the *favela*. This preoccupation with anal sex in Brazil is the only way to understand the culture of the *travesti*. They feature in straight porn films and Mr One Hundred Per Cent Heterosexual Fábio Scorpion was famously married to one without his masculinity being seen to diminish. The *travestis* are not just transvestites; they are not ex-men who've had the op: they are men who have kept their male genitalia intact and have grown breasts, aided by implants. In other cultures, *travestis* are looked upon as freaks; in Brazil, they are worshipped as goddesses, because the biggest sexual turn on is the *bunda,* not the breast.

The *bunda* is there, paraded openly on the beach of Copacabana where organised prostitution envelops the gringo lying in the sun; it's there swaying on the bandstand of the *trio elétrico*, revered like a Dionysian deity during *Carnaval*; it's paraded out of sight, clandestine in the foliage of parks of Porto Alegre and São Paulo. Sex is the defence of the poor, and the ultimate attempt of control by the rich: seduction as the only means of bridging the unbridgeable. This is how the *favela* boys and girls, desired and sought at last, can exact their revenge for their lack of social opportunity. Casual sex and random death, as Woody Allen might be prone to philosophise, are elevated in equal measures in Brazil for a simple reason: they are the only great levellers available. In such an unequal society it is only in the bed, naked, or in the grave, swathed, that we are all finally equal.

*****

The annihilation of the two missions against Canudos coincided with the transfer of power to the first civilian president, Prudente de Morais, after the military coup that deposed Dom Pedro II. The generals at the Military Club in Rio shook their heads. Look at how the politicians screwed up. To pacify them, the third expedition against Canudos was headed by Colonel Antônio Moreira César, the 'butcher of Santa Catarina', who received this nickname because he slit the throats of the local royalist rebels in Florianópolis. He was accompanied by 1,300 well-trained men, heavy artillery, cavalry and 60,000 rounds of ammunition. He left Salvador on 8 February 1897. By then, Canudos had been fortified and the nearby populace was sympathetic to the villagers' plight: not only were Moreira César's movements and route known to his enemies, but Canudos itself had received many reinforcements.

Moreira César took the long, flat route rather than the short mountainous one of the earlier expeditions. He moved rapidly to effect a surprise that never came; instead he was harassed by quick raids. He reached Canudos and started bombarding the town from the hill opposite. It was his arrogance that lost him the battle. He was dismissive of the villagers, and, instead of battering them with his cannon, he decided to attack. But once inside the narrow streets of Canudos, he lost any advantage. Cavalry requires manoeuvre; machine guns call for an open field. In the winding, unfamiliar Canudos street maze the religious fanaticism of man-to-man combat was superior weaponry. After five hours of conflict Moreira César was mortally wounded; he died the next day. His second-in-command, Colonel Tamarindo, decided to tactically withdraw. But he did not expect the villagers to come after them, incensed at the destruction of their church. The soldiers threw their munitions away and ran. Tamarindo was shot and killed. It was a massacre.

*****

Familiar London weather awaited me next day; cool and rainy. I was determined to make a day out of it, so I went to see two films at the São Paulo Film Festival.

Many people – including myself – first came across Brazilian cinema with the 1981 film *Pixote*, a Cannes Film Festival stunner. The director was an Argentinian, Hector Babenco, who went on to direct the more successful *Kiss of the Spider Woman*. Shot with real *favela* kids turned actors, *Pixote* was a bare-knuckled docudrama of the miserable life of São Paulo youngsters; it gripped millions of viewers worldwide as it exposed the summary justice and routine torture by the police, the medieval prison conditions, the corruption and day-to-day violence in São Paulo and Rio. When the military authorities first watched the film, they wanted to prosecute the director for inciting the corrupting of minors and advocating drug use: was the 10-year-old Pixote sniffing real glue or pretending? The film, relentless in its bleakness and never pulling the strings of tearful bathos, starts with a homosexual rape observed by Pixote, who goes on to participate in a prison riot, escape, steal, mug, deal drugs, pimp a whore, assault and kill friend and foe alike. Babenco admitted that the actors rewrote the script with their experiences and improvised about 40 per cent of the dialogue, turning the venture more into *cinema verité*. Fernando Ramos da Silva played Pixote, worth three Julia Roberts' Oscars, but what happened to him after the film is perhaps grimmer than what shocked the art-house crowd on celluloid.

Fernando was 11 when he was selected out of 1,300 applicants to star in *Pixote*. His father had died when he was eight and his mother received a pension of just $10 a month to feed ten children in Diadema, São Paulo. But then came Hector Babenco, offering the ultimate dream: to make it big in the movies. Moved by *Pixote*, the mayor of Duque de Caxias, a working-class town north of Rio offered Fernando a scholarship to an acting school and his family a proper house. Could someone who has lived in the margins of society return back to its bosom? Do miracles happen?

Fernando did not have the middle-class discipline and attention span for attending classes; he couldn't read properly for a start. He dropped out of school after two days. His family left Rio and moved back to São Paulo, not far from the racing circuit of Interlagos. He managed to get a few parts. He appeared in a soap opera. He advertised UNICEF Christmas cards. But his image as Pixote had stuck and the fable merged into reality. Fernando started being harassed by police in real life as much as was his fictional alter ego. In 1985 Fernando married a girl of 16 from Minas Gerais and had a daughter. On 25 August 1987, six years after his big success, he was killed by the military police. Their story is that he was resisting arrest when surprised during a hold-up and had opened fire. A forensic examination showed that he had been killed lying on the ground. The three policemen who killed him were merely dismissed from the force; two of them started a successful security firm in Diadema. One of Fernando's brothers was subsequently shot and killed. Two more of his brothers fled the area in fear of their lives. His wife published a ghostwritten tome trying to milk the sympathy of the Brazilian public as long as it lasted. A lesser film based on Fernando's story, *Who Killed Pixote?* was released in 1995. But some more staggering crimes by the authorities – massacres at Carandiru and Candelária – buried Fernando's memory.

Only *Pixote* remains.

*****

The newspapers had a field day. Antônio Conselheiro's mob were planning the destruction of the Republic and were in cahoots with the monarchists. This was Restoration! The Return of Slavery and Colonialism! The President should arm every republican man and send him to fight in Bahia!

From a lieutenant to a captain to a colonel, now a general: Artur Oscar led the fourth expedition with six brigades from eleven different states, approaching Canudos in two columns with 5,000 soldiers in total. He himself was in charge of one column comprising a Whitworth 32 cannon weighing 1.7 tons and thousands of rounds of ammunition. Oscar left Monte Santo on 7 June and sent a message to the other contingent under General Claudio Savaget to meet him in Canudos in 20 days. During the march Oscar's troops were continuously harassed by opportunistic raids; the wells were filled in; the regiment's animals were killed by arrows that spread poison and made the meat inedible. By the time Oscar passed Pitombas, strewn with the cadavers of the third expedition, the soldiers were already spooked. They were spooked even more when they reached the hill opposite Canudos at night and found themselves surrounded by the villagers who had been hiding in trenches. They could see Canudos, but they were stuck in an impasse. Where were the other three brigades?

The answer was: fighting the *sertanejos* in Cocorobó, three days away, three days over which Oscar's first column was being slowly bled. When Savaget finally arrived, he saw to his astonishment that Oscar was in dire straits. He charged up the hill and joined him. But instead of them surrounding the village, it was their 5,000 men who were surrounded on all sides. The villagers had sacked boxes and boxes of ammunition. They had food. So they waited.

By 2 July Oscar's victuals had virtually disappeared. He tried counter-raids in search of food to no avail. By 7 July his wounded stopped receiving any rations. Oscar gave the order to advance in a desperate attack against the town. The villagers had succeeded in engaging the enemy in hand-to-hand combat again. The army occupied part of the town where no food was to be found – so what? Instead of being surrounded, hungry, on the hill, they were surrounded, hungry, in the town.

On 10 August after losing 2,049 men Oscar managed to retreat to Monte Santo. He requested another 5,000 men by telegraph to complete the task.

*****

For my last evening, I went to Finnegan's, the gringo bar in São Paulo. It's a friendly Irish pub opposite Massivo. The owner was ...

'Irish?' I ventured.

'No, Turkish,' he answered. Like Gabriela's husband, he was in fact Syrian, but in Brazil all Middle-Eastern immigrants are 'Turks'.

The owner introduced me to four British and Canadian engineers who were building up São Paulo's cellular phone network. In the last five years of the twentieth century the state received 82 billion dollars' worth of investments from abroad. (Where, you ask, did it all go? It certainly didn't improve the quality of life or at least the length of the life of its people.)

'The allocation of government contracts in Brazil,' said a tall, nerdy Canadian, 'is just a matter of the biggest kickback. Ours wasn't the cheapest or the most technically advanced bid, but we offered the biggest bribe to the state officials. That's how you do business here.'

I feigned surprise.

'I hate this city,' the Canadian continued. 'I've been here six months now, and I have to go all over the state to install the mobile cells and survey the area: hills, valleys, *favelas*. There are some places in São Paulo where we are escorted by police. And believe me, I feel more uncomfortable in the presence of the police than without them. The druglords in the *favelas want* mobile phones! They are on *my* side.'

He bought me a drink, which ensured my unabated attention.

'I hate this city,' he repeated. 'If you see how some people live, it turns your guts. No water. They drink from muddy wells. No sanitation. They shit on the side of the road. Some of them don't even look human – skin diseases. It's like Africa, but only a few miles away from where we are now. Did you know that there are native Indians around São Paulo? Real Indians like in the Amazon? I've seen them.'

This was one of the wildest claims of a drunken Canadian – and yet I checked it later, and he was right. The Pankararu, a tribe native to Pernambuco migrated wholesale to São Paulo in the 1950s; they live in their hundreds near the neighbourhood of Real Parque and, like migratory birds, spend six months in the capital and six months back in Pernambuco. Their story became big because they were discovered by the media. Their *favela* has now been recognised as a reservation and bilingual schools were built. But because of their location, they don't receive aid like other Indian groups in Brazil for their own safety. Other *favela* denizens might assault and rob them. São Paulo is no less of a jungle than when Ramalho first stepped in.

'I like São Paulo,' I said – and it was the first time I had uttered these words.

The Canadian looked at me, astonished. 'What do you like about it?' he asked.

'This place. The Jardins. The New York feel. The nightlife. The occasional rain and cold,' I heard myself say, feeling more surprised by the minute.

Well, yes, John, this is the only truly cosmopolitan city in Brazil. This is a city to live in: not too hot, not too cold, unlike steamy, rainy and quintessentially Brazilian Rio de Janeiro, a place to holiday in rather than work. Peter Matthiessen wrote in *The Cloud Forest*: '*São Paulo is perhaps the most truly modern of all the cities that I saw [in South America]; it is not a handsome place, but there is a sense of experiment and life which is well suited to this huge new nation.*'

'Why not Rio?' asked the Canadian.

Why not Rio, indeed.

'Because,' I said, 'wherever you go one-third of Brazilians are employed in defending one-third of Brazilians from the other one-third who want to mug them' – this little ditty of mine drew approving grins from the Finnegan's regulars – 'but unlike Rio where *favela* meets high-class condo face-to-face, São Paulo has its neighbourhoods very much segregated. You can spend all your life in São Paulo and never stray into a *favela* – not so in Rio.'

'And that is good?'

'I don't know. But it makes São Paulo more liveable and a little less dangerous. And the work rhythm of the city gives you the confidence that should your washing machine need servicing, there will be a plumber capable enough to fix it. What more do you want?'

'What about the people? Cariocas are such fun.'

'They are. They are lovely. But there it's all beach life: sun, sea, sex and semi-naked men and women with their tanga swimsuits and their aerobically perfect super bodies. I'm an owl with an average build who likes the nightlife and the international vibe.'

I stopped, surprised at my outburst. 'And you know what?'

'What?'

'I'm coming back!'

*****

The end, when it came, was drawn out.

The fifth expedition against Canudos was composed of 3,000 men headed by Eugênio de Andrade Guimarães, brother to Artur Oscar. A permanent base of operations was established at Monte Santo from where short expeditions were made. There was continuous cannon bombardment and a war of attrition in which the regular army had a proper logistical post. The Canudos leaders who had outfoxed the Brazilian military were killed off one by one. Worse, on 22 September 1897, Antônio Conselheiro passed away, having predicted his own death. Some say it was tuberculosis, others a heart attack. In his last prophesy, he asked his followers to flee. They refused: now their Counsellor was with the angels, he was even more powerful; he would muster help. On 24 September they made a break for it. It took the soldiers a week to bring them to heel. On 2 October, 300 women, children and old folk surrendered. The men had decided to fight to the end. By 5 October Canudos only had four inhabitants left who were caught by the soldiers: a child, two males and an old man. Next day they found Antônio Conselheiro. We have a picture of the exhumed body, head cut off post-humously as if he were Count Dracula. He bears a remarkable similarity to Jerry Garcia without the glasses. He wears sandals. His left arm has rotted away. Not until Che Guevara would anyone rise like that against a South American government.

The victorious foot-soldiers who had fought in Canudos returned to the capital, to another hill, like the one they'd fought on. They called their settlement Favela, for that was the original name of the hill opposite Canudos where so many of their number had breathed their last. In Rio de Janeiro they had no prospects. They didn't find work. The Republic did not recompense them for defending its existence. Favela disintegrated and its name became synonymous with an overpopulated, dirty slum.

That is the word Canudos bequeathed the world.

– 66 –

François

Someone once said that historians are unsuccessful novelists, but maybe that description should be left for travel writers. When one travels, the normal rules of life are suspended; life becomes a tale you control. When on a journey, we make our own fiction; with a beginning, a middle and an end, a journey is real life in miniature. And, as Canudos or Pixote remind us, life is much stranger than fiction. Isn't this why you are still reading?

The third time I returned to São Paulo was during that trip in Brazil's 500th year. I stayed for a weekend, just to catch the plane to return to London. I had been to Rio's *Carnaval*, the Nordeste and Brazil's south – so the streets of the Jardins seemed like coming home.

On my last night there, when I returned from Florianópolis, I met François.

In the past five years the prices had stabilised and the country looked up for the first time in two generations. The Brazilians themselves didn't appreciate it, but journalists started exposing the corruption endemic in the system: politicians with parliamentary immunity, police in cahoots with criminals, self-perpetuating business empires involving day-to-day bribes and backhanders. The mayor of São Paulo was being denounced by his wife and resigned; the largest scalp since Collor himself. Yes, such powerful people were not uncovered by fearsome investigative journalism – in their stead estranged brothers or furious wives played their part – but the press was at last there to follow it up with teeth. But some statistics worsened. As late as 1995 the murder rate per 100,000 inhabitants in São Paulo was 17 (Northern Ireland: 10). In the next five years it more than doubled to 35, with half of them shot by the police, whereas in the US it crashed down to 9.

Finnegan's was now called O'Malley's. The gay scene, following capitalist patterns, had concentrated around Consolação. Ecstasy had arrived in the clubs of the Jardins which were now booming. Nostro Mundo had undergone a facelift and was advertised as Mondo 2000.

Clubs B.A.S.E., A Loca and SoGo were the craze. Hard house ruled and Paulistas had learned how to shake their booty to the 4:4 beat.

You could have mistaken SoGo as an extension of the Ritz with its elegant clientele chatting and smoking over expensive caipirinhas, discreetly eyeing each other. They were all white, for the capitalist patterns had also split the gay scene into a mostly white, expensive section and a cheaper, mixed, non-Jardins set. It was full of young people who had started coming out in droves since that first São Paulo Gay Pride march in 1995. Visibility was up. Aids warnings were everywhere and free condoms were available. One part of São Paulo – the one that owned cars – was becoming indistinguishable from the rest of the First World. I had no idea any more what was happening to the other: out of sight, it was slipping out of mind. The more you get involved, the less you see.

Some specialist tastes had also arrived.

You climb to the Dungeon upstairs from SoGo. As you enter, you see this big sign: 'Strict Dress Code: Leather, Rubber, Army, Underwear. Strictly Over 18!' Damn! I had nothing to wear! I resigned myself to having to take off my clothes and parade in my Y-fronts. I was already moaning that my black socks clashed with my Nike shoes as I paid my 10 reais entry.

The doorman took a quick look at me.

'You can't go in like that!'

I swallowed hard. The guy's voice was soooo, well, *masterly*.

'Will I have to take my clothes off?' I asked, excited.

'No,' he said. 'Take off your T-shirt.'

'MY T-SHIRT?'

'Yes, your T-shirt.'

I was incensed.

'You call this a strict dress code? I take off my T-shirt everywhere! It doesn't count.'

I smiled.

'How about my trousers?' I ventured.

'No, just your T-shirt.'

Oh, well, if I must ...

It was there, through the maze of semi-lit dungeon cabins peppered with glory holes and CCTV broadcasting hardcore videos that I met François. He was leaning against the upstairs bar, fair, brown-eyed and youthful, radiating presence like the central figure of a tenebrist painting, his beauty intensified by the sordid surroundings. How come he was alone? Sometimes being too good-looking has its downside. I stood next to him and our eyes met. That was enough. Before long we were kissing.

'Not here,' I told him.

'OK,' he said.

'My hotel?' I asked. 'It's not far, down Frei Caneca, the other side of Avenida Paulista.'

'Cool,' he said again.

That was my night with François.

....

The unreality of São Paulo remains to the moment of touchdown when the engines cut.

Back at the coast there is only jungle below, a trail here and there, or a clearing with a red-tiled house – no suggestion of a metropolis of five and a half million people. The escarpment rises and suddenly there is a rolling, partially wooded plain and a moment later the raw wounds of fresh red earth where the city has formed its latest boundary. It is forty miles in from the coast and the plane flies twenty of them over industry and housing. The scale and extent after the desolate emptiness between here and Rio is a jolt to the uninitiated. Here are eight car factories, petroleum refineries, chemical works and the ten thousand little industries that enable the Industria Brasileira *label to be put on almost every imaginable product needed by man in the mid-sixties. At a glance one can see that São Paulo is indeed what the Paulista claims – the engine that hauls the empty carriages of Brazil. For all that it is an uninviting prospect. Smoke haze hangs over the city and though it is nothing as bad as the Ruhr or the English Midlands even from the air one gets the impression of a seedy drabness. Then as the aeroplane banks to come into the Congonhas airport, two miles from the city centre and one of the busiest airports in the world, there is a brief glimpse of São Paulo's Manhattan, a skyscraping concrete core, white in the pellucid light, rising far above the city's exhalations. And behind, magically, are the mountains.'*

– The academic Malcolm Slesser giving us his views on São Paulo in 1967, when the city was still only a third of what it is today.

....

'François is not a Brazilian name.'

'My mother is Italian,' he said in perfect English. 'My father's Brazilian.'

'François isn't Italian either.'

'Somewhere in my background there is French blood,' he said and shrugged his shoulders.

I feasted my eyes on him lying on my bed, naked, the perfect specimen of New World blood admixture. If this is the future of a mankind falling in love without barriers, I want to beep myself two centuries ahead.

He lived in a luxury apartment in the Jardins.

'You mean SoGo is your local?'

He laughed: 'He-he-he, my parents never thought ten years ago that they would be buying property in the middle of the future gay area.'

'I presume they don't like it.'

'They complain about the noise.'

'Are you out to your parents?'

'From the age of sixteen,' he said.

Since he lived in one of the most exclusive areas of São Paulo …

'My family has land,' he said simply.

So my François was part of those elites I kept hearing about – and never did they look so gorgeously seductive. He had learned his English jet-setting between Florida and LA and was a champion skateboarder, top in Brazil, top ten in the World Games, the X-games …

'Fifth in the world, he-he-he,' he said, not without embarrassment. 'But there are hardly any facilities in Brazil compared to the States or Europe. No Nike sponsorships. I tried.'

Unless you are a footballer.

'Isn't skating dangerous?' I asked.

He showed me his party trick by displacing his wrists.

'Look, he-he-he, I've broken both,' he said with his trademark curt laugh.

I looked away for multiple reasons.

'You realise that I have to leave for London tomorrow afternoon.'

'That's cool,' he said and lay back.

'You have to give me your address,' I said.

He wrote it down immediately, as if he hated to say no.

I wondered if my Finnegan's Canadians had succeeded in wiring the capital completely.

'Are you on the Internet?' I asked.

He gave me one of his 'Here Comes The Sun' smiles we associate with Beatles' acoustic guitars.

'I'm permanently on,' he replied.

How strangely things turn out.

*****

And so my night with François became a long-distance friendship. For the next ten months we emailed each other like old friends, his exuberance and his Americanisms (no one but he dares call me 'dude') lighting up my inbox on a frequent basis. Christmas came and went and a fourth trip to Brazil was the last thing on my mind after the North-South marathon on its 500th year. But before twelve months were over, I changed my mind.

I emailed François.

'Hey … so u r coming to Brazil? Coooool … but, when? like, what days? Right now i'm in Sydney, Australia … isn't that cool? he-he, i just got back from Cairns, i went to the barrier reef …

Well, i've been here for 2 weeks already, and this will be the last one. Sunday i'm going back to Sao Paulo … for CARNIVAL!! UHUUUUU he-he-he-he

Gotta go now, have to go to dinner and get ready and everything … c ya later.'

This time, during my fourth trip, I would be in control of my own fiction.

We're entering the immediate present.

Sandstorm

The fourth time I returned to São Paulo could not be more at odds with my first view of the *favelas* through the windows of a Guarulhos taxi, one eye kept firmly on the meter. I knew exactly which area and hotel to aim for. I knew how long the trip into town would take. I was keen to eat *palmitos* at Bovinu's. I was going to party at B.A.S.E. And finally, I had someone waiting for me.

*****

A smiling, grinning François arrived to pick me up at Pamplona Palace. I had forgotten how his aura could light up the evening. Close-up it was so difficult to view him just as a friend. We embraced awkwardly.

'Dude, wow, you have come on a cool weekend,' he said. 'There's a combined party tomorrow in Pinheiros. X-Demente from Rio and Ultra-Lounge from São Paulo: Ultra-Demente!'

I looked at the flyers: starting at 23.59 with DJs Douglas, Herbert Tonn, Renato Lopez, Tatá: the DJ as the master of the universe.

'About time,' I said. 'I missed their party last year during *Carnaval*.'

'I'll drive us to Allegro,' he twittered. 'We have to get tickets in advance to avoid the line.'

Allegro was the latest 'in' gay bar-restaurant in the Jardins. François filled me in: 'SoGo is closed. Massivo is straight. The Ultra-Lounge has opened on Consolação.'

I pointed at the Range Rover parked outside.

'This car is yours?'

'Nah, my father's. He-he, I passed my test and can drive now,' he said as he switched on a techno CD to max: we were ghetto-blasting down Alameda Jaú – if the Jardins could be called a ghetto.

There was one notable change in his body he had boasted about in the emails.

'So?' he asked proudly.

I touched his pecs.

'Very good,' I said. 'How often do you go to the gym now?'

'Five times a week,' he replied. 'I'm always there five to seven in the evening.'

The gym was a block away. His *vestibular* classes were a few streets away. Allegro, Ritz, the Ultra-Lounge and the late SoGo were a few strolls down the road. François never left the Jardins.

'Well, I have to drive to B.A.S.E.,' he corrected me, tongue-in-cheek. 'And the shopping centre.'

By then we'd reached his apartment block where we parked the car in the underground garage. We took the lift up to street-level.

'What's this?' I cried.

I read a notice in Portuguese: '*It is forbidden under penalty of a fine to discriminate by virtue of race, sex, colour, origin, social circumstance, age, disability or illness non-contagious by social contact, of the access to the elevators of this building.* Municipal Law 11.995 of 16/1/96, São Paulo.'

I must have looked astonished – and I was – because François looked at me puzzled.

'You can't discriminate against anyone in São Paulo,' he said matter-of-factly.

I didn't know whether the mere existence of the law was a greater indictment of the Paulistas than its absence. I still don't. If a society needs to legislate specifically for elevator access, what was it like before the law was passed?

*****

Allegro was spacious, modern, rich and the clientele as chic as they come. Like the Ritz or Nick Havana's, the menu was innovative and the service of the highest standard. Some corners of Brazil could be transplanted lock, stock and barrel to Los Angeles or Florida and no one would notice.

François had been far chirpier behind the wheel than one-to-one at a table in Allegro. Our predicament, after the initial rush of emotion, was obvious to both. We had spent a grand total of one night together nearly a year ago. Exactly what was our status? Friends – who had never had a friendly chat face-to-face? Ex-one-night stands? Internet acquaintances? I had even forgotten his face, which had become more manly and broad, but was still as stupendously beautiful as you find them this side of Hollywood. I was dreading that the cultural, work-status and age differences would create a chasm between us. One thing he made clear from the start: he had just split with his boyfriend who was, unsurprisingly, my age. Long-distance relationship as well: the boyfriend was Dutch.

'He keeps calling me and leaving messages and saying how sorry he is,' François said with a shrug of the shoulders. 'And yet he kept shouting at me – that he didn't trust me, that I was unfaithful to him. He was so jealous, it was intolerable. I'm supposed to be the young one!'

I listened to his woes with fascination. How sexy are the ones who don't fully comprehend their own attractiveness. I remembered Isaías and a steel hand gripped my heart. In a relationship with a large age gap, it's always the older party who feels the pressure. Then, as now, it was the younger party who was unselfconsciously bridging that gap with remarkable maturity.

'So what happened?'

'We had a row during *Carnaval*, and I'd had enough.'

'I'm sorry.'

'I had a terrible start to the year,' he continued, bringing me up to date. 'I wrote to you about my accident.'

No, he hadn't. But he had disappeared for a while.

'It was a month ago. I was in this grand skating competition broadcast nationally on a Sunday morning, 11 o'clock, on *Globo* when all my friends and family were watching. And I fell! I couldn't believe it. They were all watching, and I fell badly and I burned my arm – look, almost healed.'

'You *burned* it?'

'When you slide down the ramp you get burns. This is the first weekend I've been able to go clubbing for a month.'

We were gossiping about the sexual proclivities of the X-Games skating participants when Ford rushed in.

'*There* you are, *bicha*! You *never* called! I knew you'd come here on your first night.' And turning to François: 'Who's this?' – then back to me: 'You've picked up *already*?'

It was Ford who provided the sanity during that encounter between myself and François. Here was someone with a relationship we could all relate to: the old friend. I had met Ford (named in honour of the *Star Wars'* star) in London, and we had become good mates over two years while he was studying.

'So you're going to Porto Alegre and Brasília this time,' Ford said with disbelief. 'What for?'

I couldn't really tell him I had returned to complete my quest for the soul of Brazil, so I let it pass with a shrug.

'And returning to Belo Horizonte. I have some ghosts to exorcise.'

'Go anywhere you like. But tomorrow, Friday,' said Ford, 'you'll come with me.'

'We can all go to Ultra-Demente,' added François.

Our eyes met and reassured each other.

'I'll go with you, but I won't leave with you,' François added with a smirk. 'He-he, you know me.'

This is a funny relationship we're in, but we'll make it work.

*****

'So what's up with François?' asked Ford. 'You never told me about him. He seems a very nice guy.'

It was early evening, and we were walking in Ibirapuera Park. Its obelisk was a reminder of the 1932 anti-Vargas revolt that defined the city, a monument to the big compromise which ensured its meteoric success. Ibirapuera means 'place that used to be jungle'. This had been thick bush where the jaguars roamed. Now we have muggers instead: a sign of the times.

'We spent one night together last year,' I said.

'Is that all?' He sounded surprised.

'That's all.'

Ford gave me a quick glance.

'Oh. But this year it's different, is that it?'

He got it in one.

'We kept in touch regularly through the Net. I mean regularly. I knew what he was doing every month. We've been through affairs in the meantime. We've discussed them together.'

From the small lake there is an uninterrupted view of the skyscrapers in the centre, aglitter in their artificial light. A long horizon is a rare prospect in São Paulo.

'I have a lot of time for François. I've never met anyone so together, so sure-footed. He knows what he wants. And he's so young, it's frightening.'

'It's best to leave it like that,' said Ford.

I had forgotten Ford's own focused intensity: London education, world travel, job hunt – another example of Paulista vigour. Several years older than François, Ford had his own seductiveness and drive. He had already moved twice in the job market, positioning himself higher and with larger salaries within the marketing departments of high-tech companies.

'And you? How are you finding it here?'

Ford sighed.

'Brazil – ah, Brazil. It's so tough to look for work, for a flat, for a car.'

Before a job and before a flat, Ford had bought a car along with millions of other Paulistas. Despite a metro system, São Paulo's public transport stinks. And today the buses were on strike.

'You've lost weight.'

'No time for the gym. I'm staying with family in Liberdade,' said Ford. 'But I must go. I'm being a burden.'

Paulistas were jogging around us in the latest sportswear, some followed by anti-mugger Dobermanns.

'I'm looking for a flat in Pinheiros. Reasonably OK area, not too far from the Jardins.'

'And London?'

'I miss London. I would like to work there.'

Our walk was over. We were back by the car.

'But I probably have a better chance here,' he said softly as we got inside.

Brazilians started leaving their country during the military dictatorship. But many of them returned, unable to break the umbilical cord with a lifestyle, a climate and a country less austere.

'I've often wondered what it is that makes São Paulo so stimulating,' I said. 'There is injustice, hardship, crime, poverty. And yet ...'

I left the sentence hanging.

And yet you returned. I returned.

Our car stopped in traffic over an aqueduct. This was the evening rush hour. Below us the cars were immobile like a freeze-frame from *Koyaanisqatsi*. The air was cool and, Brazilian-style, the slow-moving traffic seemed relaxed.

'São Paulo is an ugly city,' said Ford to no one in particular, certainly not to me. 'You drive in the morning and you think "This is the worst shithole I've seen". And then –'

We moved for a few seconds and stopped again.

'And then night comes and something happens to the city,' he whispered whimsically.

I looked out of the window into the distance, following the giddy reflections of a bright motion picture being developed in front of me. This was *Blade Runner* shot in Gotham City starring characters from *Akira* and *Necromancer*.

'The lights,' I said, agreeing.

'Yes,' Ford echoed me, 'the lights.'

The traffic moved on.

*****

Ultra-Demente was cancelled at the last minute. It's probably my fate never to club it at one of those famous parties. Our tickets were thankfully valid for the Ultra-Lounge, a sparkling dance club with plush sofas, four-poster beds and an artwork of a toilet. François was in his element: life was a big, grand party, and he had an exclusive VIP ticket.

Ford was already inside. 'We were early,' he said, introducing a friend. 'Everyone from Ultra-Demente is coming here, and there are more of them than can fit in. I suppose you got in because of that cute friend of yours.'

'FRANÇOIS!' I shouted.

He turned to us, leaning on the bar.

'How did we get in?'

'John pushed in the queue and started chatting to the doorman,' François said. 'Something about having come all the way from London.'

Ford smirked.

'You should have trusted your friend more,' I said to him, mock-insulted.

He bowed I-am-not-worthy.

In the Ultra-Lounge the DJs were up to date with the latest tunes, whether Euro-Trance or Tribal Techno, Old School or Trip House in a way that put Rio's handbag house in perspective. François was getting out of it and removed his top, revealing a washboard stomach and a firm muscular chest. I followed suit.

'You've put on good weight since last year,' he said and winked.

I said nothing. I felt fat like I always do. And next to François I felt even more self-conscious. Ten hours a week in the gym had turned his body into a sculpted specimen.

We were standing near the bar when a frisky François suddenly pinched me in the groin.

'Come,' he said and took me onto the dance floor.

I swallowed hard. My mind was not working well. I touched his nipples.

'No, no, no, no,' he said. 'Please.'

We danced.

'I like you a lot, John,' he said.

'I like you, too.'

'Sandstorm' played over the speakers.

'Wuoooehh,' cried François. 'I saw him. DJ Darude. In Sydney.'

'Saw whom?'

'The DJ who made this music.'

'Oh, the Finn.'

A woman started playing live percussion to the beat, adding a Brazilian twist to the house-blasting track.

'Didn't like it. He stopped after every *music*' – François called every track 'music', translating the Portuguese *música* directly – 'and went "Wowowoow – HELLO SYDNEY!" I was all dancing and ready for it and he was stopping! "HELLO SYDNEY!"'

'I hate star DJs,' I said. 'It goes to their heads.'

'It does,' he agreed. 'But I still love this.'

We danced until the end of the track. François turned to me, elated.

'John, this is the first time I'm out after my accident. This is the first time without a boyfriend. Please understand.'

I said nothing. I did not expect this. Complex feelings I had buried deeply were coming to the fore.

'I mean I was here last time with my boyfriend, and he became jealous because I was in the toilet for too long.'

I ran my finger down his back.

'Not now. Tomorrow,' he said. 'We'll have sex tomorrow.'

And with that he disappeared, leaving me with a bundle of contradictory emotions.

After an hour or so, Ford realised there was something wrong.

'You are missing François,' he said.

I felt a pang.

'There he is.'

I saw François, a strange grin on his face.

'Wow,' he said. 'Wow. I met a guy from London. Old, but sweet, so sweet. I can't believe, I can't believe I met someone from London *again*. Do you want to talk to him?'

I said no.

'OK. I'll see you later. Call me.'

I stood there and watched an English-looking guy escort François out of the club, my gut beating in sync with the throbbing rhythm.

Ford was watching the green shadow in my eyes.

'I bet you aren't interested in coming to Campinas with me tomorrow,' he said.

*****

Ford was right. I turned down a trip to Campinas to meet his boyfriend. I would have done under normal circumstances anyway: Campinas, an industrial and university town one hour north of São Paulo, is no Ouro Preto; I would have felt like piggy in the middle, and the circumstances were extraordinary as they were.

That Saturday I woke up at midday tired, hung over and with that funny feeling, part-anxiety, part-hunger, part-dread deep in my ribs. I called François.

'And how was last night?' I dared ask.

'Wow, very enjoyable, he-he-he,' he replied, smiley emoticons beaming down my phone. 'I got no sleep, he-he-he.'

'Are you tired? Are we still going out tonight?' I asked.

'Yeah, sure. We're going to B.A.S.E.'

I checked the waters.

'What time are you coming over?'

'I'm cutting a CD for a friend,' said François. 'Meet you at Allegro at midnight?'

At midnight?

'Pop over here at eight-thirty,' I suggested.

François was slow to reply.

'Hello?' I asked.

'OK,' he said simply.

That Saturday I walked around São Paulo and couldn't turn the clock forward quickly enough. At Praça República, Hotel Amazonas and all its artful inlaid wood panelling was being demolished. I ventured to São Bento, over the Anhangabaú, where no dog was being tenderised this time, on to the Praça da Sé where there were no more interrogation booths, although the crowd was as sickly and menacing as always. I recognised the folk music an old, blind man with an accordion was singing at the edge of the Cathedral stairs: *'Música sertaneja,'* I whispered to myself. I visited an Internet café in an old gem of a house on Avenida Paulista 1919, a *casarão*, an upstairs/downstairs affair with wood parquets, hexagonal mosaics and a carved wooden ceiling. How come these grand mansions have escaped the clutches of the developers? Just the income from turning them into car parks would be enough to live luxuriously in another town. There are a few scattered in the Jardins – my favourite being on the corner of João Manuel and Alameda Santos – a reminder of the coffee-baron era of the early 1900s. What is the architectural style future generations will inherit from the turn of the millennium? High fences and conspicuous security devices incorporated into an aesthetic whole? Decorative sharp bars on railings? Sealed-off porticos and windows with no access to the street?

I returned to my room. I tried to sleep but couldn't. I turned the telly on.

Rita Lee was on singing her latest hit. This was the first time I had actually watched her perform rather than heard her on CD. Like a proper Brazilian personality, she has kept her looks into old age. She is descended from a group of Confederate settlers who arrived in Brazil after the American Civil War because the country still allowed slavery at the time. Dom Pedro II had welcomed them with open arms, guaranteed them freedom of religion and sold them the red fertile land of São Paulo at 22 cents an acre. The result is Americana, a town of 250,000, a textile centre today – after all, it is cotton plantations they had left behind. Do they regret the move? Certainly not Rita Lee, now in her fifties, a grande dame of Brazilian pop, the Os Mutantes experimentation a distant cult memory. Brazilians worship old artists – especially if they have managed to stay out of jail.

At last night dawned and the city came alive once more.

*****

My phone rang and woke me from my torpor.

'Someone at reception for you.'

'Ask him to come up.'

I checked everything in my room, which I had tidied up earlier, and opened the door to meet François. He was wearing surfer shorts and looked younger than his age. He held his car keys high.

'I need to go to give the CD to a friend,' he said.

I knew then that nothing would happen.

'Did you pick up last night at Ultra-Lounge?' he asked to make conversation.

'No,' I shook my head.

Perhaps out of respect to a distant memory.

I sat on my bed.

'I need to know where I stand, François,' I said.

He looked at me.

'I don't understand.'

'I need to know what you think of me.'

'You are a friend. A good friend. I like you very much.'

He lowered his gaze.

'You wanted more,' he whispered.

It had bothered him, too.

'I think the world of you François,' I started. 'I admire you. You have the mind of a champion.'

Being young, pretty as they come, gay and rich and living in the Jardins must do something to your head. He could be so spoiled – and yet he was so down to earth.

'I didn't expect anything when I first came. How could I? What are we really? Internet acquaintances?' I hesitated. 'But last night …'

He looked at me, pained.

'Last night I was drunk,' he took up my cue. 'I'm sorry about what I said.'

You think you can control your fiction, but you can't.

I lay on my bed facing the ceiling. This didn't feel too bad. It was as if a weight was being lifted off my shoulders. I could have my life back.

François was looking at me helplessly.

'I really like you,' he repeated softly. 'As a friend.'

'Actually, I feel relieved,' I said. 'Part of me is disappointed, but a greater part of me is relieved.'

It would have complicated things so much otherwise.

'Are we still going out tonight?' I asked him.

His face brightened up.

'Yes.'

'B.A.S.E?'

'Cool.'

I stood up.

'I feel like picking up tonight,' I said to him and winked.

'I feel like it, too,' he said teasingly back.

'We'll have a great time,' I promised him.

'We will.'

He clunked his keys.

'When is your flight on Monday? I can drive you to the airport.'

'Too early. Have to be there for seven.'

He looked disappointed.

'I have to go to school,' he said.

It always threw me whenever he mentioned school, an Americanism; he meant *vestibular* prep College.

'I'm coming back to São Paulo before I leave for London,' I said. 'It's a night flight.'

It was as if I had given him a present.

'Cool – he-he-he. I'll drive you then,' he said.

I checked my watch.

'Meet up in Allegro at midnight?' I asked.

'Cool,' he replied.

This is why François wins contests, and I don't. But then, I write stories like these for you. It's better this way.

*****

I went to Allegro earlier than usual for a few drinks on my own. François was being overtly thoughtful and phoned the manager at midnight to leave a message that he was going to be half an hour late. When he arrived, we were off to B.A.S.E., a vast multi-chambered, multi-level club blasting Positiva trance anthems. We met his mates inside, we chatted, we danced, we drank. François never made me feel that we were anything less than the best of friends, and he enjoyed himself as only he knows how, or rather as only *we* know how, for there is, after all, a bond between us – we know how to party, and that night we were taking each other out, making sure the other had a good time. Only once did I try to contemplate what would have happened *if* – and dismissed the thought immediately. I felt light and I felt merry and I felt pleased when François picked up again. Ever considerate, he indirectly asked whether he could leave earlier with his new conquest – of course he could! Because when he finally left I was alone again, unattached and unburdened with emotion and that is a great feeling in São Paulo. Clubs may come and go, murder rates can soar, faces may fade, but the buzz, the *joie de vivre* that envelops you at night is still the same. There is no worse place to be lonely than São Paulo, and yet no better place to be alone. The city demands you hold her in a tight embrace where there is no room for anyone else. You cannot live in São Paulo and not surrender unconditionally, because in submission there is power, and the more you submit to its allure, the stronger you get and the higher you soar.

My eyes met Dárcio's, as 'Sandstorm' played again over the PA. Pity François missed it.

The eighth deadly sin is to be poor.

No, Isabel. You were obsessed with money. The eighth deadly sin in this city is to be weak, for Paulistas have inherited the earth through sheer bloody willpower.

I didn't take Dárcio home; we finished there and then: in B.A.S.E. He wanted to spend the night with me. He wanted to buy me a drink. He wanted to hold my hand. He wanted us to dance together. He wanted my address, a contact number, something, but after a few intimate moments in a darkened corner, I slipped away, and for that I felt impregnable.

Like a proper Paulista.

Chapter 15

Being Different (Porto Alegre, Missões)

An old, weathered sepia photograph shows four men. One, black, is holding a foot-long machete in his right hand. His left is pulling up the chin of a fair-haired white young man seated in front of him, tied up tightly. We cannot see the prisoner's features – he is looking up, his throat exposed to the blade, which just touches the side of his Adam's apple, the focal point of the macabre composition. The other two, one black, one white, flank the two central characters and stare disengaged at the camera. The expression of the would-be killer is one of obedience – to the photographer, and by implication to you, the onlooker. The unspeakable horror of the scene resides in the question in his eyes: 'Are you done? Is it OK if I cut his throat now?' You want to shout 'NO!' even though you are aware that the final act of the drama has been concluded long ago; this wasn't staged: the camera's click sealed the victim's life.

You think you know Brazil, and then you come to Rio Grande do Sul.

The Words You'll Need

baile = *dance*
cacique = *Indian chief*
carinho = *sweetie*
chimarrão = *the practice of drinking an infusion of maté tea and boiling water*
facão = *machete*
fidalgo = *a noble*
frigobar = *hotel fridge and bar*
grande putaria = *freely translated, it means 'loads of prostitutes'*
Lagoa dos Patos = *the Duck Lagoon, although the name comes from the Patos tribe (who also helped name Patagonia)*
litoral = *coast*
Nossa Senhora! = *an expression equivalent to 'Goodness gracious' or 'My, my'*
Parabéns pra você = *a Brazilian song equivalent to 'Happy Birthday'*
serra = *mountains*
sobrado = *a country villa over two storeys high*
tem cabeça dura = *he's inflexible (hard-headed)*

You'll need some Spanish, too:
Acabo de terminar mis exámenes = *I have just finished my exams*
Aprender inglés = *learn English*
cabildo = *congregation*
caudillo = *leader*
Es verdad = *it's true*
Mi error = *my mistake*
No estoy trabajando ahora = *I'm not working at the moment*
Vamos a ver = *we're going to see*
Ver el mundo entero = *see the whole world*
Voy a aprender = *I'm going to learn*

....

– 68 –

I have a question for you.

North Dakota shares one of those made-by-ruler borders with South Dakota. Demilitarised, mined or not, South Korea has a kind of border with North Korea. I may not remember its capital city, but I sure as hell know North Carolina borders its southern counterpart. So why is Rio Grande do Norte below Ceará and Rio Grande do Sul bordering Uruguay? Whaddayamean 'historical reasons'? Did they insert all these states afterwards?

The irony did not escape my funny bone: I arrived in Porto Alegre, the capital of the southern and strongly separatist state of Rio Grande do Sul on 22 April. This is the birthday of Queen Isabella of Spain (1451) and the day of the beatification of Dom Bosco (1929), but most famously the day in 1500 Pedro Álvares Cabral arrived with his Portuguese fleet in Bahia and first set eyes on the new continent.

Porto Alegre is the biggest metropolis between Rio and Buenos Aires and grandiosely calls itself the capital of Mercosur. It is a river port at the end of the Rio Guaíba, which feeds into the Lagoa dos Patos. Legend has it that when the Jesuits arrived in this part of the world, they asked the king of Spain to grant them the Lagoa 'so that we can breed some ducks to feed ourselves'. The king consented but soon discovered that the Jesuit's 'duck pond' was the undersell of the millennium and revoked his edict: the Lagoa dos Patos is the largest inland lagoon in the world, a third the size of Belgium. As it is navigable, it allows ships to dock safely at Porto Alegre. This unusual geography is the reason not only for the city's existence and prosperity, but for much of the gaucho financial independence. Under the First Republic which followed the abdication of Dom Pedro II, all income from the ocean ports – from Recife and Salvador to Santos and Paranaguá – was federal income. But the gauchos successfully argued the semantics: Porto Alegre was a *river* port, so any earnings from the customs house should be kept wholly by the state.

I wanted to try my Belo Horizonte trick again: stay within walking distance of the main bus terminal, but the area around the PoA *rodoviária* (you just *knew* there would be some abbreviation for the city) was the uninspiring hub of a spaghetti-tangle of motorways and unending avenues teeming with bored, streetwalking prostitutes – and it was still late afternoon.

'Is the area by Farroupilha Park any better?' I asked a taxi driver.

'No,' he replied. 'It's more dangerous. At least here there's only the girls. You don't have the junkies.'

I consulted my guide again. 'Let's try downtown. Hotel Ornatus.'

I waited for the inevitable comment.

'That's also dangerous late at night.'

'But it doesn't have junkies.'

'No.'

'Or prostitutes.'

'There are some,' the driver said.

I'd chance it.

In fact, Hotel Ornatus was decent and inexpensive, dead in the commercial centre of Porto Alegre, and eerily empty on a Sunday. The receptionist looked at me, at my passport and started an interrogation.

'You are here for *tourism*?' he asked.

I was.

'It's going to *rain*,' he said with evident *Schadenfreude*. 'It's going to rain *all week*.'

He gave me a key.

'You must pay in advance.'

Fine.

'And please read the hotel rules.' He pointed at a list of regulations on the wall – all innocuous but one: '*No visitors in rooms*.'

I wasn't planning any hanky-panky as I moved out to indulge in the most celebrated gaucho culinary offering of all, the *rodízio*: for a fixed price you can eat as much as you like from a range of side salads and divers cuts of meat proffered in rotation by waiters. With one warning: from the Nordeste to Porto Alegre and from Recife to Corumbá, I have never liked the look of those lardballs that masquerade as Brazilian sausages. They taste so vile and seem so sinister, I bet only my left bollock is missing from the ingredients.

In Galpão Crioulo, a Porto Alegre institution – a cross between a French *rotisserie* and a Bavarian *Bierstube* – the choice was staggering, with over 30 salads and cuts of meat from chicken hearts to filets mignons, as well as *comida campeira*: variations on beef casserole. There was an exhibition of *chimarrão*, with gourds – *cuias* – that contained the green maté tea, meant to be imbibed slowly through a metallic straw, the *bomba*. I tried it and the surprise was greater than the tastebud shock. Bitter! They drink their tea bitter – no wonder gauchos distinguish themselves from other Brazilians. At last no one will ask me whether I am diabetic for drinking my coffee neat – here only women put sugar in their maté. I could develop a taste for maté, especially since it's supposed to be an upper, but I decided I was not going to bother to learn the ritual, buy the accessories and carry around a thermos flask. Plus I burnt my lips on that thermoconducting silver straw. If I sipped any more maté, my lips would swell like a collagen prosthesis.

There was folklore to boot. I commend the gaucho men's attire: *bombachas* (loose breeches tucked into the boots) held tightly by a sash, a waistcoat, a New Romantic white shirt underneath and a bandanna, the *lenço*, tied with a knot around the neck, its ends dropping symmetrically all the way to the stomach. The women looked dressed for the Seville April Féria: their lace-bordered frocks looked positively Andalucian. The music sounded like samba-gone-carousel with a smattering of tap-dancing – in boots – thrown in. Still, it was the kid who turned up with a pair of *boleadeiras* who stole the show. These *boleadeiras* are a set of three leather thongs, each ending in a round stone; a simple but formidable weapon, the perfect ancilla for cattle control inherited from the Guarani Indians: by swinging the *boleadeiras* and flinging them like a lasso, a galloping cowboy can bring down a charging bull. As there were no obvious cows in the audience – I say that with a straight face – the boy chose a beautiful young woman for his act. She stood bravely immobile with a lit cigarette in her mouth as he started swaying the *boleadeiras* above his head. The drums rolled and *snap!* Applause, not least for the foolhardy woman herself who had put her life on the line – I mean, what do you call smoking a cigarette nowadays? I hope she did not inhale.

Before I left, I paused by the *maîtresse d'* at the door, an elderly woman dressed like Calamity Jane.

'Is it far to walk to the Cidade Baixa?' I enquired.

'This time of night? This area is dangerous. Take a taxi.'

I was annoyed. I was all tonicked up from the maté and the wine and I wanted to walk the streets of the gaucho capital, but everyone was bent on talking me out of it. This was beginning to sound like a conspiracy.

I ordered a cab.

'Rua Vieira de Castro,' I told the driver.

It was all quiet in the Centro, but in the Cidade Baixa there were occasional patches of people in bars and cafés. I spotted club 'W' in Rua Venâncio Áires where a *travesti* hostess was parading up and down trying to drum up attention.

'Stop!' I said to the driver. 'Let me walk from here.'

'We're away from the Vieira de Castro,' he said. 'It's dangerous to walk around here alone. *Grande putaria*.'

I looked at the girls. They appeared as threatening as my grandmother.

'I know,' I said. 'I can handle it.'

I paid the taxi and faced a gaggle of pouting prostitutes. I felt a rush, merging as I was with the crepuscular world: hell, I was one of those people my mum warned me about.

I walked back to 'W' and the tall *travesti*.

'Hi,' I said and added for good measure: 'You look great tonight.'

The TV acknowledged me with glee as they all do when you tell them they look gorgeous.

'Hmmm,' she said. 'I don't know you. First timer?'

'Tourist,' I said.

She picked up her Spanish black fan and waved it teasingly.

'Tourist? In Porto Alegre? Are you mad?'

'Well, I've been everywhere else in Brazil,' I said. 'I had to come here because I heard that Rio Grande do Sul is so different.'

She looked down at me again.

'Where are you from then?'

'London.'

She liked that and smiled conspiratorially.

'I'll tell you the truth. You've come too early for this place. They're all still at Veneziano's.'

'Veneziano's?'

She gave me directions and winked. 'Come in at midnight. It will be full.'

'Your name?'

'Charlene,' she said.

'*Enchanté*,' I said and kissed her hand.

She hopped on the spot, jumping an invisible rope.

'I like you,' she cried as I walked away.

Veneziano's was a small bar on two floors; it was difficult finding a space on the wall to lean on or a beer-mat-sized square on the bar to leave your glass. I stood at the bottom of the stairs, trying to avoid the constant inter-floor traffic. It felt like being in the Serengeti during the migration of the wildebeest: gay men rarely stay in one spot, although I have never fathomed where they all go – and I'm one, so I should know.

So these were the gauchos. The word comes from *cauchu* (nomad, vagabond) and is one of the few international vocabulary contributions of Araucanian, the language of the Mapuche Indians who resisted Argentinian and Chilean domination until well into the twentieth century and gave the cowboy residents of the Patagonian cone – and by extension, southern Brazil – their world-famous name. The buzz of a bar notwithstanding, my gauchos seemed quieter and less forward than other Brazilians. They're certainly good-looking: many green and blue eyes, oval faces and what must be a peculiarly local characteristic: women immigrants must have found bushy eyebrows very sexy for the natural selection process was faster than shouting 'transgenic mice'. They were all milk-white, of good Italian and German stock; I was darker skinned than anyone else – or so I thought until I walked to the mezzanine floor for the queue to the toilets and looked through the kitchen window. Three employees were washing the dishes and preparing sandwiches and salads out of sight: all three were black.

The first to address me was the woman behind the bar. Her name was Vera and she was the owner. She looked more recognisably a lesbian: gone was the Nordeste vampish mien and in came the European boyish short crop. The whole bar slowed down perceptibly as I recounted my São Paulo experiences to her – you always talk about the last town when you're travelling – and how I had reached industrial Porto Alegre to check out this least visited part of Brazil out of pure interest.

A party upstairs started singing '*Parabéns pra você*'.

'A birthday?' I asked Vera.

'Flávio,' she said. 'A regular.' And then after a pause: 'How long are you staying for?'

'I'm going to the *serra* tomorrow,' I explained, 'and then to the Missions. I'll be back next weekend.'

'Never been. Be sure to return and tell me all about it.'

*****

I walked the couple of hundred yards back to 'W' which, as Charlene had promised, was full. Two large rooms, one bar, one dance floor and upstairs, oh how sweet, a snogging corner. Charlene recognised me and introduced me to her entourage.

'John is a *tourist*,' said Charlene with exaggerated emphasis. 'We have to give him a gift.'

She gave me three condoms.

'There,' she said to me with a wink. 'Enjoy Porto Alegre.'

The dance floor looked and sounded like a university disco: an amateurish PA system plagued by constant distortion. I walked back to the bar and exchanged glances with a guy who focused on me before he unfocused to infinity again.

'Hi,' he burped in my general direction. 'It's my birthday today.'

'Hi,' I replied. 'Were you at Veneziano's?'

'I was.'

'You must be Flávio.'

The guy seemed to gel, his inebriation evaporating instantly.

'And *you* have been doing your homework,' he joked.

'How old are you then?'

'Twenty-five today.'

'I like birthdays,' I said. 'They remind me I'm not dead.'

That made Flávio laugh. He was an architect/surveyor and an interesting mix: Mexican and Brazilian German. He had curly hair, a round face and a Cheshire Cat smile leering through a pair of Mick Jagger lips; he must have sipped too many boiling *chimarrão* drinks through those metal straws.

'Happy birthday, Flávio,' I mumbled and kissed those lips.

A kiss that lasted several minutes …

'Where are you from?' he asked me when we both recovered our composure.

From Fortaleza to Florianópolis, the surprise comes from my

speaking Portuguese. In Porto Alegre it arose from the sheer fact that I had ventured such a long way. For the next half hour I had him hooked.

Flávio finally yawned, stood up and clicked a bunch of car keys.

'Come with me,' he said. 'I'll take you home.'

Charlene was passing by and winked at me.

'You're drunk,' I told Flávio.

'I'm fine. Come on.'

I followed him to his all-mod-cons Toyota. He opened my door first. Ah, a gentleman. Still I wavered.

'Let me show you Porto Alegre,' he said.

I won't make any more jokes about pissed Brazilian drivers, although I should.

Flávio drove south of the dark and menacing Farroupilha Park and followed Avenida Ipiranga the length of the canal to the Praia de Belas until we reached the Rio Guaíba.

'It's like New York and New Jersey,' Flávio said, pointing at the illuminated installations across the river that provided a dazzling industrial spectacular for our eyes, their mute sparkle intensified in the balmy night.

'It is,' I said; it didn't matter whether I agreed or not.

Flávio parked. 'Come out,' he said.

I followed him.

'Where are we now?'

'The centre,' Flávio said and traced an imaginary circle above his head with his index finger. 'This is my town.'

We had stopped over a viaduct on Rua Duque de Caxias. Behind us there were deserted municipal buildings in that stiff, buttoned-up thirties' architecture I call 'mid-period Mussolini'. Below us there was the long avenue of Borges de Madeiros with shops, parked cars, blinking traffic lights and no people. I felt as adrift as in the middle of the Amazon in a latter-day, empty, no-ghost ghost town.

'I come here alone sometimes,' said Flávio softly. 'I like the city. I like buildings. I don't like people that much. At this time of night, I feel as if Porto Alegre was built for me alone.'

Architects can be such sops.

'And now,' he continued, 'it is yours, too.'

I surveyed the inert urban landscape through his eyes.

'You're not a real gaucho,' I said. 'You're supposed to be a rough-and-rude cowboy, eating raw meat, scratching your crotch, chewing tobacco and lassoing defenceless animals.'

Flávio pointed at the city surrounding us.

'The reality is very different, isn't it?' he said.

A slight breeze from the lagoon made the air seem clean, unpolluted. Flávio touched my hand.

'Shall I come to your hotel?' he asked.

I remembered His Imperial Crabbiness at reception.

'Listen,' I said. 'I would very much like you to sleep with me tonight –'

He didn't wait much longer to shut me up with a kiss. It felt good, kissing openly in the middle of town with no one around.

'– but I think the people in the hotel are funny.'

'What?' Flávio asked. '*What?*'

'They warned me against bringing anyone home. Explicitly.'

Flávio opened the car door on my side.

'Don't worry,' he said with a dismissive gesture. 'This is Brazil.'

Oh, is it now?

– 69 –

Gauchos like to parade their – and I have to invent a new word here – their *differentness* from other Brazilians in their every step and gesture. Frontier areas are like that: think Texas and Montana; think Alsace and Lorraine. I am reading a book about gaucho customs on my way to the twin towns of Gramado and Canela just over an hour north of Porto Alegre. This is the *serra* – a continuation of the mountains of Santa Catarina, dwindling slowly into grassy hills in the Missions district and finally into the Pampa, the flat cattle-raising plains which stretch all the way to Uruguay, Argentina and down to Patagonia. It is only in this last third of the state – the borders of the borders – that the real gaucho cowboy gallops with his horse, his *facão* and his gourd of maté. Yet it is as if the leading intellectuals of Rio Grande do Sul have picked the gaucho cowboy as an emblem and are constructing a kind of state nationalism which has recently raised its voice to call for outright independence. Such independence requires people who not only feel different, but have also been told again and again that they *should* feel different. Which is the chicken and which is the egg in this conundrum?

Everywhere there is a fixation with language, the major component of national awareness. Even Galpão Crioulo serves you with paper trays proudly displaying the spectrum of gaucho vocabulary. Yes, there are many local idiomatic expressions, as you would expect; some words denote particular garments, like the *bombacha* or the *guaiaca*. Some like *guri* (which means 'boy') are of Tupi/Guarani origin, and some, *guapo* being the obvious example, are downright Spanish. But I counted at least six different dictionaries of the special gaucho 'language' which are just idiomatic expressions strung together. No matter that expressions like '*Nossa Senhora!*' or '*tem cabeça dura*' are heard throughout the length of Brazil; here they are 'local slang'. If this is a language, then the people of the *sertão* who not only have a different vocabulary, but also use archaic grammatical forms (*tu* instead of the *você*) and have an Amerindian-like singing accent, should have universities teaching in the local idiom. The festival of Bumba-meu-boi which everyone associates with Amazonas is discussed under gaucho folklore, like the Oktoberfest celebrations and, mind-bogglingly, the Procession of Corpus Christi. But isn't the quintessential gaucho feast day of Nossa Senhora dos Navigantes – Our Lady of the Seamen – celebrated on the same day as Yemanjá, the Bahian candomblé deity of the sea? Even the great gaucho habit of drinking maté tea is mirrored in the Pantanal where the local cowboys – called *vaqueiros* – drink their *tereré*, a cold maté infusion, from their *guampa* gourd through *bomba* straws.

In Rua Riachuelo, a veritable Aladdin's cave for bookworms with more bookshops than the whole of the Nordeste capitals combined, the shelves on the particularities of life in the Rio Grande do Sul are at least as numerous as the racks of mainstream Brazilian history. Just one publishing company, Martins Livreiro, has a long list of books associated only with aspects of the state. The list starts with a gaucho almanac and continues with dictionaries and local geography, flowers, landscapes and history. Slow down guys! They can't all be that interesting. I leafed through a few and there was much systematic replication or downright in-your-face untruths: is building a Christmas manger an example of Riograndense folklore? It seems it is quantity that matters: if we can fill a library of books about ourselves, we justify our convictions. After all, man is an emotional animal who reaches a gut conclusion and then tries to bolster it with logic. So aim for the heart first by instilling a sense of *differentness*. Don't we all like to feel unique?

Ironically, the only tale the books didn't mention was Rio Grande do Sul's most famous. Maybe it's too cruel and harsh for propaganda. But can you be macho without being cruel and harsh?

Negrinho Do Pastoreio (The Little Negro Pasture Boy)

Once upon a time there was a rich and miserly gaucho rancher who never gave shelter to a passing visitor and never paid his seasonal workers more than a scraggy piece of chicken roast. He only had a soft spot for three living things: his bay horse, a fast, proud stallion; his son, a guri with a heart even more pernicious than his father's; and a black slave orphan boy everyone called Negrinho who was the best horseman in the area.

One day the rancher was challenged to a race by his neighbour for thirty pieces of gold. As it was a race of honour, the loser promised to give the money to the poor. The day of the race came and hundreds of people gathered to watch and place bets. Negrinho rode the rancher's bay horse against the neighbour's black mare. Throughout the race they were neck and neck. The judges strained their heads as the horses appeared on the final straight, but then the bay horse slowed down to a trot – a refusal? – several yards before the finishing line. The black mare won.

The rancher was furious and blamed Negrinho for losing on purpose. 'You'll pay me back!' he bellowed. 'You'll stay in the wild for thirty days tending my thirty horses. One day for every gold piece you made me lose.'

He left Negrinho alone with the horses on the grasslands of the pampa. Negrinho cried and cried but as the night came, tiredness overcame him and he fell asleep.

The horses dispersed.

The rancher's son, jealous of Negrinho's horsemanship, was tailing the slave and when he found him asleep, he immediately told his father. The rancher took Negrinho to the whipping post and gave him a good beating. He then threw him out.

'Don't come back before you bring back the horses!' he shouted.

Negrinho lit thirty candles and with every one he prayed to the Virgin Mary from the bottom of his heart to help him find the horses. And lo and behold – when night came, every candle became a bright star and blazed in the sky to help Negrinho spot and round up the horses. But when, after a good day's work, he fell asleep, the farmer's mischievous son opened the corral gate and let the animals out.

When the rancher arrived in the morning and saw the sleeping Negrinho in front of the open gate, he went berserk. Together with his son, he beat the poor boy black and blue with his whip. They then led him, bloodied and semi-conscious, to an anthill where they tied him up.

'Devour him down to the bone!' the rancher called to the biting ants.

The weather changed and there was a storm. Rain, wind and hail darkened the sky and continued through three days and three nights. When it passed, the rancher and his son mounted their horses and galloped to the post where they had left the slave boy to die. When they arrived, Negrinho was waiting, his skin intact and smooth. He was riding the bay stallion surrounded by the rancher's horses. For a minute, he looked at his master, and then he cantered off with dignity followed by the thirty thoroughbreds.

To this day, farmers hear the neighs of an invisible herd galloping through their lands and some claim to have seen the horses, led by a black boy on a bay stallion. And to this day, candles are offered in churches in memory of the slave martyred on an anthill, who has become the unofficial patron saint of all things lost in the grand expanse of the hills and prairies of the Rio Grande do Sul.

....

Gramado was really worth the trip. Small but quaintly formed, it was a treat, full of Hansel and Gretel houses selling Black Forest gateaux, marzipan cakes and home-made chocolate. Its Alpine charm notwithstanding, it is still a make-believe village living on tourism with back-to-back hotels, restaurants and car parks. Canela is another proposition. Its area is vast, requiring motor transport and a sturdy pair of shoes: I destroyed a good pair of Nike trainers on its sharp, stony alleys, trying to find a cheap hotel not facing the main street to Gramado with the sweet sound of cars dropping a gear. I ended up in a cosy, inexpensive *pensão*. The outside was a dream: white-coated with a sloping slate roof and red wooden sash windows, each with a plant on its windowsill, truly Mitteleuropa in *bombachas*.

One of the delights of travelling is finding out what the peculiarities of every lodge and hostel will turn out to be. Where will I sleep next? In a hammock in the Amazon or a leaky tent in the Pantanal? In an expensive air-conditioned pool hotel in Corumbá or a floor-creaking, colonial mansion in Ouro Preto? Will there be electric-shock showers like Fortaleza? Will they conceal cockroach nests á la Manaus? Employ surly receptionists as in Recife and Porto Alegre? Contain highly sophisticated apparatus that I can't manipulate like in Maceió? Be haunted with ghosts as in Salvador? I looked at my room with its massive double bed, its own clean toilet, its *frigobar* and TV, looked at the low price and wondered what would go wrong this time. I found out as soon as I flushed the toilet. It was as if a roaring alien had been buried underneath the bowl and was being choked every time water flowed down the hole. I'm sure it was trying to mate with Sigourney Weaver, for that is what it sounded like: 'ZGOUNI WEAVER, WEAVA, WIVA, WIVA, WIVA'. I hope there wasn't an alien below the toilet of every room in my corridor, or else I'd wake up at night thinking the bogey man was going to get me. This gives new meaning to *Halloween H2O*.

I didn't have time to climb up the famous Parque do Caracol, with its basalt rocks, waterfalls and Paraná pine; I had a stroll around Canela instead, which is below-par boring, but dead cheap. If Agatha Christie were Brazilian she'd choose Canela as a sleepy village shaken by a murder at the vicarage. I had a crêpe (which was really a waffle, but I wasn't going to get into an argument) and walked to the neo-Gothic – one might venture the description *English-style* – cathedral of Our Lady of Lourdes, which stands a commanding 213 feet high, impressively made out of stone. What's this in the place of honour? A grand illustrated chart of all 264 popes from St Peter to John Paul II. Suffice to say that the first 54 are saints. It all stopped apparently with number 55, Boniface II, probably because he was a Goth, therefore an uncouth barbarian, so the fine custom of sanctifying your predecessor was regrettably stopped.

Then the curse of the receptionist struck. It started to rain. I walked back to my B&B and found out that, as it was Monday, restaurants were closed: I had to commute to Gramado. I thought of Dame Agatha again. Perhaps one day I will write a detective story based in Canela. There's something about the place which inspires me to murder.

At 8.30 p.m. sharp the bus arrived. I got on and paid my fare. I saw another bus arrive in the next lane. I put my brain on park … except that, except that …

'Where are we going?' I asked the conductor. These were the remote alleys of Canela; we should have reached the Hydrangea Highway to Gramado by now.

'Planaltina,' said the driver. 'Then we return to Canela.'

'I want to go to Gramado.'

'You should have taken the other bus,' said the driver. 'We go to Gramado after we return to Canela.'

'But this said Gramado-Circular,' I said.

'So did the other bus.'

Gauchos may think they are different, but their logic is Brazilian.

'Hold on,' I said. 'You mean there are two buses, arriving in Canela at the same time *both* saying Gramado-Circular, but going in opposite directions?'

'Exactly.'

'So how can you distinguish between them? By osmosis?'

The driver went macho on me.

'You ask the conductor,' he barked.

I'll take my revenge right now:

....

Things I Don't Like About Brazil #15: Local Buses

From Fortaleza where the local bus to Cumbuco kept its own idiosyncratic timetable, to Natal where the bus to Ponta Negra avoided the direct route and zigzagged around every dirty backstreet; from Rio's frightening buses speeding down Avenida Copacabana, to São Paulo's once-every-thirty-minutes-if-you're lucky-and-we're-full public transport: local buses suck in Brazil, with Curitiba being the notable exception. Long-distance buses are comfortable and safe but they take their time, stopping frequently en route at the driver's mates' cafés for a ten-minute break often extended to half an hour. I have already complained about the conductors' attitude to change ('We don't have any') but how about the attitude to passengers? A Brazilian expatriate I met in Santa Cruz told me that he had fallen asleep during a 24-hour journey back to Cáceres when his bus broke down. When he woke up he was in the middle of the Pantanal, in an empty broken-down bus with only the snoring driver for company: another bus had come to pick up the passengers and his luggage while he was asleep.

....

In Gramado I took shelter from the rain in the nearest *churrascaria*. The delay in arriving and the odour of cooked meats conspired to increase my appetite. I was famished, and this was the place to be: all the meat you can eat, as far removed from nouvelle cuisine as possible. Casillero del Diablo was on the menu.

'Do you have a half-bottle?' I asked the waiter.

'I'll check,' he said.

I served myself a plate of *palmitos* before he returned.

'We do,' he confirmed. 'Less than half a bottle – 250 ml.'

'How much?'

'Eight reais each,' he smiled.

I checked the menu again: Casillero del Diablo 700 ml, 29 reais. I performed the multiplication mentally.

Oh, Brazil eternal …

'The small bottle will do,' I told the waiter as I accepted a breast of roast chicken. 'If I want more I can have a second one.'

Guess what? I had three.

– 70 –

'The last seat?' I asked the Rio Sul employee with surprise.

'You *are* lucky,' she replied.

There was rain all over the *serra* and the *litoral*. The prediction was for dry weather only in the far interior of the state. I made a snap decision to forget hiking in the Parque do Caracol, leave Canela immediately, return to Porto Alegre and fly off to the capital of the Missions district. But who wants to travel to Santo Ângelo on a rainy Tuesday night? Our small Cessna was full of suits tapping away on their portable computers. I glanced obliquely at my neighbour. He was writing an article. A reporter?

When we arrived I realised that someone big was on the plane. *Really* big. The camera flashes and the anticipation in the local dignitaries' faces were not for my reception. A tall, congenial fellow in his forties with a prominent nose and a weighty demeanour, not unlike Argentina's Carlos Menem, monopolised the attention of everyone with suave bonhomie. My eye was drawn to that day's local *Tribuna Regional*; there he was, my VIP co-passenger, in a picture on the front page, under the headline: *Ciro Gomes hoje no Verzeri* – 'Ciro Gomes today at Verzeri [College]'. So, this was Ciro Gomes, ex-minister, ex-governor of Ceará, IMF associate, one of the mentors of Cardoso's Real Plan which had steadied the Brazilian economy, and a Socialist Party (PPS) presidential candidate. As it was pre-election year in Brazil, he had been invited by the wonderfully named Renaldo Stümpfle, president of the local Commercial, Industrial, Agricultural and Services Association – which sounds pretty inclusive to me – and he was speaking that same night in Santo Ângelo on 'The Economic and Political Situation in Brazil'. Well, that should last several hours.

I observed the Santoangelense assembly gyrate about the politician like a swarm of bees around an apiculturalist's hood; the hubbub moved on, squeezed into black cars and drove off, in order of importance. I remained aloof. I have travelled in the same aeroplane as Princess Margaret and cheered Princess Diana on one of her visits to Help the Aged; I have an autograph from Robert Plant; I have interviewed Bryan Ferry; I have been in a junket with The Cure and I have pissed in a urinal next to Ali McMordie from Stiff Little Fingers: see, I'm immune to celebrity.

The airport had now cleared. There was me, my luggage, a few airline employees and –

'Do you want a ride into Santo Ângelo?' the old guy asked.

'Are you a taxi driver?'

He produced a card. *Edilson. Taxi do Aeroporto. Viagens e Turismo. Carro com Ar Condicionado.* Edilson was a man in his forties, and as Argentina was closer than Porto Alegre, looked very much the Castilian aristocrat.

'Come for the ruins of São Miguel?'

'Indeed. Planning to see the Sound and Vision show tomorrow.'

'Seven-thirty in the evening. You won't be able to return to Santo Ângelo. The last bus will have left.'

I had already discovered that from my guidebook.

'I can take you there, wait for you and bring you back for 60 reais.'

I said nothing. Edilson coughed, signalling his willingness to negotiate.

'For a bit more, I can take you to two other Missions: São João and São Lourenço. A half-day trip for 90 reais. Nobody ever goes to them. And they are monuments by themselves.'

'Throw in São Nicolau, and I'm in,' I said.

'For São Nicolau, 120 reais,' he said. 'It's very far. It will be something like eight hours altogether and 250 kilometres there and back.'

Done.

*****

I might be missing the twentieth century, but such is the stroppiness of history that I have to zoom back to the sixteenth to explain it. On 15 August 1534, seven theology students at the Sorbonne decided to form a society to preach the word of God in the Holy Land under the leadership of the eldest: Iñigo Lopez from the small town of Loyola in the Basque province of Guipúzcoa, on the hills around San Sebastian. The members of the society could not travel to Palestine because superpower Venice was at war with the Turks (eternal conflict, different faces) so they decided to quench their proselytising ardour in the newly discovered continent. They were the right people at the right time, and the time was the Age of Discovery. Pope Paul III believed – and would later decree – that the American natives were sentient beings, and thus their souls were redeemable if they had the gospel preached to them. He gave the new order his blessing in 1540: amidst all these European private exploration companies, this would be the Company of Jesus. Iñigo latinised his name and remained in history as Ignacio de Loyola while his order, the Company, became famous as the Jesuits.

It was a Jesuit, Manuel de Nóbrega, who accompanied Tomé de Souza, the first Governor of Brazil, when he founded Salvador. It was a Jesuit, Padre Anchieta, who founded São Paulo. It was the Jesuits who brought baroque to Brazil and supervised the architectural masterpieces of

Pernambuco and Bahia. But it was in settling the native question that the Jesuits became indispensable. Padre Anchieta's unified *língua geral* made both catechism and conquest possible. The Jesuits collected all the natives in large *aldeias*, villages or 'reductions' as they came to be called, and kept them working in the fields or taught them manual trades. In so doing, they indirectly helped their extermination, as Old World contagious diseases for which the Indians had no immunity decimated them in their packed surroundings. Brazil, with its plantation-based, slave-thirsty economy, was particularly hostile to the Jesuits who protected the Indians, and the *bandeirante* slave-raiding parties pushed the *aldeias* to the margins of the Portuguese dominions: today the most important historical Mission sites are within Paraguay, Argentina and Bolivia near the Brazilian border.

Except that I am inside Brazil now.

In 1494 the Pope divided the New World between Spain and Portugal with the Treaty of Tordesillas, inspiring the playwright Gil Vicente to declare prematurely the end of all wars. Rio Grande do Sul and much of Santa Catarina should have been Spanish as a quick look at the treaty map can ascertain. However, the reality was different on the ground as the Paulista *bandeirantes* were busy pushing back the frontier, exploring the jungle interior for gold and silver, and manhunting for native labour. As a result, the 1750 Treaty of Madrid confirmed the status quo and defined Brazil's borders more or less as they stand today.

It had a nasty clause.

The Portuguese wanted to control the Plate river-system trade so much that they established a colony – imaginatively named Colônia – opposite the city of Buenos Aires in what is now Uruguay. The town stuck like a fishbone in the collective Spanish throat, so they most definitely claimed it for theirs in the Treaty of Madrid. What they conceded in return were the seven Jesuit reductions – the Sete Povos – on the west side of the Uruguay River which was to form the Spanish-Portuguese border, as it does today. In order of foundation these were: São Nicolau, São Miguel, São Borja, São Luiz Gonzaga, São Lourenço, São João and finally, the one which ended up as the capital of the district, Santo Ângelo. Around 40,000 Guarani natives and their priests, who had been settled there peacefully for centuries, were given two options: either to accept the rule of their traditional enemies (and a future of certain slavery) or leave their fields and march hundreds of miles to an uncertain fate.

They decided to fight.

*****

In travelling, expectation is all. You make up a mental image of a city based not only on what you've read, but also on the presumptions a name invokes internally. I had imagined Canela as a subtropical Montreux; it turned out to be a Brazilian St Mary Gray on a quiet Sunday. I had expected Santo Ângelo to be the uncouth cousin of Campo Grande, with Guarani cowboys chasing stray bulls and packs of rabid dogs barking at foreign-smelling pedestrians. It turned out to be an affable little town with inhabitants more Caucasian-looking than in Caucasus itself (not a big feat, I concede), who stayed out late in a few spacious restaurants even on a weekday when Ciro Gomes himself was passing through. I walked through the town's empty streets in the coolest night I had ever experienced in Brazil. I put on a windbreaker as I stood reading a poster advertising a *mega baile* in Santa Maria with inline skating competitions, tattoo piercing, alternative rock, techno and samba. I liked Santo Ângelo – open spaced, with its air of assured affluence and no less than four radio stations, four newspapers and a small university.

Plus its cathedral. The grandiose size of the illuminated basilica, out of proportion to everything else on the square where the original mission stood back in 1706, oozes with inexplicable magnetism. Two twin red-brick campaniles four storeys high shoot up from either side; its front is formed by five sturdy pillars supporting a large Romanesque roof over the side aisles, on top of which lies the central nave. The material of which it is built is called *itacuru* or, as they call it locally, ant-stone for the porousness of its texture resembles those anthills Negrinho do Pastoreio was left to die on. Inside, there is a rare piece of eighteenth-century Guarani art: the wooden statue of Dying Christ, a much venerated relic over an imposing choir; the Guarani were musically very talented and loved Catholic hymnody. Outside, the Missionary cross – a cross with a minor cross on the top – predominates over seven moody sculptures in the façade corniche, each representing a saint from the Sete Povos. The cathedral was built under the command of the Austrian architect Valerian von Admonovitch and is a 1929 copy of the Jesuits' Latin American Hagia Sophia: the once proud cathedral of São Miguel.

The cold air made me shiver as I felt a warm flush of recollection. *Roland Joffé. The Mission.*
Of all the sad stories in Brazil, they don't come sadder than this.

*****

Outside my hotel lobby, I checked the sky. Overcast but dry. All systems go.

A young man approached me.

'John?'

'Yes?'

'I'm your driver to the Missions,' he replied softly. 'My name is Osvaldo.'

I stared at him. Late twenties, cute, ingenuous face, delicate and dishy.

'Edilson?'

'He's my father-in-law,' he said awkwardly. 'He's working at the airport. I do the long-distance driving.'

I wasn't going to complain: Osvaldo was younger and nicer to look at. We set off for São João through green hills and grazing cattle under a foggy sky – if it weren't for the maté plantations, this could be Derbyshire. But soon I started longing for his father-in-law's chattiness. Osvaldo was a man of laconic pronouncements and was totally uninterested in me, my travels, my mastery of Portuguese or, wishful thinking, my body. I winched several sentences out of him, but most of the time was spent in silent contemplation on a quiet road.

In 1754, after several unsuccessful pleas and petitions to the Viceroyalty of Buenos Aires by Jesuit priests and Guarani chiefs, Spain and Portugal set up a joint commission to oversee the resettlement of the Sete Povos according to the Treaty of Madrid – which, parenthetically, gave the world a new legalistic term: *'demarcación'*. But then the Indian warrior José Tiaraju emerged as the marplot of the joint Iberian plans. He was an orphan, adopted by the Jesuits, who was first elected sheriff and then a leading member of the *cabildo*, the governing council. José had lost his parents to scarlet fever when he was ten, and the disease had left him with a quarter-moon scar on his forehead. Tradition tells us that the scar was illuminated by a ray – *sepé* – at night which provided the nickname by which he has survived in history: Sepé Tiaraju, or St Sepé to many.

*****

'Is this São João?' I asked the lone guard standing by the empty car park.

'Not much here, is there?' he apologised.

You could say that again. The town founded by the Missionary Padre Antônio Sepp had been obliterated. A small sign on a few scattered stones said '*Catedral*'. A tiny museum on the site contained a copper gravure from 1755 showing the extent of the settlement, which has now disappeared as if it had only ever existed on that map. Yet the town was a spillover from São Miguel, back in 1697, when the latter reduction became too populous. The extent of our knowledge about this reduction is in inverse proportion to its remains, for Padre Sepp has left a diary with many details on eighteenth-century missionary life.

I returned to the car with a long face. Osvaldo guessed correctly: 'Nothing is as barren as São João.'

Or as dangerous. At the turnoff to São Lourenço, we saw a lorry parked by the road with four gaucho cowboys, straight out of Galpão Crioulo's stage act, sipping maté from their gourds, thermos flasks corked at the ready. Do they wear any underwear under those culottes? I suppose the *bombacha* – like the Scottish kilt – is very convenient for a quick open-air squat and squirt.

My musings crashed down on the pampa when I noticed that all four were armed.

Osvaldo slowed down. 'Hide your backpack and don't speak.'

The men waved us over and someone looked inside. He stank of tobacco and his palms were as hard as his nails. All the time he eyed us suspiciously, I couldn't help looking at his hands in disgust and thinking like Patsy in *AbFab*: we *have* neglected our cuticles, haven't we?

He let us pass.

Osvaldo was stiff and nervous. As we turned into the dirt road and the lorry disappeared into our tailing dust, he let out a sigh of relief.

'Bandits?' I asked.

'More likely *contrabandistas*,' he replied, reminding me that the border with Argentina was less than 60 miles away. 'If we had turned up at the wrong time …'

His unfinished sentence sounded eerie.

But not as eerie as the ruins in São Lourenço: strangler figs had grown on trees that had taken root on the building debris; saguaro cacti merged their trunks with the walls, none resembling part of a discernible dwelling; a brightly coloured snake saw us and disappeared inside a hole in a gateway. I walked across the cemetery, which was littered with cracked tombstones, their peeled plaster exposing the brickwork underneath; some were taller than me with white sculptures of Jesus on the cross, others the colour of rust were keeling sideways where the ground had given in. As I made my way back, my right foot, too, disappeared down a cavity. I let out a cry of surprise as I found myself sliding knee-deep into a hollow recess. Was this an animal lair or an actual grave? I clenched my teeth, shook off a feeling of nausea and leapt out.

When we joined the main road, we met up with the lorry again. The contraband had not arrived yet. Or perhaps they were the contraband and were waiting for their distributors. This time they just waved us through. I waved back and made Osvaldo jump.

'Don't! They'll realise you're a gringo,' he said. He looked rattled.

'I *am* a gringo,' I corrected him.

'But *they* don't know that,' he replied.

'Even though we went to the ruins and your car says "Taxi"?' I asked. Osvaldo clearly knew more than he let on.

Whatever happened back there, I'd best remain in ignorance.

*****

Under Sepé's leadership the first round went to the Guaranis; the Europeans were taken by surprise at the extent of Indian resistance, so they left. Second summer around, it was another matter. For a start, all Jesuit priests had been recalled on penalty of excommunication – the Order of Jesuits had been founded on blind obedience. The christianised Guaranis were stunned by the complete submission of the Church to its political masters. They were to have no mass and no confessions? No final rites and Christian burials? No marriage blessings? They were to live and die in sin? A Westerner would laugh at the Indian naivety.

When the Spanish and Portuguese armies returned to the doomed Missions, they were numerous and strong. The troops of Sepé Tiaraju and the prayers of the few remaining Jesuits who had defied the orders of their superiors were no match for the well-drilled European armies – as Voltaire said: 'God favours the big battalions.' Sepé himself was killed during a routine patrol; the morale of the Guaranis was shattered. Like Moses, Sepé was buried in an unmarked grave, and he has subsequently assumed the role of holy local hero. The Missions were defeated and made the long and arduous trek westwards, leaving their churches and square grids to the harsh elements.

I rubbed the weight of centuries from my eyes.

São Nicolau, a mere 13 miles from the Uruguay River border, is different in that it is inhabited. The original ruins, complete with the obligatory eldritch strangler fig tree, stand in a paved square in the middle of a genteel town, a semi-retirement version of Santo Ângelo. This was the first of the Sete Povos, founded in 1626 by Padre Roque Gonzalez, one of three Jesuits who were martyred in the area; Pope John Paul II canonised them in 1988. Their martyrdom in the hands of the Guarani *cacique* Caarupé occurred in Caaró, in the Missions district of Rio Grande do Sul, but their remains are in Concepción, while the miraculous heart of São Roque is in Asuncion – don't ask – so they are claimed by both Paraguay and Brazil.

Unlike the other Missions, São Miguel resisted strongly and its cathedral was burned. Ironically, it was this destruction that saved it for posterity. Some villages were reinhabited for a brief period, but the building materials were recycled to construct new houses: the Silva family in São Nicolau advertise their *sobrado* to tourists as 'completely built from the old reduction ruins'. But São Miguel's cathedral was charred and useless, so it stands there as it was abandoned, the most inaccessible and tantalising of Brazil's Unesco sites.

'You've seen ruins,' said Osvaldo, 'but you've left the best till last.'

The deserted, three-pronged, photogenic, red-and-raven façade stands powerful and yet airily fragile, imposing and yet winsome, hollow but with presence comparable to the most alluring of Graeco-Roman ruins, its appeal shadowy, mystical, devout. The scale, the sheer height of the cathedral, is mind-blowing – and I have seen a few cathedrals in my lifetime. It held 2,000 people for mass and its square outside, today a meadow, could hold a greater number. This is a monument to religious devotion like no other, built a quarter of a millennium ago under the direction of an Italian priest, Giovanni Battista Primoli, for a religious order that arrived from the other side of the world. Sometimes you have to give it to those missionaries: they conquered minds and souls armed with just a book and a mountain of determination.

As I walked into the collapsed side apse of the cathedral and played with the electronic Missions game of the tourist bureau, I remembered the legend. No soldier, *fidalgo*, farmer or archaeologist has ever found anything of value in the ruins of the Missions, except the mournful woodcarvings of the Guarani, kept in the museum just outside the ruins of São Miguel. The Jesuits were a rich order and had an open tap to the Papacy's coffers. Where were the golden crosses and the silver chalices? Could it be that, hundreds of miles from their brothers in Rome, they actually lived modestly, inspired by their own principles and by the simple, four-square values of the Indians they proselytised? Or could the treasures be hidden forever, guarded by a spirit – as tradition has it – in a white house with no windows and no doors in a place no mortal will ever find?

Game over.

Around me thousands of people used to work in the Guarani Jesuit republic, which Voltaire described as 'a true triumph of humanity'. Had he known the term, he might have called it a benign communist theocracy, or a Christian socialist experiment two centuries before its time: everyone worked in the maize, cotton, maté and sugar-cane fields under the direction of the Jesuits four days a week for himself and his family and two days a week for the common good, which mostly meant building churches and carving saints' statues. Unlike other Latin American tribes, the Guarani already had a complex philosophical belief system, which, to the Jesuits' surprise included belief in one God the Creator, Tupã. As a result they were much more amenable to Christianity, and they were willing to be subject to paternalistic supervision: even to move from one village to another a Guarani Indian required the written consent of the top Jesuit governor. Within those limitations, however, there were free elections for all posts and when you compare this system to eighteenth-century absolutist regimes like France, you can sympathise with Voltaire's whole-hearted approval.

The light show started – with red and yellow spotlights on two oak trees either side of the ruins recounting the tale of the two chief demarcation commissioners: Spanish governor, the Marquis of Valdelírios and Portuguese general Gomes Freire as they ganged up against Sepé Tiaraju in São Miguel. I was half listening to the history, half concentrating on my camera setup. Is the 400 ASA film good enough? I should have brought some 800. A 30-second exposure? Shall I bracket it?

What was that?

As if answering my question, one oak tree was illuminated, the ruins were bathed in light and the voice over the tannoy shouted again. It was

Sepé confronting the joint Iberian troops back in February 1753, when it seemed he'd won the war:

'*ESTA TERRA TEM DONO!*'

This land has a lord!

It sounded like a slogan. It was. I abandoned my camera and listened more carefully as the whole weight of the centuries helped me make sense of the present.

At last, I could begin to understand Rio Grande do Sul.

– 71 –

If I had any doubts left about the Europeanness of Porto Alegre, Stoned Discos (LPs! CDs! Videos! DVDs!) on Rua Marechal Floriano dispersed them: here was a second-hand vinyl shop which would have made Nick Hornby proud. PoA loves its punk and heavy metal. On the desk there was a flyer for a Led Zeppelin tribute group; the shop assistants themselves could be ex-roadies from *The Song Remains The Same*. A fanzine from São Paulo, *Kaskadura*, advertising itself as 'Punk – Hardcore – Crust – Grind – Metal and Alternative' was being sold 'for one real or the equivalent in stamps'. A poster announced the change of show in a garage venue called Hermética: the band Garage Fuzz would not be appearing. In their place Dysfunction Magazine and the fabulously named Corel Draw Youth Crew would present Simplez Refri. I closed my eyes and I was at Rough Trade in Portobello in the eighties searching for Joy Division bootlegs. I didn't particularly want to, but I bought a Mutantes CD for Rita Lee's sake and the memories.

I struggled vainly to make something out of my washed-out weekend in Port Alegre. Cisne Branco, the catamaran operating from the Caís do Porto offering passages up and down the Rio Guaíba, was not running because of the constant rain. The art galleries in the Usina do Gasômetro were uninteresting, although the whole edifice, with its sharp geometric lines and 120,000 square feet over six floors merging intricately with one another, is worth visiting for its own sake. It was established in 1890 by a little-known Italian company called Fiat Lux – Latin for 'let there be light' – to provide thermoelectric power. Today's cars which roll out of Turin still owe their name to that original power-generating concern. The Usina maintains the old furnaces on the ground floor (used for an exhibition on Brazilian wines – unfortunately without any tastings), a library, a cinema, space for exhibitions and an arrangement of open workshops. Like Manchester, Porto Alegre dresses its manufacturing past and present in a subtle artistic veil, which has to be – that word again – unique in the context of Brazil. In my book more rain means more museum visits and PoA has its fair share: a neat little Industrial Museum with old Marcaant calculators, Ericsson telephones and Siemens telephone operating centres, an Electricity Museum, a Police Museum and a Varig Museum since it originated from here. But the State Historical Museum, open almost round the clock in the Praça da Alfândega with its audio-visual computer aids is the most inviting. There are two parallel-running history timelines: one for Brazil and one for Rio Grande do Sul. By then I was used to the idea that gauchos think they are different: even the tourist office brochures have a map with Brazil in one colour, the rest of South America in another and Rio Grande do Sul, sticking out prominently, in a third. I calculated that if this region of 10 million-odd people and 100 million-odd sheep became a sovereign state, it would be larger than Uruguay or Ecuador – and if you were in the museum you'd be excused for believing that it had just gained its independence.

Porto Alegre itself was the result of immigration by militant and aggressive settlers originally from the Azores. Although the coast was overwhelmingly Portuguese, the interior had a Guarani/Spanish influence, with ranchers rearing cattle in the manner of their Uruguayan and Argentinian neighbours. Slavery existed, but how can you pin down a slave on the saddle of a horse? A better model would be the North American Wild West with cowboys and peons living in common quarters, following their masters' orders and administering his law with gun-battles over territory or stolen cows and horses. Their main product was *charque* – dried beef, which we have come to mispronounce as 'jerky' – the staple food of the slaves in the plantations of the Nordeste. If there is one defining distinction between Rio Grande do Sul and the rest of Brazil it is this – the other states were exporting commodities to the world: coffee, gold, sugar cane; but *charque* had an *internal* market and was thus shielded from commodity price fluctuations, which allowed for long-term economic planning.

The first rupture between Brazil and the state was when Dom Pedro I lost Uruguay after a five-year war with the United Plata provinces – early Argentina. Rio Grande do Sul faced stiff competition and lost its beef jerky monopoly. The result was the Farroupilha Revolution under Bento Gonçalves which lasted from 1830 to 1845 – the longest a province has remained independent from Brazil. It spread into Santa Catarina via the Alexandre Dumas-romanced Italian adventurer/freedom-fighter/ terrorist (delete where applicable) Giuseppe Garibaldi, who famously, and oh, so romantically, found love on the battlefields of Laguna in the person of feisty Anita, the future Mrs Garibaldi. Although much has been made of that revolt to bolster narrow gaucho patriotism (It lasted 3,466 days! It involved 56 battles! It left 3,000 dead!), the truth is that it eventually fizzled out with a whimper and that the rebels were consigned most of the time to the Uruguayan border area in the southern pampa. If a gaucho could please tell me what it was about …

The real bloodshed came later in 1891, during the only revolution in the history of Brazil that arose from mostly ideological reasons, although many have observed that it also coincided with the abolition of slavery which diluted the market for *charque*.

And so it was that I froze in front of that old, weathered sepia photograph, the 1890s equivalent of a modern snuff movie. The *degola* as it is known, was the preferred method of execution in the revolt of 1891–93: the killer sat down, put the man's head between his knees and slit his carotid artery like slaughtering a sheep. The revolution of 1891 pitted the new constitutional order, exemplified by pox-faced Julio de Castilhos (there's a museum about him, too) against the old monarchist parliamentarians under Gaspar Silveira Martins, one of the principal politicians in the Empire. This was a civil war with federal troops assisting Castilhos, described as a mob-rousing Danton and purist Robespierre in one, and southern ranchers – one of whom, Aparício Saraíva, ran for President of Uruguay, just to give you an idea of the confusing loyalties. His brother Gumersindo (whose best language was Spanish) took the fighting all the way to Santa Catarina, Paraná, and would have marched into São Paulo but for lack of backbone. It was then that Desterro became Florianópolis: after its recapture by Brazilian troops under Colonel Antônio Moreira César (the one who subsequently died in Canudos), the city grandees wanted to confirm their credentials and voted to change the name in honour of President Floriano Peixoto. The atrocities by both sides left a legacy of semi-lawlessness and Sicilian-style vendettas in Rio Grande do Sul which would continue for another twenty years. They also reinforced the image of a barbaric, unrefined gaucho to the rest of Brazil: they only picked up from where Tomás Gonzaga left it. The starting verse of 'Marília de Dirceu' is, after all: *'Marília, I'm not a vulgar cowboy.'*

The effect on Brazil was far-reaching. Pinheiro Machado, who finally defeated the rebels in Passo Fundo, rose to become the *éminence grise* of the First Republic for 20 years. His key parliamentary position was to validate votes during elections. The old property requirement of the monarchy was easy to administer by any tax-collecting administration. The new, post-abolitionism requirement of literacy – we won't have *them* vote – was open to abuse. One could say Machado started the endemic corruption of the Brazilian political system, because he could render votes cast by 'illiterates' as invalid and subvert the electoral will – which he often did. This literacy requirement has been the biggest political mistake of the Brazilian ruling classes. Not only did it practically beg for abuse, but it was also the main reason why the industrialisation which resulted in the ninth largest economy of the twenty-first century occurred within a social substratum similar to that of, say, Bangladesh, as the masses were as politically disenfranchised as South African blacks under apartheid.

Pinheiro Machado in the Senate and Julio de Castilhos with the Army in Rio Grande do Sul transformed politics in Brazil's First Republic. Population didn't matter anymore; property and education did. The Nordeste had large farms in the hands of a few and masses of newly liberated non-voting slaves. On the other hand, the south had many small farm holders and, as Castilhos funded schools, he produced not only educated citizens, but more importantly, registered voters. Voters meant favours, public works, money diverted to the state, an increase in prestige. Pinheiro Machado routinely dispensed with 'invalid' votes from Bahia and Pernambuco to boost Rio Grande do Sul's influence. By 1920, the state was third in number of eligible voters, behind only Minas and São Paulo. It is generally accepted that these two latter states stitched up the spoils of patronage in the First Republic between them in an alliance called *café com leite*: namely, coffee (from São Paulo) with milk (from Minas Gerais). Outside the presidency, however, an examination of the length of time politicians held ministries between 1910 and 1930 shows the gauchos in top place. Until, that is, the whole of the First Republic disappeared in smoke after the 1930 coup by Getúlio Vargas, himself a gaucho from São Borja, the seventh of the Seven Missions way out on the Argentinian border, too far for Osvaldo to drive me there.

The wars and revolutions turned this frontier state into a military garrison with at least a quarter of Brazil's officers of gaucho descent. Like Machado and Castilhos, they were influenced by the radical secularism and technocracy of Auguste Comte's positivism which became a new religion, firstly in the state, and then in the whole of Brazil, as Catholicism, retreating even under Dom Pedro II, lost its grip. The First Republic incorporated the military's positivist dogma in the Brazilian flag where it still stands: Order and Progress. Yes, the eye can trace the flow, oh so clearly, in the state museum in Praça da Alfândega: Pinheiro Machado, positivism, Vargas and his followers, the fascism of Estado Novo, the dictatorship in the sixties with no less than three military presidents drawn from Rio Grande do Sul (da Costa e Silva, Médici, Geisel). Before the dawn of the twentieth century, before that chilling *degola* photograph was taken, Rio Grande do Sul was a forgotten corner of Brazil; but then the state's history merges with that of Brazil, like its sky and grassland meet in its spacious pampa horizon.

In fact, it defines it: Rio Grande do Sul has always been in the forefront of political discourse. It provided the country with the grand dictator Vargas. Luis Prestes, whose left-wing lieutenants' column trekked up and down the country in the 1920s stirring the masses, started his long march from Santo Ângelo. The MST movement, which demands rights for the landless, is one of the most influential worldwide anti-globalisation organisations. And a coalition of trade unionists, socialists and greens has governed Porto Alegre since 1988 with a unique urban experiment. And it is on this budgeting success that Lula's eventual 2002 presidential triumph was founded.

....

Things I Like About Brazil #15:
Participatory Budgeting

For the second time, after Curitiba, southern Brazil leads the world in urban city management. This one is not about transport, it is about the city budget, now exported to places like Montevideo and other Mercocities. The budget is set by the citizens of Porto Alegre through a series of political structures which involve several elected assemblies. These are composed firstly of temporary representatives of interested parties like neighbourhood associations, trade unions or sports centres, secondly of government institutions, and thirdly of co-ordinating technocratic bodies. The city is divided into sixteen regions and five budget committees (Transport, Education and Leisure, Health, Taxation and Urban Development). The number of delegates elected from those local neighbourhood meetings depends on the participation of the locals – a larger issue which brings together a larger crowd sends more delegates. These first-round meetings also prioritise five items out of twelve spending areas ranging from sewage to culture. The delegates meet weekly to discuss how to implement their decisions with the council engineers, accountants, lawyers and elected politicians. A formula then distributes funds in the sixteen regions according to each region's defined priorities, population and need.

The implications of all this are staggering: involvement of citizens in the assemblies from the favela marginal to the upper-class businessman; a sense of participation and satisfaction with the authorities; a new approach for the sour-faced technocrats who need to explain legal and technical problems to the uninitiated; revenue increase with taxpayers motivated to pay more; a two-way dynamic flow of information leading to a wide consensus; and most dramatically the by-passing of the elected politicians themselves. In Brazil a mayor puts forward the budget to the city chamber of deputies and they vote it in or out. But after all this process, they can only vote for it; so at a stroke, the old careerist and corrupt local politics have been neutralised. The delegates in the budget approval process – who are volunteering their time and are not even paid travel expenses – cannot be re-elected after two years. This limits any political orientation or personal empire-building of the citizen-delegates, and every time the issue has arisen, the committees have themselves voted against holding office longer. The opposition parties and the almost universally hostile media cried 'Manipulation! Communism! The budget arrives at the chamber in a cast! WE are the legislators.' But for a population whose politicians regularly fail them, that may not be a bad thing.

The results? Participation increased from 1,000 citizens in 1990 to tens of thousands with more than 20 per cent being women. Viamão, a small municipality next to Porto Alegre tried – without success – to merge with the capital in order to benefit from its prosperity. The revenue earmarked for public investment in 1990 was only 3.2 per cent of the budget; in the late 1990s it was around 20 per cent. In 1989 only 49 per cent of the population had proper running water; in 1998 the proportion was 98 per cent. The assemblies are also flexing their muscle and their scrutiny has left even the ruling coalition in discomfort. As a political analyst put it, they moved from a techno-bureaucracy to a techno-democracy.

If this is communism, it is dangerous, for it works.

....

I had met Gilberto at Veneziano's, but hadn't spoken to him until club C-Clone. It was difficult to ignore him: he was an exhibitionist through and through, taking his top off at the first opportunity to reveal a muscular body to kill for, with a tiger tattoo on his shoulder and a lion on his back. He had dimples when he smiled, and his small pencil moustache crowned a Tom Cruise flash of teeth.

'I'll be in London in six months' time *amigo*,' he said to me with a disposition as sunny as I hoped Porto Alegre would turn out to be, even for one day. '*Es verdad*.'

He kept dropping a few Spanish words here and there for my dubious benefit.

'What will you do there?'

He shrugged his shoulders.

'Wash plates, work in bars. *Vamos a ver*.'

'Without speaking the language?'

'*Voy a aprender*. That's why I want to go. I have saved some money and will be coming to London. Learn English. *Aprender el idioma inglés*. That's the only way to find a job in Brazil nowadays.'

'And what do you do?'

'I have just studied law. *Acabo de terminar mis exámenes*.'

I looked at him, surprised.

'You're a solicitor and you're going to London to wash dishes?' I asked in disbelief.

'I want to see the world. *Ver el mundo entero*.'

'But what a life!'

'Better than here, for sure.'

'You are leaving the life of a professional and going for manual work?'

'*No estoy trabajando ahora*,' he said. 'You think it's easy finding work in Brazil?'

'Gilberto, you realise I have been speaking to you in Portuguese all this time.'

'Oh yes. Of course. *Mi error*.'

I saw Charlene coming with three drag queens.

'Here is my friend from London who has come all this way for our Latino party,' she said, smiling to the girls. 'John, this is Blush, a drag queen from Mexico.'

Goddess, how ugly, I thought as I kissed her on the cheek.

'This one is Lady Nicollete, the Barbie of Paraguay.'

Mwah, mwah, frightening.

'And Swan, La Reina de España!'

This one I didn't even let come near me. I blew her a kiss instead.

Charlene, satisfied with my performance, led the drag queens to another victim and gave me a drinks voucher.

C-Clone was in a different constellation to any other club in southern Brazil. It was situated in a plush residential area in the hills of Boa Vista with villas and luxurious apartment blocks enjoying super views of downtown and the river. The people who frequented it – young, white, middle-class, well-off, snappily dressed – made the clubscape look like a snapshot from a night in Milan or Barcelona. The music was also a novelty: two rooms – a small dance floor with the Top 40 courtesy of DJ Harrison, and a larger room with house from a Uruguayan guest DJ.

Pardon me?

'Uruguay is the new Goa,' Charlene said.

No.

'The new Ibiza.'

What did she know about Ibiza?

She smiled cryptically.

'What do you know about me?' she said. 'Do you know I was once Miss Venezuela?'

OK, you win.

'The stretch of beaches around the Punta del Este,' said Charlene, 'attracts South America's ravers in the summer with never-ending beach parties. They come from places as far as Caracas. The gringos have caught on now, and we are getting students from the United States bumming around.'

I know where I'll be going soon.

'There's your friend,' Charlene said, pointing at a gyrating Gilberto on stage. 'You have good taste in men.'

She pointed at a sleeping figure on the sofa.

'And there's your *other* friend,' she said and tapped her fingers, pretending annoyance. 'Snoring in *my* club.'

I sat next to Flávio and woke him up with a kiss.

'John! You're back!' he said, yelling to be heard over the music.

'It's uncool to fall asleep,' I said. 'How can you anyway, with all this noise?'

'I am soooo drunk,' he said.

'I've never seen you sober, Flávio.'

'Mmm,' he said and dozed off again.

*****

I was recounting all this to Vera back at Veneziano's.

'Another rainy day for you,' she said, busy as ever behind her bar on the Sunday. 'It could be worse. Pelotas is flooded.'

She paused.

'You know what they say about Pelotas?'

Yes, I did. There is many a TV show in Brazil with an effeminate character from Pelotas, one of the most southern cities in Brazil. All men there are supposed to be homosexuals. Male inhabitants routinely hide their provenance when they leave their hometown. Sociologists trace this deeply entrenched prejudice back to the reign of Dom Pedro I, when the up-and-coming nouveau riche *fazendeiros* sent their sons to Europe for scholarship and cultural refinement. When they returned, their bearing francified, their speech genteel and their table manners aristocratic, they stood out amongst the sawdust-and-spittoon manners of their gaucho peers – and gained this reputation.

'I have to apologise for the whole of Porto Alegre,' continued Vera. 'You must have found us very boring, being stuck in your hotel room.'

'Actually it was OK,' I replied. 'I have lived by night. If the sun came up suddenly I'd turn to ashes.'

'I hear you took Flávio home on his birthday,' she winked at me.

Big town, small world.

'After twenty-five years, he deserved a big present,' I remarked.

She gave me a caipirinha with enough cachaça to drown a kitten. It made me cough as the alcohol evaporated into my lungs.

'I did manage to do something today,' I told Vera. 'I walked around the municipal buildings. The skaters were out for the few hours of dry weather at lunchtime in the Praça Matriz. You know what I found odd?'

'What?'

'The monument to Tiradentes. In other cities you have sky-high sculptures in the central square. Here, you have just a plaque set on a small mound of earth from Minas Gerais.'

They don't care much for Tiradentes in Rio Grande do Sul; Sepé Tiaraju is lionised instead. The fissiparous elites require a hero to instil a sense of patriotism, and it looks like they have conveniently found their man: someone who is not Portuguese (and certainly not Spanish), a native American Indian who fought against both. 'This land has a lord,' has connotations which narrow-minded politicians want to dissect and promote. There are books, even comics for boys, which describe Sepé's life with hagiographic adulation. In all accounts he becomes a native marshal of strategic genius, a Latin American *caudillo* fighting against treacherous colonial regimes. Another figure is also emerging, that of São Roque whose canonisation also played into the hands of those who would see the state independent. Now they have a local hero, a saint, a 'language' and a multitude of books celebrating their *differentness*. The Sound and Vision show in the ruins of São Miguel was as unashamed a call for independence as can be uttered in the current political climes. The stage is set – for what, no one knows.

'Has it really been a week?' Vera asked when she took a breather from serving.

'Time passes.'

'How true. I took over this bar two years ago when the Cidade Baixa didn't have the bohemian atmosphere it has now – it was more like a red-light district.'

Impressive.

'We cleaned it up and started attracting a better kind of crowd. Students, professionals. It now seems like I've spent all my life behind this counter.'

Gilberto walked in. I had started talking to a young artist, a sculptor/painter who had lived in Paris and Barcelona for two years. So many gauchos have made the trip to the Old World.

'It's the family ties,' said the artist. 'You find more southern Brazilians in Europe because we can get residency from our parents and grandparents. Italian, German, Spanish, Portuguese …'

'*Hola amigo*,' Gilberto said to me. 'Going to "W" later?'

'Yes, I have to say goodbye to Charlene.'

I turned to Vera and whispered: 'He keeps talking Spanish to me.'

'He thinks every foreigner speaks Spanish,' she whispered back.

I see.

'Is he really a solicitor?'

'Oh yes.'

'And he wants to come to London to wash dishes?'

If Brazil is such a paradise why does everyone want to leave?

'Life is easier in Europe,' said my artist. 'You come to Brazil for a holiday and you think – wouldn't it be great to live in this country? But here everything – from how you get a job, how you get a flat, even how you get a document you are entitled to, like a passport – depends on who you know. Networking is everything and family ties run deep.'

We all concentrated on Gilberto, noticing the excitement in his every move.

'He's about to see the world. I was like this. I was thrilled and proud and ready to live the life of an artist in France.'

'But you're back,' I retorted.

'When you discover the world, you realise the world knows nothing about Brazil. Everyone wanted to have sex with me because Brazilians have a reputation for sleeping around.'

He lowered his gaze.

'And who cares for the work of a Brazilian artist in Europe?'

This travelogue is finishing, and I have to start making some points.

*****

The recognition that I was a member of a persecuted, shunned and much-reviled minority has been the most humanising factor in my life. The act of coming out as gay is unique, because it forces an inner honesty and challenge of convention which heterosexuals have no concept of. You look at your parents, who want themselves perpetuated in your image and you don't fit their world of white bridal gowns and conventional family values: you are one of those your mother warned you against. But she, and the rest of the world, maintained you were evil – could she have been so wrong? So you look it up in encyclopaedias and try to analyse what went amiss, if there is a way you can solve your problem. Alternatively you suppress your feelings and live in denial. You laugh at homophobic jokes, you sneer at queers, and you sometimes get a girlfriend because even second best is better than nothing at all. And all of this you do alone for to share your secret with someone is to admit it to yourself. It is an act of extreme bravery for one who has been brought up in a world full of cowboys and Indians – of gauchos and Guaranis – to admit that he or she is an Indian. Like good ol' Galileo, you must turn against the world and challenge its orthodoxies. Moreover, you do not fit the straitjacket of presumption. Films and novels portray gay men as outsiders to be tolerated for their bitchy camp wit, as victims whose emotional instability has marked them for inner torture, or as predatory psychopaths. The stereotypes may change but they are still there: opera-lovers, cat-owners, Aids sufferers – boy, if we believe Hollywood, gay men are now an important accessory in a liberated woman's boudoir; they are a girl's best friend, better than a cocker spaniel. But no one, no one reading this travelogue will leave with a one-dimensional stereotyped image of me.

Or Brazil.

Because, yes, it takes a gay man to see through the spin and the chaff and try to bring out the true nature of an often-ridiculed and misunderstood country. A gay man can appreciate the feelings of every Brazilian who has travelled in the West and was not taken seriously because of his or her origins; if only the gauchos knew that it is only abroad they are verily different. I know, because I understand the nature of prejudice: do Brazilians live in cities? Do they play football and dance all day? Is there such a thing as Brazilian art? Are there any Brazilian writers? Any nice buildings or is it all hovels? Are their women loose? Aren't they all black? Will I get mugged as I leave the airport or will they wait until I reach my hotel first? Which Brazilian emigrant has not been subjected to questions like these? Prejudice is based not just on ignorance, it's also an act of intellectual laziness bred by the erroneous certainty of First World imperial arrogance: 'I know all about Brazil – I've been to Rio. Brazilian art? I bought that lambada record ten years ago.' If countries were people, Brazil would be a gay man: stereotyped, snubbed, reported only to reinforce existing prejudices, desperately trying to assert a separate identity within a cacophony of indifference, striving to be taken seriously with his own special background. A gay man can identify with that, so no – nobody reading this travelogue will leave with a one-dimensional stereotyped image of Brazil.

Or me.

*****

At midnight I left Veneziano's, my corner away from home in PoA.

'Come back soon,' Vera said and hugged me. 'Even though it's a long way, it's nice down here.'

I kissed Vera, Gilberto, the artist and two cute eighteen-year-olds for good measure. Vera wouldn't go away.

'Will you come back?'

'I will,' I said. 'I like it here. You know, like Bahia …'

She frowned.

'What about Bahia?' she asked.

I had better not tell Vera.

'Nothing,' I said. 'I'll come back. I promise.'

*****

Charlene was at the door of club 'W'.

'You're leaving,' she repeated, as if only hearing the fact from her own lips would make it real.

'Tomorrow,' I said.

'Tomorrow,' she repeated.

Silence.

'So when are you going to return?'

That again.

Charlene patted my head with her gloved hand.

'You are always welcome in my clubs, *carinho*,' she said.

Silence.

Charlene remembered our very first discussion.

'So, are we that different here in Rio Grande do Sul?'

'No, you're not,' I said. 'I'm different. *You're* different.'

I looked at her. She was wearing lesbian chic today. A man dressed as a woman pretending to be dressed as a man.

We're all different.

'You look gorgeous as ever,' I said, frog in my throat.

She focused on me, moaned with pleasure at the compliment and took a step outside.

'Get in!' she shouted with emotion. 'Do you know how long it took me to put this make-up on?'

*****

The club seemed familiar now, its clumsy sound system, its dark sofas, the bar which also served as a coat-check.

To my eyes one silhouette shone darker than the others.

'Hi Flávio.'

'Still here?' he asked.

'I'm leaving tomorrow.'

'I'm glad your last impression of me wasn't from C-Clone yesterday,' he said.

'You were out of it.'

'Just drink,' he protested.

We were both silent. He spoke first.

'We didn't … ahem, *again*.'

I nodded.

'Not after that first time.'

467

More silence.

'I have my car with me today,' he said.

Architects can be such sops.

'You want to show me your town again?'

His eyes lit up and his fleshy protruding lips parted slightly.

'Yes.'

I looked at Flávio and what might have been.

'I think I know it better now. Let's leave the memories intact.'

He gulped down his beer.

'Will you be coming back?'

Yes, I would. For what I didn't tell Vera or Flávio or Charlene or Gilberto was that despite the gauchos' self-imposed prejudices there are only two places in Brazil where I have made so many friends whom I long to meet again: Rio Grande do Sul – and Bahia.

If there are differences, they matter not.

Chapter 16

The Believers (Brasília)

Let us sing from our heart
The Maltese Cross our standard
You hold the name of a hero of Portugal
Vasco da Gama, your fame is his equal
　　　　　　　　　 – Vasco da Gama football supporters' chant

....

The Words You'll Need

câmara = chamber
Praça dos Três Poderes = Square of the Three Powers
Presença Divina = Divine Presence
Pretos Velhos = literally, 'Old Blacks'; the collective name for slave 'saints'
　　worshipped in Brazil
Salão Negro = Black Hall
Seta Branca = White Arrow
veado = queer (in case you forgot)

....

– 73 –

Many a commentator has observed that there never was a better year for being Brazilian than 1958. There is even a book about it: *Happy 1958 – The Year That Shouldn't End* by Joaquim Ferreira dos Santos. This was the year of the bossa nova sound which later begat 'The Girl from Ipanema', a worldwide hit not to be matched until the lambada invasion of the early nineties. It was the year of the publication of Amado's *Gabriela*, which reflected the optimism of a nation to be built by Brazilians and immigrants alike, united after the Vargas nation-shaping reforms. It was the year of Brazil's first World Cup win where an 18-year-old prodigy called Pelé entered the world stage. Finally, it was the year halfway to the inauguration of Brasília under the presidency of Juscelino Kubitschek. As a Brazilian saying has it: *Brazil is the country of the future*. Never did the proverb sound more true than in 1958 when Brasília was being erected under the auspices of architect Oscar Niemeyer and town planner Lúcio Costa.

The building of Brasília in the hot savannah of the central plateau was equivalent to Australians building Canberra in Alice Springs instead of midway between Sydney and Melbourne: an act of monumental financial folly. Brazil was bankrupted in order to build the new capital quickly and remotely. The spiral of inflation sparked by printing money resulted in the military coup of 1964 and 21 years of dictatorship. But this was also an act of faith and more; an iconic act of penance to the rebels of Canudos: we will conquer the interior for the sake of the destitute backlanders and bring prosperity and hope where previously there was none. In line with the 1969 moon landings, it was the twentieth-century equivalent of those daredevil adventures of the conquistadors: the colonisation of the uninhabitable, the taming of a frontier, a leap into the unknown for the leap's sake. As the 1966 edition of the *South American Handbook* says: '*It is not in the nature of Governments to turn their backs on luxury and make for the wilderness.*'

Others were less circumspect. Andrew Marshall, a Reuters correspondent, called Brasília '*inspired lunacy*'. The critic Robert Hughes shouted '*Utopian horror*'. The writer Peter Matthiessen called it '*less inspired than pretentious, a brave new city cunningly disguised as a World's Fair*'. Gilberto Freyre, the great Brazilian sociologist, called Brasília '*un-Brazilian*'. Yuri Gagarin, the astronaut, said he thought he had arrived on another planet. More acerbically, Lonely Planet's *South America on a Shoestring* 1977 original starts the relevant section with an exclamatory '*Brasília is a vast architectural wank*' – an appellation expunged from later editions. Yet in 1987 Unesco declared the whole planned town a World Monument, like Ouro Preto and Olinda several centuries too early.

Whether you like it or not, you haven't been to a city like Brasília, nor are you likely to visit another. It is shaped by Lúcio Costa like an aeroplane with the 'cockpit' facing east. This cockpit is the power centre: it contains the focal point, the huge Square of the Three Powers with the modernist structures of the High Court, the President's Palace and the Congress (bicameral like the US equivalent). Sports clubs and a huge artificial lake almost as large as the city itself called Paranoá (calm down, it's a Tupi root) envelop this eastern tip. The body of the plane (called the Monumental Axis, pointing west to east), thin and long, contains the ministries, the theatres, museums, the cathedral, the banks, the hotels, the entertainment complexes and tails into the inter-city *rodoviária* (a perennial Brazilian touch: as far away as possible from civilisation). The wings (pointing north to south) are composed of the *superquadras* – superblocks which include residential buildings, local shops and restaurants each connected with symmetrical access roads; the town cemeteries are in the wing tips so that the centre is spared the sight of hearses. Theoretically, you look at the map and off you go.

Except that it's not as easy as that. For a start, the addresses: my hotel, Hotel Bristol, gave its location as SHS Q4 Bl F. Go find that!

Start again: my hotel was at the Southern Hotel Sector (SHS), 4th Quarter (Q4), Block F. There is also a Northern Hotel Sector (SHN), and like everything else there is north and south: a Tourist Hotel Sector North is SHTN, a Sector of Clubs South SCES, the Sector of Banks North SBN, the Entertainment (*Diversão*) Sector South SDS, and so on. Within those there are quarters and within those there are blocks. The fabulous touch to top it all is that the only ineffectual indication (if any) of which block or quarter is which, is a small letter hidden away in an unlit corner, a doorway corniche or maybe the lawn. If you thought the Japanese system of naming buildings in a street according to seniority (the oldest being number 1) and renaming them should one disappear because of fire, earthquake or demolition (the number 2 becoming number 1, number 3 becomes number 2 and so on) was complicated enough, you have not sampled the delights of Lúcio Costa's brainstorming.

It's in the residential blocks where it gets *really* interesting. These are called SQS and SQN for SuperQuadras South and North respectively, numbering 100–116 up to 900–916, and they recede like wings from the 'fuselage', 101 being the closest and 116 the furthest. The even hundreds are below the aeroplane wing axis whereas the odd ones are above. So below the right wing of the plane (pointing south as cockpit point east) you have what? But of course 202, 402, 602, 802 SQS! Above the left wing you have 102, 302, 502, 702, 902 SQN! Easy, if you also remember that they all start at 102, 202 as the 101, 201 superblocks are subsumed by the Hotel, Bank Sectors et al closest to the plane axis. There is an exception to this exception: there is 801 and 601. (There is an explanation for this – believe me, I can bore you.) If you are really advanced you will know that 102S–116S is ERLS, 903S–914S is SGAS (but that SGAS also reappears between 602S to 612S, jumps 613S and 614S and recomprises 615S and 616S) or that after 116N comes SHLN but its southern counterpart SHLS follows 715S and is not symmetrical. Of course the intermediate side-avenues parallel to the axes are called names like W3 and W7. Trust the architects to use a letter (W) which does not exist in Portuguese.

Did anyone consult the users in all this? I have not been so impressed since my trip from Biarritz to Toulouse with SNCF French railways. Admire their seating plan:

21	23		27	25
22	28		24	26

But that was a railway compartment and this is a city where you need an algorithm to walk about. If a computer programmer could have contrived a town, Brasília would be it, with the bugs designed-in forever and the software patches revealed in all their glory.

I bet the ones who are impressed are the ones who are being chauffeured around, because the revelatory truth about Brasília is that it's not designed for people. It's designed for cars. First of all the curves joining the huge lanes running across it are highly aerodynamic with a 1:3 decline giving you several g's worth of extra weight: Brasília can only be truly experienced driving around in an automobile. Then the pedestrian cannot possibly cross those murderous six-laners; he or she has to double the already enormous distances on foot in order to traverse the few pelican crossings sprinkled irregularly and always in deference to the motor car. At the intersection of the two axes there is the local bus station used for commuting within the town: the E–W axis runs below, where the buses are; the N–S axis runs above. In order to cross you have to climb up and then down again. Of course, no one does and, as people try to negotiate the dangerous crossing, they become accident statistics. It's as if the city is a vast Darwinian contraption trying to speed up natural selection by weeding out the attention-deficient, the easily distracted, the drowsy and the downright dim. They should hand out a T-shirt at the airport Departures Gate: *I survived Brasília*.

*****

Gagarin's comments came to mind as I stood under the relentless afternoon sun of the centre-west which renders the curves of the buildings in the Square of the Three Powers extraterrestrial in their luminosity. This is a flat plain, and there are no natural distractions for Niemeyer's compositions. Here, there is abstraction in place of function: shiny glass fronts, geometric patterns, modern sculptures, lines intersecting at obtuse angles. This is a negation of Euclidean space; this is living inside a warped Lobachevsky continuum. It is in the Square of the Three Powers that the Unesco decision appears justified. The

Ministry of Justice with sheets of water running down its sides in permafall; the elegant, airy Supreme Court packed by reporters and TV cameras; the President's Palace, the *Palácio de Planalto*, low-lying and remarkably approachable with its inviting ramp entrance; the most famed sculpture in all Brazil, *Os Candangos* by Bruno Giorgi, a tribute to the pioneers who built the capital in squalid conditions; the strange Sydney Opera House-like Pantheon at the tip of the square, looking like two concrete turtles engaged in permanent coitus; and that imposing Congress building: a tall H-structure in front of two dishes, one facing up and one facing down to symbolise the complementary nature of the two elected houses in Brazil, the Senate and the Chamber of Deputies.

It is a myth that Brasília is the last capital of the twentieth century – Pakistan's Islamabad was inaugurated six years later. It is a myth that Brasília was completed within four years. Outside the governmental buildings on the Monumental Axis, upon inauguration only SQS 105, 106, 107 and 108 were ready. In SQN there are empty plots where superquadras are still waiting to be built. The famous cathedral was only finished in 1970. And, finally, it is a myth that it is a futuristic city. No, it is what a futuristic city was supposed to look like in the 1960s. And what looked sci-fi then looks cartoon pop-art now, rendering Brasília a Nebula Award prime candidate for Best Cinematic Shlock Attempt to Reconstruct Judge Dredd's Mega City One.

You can detect that sixties' feel in the Avenue of Ministries where you have those boring rectangular green-windowed monstrous towers, which remind me of London's Centre Point in duodecuplicate. You can see it in the deification of the automobile from an epoch of seemingly everlasting energy resources. You can see it in the plan of the original where the architects foresaw an upwards rather than lateral expansion of the town, like all sixties' housing projects. A real town adjusts itself over decades and centuries and is the sum total of what architects and engineers have imposed upon it – even a boomtown like Ouro Preto was not built in a decade. The original Lonely Planet reaction appears now justified. Hell, Lúcio Costa even attempted to regulate the exact type of taxis that would be allowed (DKW, dark grey, four-door), the earth that should be used in the cemeteries, and the illumination of the roads. And lest we forget, this is a city of politicians, lobbyists, civil servants and media types. What an exciting mix!

And yet the bitch is photogenic.

I found shelter from the tropical sun inside the Congress. On my right Amanda from Bahia was the guide to the Chamber of Deputies. On my left Teresa from Maranhão was waiting to start a tour of the Senate. Neither noticed me as I walked into the Salão Negro where lobbyists were handing out their info: a copy of an article in *Science* magazine on the future of the Brazilian Amazon. Brazilians are very suspicious of talk of internationalisation of the rainforest, smacking as it does of loss of sovereignty.

'Debate today in the auditorium Petrônio Portella,' the girl smiled at me. 'See you there, sir.'

I tried to maintain a sense of gravitas as I walked towards an open door leading into the Chamber of Deputies. A guy in a grey suit (grey suits are in vogue in Brasília, perhaps in deference to those planned-for DKW taxis) stopped me politely.

'The *câmara* is in session,' he said.

In session? One step forward and I would have entered the floor of the House! I thought there would be more restrictions to my movements, but this is not a country which assassinates its elected representatives – at least openly – and there is no terrorist threat. Well, relatively speaking: in the lobby a large exhibition titled 'Exodus', by Brazil's most famous photographer, Sebastião Salgado, was documenting the plight of the MST.

Some people consider the *Movimento dos Trabalhadores Rurais Sem Terra*, MST (Movement of Rural Workers without Land), a terrorist organisation, but it does not quite fit the picture, though its politics, unashamedly Maoist, have scared the elites and the middle classes. If you allow me a Marxist view of Brazil's problems, it is of course such alignments of the middle classes with the elites, whenever the formers' privileged position is threatened, that summon such perils to their front door in the first place. Brazil has a small elite class – descendants of the old latifundiary landowners, now controlling politics, the state apparatus, the judiciary and the boardrooms of industry – comprising less than 5 per cent of the population, and a small middle class of about 20 per cent. The working class and the illiterate *lumpenproletariat* together comprise the rest of the population and unlike in other countries, say the United States, they do not aspire to be middle class – on the contrary, they are alienated from it. That is the class chasm in the centre of Brazil's social problems.

It is hard to oppose the MST: it is a movement that started – unsurprisingly – in Rio Grande do Sul under the auspices of the liberation theologians of the Catholic Church based on the fact that 60 per cent of Brazil's farmland lies idle (the statistic is hotly disputed because large tracts of *potential* farmland in the Amazon and Mato Grosso are included or excluded at will). In 1985 hundreds of landless peasants took over empty land in Rio Grande do Sul where the movement took shape and acquired momentum. Is that a Mugabe-like disregard of the landowner classes? How come then that, by Brazil's 500th year, state governments have allocated land tithes to 250,000 families after MST take-overs? Is that terrorism?

This is better answered when one looks at who kills whom. The MST has suffered to the tune of 1,000 murders in the past 10 years with one massacre in Pará on 17 April 1996 occupying many Amnesty International dossiers: 19 peasants were shot dead – three at point-blank range – after a 1,500-strong demonstration by MST activists was fired at by state police. It is a strange terrorist organisation indeed, whose unarmed members die like flies in front of state security forces – and this happens not just in the rural north and the Nordeste: one of the worst offenders in using violence against the MST has been Governor Jaime Lerner of Paraná, the brains behind Curitiba's renaissance.

The MST has now grown. It is part of the 'No Logo' anti-multinational, anti-GM food, anti-IMF globalisation movement that clashed with police in Genoa and Seattle. It has produced an alternative report for the World Bank to redistribute land and stop world hunger. However, more mundanely, it has started to act like Another Brazilian Party: prone to exaggeration, flirting openly with the media, unable to give praise, but instead shooting randomly at the federal government record, especially Cardoso's neo-liberal policies of privatisation. So, although my heart embraces the lobbying on behalf of the landless poor, my brain tells me that there are enough parties on the Brazilian Left already.

*****

I chose to visit the Senate first, the upside-down of the two Niemeyer dishes. Teresa and I walked up the left corridor past a revolving door. We walked into an amphitheatre, looking through a glass partition to the chamber below. A single senator was speaking. There were only seven souls in the Senate, all sitting to his right, on the podium.

'Who are they?' I asked *sotto voce*.

'They are the first and second vice-speakers,' she replied in her normal voice. 'And stenographers. There is no need to whisper, the glass is soundproof.'

'Why is the glass there in the first place?'

'Because sometimes audiences disrupt the proceedings.'

'Shouting slogans and the like?'

Teresa looked me in the eye.

'No, throwing things.'

'Like what?'

'Fruit.'

Cool.

'Who is he?' I asked, pointing at the speaker.

'Pedro Simon, Rio Grande do Sul, PMDB,' she said. 'He is touted as a future presidential candidate.'

We listened in for a few minutes. Pedro was speaking forcefully against drugs.

'Why are there no others in the audience?'

Teresa looked at her watch.

'It's too early. Proceedings start at two-thirty. He's speaking on a preliminary motion for TV and radio to be on record. Senators will read the eventual printed text.'

I thought we were alone in the amphitheatre, but I noticed four journalists and two camera operators in the circle below us. No pictures and no recordings of the proceedings are allowed outside those of the accredited correspondents.

'How many senators are there?' I asked.

'There are three from every state; there are twenty-six states plus the federal district, Brasília, so eighty-one in all.'

'How many women?'

'Five – no, six.'

Teresa led me out along another corridor called the Time Tunnel, containing a permanent exhibition of the Senate's history. It is the oldest current political institution in Brazil, having been first invoked by Dom Pedro I upon independence. It survived the monarchy with appointed members (44 viscounts, 26 marquises, 18 barons, 2 earls and a duke). It survived the constitution of the Republic modelled on the US Federal model. Finally it suffered but still emerged rejuvenated after Vargas and the military.

'You can visit one of the committee rooms,' Teresa said and opened a door.

'Small,' I said. 'There are only two chairs.'

She looked at the plaque outside: *Francelino Pereira, (PFL, MG)*.

'Oh,' she said, 'this is the office of a senator. Better leave.'

'You're not a regular guide?' I asked.

'No, I'm a student,' she said. 'I'm studying politics and I'm doing a year in the senate here as part of the course.'

Oh, I thought, an *intern*. How Monica Lewinsky.

'How many people work here?'

'About two thousand five hundred. There is also a post office inside, several restaurants and bars, banks, a library, doctors, even a hairdresser.'

I pointed at a collection of old chairs questioningly.

'From the original Senate. Some people say the original building, the Monroe Palace in Rio, was demolished by the military government in order to force the senators to leave and come here.'

Rather drastic, but having strolled around Brasília, I empathised.

*****

Teresa passed me on to Amanda who asked me more questions than I asked her.

'*Greece?*' she said. 'Born in *Greece*? The birthplace of democracy? What's it like in Greece?'

'In fact,' I replied, 'much as it is here in Brasília. Dry heat. I quite like this climate.'

Indeed, the most pleasant thing about the capital was the near-zero humidity which made the heat oh-so-tolerable. It reminded me of Athens without the smog.

The Bahian girl looked at me apoplectically.

'But the skin dries out quickly,' she complained. 'Not good for you. I have to use so much moisturiser.'

You can't win them all in a democracy.

The Chamber of Deputies with 513 representatives was much larger, and it should be, as elected members are proportional to a state's population. It was, as I already knew, in session.

'There is no glass partition,' I whispered and this time I had to.

'There is no need,' Amanda whispered back.

The Senate must attract a wilder kind of audience.

Amanda, a public relations student, spoke volubly about committees, parliamentary procedure and passing laws, which went over my head. I had made my choice. I didn't like the anonymity of the Chamber of Deputies. I was one for the Senate. It sounds fab to have people throw fruit at you – for free! I suppose it depends; with pineapples, I'd be worried.

Besides, the Senate is less crowded and you are guaranteed a seat, whereas in the Chamber of Deputies –

'There are only four hundred seats but five hundred and thirteen representatives,' I asked. 'How do they sit down?'

'They don't,' she said. 'Whoever comes in picks a desk. Voting is done electronically with a button and anyone can log in anywhere and vote with their own password.'

'So if I give someone my password, he can log in and vote for me even if I'm absent?'

Amanda was quick to respond: 'That never happens.'

In fact, it does or rather did. The system was shown to be notoriously abused during a special enquiry shortly after I left Brasília.

'Why don't you build more desks instead?' I asked.

Amanda's grimace said it all.

'Because it's Niemeyer's?'

How arrogant to presume that a few technocrats could determine not only the present but the future, too. Talk about imposing a museum straitjacket in the most modern of capitals. This is not a city, it is a giant museum and no one can touch any part of it in spite of the obviously dated restrictions. When in the 1970s the inferior fluorescent outdoor illumination was modified to mercury lamps, the wide spacing and low height of the original posts was maintained and as a result the highways of the capital are darker at night than Rio's or São Paulo's and more dangerous for both vehicles and pedestrians. Imagine astronauts having to live aboard *Mir* because it had been declared a Unesco site. The Russians did well to sink the bugger.

Aside from the Praça dos Três Poderes, the other grand building of note is Niemeyer's cathedral, shaped like a crown of thorns, as sixteen sharp, bent concrete stakes support an airy internal structure. This must be the only church in Christendom with a designed-in car park. Why?

Did Aleijadinho lay out his churches with a horse-stable annexe? I wonder what Lúcio Costa's vision of a future Palm Sunday procession was: the devoted cruising in their convertibles waving large palms, with the priest officiating in an open limo with a ghettoblaster?

I heard flapping.

The church was full of pigeons, or, since we're in Brazil, probably something ten times worse. To top it all, the abstract stained glass tiles were falling down, just like in the great arch of La Défense.

They don't build them like they used to.

*****

In the evening I asked at my hotel if there was a street with restaurants I could walk around in.

'Yes, blocks 404/405 SQS,' I was told. 'It's called the *Rua dos Restaurantes*.'

I needed a taxi, but I didn't need to search far: the concentration of hotels in one sector has had two major side effects. Firstly, all taxis in town are parked outside with on-the-spot driver assemblies discussing politics like everyone else in Brasília. The second side effect I noticed as we turned into the South Wing via one of those rollercoaster ramps: by setting aside a sector for hotels, Lúcio Costa indirectly created the red-light district.

One plumed lady of the night tried to wave us down.

'*Veado*,' said my taxi driver, pointing at a TV and winking. 'These are all men.'

By now I was immune to the sight, but concerned about the direction.

'Shouldn't you be turning right and right again?' I asked the driver. 'I want 404S.'

I saw a sign: *Zona Bancária*. Wrong turn.

'You aren't local?' I asked.

'No,' the driver said with a singing north-eastern accent. 'I've only been here a few months. I'm from Bahia.'

'We're in the banking zone,' I informed him. 'I think we have to go up to go down again.'

We hit a cul-de-sac. I bet Lúcio threw some in for fun.

'Oh, no, you can't turn from 205 to 206,' he exclaimed.

'We must get back on the W3,' I ventured.

Out of the corner of my eye I saw a restaurant called Líbanos.

'Leave me here,' I said, resigned.

'Are you sure?' he said. 'This must still be 205.'

'206,' I corrected him. 'Let it be.'

'But we are not yet in 406.'

'404. I'm not sure we'll ever get there.'

I paid him quickly.

He gave me his card. 'If you want me again for anything.'

I didn't take it. He seemed dejected.

'You are not happy with me,' he said.

What a Brazilian thing to say.

– 75 –

From Líbanos to Bar Beirute.

Actually Beirute was not a bar at all; it was a full-blown restaurant, although you could sit outside and sip a beer. It was supposed to be 'mixed' GLS but it seemed all too straight. There was only one table free, awkwardly positioned on a slope – at least it was next to a couple of guys who might just be reading from the same bookshop, so to speak. One of them with a carefully groomed goatee made eye contact.

I drank a large bottle of Brahma, enjoying the cool of the night. Brasília can desiccate you during the day, but it compensates for its behaviour after sunset, unlike the coastal cities' hammam-by-day, hammam-by-night tortuous monotony. I checked the goatee and caught him looking. I ordered a second beer. My two neighbours were talking animatedly. I listened in. The goatee asked something and his burly friend answered: 'It's up to you whether you still want to be friends with him or not ...'

Boyfriend trouble.

After my second bottle I felt sleepy, so I decided to pay up. As soon as I asked for the bill, there was commotion at the next table. The goatee's friend asked me casually: 'You are leaving? Already?'

'I'm tired.'

'Why don't you join us for a last one? On us. It's still early.'

I tried to suss them out. Hell, why not?

'I'm Raul,' the goatee introduced himself as I sat next to him. 'This is my friend Rubem.'

My European provenance combined with my Portuguese caused a stir once more. I need a title: JohnM, Freaker-Out of Brazilians Everywhere.

Things I Like About Brazil #16: Portuguese

OK, let's hear it for the language. If you are coming from Castilian Spanish, like me, you tend to agree with Peter Matthiessen who described the Portuguese accent as that of a 'person angered, while eating macaroons'. The shock of reading the same words and pronouncing them as if you're pinching your nose while sipping some hot and bitter beverage is, I'm afraid, irreconcilable. I hated Portuguese at first and would have stopped at the regulation tourist phrases had it not been for the people. It's for them I made an effort to listen, understand and try to imitate those impossible nasal intonations. Goddess, did I use a lot of spit in the process!

Instead of switching off in front of the TV, I agonised to pick up the odd word – and felt like a million dollars when I could comprehend a whole sentence. I memorised phrases. I bought self-study grammar books and graded myself on the exercises, tried the accents, declined the verbs. It was during the eight-hour ride to Bonito with my zebu vet that my tongue took a turn of its own, my ear floated over the syllables and my brain became engaged in a two-way serious conversation. I still count that day as the day my Portuguese finally gelled and the stroppy tongue-twisters turned stirring, musical, harmonious.

Every language gives you an incomparable insight into the mindset of a people; and the people of Brazil paid me back in triplicate. I discovered a whole new literature. I submerged myself into new political thinking. I met tender lovers and made new unwavering friends. They were all grateful and flattered that I had made the effort to cross the barrier. For an effort it was: a language with four different accents that declines its infinitive is not to be taken lightly.

'You were a bit agitated earlier on,' I said, steering the subject away from myself.

Rubem picked up on the lead.

'Raul here is upset. He split last month with his boyfriend of two years.' And then, carefully: 'You *do* understand?'

Fortaleza déjà vu.

'Perfectly,' I replied. 'I remember how I felt when I split with mine.' You could sense Raul's relief.

'Is there nothing you can do?'

'Not much. He left Brasília for São Paulo.'

Raul's ex-boyfriend was a senior manager in a big Brazilian bank, posted for a period of two years to the capital. Promotion came simultaneously with his travel orders.

'So we never really split,' he said. 'Fate did it for us.'

'Couldn't you go with him and live together?'

Raul shook his head. He was a rare thing – an introverted Brazilian. Only his penetrating brown eyes divulged a fiery inner self.

'I have a job in Brasília. My mother is in Brasília. I can't leave everything and be dependent on him in São Paulo. I wish he'd stayed for my birthday, though.'

'When is that?'

'Two days' time.'

Not another one! Rather rudely, I said I didn't believe him. Raul took out his ID card and showed me.

Not just any birthday, but –

'Your twenty-first birthday!' I exclaimed.

He nodded an embarrassed yes.

'Good grief. I could have sworn you were older. At least twenty-five.'

He liked that. It must be the goatee.

'Will you come to the party?' he asked, averting his eyes.

I finished my beer.

'Of course, I will.'

Raul lowered his head and his leg touched mine.

Rubem coughed.

'Raul seems to be taken with you already,' he said bitchily. 'He hasn't asked you yet.'

'He's a foreigner,' replied Raul, shifting in his chair.

'Asked me what?'

'He always asks people the same question,' continued Rubem. 'And depending on the answer you give, Raul likes you or not.'

'He's a gringo!'

'What question?' I was starting to get annoyed.

Rubem sat back, pouting with pleasure. Raul, once more, looked down.

'ASK ME!'

Raul looked up.

'Do you like football?'

'Yes.'

'Which football team do you support?'

'Tottenham Hotspur,' I replied.

Raul turned to Rubem: 'I told you,' he said. 'I don't even know them.'

'Why?' I replied. 'What's your team?'

Raul turned to me: 'Vasco,' he said. 'Do you know Vasco?'

'Juninho, Romário,' I said, mentioning Vasco's star players.

Raul beamed.

'You said the right thing,' he said and placed his arm around my shoulders.

*****

Of course I knew of Vasco da Gama.

The club's biggest coup ever was bringing to Rio a small player from Cruzeiro in Belo Horizonte. Nowadays Romário and Juninho command fees much larger than $520,000 a year. But that was a record fee for a footballer, for the time was 1971 and the player's name was Eduardo Gonçalvez de Andrade. He's better known as Tostão.

Tostão was one of the heroes of the Brazilian 1970 World Cup-winning team which coined that cliché *'the beautiful game'*. (Beautiful? Sophia Loren is beautiful. A game? Are you serious? Darts is a game.) Tostão was only 23 at the time and with 10 goals the hero of the qualifying round. He suffered a detached retina in a Corinthians versus Cruzeiro clash in September 1969 and had eye surgery soon after. In April 1970 he woke up before a friendly with his eye socket dripping blood. Just before the World Cup itself he suffered from conjunctivitis. Still, he played after the team physician vouched for him and his crowning movement was nutmegging Bobby Moore to pass the ball to Pelé who gave it to Jairzinho to score the single goal against England in that famous game in Guadalajara.

And one little boy saw it all.

Tostão had a relapse of his eye injuries, retired in 1973 and took refuge in being Professor of Medicine in Belo Horizonte where, ever a Mineiro, he still lives. Only in the 1990s did he return to football by becoming a commentator for the 1994 US World Cup and a subsequent TV and newspaper pundit. It took him 20 years to shake off the weight of the memory of that win. Brazil and the world still haven't.

Neither have I.

*****

Raul was a Carioca who had moved to Brasília at the age of eight with his mother ('My father left us,' he said simply). He was also very athletic; if he were yogurt he would be the zero per cent fat variety.

'Do you go to the gym?' I asked.

Raul sniggered.

'Gym? I play football with a local club every week.'

'What position?'

'Centre midfield. And I'm a three-time judo champion.'

Judo champion?

'What kind of champion?'

'State champion.'

'The Federal District of Brasília is a small state,' said Rubem sarcastically.

'Third in Brazil for under twenty-ones.'

Wow.

'I won six bouts, lost one,' said Raul. 'Against a Japanese-Brazilian from Amazonas. He went on to win the gold.'

'It shouldn't be allowed,' I said. 'I mean the Japanese have an advantage in judo, don't they?'

The memory made him light a cigarette.

'An athlete and you smoke?'

'I started four months ago. Boyfriend stress. I'll give it up soon.'

Commotion. A fourth guy arrived.

'My flatmate,' said Raul, and with that he passed me a sheet of paper. He'd written '*I am crazy about you*' in English. When our eyes met, he looked away coyly. Raul was a dish.

Raul's flatmate had arrived to take us away.

'Where are we going?' I enquired.

'To the only 24-hour establishment in Brasília,' said Raul.

'I can't drink any more,' I said. And lowering my voice: 'Are you coming to my hotel with me?'

Raul squeezed my hand reassuringly.

'I need to wake up a bit with some food first. Come, you don't have to eat.'

'How are we going to get there?'

'In Rubem's car.'

'Rubem will drive after all this drink?'

'Rubem can drive with his eyes closed.'

Good practice for now.

*****

Brazilians like to give their footballers pet names. The 1970 squad was full of them: Felix the goalkeeper was 'the Cat', Rivelino was 'Ears', Piazza was 'Pepe', Brito was 'the Horse', Clodoaldo the untranslatable '*Corro*', Jairzinho was 'the Hurricane', Carlos Alberto 'the Captain' (which he was), Gérson 'the Parrot', Tostão 'Penny Coin', and Pelé – itself a nickname – was 'the King' although for the team members he was the politically incorrect 'Negrão'. The explosion of virtuosity of this Brazilian team in a sport as yet untainted by big business and still pure in its athletic essence was broadcast around the world with the advent of live colour television. The 1970 Mexico World Cup was the first truly global media event and the Brazilian team of Tostão, Pelé, Rivelino, Gérson, Carlos Alberto and Jairzinho fired the imagination of millions of fans in a way no other squad has done since. Brazilians 'in the know' claim that the 1958 national selection of Didi, Zagalo and Pelé was superior, but no video camera ever captured its progress and carved it into posterity: for that is how images in the planetary subconscious are created and how Brazil has become synonymous with football.

You will read that English merchant sailor Charles Miller organised the first official tournament in Rio between teams from the São Paulo Gas Company, the London and Brazilian Bank and the São Paulo Railway back in 1895, and clubs from those two states still predominate. What you may not read is how football was promoted relentlessly by the dictator Vargas – not that Brazilians needed too much prompting – in the same way that Hitler and Mussolini did in Europe. Stadiums were built, stipends given, clubs subsidised.

A world audience is one thing, a domestic one is another: in 1970 a third successive four-star general, Emílio Garrastazu Médici, was president, in charge of repression and sloganeering. Médici was fully aware of the popularity boost of a World Cup win and interfered even in the team selection. The coach Saldanha famously uttered the words: 'I do not choose the Cabinet and he [Médici] does not choose the squad.' He was summarily sacked just before the World Cup in favour of Zagalo.

Brazil won the 1970 World Cup because it was the best team – but often best teams don't win. As Garry Jenkins informs us in his excellent book *Beautiful Team*, its strategy was quasi-military with Médici taking special interest through his envoy Admiral Bastos: three months in preparation, six weeks in altitude in Mexico, shirt and shorts tailored to avoid friction, impressions of feet taken to create individual studded shoes with the correct weight distribution, athletic facilities for NASA astronauts to envy, a payment structure that gave the players little if they progressed but all if they won the final plus exemption from custom duties for all they brought back. And when Brazil finally won, the dictatorship made sure they identified themselves with the popular winners through posters and slogans, dinners and staged photographs. Argentina's generals further south took note. Word is that on the same night in 1978 when they, too, won the World Cup with the team of Luque, Kempes, Ardiles and Villa, they took the final decision to invade the Falklands four years later.

*****

We arrived at the owl's den somewhere off the Zona Bancária. I stumbled out of the car, mega-tired. I was getting sleepier and sleepier while the Brazilians ordered food. Then I smelled *it* and my hair stood up.

'*Tripe?* This is a *tripe* shop?'

'Have you ever tried it?' asked Rubem.

'NO!' I said in horror. 'Even the *thought* makes me puke.'

'It's great after a long drinking session,' said Raul. 'It wakes you up.'

I pulled myself together and tried to make conversation.

'I've met people from all over Brazil,' I said. 'Rio, Bahia, Maranhão, Minas. No one from Brasília. What do you call someone from Brasília anyway? Brasílian?'

Rubem raised his arm.

'Brasiliense,' he said. 'I'm one.'

'You don't get many of them.'

'Not yet. But soon there will be more.'

'You mean you like it here?'

All three looked at me surprised.

'Yes, of course. There are jobs, the standard of living is high, there isn't much crime.'

'But, but everyone else hates it.'

Rubem made a dismissive gesture.

'They don't bother finding out about it.'

'We get to see all the rock groups just like São Paulo and Rio,' said Raul's flatmate. 'We get all the latest movies. We have excellent restaurants. There are three million people in this city, and we all have jobs. *Jobs*. Do you understand?'

The tripe arrived, and I felt queasy. When I saw them tucking in I felt like throwing up.

This is it.

'I need some fresh air,' I said and walked out.

The dewy night air eased my churning stomach as I leaned groggily on Rubem's car.

I want to go home. How can I find a taxi?

I saw a silhouette move out of the restaurant. It was Raul.

'You are OK?' Raul asked.

I shook my head.

'No, I can't stand it in there any longer. I want to go home. Raul, you have to choose: it's the tripe or me.'

He squeezed my hand.

'I already have,' he said. 'I came out, didn't I?'

That felt better. Raul was still avoiding my gaze.

'I'm sorry you didn't like the idea of coming here. I understand if you don't want to go home with me. You don't know me,' he continued. 'But I still want to see you and meet up with you, and I want you to come to my birthday do.'

John, this is a three-time judo champion apologising here.

'You said just the right thing,' I said, echoing his earlier words. I kissed him on the nape of the neck, my mood rebounding like a trampoline.

*****

Did the 1970 World Cup win prolong the grip of the military dictatorship on Brazil? The superficial answer would be 'undoubtedly'. The honest one would be 'about ten years'. Everything has a price in this world.

When Pele's team returned to Brazil they were received in Brasília by President Médici who translated the success of the national team to the military's cry for patriotism, bravery and moral certitude. Tostão, a left-wing intellectual himself who had been quite outspoken about the situation at home, toyed with the idea of boycotting the Médici reception, but in the end fell foul of the myth that sport and politics do not and should not mix, normally perpetrated by the chief desecrators themselves. It must have jarred him to see his name in a song '*Marcha do Tostão*' ('Tostão's March') used for government propaganda. Maybe that's why he left sport for those 20 years.

The untouchable Pelé, another Mineiro like Tostão, was even indirectly accused of 'having set a bad example'. Had he said that the Brazilian people were 'donkeys' and that they didn't know how to vote? Pelé said he was misquoted, although he might have had Cacareco the rhino in mind.

In 1993 a *Playboy* interviewer received an oblique apology:

Playboy: You really hadn't known about the tortures carried out in Brazil?
Pelé: No, I heard some things. On trips with the Santos team, with the Brazilian team, we had some contact occasionally with exiles. Even the mayor of Rio, César Maia, the other day thanked me because I received him once, in Chile. But I was vague about these things. I didn't talk about politics. For this reason I thanked the struggles of Chico Buarque, Gilberto Gil, Caetano Veloso, and Geraldo Vandré, those that figured things out before I figured things out, because I was travelling the world playing soccer for Brazil, for my people.

– Juca Kfouri, *Playboy Brasil*, 1993

– 76 –

'It's Cariocas and Paulistas who are crazy about football,' said Raul. 'The rest of the country only wakes up when there's a World Cup.'

We were sitting on the top floor of the Pátio Brasília in the South Commercial Sector by the Praça de Alimentação. This is a tourist's dream, present in every Brazilian shopping centre: a string of self-service restaurants all within an eyeview's span, embracing a gamut of dishes and sharing a common set of tables and chairs. Raul and I were sitting in front of the House of Seafood but eating the fare of Bom Grillê, specialising in steak and chips. McDonald's had set up shop opposite, but the US multinational was being given a run for its money. Who could resist the Ta Pau next door, a gourmet Chinese self-service where you could choose a little bit of everything, the dream of every glutton confronted with all those sauces; Stroganoff, whose moot sales point was exactly the opposite: different meats – and vegetables – all in the same sauce; Giraffes, a toast-and-grill-shop; Pastine's, specialising in pasta and crêpes; Pizza Mille, the obligatory pizzeria; the Salad Club for the health and butt-conscious and, of course, Torta Bella, where you could buy ultra-saccharine Brazilian sweets by the kilo.

Raul had not stopped talking about football. Although I'm a big fan myself, it *really* felt like having a husband.

'There are very few teams which have mass appeal like your

Manchester Uniteds,' he said. 'Botafogo, Fluminense, Flamengo and Vasco da Gama in Rio de Janeiro and Corinthians or Santos in São Paulo attract the biggest crowds and have a nationwide fan base. But Vasco is the greatest. Do you know its history?'

I admitted defeat.

'It was founded in 1898,' he said.

That old?

'Yes. It is the team made out of the Portuguese immigrants of Rio, which is why it's named after a Portuguese hero,' he said.

I couldn't believe the Brazilians played organised football so early.

'It wasn't a football club then. It was a *sailing* club. In 1915 it merged with another immigrant club, the Lusitânia, and the football club emerged. It moved to the Premier Division in 1923 and won the title. And you know what happened then?'

'What?'

'The rest of the clubs moved to expel Vasco after an investigation into the "social status" of twelve of its players. Vasco had fielded black players and they were good. They were also illiterate. The elites of the other all-white clubs passed a rule not to allow players who couldn't sign their names.'

'What happened?'

'Vasco's chairman paid teachers, and they taught the players how to sign their names. So the other clubs moved to another league and left Vasco out, because they claimed our stadium was sub-standard.'

Raul was as furious as if the incident had happened yesterday.

'But Carioca support made Vasco the most popular team even though it competed in a second-class league. Money poured in to build a new stadium – São Januário, the best and biggest ground in Brazil until Maracanã. Then the other clubs let us in at last.'

I couldn't stop him.

'Vasco is a historic club. It was the team of Getúlio Vargas and Juscelino Kubitschek. The first Brazilian who held the World Cup was a Vasco captain, Bellini, in 1958.'

Oh, that Jules Rimet Golden Cup again.

*****

Upon the referee's final whistle in the Azteca Stadium in 1970, the world erupted. Rivelino fainted. Fans invaded the pitch and took all of Tostão's clothes, stripping him down to his underwear. Paulo César ran to the ball and hid it away. Gérson, deeply religious, cried. Clodoaldo donated his shirt to the church of Nossa Senhora Aparecida. Carlos Alberto lifted the Jules Rimet trophy to be forever Brazil's, having been won – with Pelé in the squad – three times: 1958, 1962 and 1970. It was the last glimpse the world would have of it for the solid gold trophy was promptly stolen. A copy of it was recently bought in an auction by the English FA for $250,000. The original is priceless, but where is it?

There is a persistent story that I have heard recounted a few times. It involves Franz Beckenbauer or Johan Creuff or David Beckham or whichever foreign football ace happens to pass through Rio. Let's choose Beckenbauer: he is kidnapped from his room by three well-dressed men at night. They show great deference and promise they will treat him well. They blindfold him and take him to a car. Next thing Beckenbauer knows, he is in the unlit backstreets of a *favela* stumbling over rubbish and loose stones; he will never be able to recognise the route from the dark maze of streets leading to the unassuming shack he is pushed into.

Inside a man awaits him in semi-darkness. He wears dark glasses, his hands are covered with golden rings and his chest with pendants.

'Welcome Mr Beckenbauer,' says the man in English. 'I've been your fan for a long time. I'd like a picture of you. Please move there.'

Beckenbauer moves to a spot which is suddenly illuminated, and there he is standing next to the stolen Jules Rimet trophy. *Click!* He has his picture taken.

'Thank you Mr Beckenbauer,' says the man again. 'We will let you go now. But if you whisper anything to anyone about this, you and your family will die.'

Urban legend or not?

Well, think: *someone* owns that stolen cup. Who can it be?

*****

The name of the venerable Dom Bosco is once again highly visible in this corner of the centre-west – with reason. On 30 August 1883, he had a dream: *'between the 15th and 20th parallels there will rise a promised land, bringing forth milk and honey with inconceivable riches.'* He was spot on – or was it that maybe Kubitschek had heard of the prophesy and realised it for pertinent religious endorsement? (Kubitschek himself bought land and

made himself rich, but that's another story.) Whatever, one of the first monuments to be inaugurated in Brasília – on New Year's Eve 1957 – was a memorial to the founder of the Salesian Order dead on the 15th parallel. The hype has now reached hysterical proportions: city brochures even speak of a 'new civilisation'. Perhaps because of this, the most striking non-Niemeyer building in Brasília is the Sanctuary of Dom Bosco in 702 SQS, a chapel whose walls consist solely of blue and purple stained-glass arched windows with three sets of white slats open to let in air. It seems that Oscar set a tone for the city, after all: only a large Christ on the Cross reminds you that this is a Christian place of worship, all the more so for the shouts of the pupils outside playing football with less than charitable intentions.

Kubitschek's decision to materialise Dom Bosco's dream turned Brasília into a South American Glastonbury with all the kooky New – and not-so-New – Age cults converging on its magnetic ley lines to be headquartered. The capital's bookshops are awash with titles like *Practical Somnambulism* and *Immortality and Reincarnation*. This is the place with the most UFO sightings outside the United States: there's a particular stretch of the Federal District Highway which apparently all but guarantees you a fleeting sight of a flying saucer.

Raul had by now come out of his shell and was being very competitive even as we walked around the shops of the Conjunto National, the largest shopping centre in Brazil.

'So you've been around the world?' he asked. 'What's the capital of North Korea?'

Hmmm. Not on my list of destinations.

'Pyongyang,' he shouted aloud. 'Now it's your turn.'

'What's the capital of Bolivia?' I asked.

'La Paz,' he said without hesitation.

This trick question gets everyone.

'It is actually Sucre,' I said. 'La Paz is the de facto capital, but in law it is Sucre.'

He looked at me in disbelief, his goatee pointing to the left.

'I don't believe you.'

'Well, I've been there. The first sign you notice approaching the town is *"Welcome to the Capital of Bolivia"*. Then you notice the graffiti against the President.'

Tottenham Hotspur: 1 – Vasco da Gama: 1.

We stood outside a record shop.

'What music do you like?' he asked me.

'Whatever the latest, newest and most interesting music is,' I said. 'Always non-commercial.'

'So you like dance music,' he guessed correctly.

I was going to justify my decision in theoretical and pop-musical dialectic terms but I lacked the vocabulary.

'Yes,' I replied.

'I like hard rock,' he said. 'Have you heard of Legião Urbana?'

I saw a CD in the window recorded during the group's recent live tour.

'Them?' I pointed.

'Yeah. They're great.'

'What do they sound like?'

Raul thought for some time. 'Mmm – like U2, I suppose.'

'Don't you like foreign groups?'

He shook his head.

'No. I'm a Brazilian. I don't understand the lyrics.'

I made a mental note to buy Raul the CD as a present.

....

Things I Don't Like About Brazil #16: Record Shops

I've been to dozens of music shops all over Brazil, and I have despaired every time. Whenever I found a record to buy it has been by pure luck. No record shop – or bookshop for that matter – has discovered the alphabetical display system yet. All CDs – vinyl is rare – are mixed up under the most general of headings such as 'MPB' or 'Foreign Groups'. It's like browsing through someone's personal record collection in a temporal state of disarray due to a house move. If you know what you are looking for, you ask the shop assistant, who has been attending the same corner for years, and who picks out the 77th of a random pack, which miraculously happens to be what you asked for. Maybe that's what I'll do: go to São Paulo, open a record shop and introduce the novel notion of filing under A to Z. Since customers might actually find what they want, I'll make a packet.

....

'So where are we going tomorrow for your birthday?' I asked.

'There's another Lebanese restaurant called Líbanos,' he said. 'It's at …'

'I know where it is,' I interrupted him. 'SQS 206.'

He was impressed.

'How long have you been in Brasília, did you say?'

'Only a few days. But the only other restaurant I have been to is Líbanos.'

Some coincidences I couldn't make up if I wanted to.

'But tomorrow I'll be back late,' I continued. 'I'll be visiting the Valley of the Dawn.'

Raul stopped and made a finger-turning gesture against his temple.

'You are mad,' he said. 'You're going to meet those people? They're not going to let you leave.'

'They can't do that,' I said.

'Oh yes they can,' he said. 'I'll never hear of you again.'

– 77 –

The *Vale do Amanhecer* – the Valley of the Dawn – is, without any rivals, the wackiest place in Brazil, way over the top even for the hippy goofiness of New Age Brasília. This is a community of 20,000 souls outside the city of Planaltina, one hour by bus from Brasília through the scrub and spindly trees of the flat, red-brown, sun-baked earth of the central *cerrado*. I travelled with two guitar-strumming Brazilian students from Belo Horizonte who had an impromptu bus argument about their favourite saint. ('St Francis of Assisi!', 'No, St Paul is best!', 'St Francis!', 'St Paul!') They were so absorbed, they didn't even blink as we approached the Disney-park setting of the village. Once in, however, they were as bemused by the spectacle as I was. They should paraphrase Dante and put up a sign at the entrance: *'Abandon All Reason Ye Who Enter Here.'*

A giant white – and rusting – hexagonal star with an arrow through it was supported haphazardly on two green metal poles next to a yellow-purple elliptic 0 with an Indian cartoon face at its bottom. They were both overshadowed by a giant cardboard image of Jesus. We were surrounded by several gaudily painted, crudely created 'temples', clashing wildly with each other as if an infant had been let loose with plywood, glue and several buckets of paint. And I haven't described the people yet.

Before I could gather my thoughts I was approached by an elderly bespectacled woman in a long red skirt and plimsolls. She was wearing a yellow and purple sash across her black blouse on which several badges were sewn or pinned. I immediately sensed she was harmless.

'Are you a visitor?' she asked.

'I am,' I said. 'All the way from London. My name is John.'

She puffed up. 'From London?' she repeated.

'Indeed.'

'And you want to find out about the Valley?' I could see she was overwhelmed.

'I do. And I want to take pictures if I can.'

'You can outside. But not inside the temple. Flashes will affect the mediums.'

I started snapping at a gathering of people holding hands around a table on which two large candles were lit. The men wore either brown and yellow capes or black and white waistcoats with a black cross wrapped in a white band at the back. I could be forgiven for thinking that they were Vasco supporters wearing the club's colours.

'What are they doing?' I asked. 'And why are they dressed so …' – I coughed while the right word dropped on my tongue – '… *unusually*?'

'My name is Maria,' she said, reading from a mental script. 'I'll be your guide. I'll tell you everything about us – the laws, the keys and the ceremonies. Tonight we have a complex ceremony called randy.'

'Randy?'

'Yes. These men are Jaguars. The women are Nymphs.'

'Are you a Nymph?'

She turned to me with what-does-he-know condescension.

'No, I'm a Centurion,' she explained patiently.

'As in ancient Rome?'

She beamed.

'Exactly! Here we believe in Jesus, but we also believe in the religions of the ancients and of the African slaves.'

'You believe in everything.'

'Exactly.'

An old woman passed by, a dream in her purple dress adorned by sewn-on white Stars of David and – rare sartorial feat in this environment – a *matching* witch's hat.

'Is she a Nymph?' I asked.

Maria beamed.

'She is,' she said. 'You are learning quickly.'

The whole tawdry cheapskate spectacle of the Valley of the Dawn, which still packs them in from the Nordeste and the centre-west, is the creation of a self-styled clairvoyant called Tia Neiva, born Neiva Chavez Zelaya in Sergipe and remarkably a lorry driver by profession. Her 1970s self-erected house is being preserved by the cult as a museum. It is pretentiously called the Casa Grande despite its sloping ceilings, leaning

walls and cement floors. I mean the loo itself had not been up to scratch even in the seventies, but compared to holes in the ground, a sitting toilet is a throne.

'Isn't she lovely?' Maria asked me in the bedroom, pointing at a full-length picture of Tia Neiva next to a Siamese cat lampshade. The bed was scarlet red – like Tia's lipstick.

'Yes,' I lied. I could only see a vain old battleaxe who applied her make-up with a spatula and whose frock, tight on her hips, made her look like a baby Zeppelin. I wondered how she could fit that bottom on that paltry toilet seat.

'Tia Neiva heard the call of Father White Arrow in 1957,' started Maria.

'Who is Father White Arrow?'

'*Pai Seta Branca* is the spirit we believe in.' She showed me one of her badges. 'White Arrow is a Spirit of Light, like Jesus, Krishna and St Francis of Assisi. Tia Neiva founded the Church of White Arrow in 1959, two years after she had her grand enlightenment at the holy age of thirty-three.'

'When did Tia Neiva die?' I asked.

'She *desincarnated*,' Maria emphasised the word, 'on the fifteenth of November, 1986. But we still adhere to her teachings.'

'And what might these be?'

'We believe in the unification of beliefs, separation of the spirit from the soul, and the scientific view of religion.'

'Scientific?' I exclaimed.

'Yes, the ectoplasm.'

'The ectoplasm?'

'Exactly. The ectoplasm is the energy responsible for the contact between the physical world and the spiritual world. Its manipulation is purely technical.'

We left Tia Neiva's house, heading to the main temple. I noticed several girls dressed as bumblebees who were pestering some cult members.

'What are they doing?' I asked.

'They are collecting signatures from the spirits to release themselves from their bodies,' replied Maria and gracefully accepted the ruled notebooks the bumblebees eagerly placed in her hands. 'They need 2,250 completed sheets for their souls' liberation.'

'Can I sign it?' I asked.

'I'm afraid not. You are not a liberated spirit.'

'So what happens if the same person signs the notebook twice?'

Maria thought for a little while.

'That never happens,' she finally decided.

I've heard that one before …

*****

I can't wait to pass the bone of wisdom on and explain the doctrine which centres around the messages White Arrow kept beaming down to Tia Neiva every New Year's Eve until her 'desincarnation'.

It seems that 32,000 years ago a group of missionaries arrived on Earth, called the Equitumans. They were 10–13 feet tall and set up the planetary system for us, including the zodiac. They lived in the Andes but disappeared during a cataclysm which destroyed their civilisation, centred around Lake Titicaca. Around 5,000 years later we had the civilisation of the Tumuchis. These were beautiful people who harnessed all cosmic forces in the triangle Earth-Sun-Moon. All signs of their presence were covered by the Pacific Ocean and only one point of their culture still exists: Easter Island. The giant heads they left behind match the pyramids in Egypt and Central America and are celestial machines. After 6,000 more years another race, the Jaguars, came about. As the Equitumans ruled over the physical world and the Tumuchis over the cosmic energy, the Jaguars came to impose discipline. We have Rome and Ancient Greece, Spain, Portugal and the conquistadors. The great spirits then were Jesus Christ and St Francis of Assisi (hey, the guy's, like, top billing in Planaltina) who were the reincarnations of the Big Jaguar, also later reincarnated as the Indian *cacique* White Arrow. He taught us, through Tia Neiva, about the three Kingdoms of Man's Nature: the physical plexus, the micro plexus and the macro plexus – body, spirit and soul.

'So White Arrow was an Indian?'

'Exactly! An Indian who lived in this area.'

I could now recognise an Indian headdress on her badge. I thought it was a badly drawn cartoon.

'He's the one who, with love, stopped the conquistadors coming to Brazil, keeping it Portuguese,' Maria added gleefully.

Now the period of Christ and St Francis is coming to an end. A New Age will rise and those guided by the Church of White Arrow will see the Light of the Equituman force, the Tumuchi science and the Jaguar actualisation. Maria pointed triumphantly at the hexagonal star, shining under a good cover of aluminium foil.

'How did Tia Neiva know all this?' I asked.

'She studied in Tibet,' replied Maria. 'Many times. With Grand Master Humaham.'

My respect for Tia Neiva climbed a few notches.

'That's cool,' I said. 'Especially now that the Chinese are occupying it. It must have been so difficult to get a multiple entry visa.'

Maria squirmed.

'Tia Neiva did not need a visa,' she said. 'She was transported to Tibet in her sleep.'

I see.

*****

Inside, the temple was hot, sweaty and full of pastel colours, lights and curtains. As soon as I got my bearings I had to move aside to let pass a cortège of twelve chanting nymphs with plastic lances.

'They keep the place cleansed,' said Maria, answering my puzzled look.

She pointed at some chairs on the wall. 'Here we work,' she continued. 'Those are for mediums who await their call.' In an enclosure 'patients' were sitting while berobed cult members held their hands over them. 'Anyone can come here for a consultation. It costs nothing. We ask for nothing. We respect all religions: we treat Catholics, Evangelicals, Umbandistas.'

'Can't they go to the doctor?'

'They can't afford a doctor.'

'What if there is something physically wrong and they need an operation?'

'Our work is complementary. We heal them spiritually and sometimes this is enough.'

One member sat on a high chair looking a bit spaced-out.

'The President of the Day,' she said. 'We have a different one each day. He concentrates for everyone else.'

She opened a curtain.

'And here is Father White Arrow. *A Presença Divina*.'

I looked astonished at the mixture of an Egyptian god in a Sioux feather headdress holding a white lance. It didn't look imposing. It looked as cheap as the trinkets in the Temple of Oxumarê in Salvador.

'Oxalá, St Francis of Assisi, White Arrow – they are one,' she said.

'And those?' I pointed at seven paintings of women on the wall.

'The seven princesses of Mãe Yara,' sighed Maria. 'They lived once all together in Pompeii, but were buried under the ashes of Vesuvius: Julema, Janaina, the Twin Souls, Vovô Agripina and Vozinha Marilú. Plus,' she stopped for emphasis, 'Princess Iracema. Isn't she lovely?'

A literary character by a writer of Ceará, a name for a little black girl in the streets of Salvador, a revered saint in Brasília. Is this one culture or many?

I moved aside to let the chanting cortège pass once more.

'This is the Recovery Room, where patients recuperate,' she said, opening another curtain. Several tired faces looked away. 'And here is the Red Room of the Induction where magnetic currents take away the vibes of envy and evil. They polarise the positive and the negative.' Where she saw giant magnets I saw carelessly drawn meanders, peeling cracked benches and a Jesus portrait of dubious artistic merit – put mildly, not quite stuff to display next to a Michelangelo.

We stepped outside. The randy ceremony was proceeding more slowly than a t'ai chi exercise set.

'What are they doing?' I asked.

'They are observing karmic law,' said Maria.

I looked at my watch. It was getting dark, and I had Raul's meal to go to.

'I have to catch the bus back,' I said.

'Oh, but you won't see the lake of Yemanjá,' she said plaintively.

'Yemanjá?'

'Yes, up the hill. We also have the lake of the Estrela Candente where we perform the Rite of Unification.'

I was out-kitsched.

'I'm going to a birthday party,' I said.

Maria, as a Brazilian, could empathise with that.

'Is there anything else you want to know?'

Actually there was.

'What about you, Maria? Where do you come from?'

She smiled.

'Pernambuco. Recife. I left ten years ago to join this community.'

'Any children?'

'Five sons. Two in São Paulo. Three here.'

I made a point of giving her some money.

'No, thank you. We don't accept money.'

'How do you live?'

'We are self-sufficient,' she said.

Like ... like ...

The sun was setting, and I could see the bus coming along.

This must have been what Canudos was like more than a century ago ...

'And are you happy?'

'Yes,' she said emphatically and smiled sweetly.

Of course. You come from a poor background and you get to be part of a community with a purpose. You get to dress in bright clothes and play *Carnaval* every day. You are a Nymph or a Jaguar, a Healer or a Centurion. You get to save people because, yes, miracles may not happen, but people who experience miracles do exist. You are not nobody anymore – oh, no, instead you're *better* than everyone else because you are part of the select few who comprehend and experience the karma of the universe.

Tell me, what's wrong with that?

– 78 –

The birthday table at Líbanos had three girls all on one side. On my right sat Raul with Rubem and at the head of the table, as if to say grace, sat a stocky middle-aged man. I gave Raul the CD and felt his emotion.

'*Legal*,' he said, beaming, and showed it to the girls.

'*Legal*,' they agreed and stared at me deeply in that inimitable female enquiring manner.

'I'm not out to the girls,' Raul whispered. 'Only the blonde one knows because she is good friends with Rubem. I don't really know the others.'

I shook my head.

'You tell one, you tell all,' I said.

'You think so?'

'I think so.'

'And him?' I pointed at the stocky man.

'Oh, Silvano is gay,' said Raul. 'He's a priest.'

'Everyone's a priest here,' I countered.

'He's a *Catholic* priest.'

I turned my attention to the priest. Perhaps he would say grace after all. But no, the *kibbés* arrived and he remained silent, thank god. Or, I suppose, *not* thank god.

'Difficult to tell without a cassock,' I said.

'Rubem knew him from the gay scene,' said Raul. 'And then Rubem turned up at a wedding and Silvano was conducting the ceremony.' He chuckled. We both chuckled.

'How do you know Raul?' one of the girls asked me.

'I … met him here,' I said.

The priest spoke.

'He's Raul's boyfriend,' he said.

Confession can't be how I remember it.

I pinched Raul's thigh under the table.

'Your secret's out,' I whispered. 'Silvano –'

'I heard,' he said. 'That's OK.'

'And I'm your boyfriend, now, am I?'

'Why, do you mind?'

The girls saved us both from a domestic.

'We'd already guessed,' they said. 'A CD. Such an expensive present. How long have you known each other?'

'A few days.'

They exchanged knowing looks.

'And I'm leaving Brasília tomorrow,' I added.

More looks confirmed they were right first time: *now that won't last.*

'Are you coming back?'

That was a difficult question.

'It's here that Brazil truly exists,' said Rubem.

They all nodded in agreement like members of a cult.

'What do you mean?'

'Here is where you can meet people from all corners of the country.'

'But do you know how other Brazilians view Brasília? As an expensive mistake, which has created another elite cut off from real life.'

'Brasília is a wonderful place,' said Rubem. 'It's now a large city but you have space, the traffic moves, we now have a metro and we're equally close to São Paulo and Rio, Salvador and Belo Horizonte –'

'You're equally *far* from everywhere,' I corrected him.

'Whatever. Life is good here. I would never move.'

'So why do people rush to the airport on Friday evenings to leave town for the weekend and return home? That's what the guidebooks say.'

'This is untrue. I've never seen it. The clubs are full every weekend.'

The priest intervened.

'But more than this,' he said, 'Brasília *was* Brazil from the day it was built.'

I shook my head. 'I have seen Brazil,' I said. 'And Brasília is not it. It is only part of the mosaic.'

And part of the rebus I have created.

'So,' said Raul who, like the others, was annoyed at my questioning tone, 'what do you think of Brazil?'

I side-stepped the question.

'What do *you* think?' I asked.

'It's my country. I love my country. Brazilians love their country more than anything else.'

'I don't like it when people say you have to love your own country more than anything else. It's too exclusive,' I countered.

For where would that leave me?

'No,' said Raul, burping the beer he'd just gulped, 'really, what do you think of Brazil? You have been all over. You must have an opinion.'

'It's a wonderful country with wonderful people,' I said. 'But it has problems, like all Third World countries.'

'You think Brazil is Third World?'

'Undoubtedly.'

'BRAZIL IS THE LAND OF THE FUTURE!' cried Raul, chest rising as he uttered the famous slogan-cum-conviction.

' ... and always will be,' I added the ironic coda affixed by the cynics.

No one was laughing. Goodness – there are still believers in Kubitschek's dream after all. I can't remember what I said *exactly* that night as we drank more and more, but the feelings had nestled inside my chest for so long that the words came out like a *sertão* flash flood ...

*****

Brazil is, by all comparisons, an industrialised country. In terms of GDP it is bigger than Russia or India and has reached the top G10. But it turns round on their heads those twentieth-century beliefs that industrialisation means progress. In Brazil's case it meant enrichment for the elites and for the foreign lenders. Its debt, restructured and re-restructured, accounts for more than $200 billion and the interest on it is nearly $50 billion every year. The military borrowed heavily when rates were low; but now the chickens that are coming home to roost are all feeble and unhealthy and worse: the chicken coop itself is mortgaged to some absent landlord. The poor masses do not have savings in order to create capital for native banks to substitute the foreign lenders. Social justice is not only a moral duty as the MST asserts – it makes overall economic sense. It is in Brazil's interests to see the enrichment of the poor through tax policies; they won't be buying Calvin Klein underwear – they will be spending their money on cheap local goods. Turning the poor into aspiring middle classes will bridge the abyss of fear and mistrust apparent even to the most casual of observers and will strengthen the democracy, for in Brazil it is the powerful who fear the weak.

This democracy, on paper, is remarkable: the best youth laws in the world; the most modern of constitutions; a surprisingly effective and proactive Aids programme for the Third World to envy; exceptional native protection legislation; colour integration in the society ahead of any other country; non-discrimination laws which would make many European countries blush. But herein lies the problem: this is all on paper. There is a vast difference between what is written in law and how things work in reality, for in day-to-day life everything operates with brown envelopes. Corruption is institutionalised: from the policeman in Rio in cahoots with the *favela* drug lords to the São Paulo businessman who fiddles his taxes and from the Brasília civil servant who expects tips to supplement his or her income to the Nordestino politician who siphons money to private accounts. This is also a society based on fear of loss of relative power which turns routine petty corruption into matters more sinister: embezzlement, murder, massacre.

To top it all, what laws are adhered to in Paraná are ignored in Pará, so to speak. Brazil was kept united, but regionalism thrives. Maybe the common recollection of the fictional story of Iracema or the historical martyrdom of Tiradentes has created a common culture – but they are far from creating a common mentality. Laws are passed in Brasília and, like the Portuguese laws of old, ignored in the periphery. An equilibrium between central and state power has been reached, but only temporarily. There are few truly national party machines, which makes personality-based coalitions between local power-brokers disruptive, disabling and disengaging. It is no wonder that it is only in Brasília that I found people whose heart first encompasses Brazil; there is not much else locally in space or in time to compete with one's loyalties.

*****

'So there's nothing good about Brazil?' said a long-faced Raul after I'd finished.

I went back to the Valley of the Dawn.

*****

I stood inside the technicolor crime-against-taste that is the room of the *Pretos Velhos* listening to Maria. 'You worship the old slaves who died?' I asked. 'Like candomblé?'

'Every religion should worship such beings,' said Maria. 'These were spirits who, against the odds, reached spiritual fulfilment in the harshest of conditions.'

It was then that the cynical gringo stopped jotting things down in his pad and looked up. For the first time Maria seemed less daft and more sagacious as she touched upon an extraordinary philosophical domain where candomblé meets Zen, Brazilian-style.

This is the tale I heard.

Among the slaves there were a number of reincarnations of Jaguars, Equitumans and Tumuchis because – and here comes the crunch – slavery was ultimately *liberating*. The elimination of personality with hard work, the corporal pain through the whip, and the loss of identity through humiliation, contributed to the internalisation of the spirit and the discovery of the Jaguar within.

We don't know who they were, but we know that two benefic spirits, Pai Zé Pedro and Pai João were slaves in two incarnations, each within 372 years. They appeared to their masters as useless, ill, waiting to die, yet continuously slipping from the claws of the Reaper. In reality they reached inside their souls to their past lives and became experts in magic charms. They inspired slaves in the whole of Brazil during their African rituals through telepathy, possession and dance. Although in *fazendas* hundreds of miles away from each other, Pai Zé Pedro and Pai João communicated regularly between themselves: Pai Zé Pedro was the mystic; Pai João the practical mind. They preached among the slaves and led them to the True Path: they showed them that Christianity and the African religions are one and the same and that their suffering made them stronger, not weaker. This is why the slaves died so quickly, within an average of seven years; not because they had been worked to death, but because they had been perfected. This wasn't a period of darkness – it was a period of greatness.

I flinched. Only in Brazil, with that logic-defying optimism of its people, would the slaves be seen as anything else but exploited human cattle. What Maria was saying was that certain slaves, through suffering, became Buddhas. And because we don't know who they were, we worship them all, like the Tomb of the Unknown Soldier.

So, ladies and gentlemen, here is the quintessence of Brazil: the magical ability to turn the bleak into the brilliant.

*****

'Are you coming in?' I asked Raul as Rubem parked his car outside Hotel Bristol. Our 2 a.m. arrival attracted the attention of the half-sleeping taxi drivers and our voices aroused the curiosity of the streetwalking prostitutes touting for clients. Behind the hotel doors, I saw the guards pin us down with their gaze.

'No, I don't think so. You're leaving tomorrow, aren't you?'

'Yes. To Belo Horizonte.'

Raul looked at me sleepily.

'Will you call my mobile when you arrive at the airport tomorrow?'

I shrugged my shoulders.

'OK. Why?'

'I want to feel the moment,' said Raul.

Silence. Every parting brings an alternative universe to mind; Univers04/05/06. Everything has a price in this world, and I have also paid mine.

'Thanks for the present.'

'This way you'll never forget me,' I said.

'Don't *you* forget *me*,' he said.

'I won't.'

Raul passed me an empty Carlton cigarette packet. On it he had scribbled a poem.

> For all that I cried
> I still cry.
> But I am crying
> So that you don't have a commitment.

'You know,' I said awkwardly, 'I don't really support any Brazilian team. I might as well start supporting Vasco.'

Raul grabbed my hand and, with all the might of a three-time judo champion, pulled me close to his body, embraced me and kissed me passionately under the curious eyes of the prostitutes, the hotel porters and the taxi drivers, until Rubem put an end to it by honking his horn.

'Now you won't forget me,' said Raul and sat next to Rubem, who sped away rapidly.

*****

Next day Vasco beat Botafogo 7–0 in a historic Maracanã win and my heart quivered with unfamiliar longing.

Chapter 17

Closure – The Dance (Rio Reprise)

So to my will-o'-the-wisp: what is there in Brazil we are missing in the West?

You must surely now ask in return – which Brazil? There are many to choose from, and I have provided you with a dozen different answers. Even to have asked that early question seems now as futile a generalisation as saying that Brazil is *Carnaval*, the Amazon, coffee and football: the nation's one-dimensional stereotype.

And yet there is a single unmistakable attribute.

....

The Words You'll Need

borrachudo = *tick*
cais = *dock*
Faço programa = *I'm on the game*
feijoada = *black bean stew, a staple of Brazilian Sunday lunches*
Lançamento da Exposição Fotográfica = *inauguration of a photo exhibition*
maconha = *marijuana*

....

– 79 –

The practical reason Kubitschek built Brasília followed the same argument as the creation of Belo Horizonte, taking over from Ouro Preto many decades earlier: Rio, the old Brazilian capital, could not expand. Yes, it was still a cultural springboard and a most desirable place to live, but it was this natural beauty that became its downfall. Hemmed in by hills and surrounded by *favelas*, its old centre around Praça 15 Novembro reeking of the musty smell of cobweb anachronism, Rio in the 1950s was thought to follow the example of Recife and Salvador: a city of yesterday unworthy of leading the 'country of the future' into its sixth century of existence. The 1965 edition of the *South American Handbook* reflects the prevalent thinking: '*On April 21 1960, Rio de Janeiro ceased to be the federal capital of Brazil; it had outrun its water and power supply and had not another foot of soil to build upon.*' In the same edition, a map of central Rio casually displays the roads around Avenida Rio Branco and Avenida

Presidente Vargas; Flamengo and Botafogo were middle-class residential suburbs no traveller would be interested in. Under 'excursions near Rio de Janeiro' the first item is a day-trip to the beach in Copacabana. Ipanema and Leblon do not even feature in a map of the surroundings; that Girl from Ipanema must have been walking lonely, indeed. A picture of Barra da Tijuca by Malcolm Slesser from 1967 shows another empty coastal strip. *'The Barra is a sand-bar of twelve miles cradling a swampy lagoon. A river emerges at one end of the Barra. Off shore stand a number of rocky islands and leftwards towards Rio city huge moss-hung walls of rock soar in one sweep to the shoulder of Pedra da Gavea even more dramatic from here than from seaward [...] The beach is quiet compared with the city's other eighteen beaches.'*

Today almost half of Rio's population live in condominiums beyond that Pedra da Gavea; the four-block strip of Copacabana has one of the highest densities of inhabitants per square mile in the world; and tourists may never venture north of the Rio Sul Shopping Centre except to climb Sugarloaf Mountain and Corcovado. The same technology that built Brasília breathed new life into Rio: the restrictive hills were burrowed through to make large tunnels. In the 1930s the Copacabana Palace stood alone; the drilling of the first Old Tunnel in the 1940s pushed the population southwards and weekend villas started appearing nearby. More tunnels were constructed including the massive Rebouças below Corcovado to Ipanema and the smaller, yet all-important, Joá Tunnel to Barra. Brasília was designed to function around the automobile, but the same automobile freed Rio from its confines and allowed the population to vote with their feet. The planners were wrong: Rio proved to be alive and kicking. Its centre of gravity moved to the Zona Sul; the professional classes relaxed in Barra, safe in the thought that the lack of public transport kept the poor out of sight; the tourists came in their thousands to bathe at Copacabana; the bohemian set moved from Lapa to Ipanema. Rio de Janeiro kept its pre-eminence as the core of Brazil's soul and increased its bewitching allure.

There is one particular place I cherish the most. Every time I've been to the city of all marvels, I end up on a bench facing Corcovado at the edge of Lagoa, and as I see the sun disappearing behind the statue of Christ and the lights come on in Gavea and around the lagoon, I make a solemn promise to myself: that I will return once more.

So here I'm back where it all began.

I arrived in Rio on the eve of May Day. Jim and Glória weren't home; I found out later they had taken a vacation in Búzios. They weren't expecting me as I had returned on impulse: I was supposed to be flying to São Paulo and back to London, but I had changed my plans at the last moment. I tried to call François who was waiting for me in São Paulo – not there. Ford: not there. I booked myself into an Ipanema hotel, negotiating a good deal since it was covered with scaffolding.

The receptionist thought I would be satisfied with his reassurance: 'They finish at six in the evening and don't start until ten in the morning,' he said.

'That's precisely when I intend to be asleep,' I informed him and cut another 100 reais from the overall package.

Everywhere I turned there were posters for B.I.T.C.H., one of the big happenings in the Terra Encantada Park outside Rio; tens of thousands were expected in a rave to beat all raves with a ghost train, rollercoaster rides and a tropical surf swimming pool. I was tempted, but how would I get there at midnight and, more importantly, how would I get back?

I went to Le Boy instead, which was packed to the rafters. I had to peek through a go-go dancer's legs at the bar to get served.

*****

You may have sailed in the bay of Istanbul and taken a trip up the Bosporus and down the Sea of Marmara admiring the onion domes of the mosques in the seven-hilled old town; you may have gazed upon San Francisco Bay and the fog-covered Golden Gate Bridge on a balmy night enhanced by the skyscraper lights; you may have been smitten by the winding shore of Sydney Harbour or the Nordic patrician charm of the islands that make up Stockholm: you have seen nothing if the sea breeze has not caressed your brow in the Bay of Guanabara, its sensual mountain curves emphasised by the lambent luxuriance of the vegetation, the celebrated beauty of its beaches and the colours of its coves dancing in front of your eyes.

Visitors flock to the jagged peak of Corcovado not to kneel in front of the 125-foot-high statue of Christ the Redeemer but to admire the view from Maracanã to Leblon. 'Corcovado in the morning, Sugarloaf Mountain at night' is the standard tourist mantra. Whether below in the bay, or from a bird's view up high, the visual experience of Rio is so overwhelming, it has drowned Brazil itself in the same way that the Amazon has become the focus of rainforest activism: it inspires images and invokes ideas implanted upon us from myth, legend and hearsay.

Rio has a similar fabled quality that towers over the rest of Brazil: Copacabana, Ipanema, Flamengo, Sugarloaf Mountain roll off the tongue as familiar as Piccadilly, Hyde Park, Victoria and Soho. Yet a foreigner's Rio is very different today from 100 or even 50 years ago. This was what our Charles Domville-Fife had to say as he took a walk in the centre of 1905 Rio – a walk which would still be familiar to a tourist in the 1950s:

Towards the centre of Rio runs Rua do Ouvidor, the Regent Street of Rio de Janeiro. It is a very narrow thoroughfare and the buildings are of a mixed character, the majority being palatial modern structures typically European in style though here and there one comes across a dilapidated and doomed habitation of the colonial days. The paving of this street is very good. It is here that the Brazilian ladies do their morning shopping. Tailors, dressmakers and jewellers or general stores occupy the ground floor of almost all the houses [...]

From narrow though busy Rua do Ouvidor let us pass into the new Broadway, known as the Avenida Central which completely traverses the City. This fine thoroughfare is 35 metres wide and just over two thousand metres in length. It is well paved and lighted by electricity. Down the centre of the roadway are small shelters similar to those which form such a useful feature of London's traffic-blocked streets. Within these refuges trees and arc lamps are placed alternately. The sidewalks which are illuminated electrically and by gas will shortly also be given the shade of foliage. The houses fronting on the street are all that can be desired as regards size and architecture and the general aspect of the avenue with its domes and parapets is strongly reminiscent of a London thoroughfare.

The Avenue terminates on the sea-front where it joins the more picturesque marine wall which follows the contour of the bay for over six kilometres. Avenida Beira-Mar or the sea-side avenue is as fine a promenade as one could wish to see. Beginning at the commercial end of the city and stretching along the front of the bay to Botafogo, the Kensington of Rio, this drive is an immensely broad level way upon which no less than four parallel footpaths or drives have been constructed. Three separate rows of trees line both sides of the two main walks and in the centre are gardens and lawns prettily laid out. In the foreground shine the blue waters of the bay sheltered by the rugged coast and surmounted by the great cone known as the Sugar Loaf, while in the far distance worthily framing so fair a picture rise the green hills and beyond them the rugged scales of the Cordillera do Mar. At the West End of this magnificent promenade, which like the Avenida Central is lighted by electricity, there runs at right-angles to the seafront another magnificent roadway, the fine Botafogo Avenue.

Today Avenida Beira Mar does not go by the seaside anymore. Santos Dumont Airport has been built on reclaimed land and the island of Vilegaignon – now the Brazilian Naval College – is connected with the mainland by a landfill, its name the sole reminder of the dream of an Antarctic France. Beira Mar passes by the picturesque marina of Glória where catamarans leave for Guanabara Bay trips and past the simple monument to the dead of World War II containing Brazil's Tomb of the Unknown Warrior. It hugs the open park of Flamengo where Cariocas cycle, jog or hustle on 250 acres reclaimed from the sea in 1965. The Avenida ends in the bay of Botafogo, the poor man's bathing ground. If you follow the coast around you reach Urca, which is possibly the best example of suburban Rio before industrial exploitation, poverty, overpopulation, immigration and crime transformed the urban environment. Urca is a low-rise, open-balconied, small-rainforest-in-your-backyard suburb which has been unable to expand because it stretches under the weather-beaten granite rock of Sugarloaf Mountain. As for the famous Broadway, the Avenida Central – it has been dwarfed by the Avenida Vargas which trawls masses of workers to the poorer western suburbs and finishes in the legendary Maracanã, a great disappointment: cement never looked so septic for lack of upkeep outside the old Iron Curtain.

....

Brazilian Anecdotes #1: A Game of Football in Moinhos Do Vento

This is the chic park in Porto Alegre in the smart part of town where the streets are called Goethe and Schiller rather than Aranha or da Silva. This is where I was supposed to find the Brazil-Aryan beau-monde jogging in their expensive designer tracksuits, T-shirts clinging sexily with sweat. With my luck I bumped into a group from the local Fatbusters chapter who nearly ran me over – their stopping distance once on the trot is considerable. I relaxed among flowerbeds and ducks in landscaped lakes. Moinhos do Vento was pleasant, green and musty with a windmill providing a Dutch touch, like Amsterdam's Vondelpark without the marijuana clouds. There, a gaucho love triangle: a boyfriend, girlfriend and their *chimarrão* thermos flask were walking the dog; they were sitting on a bench sipping their maté and kissing each other (exclude the dog, but include the thermos flask).

On the other side of this oddly shaped park there were playing fields and oh – a football match was on. The stands were filled with a few hundred fans in a state of animation. Maracanã this wasn't, but the spitting and shouting supporters didn't care.

'Who's playing?' I asked the one who expectorated the least.

'Juventus and Milan,' he told me impatiently.

I smiled uncomprehendingly. His more fearsome neighbour took more time to explain: 'Juventus *Alvorado* versus Milan *Santa Rosa*.'

It was nil–nil and quite exciting. The Moinhos do Vento pitch consisted of perfectly groomed grass tapering down into a surrounding ditch. There was seating for about 500 spectators, a barbed-wire fence running around the field and proper changing rooms and toilets. This was a lower division cup match; the labyrinthine Brazilian football schedule is full of Cups, national and local. I asked why there were two referees and no linesmen playing, and I received a long answer in staccato gaucho, which I didn't understand. And then …

'Goooooooooooooooooooooooooooooooooooooooooooooooooooooooooooooooooooool!' my neighbour roared – the final 'l' suspected rather than pronounced, since in shouting it's the vowels that matter.

A good move by Juventus Alvorado had ended with the ball being headed in by No 9 who desperately needed a haircut. Around me the Alvorado fans were delirious. I was thrilled. The goal had ignited the play. Milan Santa Rosa won a corner. I moved closer. Corner taken. The Juventus defence blindly kicked the ball out of play to the spectator stand.

In front of one spectator in particular.

As the ball landed by me, I stopped it instinctively with my foot.

The two referees, the 22 players, the managers, subs and 200-odd spectators looked at me, and I wished the earth could swallow me *now*.

I tried to throw the ball onto the pitch – and I would have done, dear reader, I would have done, if it weren't for that odd wire sticking out on top of the fence. As it happened, the ball hit the wire and fell down into the surrounding ditch with a large *splash*! The players made sour faces. One spectator who had been drenched by the splash picked up the ball and more manfully kicked it onto the pitch.

My only involvement in a Brazilian football game and I fuck up royally. Thankfully, help was at hand.

'*Argentino*?' asked the guy next to me.

'*Si*,' I replied and clapped. '*Boca Juniors! Maradona!*'

He laughed mockingly.
I am a master of disguise.

....

I'll stick my neck out and claim that the most artistically significant building in the whole of Rio is the monastery of São Bento, sandwiched between the modern seminary grounds, a steep climb from Praça Mauá. Inside, you can find *O Salvador*, the masterpiece of Brazil's first major painter Frei Ricardo de Pilar, and the work of the most important pre-Aleijadinho sculptor, Portuguese-born Domingos de Conceição. São Bento has the best examples in Brazil of the original European baroque, which preceded the Mineiro flourish of the eighteenth century: the gilded wooden sculptures of Madonna and Child on the temple, São Bento himself and the later retable of St Gertrude. Sadly a garish restoration in 1875–1878 almost destroyed the interior, but if you want to whet your appetite for Ouro Preto and Olinda, spend some time in exploring Rio's Benedictine monastery.

The *fin-de-previous-siécle* buildings in Rua do Ouvidor have fallen into disuse and now feel like Domville-Fife's dilapidated colonial buildings did in 1905. I walked in the opposite direction towards Praça 15 Novembro, *Praça Quinze* as it is popularly known, still one of the most impressive parts of old Rio. The palace of Ilha Fiscal – now a navy base – green and Cinderella-dainty, lies across the barrier where a soldier requests your papers to let you pass. This is where Dom Pedro II gave his last great ball on 9 November 1888. The crème de la crème of Rio – 4,500 of them – attended the dinner, prepared by 90 chefs and served by 150 waiters: 18 peacocks, 500 turkeys, 64 pheasants, 800 kilos of large prawns, 300 hams, 1,300 chickens, 1,200 boxes of asparagus, 800 truffle jars, 12,000 ice creams and 500 plates of assorted sweets were consumed and 10,000 litres of beer and 258 cases of champagne were drunk. Dom Pedro II himself stumbled drunkenly and joked: 'The Monarchy trips but never falls.' Six days later he was deposed – on the date that gives its name to the square. I want to believe that the generals postponed the coup d'état until after the ball so that they could all have a last extravagant party. It would be the Brazilian way.

I turn north to the best-known church of Rio: Nossa Senhora de Candelária at the bottom of Avenida Vargas. This time it's not the church I've come to see. Outside, in a small, landscaped traffic island stands a cross. On 23 July 1993 a gang of vigilantes opened fire on fifty street children and youths sleeping rough, right here. Paulo Roberto de Oliveira (11 years old), Anderson Tomé Pereira (13), Marcelo Cândido de Jesus (14), Valderino Miguel de Almeida (14), 'Gambazinho' (17), 'Nogento' (17), Paulo José da Silva (18) and Marcos Antônio Alves da Silva (20) all died. Four boys died in their sleep. Another as he ran away. Three were abducted and then shot dead nearby. One, Wagner dos Santos, was left for dead, but revived and was the main prosecution witness years later. A rare prosecution, I should add, for unlike other shootings, this was very high-profile because of the symbolic significance of Rio's most beloved church. Nine men, all but one military policemen, were implicated. One gave himself up, but the rest were identified by survivors. No protection was given to the witnesses who continued to sleep rough, threatened by police, until a further attempt on Wagner dos Santos's life, which left part of his face paralysed, persuaded the authorities to find him a new identity abroad. During the subsequent investigation a nasty figure emerged, a nefarious policeman called 'Friday the 13th' because of his blood lust and the terror he instilled in his child victims. Four arrests, two trials, several Amnesty International reports, and many years later, only two policemen have been convicted and sent to jail. So this is the last thing I don't like about Brazil: the hunting of the street children and their systematic extermination by vigilantes and death squads with the passive collusion, the connivance and sometimes the applause of the public.

With the tumult of the cars reverberating in my ears, I read a plaque under the cross that said: '*In the early morning of 23/7/93 in this square eight adolescents were assassinated while they were asleep. This cross was erected by the children of St Martin's and is a symbol of hope and resurrection.*' To die in your sleep on a noisy traffic island in the middle of town next to Rio's famous landmark – how pathetic and how pointless. I tried to enter the church. Its door was closed today, keeping out the ghosts.

Not all of them live in Minas Gerais.

....

Brazilian Anecdotes #2: The Legend of the Vira-Saias

I stood at the famed Ouro Preto crossroads and looked up at the corniche. Which way does the Madonna look?

I closed my eyes. This story would make a great costume drama starring John Malkovich.

Around the time of the Inconfidência Mineira, Antônio Francisco

Alves was killed in his house in Ouro Preto by the bullet of an arquebus while he was lunching. Unknown vigilantes abducted and repeatedly gang-raped his wife and two daughters in a nearby field – within a day all three were dead. On the same day, apparently unconnected, a mysterious Spaniard was speared to death on the Morro das Lages where a lone cross still marks the spot.

If you guessed that gold was the reason, you are correct.

Bandits and highwaymen abounded in the *serra* that separated Ouro Preto from the sea, for the lure of the loot from caravans carrying the royal fifth to Rio was too strong to resist. The Vira-Saias was an outlaws' club with tentacles extending to the highest places. Any scruples the upper classes might have had in robbing the Crown disappeared after the devastating Lisbon earthquake of 1755. The quasi-dictatorial advisor to the king, the Marquis de Pombal, vowed to rebuild the capital stone by stone. For this he needed money, tax money. So the Marquis imposed a tax on assumed – not actual – mined ore, causing discontent and revolt because by then the mines were nearly depleted.

The caravans were being robbed whichever route they followed. Decoys were useless. The outlaws knew which the real caravan was and were waiting patiently. The authorities despaired and started offering rewards; spies and informers poisoned the social life of Ouro Preto. It was a Spaniard, whose name has not survived, who gave the authorities their first clue: a silent observer should hide near the corner of the Rua Barrão de Ouro Branco and Santa Ifigênia and make note of what happened around midnight.

The hidden observer saw a ghostly shadow leave Antônio Alves' house, climb up to a corniche by the crossroads and turn the head of the statue of Nossa Senhora das Almas. The Spaniard explained: this was the direction the caravan would leave next day and the beauty of the plan was that no clandestine meetings or private communications were necessary; it was open to anyone walking in the street who knew where to look and how to interpret what they saw. And, legend has it, Antônio Alves, the respectable landlord *fidalgo*, had been informing the bandits of the various routes and was the chief of the band of Vira-Saias. Vira-Saias sounds like 'skirt-lifting' in Portuguese, but it's a corruption of the command *'vira e sai'*: turn (the statue, that is) and leave. The Portuguese Crown's revenge was swift and drastic as we saw, but so was the Vira-Saias vendetta killing of the Spaniard on the Morro das Lages.

It is hard to split fact from fiction: the band certainly existed, for there are records referring to them in 1797, 1799 and even 1803; Antônio Alves' house exists with an ancient plaque which confirms that he built it in 1741; the lone cross on Morro das Lages is still popularly known as the Spaniard's cross.

And today the Vira-Saias are a male-only fraternity at the Ouro Preto School of Mines, with skirts rather than plunder foremost in their minds.

....

– 80 –

The fast pace of change in Brazil makes me look for constants. If there has been one in my travels it is Incontru's: bringing back memories and generating future ones. Frankly, it's a dive in a bad corner of Copacabana, and its clientele is mixed: bemused tourists, predatory hustlers and wide-eyed students, attracted by the free-entry-before-midnight policy. It was on my way back from this club that I was threatened with a knife on my first trip to Rio; it was here during *Carnaval* that I started my quest. Yes, I'm secretly fond of this dump, and I was relieved to re-enter the familiar surroundings. There was a youthful vibe in the place, lacking in the super-glitzy clubs and surprisingly, since by entering Copa you're entering rip-off-land, the caipirinhas were alcoholic and inexpensive. A drag act was on, and I remembered the food-fight I had here with my trolley-dollies. Then I saw David.

I have met my fair share of pretty young things in Brazil, but David was exceptional. He was blond but brown-skinned and boyish yet rugged, like a just-woken-up Leonardo de Caprio. The elaborate white shell necklace he was wearing made the resemblance more accurate. He was leaning on the balcony upstairs, cool, detached, oblivious to his admirers around him, shaking his head rhythmically and absorbing the beat like a sponge. He was so out of my league I wasn't too fussed about rejection, so I made a move and stood next to him, looking down on the disco floor. Our elbows touched. And then our arms. I turned my head towards him. He didn't acknowledge my presence.

'What's your name?' I asked him with accumulated Dutch courage.

'David,' he replied with the accent on the last syllable.

He didn't offer to ask mine back.

'Where do you come from?' I tried again.

'Nordeste,' was his laconic answer.

'Oh, I've been there. From where?'

'Paraíba,' he said, uninterested.

'I've been to Natal,' I said, trying to compensate.

....

Brazilian Anecdotes #3: The Novo Airport in Natal

The *novo* airport in Natal had to be inaugurated on time, even if it was criminally unfinished: workers were hanging from the ceiling, oxy-acetylene torches in hand, soldering beams while the sparks fell on the travellers below. You were lucky if only a spark landed on your clothes and slightly scorched them; a large sign fell on the floor from some scaffolding, scaring an old lady into a fit. I hope she next plays the lottery.

There was no air conditioning. There was no allocation of seats at check-in. There were no luggage conveyor belts. There were no departure and arrival boards, no X-ray machines or metal detectors. So many of the things we take for granted in airports had disappeared in Natal.

There was only one gate open – smelling heavily of paint – with a waiting room for 150. We all had to stand looking enviously at the empty room next door with carefully laid out armchairs. No member of staff could find the key.

An announcement was made for a Varig flight to Fortaleza. Everyone started boarding. I was told by a fellow passenger I should ignore it; it was our flight to Recife. Yes, there was a flight to Fortaleza, too, but not with Varig.

I asked a stewardess on the ground. She concurred.

'Do you see that aircraft?' she asked me in English and pointed at an aeroplane at the end of the building.

I did.

'That's the one going to Recife,' she said. 'It's the only Varig aircraft, you can't miss it.'

'Oh,' I said angelically. 'Natal's new airport is like a bus stop.'

She checked with her eyes whether I was being sarcastic.

'No, that's cool,' I said. 'I can relate to that. As long as we don't have to stand until someone jumps off and a seat becomes available.'

Well, yes, I was.

....

Back in Incontru's I was fighting a losing battle as David's daisy eyelashes were kept half closed and distant.

'Do you want a drink?' I made a last effort.

He did not reply.

'That's OK,' I said and walked to the bar downstairs, thinking nothing ventured, nothing gained. I was ordering myself a drink when I saw David come down smiling at me.

'You left,' he said. 'I was going to say yes, thank you. Can I have a Coke please?'

I was over the moon as David proved to be a very likeable guy – and cheap. Someone offers to buy you a drink and you ask for Coke?

'I'm sorry I was so quiet before,' he said. 'I was thinking.'

'What about?' I asked as I gave him his drink.

'This and that,' he responded.

I didn't push.

David, like Isaías and François, was doing his *vestibular*. His relatively advanced age – late twenties – disclosed a certain degree of poverty. He had left Paraíba only recently to join the Nordestino migration south for work and a better life; he lived with his brothers 'nearby', which four streets up could certainly mean a *favela*.

I touched his white shell necklace. It bestowed on him the air of a beautiful beach bum. He touched my neck. I was wearing Christoff's *figa*, like I do in Brazil.

'Where did you buy that?' he asked.

'It was a present from a friend in Iguaçu,' I replied. 'Many moons ago.'

'Can I wear it?' he asked.

'You can try,' I said. 'Nowadays it takes me ages to put it on.'

He loosened it expertly. I made a move to help, but to my surprise it took him only one second to tie it around his neck.

'There,' he smiled.

'It takes me half an hour and two mirrors,' I complained. 'You're a natural.'

He put his necklace around my neck in return. 'There,' he said again. I nearly swooned.

Not long after, I asked him home.

'Where?' he asked.

'Ipanema.'

'How do we go there at this time?'

'By taxi.'

'There is a motel nearby.'

'I don't do motels.'

He sized me up.

'How do *I* come back?' he asked.

Does he want money?

'Stay the night.'

'I have to go to school tomorrow.'

'OK, I'll give you the taxi fare. We'll see how much it is on the way there.'

He thought about it and said 'Fine.'

This, John, was truly a conquest.

*****

David stayed until noon. We said we'd meet again that afternoon outside Copacabana Palace. The taxi fare was twelve reais and I gave him fifteen, although I knew he could and would take the bus instead. Surely that wasn't paying for sex, was it? I was inwardly debating this as my gaze fell on the commode.

There, curled inside an ashtray, lay David's white shell necklace right next to my *figa*.

– 81 –

There is another place in Rio which should be on everyone's itinerary: the palace in Catete whose shady gardens are one of Rio's most agreeable haunts. The surfers go to Ipanema; the tourist-fleecers to Copacabana; the joggers to Flamengo – but the older, more genteel crowd prefer the benches of the gardens of Catete. Yet it is the palace that will astound the tourist who has no time to travel to Petrópolis, a palace which is now a museum dedicated to its most famous resident, Brazil's foremost nation-shaper.

Getúlio Vargas has split historians like no other Brazilian figure. A protégé of Pinheiro Machado from São Borja in the Missions and later a governor of Rio Grande do Sul himself, he rose to power in 1930 with that coup, which he labelled revolution, and ruled for 15 long years. He is difficult to categorise: nationalist to the core, he forced all linguistic minorities to assimilate; populist, he introduced social and labour legislation to protect the working class; authoritarian, he banned political parties and persecuted both the Communists on the extreme left and the fascist Integralists on the extreme right; cruel and vindictive, he approved the extradition of the German-born wife of the Communist leader Luis Prestes to Nazi Germany where she died in a concentration camp; overly suspicious to the point of paranoia, he denounced Socialists, Communists, Jews, Masons, the Rotary Club and the YMCA;

centraliser, he antagonised São Paulo, but pragmatist, he supported its growth; calculating, he joined the Second World War on the side of the Allies, extracting enough American capital to build the steel works in Volta Redonda and kickstart Brazil's industrialisation; statist by nature, he created quangos and nationalised industries, one of which, Petrobras, became his nemesis. Vargas had a complex about his height (five foot two), was superstitious, and suffered from chronic arthritis. He was also suicidal as entries from his diaries show, starting from 1930. Yet this is someone who, like it or not, put his stamp on Brazil, which is still discernible half a century after his death – in this he is more akin to Turkey's Kemal Ataturk than to Spain's Francisco Franco.

Brazil joined both World Wars on the side of the United States. During the first one, it was the only South American country to declare war actively against Germany. Unfortunately its expedition force was decimated by the great flu epidemic while stationed at Dakar en route to Europe. They also opened fire against a school of dolphins which were mistaken for German U-boats. This may have been the only time they fired live ammunition – the fleet eventually reached Gibraltar one day after Armistice Day. Well, it's the thought that counts.

A rather fuller participation was in store for the Brazilian Armed Forces during the Second World War. And by that I don't mean the audience participation in the Glenn Miller concert at the Teatro Alberto Maranhão in Natal (he played everywhere, bless him). No, the Brazilian Expeditionary Force, numbering more than 25,000 souls, saw combat in Italy in a campaign that lasted from September 1944 until the end of the war and resulted in 457 fatalities. They fought in Massarossa and in San Quirico, they seized Monte Castello, fighting in what must have seemed to them deep-space temperatures of -20 °C, and they captured the city of Montese where you can sip a cappuccino in Piazza Brasile, named in the liberators' honour.

All wars have unexpected consequences but this one's were more unusual than most. In 1944 an American plane flying over the Amazon Basin reported a pretty big mountain that wasn't on the maps. It was in unexplored Serra Imeri, the source of the Rio Negro near the Venezuelan border. The mountain was permanently obscured by clouds, which is why it was called Pico da Neblina, Foggy Peak. At 9,888 feet it turned out to be the highest mountain in Brazil, eclipsing the Pico da Bandeira in the Serra de Caparaó, a mere 9,478 feet. This was rather upsetting since the mountain had been Espírito Santo's only claim to fame. The emotional shock was greater when Serra Imeri divulged a second highest mountain: the Pico 31 de Março stood at 9,816 feet and demoted Pico da Bandeira to a bronze within months.

The other development was the end of the Estado Novo: how can you fight against one dictatorship abroad while sustaining another at home? Vargas was forced to call elections by the military when the war ended in 1945. He lost and there followed a wave of Vargas statue-toppling on par with Lenin's in post-1989 Eastern Europe.

But Catete is the biggest monument to Vargas, or better, to his ghost. One of the first rooms of the palace contains his English handmade golf clubs, his spectacles, his hat, his first-class tram pass for 1945 issued by Central do Brasil in the name of Getúlio Domelles Vargas – did he ever get to use it? In the corner a pianola spookily plays sad forties' songs alone. Leather wraps and small packets of matches are displayed with the inscription '*Ele voltará*' (He will return). Despite the oppression, the union bosses and the working class considered Vargas one of their own. He triumphed on their shoulders in the presidential elections of 1950, where he received 49 per cent of the popular vote in a multiple-candidate field, making a comeback at the age of 68. There are pictures of him with Franklin D. Roosevelt, with Queen Elizabeth II whose coronation he attended, and with several of his contemporaries. There is a picture of his burial which silently betrays his influence as you recognise three future Brazilian presidents as pall-bearers: Juscelino Kubitschek, Jango Goulart and Tancredo Neves. A virtual library is projected on a dark, gloomy room with a hologram of his funerary mask and a slew of decorations – I counted 30 before I stopped. Brazilians named after Getúlio star in a non-stop video talking about themselves on multiple screens, young and old, rich and poor, for such is the magnetism of the memory.

Here is his Colt 38 revolver with a mother-of-pearl handle, the very same one he used to –

I move away from the Vargas exhibition to the art nouveau of Catete Palace. The Cabinet Room, with thirteen seats, a dark and light zebra parquet floor, Bacchus and Ariadne on the ceiling. Pictures of old presidents are on the wall: Floriano Peixoto, the scourge of Santa Catarina, moustache, goatee and mole giving him a sinister appearance; Prudente de Morais, the defeater of Canudos, an Abraham Lincoln lookalike; Afonso Pena, Campos Salles and Rodrigues Alves all looking as if permanently rehearsing for the stage role of Mahatma Gandhi. A red carpet leads up the main staircase – prefab in Germany – with black, gold and red columns amid faded yellow marble frescos and stucco meanders framing copies of Rafael's work in Villa Farnese. This is the Azure Hall with the grandest of chandeliers and the largest of mirrors, opposite which a balcony overhangs the garden and the congregated Carioca elders. Afterwards it is the turn of the Noble Hall, the major reception room. Its opulence is awe-inspiring with Olympian gods on the ceiling and Pompeian murals on the walls. Then comes the Venetian yellow room in Renaissance style and a grand chandelier hanging below a circular cornice; the Arab Room based on the Alhambra, with Moorish statuettes and painted arabesques; the Banquet Room with panels of sculpted food and hung game under a 20-foot-high ceiling with paintings of the goddess Diana …

Upstairs is the room where it all happened.

The democratic election of Vargas split Brazil. He was seen as an autocratic despot (which he was), a syndicalist control freak (which he was) and as a friend of the workers (which he was). He could be all things to all people: father to the poor and mother to the rich went the joke. His Minister of Labour, later president, Jango Goulart suggested an increase of 100 per cent in the minimum wage and Vargas implemented it in full, delighting the masses and alarming the elites. His creation of Petrobras was the thin end of the wedge on which the ideology of free enterprise of the opposition clashed with state intervention and protection which, like Argentina's Peron, he imbued with nationalist colours. But this was the final battleground in a background of falling coffee prices initiated by the United States, alarmed with Vargas's policies and his unexpected refusal to send troops to Korea. With inflation rising and a squeezing of foreign credit, Brazil had to resort to the newly formed IMF with predictable reactions: Carlos Lacerda, a politician-journalist, started attacking Vargas with a degree of innuendo, rumour and vitriol the world would not see again until Bill Clinton's tenure in office.

High noon.

An attempt was made on Lacerda's life. The culprit was one of Vargas's servants: a big, simple black Carioca called Gregório Fortunato whose vacant expression in the Catete newsreels betrays the innocence of manipulated victims everywhere. Had Vargas ordered the failed assassination? We'll never know. Even if he had not, there were clearly elements close to him who accepted no dissent. 'Resign!' shouted the papers. As with Fernando Collor 40 years later, the mood of the nation turned ugly.

But then the beleaguered President turned the tables on his enemies in an act worthy of an *orixá* – and yes, I'm thinking of Ogum: he shot himself through the chest at 8:35 a.m. on 24 August 1954 in this very room, leaving a final '*J'accuse*' which every schoolchild in Brazil knows by heart. The mood of the country rotated 180 degrees: the villain of yesterday became the hero of tomorrow.

The bedroom is as Vargas died in it. It's sparsely furnished and the mosquito netting gives it a macabre appearance. There is a statue of Nossa Senhora Aparecida, a large bed for such a small guy, a mock baroque table clock, a pair of brown and yellow striped pyjamas with his monogram, a sofa, two small round chairs, two round flowerstands and a reclining leather chair in front of a low marble table. There is a small en suite bathroom with a grandiose shower – and, look, a bidet. Finally, there is the bullet itself that killed Vargas but ensured the defeat of his enemies and their laissez-faire ideology for another 40-odd years. Kubitschek was elected and built Brasília to unite the country in an optimistic, reconciliatory move; Goulart followed and was ousted by the generals in 1964 who pursued an interventionist, state bureaucratic model Vargas would have been proud of. Lacerda fled abroad but returned to be elected as a governor of the state of Guanabara in 1960. He supported the junta initially, and then opposed it with the venom he had showed against Vargas. He was stripped of his political rights but did not leave the country; he died in Brazil in 1977. The rest, as they say, is history – or not, for Vargas still lives in the consciousness of Brazilians and especially in the labour legislation he passed.

On 15 January 1997, his last son Manuel Antônio Vargas committed suicide just like his father, with a bullet through the chest, adding another twist to the tale.

....

Brazilian Anecdotes #4:
Hotel International, Corumbá

Sun lotion, portable CD player, goggles, towel, sunglasses – let's try the hotel swimming pool. It was too hot to lie on the mock marble floor even after I spread my towel, so I sat on a deckchair. After five minutes of sunbathing I moved into the shade, for the heat was unbearable. I watched a kingfisher dive into the water and take its bath twittering happily:

everyone's too hot today. I dipped into the pool; after a dozen lengths, I saw through my goggles a cross between a large beetle and a giant cockroach swimming deftly below water towards me like an extra from *Starship Troopers*. I felt like Captain Kirk beamed down onto a strange planet. And I acted like Dr Spock: I got out of the pool sharpish. Oh, the excitement of finding disgusting life forms, inches in front of your face …

Only in Brazil.

………………………………………………………………………………

David was not on the beach as planned; but then again my rendezvous outside Copacabana Palace might as well not have been made at all: I never found Alex last *Carnaval*. I put my lucky charm around my neck in a procedure that lasted the best part of an hour – such a pain – and the shell necklace in my pocket just in case. Go back to Incontru's? But there were new bars and clubs to discover …

… like the Galeria in Ipanema, only a stone's throw away from my hotel. There was a sign outside: *Lançamento da Exposição Fotográfica* – 21.00. I looked at my watch: 21.30. A private launch. There was no one outside. I opened the door, walked in and pinched myself.

Oh, the *talent*.

Galeria was a chrome industrial two-floor club with a spiral staircase, two bars, an assortment of throne-like armchairs and chill-out Goa house emanating from the DJ booth. Pictures of naked and half-clothed male models were plastered around the walls vying for my attention with the plastic-beautiful crowd dressed in expensive designer attire. Trust me to go out in my Hot-Buttered Aussie shorts and bump into Rio's jet-set. When you don't know what you're doing, do it elegantly, so I made for the bar lest they discovered the gatecrasher. Oh, no, how terrible, drinks and sandwiches are free until eleven! Now is the time to order an expensive Sloe Comfortable Screw.

This was an exhibition by photographer Leonardo Falconi called '*Meninos do Rio*' inaugurating a tour which would also comprise São Paulo, Belo Horizonte, Curitiba, Brasília, Madrid, Amsterdam, London, Paris and Milan. That's it! The gorgeous men around me were the models depicted in the photos – so *that's* what they look like with their clothes on. The pictures? Well, I come from the National Geographic school of technique, and I'm a stickler for sharp focus, although those of nude men holding exotic fish were quite inventive; I hope the fish didn't suffer.

I had the barman spot Leonardo for me, as good-looking as his models himself.

'Good work,' I said to him with confidence.

He thanked me politely.

'Were these models or passers-by from the street?' I asked.

'Models,' he replied, taken aback.

No Warhol this.

'I see you're going to London,' I said.

'We should be there in August.'

'I might see you there. That's where I live. Where are you exhibiting?'

He was flustered. 'Erm, I don't know yet. Some gallery or other.'

Someone dragged him away.

'See you there,' I shouted so that they could all hear me. I was now part of the crowd and could ask for another Screw with impunity. Hey, meeting Leonardo in London would be fab. However, as much as I scanned the art news that August, I never read anything about such an exhibition. I remembered Leonardo being caught wrong-footed by my question and I wonder …

Back in Galeria, I kept on slurping my Screw sloely and comfortably until two guys, not part of the gorgeous crowd, drunkenly spoke to me.

'Hi.'

'Hi.'

'Who do you know here?' they asked to make conversation.

'Leonardo,' I said. 'I will be meeting him in London for his exhibition.'

They were Leandro and Xavier, both hairdressers in an exclusive coiffeur's in Ipanema. Leandro was a broad-shouldered African Carioca and Xavier a camp, plump, peroxide blond with make-up that was melting in the heat. They had come as friends of a model. Which one? Leandro pointed at a picture of a semi-clad blond surfer.

'Him,' he said. 'I don't know where he is at the moment.'

'Pity,' I said, still slurping after seeing the photo. 'I would love to be introduced.'

'He's straight,' Xavier informed me. 'He's been going out with this girl for years.'

I took another look at the picture and registered disappointment.

'What a waste,' I said.

They nodded in agreement.

Hairdressers know the best gossip, so they gave me the low-down on several of the guests. Eleven o'clock came and passed and the regular crowd walked in as Leonardo and his models left. Twelve o'clock and Leandro thought it was time to move.

'Come with us,' he said.

'Where?'

'Home. We're sharing. Not too far.'

Xavier touched my arm. 'Come,' he said.

'I should really meet someone,' I said.

'Friend of yours?'

'Met him last night.'

Xavier pursed his lips. Leandro chuckled.

'Where?'

'In a club. Incontru's.'

They rolled their eyes.

'No. The place is full of escorts.'

'I didn't pay for him.'

Xavier tapped his fingers theatrically.

'Hand on heart?'

'I didn't pay.'

'You must have done. Did you buy him an expensive drink? Did you give him a present?'

'No. I bought him a Coke. And I gave him no present.'

They didn't believe me because there was a shadow in my eyes.

'I just gave him money for the taxi.'

That was the cue they were waiting for.

'Told you so,' they said in unison.

'I promised him. It was a goodwill gesture,' I said. 'The fare from my hotel to his home. Politeness. It was only fifteen reais.'

'Those kids will go to bed for a bowl of *feijoada*,' said Xavier dismissively.

I didn't like his tone.

'If anything, it was him who left something behind,' I said and took out the necklace.

They approved.

'Keep it,' said Xavier. 'It's very nice.'

'I was supposed to meet him this afternoon in Copa, but he didn't turn up.'

'You'll never see him again.'

'I bet he'll be in the club tonight.'

Leandro put his arm around my waist.

'Come with us,' he said. 'You'll enjoy the night. Forget your piece of dirt.'

'David is very nice actually,' I said. 'He never said anything about money. And he looks like a tanned Leonardo de Caprio.'

Xavier squeezed my hand.

'Come with us. We have *maconha* at home. We'll get stoned.'

They dragged me to the exit. As we paid our bills, I saw Leandro slip his drinks card to the cashier, pointing at me furtively.

'I haven't offered,' I said, surprised at his impudence.

Leandro bit his lip; I wasn't supposed to see that. The cashier looked at me questioningly.

'I'm paying my own,' I shrugged my shoulders.

We walked out silently into a temperate Rio midnight. Leandro stopped a cab.

'I'm not coming,' I said. 'I don't like what happened in there.'

Xavier got heavy.

'All this chatting up for nothing? For nothing?'

'At least give us fifteen reais for the taxi,' said Leandro.

I was aghast. 'Why?'

'For keeping you company for two hours.'

I started walking away. Xavier followed me shouting insults.

'We're more expensive in Ipanema than your Incontru's piece of shit,' he said.

Dear me.

'Where are you going? You're going to walk there?'

Leandro's cab cruised by.

'Xavier, jump in. You're wasting your time with the gringo. He's going back to his rent boy.'

I was gritting my teeth.

'I'm going to Le Boy,' I said.

'So am I,' said Xavier and turned to Leandro. 'You can go.'

The taxi sped away and Xavier turned to me.

'Now see what you've done. I have no money to go home now. I need fifteen reais.'

'Xavier,' I said. 'You're on your own.'

I walked away. What upset me the most was that Xavier and Leandro were reinforcing my hidden fears. Someone as beautiful as David must surely make money from his looks – and I didn't see his picture on the Galeria walls.

'You could pay for me in Le Boy,' Xavier shouted behind me.

I saw a cab approaching. I jumped in and gave him directions for Incontru's.

*****

So here I am again, finding solace in the grime.

Once more, Incontru's was livelier than the brash, bemuscled silhouettes of Le Boy or the chilled sophisticates of Galeria. If there is an indication of atmosphere in a club, it is the energy unleashed on the dance floor.

Almost at once, my eyes met David's across the bar. He ran towards me.

'Did you remember –'

I pulled out his necklace and David's eyes flashed with joy. Why is it that some people are so easily happy and some are born to be miserable?

David hugged me tightly.

'I slept through the afternoon. I was tired from last night. Sorry I didn't meet up with you in Copa,' he said. 'What kept you?'

I felt guilty. Very guilty.

'It's nearly one o'clock. I thought you'd never come.'

'Take the *figa* from around my neck,' I said.

Puzzled, he helped me take it off.

'Put it on,' I said.

He put it around his neck without a problem, as if he had owned it forever.

'I want you to have it,' I said.

His face brightened.

'Why?' he asked.

'Because I came late,' I said.

He kissed me, but Xavier's poison had already spread.

'David,' I said.

'Yes?'

'I'm going to ask you something, and I want you to give me a true answer.'

'OK.'

I could tell he knew what the question would be for he looked down and then away.

'Are you an escort?'

'What does it matter?' he attempted to whisper over the hard house sound of the DJ and with that I knew what the answer was. I still wanted to hear him say it.

'Yes, it's important.'

He looked me straight in the eye, last night's inexpressiveness making a comeback.

'*Sim. Faço programa.*'

Uttering the words caused him obvious discomfort.

'But,' he added, 'I am much more expensive than fifteen reais.'

We stood there for a few minutes, an abyss between us, neither one able or willing to bridge it. I broke the silence.

'So long then, David,' I said.

'So long,' he replied.

As I turned my back and left, I hoped he was following me with his eyes, though I wouldn't bet on it.

– 82 –

When King João VI arrived in Rio, he instituted the Botanical Gardens as there were many fortunes to be made from the discovery and breeding of exotic plants. There are over 8,000 kinds of plants over an area of 137 hectares which include two museums, a library, a cactus collection, a *lanchonete*, several romantic alleys, ponds with giant Victoria Regias and two grand glasshouses for orchids and bromelias.

Quiet. How strange it is to find peace in the frantic throb of Rio.

I passed the meditative Japanese rock garden complete with lotus flower ponds and miniature bridges, mini bonsais and mighty cherry trees in whose blossom Princess Sayako, daughter of the Japanese Emperor, inaugurated the grounds in November 1995; oddly they planted it next to a patch of Amazonian rainforest. *Snap!* There are even mosquitoes here. How authentic. It would be funny if I escaped malaria in the Amazon and the Mato Grosso only to catch something in Rio. Dengue fever, here I come.

The pain in my hand indicated this was no mosquito. I checked. A tiny blood circle had formed below my index finger. It itched and hurt like burning acid. Within minutes it had swollen up like my ankle in Manaus. Whichever species causes this, I am its perpetual prey. I swore loudly as I pushed large waxflowers taller than me out of the way. I walked under mango trees and banana bushes with marmosets and *serelepe* long-tailed squirrels climbing rapidly up their branches as soon as I appeared. I squinted through the leaves of 65-foot-high cannonball trees with their cascading large brown fruit, rare red aromatic jasmine spilling onto their roots, and the Dutchman pipe flower, ten inches of purple and white veins obstructing my view of a guard. A guard!

I showed him my swollen hand.

'*Borrachudo*,' he exclaimed. 'Ha-ha – it's very painful.'

I asked if there was anything he could do.

'No,' he shook his head. 'It's just very painful.'

I felt like kicking him in the groin, but then I glanced at the greenhouse in front of me.

If orchids are the world's most glamorous flowers then Rio's orchidarium is a veritable Versace of glasshouses: flamboyant and exotic like its contents, it contains some of the most extraordinary examples of orchiddom. Orchids are the most evolved of flowers: they have adapted so that out of millions of insects only one species can pollinate them. This specific insect determines the size of the flower, the colour, shape and odour of the lip and even when the fragrance is emitted (night or day depending on the insect's habits). Orchids range from tropical scented varieties – vanilla itself is classified as an orchid – to minute seedlings that sprout in snow-clad Siberia. Victorians were notoriously fascinated by orchids and started hybridising them for fun. There were famous orchid-hunters like the Czech Benedict Rözl who spent 40 years in the tropics and sent back 800 species; his statue stands in Prague holding a *cattleya* flower. Frederick Sander's *List of Orchid Hybrids*, launched in the nineteenth century, now contains 100,000 entries. The *Orchid Review* by the Royal Horticultural Society is issued six times a year – you can now buy the lot on a CD-ROM and trace your flowers to the originals like a pedigree Arabian stallion. The last sensational orchid to have been discovered in the wild was in Peru in 1980, a flower so red and bright that one marvels it was not discovered earlier. I would add that most orchids are bisexual, but I'm sure you knew that already; I did mention they were highly evolved.

I walked out of the orchidarium and bumped into a group performing t'ai chi by the ruins of an old gunpowder factory which existed before the Botanical Gardens took over; I liked the concept of flowers overrunning a building dedicated to warfare. I looked at my watch. Damn. I wanted to check out the 1,700 species in the bromeliarium next door, but I was miles away from the entrance gate which was closing in half an hour and, well, I still had not found what I'd come for. I rushed through bromelias ranging from mutant pods with white fur to wide-leafed, harpoon-tipped, red-centred spikes to large mauve watermarked tubers the size and texture of watermelons.

Where is it?

The Victoria Regia pond was drained; the Burle Marx promontory was being reinforced; the cactarium had already shut. The garden for the sightless was a distraction: a touch-and-feel area with signs in Braille containing plants from rosemary and oregano to ginger, basil and cloves. No one but me, I suppose, had the evil thought of incorporating some cacti next to the gardenias. What's the time again?

Ten minutes to go. I'm lost and I haven't found it yet.

This is the sundial and the Mesa do Imperador where Dom Pedro II used to take a picnic; wrong way. This is João VI's bust and the carnivorous plant section. Quick look at the map.

There it is.

Sweaty and breathless I stood still, as if to pay homage in front of an unassuming tree hidden under the thick cover of lianas. It was about 30 feet tall, although I had read it can reach up to 90 feet in the wild. It blooms from September to December with lovely yellow flowers. This tree used to reign in the coastal forest in Brazil's Year Dot; 500 years later, like so many languages and people, plants and animals, it is almost extinct. Its yellow-green bark had been stripped to show a soft reddish interior the colour of a red coal, in Latin *brasa*, the same root as our brazier. So this is the *pau-brasil*, the brazilwood tree so prized in the markets of Lisbon. The name 'brazilwood' was a generic term used for red dye-wood: Marco Polo himself gave an account of the brazilwoods of Sumatra; Tercéira in the Azores was once called Island of Brazil for the same reason.

And yet, it's this one that baptised a country.

I closed in. I'm not the kind who speaks to flora, but, partly moved, partly curious, partly regretful, I stroked its red flesh which, true to its nature, left a slight crimson hue on my fingertips, like faded blood. For so much blood was shed: the explorers and the *bandeirantes*, the masters and the slaves, the Jesuits and the Indians, French pirates and Dutch princes, Iracema and Gabriela, Mineiro baroque and Niemeyer modernism, samba and mangue-beat, candomblé and Umbandá, caipirinhas and moquecas, camphor and quinine, colonial Brazil, Imperial Brazil, Brazil of the dictators and the presidents – history would have taken a different turning for this country of Catholic high camp cross-pollinated with tropical in-your-face sensuality but for the existence of this tree.

This is where it all began.

And this is where I'm going to close.

....

Brazilian Anecdotes #5:
The Shuttle from Rio to São Paulo

Close, yes, but not before I recount a tale of praise: a small triumph of Brazilian efficiency, a standout along with Curitiba's urban model and Porto Alegre's budget popularisation.

I left my hotel in Ipanema around 1.30 in the afternoon – I always push it as much as I can when they tell me that a new paying day starts at noon – and hopped in a taxi for the domestic airport of Santos Dumont where I arrived twenty minutes later. I walked into the reservations office of Rio Sul and asked when the next available plane was due: 14.14. I looked at my watch. It was five minutes to two.

'I suppose I'll have to catch the one after that,' I said.

'Why?' asked the girl. 'Don't you want to leave right now?'

I paid for my ticket by credit card, checked in my luggage and walked into the gate next door. In ten minutes we were boarding. At 14.14, forty-five minutes after I left my hotel without a ticket or reservation, we were off. This is not just a miracle of efficiency; it is a miracle of state subsidy, as there were only a dozen São Paulo-bound passengers, but impressive enough it *was*.

Things can work like clockwork in Brazil – and many of them do, you know.

....

– 83 –

'François?'

'JOHN!'

The scream made me move the phone away from my ear.

'I thought you'd gone back to London! Where are you?'

'São Paulo. You wanted to take me to the airport.'

'Yes, but – but you were supposed to have arrived last weekend.'

'Well, I changed my ticket. I've always wanted to do that: extend my holiday. So I did it – and went to Rio for a week. I called to let you know, but couldn't find you.'

There was a silence.

'You were in Rio? I was in Rio!'

It was my turn to shout. 'WHAT?'

'I went to B.I.T.C.H. Why didn't you come? It was fantastic. A party in a theme park with rides open all night.'

'I thought of going to B.I.T.C.H. but it was too far away,' I mumbled.

'There were buses leaving every half hour from Praça Osório in Ipanema.'

'Oh, no,' I cried. 'That's where I stayed.'

'SO DID I!'

'I can't believe we didn't meet,' I said.

'I can't believe you missed the party!' was the response.

In the timeless words of Homer Simpson: *all my emoticons have failed me.*

*****

So there I was for the final departure in Guarulhos with a François still in his tracksuit – he drove me there straight after his gym session. While we sat in a café to kill time, he broke the news.

'I'm leaving São Paulo.'

Et tu, Brute?

'Where for?'

'Sydney. I've applied for a university place, and they have conditionally accepted me if I pass my *vestibular*.'

'And your parents?'

'I told my mother yesterday.'

'What can I say?' I said. 'I'm all for learning about different cultures. Although talking of culture and Australia in the same breath smacks of – *ahem* – low standards.'

We laughed.

'Nah – Sydney will be good for you. You wouldn't like London,' I said. 'No surfing, too cold. But you'll have to visit me one day.'

'I know,' he said.

I stood back, thinking about what São Paulo would feel like without François.

'There's still Ford,' he said, my thoughts open for everyone to read. It happens so often.

'We'll keep in touch via email,' I said.

'Like we always do,' he added.

And then as an afterthought.

'What happened with that guy you met in Recife last year? Did you see him again on this trip?'

'Isaías? No. I didn't go to Recife.'

'I thought you really liked that Isaías.'

My flight was announced over the speakers. Boarding soon.

'I still do. I was totally smitten by him. The one guy I really fell for in Brazil.'

Our eyes met for an instant.

Well, maybe two.

'He called me afterwards in London. In fact, he kept calling and reversed the charges which I accepted. My quarterly phone bill was like E.T. calling home.'

'And then?'

'Then he came to Europe. Germany. Someone paid for his trip and Isaías abandoned him. He told me that the guy expected sex but Isaías wasn't so keen. So the guy took his passport. Isaías fled and was stranded in Munich. He called me from there for help.'

François was listening, absorbed.

'Isaías said that he accepted the flight offer to be nearer to me. So that we could meet again.'

François interrupted me.

'May I say something?' he asked.

'Please do.'

'Keep off.'

'I know. I didn't believe a word. And yet a part of me wants to believe that he really did befriend that German and came all the way to Europe for me.'

'That guy is trouble.'

Just what Evêncio had said.

'He is and he's not. He's only doing what you're doing: he wants to leave Brazil for some brighter future, but that's the only way he can. I understand that. That doesn't mean he feels nothing for me. I know he does.'

I took a big breath.

'You know what? I would have rushed to Munich if there was any chance we wouldn't split up again. But I couldn't go through another separation, and the odds were stacked against us.'

I was right, for Pernambuco is where Isaías ended up again. He's now learning German back in Limoeiro.

'But you also returned to Salvador on this trip, didn't you?'

'Yes. I had to see Márcio and Ari and Jorge again.'

'And worship Ogum?'

Ógun méjeje lóòde Irê.

I smiled. 'I can do that anywhere. Ogum is the god of the number seven. Sometimes I count to seven in Yoruba to invoke Him: *Òkàn, Méjì, Métà, Mérìn, Márùn, Mèfà, Mèje.* If ever I write a book, that particular adventure will be composed of seven sections following the Yoruba numbering He understands.'

My long flight back was boarding.

'I have to go, François.'

There was one thing more …

'This is something I tell everyone. That book I mentioned. You know I'm going to write about Brazil and about us, don't you?'

He grinned a coy yes.

'You're not going to write about *everything*, are you?' he said, not without apprehension.

We kissed goodbye.

'Of course not,' I replied. 'Of course I'm not going to write about everything.'

And I haven't.

– 84 –

Let's finish with the last thing I like about Brazil. For this I'll need the help of a quote by the Frenchman Jean de Léry describing the Tupi in the 1550s: '*This people hath not any knowledge of their Creator, nor of anything of heaven, nor if there be any paine or glory after this life […] but they know that they have soules and that they dye not; and they say that the soules are converted into devils and that after their death they go to certain fields where are many figge trees along by a faire River, and altogether do nothing but dance.*'

In their heaven they do nothing but dance …

*****

Back in the 1950s Anthony Quinn made his name – and received the title of honorary Greek – for his on-screen portrayal of the eponymous hero of Nikos Kazantzakis's novel, *Zorba the Greek*. Not until *Captain Corelli's*

Mandolin would a Greek locality or personality achieve such worldwide exposure. Nikos Kazantzakis was, like Jorge Amado, a Marxist and one who rejected his traditional religion for an alternative. Amado chose candomblé, Kazantzakis chose Buddhism. His novel *The Last Temptation of Christ* was put on the Roman Catholic Index of Forbidden Books in 1954; it also drew protests and criticism when its turn came to be filmed. Like Amado, Kazantzakis was put forward for, but never received, the Nobel Prize for Literature. He was born in Crete and is buried there on a hill overlooking the sea. His epitaph is very Zen: *'I hope for nothing. I fear nothing. I am free.'*

In the film, Zorba takes a recently arrived, hemmed-in, buttoned-up English teacher – Alan Bates – by the scruff of the neck and lands him in a world of sensuality, earthiness and zest for life. Alan Bates is amazed by the spirit and the wisdom of Zorba, and his world is turned upside-down as emotions he never knew he was capable of are brought to life. An Englishman in the 1950s facing a less sophisticated Greece wondering what it is that Britain has lost and Greece still harbours – sounds familiar?

I'm in a club in the middle of a hopping throng and I'm moving spasmodically to a hard-house rhythm where there are no lyrics and the sameness of the beat *is it* – anticipation of the next is all. In comedy and in music, knowing or suspecting what's next is paramount, which is why pieces of music and snatches of film comedy can be listened to again and again. This is music I have never heard, but I know the format. So I'm waiting for that thundering drum roll which will presage an equally mind-blowing beat – sometimes there is a small interval in continuity to tease you, heightening your expectation even more. Snatches of phrases are repeated over and over again: 'injected with a poison', 'this is not over yet'. Acid techno is on the speakers now and my head is in the spin-drier of the local launderette, the sound cavernous and sweet: give me turbofans, give me hoovers or lawnmowers! The sound is angry and it takes all my anger away from me. The repetitions are now slow, phrases are woven in to blend the beat and the climax when it comes sends that boy with the phosphorescent green glowsticks into a paroxysm of leaps. I point at people with my water bottle and they become visible. A guy stares at me intensely and I stare back as our bodies reinforce each other's movements. We are both in this together and we are both on our own, each one inside his own headspace. He slips away. I dance and I don't care. With every idiotic move I shake off all concerns for tomorrow, with every quake of my waist I shed my inhibitions, with every flap of my arms I am a tall, proud macaw soaring in the jungle, and with every quiver of my head I feel divine, unbeatable, unique. The dance gives me sexual energy, the dance keeps me young, the dance helps me forget yesterday's adversities and tomorrow's calamities. Who said dismissively that writing about music is akin to dancing about architecture? Do you know a better way to describe Niemeyer's creations?

Forget National Insurance and the Welfare State, the Internet and virtual worlds, abstracting in religion and killing by proxy. We in the West have ultimately forgotten how to dance – be it at a village barn-dance, a high-society waltz, a speakeasy foxtrot or a school prom rock'n'roll. It's only the young now who dance, and, hey, they need drugs for that. Brazil hasn't forgotten how to dance. Gay men haven't either – that is something we know, too.

'*If there is a Garden of Eden, it can't be far away from here*' – well, I have news for you, Amerigo. There is a Paradise everywhere and it's easy to get into. Brazilians still have the key – they are still true gatekeepers, like Zorba was fifty years ago: you know what Anthony Quinn said to Alan Bates when asked a complex philosophical question?

'*I don't know how to explain it to you, so I will dance it for you.*'

And he starts on a solo *zeibekiko* by Mikis Theodorakis, dancing about architecture and history and love and pain because this most physical of all expressions is what binds us with the earth and all the living things around us. In fifty years, Zorba's zest for life has also been lost in efficiency and comfort and here's a traveller with Greek blood and a British mind strolling in a different country, musing over the very same question and arriving at the same answer.

So let me dance Brazil for you for the last time.

I'm sitting in the restaurant of Yemanjá in Ipanema, and I'm eating a very expensive *bobô de camarão*. I look at the pictures of Pelourinho on the wall and I'm sinking into my memories: I want the carpet under my feèt to fly me to Porto da Barra in Salvador where I can watch the street urchins jump laughing into the sea from the pier at sunset, kiss Ari's lips on the beach and taste an *acarajé* from a stall with Márcio; I want to savour the studied arrogance of Pernambucans and press Isaías's body next to mine under a red moon in Porto de Galinhas; I want to return to Manaus on that night when Martin proposed and I was too scared of the consequences to accept, for there is no sorrier feeling than unrequited desire; I want to get drenched by the falls in Iguaçu or clamber, sweating, up the steep *ladeiras* of Ouro Preto and be humbled by genius; I want to feel part of the gang in Vera's Veneziano's, my own private 'Cheers'. I want to dance – party with Emílio during Rio's *Carnaval*, dance with Miranda in Fortaleza the *forró* that never ends, and enjoy Gabriela's videoke in Ilhéus; I want to boogie back in Curitiba without Max, without Glauber, without fear; I want to bop with François down the darkest recesses of B.A.S.E. in the city where all that glitters is nothing but gold. And I want to swim – to fight off the waves in Ipanema and the *jacarés* in the Pantanal; I want to *pah-pah* the dourados of the Rio Peixe in Bonito; I want to crawl from beach to beach in Florianópolis, ride the sand-dunes on a buggy in Canoa Quebrada and stare forever at the amethyst gem that is the sea in Maceió. I look up at the sky and I am jealous for I know that God made Himself omnipresent so that he can do what I can't – be everywhere in Brazil at once. Then I realise that yes, I can, I am everywhere, for God, Tupã, Oxalá or Seta Branca gave me a powerful weapon: my mind can travel and defy natural laws and I have finally learned how to use it for I have been blessed with discovering the Key; I can lose myself in dance.

I am a gatekeeper, too.

So I return to my spot in Lagoa, facing Corcovado just when the precious short dusk sets in triumphant under a fierce orange sky and, as the lights around the lake assure me that there is no greater spectacle than this, I cry out my promise to return.

References

http://www.scroll.demon.co.uk/brazil/index.htm
My site, with pictures from the places you have read about in this book
plus a complete list of references. Here is a shortened list of the more
important ones.

In English

Allen, Stewart Lee *The Devil's Cup: Coffee, the Driving Force in History*
(Canongate, 1999)

Amnesty International *Brazil: Candelária and Vigario Geral, Justice at Snail's
Pace* AI Index AMR 19/011/1997
Candelária Trial AI Index AMR 19/020/1996
Crime Without Punishment: Impunity in Latin America AI Index AMR 01/
008/1996

Bradbury, Alex *Guide to Brazil*, 2nd edn (Bradt Publications, 1997)

Bramly, Serge *Macumba* (City Lights, 1975)

Burton, Isabel *The Romance of Isabel Lady Burton: The Story of Her Life Told in
Part by W. H. Wilkins* (Hutchinson, 1897)

Cheke, Markus *Carlota Joaquina, Queen of Portugal* (Sidgwick and Jackson
Ltd, 1947)

Domville-Fife, Charles W. *The United States of Brazil* (Francis Griffiths,
1910)

Eakin, Marshall *Brazil: The Once and Future Country* (Macmillan, 1997)

Freyre, Gilberto *The Masters and The Slaves*, 2nd edn (in translation),
(Alfred Knopf, 1956)

Gheerbrant, Alain *The Amazon: Past, Present and Future* (Thames and
Hudson, 1992)

Hemming, John *Amazon Frontier: The Defeat of the Brazilian Indians* (Pan
Macmillan, 1987)
Red Gold, The Conquest of the Brazilian Indians (Pan Macmillan, 1978)
The Search for Eldorado (Michael Joseph Ltd, 1978)

Jenkins, Garry *The Beautiful Team* (Simon and Shuster, 1997)

Koster, Henry *Travels in Brazil* (Longman, Hurst, Rees, Orms & Brown,
London, 1817; Southern Illinois University Press, 1966)

Levine, Robert M. and Crocitti, John J. (eds.) *The Brazil Reader* (Latin
America Bureau, 1999)

Love, Joseph L. *Rio Grande do Sul and Brazilian Regionalism 1882–1930*
(Stanford University Press, 1971)

REFERENCES

Machado de Almeida, Lúcia 'Strolling round Ouro Preto' *Coleção Reconquista do Brasil*, Vol 32 (1980)

McLynn, Frank *From the Serras to the Pampas: Richard Burton's Travels to the Americas 1860–69* (Century, 1991)

Ritterband, Charles *Neue Zürcher Zeitung*, 13 June 1998
Article on the Ciudad del Este illicit markets.

Santos, Boaventura de Sousa *Participatory Budgeting in Porto Alegre: Toward a Redistributive Democracy*, *Politics & Society* (Stoneham, 1998)

Skidmore, Thomas E. *Brazil – Five Centuries of Change* (Oxford University Press, 1999)

Slesser, Malcolm *Brazil, Land Without Limit* (Barnes and Co. Inc., 1970)

Spotte, Stephen *Candiru: Life and Legend of the Bloodsucking Catfishes*, (Creative Arts Book Company, 2002)

Trevisan, João *Perverts in Paradise* (in translation) (Gay Men's Press, 1986)

Uys, Errol Lincoln *Brazil* (Pan, 1986)

Wittbecker, Alan E. 'Recognizing Primary Cultures as Independent Nations and Creating a Framework for Them', *Pan Ecology*, Vol 6, No 4 (1991)

In Portuguese

de Amorim, Aluízio Batista *Nazismo em Santa Catarina,* (Florianópolis, 2000)

Bazin, Germain *Aleijadinho* (Edition du Temps, 1963) Portuguese translation by Mariza Murray (Editora Record)

Arruda, Roldão 'Judiciário amplia direitos de homossexuais, article in the *Estado do São Paulo*, 9 April 2001

Camargo, Lucila (ed.) *Almanaque Abril 2000 Brasil* (26th edn) and *2001* (27th)

Cheuiche, Alcy & Melgar, José Carlos *Sepé Tiaraju* (Martins Livreiro, 1994)
Sepé's life.

da Câmara Cascudo, Luís *Lendas brasileiras* (Ediouro, 2000)

Drey, Vilmar *Guia Caminhos da Serra do Mar e Ilha do Mel* (Curitiba, 1999)

Duarte, Marcelo *O Guia Dos Curiosos* (Cia das letras, 2000)

Fátima, Maria de Portugues das Neves *Documentos sobre a Escravidão no Brasil* (Editora Contexto, 1991)

Fatos e Fotos, *Especial deluxo Gay Carnaval 2000* (Bloch, 2000)

Martins Filho, Ives Gandra *500 Anos de História do Brasil* (Editora LTR São Paulo, 1999)

Leite, Basílisso 'Generalidade das Missões Jesuíticas' *Jornal das Missões* (6th edn, 1998)

Milko, Peter (ed.) *Pantanal and Bonito* (Guias Philips, Horizonte Geográfico, 2000)

Neiva, Tia *Vale do Amenhecer Sob Os Olhos da Clarividente Tia Neiva* (Editora Vale do Amanhecer, 1999)

Novães, Carlos Eduardo & Lobo César *História do Brasil para Principiantes* (Editora Ática, 1998)

Soares, Daso *Revista dos Orixás: Origens and Lendas Vol I-IV* (Editora Provenzano, 1999)

Sola, José Antônio *Canudos – Uma Utopia no Sertão* (Editora Contexto, 1997)

Zeca, Ligiéro *Iniciação ao Candomblé* (Nova Era, 1999)

Websites

http://www.tolweb.org/tree?group=Callichthyidae&contgroup=Siluriformes
The passage on armoured catfishes by Roberto E. Reis.

http://www.geocities.com/Vienna/studio/3006/forro.htm
Etymology of *forró*.

http://www.brazzil.com (with two *z*'s)
Possibly the best English site about Brazil, the web site of *Brazzil* magazine with a plethora of articles and commentary about the country.

http://www.sil.org/ethnologue/countries/Braz.html
Extinct Brazilian languages.

http://www.ggal.al.org.br
Grupo Gay de Alagoas. Renildo Santos torture facts.

http://www.newadvent.org
The Catholic encyclopaedia online information about Dom Bosco.

http://www.religioustolerance.org/chr_slav.htm
Christianity and slavery article.

www.geocities.com/Wellesley/4328/history.htm
History of the Sisterhood of Boa Morte.

http://www.solstice.crest.org/sustainable/curitiba/index.html
Curitiba traffic.

http://www.nytimes.com/2001/07/04/world/04BRAZ.html
Article on Pelotas and its reputation.

http://www.infobrasilia.com.br
A good historical site about Brasília.

http://www.netvasco.com.br
The official Vasco da Gama football site.

Bon Courage!

A French renovation in rural Limousin
by Richard Wiles

£7.99 · paperback · 1 84024 360 0 · 129 x 198 mm/320 pp

A hilarious and heartwarming tale of obstacles overcome and dreams fulfilled.

A dilapidated, rat-infested stone barn set amidst thirteen acres of overgrown woodland might not be many people's vision of a potential dream home. But for English couple Richard and Alison, the cavernous, oak-beamed building in a sleepy hamlet of the French Limousin region is perfect. Tussles with French bureaucracy allied with fierce storms that wreak havoc on the property do little to dampen their resolve as they immerse themselves in the *calme* of this quiet corner of France, getting to know the eccentric neighbours, taking trips in Richard's balloon and starting their very own llama farm.

Corfu Banquet

A Seasonal Memoir with Recipes
by Emma Tennant

£12.99 · hardback · 1 84024 366 X · 129 x 179 mm/208 pp

Corfu Banquet celebrates the tastes, smells and colours of an island where the cooking is seasonal and the flowers play changes on the theme of a year-round spring.

A memoir set to the rhythm of the seasons of Corfu, *Corfu Banquet* tells stories of the house of Rovinia, built in the sixties by Emma Tennant's parents, and entwines recipes and fond recollections in prose.

www.summersdale.com